SIXTH EDITION

Principles and Practice of
SPORT MANAGEMENT

Edited by

Lisa P. Masteralexis, JD

Associate Dean for Faculty and
Administration

Associate Professor of Sport Law

Isenberg School of Management

University of Massachusetts Amherst

Amherst, Massachusetts

Carol A. Barr, PhD

Senior Vice Provost

Dean of Undergraduate Education

University of Massachusetts Amherst

Amherst, Massachusetts

Mary A. Hums, PhD

Professor

Department of Health and Sport Sciences

University of Lousville

Lousville, Kentucky

JONES & BARTLETT
LEARNING

World Headquarters
Jones & Bartlett Learning
5 Wall Street
Burlington, MA 01803
978-443-5000
info@jblearning.com
www.jblearning.com

Jones & Bartlett Learning books and products are available through most bookstores and online booksellers. To contact Jones & Bartlett Learning directly, call 800-832-0034, fax 978-443-8000, or visit our website, www.jblearning.com.

15986-8

Production Credits

VP, Product Management: David D. Cella
Director of Product Management: Cathy L. Esperti
Product Manager: Sean Fabery
Product Assistant: Andrew LaBelle
Director of Production: Jenny L. Corriveau
Senior Production Editor: Nancy Hitchcock
Director of Marketing: Andrea DeFronzo
Production Services Manager: Colleen Lamy
VP, Manufacturing and Inventory Control: Therese Connell
Composition: Exela Technologies, Inc.

Cover Design: Kristin E. Parker
Text Design: Scott Moden
Director of Rights & Media: Joanna Gallant
Rights & Media Specialist: John Rusk
Media Development Editor: Shannon Sheehan
Cover Image (Title Page, Part Opener, Chapter Opener):
    © Shutterstock, Inc./Danilo_Vuletic
Printing and Binding: LSC Communications
Cover Printing: LSC Communications

Library of Congress Cataloging-in-Publication Data

Names: Masteralexis, Lisa Pike, editor. | Barr, Carol A., editor. | Hums, Mary A., editor.
Title: Principles and practice of sport management / edited by Lisa Pike Masteralexis, JD, Associate Dean, Faculty & Administration and Associate Professor of Sport Law, Isenberg School of Management, University of Massachusetts Amherst, Amherst, Massachusetts, Carol A. Barr, PhD, Senior Vice Provost and Dean of Undergraduate Education, University of Massachusetts Amherst, Amherst, Massachusetts, Mary A. Hums, PhD, Professor, Department of Health and Sport Sciences, University of Louisville, Louisville, Kentucky.
Description: Sixth edition. | Burlington, Massachusetts : Jones & Bartlett Learning, [2018] | Fifth edition: 2015. | Includes index.
Identifiers: LCCN 2018025737 | ISBN 9781284142136
Subjects: LCSH: Sports administration.
Classification: LCC GV713 .P75 2018 | DDC 796.06/9–dc23
LC record available at https://lccn.loc.gov/2018025737

6048

Printed in the United States of America
23 22 21 20 19   10 9 8 7 6 5 4 3

Contents

9   International Sport   211

Mary A. Hums and Per Svensson

13 Event Management 351
Carol A. Barr

Preface

As the sport industry evolves at a dramatic rate, the goal of providing a comprehensive, current, and innovative introductory textbook on sport management becomes a challenging task. Yet we have attempted to do just that by providing our readers (students, professors, and practitioners alike) this sixth edition of *Principles and Practice of Sport Management*.

This text is intended for use in introductory sport management courses. The focus of these courses, and this textbook, is to provide an overview of the sport industry and cover basic fundamental knowledge and skill sets sport managers need, as well as to provide information on sport industry segments for potential employment and career choices.

Directed toward undergraduate students, this text has three distinct sections:

- Part I provides an overview of basic knowledge areas for the successful sport manager, presenting fundamental principles and key skills, information on current issues, as well as case studies intended to spark debate and discussion.
- Parts II through V present overviews of major sport-industry segments in which a sport manager could work, followed by case studies.
- Part VI provides the reader with the basic career strategies for breaking into the highly competitive sport management industry.

Where appropriate, we have included an international perspective to give readers a broad view of sport management in the global context, which they will need as the world grows increasingly "smaller" in the decades to come. We would like to draw special attention to Chapter 9, "International Sport," which guides the reader through the global "sportscape" by examining the burgeoning sport industry around the world. The chapter makes the point that the reader should not confuse "globalization" of sport with the "Americanization" of global sport and reinforces the notion that sport managers who embrace the international nature of the sport industry will be leaders in the field, while those who do not are destined to be left behind in the global marketplace.

New to this Edition

This *Sixth Edition* offers a mix of contributions from scholars and practitioners. Based on feedback from faculty using the text, each chapter has undergone a thorough review and revision, and chapter authors have been attentive to providing new material and the most current information and data. Key changes focus on the following topics:

- Social media's prevalence today and its usage, role, and impact on sport.
- Sport safety concerns, with a focus on the attention concussions are receiving from youth sports to professional sports and the NFL.

- International sport, with the chapter on this topic having been completely rewritten.
- Examples of ethical issues confronting sport managers, which have been woven into the text in order to prompt classroom discussions.

Additional updates include the following:

- **Case Studies** have been incorporated into Chapters 1–6.
- **Learning Objectives** have been revised to correspond with Bloom's taxonomy.
- **Chapter 8, "Collegiate Sport,"** discusses the "Pay for Play" debate and the movement for the unionization of college student athletes.
- **Chapter 9, "International Sport,"** includes a new section on the emerging area of Sport for Development and Peace whereby managers use sport as a tool to address social issues in communities worldwide.
- **Chapter 13, "Event Management,"** explores the emergence of new events involving niche and extreme sports, including a discussion of their spectator appeal.
- **Chapter 16, "Sport Analytics,"** is a new addition, introducing students to the concept of sport analytics and its growing use in all aspects of sport business and player development.
- **Chapter 19, "Recreation and Golf Club Management,"** brings together content that was previously presented in two distinct chapters, emphasizing the commonalities between golf club management and recreational sport.

Overall, this text allows the reader to learn both the foundations and the principles on which the sport industry operates and offers an opportunity to apply those foundations and principles through interactive case studies and chapter questions. This text offers historical perspectives as well as thoughts about current and future industry issues and trends. For all these reasons, *Principles and Practice of Sport Management* will prove a valuable resource to those seeking employment in the sport management field, as well as those whose role it is to educate future sport managers.

Resources for Instructors

As with previous editions, this edition offers instructors a wealth of resources to aid in the teaching of this material. These include the following:

- Test Banks
- Slides in PowerPoint format
- Answer Keys for Case Study questions
- Sample Syllabus

Resources for Students

This edition is accompanied by online resources that assist students in reviewing the content. These include the following:

- Interactive eBook with embedded Knowledge Check questions
- Interactive Flashcards
- Slides in PowerPoint format
- Web Links

Acknowledgments

We would like to acknowledge the efforts of some individuals, without whom this text would not be possible. First and foremost, we express our deep appreciation to our contributing authors. Each author contributed his or her valuable expertise and experience to create a work that provides a wealth of knowledge to the sport management student. Through the editorial process, we have gained from them a greater understanding of the sport industry and our introductory sport management curriculum.

We have made some changes to the chapters and contributing authors since the last edition of this book. You should note we have left some chapter contributors' names from the previous editions to reflect the significance of the material carried over from those editions to this *Sixth Edition*. We would like to thank those authors who did not participate in this edition, but who contributed to previous editions and whose original work may still be included in this *Sixth Edition*. These contributors over the years and previous editions of this textbook include Tim Ashwell, Kevin Barrett, Nancy Beauchamp, Gregory Bouris, Adri Broeke, Stephen Bromage, Howard M. Davis, Timothy D. DeSchriver, Sheranne Fairley, Kevin Filo, Troy Flynn, James M. Gladden, Betsy Goff, Virginia R. Goldsbury, Michael Graney, Laurie Guillion, Dennis R. Howard, William Howland, Mireia Lizandra, Mark A. McDonald, Andrew McGowan, Robert Newman, Berend Rubingh, Tracy Schoenadel, William A. Sutton, Rod Warnick, Jo Williams, and Glenn M. Wong.

We also thank everyone at Jones & Bartlett Learning for their efforts in seeing this project through to completion. Their enthusiasm for the text was a wonderful motivation for tackling the *Sixth Edition*.

Finally, we thank undergraduate students Tim Jablonsky and Matt Polimou at the University of Massachusetts, who provided help in editing a few chapters.

Reviewers

We also thank those faculty members who have adopted *Principles and Practice of Sport Management* for their classes and whose feedback we have incorporated into this edition. Specifically, we thank the following reviewers whose feedback helped shape the *Sixth Edition*:

- **John DeSpagna, MS, MBA, SDBL,** Nassau Community College
- **C. Keith Harrison, MA, EdD,** University of Central Florida
- **Thomas Kernodle, PhD,** Empire State College
- **Katie Lebel, MA, PhD,** Ryerson University
- **Jon A. Oliver, PhD,** Eastern Illinois University
- **Marc Postiglione, MA,** Union County College
- **Regina G. Presley, MS,** University of Louisville
- **F. Michelle Richardson, PhD,** The Citadel
- **Linda J. Schoenstedt, EdD,** Xavier University

Contributors

Editors

Lisa P. Masteralexis, JD
Associate Dean of Faculty &
    Administration
Associate Professor of Sport Law
Mark H. McCormack Department of Sport
    Management
Isenberg School of Management
University of Massachusetts Amherst
Amherst, Massachusetts

Carol A. Barr, PhD
Senior Vice Provost and Dean of
    Undergraduate Education
University of Massachusetts Amherst
Amherst, Massachusetts

Mary A. Hums, PhD
Professor and Coordinator of the Sport
    Administration PhD Program
Department of Health and Sport Science
University of Louisville
Louisville, Kentucky

Chapter Authors

Nola Agha, PhD
Associate Professor
Sport Management Program
University of San Francisco
San Francisco, California

John S. Clark, PhD
Professor and Director of the MBA
    Program
School of Business
Robert Morris University
Moon Township, Pennsylvania

Dan Covell, PhD
Professor of Sport Management
College of Business
Department of Sport Management
Western New England University
Springfield, Massachusetts

Todd W. Crosset, PhD
Associate Professor
Mark H. McCormack Department of Sport
    Management
Isenberg School of Management
University of Massachusetts Amherst
Amherst, Massachusetts

Tara Q. Mahoney, PhD
Associate Professor
Sport Management Department
State University of New York College
    at Cortland
Cortland, New York

James T. Masteralexis, JD
Associate Professor
Department of Sport Management
College of Business
Western New England University
Springfield, Massachusetts

Stephen M. McKelvey, JD
Associate Professor and Graduate
    Program Director
Mark H. McCormack Department of Sport
    Management
Isenberg School of Management
University of Massachusetts Amherst
Amherst, Massachusetts

Jim Noel, JD
Practicing Attorney

William Norton

Lecturer and Director of the
    Mark H. McCormack Center for
    Sport Research and Education
Mark H. McCormack Department of Sport
    Management
Isenberg School of Management
University of Massachusetts Amherst
Amherst, Massachusetts

Regina Presley, MS

Instructor and Director of the
    Undergraduate Sport Administration
    Program
Department of Sport and Health Sciences
University of Louisville
Louisville, Kentucky

Per G. Svensson, PhD

Assistant Professor
School of Kinesiology
Louisiana State University
Baton Rouge, Louisiana

About the Authors

Editors

Lisa P. Masteralexis, JD

Lisa P. Masteralexis is the Associate Dean for Faculty and Administration and an Associate Professor of Sport Law in the Isenberg School of Management at the University of Massachusetts Amherst. She holds a JD from Suffolk University School of Law and a BS in Sport Management from the University of Massachusetts. She has taught courses on Sport Agencies, Sport Law, and Labor Relations in Professional Sport. Her primary research interests are in legal issues and labor relations in the sport industry.

Professor Masteralexis is the lead editor of *Principles and Practice of Sport Management*, now in its sixth edition. She has contributed many of its book chapters, as well as other chapters in textbooks and scholarly books on sport law. Her scholarly work also includes contributions to the *Journal of the Legal Aspects of Sport*, *Journal of College and University Law*, *Jeffrey S. Moorad Sports Law Journal* (Villanova), *Marquette Sports Law Review*, *New England Law Review*, *Journal of Sport Management*, *Journal of Sport and Social Issues*, and *European Journal for Sport Management*. Professor Masteralexis has made over 60 presentations in the United States and abroad before the American Bar Association, the Sport and Recreation Law Association, the North American Society for Sport Management, the European Association for Sport Management, Women in Sports and Events, and numerous law schools and business schools.

In 2000, Professor Masteralexis coauthored an amicus brief to the U.S. Supreme Court on behalf of disabled athletes and in support of professional golfer Casey Martin. She is a member of the Massachusetts and U.S. Supreme Court Bars.

Professor Masteralexis has received the College Outstanding Teacher Award three times and has been nominated twice for the University Distinguished Teaching Award. In 2016, she received the Academic Achievement in Sport and Entertainment Award from Sport and Entertainment Venues Today and the University of South Carolina and was a 2010 recipient of the Harold J. VanderZwaag Distinguished Alumnus Award from the Mark H. McCormack Department of Sport Management. She has served on the Board of the National Sports Law Institute and was part of the Women's Sports Foundation. Professor Masteralexis is one of a few women to have been certified as an agent with the Major League Baseball Players Association and is a consultant with DiaMMond Management Group, a professional athlete management firm.

Carol A. Barr, PhD

Carol A. Barr currently serves as Senior Vice Provost and Dean of Undergraduate Education at the University of Massachusetts Amherst. In this role, she provides overall leadership for undergraduate education programs on campus. She works closely with the campus leadership to develop a comprehensive plan for undergraduate education reflecting best practices related to teaching and learning, promotion of undergraduate academic success, and campus initiatives impacting student learning and student success. Dr. Barr holds a BS in Athletic Administration from the University of Iowa (4-year letter winner in field hockey) and an MS and PhD in Sport Management from the University of Massachusetts Amherst. She joined the UMass Amherst faculty in 1991 and is a tenured faculty member in the Mark H. McCormack Department of Sport Management.

Dr. Barr's research interests lie in the areas of management issues and gender equity within collegiate athletics. She has published articles in the *Journal of Sport Management*, *Sport Marketing Quarterly*, *Journal of Higher Education*, *Journal of Business Ethics*, *Sex Roles*, and the *International Sports Journal*. Dr. Barr has published more than 40 articles for sport practitioners in publications such as *Athletic Business* and *Street & Smith's SportsBusiness Journal*. Dr. Barr has performed consulting work for the National Collegiate Athletic Association and has been involved in legal research surrounding gender equity, concentrating on its application to the collegiate athletic arena.

Within her academic association, Dr. Barr has served on the Executive Council of the North American Society for Sport Management (NASSM), serving as President in 2006–2007. She was a 2011 recipient of the North American Society for Sport Management Garth Paton Distinguished Service Award. She has also served on the editorial board of the *Journal of Sport Management*.

Mary A. Hums, PhD

Mary A. Hums is a Professor in the Sport Administration Program at the University of Louisville, where she coordinates the PhD program. She holds a PhD in Sport Management from Ohio State University, an MA in Athletic Administration and an MBA from the University of Iowa, and a BBA in Management from the University of Notre Dame. In addition to being a past President of the Society for the Study of Legal Aspects of Sport and Physical Activity (SSLASPA; now Sport and Recreation Law Society [SRLA]), Dr. Hums is an active member of the North American Society for Sport Management (NASSM) and the International Olympic Academy Participants Association (IOAPA).

Prior to coming to the University of Louisville, Dr. Hums served on the Sport Management faculty at the University of Massachusetts, Amherst; directed the Sport Management Program at Kennesaw State University in Atlanta; and was Athletic Director at St. Mary-of-the-Woods College in Terre Haute, Indiana. She worked as a volunteer for the 1996 Summer Paralympic Games in Atlanta, the 2002 Winter Paralympic Games in Salt Lake City, the 2010 Winter Paralympic Games in Vancouver, and the 2015 Para-Pan American Games in Toronto. In 2004, she lived in Athens, Greece, for 5 months, working at both the Olympic (softball) and Paralympic (goalball) Games.

A past Editor of the *Sport Management Education Journal*, her scholarly contributions also include publications in the *Journal of Sport Management*, *European Sport Management Quarterly*, *Journal of Business Ethics*, *Journal of Sport and Social Issues*, *Sport Management Review*, *Journal of Legal Aspects of Sport*, *International Journal of Sport*

Management, VOLUNTAS: International Journal of Voluntary and Nonprofit Organizations, Adapted Physical Activity Quarterly, and *Advancing Women in Leadership.* The lead author on the textbook *Governance and Policy in Sport Organizations,* Dr. Hums has also made more than 200 scholarly presentations in the United States and abroad.

In 2006, Hums was selected by the United States Olympic Committee to represent the United States at the International Olympic Academy's Educators' Session. In 2008, Dr. Hums was an Erasmus Mundus International Research Fellow at the Katholieke Universiteit of Leuven, Belgium. She is currently a Research Fellow with the Institute for Human Centered Design, which is based in Boston.

In 2009, she was named the Earle F. Zeigler Lecturer by NASSM. In 2014, she received the NASSM Diversity Award and also the Southern Sport Management Association Scholar Achievement Award. She is an inductee into the Indiana ASA Softball Hall of Fame and also the Marian High School (Mishawaka, Indiana) Athletic Hall of Fame.

Contributors

Nola Agha, PhD

Nola Agha is an Associate Professor in the Sport Management Program at the University of San Francisco. She holds a BS from Indiana University Bloomington, an MA in Sport Management from the University of San Francisco, and a PhD in Management from the Mark H. McCormack Department of Sport Management at the University of Massachusetts Amherst. Dr. Agha's primary research focuses on the economic impacts of teams and stadiums, the efficiency and equity outcomes of stadium subsidies, and a variety of issues related to minor league baseball. She brings a multidisciplinary approach to her research, combining her training in both economics and management. She has published sport-related articles in journals such as the *Journal of Sports Economics, Sport Management Review, Managerial and Decision Economics, Contemporary Economic Policy, European Sport Management Quarterly,* and more. Dr. Agha worked in international business operations for several years and has also consulted to the sport and fitness industry by conducting economic impact studies; competitive analyses; and feasibility studies for clients in the MLB, the NBA, and minor league hockey.

John S. Clark, PhD

John S. Clark is a Professor of Sport Management and Director of the MBA Program in the Robert Morris University School of Business. He received his MS and PhD in Sport Management from the University of Massachusetts Amherst and a BA in English Literature from the University of Wisconsin-Eau Claire. Dr. Clark's research has been published in both sport management and business journals, and focuses on sponsorship, cause-related marketing, and sport consumer behavior.

Dan Covell, PhD

Dan Covell is a Professor of Sport Management in the College of Business at Western New England University. He earned his undergraduate degree in Studio Art from Bowdoin College in 1986 (where he also lettered in football).

After working in public and private secondary education as a coach, teacher, and athletic administrator, Covell earned his MS in Sport Management from the University of Massachusetts Amherst in 1995. After a 1-year administrative internship in Harvard University's athletic department, Covell then earned his PhD from UMass in 1999.

His primary research interests are management issues in intercollegiate and secondary school athletics, with a recent track toward historical perspectives on these issues.

Todd W. Crosset, PhD

Todd W. Crosset is an Associate Professor in the Mark H. McCormack Department of Sport Management in the Isenberg School of Management at the University of Massachusetts Amherst. He holds an MA and PhD in Sociology from Brandeis University, as well as a BA from the University of Texas, Austin where he was an All-American swimmer and a member of a national championship team. Prior to arriving at the University of Massachusetts, he held positions as Head Coach of Swimming at Northeastern University and Assistant Athletic Director at Dartmouth College. Dr. Crosset's academic interests include gender and racism in sport management and sexual assault in sport. His book, *Outsiders in the Clubhouse*, which is about life on the LPGA golf tour, won the North American Society for Sport Sociology Book of the Year Award in 1995.

Tara Q. Mahoney, PhD

Tara Q. Mahoney is an Associate Professor in the Sport Management Department at the State University of New York College at Cortland. She earned her PhD in Educational Leadership and Organizational Development with a concentration in Sport Administration at the University of Louisville. She also earned an MBA from West Virginia Wesleyan College and a BA from Nazareth College of Rochester, where she played volleyball.

Prior to pursuing a career in academia, Dr. Mahoney worked in various sectors of the recreation industry, including municipal, campus, and outdoor recreation. Dr. Mahoney's research interests are in the areas of charity sport participation and the use of social media to facilitate sport participation.

James T. Masteralexis, JD

James T. Masteralexis, JD is an Associate Professor of Sport Law at Western New England University, where he teaches courses in Sport Law, Business Law, and Player Development and Scouting. He received his law degree from Suffolk University Law School. Prior to working in academia, he practiced labor and employment law and litigation for 18 years. Professor Masteralexis also represents major and minor league baseball players in contract negotiations and salary arbitration. He has been a certified agent with the Major League Baseball Players Association. He received his BA from the University of New Hampshire, where he was a catcher on the Division I baseball team.

Stephen McKelvey, JD

Stephen McKelvey is an Associate Professor in the Mark H. McCormack Department of Sport Management at the University of Massachusetts Amherst. Professor McKelvey holds a BA from Amherst College; an MS in Sport Management from the University of Massachusetts Amherst; and a JD from Seton Hall School of Law. He brings a unique perspective to the department, combining his sport industry experience in marketing, sales, and the law to provide students with valuable insights. His research focuses primarily on the legal and practical application of intellectual property issues to the sports marketing industry. He has authored articles on sport marketing, sponsorship, and the law for a number of publications, including the *American Business Law Journal, Virginia Entertainment and Sport Law Review, The Journal of Legal Aspects of Sport, Journal of Sport Management, Sport Management Review, Fordham Intellectual Property, Media & Entertainment Law Journal, Seton Hall Journal of Sport Law, Entertainment and Sports Lawyer*, and *Sports Business Journal*, among others. A noted authority on the topic of "ambush marketing," Professor McKelvey has more than 15 years of industry experience, both on the sport property and the agency side. From 1986–1991, he worked in the Corporate Sponsorship department of Major League Baseball, and later was responsible for building an in-house sports sponsorship consulting agency within PSP Sports, a New York City–based sports publishing company. In 1999, McKelvey conceived, sold, and managed two of the year's most innovative sport marketing programs: Century 21's "Turn Ahead the Clock" promotion (baseball's first-ever league-wide series of futuristic-themed baseball games, featuring games with players outfitted in futuristic-styled uniforms) and the first-ever promotion allowing consumers to vote for the Heisman Trophy Award winner (the linchpin of Suzuki's Heisman Trophy sponsorship).

Jim Noel, JD

Jim Noel has been a sports and media lawyer and executive for 39 years. Half of his career was spent at ESPN as Vice President, Business Affairs and Associate General Counsel, where he was the lead contract negotiator for all network programming transactions (including with the NFL, MLB, NASCAR, NHL, MLS, Wimbledon, America's Cup, PGA Tour, and USTA). He also negotiated distribution agreements with major cable companies, oversaw the creation of the legal framework for ESPN.com, and provided editorial counseling for SportsCenter and the Outside The Lines program series. At other times, he was Chief Legal Officer of the USGA, Assistant Counsel to the Commissioner of the NFL, and Senior Legal Counsel for AT&T Sports Networks. He also practiced sports law at the Seattle-based law firm of Davis Wright Tremaine, where his clients included the Seattle Seahawks.

He is a graduate of the University of Alabama School of Law and the University of Oregon School of Journalism.

Will Norton, MBA, MS

Will Norton is a Lecturer and the Director of the McCormack Center for Sport Research & Education in the Mark H. McCormack Department of Sport Management in the Isenberg School of Management at the University of Massachusetts. Will has 10 years of experience in the sport industry across a variety of sectors. He served as a data analyst and professional scout with STATS, LLC, managing the firm's NBA SportVu data collection as well as MLB, NFL, and NBA data contracts, before transitioning to a corporate partnerships role with the Boston Celtics and a brand sponsorship strategy and measurement position with full-service marketing firm Epsilon. His research and teaching interests include data-driven insights in the professional sport industry, digital media in sports, and sport finance. Will holds an MBA and an MS in Sport Management from the Isenberg School of Management and Mark H. McCormack Department of Sport Management.

He also holds a BA in Political Science and International Relations from The College of Wooster.

Regina Presley, MS

Regina Presley is an Instructor and the Director of the Undergraduate Sport Administration Program at the University of Louisville. Presley earned her MS in Sport Administration from the University of Northern Colorado and her BA in Sport Industry Operations from Metropolitan State University of Denver. Prior to arriving at the University of Louisville, she was a faculty member at Metropolitan State University of Denver and worked in the College of Business. As a small business entrepreneur, Presley owned and operated her own business for more than 10 years and has worked with students and professionals in career and professional development. In addition to her work in the classroom, where she has been recognized as a UofL Faculty Favorite and also a UofL Red & Black Scholar Athlete Mentor, Presley co-authored the 2016 textbook titled *Issues & Ethics in Sport: A Practical Guide for Sport Managers.*

Per G. Svensson, PhD

Per Svensson is an Assistant Professor in Sport Management in the School of Kinesiology at Louisiana State University. His research is primarily focused on organizations operating sport-based programs aimed at addressing social issues in low-, middle-, and high-income countries. Specifically, his work examines organizational capacity and innovation in Sport for Development and Peace. Dr. Svensson's research has been published in a number of academic journals, including the *Journal of Sport Management*; *Sport Management Review*; *Nonprofit and Voluntary Sector Quarterly*; *VOLUNTAS: International Journal of Voluntary and Nonprofit Organizations*; *Sport, Education, and Society*; *International Journal of Sport Communication*; *Sport in Society*; *Journal of Sport for Development*; and the *International Journal of Sport Management and Marketing*. In addition, Dr. Svensson's industry experiences include working with the PGA TOUR, PGA of America, and Special Olympics.

© Shutterstock, Inc./ Danilo_Vuletic

Part I

Foundations of Sport Management

Chapter

1

Todd W. Crosset and
Mary A. Hums

History of Sport Management

Learning Objectives

Upon completion of this chapter, students should be able to:

1. Demonstrate knowledge of the roots of our modern sport management structures and how most have grown in response to broader social or sport industry changes.

2. Evaluate the impact of different cultures on sport and the unique contribution of American management to the development of sport.

3. Assess the methods that successful sport managers developed in the late twentieth and early twenty-first centuries that promoted honesty.

4. Appraise the effect that the many "honesty crises" (e.g., Black Sox scandal or National Collegiate Athletic Association [NCAA] college basketball gambling scandal of 1951) have had on the sport industry.

5. Assess the historic tension in American sport between democratic ideals and race, class, and gender segregation, and describe how, in the context of American society, these limitations were used to promote social divisions.

6. Estimate the effects of exclusionary practices such age limits, performance criteria, or geographical/citizenship criteria that teams and leagues impose on their membership.

7. Explain how aristocrats in eighteenth-century England, who held thoroughbred races, formed jockey clubs, and allowed the masses to be spectators, can be viewed as precursors to modern sport managers.

8. Identify the reasons why American baseball and the Olympics have their roots in English culture.

9. Compare and contrast the ways in which unique "American" culture resulted in sport structures that differed from European models, and discuss how harness racing, professional baseball, and professional golf tours in the United States developed differently from each other and from European models.

10. Assess the important role that women and people of color have had in the growth of the sport industry.

11. Identify some of the innovative sport managers who shaped the industry.

12. Describe the need that sport organizations have for trained sport managers, and explain how this need grew from a cooperative idea between practitioners and academics.

13. Recognize that academic sport management programs exist around the world, and that although these programs may share similar curricular topics (e.g., sport marketing or sport law), each country trains its sport management students in a manner appropriate for its domestic sport industry.

14. Describe the role of the North American Society for Sport Management (NASSM) and the Commission on Sport Management Accreditation (COSMA) in the growth of sport management research and education.

Introduction

The contemporary sport industry is complex and has unique legal, business, and management practices. As a result, many of the ways this industry is organized are unique, too. The organization of sport has developed over the past 150 or so years and continues to evolve. In recent years, for example, sport managers have been tinkering with structures such as conference alignments, drafts, and playoff systems.

This chapter explores the roots of our modern **sport management structures**. The management structures of sport reviewed in this chapter are **clubs**, **leagues**, and **professional tournaments**. These structures help managers organize sport and are the basic building blocks of many of our sports today. The chapter discusses how women and racial ethnic minorities have made their mark on the industry. Finally, the chapter addresses the development of the sport management academic discipline, which evolved as the need for trained sport management professionals became apparent.

The primary theme of this chapter is that sport management structures grow in response to broad social changes and/or to address specific issues within a segment of the sport industry. The evolution of these structures illustrates that sport managers need to be creative in the ways they run their sport organizations. One "catch-all" management structure will not work for all situations. History suggests that successful sport managers are flexible and have the ability to adapt to broader changes in society. This chapter also gives a few examples of innovative and successful sport managers.

Many events have shaped the world of sport and the sport industry. While it is nearly impossible to create a timeline that hits all the highlights, one is included at the end of this chapter for your reference. This timeline includes the founding dates of many sport organizations as well as a number of "firsts" in the sport industry in terms of events. Try thinking about events or people you would add to the timeline—it is a great class discussion starter!

Two secondary themes run throughout this brief examination of the history of sport management structures: honesty and inclusion. The legitimacy of modern sport demands honest play, or at least the appearance of honest play. Nothing in sport is more reviled than the athlete who does not try. An athlete who does not exert an honest effort is a spoilsport. Players who throw games are sellouts. So critical is the perception of an honest effort that sport managers will ban people from their sport for life if they tarnish the game through the mere possibility they bet on their team to lose (e.g., Pete Rose).

The appearance of an honest effort is one of the most important precepts organizing modern sport. It is more important, for example, than fair play or equality of competition. Although some structures have been implemented to level the playing field (e.g., drafts, salary caps), disparities among teams remain, giving some teams advantages over others. The public is much more tolerant of players breaking the rules when trying to win than it is of players throwing games. The public's notion of what ensures an honest effort also changes over time. One issue addressed throughout this chapter is how sport managers have changed or adapted sport to ensure the appearance of honesty as broader structures within society have changed.

Another issue this chapter explores is the tension between democratic inclusiveness and the regulation of participation. The desire to create a meritocracy is implicit in modern sport—if you are good enough, you should play. This is illustrated nicely by the slogan and campaign, "If you can play . . . you can play" (You Can Play Project, 2013). But, by necessity, any form of organized sport includes rules limiting who is allowed to participate. For example, most contemporary sport leagues or teams have age and gender requirements. International governing bodies, as well as local leagues, have citizenship and residency requirements. On this basis, athletes who have just moved to a new nation or town are sometimes excluded from participating in sports.

Answering the questions "Who gets to play?", "Who is encouraged to watch?", and "Who is left out?" requires an understanding of both sport-specific issues and broader social issues. When it comes to who gets to play, what seems "fair" at a particular juncture in history often reflects broader social beliefs. For example, not long ago it would have been unthinkable for girls to play Little League Baseball or for women to compete against men on the Professional Golfers' Association (PGA) TOUR. Although it is still unusual, women have competed in PGA tournaments. Michelle Wie, for example, played against men in 14 tournaments, including eight PGA TOUR events. Both Wie and Si Re Pak have made the cut in Asian men's competitions as well.

Historically, the groups with the most power in a society define the limits of participation, usually to their benefit. Sport in the first half of the twentieth century, for example, developed along with the eugenics movement, legal racial segregation, and an ideology of white racial superiority in the United States and South Africa. Thus, for many generations, mainstream sport structures in the United States and South Africa either excluded or limited participation by people of color.

Many of these practices now seem antiquated and are perceived as unfair. Given that notions of what makes for honest play and who should be allowed to play or watch sport change over time, sport management likewise has evolved to reflect changes in the broader society.

The Club System: Sports and Community

England is the birthplace of modern sport and sport management (Mandell, 1984). The roots of most Western sports, including track and field,

all the variations of football, and stick-and-ball games such as baseball, field hockey, and cricket, can be traced to England. The broad influence of England's sporting culture is the result of the British Empire's imperial power in the eighteenth and nineteenth centuries. Britain had colonies all over the world, and British colonists took her sports to all of them.

The continuing influence of the British sports tradition after the empire's demise has as much to do with how the English organized sport as it does with England's political and cultural domination. Even sports that originated outside England, such as basketball, gymnastics, and golf, initially adopted English sport organizational structures.

In the eighteenth century, the English aristocracy, made up of nobles and the landed gentry, began to develop sports clubs. Membership in these clubs was limited to the politically and economically powerful of English society. The earliest clubs simply organized one-time events or annual competitions and brought members together for social events. By the nineteenth century, clubs standardized rules, acted to settle disputes between teams or horse owners, and organized seasons of competitions.

Thoroughbred racing was one of the first sports transformed by the club management system. Other English sports, such as cricket, rugby, and soccer, also adopted a similar club management structure. The focus here is on thoroughbred racing simply because it is the earliest example of club management.

Thoroughbred Racing

Early horse races were local events, often associated with holidays or horse sales. By the mid-eighteenth century, thoroughbred racing and breeding had established a broad following among the English aristocracy. Local groups of breeders organized races. Horse owners arranged the events, put up purses, and invited participants to show off their best horses and demonstrate their prestige.

At this time, horse racing was managed on a local level. The organization was essentially a volunteer system of management, controlled by the same wealthy men who owned the horses and estates. Despite the extreme stratification of eighteenth-century English society, horse races drew a broad and diverse audience, with all levels of society attending the races. The owners, who represented the elite of the community, in keeping with tradition and meeting their social obligation to entertain the masses, did not charge admission.

Even though horse races were important for demonstrating prestige, they were rarely the primary business interest of the horse owners who controlled the sport. Consequently, seventeenth-century horse racing and sport remained largely separate from the growing capitalist economy. Horse racing existed primarily for the entertainment of wealthy club members and did not have to be an independent, self-supporting financial entity. This system gave horse racing the appearance of honesty. The public believed that the aristocracy—men of breeding, culture, and wealth—would not be tempted by bribes, influenced by petty feuds, or swayed to make unfair decisions.

The local club system governed the sport successfully as long as racing remained local. Soon, however, two factors combined to create a need for more systematic management: (1) the desire of owners to breed and train the fastest horses in England and (2) the increasing complexity of gambling.

As members of the elite gained prestige for owning the fastest horses, horses were bred for no other purpose than to win races. Speed was appreciated for its own sake, distinct from its religious, military, or economic purpose—a uniquely modern phenomenon (Mandell, 1984). Races usually consisted of a series of 4-mile heats, so the ideal horse combined speed with endurance.

By the 1830s, rail transportation enabled owners to compete nationally. Local-level management governing area breeders, owners, and jockeys had worked well because of the familiarity among all involved, but national competition meant race organizers now managed participants whom they did not know very well, if at all. Thus, the management of thoroughbred racing needed to become more systematic. This also meant dealing head-on with the prevalence of gambling.

Gambling on thoroughbred horse races was common among all classes. Much as speed came to be appreciated for its own merits, betting on thoroughbred races began to be appreciated for its own value. Gambling not only provided exciting entertainment, but also offered bettors tangible evidence of their knowledge of horses and ability to predict who would win (Mandell, 1984).

Gambling also ensured honest competition. The crowd policed the jockeys. At that time, horse racing was a head-to-head competition. As noted earlier, events were comprised of a series of 4-mile runs, and the winning horse had to win two out of three races. If the crowd suspected a jockey had allowed the other contestant to win, the crowd would punish that jockey, often physically.

By the eighteenth century, innovations in the sport designed to draw larger audiences and enhance the ways spectators could wager also made the gambling system more complex. The English created handicapping, tip sheets, and sweepstakes; used the stopwatch to time races; standardized race distances; and added weights to horses. All of these innovations enhanced the public's interest in the sport. As the influence and importance of gambling grew and the systems of weights and handicapping leveled the playing field, the opportunity for a "fixed" race to go undetected also increased. All the enhancements and innovations made it difficult for the audience to detect when and how races were fixed. As a result, conventional methods could not be counted on to adequately police the sport (Henriches, 1991).

The Jockey Club: The Birth of Club Governance

The roots of the management system in thoroughbred racing can be traced to around 1750, when a group of noble patrons in Newmarket established the Jockey Club. This group's responsibilities were to settle disputes, establish rules, determine eligibility, designate officials, regulate breeding, and punish unscrupulous participants. The club organized, sponsored, and promoted local events (Vamplew, 1989). Like other local clubs, members of the Newmarket Jockey Club put up the purse money and restricted entries to thoroughbreds owned by club members.

The effective organization and management of thoroughbred racing in Newmarket made it a national hub for the sport. Local champions faced challenges from owners outside their region. The Jockey Club sponsored prestigious races that attracted horse owners from across England. As the need grew for a strong national governing body to establish rules and standards and to create a mechanism for resolving disputes, the Jockey Club from Newmarket emerged to serve those functions (Henriches, 1991).

Some of the lasting contributions the Jockey Club made to racing included sponsoring a stud book listing the lineage of thoroughbreds, thereby helping ensure the purity of the breed; promoting a series of race schedules; announcing, regulating, and reporting on horse sales; and restricting the people involved with thoroughbred breeding and racing to the English elite. The Jockey Club served as a model for wider sport management practices in England.

Cricket, boxing, and other English sports eventually adopted the management and organizational structures developed in thoroughbred horse racing. In each case, one club emerged as the coordinating and controlling body of the sport, not out of a formal process but by collective prominence. The Marylebone Cricket Club, for example, revised the rules of cricket in 1788 and became the international governing club for the entire sport (Williams, 1989). In 1814, the Pugilist Society was formed by a group of gentlemen to regulate bareknuckle boxing and guarantee purses. Even sports such as association football (soccer) and rugby, which were organized much later, adopted the club organizational structure (Henriches, 1991).

Club structure depended on the appearance of fairness, loyal support, and volunteer management for its success. The aristocrats who managed and sponsored sport were presumed to be honest and disinterested, giving spectators the sense that competition was fair. Fairness was cultivated through the reputation of sport organizers and their nonprofit motives. Loyalty to specific clubs was cultivated through membership.

The Modern Olympic Games: An International Club Event

The club structure is also the foundation for the **modern Olympic Games**. Indeed, the early Games can be viewed as an international club event. Created at the peak of the club system, the modern Olympic Games resemble international club events much more than they do the ancient Games for which they are named. The ancient Games, at least initially, were part of a larger religious ceremony and were initially only for the viewing of, and participation by, free, able-bodied, male Greek citizens. These Games existed for 1,169 years and over time became an international gathering of athletes. They were discontinued in AD 393, although they were held sporadically in some form until AD 521 (Ministry of Culture–General Secretariat for Sports, 1998). Almost 15 centuries passed before the international Olympic Games were revived in another form.

Although 1896 marked the first official staging of the modern Olympic Games, Olympic-like festivals and revivals had been organized on local levels in England much earlier. The most important of these events in the revival of the Games was the annual festival at Much Wenlock, Shropshire, started in 1850 by Dr. William Penny Brookes. As a logical extension of his annual games, Brookes organized the Shropshire Olympian Association in 1861, which led to the founding of the National Olympian Association four years later (Young, 1996).

The current International Olympic Committee's founding conference for the modern Olympic Games was held in 1894. **Pierre de Coubertin**, a young French physical educator who was influenced by Brookes' vision of an international Olympic Games, Professor William Sloane of Princeton University, and Charles Herbert, Secretary of the (British) Amateur Athletics Association, were the driving forces behind this meeting, which they dubbed an "international athletic congress." More than 70 attendees representing 37 amateur athletic clubs and associations from at least a dozen different nations attended the congress. The primary focus of this meeting was to establish the meaning and application of amateurism. De Coubertin—inspired by the English Olympic revivals, chivalry, Victorian notions of character development through sport, and the notion of an international peace movement—argued for an Olympic-like festival at the meeting. These Games, he suggested, would be held every four years, in rotating sites, and participants would need to be chivalrous athletes—men who competed with grace and for the honor of their club and country. He proposed that the first Games be held in Paris in 1900. The attendees were so receptive to the idea that they voted to convene the Olympic Games earlier, in 1896 in Athens, Greece.

The first modern Olympic Games were a 9-day event and drew 311 athletes from 13 nations. The participants were exclusively amateurs. Most entrants were college students or athletic club members, because the concept of national teams had not yet emerged. Clubs such as the Boston Athletic Association, the Amateur Athletic Association, and the German Gymnastics Society sent the largest delegations. Spectators filled the newly built Panathinaiko Stadium to watch the Games, which featured nine sports: cycling, fencing, gymnastics, lawn tennis, shooting, swimming, track and field, weight lifting, and wrestling (Ministry of Culture–General Secretariat for Sports, 1998). In several subsequent Olympic Games (Paris, St. Louis), however, the event floundered. The Games did not hit solid footing until—perhaps not surprisingly—London hosted them in 1908.

The Club Structure Today

Many contemporary sports and events have organizational roots in the club sport system. These include U.S. collegiate athletics and European football. Although the club system for the organization of elite sports is fading in some places, it is still a popular way to organize sport and recreation.

Some clubs remain committed to serving their broad membership and managing an elite sports enterprise. Many European football clubs and the Augusta National Golf Club, host of the Masters Golf Tournament, are examples of contemporary club governance. Larger clubs such as Olympiakos or Panathinaikos in Athens, Greece, provide recreation for members in addition to managing their high-profile teams or events. Clubs often organize youth teams and academies, adult recreational leagues, and social events such as dinners and dances for their members. Some club sports, such as association football in Europe, have large built-in memberships and loyal fan bases and consequently rarely have a problem attracting crowds for their matches.

Once the dominant management structure of elite sport, the club system is now slowly being replaced by other sport management structures. Clearly, the Olympic Games have changed dramatically from the early days; they now resemble the tournament structure discussed later in this chapter. Probably the most dramatic change was the decision to allow professional athletes to play in the Games. Beginning in the 1970s, amateurism requirements were gradually phased out of the Olympic Charter. After the 1988 Games, the International Olympic Committee (IOC) decided that professional athletes would be eligible to compete at the Olympic Games. Without amateurism, the last remaining vestige of chivalrous, fair, and clean sport is the IOC's rigorous drug testing of athletes, although it is even being called into question in recent years.

European football—once a prime example of the club system—is changing, too. Today, it looks more like the league structure described later in this chapter. A major change occurred in 1995 when the European Court of Justice ruled in favor of Jean-Marc Bosman, a professional footballer who argued that his Belgian team was restraining free trade when it refused to grant him a transfer to another club. This opened up the market for the movement of talented soccer players. Now elite European club teams such as Manchester United, Real Madrid, and Olympiakos are increasingly controlled by wealthy individuals, pay handsome salaries for the best players, and operate like entertainment/sport businesses (King, 1997).

Clubs are also no longer local in nature. Today's large clubs feature players from all over the world. For example, in the 2010 World Cup, members of the French national soccer team played for clubs in several different countries, not just clubs in France. A look at the roster of the Real Madrid team lists players from not only Spain but also Brazil, Germany, and Argentina.

The emerging European sport management system has its roots in the U.S. professional sport league system that appeared in the nineteenth century. The league system in the United States developed when the English club system proved poorly suited to the economic and cultural atmosphere of nineteenth-century United States.

Sport Structures in the United States: Sport Clubs Adapt to a Different Culture

Courtesy of Library of Congress Prints and Photographs Division, FSA-OWI Collection [LCUSF34-055212-D DLC]

In the early 1800s, upper-class sports enthusiasts in the United States attempted to develop sports along the lines of the English club system but had only limited success. The wealthy elite formed clubs throughout the nineteenth century, complete with volunteer management, but these clubs were not able to establish a place in U.S. culture in the same way that clubs had in England and throughout Europe.

Whereas European clubs emphasized sport to attract large and broad memberships, the most prestigious clubs in the United States

were primarily social clubs that did not sponsor sporting events. Athletic clubs, such as the New York Athletic Club, did not gain prestige until late in the century, when the profit-oriented league system had already established a foothold in the cultural landscape of the United States (Gorn & Goldstein, 1993).

Nineteenth-century thoroughbred horse racing in the United States, although occasionally wildly popular, repeatedly fell on hard times. One obstacle to the club system in the United States was the country's lack of an aristocratic tradition equivalent to the one that had given the club system both its means of support and its legitimacy in Europe. Another was the political power of religious fundamentalism, which periodically limited or prohibited gambling (Adelman, 1986).

Out of the shadow of the struggling thoroughbred horse racing scene, a uniquely American sport developed: harness racing. The league structure, which today dominates sport in the United States, grew out of the success and failure of harness racing in the 1830s and 1840s. As such, it is worthwhile understanding this transition between clubs and leagues.

Harness Racing: The First National Pastime and Professional Sport

Nineteenth-century harness racing was the sport of the common person, an early precursor of stock car racing. In the 1820s, the horse and buggy was not just commonplace, but the preferred mode of transportation of a growing middle class. Many early harness races took place on hard-packed city streets, and anyone with a horse and buggy could participate. The sport was more inclusive than thoroughbred horse racing. The horses pulling the buggies were of no particular breeding. During that era, it was relatively inexpensive to own and maintain a horse, and horses that worked and pulled wagons by day raced in the evening (Adelman, 1986).

As the popularity of informal harness races grew, enterprising racing enthusiasts staged races on the oval tracks built for thoroughbred racing. Track owners—whose primary business was suffering from a lack of public enthusiasm for thoroughbred racing—were eager to rent their tracks to harness racers. Promoters began to offer participants purse money raised through modest entry fees and paid track owners rent by charging admission (Adelman, 1986).

The nineteenth-century middle class in the United States, including artisans, shopkeepers, dockworkers, clerks, and the like, was far more likely to participate in this sport than were wealthy merchants. Because harness racing lacked the elitist tradition of horse racing, the public perceived the sport as "its own" and was more willing to pay admission to subsidize the events. Promoters counted on spectator interest, and participation grew. By the 1830s, harness racing surpassed thoroughbred racing as the most popular sport in the United States (Adelman, 1986).

Although harness racing was not always as dramatic as thoroughbred racing, it was a better spectator sport. A traditional horse racing event was a 4-mile race. The races were so grueling that horses raced only once or twice a year. Consequently, it was difficult for individual horses to develop a reputation or following among fans. In contrast, harness racing was a sprint. Horses recovered quickly and could compete almost daily. Promoters offered spectators as many as a dozen races in an afternoon. Horses of any breed could race, ensuring a large field of competitors. These dynamics gave the public more races, excitement, and opportunities to gamble (Adelman, 1986).

The management structure of harness racing was also distinct from that of thoroughbred racing. Track owners and race promoters managed the sport. Unlike members of Jockey Clubs, these entrepreneurs' livelihood depended on gate revenues, so they catered to spectators. Ideally, promoters tried to match the best horses against each other to build spectator interest.

This desire for intense competition, however, created problems for harness racing promoters. Potential contestants often tried to increase their chances of victory by avoiding races with other highly touted trotters. To ensure a high level of competition and "big name" competitors, innovative promoters began to offer the owners of the best and most famous trotters a percentage of the gate (Adelman, 1986).

Unfortunately, this arrangement led some participants and promoters to fix races in an effort to promote and create demand for future races. Highly regarded trotters traded victories in an effort to maintain spectator interest. Harness races were sometimes choreographed dramas—a practice that violated the notion of honesty critical to a sport's success. Once the word got out that some races were fixed, harness racing lost its appeal with the public. Unlike members of the Jockey Club, harness racing promoters and participants lacked the upright, solid reputations to convince the public that their races were legitimate. Ultimately, spectators lost faith in the integrity of the sport, and the race promoters, no matter how honest, lacked the legitimacy to convince the public otherwise. By the start of the Civil War, harness racing had lost its appeal and its audience (Adelman, 1986).

Leagues

Harness racing's popularity and commercial promise led sport enthusiasts and managers to further refine and develop a sport management system that would work in the United States. The result was the profit-oriented league, which baseball organizers pioneered in the 1870s. Baseball was the first sport to successfully employ the league structure.

William Hulbert's National League

At first, baseball was organized according to the club system. Club leaders organized practices, rented field time, and invited other clubs to meet and play. Loosely organized leagues formed, encouraged parity of competition, and regulated competition between social equals. For example, the famous early team known as the Knickerbockers played games in Hoboken, New Jersey, to ensure they competed only against upper-class teams who could afford the ferry ride over and back from New York.

Only the best teams, such as the Cincinnati Red Stockings of 1869–1870, were able to sustain fan interest. The Cincinnati team of 1869 was the first openly all-professional team. The Red Stockings' road trips to play Eastern teams drew thousands of fans and earned enough to pay the team's travel expenses and player salaries. Then, after two seasons of flawless play, the team lost three games at the end of the 1870 season. Despite the Red Stockings' impressive record, they were no longer considered champions, and their popularity fell, along with the team's revenues. The team disbanded prior to the next season (Seymour, 1960).

In the late 1860s and early 1870s, a rift developed along social/class lines. Teams that paid their players a salary were in conflict with teams that did not. The business elite in local communities managed both types of clubs, but there were subtle and growing class and ethnic differences among the participants.

In 1871, a group of professional baseball teams formed the **National Association of Professional Baseball Players** and split off from the amateur club system. Any club willing to pay its elite players could join. This association, like other club sports, still depended on the patronage of its well-off members and consequently lacked stability. Members managed and participated in sporting activities haphazardly, and the break-even financial interests of

individual clubs carried more authority than any association of clubs. It was common for teams to form, fall apart, and re-form within a season (Adelman, 1986; Leifer, 1995; Seymour, 1960).

In 1876, **William Hulbert** took over management of the National Association and renamed the body the **National League of Professional Baseball Players**. Hulbert became known as the "Czar of Baseball" for his strong leadership of the game and his role as a major figure in the development of sport management in the United States. He believed baseball teams would become stable only if they were owned and run like businesses. Teams, like other firms, should compete against one another and not collude (secretly work together), as was the case in harness racing. Hulbert called the owners of the best baseball clubs in the National Association to a meeting in New York City. When they emerged from the meeting, the groundwork had been laid for the new National League. The initial members of the league were from Boston, Chicago, Cincinnati, Hartford, Louisville, New York, Philadelphia, and St. Louis (Abrams, 1998).

Hulbert also understood that unless there were strict rules to ensure honest competition, baseball team owners would be tempted by collusion. For the National League to succeed, authority needed to rest with the league, not with a loose association of teams. Hulbert revamped the management of baseball to center on a league structure and created strong rules to enforce teams' allegiance to each other and to a season (Leifer, 1995; Seymour, 1960).

Learning from the earlier experiences of owners and supporters walking away when a team began to lose money, Hulbert structured the National League to force team owners to take a financial risk. Previously, teams simply stopped playing when they began to lose money, much like a Broadway show which closed when it failed to attract an audience. Hulbert understood how ending a season early to decrease short-term costs eroded the long-term faith of the public. In Hulbert's league, teams were expected to complete their schedules regardless of profit or loss.

Tying team owners to a schedule resulted in costs from fielding a bad team and benefits from having a competitive team. Hulbert understood that fans like to see teams in earnest competition with one another. The public, he knew, would have more faith in a structure in which owners needed to field winning teams to make profits.

Hulbert established the league's credibility by strictly enforcing these rules. In the first year of National League play, two struggling teams, Philadelphia and New York, did not play their final series. Even though the games would not have impacted the final standings, Hulbert banned the two teams from the league (Leifer, 1995; Seymour, 1960; Vincent, 1994). The message was clear: The integrity of the league would not be compromised for the short-term financial interests of owners.

Hulbert also understood that the integrity of baseball would become suspect if the public questioned players' honesty. Baseball became popular at the height of the Victorian period in the United States, a time when large segments of Middle America followed strict cultural conventions. Many people in the United States adhered to religious rules prohibiting gambling and drinking—staples of the sporting subculture. Hulbert needed to create a cultural product that did not offend the sensibilities of the middle and upper classes. To appeal to this large market segment, he prohibited betting at National League ballparks. He also prohibited playing games on Sunday and selling beer at ballparks. The Cincinnati club objected to the no-liquor rule and was ultimately expelled from the National League (*Sportsencyclopedia*, 2002). Hulbert tried to clean up the atmosphere at ballparks further by banning "unwholesome

groups" and activities from the game. He raised ticket prices to decrease the number of working-class patrons and make the games more appealing to the "better" classes (Abrams, 1998).

Players, many of them working-class immigrants, benefited from the widely held Victorian notion that a strong athletic body signaled an equally strong moral character. The National League owners imposed curfews on their players to maintain a clean image, and Hulbert policed the sport with a vengeance. Players caught gambling were banned from the league for life (Leifer, 1995; Seymour, 1960; Vincent, 1994), a rule emphasizing the importance of the appearance of honest effort.

Central to the organization of American Victorian culture were notions of biological distinctions among ethnic and racial groups. The National League, not surprisingly, prohibited African Americans from participating. Although other major and minor leagues had blacks on their rosters in the mid- to late 1880s, by 1888 the ban would extend to all white baseball leagues.

Once the league established a solid structure and the appearance of honest play, Hulbert still needed to create a market for professional baseball. It was relatively easy to attract spectators to championships and other big games between rival clubs, but team owners needed to find a way to attract audiences to regular season games. Hulbert's dilemma was complicated by the fact that many of the independent baseball clubs (not affiliated with his league) fielded superior teams. In the late 1870s, National League teams lost more often than they won in non-League play (Leifer, 1995).

Hulbert's solution was to create the pennant race—a revolutionary idea in 1876. The success of the National League depended on spectators viewing baseball as a series of games, rather than as a single event or a tournament. A genuine pennant race requires fairly even competition. In other words, for the league to be a successful business, even the best teams had to lose a substantial portion of their games (Leifer, 1995).

A pennant race also requires closed leagues. Although local rivalries had been important in the past, Hulbert's league limited membership. A team was either in the league or not. Hulbert kept his league small by limiting it to eight teams. As such, the National League was small enough to ensure that no team was so far out of first place that winning the pennant seemed impossible.

Courtesy of Arthur Rothstein, 1915, Office of War Information, Overseas Picture Division, Library of Congress

The National League structure tied teams' appeal to community pride. The "home team" concept developed out of Hulbert's league rules, which prohibited placing more than one National League team in or near any current National League city. The rules also prohibited teams from playing non-League teams within the same territory as a National League team (Seymour, 1960). Adhering to this prohibition required discipline on the part of team owners, because non-League games, especially against local non-League rivals, generated strong short-term profits. By avoiding "independent" clubs in National League cities, the League promoted the notion that National League teams represented the community exclusively. This type of

fan allegiance was different than the English club loyalty based on membership.

The notion of a team's "territory" persists in the management of major and minor league baseball as well as in all other league sports (e.g., National Basketball Association [NBA], National Football League [NFL], National Hockey League [NHL]). Back in the 1870s and 1880s, independent teams, languishing from the National League's rules on exclusivity and territoriality, moved on to non-League cities and some attempted to create new leagues. Over time, however, spectators increasingly identified the National League teams with both their cities and superior performance (Leifer, 1995).

Other innovations that Hulbert brought to the sport significantly influenced the history and development of sport management. For example, to protect their own teams from being raided by other National League teams during the season, owners agreed to respect one another's contracts with players for one year. Other leagues could pay the National League a fee to participate in this "reservation" system and protect themselves from raids by National League teams. The practice not only helped distribute talent more evenly, but also kept player salaries down. This practice eventually developed into the "reserve system," which included a "reserve clause" in player contracts and a "reserve list" of protected players on each team roster. These rules also limited the movement of players, enhancing the sense of a local team and, in turn, fan loyalty.

The league structure enjoyed a significant boost from newspapers, another rapidly expanding U.S. institution. Although the initial response to the National League by the media was generally unfavorable (Vincent, 1994), newspapers in cities with teams in the League soon warmed to the idea of a pennant race. In the 1870s, most major cities supported a dozen or more newspapers. One effective way to attract readers was to cover local sporting events. Newspapers played up the concept of the hometown team in a pennant race to hold the attention of sports fans between games. Reports on injuries, other teams' records, players' attitudes, and coaching strategies were given considerable coverage before and after games. Presenting baseball in terms of an ongoing pennant race sold newspapers and underscored Hulbert's desire to promote continuing attention to and attendance at regular season games (White, 1996).

National League teams participated in an early form of revenue sharing. Home teams were required to share their gate revenues with the visiting team—a practice that allowed even the least talented teams to receive revenues when they played away from home. Gate sharing redistributed wealth around the National League, enabling teams to compete financially for players (Leifer, 1995).

Leagues Today

The National League's successful strategy seems fairly straightforward when compared with the business strategies used by today's professional sports leagues, which take into account naming rights, licensing agreements, and league-wide television and streaming deals. Nevertheless, the basic structure persists: Successful contemporary commercial sports leagues still depend on consolidated league play with strong centralized control and regulation. League play is, in large part, designed to encourage the fans' faith that teams operate on an equal footing, both on the field and off, and that owners, managers, and players are putting forth an honest effort.

The audience has changed over time, however. The need to see teams as independent firms has faded. The most recent start-up leagues such as the Women's National Basketball Association (WNBA) and Major League Soccer (MLS) have used a single-entity structure, in which each team is owned and operated by the league, though these leagues moved away from this model as they matured. The public's perception of locus of honest effort resides more with the players than it does with the ownership structure.

Not all professional sports are organized in the league structure. Sports such as golf or tennis developed and continue to operate today using a different organizational structure. Sometimes referred to as professional tournament sports, the next section chronicles their development.

Professional Tournament Sports: Mixing Business and Charity

Professional tournament sports such as tennis and golf have their roots in the club system. Private clubs sponsored early tournaments for the benefit of their membership. By the turn of the twentieth century, professionals—usually club employees who taught club members the game—were often excluded from club tournaments. Without wealthy patrons' sponsorship of tournaments, professional athletes in some sports needed alternative financial support if they were going to compete. This was the case with golf.

Professional Golf

Many early golf professionals were European men brought to the United States by country clubs to help design, build, and care for golf courses and teach the finer points of the game to club members. By its very nature, golf was an exclusive game—one that catered to upper-class white males. Although these golfers were technically professionals, they were much different from the tournament professionals of today's Ladies Professional Golf Association (LPGA) and Professional Golfers' Association (PGA). The early golf professionals were club instructors and caddies who made extra money by giving exhibitions. Golf manufacturers hired the best-known professionals as representatives to help publicize the game and their brands of clubs at exhibitions and clinics.

Numerous attempts were made to organize golf leagues prior to the 1930s, but professional leagues failed to capture the public's interest or attract golf professionals. Professionals shunned these risky tournaments in favor of the stability of exhibitions and clinics, and when they competed they vied for prize money they had put up themselves. Professional tournaments did not stabilize until the professionals found someone else—in the form of community and corporate sponsors—to provide the prize money.

One entrepreneurial type of tournament, which ultimately failed, was an attempt to generate a profit from gate revenues for country club owners. In the first half of the twentieth century, spectator attendance was the primary revenue stream for most sports. Following the proven approach of boxing promoters and baseball owners, individual country club owners produced golf events themselves, selling tickets to the events and operating concessions.

The failure of the privately owned tournaments to catch on was the result of how the sport developed in the United States. Individually owned golf courses were rare; most clubs were either member-owned or public courses. Even if there were a consortium of course owners, as was the case in baseball, they did not control the athletes—golfers operated independently. Because these players did not need teams, managers, or promoters, they were difficult to control.

Corcoran's Tournaments

Fred Corcoran, the architect of the professional golf tournament, understood the unique qualities of golf. Golf, he wrote, "operates upside down" in comparison to other sports. "The players have to pay to tee off, and they use facilities

constructed for the use of the amateur owners who, occasionally, agree to open the gates" to professionals (Corcoran, 1965, p. 246).

To manage this "upside down" sport, Corcoran took his lead from Hollywood and advertising executives. Corcoran used athletes and golf tournaments the same way newspapers used news—to sell advertising space to the public. Corcoran never promoted golf strictly as entertainment. The golf tournament, for Corcoran, was the medium through which a celebrity, a local politician, a manufacturer, a charity, a town, or a product gained exposure—in short, he sold the event. As a result, the contemporary professional tournament, unlike other sports operating 50 years ago, was less dependent on ticket sales and more dependent on sponsorship from community groups and corporations.

In 1937, a consortium of golf manufacturers hired Corcoran as tournament director for the men's PGA circuit. He served in that capacity for more than a decade, making arrangements with public and private clubs to host professional tournaments. Then, in 1949, the golf equipment manufacturers hired him again to organize the women's tour (Corcoran, 1965; Hicks, 1956). Corcoran organized the players into associations with rules governing play and eligibility. In essence, the players governed themselves.

One of Corcoran's first contributions to the professional golf tour was the creation of the financially self-sufficient tournament. Prior to 1937, the PGA, through entry fees, had guaranteed to pay the players' purse to entice communities to sponsor tournaments. Corcoran, who had spent a decade organizing amateur tournaments in Massachusetts, understood the potential revenue that a tournament could produce for a community. He was able to convince communities to take responsibility for providing the purse by demonstrating how the revenue generated by 70 professional golfers eating in restaurants and sleeping in hotels would be three times greater than the minimum $3,000 purse (Corcoran, 1965).

Corcoran enhanced the tremendous growth in competitive golf by sharing status with celebrities like actor/singer Bing Crosby. In addition to being a famous movie star and singer, Crosby was a sports entrepreneur associated with horse racing and golf. In 1934, Crosby orchestrated the first celebrity professional and amateur (pro-am) tournament preceding a men's golf tournament to raise money for charity. The combination of a celebrity and a pro playing together on a team in a mock tournament was extremely successful. Amateur golfers, celebrities, and community leaders paid exorbitant fees to participate. Although these funds were directed toward charity, there were also spin-off professional golf benefits. The appearance of celebrities not only enhanced the athletes' status, but also increased attendance, thereby increasing the proceeds for charity and the exposure for professional golf. Since the 1930s, the celebrity pro-am has been the financial core around which most professional golf tournaments have been built (Graffis, 1975).

The financial power of this type of charity event became clear during World War II, when golf was used to raise money for the Red Cross. Under a celebrity pro-am format, Bing Crosby teamed up with movie co-star Bob Hope, professional golfers, and various other celebrities, including Fred Corcoran, to raise millions of dollars for the war effort and the Red Cross (Graffis, 1975). At the end of the war, Corcoran stayed with the pro-am tournament format, using civic pride and charities such as hospitals and youth programs to draw crowds.

Tying professional golf to charity was good business, in addition to being good for the community. Donations to charitable organizations were fully tax deductible. Local business-people not likely to benefit directly from a golf tournament were more easily persuaded to contribute to the tournaments when offered tax deductions as incentives. In addition, a good charity attracted the hundreds of volunteers and essential in-kind donations needed to run a tournament. Further, a charity with broad reach and many volunteers acted as a promotional vehicle for the tournament. Thus, Corcoran transformed a potentially costly, labor-intensive event into a no-cost operation. By appealing to the altruism of a community to host a tournament, Corcoran obtained a tournament site, capital, and event management for no cost.

A consortium of golf equipment manufacturers paid Corcoran's salary to organize the golfers into an association and to help arrange tournaments. Golf manufacturers understood that the cost of retaining player representatives could be reduced by putting a solid tournament circuit in place. Manufacturers could retain player representatives at a fraction of the cost and increase players' values as marketing tools. The better players earned their salaries through prize money. The cost of sponsoring a player on tour was far less than hiring a player full-time as a representative and paying expenses.

It was clear to Corcoran that if manufacturers could use their association with tournaments to sell golf products, then celebrities could use this relationship to add to their status, and local community groups could use the events to raise funds or gain political influence. Tournaments could also be sold as an advertising medium for non-golf-related merchandise. As tournament director of the PGA and the LPGA, Corcoran orchestrated the first non-golf-related corporate sponsorship of professional golf tournaments when he arranged for Palm Beach Clothing to sponsor men's events. A few years later, he orchestrated a transcontinental series of women's tournaments sponsored by Weathervane Ladies Sports Apparel (Corcoran, 1965).

Corcoran's adaptation of Crosby's celebrity tournaments to tournaments funded by advertising for clothing foreshadowed the immense corporate involvement in contemporary professional tournaments. Even so, professional golf was not able to take full advantage of corporate interest in athletes until the late 1950s. Up to that time, the major media wire services, Associated Press and United Press International, followed a policy of using the name of the city or town to distinguish a tournament. They argued that using the name of the corporate sponsor was a cheap way to avoid paying for newspaper advertising. In the late 1950s, however, the newspaper industry reversed its policy and agreed to call tournaments by the name of their corporate sponsors. Thus, by sponsoring a national sporting event, a corporation gained tax-free exposure to a target market in the name of charity (Graffis, 1975). In the end, professional golf, charities, and corporations all benefited from this arrangement.

Tournaments Today

Variations of the tournament structure just described can be found today in golf, tennis, track and field, and multisport events such as triathlons and the Olympic and Paralympic Games. Like Corcoran, today's tour promoters do not sell the event solely as entertainment. Instead, they promote tournaments as a medium through which a person, community, or corporation can buy exposure. Gallery seats, pro-am tournaments, and pre- and post-tournament festivities are the foci of interaction, access to which can be sold. Although communities, politicians, and radio and movie personalities have found tournaments a worthwhile investment, the corporate community has benefited the most handsomely. The golf tournament has evolved into a corporate celebration of itself and its products (Crosset, 1995).

Associations such as the PGA have long been viewed as private groups who set their own rules of eligibility. However, recent challenges to that idea, as seen with Casey Martin's successful attempt to have the PGA accommodate his disability, suggest that these associations cannot be as exclusive as private clubs. In Martin's case, he used the fact that Qualifying School (Q-School) was open to the public as a means of applying the Americans with Disabilities Act public accommodation provisions to force the PGA to allow him to compete using a cart.

In another trend that is pushing tournament management away from nonprofit private associations, today's tournaments are just as likely to be created by marketing agencies or broadcast media as by player associations. For example, the X-Games and the Dew Tour are the products of corporations. The X-Games are owned by ESPN, which is a subsidiary of the Disney Corporation; the Dew Tour is a division of NBC Sports. It is not yet clear how corporate-owned tournaments will affect older associations or if "made-for-TV" tournaments will be able to sustain their legitimacy with the public. Nevertheless, years into the X-Games and Dew Tour–type tours, the public still seems willing to follow them.

The first section of this chapter focused mainly on the historical aspects of professional sports, particularly teams and leagues. Most certainly the sport industry includes many more segments other than these two. This fact becomes obvious simply by looking at the broad range of chapters in this introductory text. Many of the basic tenets covered in this chapter are applicable across other segments as well. To learn more about the historical developments in segments such as intercollegiate athletics, high school and youth sport, recreational sport, and many more areas, the reader can turn to the chapters designed to cover those specific industry segments in-depth. Each chapter has a section devoted to the important historical events for that industry segment.

It is important to note that *how* the story of the growth of the sport industry is told is very much shaped by *who* is telling the story. While the sport industry in the United States was primarily established and maintained by white males, they are not the only people who helped the industry flourish. The next section discusses the inclusion of people of color and women in the sport industry over the years.

Inclusion and Innovators: Heroes and Sheroes of Sport Management

In this first chapter, we presented the history of the development of the sport industry. Throughout this chapter, we mentioned a number of innovative sport managers, and authors in the other chapters throughout this text will mention additional names. A text such as this brings together information across different sport industry segments so that the reader is exposed to as broad a landscape of the industry as possible.

One reason (though obviously not the only one) for studying the history of the sport industry is to provide the reader with a foundation for success. We want you to know about heroes and sheroes from the past so that you might admire, study, and emulate them.

But who are we to tell this story? And whose story gets told? History is typically written by those who win out, and it is usually the story of who won. For years, the mainstream sport industry, like business journalism and academia, has been dominated by the people in the majority—namely, white men. We want to make it very clear that women and people of color have been successfully managing sport for a long time. The accomplishments of marginalized managers of color and women often get incorporated into mainstream sport, but then their work gets forgotten. Without some intention on the part of historians, the story of their accomplishments risks being lost. We believe students—all students—deserve to see

themselves in the stories we tell about ourselves as an industry.

This section introduces a selection of innovative managers and their contributions. We cannot include all the innovators, so we feature a small diverse group from a variety of sports and time periods to give you an idea of how innovative managers have changed sport. Our intent here is to provide the future sport manager with a starting point to recognize and embrace the notion and impact of innovation—a skill that never goes out of style. Perhaps you have heard their names, but perhaps not. Here you will be introduced to the stories of E. B. Henderson, Effa Manley, Billie Jean King, and Mark H. McCormack.

E. B. Henderson may be the most significant sport manager and promoter from the first half of the twentieth century. Other promoters of the time, like Tex Richard, may be more famous, but Henderson may have actually done more to shape sport, especially amateur/college basketball. He was inducted into the Basketball Hall of Fame in 2013 for his contributions.

In 1904, Henderson was introduced to the game of basketball while a student at a Harvard summer training program for physical education teachers. As an African American, when he came home to Washington, D.C., he faced discrimination at the local YMCA. Barred from even watching the game he loved, Henderson set out to organize basketball for African Americans.

In 1906, Henderson formed the first African American athletic conference, the Interscholastic Athletic Association (ISAA). This conference promoted the game of basketball, especially in the geographic area in and between New York City and Washington, D.C. Henderson's organizational skills laid the foundation and set up a structure for league and tournament play for historically black colleges and universities (HBCUs) (Cooper, Cavil, & Cheeks, 2014). It is important to realize that Henderson was organizing black collegiate sport during the same period when historically white schools were struggling to find some footing and the Olympic Games were floundering following the disastrous games in St. Louis. The point is that many of Henderson's management practices and tournament structures predate those of pre-dominantly white organizations and leagues.

Shortly after establishing the ISAA, Henderson founded a youth basketball team at the black YMCA in Washington, D.C. After quickly turning this group into a national champion team, he petitioned Howard University to accept the 12th Y team as its varsity squad. Henderson coached the collegiate team to the 1910–1911 Colored Basketball World's Championship title (Lindsay-Johnson, 2017).

For Henderson, black scholastic sport, col-legiate sport, and amateur sport were more than games. He embraced the notion of the politics of respectability, and saw education, culture, and sportsmanship as venues in which to demonstrate that African Americans should be full members of American society (Henderson, 1911). Cultivating black scholars/athletes was a worthy pursuit in and of itself, but was also a political tactic. An advocate of physical educa-tion and sport, Henderson's love for organizing, writing about, and promoting black basketball (and black sport in general) was driven by an undying passion for racial justice (University of the District of Columbia, 2017). If you appreci-ate Henderson's highly principled approach to sport, you might also admire Branch Rickey (baseball) and Pierre De Coubertin (Olympic Movement) for their embrace of this approach in other areas of the sport industry.

Another African American who left an imprint on the sport industry was a part of Negro League baseball. The Negro Base-ball Leagues transformed major and minor league baseball. All Star games, night games, and between-inning clowning around and

entertainment were a direct result of the innova-tions in Negro Baseball Leagues. The person behind many of these additions to the industry was Effa Manley: Not only did she contribute to the success of Negro League baseball, but she was also one of the first significant modern female sport managers (O'Connor-McDonogh, 2007). As co-owner of the Newark Eagles in the Negro Baseball League from 1936 to 1948, Manley was responsible for the day-to-day operations of the ball club and was active in league management (Berlage, 1994; Luke, 2011). During the Great Depression and during World War II, she ran a successful Negro League team; then, as the sole owner of the Newark Eagles, she won the Negro League championship in 1948.

Manley tussled with Branch Rickey over the method and manner of integration of Major League Baseball (MLB) and Rickey's contention that the Negro Leagues were not organized. The Negro Leagues avoided restrictive con-tracts that reserved players from one year to the next, recognizing that such arrangements were uncomfortably close to a master–slave arrangement. When white teams began signing Negro League players, they did not compensate the Negro League teams for the loss of those players' services, arguing that MLB teams were not obligated to do so because the Negro League players were technically not under contract. Manley fought the MLB owners, insisting that it was necessary to compensate the teams that organized black baseball, honed the skills of some of the most talented ballplayers, and developed an audience for baseball. Ultimately, she received $15,000 compensation from Bill Veeck of the Cleveland Indians after he signed Larry Doby, and thereafter it became standard practice to compensate Negro League team owners when their players joined MLB.

For her contributions to professional baseball, in 2006 Manley became the first and only woman elected to the Baseball Hall of

Fame in Cooperstown, New York (National Baseball Hall of Fame, n.d.). Other women who have been successful sport managers in men's sports include Kim Ng (baseball), Lesa France Kennedy (motorsports), Michele Roberts (basketball), and Val Ackerman (basketball).

On occasion, an athlete becomes an innovative sport manager. As an example, Phil Knight, the founder of Nike, was a runner at the University of Oregon. Only rarely, though, does a superstar athlete become a managerial innovator. Billie Jean King is the exception. While perhaps best remembered for her dominance on the tennis court in the late 1960s and the early 1970s and her victory over Bobby Riggs in the 1973 "Battle of the Sexes," King also transformed tennis off the court. Just consider that King was instrumental in establishing the Women's Tennis Association (WTA) and was a founder of *WomenSports* magazine, World Team Tennis, the Women's Sports Foundation, and the Billie Jean King Leadership Institute, which was established to provide opportunities for inclusive leadership around the world (Lough, 2007; Women's Sports Foundation, 2011, 2017b).

King's executive contributions to sport grew out of her unhappiness with the pay differential between the men's and women's tennis tournaments during the late 1960s and early 1970s. In those years, men were paid four to five times more prize money than women. King, supported by some other players, threatened to form a professional women's tennis circuit if the women's prize money and tournament opportunities did not become more equitable. When the tennis establishment balked at the athletes' demands, in September 1970, King and eight other players (later called the "Original 9"), along with Gladys Heldman, the publisher of *Tennis World* magazine, started a new professional tennis circuit for women (Women's Sports Foundation, 2017a). The first sponsor was Virginia Slims, a cigarette branded for women. By the end of the year, 40 players had joined the Virginia Slims World Championships Series. The Virginia Slims circuit would later grow into the WTA (Women's Sports Foundation, 2017a).

A tireless advocate for women's rights in sport, King also led the charge for other under-represented groups as well, particularly the lesbian/gay/bisexual/transgender (LGBT) community. For her tireless work and innovative thinking devoted to improving the position of women in sport, the annual site of the U.S. Open Grand Slam event was named the USTA (U.S. Tennis Association) Billie Jean King National Tennis Center in her honor. If you admire superstar athletes who left a mark on the management of the game, you might also like to know more about John Montgomery Ward (baseball), Oscar Robertson (basketball), and Edwin Moses (track and field).

While King fought for equity for female tennis players, Mark H. McCormack radically transformed how the sport industry generated revenue. One *Wall Street Journal* sport business writer called McCormack "the man who invented sports" (Futterman, 2016). That may be a bit of an overstatement, but in the 1960s and the 1970s McCormack forced the sport industry, as well as the public, to recognize that athletes were much more than laborers—that is, they had value well beyond the game. McCormack's innovative thinking empowered athletes, grew the economic potential of the games they played, and as a result transformed sport.

McCormack started out representing golfers and tennis players, first by managing their business lives outside of the game, creating sponsorship deals and exhibitions. Later, he began creating events for his athletes. If the golf or tennis circuit did not have enough tournaments in large enough markets, McCormack created them. If the events were not filmed and sold to television, he would do that, too. Because

McCormack represented so many of the finest athletes in those two sports, the events and the television shows he developed drew substantial audiences.

McCormack also realized that old and venerable tournaments like Wimbledon needed rejuvenation. These dated tournaments were still steeped in the tradition of private clubs, and the people managing the events lacked commercial acumen. In 1968, McCormack got the go ahead from the All England Club to sell the film rights to the Wimbledon tournament. Within a few years, he had secured an advertising deal with the razor company Wilkinson Sword. As the film rights generated money for the tournament, prize money increased. Shortly thereafter, the All England Club secured television rights to Wimbledon (Futterman, 2016). McCormack sold the tournament television rights, along with his films, across the globe. Before long, companies wanting to be associated with sport were contacting McCormack to help them find the right sponsorships for their brand. Most famously, McCormack convinced the Swiss watchmaker Rolex to get involved with elite sporting events like sailing's America's Cup (Futterman, 2016).

Through his management company IMG and his production company TWI, McCormack vertically integrated sport. He put the best athletes in the most important and entertaining events. By making those events as big and profitable as possible, McCormack grew the sport industry, transforming the sport business in a fashion that was lucrative for the athletes. "Take care of the athletes," McCormack was fond of saying, "because without them you don't have a game." If you admire the way McCormack innovatively increased revenue and/or empowered athletes, you might also want to find out more about C. C. Pyle (baseball), Marvin Miller (baseball), or Pete Rozelle (football).

The Birth of Sport Management as an Academic Field

As the sport industry evolved, it increasingly took on the business characteristics of other industries. The early sport managers discussed in this chapter came to their sport management positions with some background in sport or some background in business. Very few brought a combination of the two to the workplace. However, to be a successful sport manager in today's industry, preparation in both sport and business is a necessity. The academic field of sport management began to develop in response to this need. How did this field come into existence, and what makes it unique?

Sport clubs, leagues, and tournaments are three of the more prevalent structures currently used to manage, govern, and organize sport. Management systems, including amateur bodies such as the National Collegiate Athletic Association (NCAA) and U.S. Soccer, or professional organizations such as the NBA or the Professional Bull Riders, employ some variation of these structures to produce sporting events. But contemporary sport management is far more complex than its historical antecedents. Furthermore, the growing popularity of newer and emerging sports such as eSports as well as the increasing power of global media, particularly social media, encourage the evolution of new management structures.

The continuing growth of the sport industry and its importance to numerous sponsors and institutions created demand for the systematic study of sport management practices. Since the late 1960s, the academic field of sport management has focused on the unique issues facing the people who conduct the business of sport.

As the sport management profession began to grow and prosper, it became apparent that although similarities existed between running a general business and running a sport organization, the sport industry presented its own unique intricacies and variations. Early on, sport managers learned from hands-on experiences gained in the industry. As the sport industry became more complex, however, the need to train sport managers in a more formal fashion became apparent. The formal study of sport management emerged from this need.

The concept of a sport management curriculum is generally credited to two people: **James G. Mason**, a physical educator at the University of Miami–Florida, and **Walter O'Malley** of the Brooklyn (now Los Angeles) Dodgers, who discussed the idea in 1957 (Mason, Higgins, & Owen, 1981). The first master's program in sport management was established at **Ohio University** in 1966 and was based on Mason's and O'Malley's ideas (Parkhouse & Pitts, 2001). Shortly after the Ohio University graduate program began, Biscayne College (now St. Thomas University) and St. John's University founded undergraduate sport management programs (Parkhouse & Pitts, 2001). The University of Massachusetts–Amherst started the second master's program in 1971.

The number of colleges and universities in the United States offering sport management majors grew rapidly. By 1985, the National Association for Sport and Physical Education (NASPE) indicated there were more than 40 undergraduate programs, 32 graduate programs, and 11 programs at both levels offering sport management degrees. As of this writing, there are currently 410 bachelor's, 235 master's, and 33 PhD programs in the United States (North American Society for Sport Management, n.d.). Just over a dozen Canadian universities offer programs as well. Programs across the United States and Canada take a variety of forms, such as traditional face-to-face classes and totally online courses. Programs are also housed in different departments or colleges—for example, in Schools of Business, Colleges of Education and Human Development, Schools of Tourism and Hospitality, and Schools of Kinesiology—and some are freestanding departments on their own. The growth of sport management as an academic field was prompted by the sport industry's need for well-trained managers, but it also was influenced by universities' and colleges' need to attract students. Some schools wishing to increase enrollments in a highly competitive market added sport management programs to their curricula in the 1980s.

Given the rapid growth of the academic field, concern developed among sport management educators over what constituted a solid sport management curriculum capable of producing students qualified to work as managers in the sport industry. The first group of scholars to examine this issue formed an organization called the Sport Management Arts and Science Society (SMARTS), which was initiated by the faculty at the University of Massachusetts–Amherst. This group laid the groundwork for the present scholarly organization, the **North American Society for Sport Management (NASSM)** (Parkhouse & Pitts, 2001).

The purpose of NASSM is "to promote, stimulate, and encourage study, research, scholarly writing, and professional development in the area of sport management," both in the theoretical and applied aspects (NASSM, n.d., para. 2). In the past, NASSM and NASPE monitored sport management curricula through the Sport Management Program Review Council (SMPRC). Currently the movement toward program accreditation is under way via the **Commission on Sport Management Accreditation (COSMA)**. COSMA is "a specialized accrediting body whose purpose is to promote and recognize excellence in sport management education in colleges and universities at the baccalaureate and graduate levels through specialized accreditation"

management developed as an academic field to meet this demand. To maintain quality control in this rapidly-changing field of study, the COSMA curriculum guidelines have been established. As the sport industry continues to evolve globally, the academic field of sport management will evolve as well to produce the future leaders in the industry.

Case Study 1-1

Learning from the Past, Looking to the Future

What can we learn from historical investigations of today's sport organizations? For starters, we most certainly can learn to avoid the mistakes that sport managers made in the past. Granted, sport managers were products of their times, and often, those times were neither inclusive nor forward thinking. In general, the sport industry has been slow to evolve and resistant to change and modernization. As this chapter pointed out, while there have been a few forward-thinking innovators such as Mark H. McCormack, those individuals are exceptional.

The early business practices of professional sports leagues often relied on the guidance of people who were former players or coaches rather than people with strong business-based leadership experience. In addition, sport organizations have lagged behind in having a diverse front office workforce that reflects not just the athletes who compete, but greater society in general.

This chapter described the development of several different sport systems, but there was a primary focus on the development of professional baseball, which produced North America's first professional sports league, the National League. For purposes of this case study, choose one of the other major North American professional sports leagues (the NBA, the NFL, or the NHL) and answer the questions that follow.

Questions for Discussion

1. Who were the people who played strategic roles in the formation of the league you chose, and why were they important?

2. What did the early structure of the league look like? The number of teams? Which cities? How did the league grow into the powerhouse it is today?

3. MLB was slow to integrate in modern times, with Jackie Robinson breaking the color barrier in modern professional baseball when he signed with the Brooklyn Dodgers in 1947. What did the process of integrating African Americans into the league you chose look like, and how did it progress?

4. If you were the commissioner of the league you chose, which two changes would you make to improve the business operations of the league and why would you make them?

5. Out of the four major North American professional sports leagues today, which one do you think has learned the most from its history? Explain your answer.

Key Terms

clubs, Commission on Sport Management Accreditation (COSMA), Fred Corcoran, James G. Mason, leagues, modern Olympic Games, National Association of Professional Baseball Players, National League of Professional Baseball Players, North American Society for Sport Management (NASSM), Ohio University, Pierre de Coubertin, professional tournaments, sport management structures, Walter O'Malley, William Hulbert

References

Abrams, R. (1998). *Legal bases: Baseball and the law.* Philadelphia, PA: Temple University Press.

Adelman, M. (1986). *A sporting time: New York City and the rise of modern athletics, 1820–70.* Urbana, IL: University of Illinois Press.

Berlage, G. I. (1994). *Women in baseball: The forgotten history.* Westport, CT: Praeger.

Commission on Sport Management Accreditation (COSMA). (2015). Home. Retrieved from http://www.cosmaweb.org/

Cooper, J. N., Cavil, J. K., & Cheeks, G. (2014). The state of intercollegiate athletics at historically black colleges and universities (HBCUs): Past, present, and persistence. *Journal of Issues in Intercollegiate Athletics, 7,* 307–332.

Corcoran, F. (1965). *Unplayable lies.* New York, NY: Meredith Press.

Crosset, T. W. (1995). *Outsiders in the clubhouse: The world of women's professional golf.* Albany, NY: SUNY Press.

Futterman, M. (2016). Players: *The story of sports and money, and the visionaries who fought to create a revolution.* New York, NY: Simon and Schuster.

Gorn, E., & Goldstein, W. (1993). *A brief history of American sport.* New York, NY: Wang and Hill.

Graffis, H. (1975). *The PGA: The official history of the Professional Golfers' Association of America.* New York, NY: Crowell.

Henderson, E. B. (1911). The colored college athlete. *Crisis, 2*(3), 115–118.

Henriches, T. (1991). *Disputed pleasures: Sport and society in preindustrial England.* New York, NY: Greenwood Press.

Hicks, B. (1956). Personal correspondence, LPGA Archives.

King, A. (1997). New directors, customers and fans: The transformation of English football in the 1990s. *Sociology of Sport Journal, 14,* 224–240.

Leifer, E. M. (1995). *Making the majors: The transformation of team sports in America.* Cambridge, MA: Harvard University Press.

Lindsay-Johnson, B. (2017). Edwin B. Henderson: Grandfather of black basketball. Retrieved from http://truthbetold.news/2017/03/edwin-b-henderson-grandfather-of-black-basketball/

Lough, N. (2007). Women in sport-related business. In M. A. Hums, G. G. Bower, & H. Grappendorf (Eds.), *Women as leaders in sport: Impact and influence* (pp. 191–206). Reston, VA: National Association for Girls and Women in Sport.

Luke, B. (2011). *The most famous woman in baseball: Effa Manley and the Negro Leagues.* Washington, DC: Potomac Books.

Mandell, R. (1984). *Sport: A cultural history.* New York, NY: Columbia University Press.

Mason, J. G., Higgins, C., & Owen, J. (1981, January). Sport administration education 15 years later. *Athletic Purchasing and Facilities,* 44–45.

Ministry of Culture–General Secretariat for Sports. (1998). *Greek athletics: A historical overview.* Athens, Greece: Author.

National Baseball Hall of Fame. (n.d.). Effa Manley. Retrieved from https://baseballhall.org/hall-of-famers/manley-effa

North American Society for Sport Management (NASSM). (n.d.). Purpose and history. Retrieved from http://www.nassm.com/NASSM/Purpose

O'Connor-McDonogh, M. (2007). Professional sport. In M. A. Hums, G. G. Bower, & H. Grappendorf, *Women as leaders in sport: Impact and influence* (pp. 233–250). Reston, VA: National Association for Girls and Women in Sport.

Parkhouse, B. L., & Pitts, B. G. (2001). Definition, evolution, and curriculum. In B. L. Parkhouse (Ed.), *The management of sport: Its foundation and application* (3rd ed., pp. 2–14). New York, NY: McGraw-Hill.

Seymour, H. (1960). *Baseball: The early years.* Oxford, UK: Oxford University Press.

Sportsencyclopedia. (2002). William Hulbert (1877–1882). Retrieved from http://www.sportsencyclopedia.com/mlb/nl/hulbert.html

University of the District of Columbia. (2017). UDC: We are Black history: Dr. Edwin Bancroft Henderson. Retrieved from https://www.udc.edu/2017/02/04/udc-we-are-black-history-edwin-bancroft-henderson/

Vamplew, W. (1989). *Pay up and play the game: Professional sport in Britain, 1875–1914.* Cambridge, UK: Cambridge University Press.

Vincent, T. (1994). *The rise and fall of American sport.* Lincoln, NE: Nebraska University Press.

White, G. E. (1996). *Creating the national pastime: Baseball transforms itself, 1903–1953.* Princeton, NJ: Princeton University Press.

Williams, J. (1989) Cricket. In T. Mason (Ed.), *Sport in Britain: A social history* (pp. 116–145). Cambridge, UK: Cambridge University Press.

Women's Sports Foundation. (2011). Billie Jean King. Retrieved from http://www.womenssportsfoundation.org/home/about-us/people/founder

Women's Sports Foundation. (2017a). The "Original 9." Retrieved from https://www.womenssportsfoundation.org/education/the-original-9/

Women's Sports Foundation. (2017b). WSF founder Billie Jean King announces launch of the Billie Jean King Leadership Institute. Retrieved from https://www.womenssportsfoundation.org/sports/wsf-founder-billie-jean-king-announces-launch-of-the-billie-jean-king-leadership-institute/

World Association of Sport Management (WASM). (n.d.). About. Retrieved from http://2012gsms.sport.au.edu.tw/wasmweb/page/about.html

You Can Play Project. (2013). Mission statement. Retrieved from http://youcanplayproject.org/pages/mission-statement

Young, D. (1996). *The Modern Olympics: A struggle for revival.* Baltimore, MD: Johns Hopkins University Press.

SPORT MANAGEMENT TIME LINE

BC 776	First ancient Olympic Games
AD 393	Last ancient Olympic Games
1750	Establishment of Jockey Club in Newmarket
1851	First America's Cup (sailing)
1869	Cincinnati Red Stockings become first professional baseball club
1871	National Association of Professional Baseball Players founded
1875	First running of Kentucky Derby (horse racing)
1876	National League of Professional Baseball Players established
1892	Basketball invented
1894	International Olympic Committee founded
1896	First modern Olympic Games in Athens, Greece
1900	Women first compete in Olympic Games
1903	First Tour de France
1904	Fédération Internationale de Football Association (FIFA) founded
1906	Intercollegiate Athletic Association of the United States issues first constitution/bylaws
1910	Intercollegiate Athletic Association of the United States changes name to National Collegiate Athletic Association (NCAA)

© Corbis/age fotostock

(continues)

SPORT MANAGEMENT TIME LINE (*continued*)

1911	First Indianapolis 500
1912	International Association of Athletics Federation (IAAF) began
1916	First Professional Golf Association (PGA) Championship
1917	National Hockey League (NHL) established
1920	National Football League (NFL) began/National Federation of State High School Associations (NFSHSA) founded
1924	First Winter Olympic Games in Chamonix, France/International Association of Assembly Managers (IAAM) established
1930	First FIFA World Cup (soccer) in Uruguay/First Commonwealth Games
1933	First NFL Championship
1939	First NCAA basketball tournament/Baseball Hall of Fame inducts first class
1943	First women's professional baseball league (All-American Girls Professional Baseball League)
1946	National Basketball Association (NBA) (originally known as Basketball Association of America) established
1947	Jackie Robinson integrates Major League Baseball (MLB)
1950	First Formula One Championship (F1)/Ladies Professional Golf Association (LPGA) founded/National Intramural-Recreational Sports Association (NIRSA) began
1951	First Asian Games/Bill Veeck sent Eddie Gaedel up to bat
1959	First Daytona 500
1960	First Summer Paralympic Games in Rome, Italy/Arnold Palmer signed as the International Management Group's (IMG) first client
1961	International Olympic Academy officially inaugurated in Olympia, Greece
1966	Marvin Miller appointed Executive Director of Major League Baseball Players Association (MLBPA)
1967	First Super Bowl
1971	Nike Swoosh designed by Carolyn Davidson
1972	Title IX passed
1974	UCLA men's basketball team loses for the first time in 88 games, setting the longest win streak in NCAA college basketball history/Women's Sports Foundation founded by Billie Jean King
1975	Arbitrator declares MLB players Andy Messersmith and Dave McNally free agents
1976	First Winter Paralympic Games in Örnsköldsvik, Sweden
1978	First Ironman Triathlon
1982	First NCAA women's basketball tournament
1985	North American Society for Sport Management (NASSM) established/First Air Jordan shoes debut at retail/The Olympic Partner (TOP) Program created
1988	The International Olympic Committee (IOC) decided to make all professional athletes eligible for the Olympics, subject to the approval of the International Federations
1990	Americans with Disabilities Act signed into law
1991	First FIFA Women's World Cup
1992	NBA players first played in the Summer Olympic Games

SPORT MANAGEMENT TIME LINE (*continued*)

1994	NFL salary cap came into effect
1995	European Court of Justice ruled clubs restrained trade opening the transfer market in European football
1996	Women's National Basketball Association (WNBA) founded
1998	NHL players first competed in the Winter Olympic Games/First college football Bowl Championship Series (BCS) games played
1999	World Anti-Doping Agency (WADA) established
2001	Beijing, China awarded Olympic and Paralympic Games for 2008/U.S. Supreme Court ruled golfer Casey Martin allowed to use a cart in PGA events
2003	Nike acquires Converse
2004	William Perez succeeds Phil Knight as President and CEO of Nike/Athens Organizing Committee (ATHOC) becomes first Organizing Committee for the Olympic Games to jointly manage both Summer Olympic and Paralympic Games/Nextel takes over sponsorship of NASCAR's Winston Cup
2005	Under Armour Inc. makes its debut as a publicly traded company/Adidas acquires Reebok/NHL labor problems cause first postponement of an entire major professional league season as NHL suspends operations for 2004–2005 season/ MLB Players Association and owners announce new drug testing agreement including suspensions and release of player names/United Nations designates 2005 as the International Year of Sport and Physical Education
2006	Germany hosts successful World Cup, featuring a "Say No to Racism" campaign/ First World Baseball Classic held
2007	Michael Vick pleads guilty to leading a dog fighting ring in Virginia, is sentenced to 23 months in prison/Barry Bonds becomes new MLB home run king amid steroid allegations
2008	Beijing, China hosts the Summer Olympic Games/ /Final year for old Yankee Stadium
2009	Rio de Janeiro, Brazil awarded 2016 Summer Olympic Games, marking the first time the Games will be held in South America/Tiger Woods' infidelity scandal breaks, beginning an avalanche of lost sponsorships and damaged image
2010	NCAA conference realignment: Big 10, Big 12, and Pac-10/South Africa hosts first World Cup on African continent/The University of Connecticut women's basketball team surpasses UCLA's NCAA basketball 88 game win streak, eventually falling after winning 90 straight games/LeBron James announces "The Decision" to leave Cleveland to play with the Miami Heat
2011	Reebok rebrands its logo for the company's second time in history, simultaneously signing a 10-year deal as the main sponsor of the CrossFit Games/Former Pennsylvania State University Assistant Football Coach Jerry Sandusky child abuse scandal comes to light
2012	London Olympic Games marked the first Games where every competing nation was represented by at least one female athlete/Lance Armstrong's seven Tour de France victories erased amid doping scandal/Legendary women's college basketball coach Pat Summitt retires after revealing a diagnosis of early-onset Alzheimer's disease/For the first time in its 80-year history, Augusta National Golf Club allows female members

(*continues*)

SPORT MANAGEMENT TIME LINE (*continued*)

2013   A terrorist attack at the Boston Marathon finish line kills three and injures hundreds/ EA Sports discontinues college sports video games in the midst of lawsuits brought forward by athletes represented on the video games alleging the NCAA and EA Sports were making profit off their likeness without permission or compensation

2014   The NCAA votes to grant autonomy to Power Five conferences: The ACC, Big 12, Big Ten, SEC, and Pac-12/The IOC and United Nations sign historic agreement aimed at strengthening collaboration between the two organizations on the highest level/IOC release Agenda 2020, a strategic roadmap for the future of the Olympic Movement

2015   LeBron James signs new "lifetime" Nike deal worth a reported $1 billion, the largest single athlete guaranteed deal in company history/Under Armour signs sponsorship extension with Steph Curry/The Ohio State University wins the first ever College Football Playoff/USA Women's Soccer wins 2015 World Cup, its third overall

2016   Russian doping scandal results in International Olympic Committee banning numerous athletes from the Rio Summer Olympic Games/International Paralympic Committee issues total ban on all Russian athletes at Rio Summer Paralympic Games/ Michael Phelps wins five gold medals in Rio, bringing his career gold medal total to 23 (28 total medals), solidifying him as the most decorated Olympian of all time/NBA and NBPA sign new collective bargaining agreement/ESPN launches The Undefeated, the premier platform for exploring the intersection of sport, race, and culture

2017   eSports annual revenues projected at $465 million/NBA plays All-Star Game in Atlanta, Georgia rather than Charlotte due to North Carolina's passage of discriminatory anti-LGBTQ legislation known as House Bill 2 (HB2)/IOC agrees to simultaneously award two Olympic/Paralympic Summer Games (2024 and 2028) breaking tradition of awarding one Games seven years in advance

© Corbis/age fotostock

Chapter 2

Carol A. Barr and
Mary A. Hums

Management Principles Applied to Sport Management

Learning Objectives

Upon completion of this chapter, students should be able to:

1. Demonstrate how knowledge of basic management skills is critical to the success of a sport organization.

2. Assess the role that people play in the success of a sport organization.

3. Compare and contrast the historical phases of management theory from scientific management to the human relations movement through organizational behavior.

4. Differentiate between the four functional areas of management: planning, organizing, leading, and evaluating.

5. Demonstrate understanding of the basic management skills needed to be a successful sport manager, include communicating verbally and in writing, managing diversity, managing technology, making decisions, understanding organizational politics, managing change, motivating employees, and taking initiative.

6. Develop a plan to stay abreast of trends occurring in the sport industry that are of concern to managers, such as workplace diversity, emerging technologies, and issues unique to international sport management.

7. Assess new and emerging theories of management such as empowerment and emotional intelligence.

8. Analyze the role that social responsibility plays in the management of sport organizations.

Introduction

It has been said that sport today is too much of a game to be a business and too much of a business to be a game. The sport industry in the United States is growing at an incredible rate. Current estimates by *Forbes* magazine of the value of individual professional team sport franchises list the average National Football League (NFL) team's value at $2.38 billion, the average Major League Baseball (MLB) franchise's value at $1.53 billion, the average value of the top 20 professional soccer teams at $1.46 billion, the average National Basketball Association (NBA) franchise's value at $1.35 billion, and the average National Hockey League (NHL) franchise's value at $517 million (Ozanian, 2017). In 2010, the National Collegiate Athletic Association (NCAA) reached a 14-year, nearly $11 billion agreement with CBS and Turner Sports for television rights to the 68-team NCAA men's basketball tournament. In 2016, that deal was extended for eight more years, through 2032, for an additional $8.8 billion (Sherman, 2016). The NFL makes more than $7 billion per year from the NFL Sunday Ticket and the NFC, AFC, Monday Night Football, and Thursday Night Football television packages with CBS, NBC, Fox, DirecTV, and ESPN/ABC (Travis, 2017). The health and sports club industry reported industry revenues worldwide in 2015 totaling $81 billion, as more than 187,000 clubs served some 151 million members (International Health, Racquet, and Sportsclub Association, 2017). Clearly, the sport industry has shifted toward a more business-focused orientation.

While keeping the financial scope of the sport industry in mind, it is important to note that in whatever segment of the sport industry they work, sport managers need to be able to organize and work with the most important asset in their organization—people. This chapter on management will help the future sport manager recognize how essential utilization of this most important asset is critical to the success of a sport organization. A manager in a sport organization can go by many different titles: athletic director, general manager, director of marketing, coach, health club manager, ski resort operator, social media manager, and so on. No matter the title, every sport manager needs to understand the basics of being a manager in the twenty-first century, while also learning about the complexities of the management function applied to the role that the manager is in. For example, managing an arena may involve complexities and approaches that are quite different from those required to manage a marketing department, although the overarching principles of management can still be applied. The purpose of this chapter is to introduce the reader to basic management knowledge areas and skills that sport managers can apply in any segment of the industry.

Definition and History of Management Principles

Management has been defined in a number of different ways, but common elements of these various definitions include (1) goals/objectives to be achieved (2) with limited resources and (3) with and through people (Chelladurai, 2009). The goal of managerial work and the role the manager plays within an organization is to get workers to perform in a way that will lead to meeting organizational goals and success in an efficient and cost-effective manner. The management process includes knowledge areas such as planning, organizing, leading, and evaluating. These knowledge areas are discussed in the next section of this chapter.

The development of management theory has gone through a number of distinct phases. Two of the earlier phases were scientific management and the human relations movement. Frederick Taylor was one of the first true pioneers of management theory. The publication of Taylor's 1911 book, *The Principles of*

(COSMA, 2015, para. 1). The first programs were accredited in 2010 and, as of this writing, 48 programs are COSMA accredited at one or more levels (undergraduate, master's, PhD).

Sport management professional organizations also exist in a number of nations outside North America. The recently formed World Association of Sport Management (WASM) includes the European Association of Sport Management (EASM), the Sport Management Association of Australia and New Zealand (SMAANZ), the Asian Association for Sport Management, the Latin American Organization of Sport Management, and the African Sport Management Association (ASMA). WASM's mission "is to facilitate sport management research, teaching, and learning excellence and professional practice" (WASM, n.d., para. 4). As sport management becomes more global in nature, universities implementing successful country-specific curricula outside North America are producing successful sport managers as well. Universities in Belgium, England, Germany, Greece, Ireland, Spain, and the Netherlands, for example, are preparing future sport managers. Programs are also thriving in Japan, and the continent of Africa is beginning to open up as well. More sport management programs are infusing study abroad programs into the curriculum. Via partnership agreements, George Washington University students had the opportunity to work at the 2018 Winter Olympic Games in PyeongChang, South Korea, while University of Louisville students worked at the 2016 European Athletics Championships in Amsterdam and the 2017 World Games in Wroclaw, Poland. Depending on program requirements, sport management students also have the opportunity to do an internship in a different country.

The value of international education in the sport industry cannot be overstated. Future sport managers need to realize that unless they embrace this global industry and a connected world, their sport organizations are destined to fall behind or fail. As the sport industry evolves, sport management curricula will continue to change to meet the needs of this global industry.

Summary

It is impossible to cover the complex history of sport management thoroughly in one chapter. This chapter discussed the historical origins of three basic sport management structures: clubs, leagues, and tournaments. Sport management structures that developed over the past 150 or so years organized sporting events in different ways to meet the specific needs of participants, spectators, and sponsors at particular points in history. The club structure, the league structure, and the tournament structure each arose in response to changes in broad social structures and addressed specific issues within a segment of the sport industry. The evolution of each of these three management structures illustrates that industry professionals need to be creative in the ways they manage sports.

Many innovators and contributors to the management of sport can be cited, including such historic figures as John Montgomery Ward, Albert Spalding, Judge Kennesaw Mountain Landis, Effa Manly, and Marvin Miller in baseball. Other notable sport managers include Peter Ueberroth in the Olympic Games, E. B. Henderson and David Stern in basketball, Pete Rozelle and Paul Tagliabue in football, Gary Bettman in hockey, Billie Jean King in tennis, Roone Arledge in sport broadcasting, and agents C. C. Pyle and Mark McCormack. These people, along with many others, have contributed to making sport one of the most popular forms of entertainment.

The three basic management structures (clubs, leagues, and tournaments) are still found in contemporary sport, but these structures now operate within highly complex organizational systems. As a result, the sport industry demands well-trained managers. Sport

Scientific Management, laid the foundation for the **scientific management** movement (sometimes referred to as "Taylorism") in the early 1900s (Taylor, 2002). Taylor worked as an industrial engineer at a steel company and was concerned with the way workers performed their jobs. He believed that through scientific study of the specific motions that make up a total job, a more rational and efficient method of performing that job could be developed. In other words, workers should not be doing the same job in different ways because there exists one "best way" to perform a job efficiently. In Taylor's view, the manager could get workers to perform the job this "best way" by offering them economic rewards.

The second major phase in management theory is known as the **human relations movement**. From 1927 to 1932, Elton Mayo was part of the team that conducted the Hawthorne studies at Western Electric's Chicago plant. In the Hawthorne studies, the workers' motivations were studied by examining how changes in working conditions affected output. Mayo found that social factors in the workplace were important, and job satisfaction and output depended more on cooperation and a feeling of worth than on physical working conditions (Mayo, 2002). The human relations movement was also popularized by the work and writings of Mary Parker Follett. Follett was a pioneer as a female management consultant in the male-dominated industrial world of the 1920s. Follett saw workers as complex combinations of attitudes, beliefs, and needs. She believed effective motivational management existed in partnership and cooperation and that the ability to persuade people was far more beneficial to everyone than hierarchical control and competition (Follett, 2002). The human relations movement was significant in that it transformed the focus of management thinking to the behavior of people and the human components in the

workplace, rather than the scientific approach to performing a task.

Today, it is common to view the study of human behavior within organizations as a combination of the scientific management and human relations approaches. **Organizational behavior** is characteristic of the modern approach to management. The field of organizational behavior is involved with the study and application of the human side of management and organizations (Luthans, 2005). Organizations have undergone numerous changes over the past decades, including downsizing to address economic recessions, globalization, installation and use of information technology, and embracing of an increasingly diverse workforce. Managers have been preoccupied with restructuring their organizations to improve productivity and meet the competitive challenges created by organizational changes. Through all the organizational changes and evolution of management thought and practices, one thing remains clear: A lasting competitive advantage for organizations comes through human resources and how they are managed (Luthans, 2005). Current management theory stresses the concepts of employee involvement, employee empowerment, and managers' concern with the human component of employees. Topics explored within organizational behavior research include communication, decision making, leadership, and motivation, among others. However, the essence of organizations is productivity, and thus managers need to be concerned with getting the job done.

In looking at the study of management theory, it is evident that the approaches to management have moved from the simple to the complex, from a job orientation to a people (worker) orientation, from the manager as a dictator and giver of orders to the manager as a facilitator and team member. Human beings, though, are complex and sometimes illogical, so no single method of management can guarantee success. Take, for example, successful football coaches Bill Belichick and Pete Carroll. Both amass wins and championships, yet each uses a dramatically different management style. The role of managers can be challenging as they try to assess the needs of their employees and utilize appropriate skills to meet these needs while also getting the job done.

© Jupiterimages/Comstock/Thinkstock

Functional Areas

Sport managers must perform in a number of functional areas and execute various activities to fulfill the demands of their jobs. Some of the functional areas used to describe what managers do include planning, organizing, leading, and evaluating (Chelladurai, 2009). Although these functional areas may be helpful in providing a general idea about what a manager does, these terms and their descriptions do not provide a comprehensive list of the manager's tasks and roles. Organizations are constantly evolving, as are managers and the activities they perform. The functional areas emphasized here describe an overall picture of what a manager does, but keep in mind it is impossible to reduce a manager's activities to the level of a robot following a set pattern of activities.

Planning

The **planning** function includes defining organizational goals and determining the appropriate means by which to achieve these

desired goals (Gibson, 2006). Planning should always be the first step in carrying out managerial functions. The planning function is often referred to as strategic planning—a term used by many organizations to describe the drafting and execution of their planning process. Planning involves setting a course of action for the sport organization (VanderZwaag, 1998). Based on VanderZwaag's (1984) model, Hums and MacLean (in press) define the planning process as establishing organizational vision statements, mission statements, goals, objectives, tactics, roles, and evaluation. It is important to keep in mind that the planning process is continuous. Organizational plans should change and evolve—they should not be viewed as set in stone. In case of problems or if situations arise that cause organizational goals to change, the sport manager must be ready to adjust or change the organization's plans to make them more appropriate for what the organization is trying to accomplish.

The planning process consists of both short- and long-term planning. Short-term planning involves goals the organization wants to accomplish soon—say, within the next couple of months to a year. For example, an athletic shoe company may want to order enough inventory of a particular type of shoe so that its sales representatives can stock the vendors with enough shoes to meet consumer demands for the upcoming year. Long-term planning involves goals the organization may want to try to reach over a longer period of time, perhaps five to ten years into the future. That same shoe company may have long-term goals of becoming the number one athletic shoe company in the nation within five years, so the company's long-term planning will include activities the company will participate in to try to reach that goal. Managers must participate in both short- and long-term planning.

The planning process also includes ongoing and unique plans. An example of an ongoing plan would be a parking lot plan for parking at every university home football game. A unique plan might involve use of that same parking lot as a staging area for emergency vehicles if the city were hit by an unexpected natural disaster such as a flood or tornado.

Organizing

After planning, the sport manager next undertakes the **organizing** function. The organizing function begins the process of putting plans into action. As part of the organizing function, the manager determines which types of jobs need to be performed and who will be responsible for doing these jobs.

An organizational chart is developed to graphically illustrate which jobs must be performed (**Figure 2-1**). It shows the various positions within an organization as well as the reporting schemes for these positions.

In addition, an organizational chart may contain information about the people filling the various positions. This chart visually shows the various roles and reporting lines within the organization, with position descriptions providing information about the activities and responsibilities of these various positions. For example, the position description for the Assistant Athletic Director for Marketing may include soliciting corporate sponsors, promoting teams or special events, overseeing the department's social media program, and selling stadium signage. Position qualifications must also be developed. They define what type of experience and skill set the person filling a particular position needs. These qualifications will depend on the organizational chart, the responsibilities of a particular position, and the authority given to a particular position. Thus, the position qualifications for the

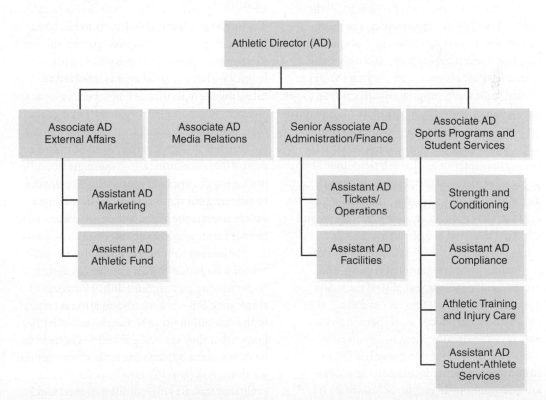

Figure 2-1 Athletic Department Organizational Chart

Assistant Athletic Director for Marketing may include a master's degree, three to five years of athletic department experience, and good written and oral communication skills.

The need for a well-developed and well-communicated organizational chart cannot be overemphasized. On numerous occasions, organizations may find that problems occur because one person does not know what another person in the organization is doing. The organizational chart can be extremely beneficial in showing employees the various positions within the organization, who fills those positions, the responsibilities of each position, and who reports to whom.

Once the organizational chart has been developed and the position qualifications established, staffing can take place. Staffing determines who will be responsible for the jobs in the organizational chart. Staffing involves the effective recruitment and selection of people to fill the positions within an organization. The position qualifications developed during the organizing function come into play here. Recruiting and selecting an employee means finding the right person, with the appropriate qualifications, to get the job done. To find that person, managers must do their homework and go through the proper steps to really get to know and understand the people they interview. These steps include appropriate advertising of the position, reviewing completed applications, choosing qualified people for the interview process, checking references, and selecting the "best fit" person for the job.

In addition to the selection process, staffing includes the orientation, training, and professional development of staff members (Quarterman & Li, 1998; VanderZwaag, 1984). Orientation introduces a new person to the nature of the organization, to organizational goals and policies, and to his or her fellow employees. Training focuses on the actual job and teaching an employee how to do it.

For example, new ushers at a sport venue may be involved in a half-day training seminar to learn about seating arrangements, locations of first aid stations and uniformed security, and procedures for checking in and out of work. Professional development involves a commitment to improving employees' knowledge, skills, and attitudes, allowing them the opportunity to grow and become better employees. Sending athletic department employees to a week-long seminar on using social media is one example of how professional development can occur. Unfortunately, many sport managers are so busy trying to accomplish their day-to-day work that they ignore the development of their employees. Neglecting professional development is unwise, however, as professional development can help lead to more efficient and productive workers.

Leading

The **leading** or leadership function has often been referred to as the "action" part of the management process. This is where it all happens. The sport manager is involved in directing the activities of employees as he or she attempts to accomplish organizational goals. In carrying out the leading function, the manager participates in a variety of activities, including delegating, communicating, managing conflict, managing change, and motivating employees. In carrying out these activities, the manager utilizes numerous skills, which are discussed in the next section of this chapter.

The leading function begins with the process of **delegation**, which involves assigning responsibility and accountability for results to employees. Effective communication is critical to the delegation process. Employees need to know what they are being asked to do, need to be assigned the appropriate authority to get the job done, and need to know how they will be evaluated for carrying out the assigned tasks.

The importance of delegation cannot be overstated, yet it is one of the most difficult skills for new managers to acquire. A person's first inclination is usually to "do it myself" so that a task will get accomplished the way the individual manager wants. Realistically, though, it is impossible for one person to do everything. Could you imagine if the general manager of an MLB team tried to do everything? In addition to making personnel decisions and negotiating contracts, that person would be broadcasting the game, pulling the tarp, and selling beer! Also, delegation plays an important part in how new employees learn to be sport managers. Just as a coach allows substitutes to slowly learn the game plan until they are ready to be starters, so, too, do sport managers allow their subordinates to hone their managerial skills via delegation. Delegation is also how you will learn about working in the sport industry through an internship; that is, a supervisor will assign you certain tasks and then provide you with feedback along the way. Such learning is possible only because someone delegates a task to you!

The leading function also requires the manager to take an active role and manage any differences or changes that may take place within the organization. Ultimately, the manager is responsible for the employees and how they perform their duties. The manager must handle any conflicts, work problems, or communication difficulties so that the employees can achieve their goals. The manager also must be ready to stimulate creativity and motivate the employees if needed. Thus, the manager takes on a very dynamic role in the operations of the organization when performing the leading function.

Evaluating

The manager performs the **evaluating** function by measuring and ensuring progress toward organizational objectives. This progress is accomplished by the employees effectively carrying out their duties. The manager evaluates the workers by establishing reporting systems, developing performance standards, comparing employee performance to set standards, and designing reward systems to acknowledge successful work on the part of the employees. Position descriptions, discussed earlier in this chapter, are important in the evaluating function as well, because they establish the criteria by which employee performance is measured.

The reporting system involves collecting data and information regarding how an employee is performing his or her job. For example, the director of corporate sponsorship for an event would collect information on how many sponsorship packages the local corporate sponsorship representative has sold. This information would then be reported to the event director. Developing performance standards sets the conditions or expectations for the employee. In the previous example, the local corporate sponsorship representative, in conjunction with the director, would determine how many local sponsorship packages should be sold and what their value should be. Employee performance can then be evaluated based on how well (or poorly) each employee did in meeting these performance standards.

Finally, a reward system should be put in place so employees believe their work is noticed and appreciated. Receiving recognition for good performance and accomplishments helps motivate employees to reach their job expectations. Employees will not be motivated to reach the performance standards placed before them if they believe they will not be rewarded or recognized in some way or if the standards are unattainable.

Sometimes employees may fail to meet the levels of performance expected of them. Managers must deal with these situations, which may be quite unpleasant. It is necessary to have a plan in place to help employees adjust their work efforts to become successful, as well as one to deal with employees who may need to be asked to leave the organization. The chaotic hiring and firing of individuals is disruptive to the organization, however, and a clear indicator of an ineffective management style. Instead, managers need to project consistency and thoughtfulness to instill any sort of confidence in their employees. The chaotic manager is clearly not a leader, but merely a stumbling block to employees attempting to accomplish organizational goals and objectives.

One form of evaluation used for mid-level managers is the 360-degree review. This involves the manager performing a self-evaluation on how he or she feels about his or her performance relative to certain standards, metrics, job responsibilities, and skills needed in the job. The direct reports or employees of this manager would also perform a review answering the same questions. The 360-degree review provides useful information by comparing the manager's perceptions of how he or she is doing in the leadership role (self-report results) with the direct reports' or employees' perceptions of their leader's performance.

Managerial functions involve a manager performing a number of activities requiring various skills. The next section discusses the skills managers use when fulfilling their job responsibilities.

Key Skills

People Skills

As mentioned earlier, the most important resources in any sport organization are the human resources—the people. The sport management industry is a "people-intensive" service industry. Sport managers deal with all kinds of people every day. For example, on a given morning a ticket manager for a minor league baseball team may have the task of meeting with chief executive officers or chief financial officers of local businesses to arrange the sale of stadium luxury boxes. That afternoon, he or she may be talking with the local Girl Scouts, arranging a special promotion night. The next morning may bring a meeting with the general manager of the team's MLB affiliate to discuss ticket sales. Before a game, a season ticket holder may call to complain about his or her seats. Managing people, both internal and external to the sport organization, is key.

Managers in professional sport interact with unique clientele. On the one hand, they deal with athletes making millions of dollars; indeed, depending on their role with the organization, managers may have contact with these athletes on a regular basis. On the other hand, they deal with the maintenance crew, who may be paid just the minimum wage. The sport manager must be able to respond appropriately to these different constituencies and keep everyone in the organization working as a team. Using interpersonal skills and promoting teamwork are two valuable ways sport managers utilize their **people skills** (Bower, 2014). Without proper people skills, the sport manager is destined to fail. Learning to treat all people fairly, ethically, and with respect is essential for the sport manager's success.

© Dmitriy Shironosov/Shutterstock, Inc.

Communication Skills: Oral and Written

The importance of mastering both oral and written **communication skills** cannot be overstated (Bower, 2014). Sport managers deal with all kinds of people on a daily basis, and knowing *how* to say something to a person is equally as important as knowing *what* to say. Communication may take place in a one-on-one encounter with employees or customers, or in a large group setting such as a team meeting to discuss that week's goals. Communication can also take place with external constituencies such as a person with a disability who calls the ticket office with questions about parking and stadium access. Sometimes people just need general information, such as when the next home event takes place. To sport managers, these types of questions can begin to seem mundane and repetitive. For the person asking the question, however, this may be the first time he or she asked it, and this instance also may be his or her first personal contact with anyone in the organization. Answering each question professionally and courteously wins a lifelong fan; being rude or uncooperative ensures an empty seat in your arena or stadium. Remember this point as well: People who have had bad experiences talk to others, which may result in the loss of other existing or potential fans.

As representatives of their sport organizations, sport managers are often asked to give speeches to community groups, schools, and business leaders. Thus, sport managers need to learn how to give a proper oral presentation to a group. To assess your readiness to give a presentation, consider the following points (Hartley & Bruckman, 2002, p. 304):

1. Do you have clear objectives?

2. Do you know your audience?

3. Do you have a clear structure?

4. Is your style of expression right?

5. Can you operate effectively in the setting?

Jacobs and Hyman (2010) offer college students 15 strategies for giving oral presentations:

1. Do your homework.

2. Play the parts (organizing your presentation into a few main parts and telling the audience what these parts are).

3. Do a dry run.

4. Look presentable.

5. Talk, do not read.

6. Take it slow.

7. Use aids (e.g., PowerPoint slides, handouts).

8. Do not bury the crowd (with massive amounts of information that overwhelms them).

9. Be yourself.

10. Play it straight (a little humor may be acceptable, but not too much).

11. Circle the crowd (make eye contact with people seated in different parts of the room).

12. Appear relaxed.

13. Finish strong.

14. Welcome interruptions (questions are not necessarily a bad thing).

15. Know when to stop lecturing (discussions are great).

No doubt in your sport management classes you will have numerous opportunities to practice and perfect your oral presentation skills! These strategies can be applied later on in your professional career as well.

In addition to oral communication skills, successful sport managers need excellent written communication skills. Sport managers must be able to write in many different styles. For example, a sports information director needs to know how to write press releases, media guides, season ticket information brochures, interoffice memos, proper tweets, business letters to other professionals, and lengthy reports that may be requested by the athletic director or university faculty. Communications via social media platforms present their own unique challenges, especially when considering the use of Twitter. Although the 140-character limitation on Twitter has been relaxed, communications via this platform should still be short and to the point. Coaches need to be able to write solid practice plans, letters to parents or athletes, and year-end reports on a team's status. A marketing researcher for a footwear company has to write extensive reports on sales, consumer preferences, and product awareness.

Remember that professional writing is *not* the same as texting or posting to Facebook or Twitter. During such communication, you should always write using complete sentences and never include texting abbreviations. Similarly, email for business communication purposes needs to follow a succinct, professional approach.

According to Stoldt, Dittmore, and Branvold (2012, p. 8), "Although the channels through which the information is carried vary from news releases to publications to blogs, the core competency remains constant—being able to write effectively." Knowing how to communicate facts and information in an organized, readable fashion is truly an art, one a sport manager must master to be successful.

Managing Diversity

Diversity is a fact of life in today's sport workplace, and there is an ongoing need to include more women, people of color, and people with disabilities at the managerial level in the sport industry. Sport managers who do so are paving their way to success in the industry. Choosing to ignore or disregard the diversity of the sport industry is at least bad business and at worst completely disrespectful of the current state of the forward-moving diverse world around us. Cunningham (2015, p. 6) defined **diversity** as "the presence of differences among members of a social unit that lead to perceptions of such differences and that impact work outcomes. This definition highlights (a) the presence of differences, (b) the dyadic or group nature of diversity, (c) the manner in which actual differences can influence perceptions of such heterogeneity, and (d) the impact diversity has on subsequent outcomes." The primary areas identified when talking about diversity include race, gender, ethnicity, disabilities, and sexual orientation, but diversity can also refer to any difference among people—including political affiliation, religion, socioeconomic status, age, language, and cultural differences, to name a few.

The organizational benefits of diversity are numerous. According to the International Labour Organization (2014, p. 10), some of these advantages include the following:

- Gains in worker welfare and efficiency.
- Reduced turnover costs.
- Improved accessibility to new and diverse customer markets.
- Higher productivity and increased revenue.
- Increased innovation.
- Development of new products and services.
- Improved enterprise reputation management.
- Greater flexibility and adaptability in a globalized world.
- Prevention of marginalization and exclusion of categories of workers.
- Improved social cohesion.
- A more positive public image.

The face of the U.S. workforce is changing rapidly. In 2015, minorities accounted for approximately 37.72% of the workforce.

Women represented approximately 29.73% of executive/senior-level officials and managers, and 39.24% of first/mid-level officials and managerial positions in the workforce (U.S. Equal Employment Opportunity Commission, 2015). Information from the National Organization on Disability (2017) indicates that approximately 80% of working-age Americans with disabilities are not employed.

As a part of the greater business community, the sport industry must keep pace with the trend toward greater diversification in the workplace and encourage the inclusion of people with diverse qualities into the management of sport. The latest data in the 2016 Racial and Gender Report Card for college sports revealed that 86.1% of Division I, 88.1% of Division II, and 91.7% of Division III head coaches of men's sports were white. On the women's side, 84.5% of Division I, 87.5% of Division II, and 91.6% of Division III coaches of women's teams were white. More than 60% of all women's teams are coached by men. In 2016, white athletic directors held 87.6%% of the NCAA Division I positions, with women accounting for only 9.8% of these positions. All of the conference commissioners at Football Bowl Subdivision (FBS) conferences are white, with one female joining the group of nine men. Ten women and two persons of color are conference commissioners in all of Division I, out of a total of 30 commissioners (excluding historically black conferences) (Lapchick, 2017a). Clearly, there is still work to do in diversifying the gender make-up in intercollegiate athletics (Hums, Bower, & Williams, 2017).

At the senior executive level at the MLB central office, 15.9% of employees are people of color, while women occupy 20.6% of these positions. At the director and managerial level, 35.1% of employees are people of color, while women fill 26.3% of these positions (Lapchick, 2017b). Results for MLB professional franchises show that 19.6% of senior team administrators are people of color, while 27% are women

(Lapchick, 2017b). To address these issues, MLB Commissioner Rob Manfred has established important diversity initiatives, including (1) the Diversity Pipeline Program to identify, develop, and grow the pool of qualified minority and female candidates for on-field and baseball operations positions; (2) a major program on inclusion, particularly with respect to an individual's sexual orientation; (3) a program for inclusion for persons with disabilities; and (4) initiatives to engage more women in baseball on and off the field (Lapchick, 2017b).

The NBA has the most diverse league office in men's professional sport, with 35.1% of the professional positions held by people of color and 38.8% held by women (Lapchick, 2017c). At the team level, people of color fill 19.5% of the team vice-president positions and 32.6% of the team professional administration positions. Women account for 24.2% of the team vice-president positions and 29.3% of the team senior administration positions (Lapchick, 2017c).

The NFL League Office has made continuous improvements over the years in the hiring of women and people of color. In 2014, 14 people of color were employed at or above the vice-president level. This improved to 21 people in 2015 and 24 people in 2016. A similar trend of improvement in the League Office can be seen for women as well, with the number of women at or above the vice president level increasing from 21 in 2015 to 35 in 2016 (Lapchick, 2016). The percentages of women and people of color in vice-president or senior administrator positions on NFL teams, though, decreased in 2016 to 10.8% people of color and 21.1% women serving as NFL team vice presidents, and 18.7% people of color and 21% women holding senior administrator positions (Lapchick, 2016). The Rooney Rule, which requires that people of color be interviewed as part of the search process for head coaches, has helped the NFL to increase the number of African American head coaches in recent years, from 3 in 2003 to 6 in 2016.

The employment process—spanning from hiring through retention through employee exit—is now a much more complex process than it was in the past. Given the small numbers of women, minorities, and people with disabilities in leadership positions in the sport industry, steps must be taken to increase opportunities for access to the industry. When undertaking to follow ethical considerations for including all qualified individuals in the employment process, each phase of the process should be examined. These stages include recruitment, screening, selection, retention, promotion, and ending employment. The following suggestions offer concrete steps that sport managers can take to successfully manage diversity in the sport industry (Ilgaz, 2015):

- Understand the true perks of diversity (see the benefits listed at the beginning of this section).
- Identify new talent pools: Be creative in the recruitment and hiring process.
- Incorporate diversity beyond human resources: Make it an organization-wide commitment.
- Make diversity part of your brand's identity: Actions speak louder than words.

The North American workforce is rapidly changing and diversifying, and sport leaders must be keenly aware of how this trend will enhance their sport organizations. By being proactive and inclusive, sport leaders can ensure that all qualified individuals have an opportunity to work in the sport industry, allowing for the free exchange of new and diverse ideas and viewpoints, resulting in organizational growth and success. Sport leaders advocating this proactive approach will have organizations that are responsive to modern North American society and will be the leaders of the sport industry.

Managing Technology

Technology is evolving more and more rapidly every day, and **managing technology**—that is, being familiar with technology and using it to one's advantage—is something every manager should strive for. Managers need to be aware of technological advances and the way technology is used in the sport industry. This includes social media; customer data collection and advanced ticketing systems; sabermetrics and data analytics; and video conferencing and multimedia presentations, to name a few. Managers must stay current and be proficient with technology as it is used in the workplace.

The recent explosion in the use of social media has had a major impact on sport managers. Every team in the Big Four (NFL, MLB, NBA, and NHL) uses social media. The National Association for Stock Car Auto Racing (NASCAR), NCAA schools, and even high school sport teams, in addition to major international events such as the World Cup and Olympic and Paralympic Games, use social media. Individual athletes are active on social media as well. Sport management students should be aware of how sport organizations are using social networking sites such as Facebook, Twitter, Instagram, and Pinterest to promote their athletes, teams, and products.

The Internet has become a pivotal source of information on a variety of subjects. Computerized ticketing systems such as Spectra (formerly Paciolan) are used on a daily basis by professional sport teams, major college athletic departments, theme parks, and museums. Spectra (2017) describes itself as "a leader in ticketing, fundraising, marketing, analytics, and technology solutions . . . powering more than 500 live entertainment organizations that sell over 120 million tickets per year" (para. 1).

Most sport organizations use a customer relationship management (CRM) system such as Microsoft Dynamics or SalesForce to manage their databases. Information on potential and current customers is logged and tracked, and the data analysis used to help identify (un)successful ticketing and sponsorship campaigns. Data analytics is also used in the player personnel area, including applications to player performance and contract negotiations.

In addition, sport managers use technology to access these data virtually anywhere and can transform the data into analyzed information for presentation to sponsors. With the ongoing integration of the Internet and other multimedia interactive technologies into everyday business practices, sport managers and sport management educators now face new challenges: how to analyze and benefit from the effects of expanding technologies on the sport industry and how to educate future sport managers who are entering into this rapidly evolving high-tech world.

Decision Making

People make many decisions every day, ranging from simple to complex. All decisions consist of two basic steps: (1) gathering information and then (2) analyzing that information. For example, when you got up this morning, why did you choose the clothes you have on? Because they matched? Because they were clean? Because they were on the top of the clothes pile? Because of the weather? Because you had a presentation to give in class? Although this is a relatively simple decision (for most people), other decisions are more complex. Think about choosing a college major: What made you decide to major in sport management as opposed to management or accounting or theater management? This choice involves decision making on a much deeper level.

Sport managers have to make decisions about how to pursue opportunities or solve problems every day. To do so, they need to have a comprehensive understanding of the

opportunity or problem and engage in a decision-making process that will lead to an effective decision. The classic model of **decision making** has four steps (Chelladurai, 2009):

1. *Problem statement/framing the problem.* This first step involves defining the goal to be achieved or the problem that needs to be solved.

2. *Generating alternatives.* The next step involves determining as many courses of action or solutions as possible. This is also known as brainstorming, where all ideas are welcome and creativity is encouraged.

3. *Evaluate alternatives.* Each alternative identified in step 2 is analyzed in this step. The evaluation may include cost determination, risk identification, and identification of the effects the alternative will have on employees.

4. *Select the best alternative.* The manager makes and implements the final decision here.

Following an organized decision-making process helps ensure consistent decision making throughout the sport organization and ensures that no piece of important information is overlooked.

There is one other consideration for sport managers when making decisions: When is it necessary to include group input and feedback in the decision-making process? **Participative decision making** involves employees or members of the organization in the actual decision-making process. There are benefits as well as drawbacks to using a participative decision-making process within an organization. According to the Holden Center for Leadership and Community Engagement (2013) at the University of Oregon, the benefits of group decision making include a greater sum total of knowledge and information, a greater number of approaches to a problem, increased acceptance due to participation, better comprehension of decisions, and greater commitment of group members to decisions. Conversely, the potential downfalls of group decision making include social pressure, individual domination, conflicting secondary goals, risk taking, and the time needed when a group is used in the decision-making process (Holden Center, 2013). No doubt you have experienced many of these benefits and downfalls when working on group projects for class assignments.

Organizational Politics

What is meant by the term **organizational politics**? Organizational politics can be difficult to identify and pinpoint, but generally refers to individuals or groups within the organization pursuing their own self-interests and personal agendas instead of the organization's mission and goals. Organizational politics is a way of life. The degree of organizational politics varies from one organization to another, but the reality is that all organizations experience some degree of internal political struggle that, if not managed appropriately, can be detrimental to employee behavior and productivity. Dealing with this struggle takes a keen awareness of the landscape, players, and rules of the political game (Bolander, 2011). Although somewhat intangible and difficult to measure, politics pervades all sport organizations (Slack & Parent, 2006).

What is most important for sport managers is that they learn to be aware of the political environment around them. What are the personalities and potential personal agendas among their employees? Who is truly the most "powerful" person in a sport organization, and what type of influence does he or she have over the other employees? Sport organizations, like all organizations, have two different types of leaders: formal and informal.

The formal leader is a leader because of his or her title, such as athletic director, director of community relations, or general manager. The formal leader may indeed be the person who holds the most power in an organization and is able to influence employees in achieving organizational goals.

Informal leaders, by contrast, are leaders because of the power they possess from knowledge, association, or length of time with an organization. Informal leaders can be very influential in terms of what takes place within an organization. For example, if the coaches in an athletic department are trying to convince the athletic director to make some sort of change, they may ask the coach who has been there for many years, knows the ins and outs of the organization, and knows how to persuade the athletic director to speak on their collective behalf. Alternatively, the coaches may ask the coach of the team with the largest budget or one of the higher-profile coaches to talk to the athletic director about making this change. Identifying informal leaders can help new sport managers understand the politics of a sport organization. By understanding personalities and personal agendas, and exhibiting transparent, honest, and mission-driven leadership and decision making, sport managers can help to minimize the impact of organizational politics.

Managing Change

Sport organizations change on a daily basis. New general managers are hired, teams move into new facilities, league policies and rules change, health clubs purchase new fitness equipment, and environmental use laws affect state or national park recreation areas. Change can be internally driven, such as when a professional sport team implements a new ticket distribution system, or externally driven, such as when changes are dictated by new government regulations or consumer demand changes.

Life is all about adapting to change—and that applies to the sport industry as well.

Although most change happens without major resistance, sport managers have to be aware that people tend to resist change for a number of reasons. Employees may fear failure, be creatures of habit, perceive no obvious need for change, feel loss of control, feel concern about support systems, be closed-minded, be unwilling to learn, fear that the new way may not be better, fear the unknown, and fear personal impact (Peter Barron Stark Companies, 2010). For example, a sales representative for a sporting goods company who is assigned to a new geographic area may resist this move because he or she is scared about getting a new territory (fear of the unknown), may be concerned that the potential for sales and commissions is lower in the new territory (the new way may not be better), may have had friends in the old territory (concern about support system), may now have a territory not as highly regarded in the company (fear of personal impact), may wonder if he or she will be able to establish new contacts (unwillingness to learn), or may just see the change as another hassle (no obvious need for change). Although not all of these reasons may be present, sport managers need to be aware of what employees may be thinking. Buckley (2013, para. 3) suggests examining five questions to determine if a change can succeed:

1. How is the vision different, better, and more compelling?

2. Are the leaders personally committed to the change?

3. Does the organization have the capacity to make the change?

4. How ingrained is the current culture?

5. Will the change actually deliver the identified outcomes?

How, then, can sport managers effectively implement change in the workplace? When **managing change**, managers should do the following (Douglas, 2017):

1. Review the process you want to change and determine exactly what you want to do and why.

2. Carefully consider the risks associated with the change and how these risks may affect your employees.

3. If the change appears feasible, consult carefully with your employees and, if relevant, their union.

4. Undertake a careful assessment, based on data and acceptable workloads (through internal and external research), in consultation with your employees.

5. Provide an opportunity for the employees and the union to read the report and comment. If there are criticisms, determine what the particular issues are and consider them carefully.

6. Amend the report, utilizing best knowledge; then, prior to implementation, walk everyone through the proposed changes, why they are being implemented, and why they are safe.

7. Implement the changes; have legal directions and a set of frequently asked questions and answers available in the event of a dispute.

8. Stay keenly attuned to how employees are responding to the change so that any resistance can be dealt with fairly and honestly.

Motivation

The ability to motivate employees to strive to simultaneously achieve organizational goals and objectives as well as their personal goals and objectives is an art form. For example, both a head coach and a player for an NBA team want their team to win. The player also knows, however, that his personal game statistics will determine his salary. As a head coach, how do you motivate a player to be a "team player" (organizational goal) while still allowing him to maximize his personal statistics (personal goal)?

Theories of **motivation** abound, with works including Maslow's hierarchy of needs, Herzberg's two-factor ideas, Vroom's expectancy theory, and Adam's equity theory (Luthans, 2005). After reviewing these and other theories, Lipman (2013) points out five practices that can raise the level of employee motivation:

1. Align individual economic interests with company performance.

2. Take a genuine interest in the future path of an employee's career.

3. Take a genuine interest in an employee's work–life balance.

4. Listen.

5. Do unto others as you would have done unto you.

Talented sport managers also recognize that not all workers respond to the same motivational strategies. For example, as more millennials enter the sport industry workplace, it is important to engage in appropriate motivational methods with them. According to Gordeau (2013, p. 1), taking these steps in the workplace can help to motivate millennial employees:

1. Explain the company vision.

2. Prioritize community service.

3. Develop in-between steps and titles.

4. Give encouragement and regular feedback.

5. Offer more flexibility.

6. Provide education and professional development.

7. Give employees time for personal projects.

Motivating employees on a daily basis is a constant challenge for any sport manager. Nevertheless, for a sport organization to be successful, it is critical for everyone to be on the same page when it comes to working to accomplish organizational goals and objectives.

Taking the Initiative

"What else needs to be done?" Sport managers should be ready to ask this important question at any time. No doubt, speaker after speaker from the sport industry has visited or will visit your classroom and talk about the importance of taking the **initiative** in his or her sport organization. This will be especially true when you do your internship. When you have the opportunity to help out with an additional task, take advantage of that opportunity. First, doing so may enable you to learn about a different aspect of the sport organization with which you are working, and learning is a valuable skill in and of itself (Bower, 2014). Second, it may allow you to meet and interact with people outside of the office where you work, thereby growing your personal network. Finally, taking the initiative shows your employer your commitment to working in the industry. Working in the sport industry is not always easy. The hours are long, the pay is low, and the work is often tedious and seemingly endless. People in the organization recognize when someone is willing to do what is necessary to make sure an event happens as it should. Remember, "first impressions last"—so leave the impression at your workplace that you are willing to work hard and take the initiative.

Current Issues

Diversity in the Workforce

As mentioned earlier in this chapter, the demographics of the North American workforce are ever changing, and sport management professionals need to stay abreast of these changes. Women, racial/ethnic minorities, people with disabilities, people from different nations, people with different sexual orientations, and people with various religious backgrounds all contribute value to the sport industry. Sport organizations that embrace diversity will be seen as leaders in the twenty-first century; those that do not will be left behind. "A commitment to inclusion is a sign and reflection of leadership. . . . We need inclusion leaders—role models and champions who promote and implement inclusion not merely as lip service or tokenism, but as a legitimate core value" (Wolff & Hums, 2015, para. 1–2). Of the major North American leagues, the NBA currently leads the way on ensuring the diversity in the front office, and the league has parlayed this position into success. According to Groves (2016, paras. 3 and 5):

> Not surprisingly, when the brain trust of decision makers is diverse, so is the product. . . . If the NFL, MLB, and NHL are as serious about economic growth as they are about maintaining ownership norms, they too will eventually diversify decision-making board members beyond the select few who view the world from the 20th century lens.

Sport managers from all industry segments can learn important lessons from how the NBA does business on the diversity front: No one can argue with the NBA's success.

Sport managers need to stay on top of the latest legislation and managerial theories in their efforts to help their organizations become truly inclusive. In addition to staying knowledgeable about the current status of diversity in the sport management workforce, it is important for sport managers to be proactive. One suggestion is for sport managers to perform a self-study of their organization to evaluate their effectiveness in terms of recruiting and employing women, racial/ethnic minorities, people with disabilities, people with different sexual orientations, and people from different nations and religious backgrounds. The development and implementation of strategies involving recruitment and employment methods can then take place to encourage diversity in the workplace.

Managing Technology

As mentioned earlier, the technology that sport managers work with changes daily. Sport managers need to be aware of how these changes affect the segment of the sport industry in which they work and how new technologies can be incorporated into the workplace. It is imperative that sport managers understand how expanding technology will improve customer relations and service. Internet sites such as Universal Sports, ParalympicSport.TV, and the Olympic Channel are changing how fans consume sport media. Social networks now heavily influence sport organizations, and many sport consumers are Facebook, Twitter, Instagram, and Pinterest users. For example, in 2016, the NFL livestreamed ten Thursday Night Football games on Twitter; in 2017, MLB featured Friday games live on Facebook. Just as the computer replaced the typewriter, and email and text messaging are replacing phone calls, so the next wave of technology will affect how sport managers run their daily business operations.

International Sport Management

Sport management is not unique to North America. Sport—and with it, the field of sport management—continues to grow in popularity throughout the world. For example, Europe has a number of successful major professional soccer and basketball leagues as well as motor sports events. The Olympic Games, the Paralympic Games, the World Cup, and other multinational events are important elements of the sport industry.

In addition, U.S. professional sport leagues are increasingly exporting their products around the world, through games being played in different countries or televised games in the United States being shown in countries around the world. The NBA has 12 international regional offices in Asia, Canada, China, Europe, India, Latin America, and South Africa (NBA, 2017). In the 2017 NFL season, four games were played in London and one game between the New England Patriots and Oakland Raiders was played in Mexico City (Seifert, 2017). MLB focuses on worldwide growth and international activities through Major League Baseball International. This international division of MLB broadcasts games in 189 countries and territories, with the telecasts being transmitted in 14 different languages (MLB, 2017). In addition, the World Baseball Classic continues to create excitement and enthusiasm for baseball among fans from many nations. The PGA Tour recently established the PGA Tour Latinoamérica.

Sport managers from North America working abroad must be aware that they cannot unilaterally impose domestic models of sport governance on other cultures. Differences exist in terms of language, culture, etiquette, management, and communication styles. Sport managers need to learn, understand, and respect these differences when working in the international sport marketplace.

Additional Management Theories

Management theories and approaches to management are constantly changing, with new thoughts and ideas taking hold on a regular basis. Two of the more recent approaches to management are empowerment and emotional intelligence.

Empowerment refers to encouraging employees to take the initiative and make decisions within their area of operations (Luthans, 2005). Workers within the organization are provided with appropriate information and resources when making these decisions. As such, empowerment encourages innovation and accountability on the part of the employee (Luthans, 2005). The idea behind empowerment is that the employee will feel more a part of the organization, be more motivated, and, in turn, perform more effectively.

In his book *Good to Great* (2001), Jim Collins conducted research on those companies that achieved long-term success and superiority. His findings support the empowerment approach to management and identify a culture of discipline common among "great" companies. Collins found that good-to-great companies build a consistent system with clear constraints, but also give people freedom and responsibility within the framework of that system. They hire self-disciplined people who do not need to be managed and then manage the system, not the people (Collins, 2001).

Emotional intelligence was first defined in the 1980s by John D. Mayer and Peter Salovey, but later received more attention with the studies of Daniel Goleman (1997). People at work may experience a variety of different emotions, both positive and negative. These emotions can be detrimental to the work process and organizational work environment. Emotional intelligence refers to the ability of workers to identify and acknowledge these emotions when they occur, and instead of having an immediate emotional response, to take a step back, allowing rational thought to influence their actions (Goleman, 1997).

Beyond the Bottom Line

In the twenty-first century, sport managers are more accountable than ever for looking at how their organizations can act in a socially responsible manner (Babiak & Wolfe, 2009; Bradish & Cronin, 2009; Cortsen, 2013). Sport managers now need to think about how their organizations will contribute to society in relation to issues such as sport and the environment, sport and human rights, and sport for development and peace (Hums, 2010; Hums & Hancock, 2011). This is especially true as an increasing number of athletes are using their public platform to advocate for improving social conditions (Schimdt, 2016; Wolff & Hums, 2017). These are new skill sets and knowledge areas for managers in the sport industry, but they are becoming ever more essential in the international sport marketplace.

Summary

Sport managers today face rapidly changing environments. One constant, however, is the necessity to successfully manage the sport organization's most valuable resource: its people. As we move closer to the middle of the twenty-first century, the workforce will be vastly different from the workforce of even the recent past. The influence of people of different cultures, rapidly changing technologies, and the globalization of the marketplace all make it necessary for tomorrow's sport managers to adapt to this evolving environment. The measures of a good sport manager are flexibility and the ability to move with changes so that the sport organization and, more importantly, the people within that sport organization, continue to grow and move forward successfully into the future.

Functional areas of management have been used to explain and prepare managers for the various activities in which they become involved in as a result of their management role. These functional areas include planning, organizing, leading, and evaluating. In fulfilling these functional activities of management, managers employ a variety of skills essential to their success. The skills discussed within this chapter include people skills, communication skills (oral and written), diversity management skills, technology management, decision-making skills, organizational politics awareness, managing change, motivating employees, and taking the initiative.

Managers in today's sport organizations need to be aware of constantly evolving management schools of thought and ideas, learn from these theories, and incorporate what works best within their organizations. Sport managers also need to think of their organizations in terms of being good corporate citizens. Management is all about finding the best way to work with employees to get the job done. The fact that there is no one best way to manage underscores the excitement and challenge facing managers today.

Case Study 2-1

Using Management's Four Functions in Daily Athletic Department Operations

College athletic departments are complex organizations, no matter whether they are at the Division I, II, or III level. College athletic administrators face a variety of challenging situations on a daily basis. In carrying out their jobs, they must be able to successfully use the managerial skills covered in this chapter, particularly the four functions of management—planning, organizing,

(continues)

Using Management's Four Functions in Daily Athletic Department Operations (*Continued*)

leading, and evaluating. In this case study, you are asked to apply each of these functions in a different setting within a college athletic department.

Big State University (BSU) is an NCAA Division I institution in a Power Five conference. Located in a major metropolitan area, its teams consistently bring home conference titles in many of its 21 sports. Success on and off the field is important, and the university highly prizes both athletic and academic success.

Using this scenario, focus on how athletic administrators in selected departments rely on the four functions of management in day-to-day situations.

Planning

Blake Austin is the Associate Athletic Director for Student Athlete Academic Services. Thanks in part to a gift from a major corporate donor, the Academic Services department will be moving into a new academic center in two years. Blake now needs to draw up the plan for the move from the old academic center to the new one. This is a very exciting time for the department, especially for the student-athletes.

Questions for Discussion

1. In drawing up the plans for the new center, who does Blake need to include in the planning meetings? Why?

2. Which specific input would each of these people or groups provide?

3. What might be some key elements or strategies Blake will need to consider?

Organizing

Gail Williams is the Assistant Athletic Director for Sports Information. The athletic department has just been given permission to add three new positions to work with social media. The new positions will be added to Gail's staff, which currently includes five staff members with specific sport responsibilities (e.g., one person is responsible for softball, field hockey, and men's tennis, while another works with women's soccer, baseball, and men's golf) as well as two television production workers.

Questions for Discussion

1. How should Gail organize the Sports Information department to best utilize these three new employees?

2. How might current job responsibilities be altered?

3. Which duties might the new members take over?

4. What might be some additional duties?

5. How will Gail prioritize these roles and positions?

Leading

Becky Slater is the Associate Athletic Director for Business Operations. As such, she oversees all the personnel decisions when it comes to hiring new staff. While BSU is located in a diverse metropolitan area, its athletic department is lagging behind the other conference members in hiring a diverse staff. Becky has been instructed by her supervisor to add more diverse staff members in the department. Using the decision-making model from this chapter, discuss how Becky will be an effective leader in this situation.

Questions for Discussion

1. How will Becky ensure the athletic department reflects the truly diverse nature of college athletics? How will this help to build success into the future?

2. Which elements from the decision-making model will Becky need to concentrate on?

3. Which type of leadership do you think will be most effective to create inclusion?

Evaluating

Taylor Stephens is the Assistant Athletic Director for Ticket Operations. The athletic department is just now completing a football stadium expansion project that will add 8,000 seats to BSU's current 50,000-seat stadium. The staff must make sure these new seats are sold via three ticket package options—season, three-game choice, or single game. The Ticket Office sales staff includes three account executives. This year's football season just concluded with the team having a 7–5 record and a win in the newly established Airbnb Bowl.

Questions for Discussion

1. Which types of expectations would be reasonable for the upcoming season?

2. How could Taylor establish an evaluation system to assess how the account executives are doing?

3. How can he determine whether the staff is reaching their sales goals for the upcoming season?

Key Terms

communication skills, decision making, delegation, diversity, emotional intelligence, empowerment, evaluating, human relations movement, initiative, leading, managing change, managing technology, motivation, organizational behavior, organizational politics, organizing, participative decision making, people skills, planning, scientific management

References

Babiak, K., & Wolfe, R. (2009). Determinants of corporate social responsibility in professional sport: Internal and external factors. *Journal of Sport Management, 23*(6), 717–742.

Bolander, J. (2011). How to deal with organizational politics. Retrieved from http://www.thedailymba.com/2011/02/28/how-to-deal-with-organizational-politics/

Bower, G. G. (2014). *A guide to field experiences and careers in sport and physical activity* (2nd ed.). Deer Park, NY: Linus Publications.

Bradish, C., & Cronin, J. J. (2009). Corporate social responsibility in sport. *Journal of Sport Management, 23*(6), 691–697.

Buckley, P. (2013, May 1). The key to managing change. *Businessweek*. Retrieved from http://www.businessweek.com/articles/2013-05-01/the-key-to-managing-change

Chelladurai, P. (2009). *Managing organizations for sport and physical activity: A systems perspective* (3rd ed.). Scottsdale, AZ: Holcomb Hathaway.

Collins, J. (2001). *Good to great*. New York, NY: HarperCollins.

Cortsen, K. (2013). The application of "strategic CSR" in the sports industry. Retrieved from http://kennethcortsen.com/sport-economy/the-application-of-strategic-csr-in-the-sports-industry/

Cunningham, G. B. (2015). *Diversity in sport organizations* (3rd ed.). New York, NY: Routledge.

Douglas, A. (2017). How to effectively manage change in your workplace. Retrieved from http://www.healthandsafetyhandbook.com.au/how-to-effectively-manage-change-in-your-workplace/

Follett, M. P. (2002). In Editors of Perseus Publishing, & D. Goleman (Eds), *Business: The ultimate resource* (pp. 988–989). Cambridge, MA: Perseus.

Gibson, J. L. (2006). *Organizations: Behavior, structure, processes* (12th ed.). Chicago, IL: Richard D. Irwin.

Goleman, D. (1997). *Emotional intelligence*. New York, NY: Bantam Books.

Gordeau, J. (2013). 7 surprising ways to motivate millennial workers. *Forbes*. Retrieved from https://www.forbes.com/sites/jennagoudreau/2013/03/07/7-surprising-ways-to-motivate-millennial-workers/#6f6d1d06c79f

Groves, R. (2016, Dec. 26). Trending NBA front office culture models how diversity makes business sense. *Forbes*. Retrieved from https://www.forbes.com/sites/rogergroves/2016/12/26/trending-nba-front-office-culture-models-how-diversity-makes-business-sense/#263c4caf24cb

Hartley, P., & Bruckman, C. G. (2002). *Business communication*. London, UK: Routledge.

Holden Center for Leadership and Community Engagement. (2013). Group decision making. Retrieved from http://leadership.uoregon.edu/resources/exercises_tips/organization/group_decision_making

Hums, M. A. (2010). The conscience and commerce of sport management: One teacher's perspective. Earle F. Zeigler Lecture. *Journal of Sport Management, 24*(1), 1–9.

Hums, M. A., Bower, G. G., & Williams, S.B. (2017, June). *A comparison of the career experiences of men and women working in intercollegiate athletic administration*. Presented at the annual North American Society for Sport Management Conference, Denver, CO.

Hums, M. A., & Hancock, M. G. (2011). Sport management: Bottom lines and higher callings. In A. Gillentine, B. Baker, & J. Cuneen, *Paradigm shift: Major issues facing sport management academia* (pp. 133–148). Scottsdale, AZ: Holcomb-Hathaway Publishing.

Hums, M. A., & MacLean, J. C. (In press). *Governance and policy in sport organizations* (4th ed.). London, UK: Routledge.

Ilgaz, Z. (2015, June 11). How to create a more inclusive workplace for your diverse employees, *Forbes*. Retrieved from https://www.forbes.com/sites/ellevate/2015/06/11/how-to-create-a-more-inclusive-workplace-for-your-diverse-employees/#613571c03f76

International Health, Racquet and Sportsclub Association. (2017). About the industry. Retrieved from http://www.ihrsa.org/about-the-industry/

International Labour Organization. (2014). Promoting equity: Ethnic diversity in the workplace: A step by step guide. Retrieved from http://www.ilo.org/wcmsp5/groups/public/—ed_norm/—declaration/documents/publication/wcms_340481.pdf

Jacobs, L. F., & Hyman, J. S. (2010, Feb. 24). 15 strategies for giving oral presentations. *U.S. News & World Report*. Retrieved from http://www.usnews.com/education/blogs/professors-guide/2010/02/24/15-strategies-for-giving-oral-presentations

Lapchick, R. (2016, September 28). *The 2016 racial and gender report card: National Football League*. Orlando, FL: University of Central Florida, Institute for Diversity and Ethics in Sport. Retrieved from http://www.tidesport.org/reports.html

Lapchick, R. (2017a, April 6). *The 2016 racial and gender report card: College sport*. Orlando, FL: University of Central Florida, Institute for Diversity and Ethics in Sport. Retrieved from http://www.tidesport.org/reports.html

Lapchick, R. (2017b, April 18). *The 2017 racial and gender report card: Major League Baseball*. Orlando, FL: University of Central Florida, Institute for Diversity and Ethics in Sport. Retrieved from http://www.tidesport.org/reports.html

Lapchick, R. (2017c, June 29). *The 2017 racial and gender report card: National Basketball Association*. Orlando, FL: University of Central Florida, Institute for Diversity and Ethics in Sport. Retrieved from http://www.tidesport.org/reports.html

Lipman, V. (2013, March 18). 5 ways to motivate—and demotivate—employees. *Forbes.* Retrieved from http://www.forbes.com/sites/victorlipman/2013/03/18/5-easy-ways-to-motivate-and-demotivate-employees/

Luthans, F. (2005). *Organizational behavior* (10th ed.). Boston, MA: McGraw-Hill.

Major League Baseball (MLB). (2017). MLB International contact information. *MLB.com.* Retrieved from http://mlb.mlb.com/mlb/international/mlbi_contact.jsp

Mayo, E. (2002). Elton Mayo: The Hawthorne experiments. In Editors of Perseus Publishing, & D. Goleman (Eds), *Business: The ultimate resource* (pp. 1020–1021). Cambridge, MA: Perseus.

National Basketball Association (NBA). (2017). Career opportunities. *NBA.com.* Retrieved from http://careers.nba.com/locations

National Organization on Disability. (2017). About: 35 years in the making. Retrieved from http://www.nod.org/about/

Ozanian, M. (2017, April 11). Baseball team values 2017. *Forbes.* Retrieved from http://www.forbes.com/sites/mikeozanian/2017/04/11/baseball-team-values-2017/

Peter Barron Stark Companies. (2010, January 12). Why employees resist change. Retrieved from http://www.peterstark.com/why-employees-resist-change

Quarterman, J., & Li, M. (1998). Managing sport organizations. In J. B. Parks, B. R. K. Zanger, & J. Quarterman (Eds.), *Contemporary sport management* (pp. 103–118). Champaign, IL: Human Kinetics.

Schmidt, S. H. (2016). Athletes and social responsibility. In G. Presley, M. Hancock, M. B. Shreffler, & S. Schmidt (Eds.), *Issues and ethics in sport: A practical guide for sport managers* (pp. 105–127). Dubuque, IA: Kendall-Hunt.

Seifert, K. (2017, April 20). Ranking the NFL's five international games in 2017. *ESPN.com.* Retrieved from http://www.espn.com/nfl/story/_/id/19203296/ranking-fiver-international-games-nfl-2017-schedule-london-mexico-city

Sherman, R. (2016, April 12). The NCAA's new March Madness TV deal will make them a billion dollars a year. *SBNation.com.* Retrieved from https://www.sbnation.com/college-basketball/2016/4/12/11415764/ncaa-tournament-tv-broadcast-rights-money-payout-cbs-turner

Slack, T., & Parent, M. (2006). *Understanding sport organizations* (2nd ed.). Champaign, IL: Human Kinetics.

Spectra. (2017). About us. Retrieved from http://www.spectraexperiences.com/ticketing/

Stoldt, G. C., Dittmore, S. W., & Branvold, S. E. (2012). *Sport public relations: Managing stakeholder communication* (2d ed.). Champaign, IL: Human Kinetics.

Taylor, F. W. (2002). Frederick Winslow Taylor: Father of scientific management. In Editors of Perseus Publishing, & D. Goleman (Eds), *Business: The ultimate resource* (pp. 1054–1055). Cambridge, MA: Perseus.

Travis, C. (2017, March 1). How much do the NFL and TV partners make a year? *Outkick the Coverage.* Retrieved from https://www.outkickthecoverage.com/how-much-do-the-nfl-and-tv-partners-make-a-year-030117/

U.S. Equal Employment Opportunity Commission. (2015). 2015 job patterns for minorities and women in private industry (EEO-1). Retrieved from http://www1.eeoc.gov/eeoc/statistics/employment/jobpat-eeo1/2015/index.cfm#select_label

VanderZwaag, H. J. (1984). *Sport management in schools and colleges.* New York, NY: John Wiley & Sons.

VanderZwaag, H. J. (1998). *Policy development in sport management* (2nd ed.). Westport, CT: Praeger.

Wolff, E. A., & Hums, M. A. (2015, June 8). Be a leader for inclusion in sport. *Huffington Post.*

Retrieved from http://www.huffingtonpost
.com/eli-wolff/be-a-leader-for-inclusion
_b_7532052.html

Wolff, E. A., & Hums, M. A. (2017, February 10).
Athletes for human rights, peace and inclusion. *Huffington Post*. Retrieved from
http://www.huffingtonpost.com/eli-wolff
/athletes-for-human-rights_b_14678822.html?

Chapter

3

John Clark

Marketing Principles Applied to Sport Management

Learning Objectives

Upon completion of this chapter, students should be able to:

1. Differentiate between sport marketing and the marketing of traditional goods and services.

2. Assess the historical development of sport marketing, with a particular emphasis on the impact of broadcasting, sponsorship, promotion, and marketing research.

3. Compare and contrast the four P's of the marketing mix: product, price, place, and promotion.

4. Differentiate between mass marketing and market segmentation, and describe the various demographic, geographic, and psychographic characteristics that can be used to identify specific target markets.

5. Analyze the importance of fostering fan identification and utilizing relationship marketing strategies.

6. Identify the key skills needed to be successful in sport marketing.

7. Evaluate social media's role in sport marketing.

8. Recognize the value of sport marketing research.

9. Differentiate between broadcast/satellite television service and over-the-top viewing and discuss the importance of each to televised sport.

Introduction: What Is Sport Marketing?

During the summer of 2017, Luther College, an NCAA Division III institution located in Decorah, Iowa, announced that it was changing its football stadium turf from natural grass to bright blue turf, similar to the turf made famous by Boise State University. When asked about the change, head football coach Aaron Hafner remarked, "Having Luther blue will be unique among Midwest colleges and provide a visible way to promote our football program, athletic department and Luther College" ("Luther to Install New AstroTurf," 2017). While one could argue that changing the football field turf to a blue color is gimmicky, it does illustrate what some sport organizations must do to attract attention and customers—in this case, student-athletes.

The Luther College situation is but one of a myriad of marketing-related issues facing sport organizations today. These issues could deal with increasing the customer base while decreasing customer turnover, deciding on the appropriate proprietary content for an organization's subscription-based website, or speeding up Major League Baseball (MLB) games. It would be fair to say that the field of sport marketing has never been so diverse or interesting.

As defined by Kotler (2003, p. 5), "Marketing is typically seen as the task of creating, promoting, and delivering goods and services to consumers and businesses." Functions such as product development, advertising, public relations, sales promotion, and designing point-of-sale materials are all covered within this definition. However, Kotler (2003) ultimately boils the marketer's job down to one action: creating demand. If the marketer can cause a consumer to want a product, then that marketer has been successful. To accomplish this goal, marketers must identify customer wants and needs and then identify ways to satisfy them. According to Ries and Trout (1993, p. 106), "Brilliant marketers have the ability to think like a prospect thinks. They put themselves in the shoes of the consumer." Demand for a product will continue only as long as consumers see it as valuable. As such, one of the marketer's greatest challenges is to obtain the best possible understanding of what consumers want.

Sport marketing, therefore, consists of all activities designed to meet the needs and wants of sport consumers. According to this definition, sport marketing includes the marketing of (1) products, such as equipment, apparel, and footwear; (2) services and experiences, such as attendance at a sporting match or participation in sport; (3) entities, such as leagues, teams, or individuals; and (4) the recruitment and retention of volunteers as a relationship marketing exercise. Further, the sport marketer must think outside of the home stadium and consider providing the optimal experience for those who attend away games, events, or tournaments through the development of sport tourism product. Much of this chapter focuses on the marketing of leagues, teams, and individuals. It also addresses the use of sport promotion to market consumer and industrial products through sponsorships, partnerships, and/or endorsements.

Historical Development of Sport Marketing

Given the multifaceted nature of the definition of sport marketing, there are a variety of significant historical developments relating to key sport marketing concepts. These developments arose as sport organizations sought to more effectively communicate with their **target markets**, the group of consumers to whom a product is marketed. In some cases these concepts were utilized as the result of experimentation, in other cases because of the intuitive nature of the sport marketer, and in still other cases because they were found to be successful in mainstream business marketing.

It is a widely held view that Mark McCormack and his agency, International Management Group (IMG), invented sport marketing in the late 1960s. McCormack and IMG created a niche in sport marketing spanning from athlete representation to event management to sponsorship rights fees and television broadcasts. IMG's influence in sports can be felt through its offices in 25 countries and its involvement in sports, entertainment, and media throughout the world. In a 1990 *Sports Illustrated* article, McCormack predicted that Southeast Asia would be the center of future sports growth, followed by South America and Africa (Swift, 1990). International sporting events have moved into those parts of the world, showing that his predictions were correct. For instance, the 2008 and 2022 Summer Olympics were both awarded to Beijing, the 2010 World Cup was awarded to South Africa, the 2014 World Cup and 2016 Summer Olympics were awarded to Brazil, the 2018 Winter Olympics was recently held in PyeongChang, South Korea, and the 2020 Summer Olympics were awarded to Tokyo. The legacy of McCormack, along with the reach, scope, and vertical integration of IMG, continues to impact the industry.

This section examines a number of the key concepts related to the emergence of sport marketing, along with the innovators responsible for these developments. We have separated the developments into four categories: (1) the evolution of sport broadcasting, (2) the growth of sponsorship, (3) the development of promotional strategies, and (4) the birth of research in sport marketing.

The Evolution of Sport Broadcasting

Beyond the actual broadcasting of sporting events, first on the radio, then on television, and now on the Internet and handheld wireless devices, one of the most dynamic changes in sport marketing was the evolution of sport broadcasting from pure, factual reporting aimed at sport fans to sport entertainment aimed at the masses. This was achieved most notably through the efforts of ABC's *Monday Night Football* television program and an ABC executive named Roone Arledge. Arledge was the first person to recognize that sport televised in prime time had to be more than sport—it also had to be entertainment. He incorporated that philosophy into *Monday Night Football* through the use of three broadcast personalities: initially sports journalist Howard Cosell; the voice of college football, Keith Jackson (who would be replaced the next year by Frank Gifford); and former National Football League (NFL) star Don Meredith. In doing so, Arledge became "the first executive who refused to let sport owners or leagues approve the announcers" (Bednarski, 2002, p. 41). Arledge also instituted more cameras and more varied camera angles, video highlights of the preceding day's games, commentary, criticism, humor, and wit. *Monday Night Football* is now a sport institution.

When asked about his approach and view that sport was entertainment, Arledge responded that his job was "taking the fan to the game, not taking the game to the fan" (Roberts & Olson, 1989, p. 113). Arledge wanted the viewer sitting in his or her living room to see, hear, and experience the game as if he or she were actually in the stadium:

> What we set out to do in our programming (*College Football*, *Monday Night Football*, *Wide World of Sports*, and the *Superstars* to name a few) was to get the audience involved emotionally. If they didn't give a damn about the game, they might still enjoy the program. (Roberts & Olson, 1989, p. 113)

Arledge's innovations—most notably, instant replay, multiple cameras, crowd microphones, and sideline interviewers—added to the enjoyment of the program.

The manner in which *Monday Night Football* (and other Arledge creations, such as the *Wide World of Sports*—a 1970s and 1980s favorite) married sport and entertainment paved the way for the success of other sports in prime time and today represents the norm. Think about it: When was the last time you saw a National Basketball Association (NBA) Finals game or MLB World Series game on TV during the daytime? This confluence of sport and entertainment is now visible 24 hours a day through ESPN. From the zany nicknames and commentary offered by Chris ("Boomer" or "Swami" depending on the persona) Berman, to the *Top Ten List* and *Pardon the Interruption* features on SportsCenter, ESPN has expanded into a global multimedia brand with nine U.S. networks (ESPN, ESPN2, ESPN3, ESPN3D, ESPN Classic, ESPN Mobile TV, ESPNU, ESPN News, Spanish-language ESPN Deportes) and 46 international networks reaching all seven continents, ESPN radio and ESPNDeportes Radio (syndicated in 11 countries), games and shopping (ESPN Shop), and popular websites (ESPN.com, ESPNDeportes.com, TEAM ESPN, and market-specific sites) (ESPN, 2013). Today, additional growth is evident in sport-dedicated networks such as the Big Ten Network, Mountain West Network, SEC Network, Versus, and Spike TV. Further, the televised experience has changed substantially in recent times with the introduction of high-definition television and three-dimensional television. The evolution of broadcasting is also international in scope. The World Cup has been televised since 1954. However, the 1970 World Cup broadcast from Mexico in color is largely credited with the growth of international sport television as a whole. During this early time, the growth of international television was also sparked by

Olympic and track and field content. Viewers can now follow almost any team, sport, or event live from anywhere in the world through an array of international broadcasting options.

Traditionally, the desire for viewers to tune into a live sporting event as it happened increased the desirability of the broadcast with networks that needed to sell advertising time. Today, however, and as we discuss later in this chapter, the current model of sport broadcasting is being challenged by the proclivity of younger consumers to view only parts of broadcasts or eschew the broadcast altogether in favor of some other means of receiving game information.

The Acceptance and Growth of Sport Sponsorship

Sponsorship is the practice of partnering with a rightsholder for the purpose of gaining some benefit of that partnership (Mullin, Hardy & Sutton, 2014). When we speak of sport sponsorship, the rightsholder can be a league, team, player, event or broadcast, and the party seeking to partner with the rightsholder is usually some business organization. While the proliferation of sport sponsorship in modern times has been noteworthy, it is not a recent phenomenon. The very first collegiate athletic event, an 1852 rowing contest between Harvard and Yale universities, was held in New Hampshire and sponsored by a railroad company. Coca-Cola has been a sponsor of the Olympic Games since 1928 (Coca-Cola Company, 2006). Sugar (1978) has documented the early roles of such companies as Coca-Cola, Bull Durham Tobacco, Curtiss Candy Company, Chalmers Motor Car Company, Purity Oats, American Tobacco Company, and Gillette in exploiting the country's interest in sport through sport promotions, contests, advertising, and the use of sport personalities as endorsers. A picture of a professional baseball stadium from the early 1900s shows many signs on the outfield wall. Although the money involved may seem insignificant by today's standards, these early activities set the tone for what is perceived to be acceptable and advantageous in today's marketplace.

There have been, and continue to be, many pioneers in sport sponsorship and corporate involvement related to sport. One of the earliest pioneers was Albert G. Spalding, a former professional baseball player who parlayed his fame into what at one time was one of the largest sporting goods manufacturing companies in the world. Spalding was the first marketer to capitalize on the term "official" as it relates to a sport product, when his baseball became the "official baseball" of the National League in 1880 (Levine, 1985). Having secured the "official" status, Spalding then marketed his baseball as the best because it had been adopted for use in the National League, the highest level of play at that particular time. In the consumer's mind, this translated to the following message: "Why choose anything but Spalding? If it is good enough for the National League, it must be superior to any other product in the market." Spalding carried over this theme when he began producing baseball uniforms for the National League in 1882. This type of practice is still prevalent today. Think for a moment: Which company makes the highest-quality football or basketball? Why is that your perception?

Whereas Spalding had the most profound impact on sport sponsorship in the latter part of the nineteenth century, two forces had a tremendous impact on sport sponsorship in the latter half of the twentieth century. The first was Mark McCormack, who built the sport marketing agency IMG from a handshake with legendary golfer Arnold Palmer in 1960 (Bounds & Garrahan, 2003). At the time, Palmer was the most popular professional golfer. McCormack capitalized on this popularity by securing endorsement contracts for Palmer, helping companies promote and sell their products.

As a result, Palmer's earnings skyrocketed, paving the way for McCormack to sign other popular golfers, such as Jack Nicklaus and Gary Player. Today, IMG represents some of the world's greatest sports figures as well as models and members of the media. IMG also manages and markets thousands of live events such as the The Open—the oldest and most prestigious golf championship in the world (IMG, 2018).

Nike was the second significant force to affect sponsorship in the second half of the twentieth century. From its beginning as Blue Ribbon Sports in 1964 (an American offshoot of the Onitsuka Tiger brand), to its emergence as an independent brand in 1972, to its dominant role in the sport products industry today, Nike has faced numerous challenges and emerged victorious on every front. One of the key elements in the history of Nike and its role in the world today was the packaging of the Nike brand, product, advertising, and athlete into one personality. This was achieved when Nike and Michael Jordan created "Air Jordan" (Strasser & Becklund, 1991). Understanding the impact of an athlete on footwear sales and having experienced disloyalty among some of its past endorsers, Nike sought to create a win–win situation by involving the athlete—in this case, Jordan—in the fortunes of the product. Nike looked at the long term and created a package that provided royalties for Jordan not only for shoes but also for apparel and accessories. In Nike's opinion, if a player had an incentive to promote the product, he or she would become a member of the "team." The result of this strategy was the most successful athlete endorsement in history, with more than $100 million of Air Jordan products being sold in a single year (Strasser & Becklund, 1991). More recently, Nike has continued to partner with not only premier athletes but also premier athletes with unique identities. Its successful endorsement of highly promoted basketball phenomenon LeBron James demonstrates that Nike regularly strives to identify with athletes who personify "the best" in their particular area.

Beyond athlete endorsements, Nike has been extremely influential in other aspects of sponsorship. In an attempt to associate its business with the best college athletic programs, Nike initiated and signed university-wide athletic sponsorship agreements with major athletic programs such as the University of Michigan and the University of North Carolina. This is a trend that has been followed by Nike competitors Reebok, Adidas, and Under Armour. Throughout the 1990s, Nike was also known for the way it increased business while not paying to be "an official sponsor." Perhaps most visibly at the Atlanta Summer Olympic Games in 1996, Nike showed its adeptness with **ambush marketing**—capitalizing on the goodwill associated with an event without becoming an official sponsor. Even though Nike was not an International Olympic Committee (the governing body overseeing the Olympics)

sponsor, many people thought it was. To create this impression, the company employed a variety of strategies. For example, Nike turned a parking garage in close proximity to the Olympic Village into a "mini-Niketown" experience that included autograph sessions and appearances from Nike athletes such as track star Michael Johnson.

Sponsorship has expanded its look and feel over the past 10 years. Whether they are larger events such as the Olympics and World Cup or a local soccer club, the dynamics of sponsorship have penetrated far beyond field signage and television mentions. The digital era is evolving sponsorship into mobile phone applications. Further, some of the sanctities of sponsorship in the United States are slowly diminishing. For example, naming rights of teams and sponsor logos on team uniforms are no longer off limits, as companies are branding teams in their image—the New York Red Bulls are a prominent example. Professional sport leagues in the United States are also following

© lev radin/Shutterstock, Inc.

suit. The Women's National Basketball Association (WNBA) allows member franchises to place sponsor logos on player uniforms, and at the beginning of the 2013 season, 7 of the 12 WNBA teams had a jersey sponsorship (Bowman, 2013). The NBA eventually followed suit, allowing teams to sell jersey sponsorships for the 2017–2018 season (Mahoney, 2016).

Emphasis on Product Extensions and Development of Promotional Strategies

The emphasis on product extensions and the development of team sport promotional strategies can be traced to Bill Veeck (1914–1986), a sport marketing pioneer in professional baseball for almost 40 years. At various times from the 1940s through the 1970s, Veeck was the owner of the Cleveland Indians, the St. Louis Browns, and the Chicago White Sox (on two different occasions). Prior to Veeck's efforts, sporting events were not staged for the masses but rather for the enjoyment of sport fans. Veeck recognized that to operate a successful and profitable franchise, one could not totally depend upon the success of the team to generate capacity crowds. In other words, Veeck believed that a team must provide reasons other than the game itself for people to attend and support the franchise.

Several philosophies guided much of Veeck's efforts and left a lasting legacy for sport promotion. First, Veeck was firm in his belief that fans came to the ballpark to be entertained (Holtzman, 1986). Veeck's promotional philosophy embraced the goal of "creating the greatest enjoyment for the greatest number of people . . . not by detracting from the game, but by adding a few moments of fairly simple pleasure" (Veeck & Linn, 1962, p. 119). Promotions and innovations attributed to Veeck include giveaway days like Bat Day, exploding scoreboards, outfield walls that went up and down,

fireworks, and the organizing of special theme nights for students, Scouts, and church groups (Veeck & Linn, 1962).

Second, Veeck recognized that to build a loyal fan base, the attending experience had to be pleasurable: "In baseball, you are surprisingly dependent upon repeat business. The average customer comes to the park no more than two or three times a year. If you can put on a good-enough show to get him to come five or six times, he has become a source of pride and a source of revenue" (Veeck & Linn, 1965, p. 20). In addition to being entertaining, part of creating loyal customers entailed ensuring the best possible attending atmosphere. As such, Veeck focused on providing a clean facility and a hospitable environment. He carried out this philosophy by enlarging bathrooms, adding daycare facilities, greeting his "guests," and standing at the exits to thank them for coming.

Finally, Veeck suggested:

> It isn't enough for a promotion to be entertaining or even amusing; it must create conversation. When the fan goes home and talks about what he has seen, he is getting an additional kick out of being able to say he was there. Do not deny him that simple pleasure, especially since he is giving you valuable word-of-mouth advertising to add to the newspaper reports. (Veeck & Linn, 1965, p. 13)

In an effort to have people talk about their experience, Veeck devised unique and unorthodox promotions such as "Grandstand Managers" night, in which a section of the audience voted on what a manager should do in a particular situation. While Veeck was often criticized for his practices (and they were quite radical), his legacy is still visible today throughout sport events.

The Birth of Research in Sport Marketing to Improve Performance and Acceptance

Although some early pioneers like Veeck communicated well with their customers through informal contacts, letters, and speaking engagements, Matt Levine is the individual most often credited with formalizing customer research in the sport industry. Like Veeck, Levine was well aware that there were marketing variables other than winning and losing. Employed as a consultant by the Golden State Warriors in 1974 and given the goal of increasing attendance, Levine developed what he termed an "audience audit" to capture **demographic** and **psychographic** information about fans attending games (Hardy, 1996). Levine was also a pioneer in using intercepts (one-on-one on-site interviews) and focus groups (discussion groups involving 8 to 12 individuals with similar characteristics discussing a predetermined agenda) to gather marketing information for professional sport franchises.

Levine's research—and, for that matter, most research in sport marketing—had the following purposes:

- To profile the sport consumer demographically, geographically, or psychographically.
- To categorize attendance behavior and segment attendance by user groups related to potential ticket packages.
- To analyze purchasing behavior as it relates to product extensions such as merchandise, concessions, and so on.
- To evaluate operational aspects of the sport product such as parking, customer service, entertainment aspects, and employee courtesy and efficiency.
- To measure interest in new concepts that may be under consideration.

- To document viewing and listening behavior.
- To understand the consumer's information network so as to determine efficient methods of future communication to that consumer and like consumers.
- To offer two-way communication with the target market.

One of the most successful applications of Levine's market research techniques involved the National Hockey League's (NHL's) San Jose Sharks. Levine used a series of what he calls **pass-by interviews** or **intercept interviews**. Pass-by interviews are on-site interviews in heavily trafficked areas such as malls. These interviews utilize one or more visual aids and assess the interviewee's reaction to the visual aid. The visual aid is usually a sample or interpretation of a product (style, color, or logo) under consideration. Levine's pass-by interviews were used to determine the reaction of people who had submitted ticket deposits for the expansion of the San Jose Sharks to a series of proposed logo and uniform designs. The results of Levine's research efforts? The color scheme under consideration was eliminated and the graphic logo of the shark was changed. In 1992, the new logo and colors resulted in estimated retail sales of Sharks' merchandise in the United States and Europe of $125 million (Hardy, 1996).

As a result of Levine's approach and success with his clients and their acceptance of his methods and findings, market research in the sport industry is increasingly becoming a common practice rather than the exception. Although consumer research remains very popular, today's research tends to focus more on sponsorship evaluations such as brand fit, commitment and loyalty, media exposure, digital impact, and—one of the toughest concepts to capture—return on investment or return on objectives.

Key Sport Marketing Concepts

The Sport Marketing Mix

As defined by McCarthy and Perreault (1988), the **marketing mix** refers to the controllable variables the company puts together to satisfy a target group. The marketing mix, then, is the recipe for creating a successful marketing campaign. The elements of the marketing mix most commonly associated with sport are often referred to as the "four P's": product, price, place, and promotion (Kotler, 2003). In sport marketing, we often refer to the "five P's," including public relations as its own P (instead of lumping it in with promotion), given the significant role it plays in sport marketing. In comparison with the marketing of a laundry detergent, soup, car, or telephone, there are some unique aspects of marketing the sport product that must be accounted for when discussing the marketing mix. Some of the most important differences are presented in **Table 3-1**. These differences and their relevance to sport marketers will be discussed throughout the rest of this chapter.

Table 3-1 Key Differences Between Traditional Marketing and Sport Marketing

Traditional Marketing	Sport Marketing
The success of any entity may depend on defeating and eliminating the competition.	In many cases, sport organizations must simultaneously compete and cooperate.
Very few consumers consider themselves to be experts, but instead rely on trained professionals for information and assistance.	Due to the preponderance of information and the likelihood of personal experience and strong personal identification, sport consumers often consider themselves to be experts.
When a customer purchases a sweater, it is tangible and can be seen and felt and used on more than one occasion.	The sport product is invariably intangible, subjective, and heavily experiential.
Customer demand is more predictable because the product is always the same.	Consumer demand tends to fluctuate widely.
Mainstream products have an inventory and a shelf life, and supplies can be replenished.	The sport product (the game) is simultaneously produced and consumed; there is no inventory.
Although other people can enjoy the purchase of a car, the enjoyment or satisfaction of the purchaser does not depend upon it.	Sport is generally publicly consumed, and consumer satisfaction is invariably affected by social facilitation.
Inconsistency and unpredictability are considered unacceptable—for example, if a particular car occasionally went backward when the gear indicated forward, consumers would be up in arms.	The sport product is inconsistent and unpredictable.
The mainstream marketer works with research and design to create the perceived perfect product.	The sport marketer has little or no control over the core product and often has limited control over the product extensions.
Only religion and politics, which in and of themselves are not viewed as products or services but rather as beliefs, are as widespread as sport.	Sport has an almost universal appeal and pervades all elements of life.

Product

Whereas marketing sporting goods is similar to marketing mainstream products because tangible benefits can be provided, marketing a sporting event (such as a minor league baseball game), a sport service (such as a health club), or even an athlete is different. There has been some debate about what constitutes the "core" product in sport marketing. On the one hand, some posit that the core product is the actual event. On the other hand, if we apply a mainstream marketing definition, the "core" product is the *benefit* that consumers seek from a product, service, or experience—a perspective that takes the focus off the actual event. Thus, for a Ladies Professional Golf Association (LPGA) event, one side would view the core product as the golfers on the course, whereas the other side would counter that the core product is the benefit that consumers received from attending the event that may or may not be related to what actually happens on the course. Spectators at the event and television viewers cannot touch or taste the product—they merely experience it. Further, spectators and viewers have no idea who is going to win the event. Such unpredictability is both an advantage and a disadvantage for sport marketers. In one sense, it allows the sport marketer to promote the fact that fans do not want to miss out on a chance to see something spectacular. From another perspective, though, the sport marketer cannot entice people to attend by promising success for a particular athlete or team. In fact, in nearly all cases relating to spectator sport, the sport marketer has little control over the core product. Again, however, this depends on what one views as the core product. The vice president of marketing for the LPGA cannot orchestrate who will win the LPGA championship. The chief marketing officer for the Dallas Mavericks of the NBA cannot do anything to enhance the chances that the Mavericks will win.

The sport marketer must account for these unique differences relating to the sport product. For example, because the sport marketer has little control over what happens on the playing field, court, or course, he or she must focus on the extensions surrounding the game that can be managed. This is where the work of Veeck, who employed a variety of tactics to enhance the attending experience beyond what happened on the field, provides important lessons. For example, if you were to attend almost any NBA game today, you would be entertained during every time-out with on-court performances and the extensive use of interactive video boards that allow fans to text messages and view themselves on the big screen.

© Photos.com

Price

Like any other product, most sport products have an associated price. A variety of products within the sport industry must be priced: tickets, health club memberships, satellite television packages, special access areas on sport websites, and so on. When attending an event, there is usually more than one price. For example, beyond the cost of a ticket, the attendee may have to pay to park or to purchase concessions or a souvenir.

Increasingly, the cost of a ticket is separated into the actual ticket price and an additional charge per ticket for access to premium services such as restaurants or waiter/waitress service. Because the sport product is usually intangible and experiential, its price often depends on the value (or perceived value) provided by the sport product or experience. Consumers can perceive a higher price to mean higher quality, but the sport marketer needs to be careful to balance perceived value versus perceived quality. Using concessions at a new MLB stadium as an example, just because a Coca-Cola costs $5, it does not mean that the consumer will perceive this deal to be a good value and of high quality. Further, in a time when both ticket prices associated with professional sport and the costs of ancillary items such as concessions have risen dramatically, sport marketers are challenged to provide attendees with more value than ever. A consumer attending an event considers the entire cost of attending when determining the value of the event. This cost includes the monetary costs (such as the ticket price, concessions, and parking), the personal cost of attending (which includes the time it takes to travel to a stadium or arena), and the opportunity cost (the other options not chosen instead of attending the sporting event).

Place

The typical mainstream product is made at a manufacturing site and then transferred to a location where it is available for customers to purchase. Further, most products have a shelf life; that is, if they are not bought today, they can still be sold tomorrow. Neither condition is true when examining team sports and events. The place where the product is produced (the stadium or arena) is also the place where the product is consumed. Further, once a game is over, the tickets for that game cannot be sold. What would happen if someone offered to sell you tickets to one of your favorite team's games that had already happened? You would laugh,

right? Because of these unique nuances associated with the place at which the sport product is distributed, sport marketers must aggressively pre-sell sporting events.

Although there are some unique differences associated with place in sport marketing, there are also some similarities to mainstream marketing. Location can be very important. People talk about going to Wrigley Field in Chicago for a variety of reasons, including the history and tradition of the facility as well as its location in a popular North Chicago neighborhood. Similarly, the location of a health club can be vitally important to its success. Referring back to Veeck again, facility aesthetics also play an important role. Veeck believed in a clean facility. From 1990 to present, MLB experienced a surge in new ballparks with "retro" features that reminded fans of baseball parks from the early 1900s. Further, the amenities available in new stadiums or health clubs can be a very important part of the place a sport product is sold. Because the sport consumption experience is a social one, most new stadiums and arenas have significant space dedicated to upscale restaurants and bars. One of the newest and most fan-friendly stadiums is AT&T Stadium (previously known as Cowboys Stadium) in Texas. Opened in 2009, it is 3 million square feet in area and seats 80,000 spectators, but it can comfortably accommodate 100,000 thanks to fan-friendly, standing-room-only spaces interspersed across the facility. There are 2,900 television screens (not to mention the largest center video board) throughout the facility, making it almost impossible to miss a play on the field no matter where a fan is seated. In 2012, MLB's Miami Marlins opened a new 37,000-seat stadium on the site of the old Orange Bowl. Marlins Park incorporates aspects of Miami and South Florida culture into the entire facility—from colorful art exhibits to aquariums—all designed to make the fans feel connected to the franchise.

This type of facility atmosphere and other traditions are a vital part of the fan experience. Vuvuzela horns at the 2010 Fédération Internationale de Football Association (FIFA) World Cup in South Africa, the Pagoda at Indianapolis Motor Speedway, and the Green Monster at Fenway Park are all fixtures of the fan experience at those facilities. As facilities expand, renovate, and/or begin new construction, the fan experience is invoked by the facility. Today, most major sporting facilities offer tours for interested fans.

Promotion

Promotion typically refers to a variety of functions, including advertising (paid messages conveyed through the media), personal selling (face-to-face presentation in which a seller attempts to persuade a buyer), publicity (media exposure not paid for by the beneficiary), and sales promotion (special activities undertaken to increase sales of a product) (Mullin et al., 2014). In undertaking sport promotion, the unique aspects of sport marketing are important to understand. Sport entities often both compete and cooperate. For example, the Tampa Bay Rays will probably heavily promote the fact that the New York Yankees are visiting in an effort to increase attendance for the Yankees series, even though the Rays are competing with the Yankees on the field. In fact, in many cases, and for the Rays in particular, a sport team's competition may help draw fans to the sporting event.

In promoting sport, the sport marketer must also take into account the unpredictable and experiential nature of the product. The Seattle Storm of the WNBA would probably promote the chance to have a good time while watching a Storm game instead of promising a Storm win. While recognizing with the experiential nature of sport, promotion can offer something tangible to accompany and drive home the fleeting experience, such as souvenirs or giveaways.

A fan who receives a Steph Curry bobblehead doll after attending a Golden State Warriors game, for example, is likely to remember that experience.

Sponsorships typically try to take advantage of all of the elements of promotion. Consider Coca-Cola's "Bracket Town" ad campaign launched in conjunction with the 2013 NCAA March Madness Basketball Tournament. As a sponsor of the National Collegiate Athletic Association (NCAA), Coca-Cola set up fan interactive zones, or Bracket Towns, in each city hosting regional games. The towns, which were hyped as the official pre- and post-tournament party sites, had many activities and prizes for fans, as well as celebrities such as basketball announcer Dick Vitale. Coke cross-promoted the Bracket Towns with print, digital, and social media buys to link its brand with the positive emotions people feel toward March Madness. Finally, Coke utilized the Bracket Towns and associated media to allow attendees to test new products and generally promote the sale of its many brands.

Segmentation

As opposed to mass marketing, where an organization markets its products to every possible consumer in the marketplace, **segmentation** entails identifying subgroups of the overall marketplace based on a variety of factors, including age, income level, ethnicity, geography, and lifestyle tendencies. Although the sport product has nearly universal appeal, it would still be foolish of sport marketers to market their product to the entire population. A target market is a segment of the overall market that has certain desirable traits or characteristics and is coveted by the marketer. These traits or characteristics can be (1) demographic, such as age, income, gender, or educational background; (2) geographic, such as a region or a postal code; (3) psychographic, lifestyles, activities, or habits; or (4) product use, such as type of beer the members of a target market drink, the car they drive, or the credit card they use most often. Using a women's college basketball program as an example, target markets could include girls age 8 to 18 (age segmentation) who play organized basketball (psychographic segmentation) within 30 miles of the university campus (geographic segmentation).

Two increasingly popular bases of segmentation are ethnic marketing and generational marketing. As of 2017, 17.8% of the U.S. population was Hispanic (U.S. Census Bureau, 2017). Recognizing that the Hispanic subpopulation is a fast-growing and large segment of the larger U.S. population, sport teams now attempt to market directly to Hispanics through such strategies as producing radio broadcasts and websites in Spanish. For example, ESPN has created ESPN Deportes, a United States–based Spanish-language network targeted to Hispanics (Liberman, 2003). Major League Soccer (MLS), in particular, pays attention to the Hispanic market. Almost half of MLS's league office staff is Latino, MLS has more Spanish-speaking TV partners than any other U.S. league, and the league hosts SuperLiga, InterLiga, and Mexican national team appearances in the United States.

Sport marketers also are expending significant energies to reach millennials (people born between 1980 and 2000). This segment is unlike others in that—in addition to mainstream sports such as football, basketball, and baseball—millennial consumers are very interested in "action" sports such as skateboarding and motocross. For sports such as MLB, this presents a challenge in creating future generations of fans.

Another basis of segmentation receiving increased attention is product use segmentation as it relates to attendance at sporting events. This tactic assumes that the consumption of people who attend a few games per year can be increased. Teams naturally have information about all people who purchased single-game tickets during a given season. Using these data, the sales force for a given team will call someone after that person has attended a game and inquire about the experience. If the fan had an enjoyable time at the game, then the salesperson will attempt to sell the fan additional games or a partial season ticket package of five or eight games. This strategy is commonly adopted by teams that have excess seats to sell.

The adoption of business analytics practices have aided these bases of segmentation across sport. The natural outgrowth of sport organizations having access to large amounts of customer data, business analytics combines traditional segmentation with advanced clustering techniques to more narrowly define market segments. For instance, the Boston Celtics subscribe to a software platform called Fanmanager that allows the franchise to capture information on fans who tweet, Facebook-like, or Instagram-like anything linked to a Celtics social media account (Nielsen, 2017). This information is combined with any franchise-related purchases by a customer. The key point is that each fan is identifiable by a Twitter, Facebook, Instagram, or email account. If the fan engages in any of these actions while having his or her location information public, the Celtics staff then knows exactly where the fan is who is engaging via social media. This allows the Celtics business analytics staff to target that fan with a specific offer based on all of the information volunteered and the behavior exhibited. For instance, one morning fans in the greater Boston metro market may hear Kyrie Irving interviewed on a local sport radio show. Any of those fans who tweet about that interview and use the @celtics hashtag would be noticed by the Celtics business analytics staff. If the Celtics had a game with available inventory that evening, the analytics staff could then send a message to these fans with special offers of tickets and an Irving autograph if they come to the Boston

Garden that evening. This type of segmentation is very effective and efficient because the amount of information shared by fans allows the organization to target individuals or groups of individuals on multiple levels, increasing the likelihood of a positive response to the organization's offer.

© Pamela Moore/iStockphoto

Fan Identification

Fan identification is defined as the sense of oneness with or belongingness to an organization (Bhattarcharya, Rao, & Glynn, 1995). In theory, the more a fan identifies with a team or organization, the greater the likelihood the fan will develop a broad and long-term relationship with that team and attach his or her loyalty to the organization. Sport is unique in the significant fan identification it engenders among its consumers. Think about it: Are you more emotionally connected to your toothpaste or to your favorite sport team? Manifestations of fan identification are everywhere. Message boards, painting one's face, and wearing logo apparel are all ways in which sport fans demonstrate their connection to a team. When you talk about your favorite team's games, do you refer to your favorite team as "we" or "they"? Many people refer to their team as "we" (especially after a team wins), even though they have no direct impact on the team's performance. This is an example of high fan identification. Beyond

teams, recent research suggests that fans may identify with an array of elements including coaches, individual players, smaller subgroups of fans, or sports in general.

Fan identification also is very important for sponsors of sporting events. Ideally, a sponsor will be able to tap into some of the strong emotional connection between a fan and his or her sport team through a sponsorship. For example, it is often thought that sponsors of National Association of Stock Car Auto Racing (NASCAR) drivers earn the business of the drivers' fans through association with the race team. Similarly, it could be argued that a sponsorship with the Dallas Cowboys or New York Yankees, each of which has a large group of vocal and loyal supporters, could result in increased business, at least in part due to the ability to capitalize on the strong identification that exists with each of these teams.

Another method of establishing fan identification is for sport marketers to adopt cause-related marketing into their marketing strategies. Cause-related sport marketing entails a sport organization forming a partnership with a charity or cause to market a product or service for mutual benefit (Adkins, 1999). If the sport organization chooses a charity or cause that resonates with its fans or desired target market, fans may develop deeper levels of identification and actively support the cause (Lachowetz & Gladden, 2003).

Relationship Marketing

If marketers adopt **relationship marketing** strategies, they can help foster identification with sport teams. According to Kotler (2003, p. 13), "relationship marketing has the aim of building mutually satisfying long-term relations with key parties—customers, suppliers, distributors—in order to earn and retain their business." Rather than looking at consumers as transactions, relationship marketing suggests that organizations seek to build long-term relationships with their customers, ultimately converting them to or maintaining them as loyal product users (Berry, 1995). Relationship marketing begins with the customer and in essence encourages the organization to integrate the customer into the company; to build a relationship with the customer based on communication, satisfaction, and service; and to work to continue to expand and broaden the involvement of the customer with the organization. In effect, this integration, communication, service, and satisfaction combine to create a relationship between the consumer and the organization (McKenna, 1991). The implementation of relationship marketing practices is often called **customer relationship management**.

In addition to sport organizations seeking to develop and sustain lasting relationships with sport fans, relationship marketing is key to the recruitment and retention of a volunteer workforce. Many sport organizations and events rely on the ongoing contributions of volunteers to run and sustain their operations. Therefore, it is critical to develop relationships with these volunteers who provide an ongoing commitment and service to the organization.

Enhanced technology has enabled sport marketers to utilize social media sites to establish and foster these relationships with fans and other stakeholders. Due to the immediacy social media offers both the marketer and fans, information can be disseminated more effectively and efficiently, problematic issues can be dealt with in a more timely manner, and the personality of the sport organization's brand takes on a new dimension. **Box 3-1** discusses the social media strategy employed by the Dick's Sporting Goods Pittsburgh Marathon marketing team. Despite the need to constantly monitor social media sites, when used properly, such sites can be an important tool for sport marketers to build and nurture fan relationships.

Box 3-1 Social Media's Role in Sport Marketing: The Dick's Sporting Goods Pittsburgh Marathon

For sport organizations of all types, engagement via social media has become a standard part of the marketing toolbox alongside the traditional marketing channels of television, radio, and print. Unlike traditional marketing channels, social media are inexpensive, give the sport marketer the ability to easily create custom messages, and, most importantly, provides an opportunity for dialogue between the sport organization and the consumer.

One sport organization that does an excellent job employing social media as part of its marketing mix is the Dick's Sporting Goods Pittsburgh Marathon (DSG Pittsburgh Marathon). The original Pittsburgh Marathon was run in 1985, and quickly became one of the top five marathons in the United States (Dee, 2009). Poor regional economic conditions led to the pullout of the marathon's top sponsor, forcing the event to go on hiatus from 2004 to 2008, when a new management team resurrected the event with Dick's Sporting Goods becoming the title sponsor. Since 2009, the DSG Pittsburgh Marathon has had more than 264,500 runners. Social media have been instrumental in that growth (DSG Pittsburgh Marathon, 2018).

The DSG Pittsburgh Marathon staff takes a three-pronged approach for their social media strategy, which is conducted both prior to and during the race weekend.

(continues)

Box 3-1 Social Media's Role in Sport Marketing: The Dick's Sporting Goods Pittsburgh Marathon (*Continued*)

Promotional Marketing

At least six months prior to an upcoming race weekend, the marathon communications director uses platforms such as Facebook, Twitter, Instagram, and Pinterest to alert runners about registration information, training techniques, the meeting time and place of informal training groups, and nutritional information. This method is also used to market other organizational activities (other races, fundraising events) throughout the year.

Sponsorship Fulfillment

Each sponsorship contract that the marathon enters into is unique, yet most of the contracts include language that deals with the use of social media to promote the sponsors. Taking care not to inundate followers with overt commercials for sponsoring businesses, the marathon staff will promote a sponsoring brand using social media only if the message adds value for the followers. For example, several months before the event day, the marathon staff use Twitter to notify followers that the official training gear can be purchased only at Dick's Sporting Goods. This tweet includes hashtags for both the marathon and DSG. Additionally, the staff will tag the Facebook page of DSG.

According to Emily Baum, the Communications Coordinator for the DSG Pittsburgh Marathon, a great deal of attention is paid to managing the marathon brand as it is perceived by its customers in relation to sponsored messages: "Our runners are very loyal to the Marathon. We don't send out messages that look like ads. We try to position the sponsors in messages that are valuable to our runners and followers."

An example of this practice can be found in messages (tweets, Facebook postings) sent by the marathon staff on training tips. This content is supplied by the University of Pittsburgh Medical Center (UPMC), an authority in the field and also a marathon sponsor.

Operational Messaging

During race week, the marathon staff utilize social media to inform the public about key race-related information and customer service activities. Staff members on the various full- and half-marathon courses monitor traffic and pedestrian activity, and then, using Twitter, text messaging, or a live chat program, convey the problem areas back to the control center, where other staffers can alert the appropriate authorities to deal with the issue. For the 2014 race, the marathon staff created a unique hashtag, #AskPGHMarathon, which fielded questions from race participants, spectators, media, and those local denizens who wished to avoid marathon-related road closures.

A key component of the DSG Pittsburgh Marathon's social media strategy was the creation of a Social Media Command Center—the first event of its kind in the United States to employ such a strategy. This center was staffed with 30 volunteers who worked a rotating schedule on the two days leading up to the marathon, as well as on the day of the marathon itself. The volunteers were trained as to the type of promotional, operational, and sponsorship-related messages they were to disseminate. Early results indicate a stunning success, with the center engaging with 93% of its followers (only 10% of whom were registered runners).

Each sport organization has different marketing objectives that can be achieved in a variety of ways. As described in this feature, traditional marketing channels can be supplemented, or even replaced, by the use of social media to engage customers and enhance sponsorship agreements.

Data from: Emily Baum, Communications Coordinator, DSG Pittsburgh Marathon (personal communication, May 7, 2014); DSG Pittsburgh Marathon, Dicks Sporting Goods Pittsburgh Marathon Showcases Steel City as One of America's Top Running Cities. (2017, May 25). Retrieved from http://www .thepittsburghmarathon.com/News-Item-DICKS-Sporting-Goods -Pittsburgh-Marathon-Showcases-Steel-City-as-One-of-Americas -Top-Running-Cities

Key Skills

Because marketing is a form of communication, the key skills involved in sport marketing are communication based and are in many ways similar to the skills required for sport management:

- *Oral communication:* The ability to speak in public, speak to large groups, and make persuasive presentations demonstrating knowledge about the product and its potential benefit to the consumer.
- *Written communication:* The competence to prepare sales presentations, reports, analyses, and general correspondence in a concise and insightful manner.
- *Data analysis skills:* The use of data to inform the decision-making process. Whether it be projecting the return on investment for a sponsorship program or analyzing a customer database to identify the organization's best customers, quantitative skills are increasingly in demand in sport organizations.
- *Computer capabilities:* Beyond basic word processing skills, expertise in all types of software, including databases, spreadsheets, desktop publishing, ticketing systems, webpage design and utilization, and social media tools. In particular, in-depth knowledge of presentation software (such as Microsoft's PowerPoint) is important to the preparation of professional presentations.
- *Personnel management:* The skills to develop, motivate, and manage a diverse group of people to achieve organizational goals and objectives.
- *Sales:* The ability to recognize an opportunity in the marketplace and convince potential consumers of the value and benefits of that opportunity. Part of

identifying opportunities is understanding the wants and needs of consumers. Therefore, listening is a very important, yet often overlooked, skill for anyone in a sales capacity.
- *Education:* A minimum of a bachelor's degree in sport management or a bachelor's degree in business with an internship in a sport setting. A master's degree in sport management or a master of business administration degree, although not essential in some positions, is desirable for advancement and promotion.

Finally, the successful marketer must understand the sport product. It is not essential for the marketer to be a dedicated follower of the sport, but the marketer must comprehend the sport product, know its unique differences, and know how these differences assist and hinder the marketing of the sport product.

Current Issues

Innovation in sport marketing practices has lagged behind innovation in other service industries, in mainstream marketing, and in business in general because the cultivation of trained sport management professionals is a relatively new phenomenon (occurring over only the past 40 years). Nevertheless, in recent years, certain approaches and philosophies have begun to be accepted and have become widespread in the sport industry. Yet, as sport moves forward in the twenty-first century, it faces a variety of challenges that will require an increased focus on marketing innovation and sophistication. Some of these challenges, as well as practices being developed to adapt to them, are discussed in this section.

eSports

Organized multiplayer videogaming events, or eSports, have become a worldwide phenomenon impacting sport marketers. According to market intelligence company Newzoo, the segment described as eSports Enthusiasts included 191 million people in 2017, with another 194 million people tuning in as occasional viewers. As impressive as the eSports viewership numbers are, the eSports economy was approximately $696 million in 2017 (Newzoo, 2017). Fifty-eight percent of eSports Enthusiasts are males age 10 to 35, while 21% of eSports Enthusiasts are female (Newzoo, 2017). These figures, coupled with traditional demographic information such as household income and education levels, make reaching the eSports audience highly desirable for marketers.

This fact has not been lost on professional sport leagues. In April 2018, the NBA 2K League held its first draft. Each of the 17 teams selected 6 players from the 102 eligible person draft pool (Bonesteel, 2018). In May 2018, the 17 NBA-sponsored eSport franchises began competing against each other using five on five matchups just like a real basketball game (Alvarez, 2017). A fan can watch these eSport games on NBA TV or on a website called Twitch (Bonesteel, 2018).

Marketers will have to adapt their strategies to this new form of sport to cultivate a fan base that may be separate from that of traditional NBA basketball. It remains to be seen if a game like NBA 2k can be as popular with viewing millennials as the more traditional eSports games such as *Call of Duty* and *League of Legends*. There is also the question of whether eSports fans will cross over and become fans of the traditional sport, or if eSports will replace the traditional in-arena experience.

Cord-Cutters

As mentioned earlier, one factor impacting the distribution of sport is the increasing use of alternative viewing methods. According to a report from eMarketer, in 2017 there were 56.6 million nonpaying television viewers in the United States (Perez, 2017). This number includes people who have stopped subscribing to a cable/satellite television package as well as those who never subscribed to a cable/satellite package. Instead, these viewers watch programming using **over-the-top viewing**— that is, by receiving television or film content through high-speed Internet connections. The over-the-top viewers use a combination of live streaming services (e.g., Sling TV, PlayStation Vue, YouTube TV), on-demand subscription services (e.g., Netflix, Amazon), and free television to meet their entertainment needs. This exodus of mostly younger viewers has led to a decrease in cable advertising spending, with television's share of the total media advertising spending budget dropping to approximately 35% of the total U.S. spending of $71.65 billion in 2017, down from 36.6% in 2016 (Perez, 2017).

While decreasing cable/satellite viewership overall is concerning, live sport events continue to deliver strong ratings for partner networks. In fact, eight of the top 10 broadcasts in 2017 were sport events (Porter, 2017). Forward-thinking leagues have partnered with social media companies to experiment with live-streaming game content. For instance, the NFL's early successes with Twitter and Amazon in 2016 and 2017, respectively, led to a bidding war for the league's Thursday night streaming package (Wagner, 2018). Other leagues and events also look to occupy the live streaming space in addition to or in place of broadcast agreements. Sport marketers must be able to differentiate the various distribution platforms in terms of price and quantity, but also ensure quality standards, as they reflect on the brand of the sport property.

The Next Generation of Fans

In 2017, MLB Commissioner Rob Manfred spoke at the Aspen Institute's Project Play Summit in support of encouraging children to play multiple sports. In this interview, Manfred cited the long-standing belief that the best indicator of sport fandom is participation in the sport as a child (Aspen Institute, 2017). As innocuous as Manfred's wish may be, it is not always easy for children to participate in organized sport, and if they do, their experience may not be a good one. The professionalization of youth sport takes its toll on many participants, who self-select out of the sport at an increasingly early age. Some may find other sporting activities to adopt, but others may find themselves behind their age group and will have no success. The cycle then continues, such that perhaps the child is never positively socialized into the individual sport culture, thereby decreasing the chance of being a fan later in life.

Of course, some sports have additional issues facing youth participation and adoption. Football has seen participation rates decline in youth leagues primarily due to parental concerns about serious head injuries (Keilman, 2017). This poses a vexing problem for the NFL and its member franchises: How do they create the next generation of fans if the next generation is not playing the game? **Case Study 3-1** addresses this very issue.

Summary

The marketing of sport demonstrates unique advantages and disadvantages when compared with the marketing of more traditional products and services. Sport benefits from the immense media coverage afforded the industry, often at no cost, yet simultaneously can suffer from the scrutiny imposed by the same media. Besides sport, there is probably no other industry in which the majority of the consumers consider themselves to be experts. Finally, the sport marketer's control over the core product offered to the consumer is often significantly less than that of his or her counterparts in other industries.

Sport marketers must not only understand the unique aspects of their own product, but also be well informed and knowledgeable about marketing innovations and practices in more traditional business industries and be able to adapt or modify these practices to fit the situations they encounter in sport. In particular, the application of such concepts as the marketing mix, segmentation, fan identification, and relationship marketing is central to the success of a sport marketer. Similarly, recognizing and adapting to current issues such as the growth of eSports and eSports leagues, cord-cutters and new ways that fans are consuming sport, and the concerns about developing the next generation of sport fans are central to most sport marketers' work. Beyond an understanding of and appreciation for these factors and practices, a sport marketer must have strong interpersonal skills, computer skills, and in many cases the ability to sell a product or concept if he or she is to be successful.

© Tom Hirtreiter/Shutterstock, Inc.

Case Study 3-1

San Antonio Firedogs Youth Marketing Initiatives*

Assume the San Antonio Firedogs are a new team in the National Football League (NFL) that began play in 2016. It has adopted a marketing strategy that focuses on growing a new fan base by providing world-class entertainment and engaging, unique experiences. The Firedogs' goal is to create a deep connection to the community and build new fans, while strengthening the fandom of existing fans. This approach will help maintain the fan base even if the team performance is off. The Firedogs believe that if fans feel a deeper connection to the team and the team has become part of their lives, they will have accomplished their goal.

As a member of a robust league, the NFL has suggested the Firedogs focus on providing access and content that is relevant to their fans' respective life stages. As you know, youth and high school football offer huge participation opportunities for young boys in Texas. The Firedogs have focused on that segment of the youth market to create an early connection to fans and their families. The team has mined data from fans' social media accounts. Their data taught them that football participation, especially as a young person, makes a person significantly more likely to become a lifelong football fan. Therefore, the Firedogs' goal in youth marketing initiatives is to drive participation in the sport of football. The Firedogs provide exclusive opportunities for youth football players. They also work with local and statewide teams and leagues to boost their offerings through an alignment with the San Antonio Firedogs.

The main youth initiative is the Firedogs "Fire Station" youth outreach program. This program has many components, all targeted at different youth through the game of football. The Fire Station and Fire Truck are key components of the program. The

Fire Station is a traveling exhibit that is a replica Fire Station and the Fire Truck is actually a Food Truck that prepares Tex Mex Food.

The core elements of this program consist of the following:

- *Team at the "Station":* This core component of the program targets existing players and teams in the San Antonio region. The Firedogs encourage youth teams in the marketing region to register as an official Firedog youth team. Enrollment is free and teams that register receive a "team pack" delivered by the Fire (Food) Truck. The package contains items to excite the players and encourage safe play. Items include Firedog-themed mouth guards, helmet stickers, bag tags, Sparky (mascot) dog tags to wear, and exclusive offers and opportunities from the team sponsors. To be a Fire Station team, the team and league are required to comply with USA Football safe coaching/Heads Up Football certification. This helps the Firedogs identify teams and leagues that may need resources to ensure they are teaching safe participation in football.

- *"Play like a Firedog" Football Clinics:* The Firedogs sponsor weekend clinics targeted at youth who have little or no playing experience. The Firedogs provide a USA Football Master Trainer to support the coaching staff to teach the kids the safe basics of playing the sport, which are skills they will need throughout their football careers. The training is focused on on-the-field as well as off-the-field lessons. They also provide a Firedogs player or former NFL player to speak to the children about the life skills they may learn from football along with why it's important to learn to play the game safely.

*The San Antonio Firedogs case study is based off of the Baltimore Ravens initiatives.

■ *High School Football Game of the Week:* This program supports high school football teams from communities throughout Texas. Each week, the Firedogs will select four upcoming games and host a poll through its media partner, *The San Antonio Herald*, to allow fans to vote on which game should be recognized as the Firedogs Fire Station High School Football Game of the Week. The game that gets the most votes on *The San Antonio Herald*'s social media page is chosen for that week's game. The Firedogs feature the game in a number of ways. *The San Antonio Herald* sends a staff member to the school to feature the team/players on social media throughout the game day by following the team through their school day leading up to kick-off and throughout the actual competition. The Firedogs' spirit staff members travel to the game with their mascot (Sparky, the Dalmatian), cheerleaders, and youth football staff. At the game they set up the Fire Station and bring along their Fire (Food) Truck. The Fire Station has team exhibits to entice the fans to learn more about the team. At the Fire Station, the staff also hands out Firedogs-branded items, facilitates giveaways to the fans in attendance, and presents a game ball and a financial contribution to each school participating in the game. The Fire Truck sets up in the tailgating area and in addition to serving Tex Mex food items, it hosts a tailgating food contest among fans. The contest is an "eat-off" where fans vote for the best tailgate chili, best tailgate appetizer, and best tailgate dessert. So far, the program has done a great job engaging communities around the Firedogs, as evidenced by the fact that in the first season they routinely have more than 1 million votes per week for the Showdown (almost 10 million votes for the season). This program is a very strong grassroots initiative for the Firedogs.

In addition to these event-based initiatives, the Firedogs communicate with parents through a monthly newsletter. This newsletter provides information on upcoming opportunities, such as hosting games at the stadium, equipment grant process, USA Football initiatives, and football safety lessons, just to name a few.

These programs are promoted through the Firedogs' social media accounts. The team's social media becomes a resource for coaches and parents. The Firedogs hope to use the platform to educate parents on safety, exercise, appropriate weight training, and other football training tips. Ideally, the team would like to provide youth football participants with tickets to games, but tickets are sold out for the season. The team's primary goal for the program is to develop these children into fans of the game and ideally fans of the Firedogs and the NFL; therefore, creating a connection with them at a young age is critical. The hope is that they watch the Firedogs on TV and when their parents can no longer keep season tickets, the children may be willing to take over their tickets.

The Firedogs use metrics to evaluate both direct (attendance, participation, higher level of engagement) versus indirect (likes, shares, comments, and other lower levels of engagement) reach. Thus, the Firedogs evaluate the youth programs by assessing how many players they are reaching. Likes on social media sites, page hits, and shares are monitored. The team carefully tracks the enrollment of football players in its programs. For instance, last year in the Team at the Station program, approximately 400 youth teams registered, and with approximately 25 players on each team, the team estimates a direct reach of 10,000 kids. More than 1,000 kids participate in the youth clinics the Firedogs host throughout the area. The High School Game of the Week received over 1.2 million votes last year. *The San Antonio Herald* viewed that as a good value and renewed its partnership with the Firedogs.

(continues)

San Antonio Firedogs Youth Marketing Initiatives (*Continued*)

Questions for Discussion

1. The Firedogs are sold out for every game, so the young people they are attempting to entice to become fans cannot attend an actual Firedogs game. What are ways for the Firedogs Marketing staff to deal with this dilemma? Can you come up with any way, despite a sold-out season, to give young people a game experience?

2. Much of the outreach discussed above is geared toward youth football teams, presumably made up of a majority of male players. What implication does that have on the Firedogs attempt to grow the fan base? What ideas do you have to grow the game among young female fans?

3. Do you agree with this statement, "We evaluate the entire youth program based on how many players we are reaching." Is that the appropriate way to evaluate a youth marketing program? How should the Firedogs build a youth fan base among those who are not players?

Key Terms

ambush marketing, customer relationship management, demographic, fan identification, intercept interviews, marketing mix, over-the-top viewing, pass-by interviews, psychographic, relationship marketing, segmentation, sponsorship, target markets

References

Adkins, S. (1999). *Cause related marketing: Who cares who wins.* Oxford, UK: Butterworth Heineman.

Alvarez, E. (2017, September 26). The NBA's big eSports push begins in May 2018. Retrieved from https://www.engadget.com/2017/09/26/nba-2k-league-draft-tryouts-interview/

Aspen Institute. (2017, December 12). MLB Commissioner: Kids, don't *just* play baseball. Retrieved from https://community.sportsengine.com/news_article/show/866095

Bednarski, P. J. (2002, December 9). Applauding Arledge: He invented fresh ways to report sports and news on TV. *Broadcasting & Cable, 132*(50), 41.

Berry, L. L. (1995). Relationship marketing of services: Growing interest, emerging perspectives. *Journal of the Academy of Marketing Sciences, 23*(4), 236–245.

Bhattacharya, C. B., Rao, H., & Glynn, M. A. (1995). Understanding the bond of identification: An investigation of its correlates among art museum members. *Journal of Marketing, 59*(4), 46–57.

Bonesteel, M. (2018, April 4). Inaugural NBA 2K League draft: Who was No. 1 pick and everything else you need to know. *Washington Post.* Retrieved from https://www.washingtonpost.com/news/early-lead/wp/2018/04/04/the-inaugural-nba-2k-league-draft-heres-what-you-need-to-know/?noredirect=on&utm_term=.65eae9eb15c5

Bounds, A., & Garrahan, M. (2003, June 26). A question of sport and image: Mark McCormack, the sports marketing pioneer, died in May. *Financial Times,* p. 12.

Bowman, J. (2013). Tulsa Shock pick up jersey sponsorship. *SB Nation.* Retrieved from

http://www.swishappeal.com/2013/1/31
/3938278/tulsa-shock-pick-up-jersey
-sponsorship

Coca-Cola Company. (2006). The Olympic Games.
Retrieved from https://www.olympic.org
/sponsors/coca-cola

DSG Pittsburgh Marathon. Dick's Sporting Goods
Pittsburgh Marathon Showcases Steel City as
One of America's Top Running Cities.
(2017, May 25). Retrieved from http://www
.thepittsburghmarathon.com/News-Item
-DICKS-Sporting-Goods-Pittsburgh
-Marathon-Showcases-Steel-City-as-One
-of-Americas-Top-Running-Cities

ESPN. (2013, January 10). ESPN, Inc. fact sheet.
Retrieved from http://espnmediazone.com
/us/espn-inc-fact-sheet/

Hardy, S. (1996). Matt Levine: The "father" of
modern sport marketing. *Sport Marketing
Quarterly, 5*, 5–7.

Holtzman, J. (1986, January 3). Barnum of baseball
made sure fans were entertained. *Chicago
Tribune*, pp. D1, D3.

IMG. (2018). Retrieved from http://imgevents
.com/property/golf/the-open/ and from
http://imgevents.com/about-img/

Keilman, J. (2017, September 5). Youth
football participation declines as worries
mount about concussions, CTE. *Chicago
Tribune*. Retrieved from http://www
.chicagotribune.com/news/local/breaking
/ct-football-youth-decline-met-20170904
-story.html

Kotler, P. (2003). *Marketing management*. Upper
Saddle River, NJ: Prentice Hall.

Lachowetz, T., & Gladden, J. (2003). A framework
for understanding cause-related sport
marketing programs. *International Journal of
Sports Marketing & Sponsorship, 4*(4), 313–333.

Levine, P. (1985). *A. G. Spalding and the rise of
baseball*. New York, NY: Oxford University
Press.

Liberman, N. (2003, June 16). Defining Hispanic
market challenges teams. *Street & Smith's
SportsBusiness Journal*, p. 20.

Luther to install blue AstroTurf in Carlson
Stadium. (2017, June 1). *The Decorah
Journal*, p. A1, A3.

Mahoney, B. (2016, April 15). NBA to begin
selling jersey sponsorships in 2017–18.
Retrieved from http://www.nba.com/2016
/news/04/15/nba-to-begin-selling-jersey
-sponsorships-in-2017-18.ap/

McCarthy, E. J., & Perreault, W. D. (1988).
Essentials of marketing. Homewood, IL:
Richard D. Irwin.

McKenna, R. (1991). *Relationship marketing*.
Reading, MA: Addison-Wesley.

Mullin, B., Hardy, S., & Sutton, W. A. (2014). *Sport
marketing* (4th ed.) Champaign, IL: Human
Kinetics.

Newzoo. (2017). 2017 global eSports market report.
Retrieved from http://resources.newzoo.com
/hubfs/Reports/Newzoo_Free_2017_Global
_Esports_Market_Report.pdf?hsCtaTracking
=5a96aa39-a810-47a6-834b-559c317775c3
%7C6a2d5758-bab2-4d87-9fbe-f82dc9ba638a

Perez, S. (2017). 56.6 million customers to go
without pay TV this year, as cord cutting
accelerates. Retrieved from https://
techcrunch.com/2017/09/13/56-6-million
-u-s-consumers-to-go-without-pay-tv-this
-year-as-cord-cutting-accelerates/

Porter, R. (2017, December 28). The 100 most-
watched TV programs of 2017: Super
Bowl LI laps the field. Retrieved http://
tvbythenumbers.zap2it.com/more-tv-news
/the-100-most-watched-tv-programs-of-2017
-super-bowl-li-laps-the-field/

Ries, A., & Trout, J. (1993). *The 22 immutable
laws of marketing*. New York, NY: Harper
Business.

Roberts, R., & Olson, J. (1989). *Winning is the only
thing: Sports in American society since 1945*.
Baltimore, MD: Johns Hopkins University
Press.

Strasser, J. B., & Becklund, L. (1991). *Swoosh: The
unauthorized story of Nike and the men who
played there*. New York, NY: Harcourt Brace
Jovanovich.

Sugar, B. (1978). *Hit the sign and win a free suit of clothes from Harry Finklestein*. Chicago, IL: Contemporary Books.

Swift, E. M. (1990, May 21). The most powerful man in sports: Mark McCormack, founder and CEO of International Management Group, rules his empire as both agent and impresario. Retrieved from https://www.si.com/vault/1990/05/21/122017/the-most-powerful-man-in-sports-mark-mccormack-founder-and-ceo-of-international-management-group-rules-his-empire-as-both-agent-and-impresario

U.S. Census Bureau. (2017). The Hispanic population 2017. Retrieved from https://www.census.gov/quickfacts/fact/table/US/PST045216

Veeck, B., & Linn, E. (1962). *Veeck—As in wreck*. New York, NY: G. P. Putnam's Sons.

Veeck, B., & Linn, E. (1965). *The hustler's handbook*. New York, NY: G. P. Putnam's Sons.

Wagner, K. (2018, February 15). Twitter, YouTube, Amazon and Verizon are competing for streaming rights to NFL's "Thursday Night Football." Retrieved from https://www.recode.net/2018/2/15/17018528/nfl-twitter-youtube-amazon-verizon-thursday-night-football

Chapter

4

Nola Agha

Financial and Economic Principles Applied to Sport Management

Learning Objectives

Upon completion of this chapter, students should be able to:

1. Critically evaluate the various estimates of the economic magnitude of the sport industry.

2. Recognize that, whether large or small, all sport organizations have a need for staff with training in financial management.

3. Identify and define basic financial terms such as revenues, expenses, income statement, balance sheet, assets, liabilities, debt, owner's equity, and return on investment (ROI).

4. Define financial risk, examine some of the factors that affect the risk of sport organizations, and discuss how excess risk may lead to default or bankruptcy.

5. Understand how the industrial organization of the spectator sport industry is fundamentally different from the non-spectator sport industry and the rest of U.S. business.

6. Assess the degree of monopoly power that professional sport leagues enjoy and the effect that it has on teams' ability to earn profits.

7. Judge the challenges that professional and intercollegiate sport organizations will encounter as the sport industry tries to continue growing revenue in the future.

8. Consider why only a few intercollegiate athletic departments generate an annual surplus and, that taken as a whole, college athletics is unprofitable.

9. Define competitive balance and illustrate its importance to leagues and teams.

10. Illustrate how techniques such as salary caps, revenue sharing, reverse-order-of-finish drafts, and luxury taxes may affect the degree of competitive balance within a league.

Introduction

The media are constantly drawing our attention to the financial aspects of the sport world. Some of the numbers that we read and hear can seem staggering to the average person. To get a sense of the magnitude of the dollar values being generated by the industry, consider these statistics:

- The average player salary in the National Basketball Association (NBA) is currently $6.2 million per season (Badenhausen, 2016b).
- The NBA's Golden State Warriors will open a $1 billion arena in 2019, and the naming rights were sold to JPMorgan Chase for approximately $300 million over 20 years (Badenhausen, 2017).
- Major League Baseball's (MLB's) current 8-year television contract with ESPN calls for the league to be paid $5.6 billion, or about $23 million per team per year (Ourand, 2012).
- The estimated market value of the Dallas Cowboys is $4 billion, up 25% from 2015, making it the most valuable franchise in the world. This is the first time since 2010 a non-soccer team has topped the list (Badenhausen, 2016a).

In college sports, the pattern is the same: The Big Ten conference received $132.5 million when four of its member schools played in 2016–2017 bowl games (Dosh, 2016); the National Collegiate Athletic Association's (NCAA's) contract with CBS and Turner Sports, signed in 2010, to televise the NCAA Men's Basketball Tournament every March will pay the NCAA about $19.8 billion through 2032 (Brady, 2016); 24 universities make more than $100 million annually, with Texas A&M topping the list at $192.6 million (Gaines, 2016).

© Mike Liu/Shutterstock, Inc.

The list could go on and on, but one thing is clear—sport is very big business.

The examples given here are from only one segment of the sport industry—the spectator sport segment. Of course, the sport industry is much broader than just the spectator side. It includes not only a wide range of service businesses related to participatory recreational activities (such as fitness centers, bowling alleys, and rock climbing gyms), but also the entire sporting goods and related apparel industry.

The sport industry is definitely a major force in North American business, although it is difficult to get an accurate, reliable measure of its true financial magnitude. According to Plunkett Research (2017), the entire U.S. sport industry in 2015 accounted for $472 billion in total spending, of which only $32.1 billion was derived from professional leagues and teams. In contrast, the U.S. Department of Commerce (2017a) estimated the combined gross economic output of the arts, entertainment, and recreation categories (which includes spectator sports) in the United States to be about $341 billion in 2016.

Part of the practical problem in measuring the exact size of this industry is deciding what to include. For example, the gambling sector derives much of its business from betting on spectator sports. So, should gambling be included? Perhaps more importantly, different methods use different variables to measure the size of the industry. For example, if a golf club manufacturer sold a set of golf clubs to a retailer for $1,000, which in turn sold the clubs to a customer for $1,500, one could naïvely (and incorrectly) add the two together and say the total output of the industry is $2,500. While this might seem like an obvious error—the $1,000 is double-counted, and the true value of the transactions is $1,500—it is surprising how often these kinds of errors are made. The point is that unless you know how someone is calculating the magnitude of the industry, you should exercise extreme caution before you put too much faith in the result.

This raises a related issue—namely, the difference between an industry's sales and its value added. For example, the golf club manufacturer in the example given earlier may have bought raw materials (e.g., graphite, titanium, rubber) from its suppliers for $300, used these materials to manufacture the clubs, and then sold the clubs to the retailer for $1,000. Although the manufacturer's sale totals $1,000, its value added is only $700, because $300 of the $1,000 sale price was attributable to those outside the industry. When one adjusts for the concept of **value added**, the numbers change considerably. For example, while the Department of Commerce estimated total output for the sport industry in 2016 to be $341 billion, it estimated the value added to be only $198 billion, which represented only 0.01% of the U.S. gross domestic product (U.S. Department of Commerce, 2017b). The concept of value added is probably the best single measure of an industry's impact.

Despite these practical complexities with actually measuring the size of the industry and the caution one must always take when interpreting the numbers, one thing is certain: Regardless of how one specifically measures it, the sport industry is both significant and growing. Many managers inside sport organizations (whether professional or college spectator sports), the recreational service sector, and the sporting goods industry are now responsible for multimillion-dollar budgets. This financial boom has created a great need in the industry for people with training in finance. Even when the sport organization operates on a more modest scale than the examples given earlier—whether it be a locally owned baseball bat manufacturer, a minor league hockey team, or a Division III athletic department in college sports—the need for sound financial management practices is no less urgent.

This chapter provides an introduction to the fields of finance and economics within a sport context. It examines what finance is and what it is not. It discusses how money flows into and out of a sport organization, and it examines the types of management decisions that must be made to maximize the financial success of an organization. From an economics perspective, this chapter looks at the structure of the sport industry in terms of competition, monopoly, and competitive balance, including how those features relate to finance. It also discusses some of the current issues facing various sectors of the industry.

Key Concepts

What Is Finance?

The term *finance* often has quite different meanings to different people. For some individuals not specifically trained in finance, it is often used very broadly to describe anything related to dollars, money, or numbers. This definition implies that almost everything that occurs in an organization falls under the broad umbrella of "finance," given that almost everything within an organization has monetary implications.

In contrast, those trained in finance tend to define the field somewhat more narrowly. Part of the purpose of this chapter is to illustrate what finance actually is and, just as importantly, what it is not. Because the finance discipline tends to intersect with other managerial disciplines—for example, marketing—it may be unclear to some where the marketing function ends and where the finance function begins.

Perhaps the best way to make this distinction is to consider that what defines finance is not really the subject matter—it could be ticket sales, merchandise sales, the signing of a free agent, or the construction of a new stadium—but rather the concepts and techniques used to solve problems and make decisions about these issues. For example, the act of a college athletic department selling a corporate sponsorship has clear financial implications: Sponsorship salespeople must be paid for their services, and the sponsorships they ultimately sell will generate revenues for the department. The act in itself is not about finance, however, but rather about sales.

Of course, finance issues could still be embedded within this process. For example, a question might arise about how many salespeople should be allocated to the sponsorship sales department. Might some of the sales staff be more effectively employed in selling season ticket packages instead of selling sponsorships? This question, while not necessarily straightforward, is crucial, and it is an example of a financial allocation decision that a sport organization must make. Allocation decisions such as these tend to occur in the course of the **budgeting** process.

The basic financial "answer" to this question is that the organization should allocate its sales staff based on the magnitude of the financial payoff that each department (tickets and sponsorships) can return for a given salesperson. In essence, the question is this: Would shifting one salesperson from sponsorship sales to ticket sales increase or decrease the overall revenue that flows into the department? In other words, finance is not as much about simply identifying where and how money flows into the organization as it is about how organizations make allocation decisions to ensure the net inflow is maximized.

In summary, the managerial discipline of finance refers to something much more specific than simply anything to do with money or dollars. While there is no single, universally agreed-upon definition, finance generally refers to two primary activities of an organization: how an organization *generates* the funds that flow into an organization, and how these funds get *allocated* and spent once they are in the organization.

Some Basics: Financial Flows in Sport Organizations

Like any other field, finance is an area that has its own terminology. Being familiar with this terminology is a necessary prerequisite to better understanding the finance function. This terminology is best introduced by thinking about the process by which funds (i.e., dollars) flow through a sport organization. Let's start with how funds flow into an organization.

The primary business of organizations in the spectator sport sector is to provide entertainment through the staging of athletic contests. The selling associated with these events is the primary way in which sport teams raise funds. These funds are called **revenues**. Revenues may come from a variety of sources—ticket sales, concession and merchandise sales, media contracts, and sponsorship revenues, to name only a few. For college athletic programs, funds may also come from nonrevenue sources, such as budgetary allocations from the university to the athletic department.

Outside of the spectator sport sector, revenues come from the sale of the organization's primary goods and services. For example, a YMCA may generate revenue from a variety of sources, such as yearly membership fees, day use fees, summer camps, after-school programs, birthday party rentals, child care, and swim lessons.

Obviously, money does not just flow into sport organizations; some also flows out. In other words, **expenses** must be incurred to generate revenues. For the YMCA, expenses might include such items as staff salaries, water to fill the pool, electricity to light the building, and insurance to protect the business in case of injuries. In the spectator sport sector—whether it be college or pro—expenses include uniforms and equipment (e.g., bats, balls, hockey sticks), player transportation and hotel accommodation for away games, and so on. Facility-related costs include ticket takers, ushers, and concession workers on game days; electricity to provide lighting and to run

equipment; a cleaning crew after an event; and expenditures for maintaining the playing surface. For major professional teams, these types of costs are all secondary to the single biggest expenditure item: player salaries.

In a basic sense, the financial success of an organization is ultimately dependent on the difference between revenues and expenses. This difference is called **profits** (sometimes referred to as **income**). Profits can be increased by increasing revenues, by decreasing costs, or both. An organization's revenues, expenses, and profits over a given time period (for example, a year) are usually summarized on a financial statement called an **income statement**, statement of activity, or profit and loss statement (P&L).

Another important financial concept is **assets**. Broadly speaking, assets are anything that an organization owns that can be used to generate future revenues. For example, the primary assets of a firm that makes wearable fitness trackers are its manufacturing equipment and production facility, while in indoor futsal center's primary assets are its building and equipment. With spectator sports, a team's stadium is an important asset because it provides the team with a venue at which to stage games, which in turn allows the team to earn various types of revenue. As we will see later in the chapter, new stadiums tend to have dramatic and immediate effects on a franchise's revenue stream.

One of the most important assets that major professional sports franchises possess is their membership in the league to which they belong. For example, in 2007, Toronto FC paid $10 million to join Major League Soccer (MLS); ten years later, in 2017, two expansion franchises each paid $150 million to join MLS (Strauss, 2016). The National Football League's (NFL's) popularity as a league is so high that the most recent expansion franchise, the Houston Texans, paid the NFL an expansion fee of $700 million (*SportsBusiness Journal*, 2006).

This fee was paid just to "join the club" and to enjoy all the future financial benefits that such membership in the NFL may bring; it did not include money for such large-scale expenditures as stadium construction and player salaries.

In essence, all sport organizations, like any other businesses, must spend money up front to generate what they hope will be even greater inflows later on. For example, an indoor futsal center cannot sign up teams until its owners first buy or lease a building and then outfit that building with courts; a wearable fitness tracker manufacturer cannot make and sell any wearable devices until it first purchases the necessary raw materials. In financial terms, any business must make an initial investment in assets to generate future revenues.

One further element can be added to the mix. Assets have to be bought, so where do the dollars come from that are invested in these assets? A new stadium, for example, may cost hundreds of millions of dollars to construct.

For some assets, such as stadiums, professional teams have been very successful in convincing local governments to pay for all or part of the costs of the facility. Among the stadiums and arenas built or renovated since 2010, 80% of those facilities received a total of $13 billion in tax-exempt municipal bonds, with the other 20% receiving other forms of public subsidies (Gayer, Drukker, & Gold, 2016).

This issue aside, professional teams can fund or "finance" assets in a number of ways. First, **owners' equity** (sometimes simply referred to as equity) can be used to finance assets. Owners' equity is essentially the amount of their own money that owners have invested in the organization. Much of this investment of funds typically occurs when the owners initially purchase (or start up) the entity, but that amount can increase if the owners reinvest any profits back into the venture, rather than removing these profits and paying themselves dividends.

In major professional sports, most franchise owners (i.e., the equity holders) tend to be either a sole individual or a small group of individuals. Sometimes, existing owners will sell part of their ownership stake in a team (i.e., sell part of their equity) as a means to bring cash into the team. For example, in 2015, the owners of the Chicago Cubs sold a minority share of the team worth $300 million to renovate Wrigley Field (Shaikin, 2017).

A few franchises are owned by corporate conglomerates. **Table 4-1** shows that Maple

Table 4-1 Examples of Sport Franchises Owned by Corporations	
Corporation	**Franchise(s) Owned**
Anschutz Entertainment Group (AEG)	MLS Los Angeles Galaxy, ECHL Ontario Reign, European hockey and soccer teams, part of the NHL Los Angeles Kings and NBA Los Angeles Lakers
Comcast-Spectacor	NHL Philadelphia Flyers, ECHL Maine Mariners, minor league baseball team in Maryland
Liberty Media	MLB Atlanta Braves
Madison Square Garden Company	NHL New York Rangers, NBA New York Knicks, WNBA New York Liberty, NBA D-League Westchester Knicks, AHL Hartford Wolf Pack
Maple Leaf Sports and Entertainment (owned by Rogers Communications and Bell Canada)	NHL Toronto Maple Leafs, NBA Toronto Raptors, MLS Toronto FC, AHL Toronto Marlies, NBA D-League Raptors 905
Rogers Communications	Toronto Blue Jays, part owner of Maple Leaf Sports and Entertainment

Leaf Sports and Entertainment leads the way among corporate owners, with ownership of teams in the National Hockey League (NHL), NBA, MLS, American Hockey League (AHL), and NBA Development League (D-League). Corporate ownership can also get very complex. For example, in 2012, Maple Leaf Sports and Entertainment was acquired by Rogers Communications and Bell Canada, two rival telecommunications companies that owned their own professional teams.

There have even been a few occasions where a franchise's shares have been publicly traded on a stock exchange. In these cases, there are literally thousands of owners of a team, most of whom own only a small portion of the franchise. At one time or another in the past 20 years, teams such as the Boston Celtics, Cleveland Indians, Vancouver Canucks, and Toronto Maple Leafs have had publicly traded shares.

In the non-spectator sector, publicly traded shares are much more common than in the spectator sector. **Table 4-2** shows some of the sport organizations whose shares are publicly traded. Publicly traded shares give organizations much wider access to investment capital, which potentially allows them to expand more quickly than they otherwise would be able to do.

Besides owners' equity, the other major way that sport organizations raise money to finance their assets is to borrow money. The amount of money that an organization borrows is referred to as its **debt** (also referred to as **liabilities**).

When organizations borrow, they are legally obligated to pay back the original amount they borrowed (the **principal**), plus **interest**. Money might be borrowed from banks, or it might be borrowed from other lenders in financial markets through, for example, instruments such as **bonds**. Bonds are financial instruments that allow the borrower to both borrow large dollar amounts and borrow this money for a relatively long period of time (usually 20 or more years). Bonds are normally issued only by relatively large corporate entities and by governments. There is usually a secondary market for bonds, meaning the original buyer (i.e., the lender) can sell the bonds to another buyer at any time prior to the bonds "maturing." Bonds are usually purchased by institutional investors, such as mutual funds, insurance companies, and pension funds.

In spectator sports, stadium construction projects are often financed with bonds.

Table 4-2 Examples of Publicly Traded Sport Companies

Name	Type of Business	Stock Exchange
Big Five	Sporting goods retailer	NASDAQ
Callaway Golf	Golf products	NYSE
Churchill Downs	Thoroughbred racing	NASDAQ
Electronic Arts	Video games	NASDAQ
International Speedway Corp	Motorsports entertainment	NASDAQ
Madison Square Garden	Venues and teams	NYSE
Nike	Shoes	NYSE
Town Sports International	Fitness clubs	NASDAQ
Vail Resorts	Skiing	NYSE

Abbreviations: NASDAQ, National Association of Securities Dealers Automated Quotations; NYSE, New York Stock Exchange.

For example, the small town of McKinney, Texas, issued bonds to build a $62.8 million high school football stadium (Whitten, 2016) and Colorado State University sold $239 million in bonds to build a new college football stadium (Oldham, 2015).

The interest rate at which any money is borrowed depends on the lender's perception of the borrower's ability to repay. In turn, this ability to repay depends on a variety of factors: the popularity of the organization's goods or services, the magnitude and stability of the organization's revenue streams, the future prospects for revenue growth, the degree to which costs are controlled and contained, the amount of debt the organization is already carrying, and so forth.

Leagues such as the NFL, NBA, and MLB maintain "credit facilities," sometimes called loan pools, and they borrow extensively in financial markets to fund these facilities. Individual teams in the league can then borrow from the credit facilities, rather than borrowing directly in financial markets. Leagues can borrow less expensively than can individual teams, simply because league loans are backed by the collective revenues of all teams in the league, whereas loans to teams are backed only by that individual team's revenues. Companies such as Fitch and Moody's "rate" this debt of major professional leagues, teams, and universities. Generally, the NFL's debt receives the highest credit rating in sports, indicating that the NFL has the lowest credit risk, which allows it to borrow at the lowest possible interest rate. For example, Fitch has rated recent debt issues of the NFL as A+ (Business Wire, 2016b); MLB received an A rating (Business Wire, 2016a).

An organization's assets, liabilities, and owners' equity at any given point are shown on a financial statement called a **balance sheet**.

College athletic programs are nonprofit organizations and can have quite different sources of funds. In college athletics, there are no real equity holders—no one "owns" these programs. Typically, outside sources of funds flow into the athletic department through budgetary transfers from the university itself. However, some athletic programs are finding very innovative ways to raise capital. For example, in 2000, Duke University created a venture capital fund to invest in start-ups; by 2012, the earnings from the investments were sufficient to permanently endow the men's basketball team (Beaton & Kyle, 2012). These attempts at innovative fundraising can also fail, such as when Oklahoma State University spent $33 million on life insurance policies for a group of wealthy boosters, only to cancel the program and lose its investment (Associated Press, 2012).

Some college programs, such as the University of Florida, are run through an outside entity that is incorporated by the state (University Athletic Association, 2017). In Florida's case, the University Athletic Association seeks revenue through corporate sponsors, media and ticket revenues, and private donors. Funding for expenses, such as student-athlete tuition and expenses, are paid to the university from the University Athletic Association. This structure is common to the Southeastern Conference and is a growing model in collegiate athletics.

Some Typical Financial Decisions

With these basic concepts in mind, let's look at some examples of financial decisions that sport organizations may face. Many of the financial decisions in a sport organization ultimately revolve around the management of assets. For example, in any given season, there may be a variety of investment expenditures that a ski resort could make to increase the value of its assets. Because investment dollars are likely limited, however, choices have to be made about which options will be the most rewarding.

One option might be for the ski resort to expand its facilities by adding new runs and lifts. Another option might be to upgrade and modernize its existing ski lifts. Still another choice might be to acquire a ski resort in a different state to diversify the owners' risk given the unpredictability of snowfall. All of these options will have different initial investment costs, and all will have different revenue potentials.

In the spectator segment, a baseball team might face similar choices. For example, one option might be for the team to go into the free agent market and sign a star player. This move would presumably increase the team's performance on the field, which in turn might lead to more tickets being sold and/or higher TV ratings. Alternatively, the team could take the money that it would have used to sign the free agent and instead upgrade the luxury suites in the stadium. By making these upgrades, the team could then charge a higher price to its corporate clients to lease the suites. Another option might be to install a state-of-the-art scoreboard in the stadium. This novelty might increase the overall fan experience, making people more likely to attend games. Furthermore, it might provide increased sponsorship and advertising opportunities for the team. Or perhaps the team might want to replace its existing natural grass field with an artificial surface. This change might reduce maintenance costs; reduce player injuries, which may increase team performance and, therefore, ticket revenues; and reduce future expenses, in that fewer players will appear on the roster during the season because fewer replacement players will be needed to take over for injured players. A new artificial surface may also increase revenues in other ways by making the venue usable for a wider range of events.

It is these types of decisions that lie at the heart of finance. Finance-trained people approach these kinds of problems by applying certain concepts and techniques. In this case, one approach is to calculate each alternative's **return on investment (ROI)**. The concept of ROI is very commonly encountered in finance. It shows the expected dollar value return on each alternative investment, stated as a percentage of the original cost of each investment. For example, an ROI of 9% indicates the team would recover all of its initial investment, plus an additional 9%.

To calculate ROI, the financial analyst needs to make two types of estimates. The first task is to calculate the initial cost of each investment: What will it cost to sign the free agent, or what will the new turf or scoreboard cost? The second, somewhat more difficult task is to estimate the magnitude of the revenues that each alternative will generate. For example, with the free agent signing, the player's on-field performance should ultimately affect (positively, one hopes) the team's winning percentage, which should in turn affect attendance and media revenues.

© ktasimar/Shutterstock, Inc.

An interesting case study has arisen in recent years that pertains to the ROI of player personnel decisions. The best-selling book *Moneyball* (Lewis, 2003) chronicles the processes that Oakland A's general manager (GM) Billy Beane uses to make player selection decisions. Beane contends that many teams in baseball often make systematic player selection errors—"overvaluing" some players while "undervaluing" others. As the GM of a small-market team, one of Beane's strategies to more effectively compete with large-market teams is to identify and acquire these undervalued players. In essence, an investment in an undervalued player produces a higher ROI than a comparable investment in an overvalued player; undervalued players create more wins per dollar of payroll than do overvalued players, and hence they make a greater contribution to team profits.

When examining free agents, a player's off-field performance must also be evaluated. That is, would he increase merchandise sales? Would she increase the overall visibility of the team?

This raises another key issue: Investments such as these require managers to think about the future. The future is notoriously difficult to predict accurately. For example, no one can know for certain the magnitude of the increased revenues that would result from a ski resort adding new runs and lifts. Many uncertainties exist: Will the popularity of skiing, relative to other activities, continue to grow? Will consumers continue to have the disposable income necessary to engage in leisure activities such as skiing? Will other competing ski resorts enter the market, thereby reducing market share for the existing ski resort? Will climate change affect the predictability of annual snowfall? Similarly, in the baseball example, no one can say for certain how much the free agent's signing will actually increase revenues. The player might not perform as expected, adding the player may affect team chemistry in ways not foreseen, the player might be plagued by injuries, and so on.

These difficulties in making accurate predictions about the future relate to the concept of **risk**. Risk is one of the most important concepts in finance. It refers to the fact that the future is uncertain, so that the future benefits of any investment made today cannot ever be known with certainty at the time the investment is made. Of course, some investments inherently carry more risk than others. Financial managers need to take into account these different levels of risk when they evaluate investment

projects. For example, investing in upgraded luxury suites may be less risky than investing in a free agent, in the sense that the future revenue payoffs from the former move are more predictable than they are for the latter investment.

Making decisions about which assets to invest in is not the only place where the concept of risk arises in sport finance. As we have seen, there is a whole other class of decisions, called financing decisions, where risk is a crucial factor. These financing decisions revolve around the degree to which financing will occur with equity versus debt. In other words, owners must decide how much of the assets of the franchise they will finance with their own money versus how much they will finance with borrowed money. There are always tradeoffs. Generally, financing with borrowed money is less expensive than equity, but it carries more risk. It is less expensive because lenders do not have any ownership stake in the organization and, therefore, are entitled to only repayment of their original loan, with interest. If the organization's financial performance is better than expected, none of this upside has to be shared with lenders, so it can be retained by the current equity holders.

Debt carries more risk because the organization is legally obligated to repay the borrowed money, with interest, at a prespecified date. If the borrower is unable to do so—perhaps because revenues are lower than expected— then the borrower is said to be in **default** on the debt. If a default occurs, the lenders may force the organization into bankruptcy. Such a scenario is not merely hypothetical in the spectator sport industry. It has occurred remarkably often in the NHL, with the Los Angeles Kings, Ottawa Senators, Buffalo Sabres, Pittsburgh Penguins, Phoenix Coyotes, and Dallas Stars. Most recently, in 2012, the New Jersey Devils defaulted on a loan, although the lenders did not opt to force the Devils into bankruptcy (Kaplan & Botta, 2012). MLB teams that have entered into bankruptcy include the Seattle Pilots (later the Milwaukee Brewers), Baltimore Orioles, Chicago Cubs, Texas Rangers, and Los Angeles Dodgers.

Similar situations have occurred in the non-spectator sport sector. For example, when athletic gear retailer Sports Authority missed interest payments on $300 million in debt, it was forced to file for bankruptcy (McGrath, 2016).

The Economics of Sport

What we have discussed up to this point falls within the realm of sport finance. The chapter reviews how managers make decisions about where to raise funds and where to spend those funds. A related area, called sport economics, is also relevant to anyone interested in the financial aspects of sport.

The general field of (micro) economics examines, among many other issues, how an industry organizes itself and how this industry structure affects competition and profits among firms in the industry. In recent years, an entire subfield of economics has developed that examines the peculiar aspects of the spectator sport industry. The focus has been on the spectator sport industry because it is organized so differently from the non-spectator industry and, for that matter, from the rest of U.S. business. In most industries, firms directly compete with each other for market share: Uber competes with Lyft, Coca-Cola competes with Pepsi, Fitbit competes with Apple and Garmin, Under Armour competes with Nike, IMG College competes with Learfield, Ping competes with Callaway. There are little or no common interests among the competitors. For example, every pair of shoes that Under Armour sells is a pair that Nike did not sell. In fact, all else equal, Nike would be better off if Under Armour did not exist, and vice versa.

In the spectator sport industry (whether college or pro), the issue is very different. While teams may compete against each other on the field, they must cooperate off the field. For example, the MLS Portland Timbers and Seattle Sounders are intense rivals (Know Rivalry, 2017), and each franchise would be less valuable if the other did not exist. Thus, the Timbers and the Sounders are not competitors in the same way that Under Armour and Nike are; in a business sense, the Timbers and Sounders are more like partners. They are both members of the Western Conference, and the existence of one franchise benefits the other franchise.

The other significant feature that differentiates major professional sports leagues from the non-spectator sport sector, and from the rest of U.S. business, is that these sports leagues are considered **monopolies**. That is, these leagues face no direct competition for the products and services they produce. For example, the NBA is currently the only seller of elite-level professional basketball in North America. Fans who enjoy watching the highest-caliber professional basketball must watch the NBA's version of the product because no other league supplies a comparable product. Again, compare this situation to the golf club industry, where a consumer shopping for a new set of clubs has a wide range of manufacturers from which to choose.

Businesses that are a monopoly, by definition, face no direct competition. This gives them greater bargaining power when dealing with stakeholders and allows the monopoly to potentially charge a higher price for its product than would be the case if it faced competitors. Thus fans pay higher prices for tickets, media companies pay higher fees for broadcast rights, corporations pay higher amounts to lease luxury suites, and taxpayers pay a large share of stadium construction costs. In short, the monopoly status of sports leagues allows them to earn much higher profits than would otherwise be the case.

North American sports leagues have not always had the luxury of this monopoly status; indeed, many leagues regularly faced competitors. The league that has faced the most competitors over the years is—perhaps somewhat surprisingly—the NFL. Since World War II, the NFL has faced serious competition from the All American Football Conference (AAFC) during the late 1940s, the American Football League (AFL) during the 1960s, the World Football League (WFL) during the mid-1970s, and the United States Football League (USFL) in the mid-1980s. In basketball, the NBA was actually formed in the late 1940s from the merger of two competing leagues—the National Basketball League (NBL) and the Basketball Association of America (BAA)—and then faced competition from the rival American Basketball Association (ABA) from 1967 to 1976. In women's professional basketball, the American Basketball League (ABL) was formed in 1996 before the Women's National Basketball Association (WNBA) began. Despite having signed most of the best talent from the gold medal–winning 1996 Summer Olympics team, the ABL could not match the marketing and financial backing that the WNBA received from the NBA; ultimately, the ABL folded after 2 years of operations. In hockey, the NHL faced competition from the rival World Hockey Association (WHA) during the 1972 to 1979 time span. Only in baseball has there not been a competitor league emerge since World War II.

The presence of these leagues rapidly and dramatically bid up player salaries. In some cases, they also forced a merger with the established league. The AFL was the most successful of all **rival leagues**, gaining a complete merger in 1966, with all eight AFL teams at the time being accepted into the NFL. The ABA and the WHA were also successful in gaining at least partial mergers, with four ABA teams entering the NBA in 1976, and four WHA teams entering the NHL in 1979.

Why have no new rival leagues emerged in nearly 40 years? Rival leagues need two elements to be successful. First, they need players, at least some of whom are talented enough to be able to play in the established league, but who have chosen to play in the rival league. Many great players are alumni of rival leagues—Joe Namath and Herschel Walker in football, Julius Erving and Moses Malone in basketball, Teresa Edwards and Yolanda Griffin in women's basketball, and Wayne Gretzky and Mark Messier in hockey, to name only a few. Before the emergence of strong players associations and free agency, players often were "underpaid," generally earning only 20% to 25% of league revenues, compared to the situation today, where 55% to 60% is the norm. Thus, players today have much less incentive to jump to a rival league.

In addition to having quality players, a second factor that rival leagues need to be successful is viable cities and markets in which to play. Over the past three decades, the major professional men's leagues have undergone successive rounds of expansion, to the point where all four currently have 30 or more franchises. This larger geographic footprint forces potential rival leagues either to place franchises in more mid-size, and probably less viable, markets, or to challenge the established league in head-to-head competition in the markets where the established league is already located. Younger leagues like MLS are currently expanding to viable cities in part to reduce the likelihood of rival competition.

The examination of rival leagues can make for an interesting history lesson, but what relevance does it have to business and finance in today's sport world? It turns out that the monopoly status of sports leagues has a great impact on financial issues. With no real threat of outside competition emerging, at least for the foreseeable future, the established sports leagues have large degrees of market power. This, in turn, allows them to have greater bargaining power with players, with broadcasters, with corporate sponsors, and with local governments regarding stadium funding issues. All else equal, this factor makes the monopoly professional sports leagues much more profitable than they otherwise would be. It also allows them to enact financial policies—such as salary caps and revenue sharing—that would simply not be possible if a league faced direct competition from a rival league.

This level of monopoly power is almost unheard of in any other U.S. business or industry. In fact, some economists argue that major professional sports leagues and their member teams are the only legal monopolies in the United States today. Some economists (Quirk & Fort, 1999) have even called for the federal government to break up the monopoly leagues, similar to the forced breakup of telecommunications giant AT&T in 1984. While a forced breakup is unlikely to occur (the spectator sport industry simply has too much political power), the industry will no doubt have to continue to occasionally publicly defend its monopoly status from challenges by economists or by certain members of Congress.

Of course, this monopoly position of leagues and teams does not guarantee financial success, nor does it guarantee that every team in every league will enjoy equal financial success. For example, even though the NFL and the NHL are both monopolies, the former is obviously a much stronger, much more successful business entity. The market power exercised by the NFL in negotiating its television deals combined with the league's revenue-sharing models for media revenues also contribute greatly to the economic success of the NFL as compared to the NHL. Even within a league, teams must still produce a quality product, and they must display sound and innovative business management practices to achieve maximum success. In the NFL, the New England Patriots went from the lowest-valued franchise in 1991 to the second highest-valued franchise in 2016, largely due to the Kraft family's purchase of the team in 1994 and the subsequent innovative management approaches that were adopted.

While the monopoly position of the major professional leagues ensures no direct competition in the same sport, teams must still compete for the broader entertainment dollar of consumers. Consumers in many cities have a wide variety of entertainment options, including major professional sports, minor professional sports, college sports, theme parks, and the increasing digital streaming entertainment options available on mobile devices both inside and outside the home.

Key Skills

The future will continue to provide many growth opportunities for sport organizations, but it will also present challenges. As sport organizations continue to increase their managerial sophistication, the need for well-trained individuals in finance will become even greater. The specific issues will likely change. The key financial issues facing the industry in 15 years may be quite different than the ones facing the industry today. Thus, managers need to understand the underlying financial principles and techniques, rather than just simply being familiar with the current issues and facts. The issues will change, but the underlying analytical tools will not.

No matter which type of sport organization is involved, the finance function is crucial. It is important to remember that finance is not defined as much by the subject matter being analyzed—it could be decisions related to ticket or sponsorship sales, team marketing, stadium operations, or player personnel—as it is by how the issue is analyzed. Academic and practical training in finance helps people to think like a "finance person" and to evaluate problems using the fundamental concepts of financial analyses such as time value of money, risk and return, capital budgeting, ROI, and asset allocation.

While finance people do need to be comfortable working with numbers, this is far from the only skill needed. In addition to formal training in corporate finance, those interested in a career in the area should have a solid grounding in managerial and financial accounting, and in the advanced use of spreadsheets (e.g., Microsoft Excel). For those with aspirations of working in the spectator sport industry, a familiarity with sports economics is also very beneficial.

The specific issues may differ depending on the setting. For example, the issues facing the chief financial officer for a nonprofit organization like Positive Coaching Alliance will be different than those faced by an athletic director of a Division II college program, which in turn will be different than those faced by a chief financial officer of a global firm like scoreboard manufacturer Daktronics. However, the common link is that financial decision making in each of these settings should be grounded in the same basic set of principles, techniques, and thought processes.

Current Issues

Can Growth Continue?

In the non-spectator sport sector, a key issue is the extent to which the recreation and leisure market will continue to grow. Much of this sector—from yoga studios to skateboarding parks to indoor pools—is driven by demographics, affluence, and societal values. Since 1970, the U.S. population has aged, our overall affluence has increased, and our societal concerns over health-related issues have grown. The effect has been increased spending on recreational

and fitness activities that has propelled the industry to new financial heights.

For individual segments of the non-spectator sport industry, predicting consumer trends also becomes a factor in their growth. For example, will consumers continue to prefer smaller TRX, yoga, and Pilates studios over larger health clubs? Will the popularity of eSports continue to grow? Will NBA teams continue to purchase eSports teams? These are crucial financial questions because capital investments (e.g., building a new health club or purchasing an eSports team) are made now, but the payoff from these investments does not occur until later. Thus, if our assumptions about the future growth of the industry are incorrect, our ROI calculations will also be incorrect. For example, if the popularity of rock climbing begins to wane over the next decade, the ROI on any new rock climbing gym construction will be lower than it has been in the recent past, and it may even be low enough to cause the investor to not undertake the new project.

Broadly similar questions exist for the spectator side of the sport industry; in particular, can the financial successes of the past continue at their same level into the future? Both the major professional leagues and the major revenue-generating college sports (Division I football and men's basketball) have seen tremendous revenue growth in the past 25 years. **Table 4-3** shows how franchise values

Table 4-3	Average Franchise Values: 1991 and 2016/17 Seasons (in millions of dollars)		
	2016/2017 Season	**1991**	**Average Annual Growth Rate**
NFL	2,388	132	12.3%
MLB	1,540	121	10.7%
NBA	1,355	70	12.6%
NHL	517	44	10.4%

Data from Ozanian, M. (2017). Baseball team values. *Forbes*. Retrieved from https://www.forbes.com/sites/mikeozanian/2017/04/11/baseball-team-values-2017/; and Quirk, J., & Fort, R. (1997). *Pay dirt: The business of professional team sports*. Princeton, NJ: Princeton University Press.

Table 4-4 NCAA Division I-A (Football Bowl Subdivision) Median Total Revenues per School, by Sport: 1989 and 2015 (in thousands of dollars)

	2015	1989	**Average Annual Growth Rate**
Football	22,837	4,300	6.6%
Men's basketball	6,102	1,600	5.3%
Women's basketball	809	60	10.5%

Data from Fulks, D. (2016a). Revenues and expenses 2004–15: Division I intercollegiate athletics programs report. Retrieved from http://www.ncaapublications.com/productdownloads/D1REVEXP2015.pdf.

in the major professional leagues have changed over this time period. Franchise values capture the future expected profitability (revenues minus expenses) of the franchise and represent the current market price of the franchise. All four leagues have shown significant growth in franchise values over the time period, largely because revenues have risen faster than expenses.

Revenues have also risen in the major revenue-generating college sports. **Table 4-4** compares total revenues in 1989 with total revenues in 2015 for football, men's basketball, and women's basketball. All three show healthy yearly revenue growth. Of the three, women's basketball grew the most, experiencing an 10.5% increase per year over the time period, although this is somewhat offset by the fact that women's basketball started with the lowest base revenue (in 1989) of the three by far. In absolute terms, football continues to lead the revenue parade, with the average Division I-A (Football Bowl Subdivision) program now earning almost $23 million per year in earned and allocated revenues. While not shown in Table 4-4, the NCAA reports that the college football program with the highest revenues in 2015, the University of Texas, earned almost $152 million (Smith, 2015).

This increased revenue in spectator sports has come from a number of specific areas: gate receipts, new stadium revenues, and broadcast contracts. The growth in gate receipts is largely attributable to higher ticket prices—these prices have increased considerably in all leagues. The increased prices reflect the growing popularity of sport, sport consumers' increased ability to pay for tickets, and the scarcity of tickets in some locations. For example, many universities require a donation to the athletic department for the rights to purchase season tickets or tickets with premium locations. The University of Louisville collected $21.7 million in such donations for its men's basketball program, while the University of Washington pocketed $19.1 million in football donations (Collins & Rubin, 2015).

© best images/Shutterstock, Inc.

New (or refurbished) stadiums have also enhanced gate receipts because the revenue-generating ability of a stadium depends not only on the quantity of seats, but also on the quality. Teams prefer luxury seating and club seating because these premium seats have much greater revenue potential than the ordinary, regular seating. Such premium seats allow teams to better target high-income individuals and/or corporate clientele, and they allow teams to capture the increased ability and willingness to pay of these groups. Older stadiums simply do not have configurations that allow for this type of premium seating. In essence, new stadiums give sport consumers many more ways to spend their money. Many new stadiums have been able to generate even more revenues by selling the naming rights to the stadium. For example, Mercedes-Benz purchased the naming rights to the Atlanta Falcons' new football stadium for $324 million over 27 years, and JPMorgan Chase purchased the naming rights to the Golden State Warriors' new basketball arena for approximately $300-400 million over 20 years (Lefton, 2016).

Media revenues have also continued to grow strongly. For example, a 7-year deal (which began in 1991) between the NCAA and CBS to televise the men's basketball tournament paid the NCAA an average of approximately $140 million per season. In contrast, a 14-year agreement signed in 2010 and an 8-year extension signed in 2016 will pay the NCAA an average of more than $800 million per year through 2032 (Brady, 2016). In college football, ESPN is paying $500 million per year for the college football playoffs (Ourand & Smith, 2012), while Fox is paying $240 million per year and ESPN is paying $190 million for shared rights to the Big Ten Network (Ourand, 2016). These contracts illustrate the shift in college athletics as nonprofit conferences use their collective bargaining power to launch conference-specific networks that reap financial windfalls for each member school. For instance, in the 2016 fiscal year, the Southeastern Conference (SEC) reported revenues of $180 million from the College Football Playoff and $420 million in television and radio rights fees, which allowed the SEC to distribute an average of $40 million

to each school in the conference (Berkowitz, 2017). Similarly, the Big Ten distributed approximately $35 million from these sources and the Pac-12 distributed approximately $27 million in 2016 (Wilner, 2017).

In professional sports, the story is the same, as all four leagues have substantially increased their total television revenues. For sports such as baseball and hockey, the growth has been particularly at the local—as opposed to national—level. In the NFL, where almost all TV money is obtained through national contracts, the growth has been the most dramatic. The NFL's contracts with Fox, CBS, NBC, and ESPN collectively will pay an average of $4.95 billion each year from 2014 to 2021, or approximately $155 million per year in revenues for each NFL team. This is an increase from $100 million per team from 2006 to 2013 and from $30 million per team in 1991 (Associated Press, 2011). All told, the media rights for the largest sports properties (NFL, NBA, MLB, NHL, Olympics, Fédération Internationale de Football Association [FIFA] World Cup, English Premier League, College Football Playoff, NCAA Division I Men's Basketball Tournament, Big Ten, SEC, Pac-12, Big 12, and Atlantic Coast Conference [ACC]) are all locked up through 2020, and in some cases until 2034 (Crupi, 2016).

This interesting trend has occurred at the same time that fan avidity is dropping among millennials (Luker, 2016) and cable companies like ESPN have lost subscribers to "cord-cutting," as consumers increasingly prefer to watch games on digital platforms (Fahey, 2016). In this turbulent environment, some leagues have benefited by diversifying onto newer media platforms. For example, the NFL sold streaming rights for its Thursday Night Football games to Twitter for $10 million in 2016 and to Amazon for $50 million in 2017 (Ourand, 2017). Meanwhile, MLBAM, the technology arm of MLB, is owned equally by all team owners, is worth

$12 billion, and generates revenues of more than $600 million annually (Ozanian, 2017). A similar entity called BAMTech is a streaming technology provider and is a joint venture of MLBAM, Disney, and the NHL. It is valued at nearly $4 billion and is engaged in a variety of partnerships: developing an over-the-top service for ESPN, streaming live League of Legends video game competitions, and working with Discovery Communications and Eurosport, the rightsholder for the Olympics in Europe, to develop distribution platforms (Ozanian, 2017).

© David Lee/Shutterstock, Inc.

Challenges

While revenues have certainly increased, the cost of doing business in the sport industry has also gone up. In the non-spectator sport sector, increasingly larger capital investments are needed to continue to generate revenues. This also applies to investments in physical assets, such as when a fitness club spends money to upgrade to the newest and most advanced exercise equipment. Likewise, it applies to investments in human assets, as when a video game maker like Electronic Arts (EA) must invest heavily in hiring and retaining the best software engineers to create its products. Thus, if businesses are to remain competitive, they must always be evaluating the quality of their assets, and they must always be prepared to

upgrade these assets to counter the competition's moves. As we learned earlier in the chapter, revenues flow from assets. If a firm's assets decline in quality, then its revenues will be negatively affected. Similar concepts apply to the spectator sport industry, where much of the revenue growth is attributable to teams playing in new or refurbished stadiums.

The financial challenge arises because these assets cost money. For example, new stadiums can cost more than $1 billion. While the scale of investment may not be as great for a local fitness club investing in new exercise equipment, it is proportionately no less significant. Usually, these large-scale investments are financed, at least in part, by borrowed money (i.e., debt). As noted earlier, debt is risky, in that interest and a proportion of the principal must be paid back to the lender at regular, prespecified intervals, regardless of whether the business meets its revenue expectations. Failure to meet these loan payments could ultimately result in bankruptcy. These debt issues have certainly been prominent in the major professional leagues, as teams have often borrowed heavily to finance their portion of stadium costs. Many new team owners have also borrowed heavily to finance the purchase price of the team.

College sports have faced some unique challenges, in large part because of the aforementioned increases in broadcast rights and associated payouts to conferences and schools. Despite the dramatic revenue growth, college athletic departments are nonprofit entities that do not pay wages to their athletes. Instead, the increased revenues have flowed to coaches' salaries and, in some cases, extravagant facilities designed to recruit the best athletes. The University of Central Florida, a school that charges each student $344 in annual fees to support athletics, is building a lazy river, sand volleyball courts, hot tubs, and a miniature golf course for its athletes for $25 million

(Hobson, 2017). Similarly, the University of Florida is building a $60 million athletic facility, and Clemson University has completed a $55 million football-only facility with sand volleyball courts, mini-golf, and laser tag (Hobson, 2017). This excessive spending, coupled with the inability to justify how these facilities relate to the educational mission of the university, have led, in part, to a series of lawsuits against the NCAA. Generically referred to as the pay-for-play movement, these lawsuits seek to affirm that athletes are employees of the university and as such are entitled to wages, medical care, and disability coverage.

To defend the status quo, the NCAA has relied on the principles of amateurism, as well as financial figures that tell a different story. In 2008, the NCAA began to distinguish between generated revenues (such as ticket sales, sponsorships, media rights, and donations) and allocated revenues (such as student fees, institutional support, and state or local funds). **Table 4-5** shows the breakdown of generated revenues and expenses by division. The table indicates even Division I schools would be, on average, in significant deficit positions with their athletic programs without the external

support of allocated revenues. The NCAA points out that the revenue-generating abilities of football and men's basketball are insufficient to compensate for the deficits that occur in the other sports. Opponents counter that the deficits occur not because of other sports, but because of the spending largess of the men's football and basketball programs.

The numbers in Table 4-5 indicate that Division I-AA (Football Championship Subdivision) schools are unable to generate the same level of revenues as the Division I-A (Football Bowl Subdivision) schools, but they still incur many of the same costs as I-AAA schools without football and certainly incur much higher costs than their Division II counterparts. The high-profile financial successes of the major revenue-generating sports often overshadow the rest of the college athletics spectrum but, taken as a whole, the values in Table 4-5 indicate college sports continue to be unprofitable without external allocations. Whether this is because of not enough revenue or excessive spending is open to debate.

Another issue relates to the financial differences between programs. Even if one focuses on just Division I-A programs, there is a very

Table 4-5 Median Generated Revenues and Expenses per School, Excluding Institutional Support: 2015 (in thousands of dollars)

Division	Median Generated Revenue	Median Expense	Difference
I-A (Football Bowl Subdivision)	47,962	66,295	−18,333
I-AA (Football Championship Subdivision)	4,047	16,174	−12,127
I-AAA without football	2,915	15,066	−12,151
II with football (2011)	727	6,539	−5,812
II without football (2011)	354	4,689	−4,335

Data from Fulks, D. L. (2016a). Revenues and expenses 2004–15: Division I intercollegiate athletics programs report. Retrieved from http://www .ncaapublications.com/productdownloads/D1REVEXP2015.pdf; Fulks, D. L. (2016b). Revenues and expenses 2004–15: Division II intercollegiate athletics programs report. Retrieved from http://www.ncaapublications.com/productdownloads/D2REVEXP2015.pdf.

unequal distribution of revenues across programs. For example, the formula used by the NCAA to pay out revenues to conferences from the men's basketball tournament is based, in part, on the success of conference teams in the tournament. Thus, conferences that are traditional powers tend to get the highest payouts, which can help to perpetuate their success while inhibiting the ability of other conferences to increase their success. In football, similar issues exist.

This issue of revenue disparities across schools and conferences is part of a larger issue that economists call **competitive balance**. The competitive balance issue is rooted in the notion that consumers of a spectator sport seek to be entertained by the game itself, with two roughly equally balanced opponents producing a better game than two unequal opponents. Research by economists reveals that this entertainment value is connected to a concept of "uncertainty of outcome": The greater the uncertainty of outcome, the greater the entertainment value for fans. This concept of uncertainty of outcome can be defined for an individual game, for a season, or over a number of seasons.

For an individual game, while local fans may prefer the home team to win, they also value competitiveness. Games that are expected to be a mismatch, where the outcome is largely predetermined, will reduce fan interest. Similarly, if one looks at an entire season rather than an individual game, fans tend to prefer situations where teams in the league are relatively closely bunched in the standings, as opposed to situations where there is a high level of disparity among the teams. In this latter situation, games played later in the season will become much less meaningful because large gaps separate the teams in the standings. Furthermore, one can look at this concept of uncertainty of outcome across seasons. Are the same teams successful year in and year out, or is there considerable change in the standings from year to year? For

example, the New England Patriots won the American Football Conference championship of the NFL every year except one from 2013 to 2017. Again, the suspicion is that fan interest will be reduced if fans enter each season believing that their favorite team's place in the standings is largely predetermined.

While the concern over competitive balance certainly is relevant to college sports, given the highly differential payouts that tend to favor the already dominant conferences, this issue has received the most attention in professional sports, particularly in baseball. Those who argue that MLB has a competitive balance problem point to the fact that large-market teams have still been more likely to make the playoffs over the past decade than have small-market teams. For example, since baseball went to the wild card system in 1995, the New York Yankees have made the playoffs in every season except four, through the 2017 season. The Boston Red Sox, another large-market team, have made the playoffs in 12 of those seasons. Contrast this with a small-market team such as the Kansas City Royals, which finally made the playoffs in 2014 after a 28-year absence.

This example highlights the economic roots of the competitive balance problem: All else equal, large-market teams have greater revenue potential than small-market teams and, therefore, will find it more beneficial (in a revenue generation sense) than small-market teams to employ higher-quality players than will their small-market rivals. To the extent that this higher level of talent ultimately translates into better on-field team performance, large-market teams should, over the long run, be able to field consistently better teams than their small-market counterparts.

Leagues have long had policies that have attempted to improve the on-field fortunes of poorly performing teams. All leagues use some form of a "reverse-order" draft, whereby those teams with the poorest records during the previous season have the top draft choices for the following season. The NFL also has used the scheduling system to foster competitive balance, by giving teams with poorer records during the previous season "easier" schedules in the following season.

These two mechanisms could be termed "nonfinancial" ways to alter competitive balance. However, neither directly addresses the root of the problem: the fact that differences in market sizes across franchises cause differences in revenue potential, which cause differences in the ability to pay players, which cause differences in team payroll, which cause differences in on-field performance.

In an attempt to better deal with these underlying causal factors, professional leagues have introduced a number of "financial" mechanisms to alter competitive balance. One of these mechanisms is a **salary cap**. Both the NFL and the NHL have "hard" caps, while the NBA and MLS have a "soft" cap. With the hard cap, the team payroll limit is an absolute and cannot be violated. A hard cap has been used in the NFL since 1994 and in the NHL since 2005. These hard caps are the result of negotiations between the leagues and their players' associations. The hard cap limit is typically set as a percentage of league revenues, usually between 55% and 60%. The philosophy behind the hard cap is that it will constrain all franchises to spend about the same amount on payroll (hard caps usually include a minimum payroll, called a payroll floor, as well), presumably ensuring that franchises are fielding relatively equally balanced teams on the field. In essence, a hard cap prevents large-market teams from using their natural financial advantage to buy the best teams.

With a soft cap, a payroll limit is still set, but teams can exceed this limit through various types of exclusions or exceptions. For example, one type of exclusion is situations in which teams sign their own free agents, as opposed to another team's free agents. Given this fairly wide array of exclusions, there is generally a much wider disparity in payrolls across teams with a soft cap than there is with a hard cap. The NBA has had a soft cap since 1984 and made history that year when it was the first league in the modern era of professional sports to implement any type of salary cap.

Revenue sharing is another financial mechanism intended to foster greater competitive balance. With revenue sharing, teams in the league agree to share certain types of revenues among themselves. For example, all four major professional leagues share national television revenues equally. However, the relative significance of this sharing revenues differs across leagues, with the NFL being the only league where national television revenues account for a large portion of total league revenues. In the other three leagues, "local" revenues (such as gate receipts and local television) are much more crucial. These local revenues can vary widely across teams, as mentioned previously, and are directly related to the market size in which the teams play. Thus, unless leagues also have a mechanism to share these revenues, large disparities in total revenues will persist across teams. Historically, there has been little or no sharing of these local revenues, but this has changed significantly in recent years. For example, under the current 2017–2021 collective bargaining agreement (CBA), MLB teams share approximately 34% of their net local revenues, although the actual amounts are determined by a complex formula, and teams in the 15 largest markets are not eligible to receive any shared revenues. In the NHL, the 2013–2022 CBA increased the amount of shared revenues by more than 30% as compared to the amount shared in the 2005 CBA.

Most economists have suggested that revenue sharing, in and of itself, will do little to improve competitive balance. The reason is that teams receiving revenue-sharing transfers may have little incentive to use the money to increase payroll. Instead, they may be motivated to simply retain the transfer as added profit. In other words, if it were beneficial (in an ROI sense) for small-market teams to increase their payroll, they would have already done so, even without the revenue-sharing transfers. This criticism of revenue sharing has frequently been leveled at baseball's revenue-sharing plan, as some small-market teams that received significant revenue transfers in recent years do not seem to be noticeably improving their on-field performance (but do seem to be improving their profitability). This is particularly a problem in baseball, because there is no payroll floor to which teams must adhere.

Revenue sharing may be more effective as a tool to improve competitive balance when it is used in conjunction with a hard salary cap. Hard caps, in addition to having a payroll ceiling, have a payroll floor. For some small-market teams, revenues may not be sufficient to meet this floor without revenue-sharing dollars. Thus, the hard cap essentially requires small-market teams to use all or part of their revenue-sharing transfers on payroll.

Finally, a **luxury tax** has been used as a mechanism to influence competitive balance. Both the NBA and MLB have a form of a luxury tax. With a luxury tax, a payroll threshold is set prior to a season. Teams that exceed this threshold pay a tax on the excess amount. In baseball, for example, team payroll thresholds under the existing CBA are $195 million in 2017 and increase each year to $210 million in 2021 (the last year of the agreement). Teams are taxed at a rate of 20% for a first violation of the threshold, 30% for a second violation, and 50% for subsequent violations, with additional penalties levied in terms of draft positions for

teams that significantly exceed the threshold (Brown, 2016). The luxury tax works somewhat differently than salary caps or revenue sharing, in that it is focused solely on changing the behavior of high-payroll teams, such as the New York Yankees. The Yankees have been the only team to exceed the threshold every season since the tax was introduced in 2003. In 2016, the team paid a luxury tax of $27.4 million, and it has cumulatively paid $325 million since 2003 (Blum, 2016). Over time, more teams have exceeded the threshold, with a record six MLB teams paying the luxury tax in 2016 (Blum, 2016).

Summary

Despite a recession in the first decade of the twenty-first century, there is no question that the past two decades have proved especially lucrative for all facets of the sport industry. An aging population and growth in the amount of disposable income available to be spent on recreation and entertainment have resulted in skyrocketing revenues in many sectors of the industry.

This financial boom has created a great need in the industry for people with training in finance. The future will continue to provide many growth opportunities for sport organizations but will also present notable challenges. As sport organizations continue to increase their managerial sophistication, the need for well-trained individuals in finance will become even greater.

The important financial issues facing the sport industry in the future may be quite different than the ones facing the industry today. Thus, managers need to understand the underlying financial and economic principles and techniques, rather than just simply being familiar with current issues and facts. The issues will change, but the underlying analytical tools to analyze the issues will not.

Case Study 4-1

A New Arena for the Golden State Warriors

The NBA's San Francisco Warriors played in San Francisco for nine seasons before relocating to Oakland, California, in 1971 and renaming themselves the Golden State Warriors. Their new home was the Oakland Alameda County Arena—a $24 million, 13,000-seat facility built in 1966. In 1997, a $121 million renovation expanded the facility to 20,000 seats; in 2007, it was renamed Oracle Arena. The Warriors won three NBA Championships in 1975, 2015, and 2017 in that facility. Despite playing in the oldest arena in the NBA, the Warriors' success on the court led to a season ticket waiting list of approximately 40,000 fans.

Oracle Arena is owned by the joint city–county governmental agency called the Oakland Alameda County Coliseum Authority (OACCA). The city and county taxpayers covered the original arena construction cost and in 1996 issued $140 million in construction bonds for the renovation. That year the Warriors signed a 20-year lease that included paying $1.5 million for rent as well as the first $7.4 million of the team's premium seating revenue to the OACCA. The OACCA retained 5% of each ticket sold, a portion of the naming rights, parking revenue, and concession revenue. The OACCA share of annual ticket revenue tripled to $6.5 million in the period between 2011 and 2016 as the Warriors' popularity grew. The OACCA also covered costs including maintenance and operation of the arena, some game-day production and marketing expenses, and approximately $22 million for the principal and interest on the loan. In 2016, the OACCA required contributions of $11 million from both the city and the county to balance its budget.

In 2012, the Warriors announced their intention to leave Oracle Arena and build a new facility on the waterfront in San Francisco. After years of opposition and ballooning costs, the team altered its plans and in April 2014 paid a reported $250 million to purchase a different plot of land south of the San Francisco Giants' AT&T Park. After several years of lawsuits from a local hospital concerned with arena crowds reducing patient and ambulance access, a ground-breaking ceremony for the arena took place in January 2017. The 11-acre development built and owned by the Warriors encompasses the 18,000-seat Chase Center arena, 100,000 square feet of retail space, and 580,000 square feet of office space. Half of the office space has already been rented out by ride-sharing firm Uber, and JPMorgan Chase paid $300 million over 20 years for the naming rights.

Despite excitement about the new arena, the Warriors are responsible for the $1 billion cost. Arenas need to book events 200 or more days per year to break even. When the Chase Center opens in 2019, it will compete to fill those 200 dates with other local arenas, including the newly abandoned Oracle Arena in Oakland, the 80-year-old Cow Palace south of San Francisco, and the SAP Center 45 miles away in San Jose. Notably, there are no other large, modern arenas within San Francisco, leading some to suggest the Chase Center will have the upper hand in booking events. As evidence of the Warriors' hopes for high profit potential, two years before opening the facility the team announced that prices for suites will range from $525,000 to $2.5 million in the Chase Center, whereas they cost only $200,000 to $300,000 at Oracle Arena.

Back in Oakland, Oracle Arena will see its average of 110 events per years decrease by about 50 because of the loss of the Warriors games. In addition, there will still be approximately $55 million remaining to be paid on the bonds that the OACCA issued in 1996.

Questions for Discussion

1. From a finance perspective, why did the Warriors allocate $1 billion to build a new arena?

2. Which new revenue streams might the Warriors generate that could cover the cost of the new arena?

3. Which specific risks do the Warriors face in taking on the full cost of the project?

4. Which specific risks does the OACCA face in paying off the principal and interest on its existing bonds?

5. If the Warriors used bonds to finance a portion of the new arena's costs, which criteria would lenders use to evaluate their ability to repay the loan?

Key Terms

assets, balance sheet, bonds, budgeting, competitive balance, debt, default, expenses, income, income statement, interest, liabilities, luxury tax, monopoly, owners' equity, principal, profits, return on investment (ROI), revenues, revenue sharing, risk, rival leagues, salary cap, value added

References

Associated Press. (2011, December 14). NFL renews television deals. Retrieved from http://espn.go.com/nfl/story/_/id/7353238/nfl-re-ups-tv-pacts-expand-Thursday-schedule

Associated Press. (2012, March 12). Oklahoma State fails to recoup $33M. *ESPN.com*. Retrieved from http://www.espn.com/college-sports/story/_/id/7678962/oklahoma-state-cowboys-lose-bid-regain-33m-fundraiser

Badenhausen, K. (2016a, July 13). Dallas Cowboys head the world's 50 most valuable sports teams of 2016. *Forbes*. Retrieved from https://www.forbes.com/sites/kurtbadenhausen/2016/07/13/dallas-cowboys-head-the-worlds-50-most-valuable-sports-teams-of-2016/

Badenhausen, K. (2016b, December 15). The average player salary and highest-paid in NBA, MLB, NHL, NFL and MLS. *Forbes*. Retrieved from https://www.forbes.com/sites/kurtbadenhausen/2016/12/15/average-player-salaries-in-major-american-sports-leagues/

Badenhausen, K. (2017, January 17). Golden State Warriors break ground on new $1 billion Chase Center. *Forbes*. Retrieved from https://www.forbes.com/sites/kurtbadenhausen/2017/01/17/golden-state-warriors-break-ground-on-new-1-billion-chase-center/

Beaton, A., & Kyle, A. (2012, October 1). Duke basketball completes its Legacy Fund endowment. *Duke Chronicle*. Retrieved from http://www.dukechronicle.com/articles/2012/10/01/duke-basketball-completes-its-legacy-fund-endowment

Berkowitz, S. (2017, February 2). Some SEC schools received $40M-plus in 2016 fiscal year. *USA Today*. Retrieved from https://www.usatoday.com/story/sports/ncaaf/sec/2017/02/02/sec-tax-return-639-million-in-revenues-2016-fiscal-year/97400990/

Blum, R. (2016, December, 17). Record 6 MLB teams to pay luxury tax. *APNewsBreak*. Retrieved from https://apnews.com/402e447f332e44dea08616e3d959ba22

Brady, E. (2016, April 12). NCAA extends tournament deal with CBS, Turner through

2032 for $8.8 billion. *USA Today*. Retrieved from http://www.usatoday.com/story/sports /ncaab/2016/04/12/ncaa-contract-extension -cbs-turner-ncaa-tournament-march -madness/82939124/

Brown, M. (2016, November 30). Breaking down MLB's new 2017–21 collective bargaining agreement. *Forbes*. Retrieved from https://www.forbes.com/sites /maurybrown/2016/11/30/breaking-down -mlbs-new-2017-21-collective-bargaining -agreement/#1e0461f111b9

Business Wire. (2016a, May 25). Fitch affirms MLB club trust securitization senior secured credit facility & term notes at "A". Retrieved from http://www.businesswire.com/news /home/20160525006537/en/Fitch-Affirms -MLB-Club-Trust-Securitization-Senior

Business Wire. (2016b, June 15). Fitch affirms National Football League ratings; outlook stable. Retrieved from http://www.businesswire.com/news /home/20160615006591/en/Fitch-Affirms -National-Football-League-Ratings-Outlook

Collins, M., & Rubin, R. (2015, February 2). College sports ticket tax break would vanish in Obama budget. *Forbes*. Retrieved from https://www.bloomberg.com/news /articles/2015-02-02/college-sports-ticket -tax-break-would-vanish-under-obama -budget

Crupi, A. (2016, June 23). The TV sports well has run dry: In locking in a Big Ten deal, ESPN and Fox claim the last big rights prize. *Advertising Age*. Retrieved from http://adage .com/article/media/big-ten-deal/304667/

Dosh, K. (2016, December 31). College football playoff payouts by conference for 2016–17. *Forbes*. Retrieved from https://www.forbes .com/sites/kristidosh/2016/12/31/college -football-playoff-payouts-by-conference -for-2016-17/

Fahey, M. (2016, December 10). ESPN isn't the only cable network that suffered this year.

CNBC. Retrieved from http://www.cnbc .com/2016/12/09/espn-isnt-the-only-cable -network-that-suffered-this-year.html

Fulks, D. L. (2016a). Revenues and expenses 2004–15: Division I intercollegiate athletics programs report. Retrieved from http://www .ncaapublications.com/productdownloads /D1REVEXP2015.pdf

Fulks, D. L. (2016b). Revenues and expenses 2004–15: Division II intercollegiate athletics programs report. Retrieved from http://www .ncaapublications.com/productdownloads /D2REVEXP2015.pdf

Gaines, C. (2016, October 13). The 25 schools that make the most money in college sports. *Business Insider*. Retrieved from http://www.businessinsider.com /schools-most-revenue-college-sports-2016-10/

Gayer, T., Drukker, A. J., & Gold, A. K. (2016). *Tax-exempt municipal bonds and the financing of professional sports stadiums*. Washington, DC: Brooking Institution Press.

Hobson, W. (2017, March 31). One school's formula for athletic success: Build a lazy river and (hope) the recruits will come. *The Washington Post*. Retrieved from https://www.washingtonpost.com /sports/colleges/one-schools-formula-for -athletic-success-build-a-lazy-river-and -hope-the-recruits-will-come/2017/03/31 /e1b7f5c8-1568-11e7-833c-503e1f6394c9 _story.html?

Kaplan, D., & Botta, C. (2012, August 13). Deadline near for Devils, but lenders unlikely to act. *SportsBusiness Journal*. Retrieved from http://www.sportsbusinessdaily.com/Journal /Issues/2012/08/13/Finance/Devils.aspx?hl =equity%20stake&sc=0

Know Rivalry. (2017). Portland Timbers. Retrieved from https://knowrivalry.com /team/portland_timbers/

Lefton, T. (2016). Naming-rights market finds more takers. *SportsBusiness Journal, 18*(43), 14. Retrieved from http://www

.sportsbusinessdaily.com/Journal /Issues/2016/02/22/In-Depth/Naming -Rights.aspx

Lewis, M. (2003). *Moneyball: The art of winning an unfair game.* New York, NY: W. W. Norton.

Luker, R. (2016, November 21). Cold reality: Growth no longer uncontested. *SportsBusiness Journal, 19*(32), 15. Retrieved from http://www .sportsbusinessdaily.com/Journal/Issues /2016/11/21/Research-and-Ratings/Up-Next -with-Rich-Luker.aspx

McGrath, M. (2016, March 02). Sports Authority files for bankruptcy, plans to shutter 140 stores. *Forbes.* Retrieved from https://www .forbes.com/sites/maggiemcgrath/2016/03/02 /sports-authority-files-for-bankruptcy-plans -to-shutter-140-stores/

Oldham, J. (2015, April 21). Football stadium arms race pushed this school deeper into debt. *Bloomberg.* Retrieved from https://www .bloomberg.com/news/articles/2015-04-22 /football-stadium-arms-race-pushes -colorado-school-to-double-debt

Ourand, J. (2012, August 28). Sources: ESPN secures MLB rights in eight-year, $5.6b deal. *SportsBusiness Journal.* Retrieved from http://www.sportsbusinessdaily.com /Daily/Morning-Buzz/2012/08/28/ESPN -MLB.aspx

Ourand, J. (2016, June 20). ESPN stays in the game: Ponies up $1.14B for Big Ten package. *SportsBusiness Journal.* Retrieved from http:// www.sportsbusinessdaily.com/Journal /Issues/2016/06/20/Media/ESPN-Big-Ten.aspx

Ourand, J. (2017, April 10). Five things to know about NFL–Amazon. *SportsBusiness Journal, 19*(49), 3. Retrieved from http://www .sportsbusinessdaily.com/Journal/Issues /2017/04/10/Media/NFL-Amazon.aspx

Ourand, J., & Smith, M. (2012, November 9). ESPN closing in on $500 million BCS media rights deal. *The Sporting News.* Retrieved from http://www.sportingnews.com

/ncaa-football/news/4307688-bcs-media -rights-deal-espn-500-million-per-season -tv-rights-contract-bowls

Ozanian, M. (2017, April 15). Baseball team values 2017. *Forbes.* Retrieved from https://www .forbes.com/sites/mikeozanian/2017/04/11 /baseball-team-values-2017/

Plunkett Research. (2017). Sports industry, teams, leagues & recreation market research. Retrieved from http://www .plunkettresearch.com/industries /sports-recreation-leisure-market -research/

Quirk, J., & Fort, R. (1997). *Pay dirt: The business of professional team sports.* Princeton, NJ: Princeton University Press.

Quirk, J., & Fort, R. (1999). *Hard ball: The abuse of power in pro team sports.* Princeton, NJ: Princeton University Press.

Shaikin, B. (2017, February 8). Want to own a share of the Dodgers? This could be your chance. *Los Angeles Times.* Retrieved from http://www.latimes.com/sports/mlb/la-sp -dodgers-sale-20170208-story.html

Smith, C. (2015, December 28). College football's most valuable teams 2015: Texas, Notre Dame and . . . Tennessee? Retrieved from https://www.forbes.com/sites /chrissmith/2015/12/22/college-footballs -most-valuable-teams-2015-texas-notre -dame-and-tennessee/

SportsBusiness Journal. (2006, July 31). Tagliabue's tenure: The NFL during Paul Tagliabue's reign as commissioner, p. 32.

Strauss, B. (2016, December 15). MLS sets timetable for expansion to 28 teams, $150M fee for teams No. 25, 26. *Sports Illustrated.* Retrieved from https://www.si.com/planet -futbol/2016/12/15/mls-expansion-don -garber-timeline-28-teams-fees-miami

University Athletic Association. (2017). Overview and history. Retrieved from http:// floridagators.com/sports/2015/12/10 /_overview_.aspx

U.S. Department of Commerce, Bureau of Economic Analysis. (2017a, April 21). Industry data: Gross output by industry. Retrieved from http://www.bea.gov/iTable /iTableHtml.cfm?reqid=51&step=51&isuri=1 &5114=a&5102=15

U.S. Department of Commerce, Bureau of Economic Analysis. (2017b, April 21). Industry data: Value added by industry. Retrieved from http://www.bea.gov/iTable /iTableHtml.cfm?reqid=51&step=51&isuri=1 &5114=a&5102=1

Whitten, S. (2016, May 10). Texas high school to build $62.8 million football stadium. *CNBC*. Retrieved from http://www.cnbc .com/2016/05/10/texas-high-school-to-build -628-million-football-stadium.html

Wilner, J. (2017, February 7). College hotline: The Pac-12's expanding revenue deficit relative to SEC, Big Ten. *The Mercury News*. Retrieved from http://www.mercurynews .com/2017/02/07/college-hotline-the-pac-12s -expanding-revenue-deficit-relative-to-sec -big-ten/

Chapter

5

Lisa P. Masteralexis and
James T. Masteralexis

Legal Principles Applied to Sport Management

Learning Objectives

Upon completion of this chapter, students should be able to:

1. Understand that sport managers should have a basic understanding of legal principles to manage risk in their day-to-day activities and to know when to seek legal assistance.

2. Define risk management and understand that legal uncertainties can wreak havoc on a sport organization.

3. Develop a risk management program using the D.I.M. process.

4. Understand why under judicial review courts may overturn the rules of voluntary athletic organizations.

5. Differentiate between the various areas of law that may affect sport organizations, such as tort law, agency law, contract law, constitutional law, antitrust law, labor and employment law, and intellectual property law.

6. Appraise how the federal government enforces Title IX, and identify some of the important cases that have shaped the law since its passage in 1972.

7. Understand how the study of law can improve analytical, communication, negotiating, leadership, listening, and ethical reasoning skills.

8. Recognize that the impact of law on sport organizations is likely to increase in the future as the sport business becomes increasingly complex.

Introduction

Sport law refers to the application of law to the sport industry. In a few instances, new **statutes** (laws) have been enacted specifically to regulate the sport industry. The following federal laws are examples: the Sports Agent Responsibility and Trust Act of 2004 (SPARTA regulates sport agents), the Sports Broadcasting Act of 1961 (sport broadcasting antitrust exemption), the Professional and Amateur Sports Protection Act of 1992 (PASPA bans betting on sporting events *except* in states where betting was already legal), and the Ted Stevens Olympic and Amateur Sports Act (regulates Olympic and other amateur sports). At the state level, 43 states plus the District of Columbia and the U.S. Virgin Islands have adopted the 2001 Uniform Athlete Agent Act (Uniform Law Commission, 2017). At least three states have their own laws regulating agents.

Over the past 50 years, the sport industry has evolved into a complex multibillion-dollar global entity with much at stake for those involved in sport business. When disputes arise, parties in sport rely heavily on the legal system for resolution. Thus, sport managers must have an understanding of legal principles to successfully manage risk and to know when to seek legal assistance.

History

Early sport and recreation cases in the United States and Great Britain were based in tort law and focused on participation in sport and games. For instance, a treatise published in 1635 in Britain and a landmark 1800s tort case, *Vosburg v. Putney*, both discuss tort liability for participation in games and horseplay (Yasser, McCurdy, Goplerud, & Weston, 1999).

Many of the earliest U.S. sport industry's lawsuits involved the business of baseball because it hosted the first professional sport league. Early cases involved baseball players challenging the reserve system adopted by owners to prevent players from achieving any form of free agency (*Metropolitan Exhibition Co. v. Ewing*, 1890; *Metropolitan Exhibition Co. v. Ward*, 1890). Interestingly, a player involved in one of these cases, John Montgomery Ward, led the first efforts to form a players union in baseball in the late 1800s and went on to become a lawyer (Staudohar, 1996). Throughout the early to mid-twentieth century, most cases in the sport industry were based in contract, antitrust, and labor law.

In the 45 years since a Boston College Law School professor, Robert Berry, offered the first documented sport law course, the legal profession has moved toward a greater degree of specialization. The amount of litigation and diversity of cases in the sport industry have increased as more people rely on the courts to resolve disputes.

Many athletic associations have adopted their own governance systems with rules, regulations, and procedures. Sport governing bodies operate much like federal and state administrative bodies. **Administrative law** describes the body of law created by rules, regulations, orders, and decisions of administrative bodies. Governance documents of sport organizations resemble state or federal laws, rules, and regulations. The constitutions and bylaws of professional leagues govern the relationship among leagues, team owners, and players who use dispute-resolving mechanisms and internal procedures for settling disagreements. The National Collegiate Athletic Association (NCAA), for example, has developed its own manual of rules and regulations, which mirror the language of statutes. When a dispute arises over the interpretation of an NCAA rule or regulation, sport lawyers often represent both the governing body and the institution, resolving the dispute through an administrative process established by the NCAA. Because many sport organizations use lawyers to draft their rules and regulations, lawyers can best interpret, challenge, or defend these rules and regulations. Indeed, lawyers have developed sport industry specialties to address the various challenges that sport managers at governing bodies may face. Some lawyers now specialize in representing schools and athletes in investigations by and hearings before the NCAA (Haworth, 1996). Other lawyers specialize in representing athletes in crises, representing athletes who have failed drug tests, and representing athletes in front of arbitration panels such as the Court for Arbitration in Sport.

Three professional associations are devoted to sport law in North America, with others found around the world in Europe, Australia, and New Zealand. The North American associations are the Sports Lawyers Association, the American Bar Association Forum Committee on Sport and Entertainment Law, and the Sport and Recreation Law Association. These associations publish journals and newsletters, as well as hold conferences. In addition, a number of law schools host sport law institutes.

While possessing a law degree is not a requirement for a sport manager, the skills provided by a legal education are certainly beneficial. Legal education teaches written and oral communication, analytical reasoning, critical thinking, problem solving, and negotiating skills. Many in the sport industry possess law degrees but work in sport management rather than practicing law. For instance, in professional sport, National Hockey League (NHL) Commissioner Gary Bettman and National Basketball Association (NBA) Commissioner Adam Silver are lawyers. Other positions held by lawyers include league and team general counsels, professional team general managers, players association executive directors and staff, NCAA officials, college conference commissioners and staff, athletic directors and compliance staff, International and U.S. Olympic Committee members and staff, national governing body members and staff, player representatives, and facility managers. While people in these positions possess law degrees, they do not practice law in the traditional sense. Instead, their knowledge of law guides their decision making and may save organizations the expense of hiring counsel. For example, a facility manager may need to understand local ordinances and codes, tort law, contract law, labor and employment laws, and the Americans with Disabilities Act, just to name a few aspects of the governance system. A facility manager also may be responsible for negotiating a variety of contracts, including leases with cities and teams, event contracts, concessionaire contracts, sponsorship agreements, employment contracts, collective bargaining agreements with labor unions, and pourage rights for the beverages sold in the facility.

Key Concepts

People turn to the legal system to resolve disputes because of the increased financial interests involved at all levels of youth and high school, collegiate, Olympic, and professional sports. On the high school and intercollegiate side, gender discrimination, constitutional rights violations, recruiting violations, use of ineligible players, and rule violations by athletes, coaches, and educational institutions are common sources of litigation (Wong, 2010). On the professional side, labor disputes, contract issues, misconduct by athletes and owners, health and safety issues (e.g., concussions), and the enforcement of and challenges to rules are the primary sources of litigation. Personal injury and product liability cases filed by recreational sport participants have increased as well. Olympic and Paralympic eligibility issues, drug testing, and ambush marketing are also topics of litigation. To make legally sound business decisions, it is important for sport managers to have a basic understanding of legal principles.

Risk Management

Risk management requires developing a management strategy to maintain greater control over the legal uncertainties that may wreak havoc on a sport business. Whatever the type of sport business, risk management plans focus on the same goals: prevention and intervention. Prevention involves keeping problems from arising, whereas intervention involves having a plan of action to follow when problems do occur. Risk management strategy encourages sport managers to develop a plan to prevent legal disputes from happening and a plan for intervening when a legal problem does arise. Through risk management, sport managers may limit their losses by avoiding becoming defendants in court actions. (Note: A **plaintiff** is a person or organization that initiates a lawsuit, and a **defendant** is the person or organization that allegedly wronged the plaintiff and must respond to the lawsuit.)

The D.I.M. process is one method used to establish a risk management program. It consists of three steps: (1) *developing* the risk management plan, (2) *implementing* the risk management plan, and (3) *managing* the risk management plan (Ammon, 2017). It is important that sport managers follow these steps to create a risk management program specifically tailored to their organizations. This risk management plan should address all potential sources of legal liability. Often people assume that risk management plans are developed solely to address the potential for tort liability—in particular, **negligence**, such as when a spectator is injured at a stadium while attending an event or a participant gets hurt while taking part in a recreational activity. In reality, this kind of plan should include the many areas of law discussed throughout this chapter. For example, adopting a risk management philosophy may keep a sport manager from losing an employment discrimination suit, an arbitration proceeding, or a challenge to an athletic association's rule. One key to

a successful risk management strategy is to have all the organization's employees be involved in developing, implementing, and managing the process. This way, employees will have "ownership" in the plan (Ammon, 2017); that is, they will know why the plan exists and what its goals are, and will be likely to follow it.

Judicial Review

Athletic administrators make decisions regarding athletic rules and regulations daily, in areas such as eligibility or recruiting. As decision makers, athletic administrators must realize that courts may be asked to review their decisions, as athletes and coaches may initiate judicial and/or administrative challenges to decisions that are not in their favor. **Judicial review** occurs when a plaintiff challenges a rule and the court evaluates that rule to determine whether it should apply. Historically, courts have tended to decline to overturn rules of voluntary athletic organizations, except where the rule or regulation meets one of the following conditions (Masteralexis & Masteralexis, 2017):

1. The rule violates public policy because it is fraudulent or unreasonable.

2. The rule exceeds the scope of the athletic association's authority.

3. The athletic association breaks one of its own rules.

4. The rule is applied in an arbitrary or capricious manner.

5. The rule violates an individual's constitutional rights.

6. The rule challenged by the plaintiff violates an existing law, such as the Sherman Antitrust Act or the Americans with Disabilities Act.

Courts have the power to grant two types of remedies: monetary damages and equitable relief. Monetary damages compensate a plaintiff and punish a defendant. Of course, money is not always the best remedy. A student ruled ineligible for a tournament, for example, simply wants to play. When a plaintiff seeks judicial review, he or she will usually also request an **injunction**—that is, an order from the court to do or not do a particular action. In cases involving a challenge to an athletic association's rule, the plaintiff's interest may be to keep the rule from applying or to force the athletic association to apply it differently to allow the plaintiff to play. An injunction is a type of equitable relief that is a better remedy than money because it provides a court order with the power to do exactly that, with the relief often being to maintain the status quo until a full trial can be held on the matter. Injunctions prevent current and future wrongs and can be used only to prevent an irreparable injury. An injury is considered irreparable when it involves the risk of physical harm or death, the loss of a special opportunity, or the deprivation of unique, irreplaceable property (Wong, 2010).

Money does not provide adequate compensation for an irreparable injury such as being barred from sport participation. For example, assume a high school provided a boys' soccer team but no girls' soccer team. A girl tried out and made the boys' team. Her play impressed the coach, and he gave her a starting position after the first game of the season. Her team went undefeated in the regular season. The night before the first playoff game, the league commissioner called the coach to tell him that the other coaches in the league had launched a complaint against the team for having a girl on its roster when they were competing in a boys' league. The commissioner stated that if the girl showed up to play in the tournament, the team would have to forfeit those games. In this situation, the coach and the female student-athlete might seek an injunction to bar the imposition of the commissioner's ban to allow her to compete in the

tournament. In this case, the plaintiffs are not interested in money. Besides, there is no way to determine how much participating in the soccer game is worth. The girl will argue that she faces irreparable harm by being denied the opportunity to play. She may never have the opportunity to participate in this type of tournament again, and even if she were to have another opportunity, it would not be the same because she has worked hard with *this* team. Additionally, the other coaches had all season to complain and they waited until the playoffs in an attempt to damage an undefeated team. No amount of money can compensate the girl for this lost opportunity. Beyond seeking an injunction, the female plaintiff here could file a lawsuit against the league for gender discrimination, seeking damages for the discrimination she faced.

© Photos.com

Tort Liability

A **tort** is an injury or wrong suffered due to another's improper conduct. The goals of tort law are to provide monetary damages to compensate an injured person (plaintiff) and to deter people (defendants and others in society) from engaging in similar conduct in the future. The sport industry is often the subject of tort claims because people participating in sport may hurt themselves or others. Tort law allows people to assess loss and allocate blame.

The defendant's intent while committing the tort helps the court to determine which tort the defendant committed and to assess any damages owed to the plaintiff. The possible types of torts could include intentional torts, gross negligence, and negligence. Intentional torts occur when one person purposely causes harm to another or engages in an activity that is substantially certain to cause harm. Assault, battery, defamation, intentional infliction of emotional distress, intentional interference with contractual relations, and invasion of privacy are all intentional torts. When intentional torts are found to have occurred, plaintiffs may be eligible for additional damages, called *punitive damages*, to punish the defendant.

Gross negligence occurs when a defendant acts recklessly. Recklessness exists when a person knows that an act is harmful but fails to realize the degree of extreme harm that results (*Hackbart v. Cincinnati Bengals, Inc.*, 1979). Gross negligence falls between negligence (discussed shortly) and an intentional tort, and is applied routinely in participant versus participant cases, except in Arizona, Nevada, and Wisconsin (*Mark v. Moser*, 2001).

Negligence is an unintentional tort and is the most common tort that sport managers encounter. Thus, the focus of this introductory chapter is on negligence and not intentional torts.

Sport managers are negligent when they commit an act or omission that causes injury to a person to whom they owe a duty to act with care. To determine whether a sport manager has been negligent, a court focuses on the relationship between the plaintiff (the injured person) and the defendant (sport manager). Before the defendant can be found liable for negligence, the plaintiff must show that the defendant owed the plaintiff a **duty of care**. A legal duty of care is more than a moral obligation. According to Van der Smissen (2007), a legal duty arises from one of three origins: (1) a relationship inherent in a particular situation, (2) a voluntary assumption of the duty of care, or (3) a duty mandated by a law.

For example, assume a college track coach was conducting a private training session with her top athlete. After running 500 meters, the athlete collapsed. Due to her special relationship with the runner, the coach has a duty to provide the athlete with prompt medical assistance. Now assume that a citizen of the community who has no connection to the team is exercising at the facility. The citizen may be morally obligated to help the athlete, but the citizen has no relationship to the athlete and, therefore, no legal duty to render assistance. However, if the citizen ran over to the collapsed athlete to help the coach administer cardiopulmonary resuscitation (CPR), the citizen would then voluntarily assume a duty of care toward the athlete. The law may also impose a duty of care on certain individuals due to their special training or skills. Assume further that the citizen is an off-duty emergency medical technician (EMT) and the state where the incident occurs requires all certified EMTs to respond to emergencies. Such a law would create a relationship between the collapsed athlete and the EMT. In such a case, if the EMT did not respond, the EMT could be accused of negligence. To be found negligent, a defendant must also be the actual cause of the injury and the injury must be a reasonable, foreseeable consequence of the defendant's action.

Negligence imposes a duty to refrain from careless acts. A good risk management plan will help a sport manager avoid lawsuits based on negligence. To develop such a plan, sport managers must consider potential problems the business may face and contemplate what is reasonable and foreseeable. If the sport manager then implements a plan to avoid reasonable and foreseeable injuries, he or she is working to establish an environment free from negligence. In this way, the sport manager will also reduce the risk of a successful negligence claim.

An issue that arises often in the sport context is the liability of teams and facilities in regard to spectators who become injured while attending games. Some courts have adopted a "no duty" or "limited duty" rule to limit negligence cases, particularly in baseball. For example, in *Thurmond v. Prince William Baseball Club, Inc.* (2003), the court held that when an adult spectator of ordinary intelligence and a familiarity with the sport attends a game, he assumes the normal risks of watching a baseball game, such as being hit by a ball when sitting in an unscreened area. In a foul ball case involving a Major League Baseball (MLB) club, *Costa v. Boston Red Sox* (2004), the Massachusetts Appeals Court found that the Red Sox did not have a duty to warn their fans of the open and obvious danger of a foul ball. Similarly, in *Turner v. Mandalay Sports Entertainment* (2008), a minor league baseball team did not provide a protective screen around its concession area. A patron who was sitting in the concession area was hit in the face with a ball hit from the field of play. The court found that the baseball team had a "limited duty" to the plaintiff and that the plaintiff had been unable to demonstrate that the area in which she was seated constituted an "unduly high risk of injury."

However, in *Crespin v. Albuquerque Baseball Club* (2009), a New Mexico appellate court declined to adopt the limited duty rule, holding that the team and the city owed a general duty of reasonable care to all spectators, and determinations regarding whether they breached the duty should depend on the facts and circumstances of each case. The court found no compelling reason to adopt the limited duty rule due to the state's comparative negligence statute, under which juries could evaluate risks that spectators accept while attending games. Applying traditional tort law principles, the court found the trial court's granting of summary judgment (due to the limited duty rule) inappropriate, emphasizing that a jury should determine whether the team and the city breached their duty to the spectator by failing to screen the picnic area or warn that batting practice was under way. In dismissing the claims against the Houston Astros and the minor league player, the court noted that the player was merely practicing to perform in a manner consistent with the rules of the game, under which his team would be rewarded for home runs. Incidentally, as a result of the mounting number of serious injuries to fans who sit close to the fields in Major League Baseball, teams are extending the netting along the first and third base lines. Prior to the start of the 2017 season, 10 teams had expanded this protection, and by season's end an additional 4 announced netting extensions for the 2018 season, with others considering making the change over the off-season (Brown, 2017). By January of 2018 with the addition of the Arizona Diamondbacks and Tampa Bay Rays, all teams will now have extended netting from behind homeplate to behind the dugouts in time for the start of the 2018 season (Matthews, 2018).

Contact sports pose an interesting question for the court when deciding whether a tort has occurred, given the fact that participants in sports such as football are agreeing to and purposely tackling and striking each other on every play. As noted previously, most courts adopt a gross negligence standard of liability for coparticipant torts. In *Noffke ex. rel Swenson v. Bakke* (2009), the court found that cheerleading should be considered a contact sport and that a male cheerleader's inability to prevent the plaintiff's fall was not an act of negligence. In other words, if a sport is a contact sport, then a defendant must act in a grossly negligent manner for liability to attach to his or her action.

Vicarious Liability

Vicarious liability provides a plaintiff with a cause of action to sue a superior for the negligent acts of a subordinate. Often lawsuits arise when an employee commits a tort and a plaintiff seeks to hold the employer responsible because the employer has a greater ability to pay damages. Under vicarious liability, the employer need not be negligent to be liable. The employer is legally responsible provided the employee is, in fact, an employee and the employee committed a tort while working for the employer. If the employer is also negligent for hiring an unqualified individual or not providing proper training, the employer's negligence may provide an additional legal claim.

Three defenses are available to an employer that faces a vicarious liability claim. First, if the employee was not negligent, the employer cannot be held liable. Second, the employer may argue that the employee was not acting within the scope of employment, as is the case when an employee acts on his or her own. Third, the employer may argue that the employee is an **independent contractor**. An independent contractor is an employee who is not under the employer's supervision and control. Examples of employees who may be independent contractors include freelance sportswriters or photographers, sport officials, part-time fitness instructors, personal trainers, team physicians, and athletic trainers.

Agency Law

The term **agency** describes "the fiduciary relation which results from the manifestation of consent by one person (the **agent**) to another (the **principal**) that the other shall act on his behalf and subject to his control and consent" (*Black's Law Dictionary*, 1979, p. 58). The law of agency affects all businesses, including those in sport. Try not to think just about sport agents when hearing the term "agency law"—agency law is broader than that and impacts many aspects of business.

The primary purpose of agency law is to establish duties that the principal and the agent owe to each other. While the principal and the agent often have an underlying contract to establish their relationship's parameters, agency law is not concerned with promises established by contract, as they are governed by contract law. Fiduciary duties are inherent in the principal–agent relationship and are imposed on the parties in accordance with agency law, regardless of what a contract between the parties specifies. The term **fiduciary** comes from Roman law and means a person holding the character of a trustee. A **fiduciary duty** obligates a fiduciary to act with trust that one will be loyal and act in the best interest of the other (*Black's Law Dictionary*, 1979).

A second purpose of agency law is to hold the principal responsible to others for actions of the agent, provided the agent is acting under the authority granted to the agent by the principal. A good example of a principal–agent relationship, outside of the sports agent example, is the employer–employee relationship. In such a case, the employer is the principal and the employee is the agent.

Under agency law, the principal owes the agent three duties:

1. To comply with a contract, if one exists.

2. To compensate the agent for his or her services.

3. To reimburse the agent for any expenses incurred while acting on the principal's behalf.

The agent owes the principal five fiduciary duties (Howell, Allison, & Henley, 1987):

1. To obey.

2. To remain loyal.

3. To exercise reasonable care.

4. To notify.

5. To account (for information and finances on a reasonable basis).

This list of fiduciary duties is fairly self-explanatory. However, the second duty—to remain loyal by avoiding conflicts of interest—may need clarification. Because conflicts of interest arise so frequently, an agent can continue representing a principal when a conflict of interest is present, provided the agent fully discloses the conflict to the principal and gives the principal the option to work with a neutral party in the agent's place. For example, assume a player representative has two MLB clients who are all-star catchers and free agents. Both have similar defensive skills and are power hitters. Assume the Atlanta Braves are in need of a top-shelf catcher. The player representative may be in a position of favoring the interest of one free agent over the other, as the Braves will need just one of the players. In such a case, the agent and catchers need not end their relationship, but the agent should disclose the conflict to both catchers to give one of them the option of finding another negotiator for the contract negotiation with the Braves.

Another example that occurs quite frequently in the sport industry is when a sport management agency represents both an athlete and the event in which the athlete is competing. For a major event, the athlete may receive an appearance fee that is negotiated by the event division of the agency and the athlete's agent, both of whom work for the same parent company.

Agency law is an important component of the sport representation industry. Athletes and coaches hire sport agents to gain a level of parity in negotiations with more experienced negotiators, such as club management or university representatives (Shropshire & Davis, 2003). Sport agent relationships are based in contract law, but are also governed by the law of agency and its imposition of fiduciary duties. Thus, when lawsuits do occur between agents and clients as well as between agents and their current,

past, or prospective firms, those disputes often involve claims under contract (*Hendrickson v. Octagon, Inc.*, 2016; *Total Economic Athletic Management of America v. Pickens*, 1995; *Williams v. CWI, Inc.*, 1991; *Zinn v. Parrish*, 1981), agency law (*Buse v. Vanguard Group*, 1996; *Detroit Lions, Inc. and Sims v. Argovitz*, 1984; *Hillard v. Black*, 2000; *Jones v. Childers*, 1994), or torts when fraud, misrepresentation, or tortious interference in contracts/economic advantage is alleged (*Hendrickson v. Octagon, Inc.*, 2016; *Vick v. Wong*, 2009; *Brown v. Woolf*, 1983), A case involving contract, agency, tortious interference, invasion of privacy for hacking into an agent's private email account, plus other torts and business law claims (*Mintz v. Mark Bartleson and Associates, Inc.*, 2012).

Contract Law

A **contract** is a written or verbal agreement between two or more parties that creates a legal obligation to fulfill the promises made by the agreement. A contract has also been defined as a promise that the court will enforce. Every aspect of the sport industry uses contracts. Sport managers use contracts for employing players, officials, and other staff. Contracts are also used for broadcasting deals; licensed property; merchandise, equipment, uniform, and ticket sales; facility leases; sponsorships; concession arrangements; memberships and scholarships; purchasing; scheduling arrangements; and the like. Many sport managers negotiate and enter into contracts regularly. It is essential that sport managers have a basic understanding of contract law to limit their liability and that they know when to engage a lawyer for help. Sound contract drafting and analysis should be part of a sport manager's risk management plan. **Figure 5-1** depicts the formation of a contract.

To have a valid contract, all five elements of a contract must be present: offer, acceptance,

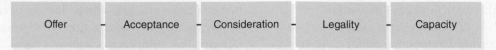

Figure 5-1 Contract Formation

consideration, legality, and capacity. If any of these elements is lacking or nonexistent, a valid and enforceable contract does not exist. A valid contract must have **mutual assent**, which is an offer by one party and an acceptance by another party. A contract also requires both parties to give **consideration**. Consideration is something of value, such as money or property, but could also be something intangible. For example, consideration in a coach's contract may include perks received by the coach, such as a car or country club membership (*Rodgers v. Georgia Tech Athletic Assoc.*, 1983).

People entering into contracts must have the **capacity** to understand the nature and effects of their actions. Generally, individuals older than the age of 18 possess capacity. Under contract law, minors and mentally incompetent individuals may enter contracts but also may **disaffirm** (opt out of) them at any time. Thus, sport managers agreeing to appearances or endorsements with athletes younger than age 18 enter into those contracts at their own risk. They should know that minors may disaffirm the contracts provided they return anything of value that was not earned. The subject matter of a contract must be legal, which means it cannot violate laws or public policy—a concept known as **legality**.

If a contractual promise is broken, it is considered a **breach**. A full breach occurs when the contract is entirely broken, whereas a partial breach occurs when one or more, but not all, of the provisions in the contract are broken. The remedy for a breach is usually monetary damages to compensate the injured party, as money will usually enable an individual to

fulfill his or her expectations elsewhere. In rare cases, the remedy of an injunction may be used to force a party to comply with a contract. Most often this remedy is available only when the subject matter of the contract is so rare, unique, or a one-of-a-kind opportunity that no amount of money will provide an adequate remedy. For example, if a sports memorabilia collector entered into a contract to purchase the only mint-condition Honus Wagner rookie baseball card in existence and the seller backed out of the deal, the collector could go to court to obtain a court order to force the seller to comply with the contract.

Waivers and **releases of liability** are contracts that may form an important component of a risk management plan. You might be familiar with these contracts if you ever signed one before participating in activities such as a Tough Mudder event, bungee jumping, or a paintball tournament. Through waivers, parties agree contractually to give up their right to sue for negligence. Waivers cannot be used to waive a right to sue for gross negligence or intentional torts. A waiver is signed before the person participates in the activity for which that individual is giving up the right to sue. A release of liability is similar to a waiver but is a contract that a party signs after an injury occurs, under which the injured party gives up the right to sue later, usually in exchange for a financial settlement.

Jurisdictions vary regarding whether a waiver will be upheld. When using a waiver, a sport manager should draft it carefully so that it will be enforceable. Flawed language in a waiver may lead a court to conclude that the

© Photos.com

Cotton (2017) has found that 24 states do not enforce parental waivers. More recently, however, 25 states have enforced parental waivers in "some or all circumstances." In another 19 states, there is insufficient information, according to Cotton, to predict whether the parental waiver will be enforced. A sport manager or practitioner must check the law of his or her particular state or jurisdiction to understand the state of the law regarding parental waivers.

That said, some courts have ruled waivers invalid as a matter of **public policy**. Generally, a waiver violates public policy if (1) the activity involves an essential service or the public interest; (2) the waiver conflicts with a statutory duty; (3) the waiver is ambiguous; (4) the waiver is between parties of unequal bargaining power; or (5) the waiver is too broad or attempts to waive gross negligence or reckless conduct (Cotton, 2017). For example, the mandatory use of waivers to bar negligence claims by high school athletes was found to violate public policy in Washington (*Wagenblast v. Odessa School District*, 1988).

Constitutional Law

The U.S. Constitution is the supreme law of the land in the United States. It is a document where "We the People" of the United States grant to the government the authority to govern them and specifically define the powers and duties of the president, the U.S. Congress, and the U.S. Supreme Court. **Constitutional law** is developed from precedents established by courts applying the language of the U.S. Constitution and state constitutions to the actions and policies of governmental entities. With regard to state constitutions, each state must give at least the protections afforded by the U.S. Constitution, but may choose to give their citizens greater protections. The constitutional challenges that tend to arise in the sport

individual signing the waiver did not knowingly and voluntarily agree to waive his or her right to sue. A waiver should be drafted with clear, unambiguous, and precise language that is easily understood by non-lawyers. Waivers should also be printed in large, readable font, preferably 10- or 12-point type. According to Cotton (2017), "in at least 47 of the 54 jurisdictions (the 50 states, admiralty law, Puerto Rico, the Virgin Islands, and Washington, D.C.) a well-written, properly administered waiver, voluntarily signed by an adult, has a reasonable chance of protecting the recreation or sport business from liability for ordinary negligence by the business or its employees" (p. 106).

In the past, parental waivers and releases of indemnity were deemed ineffective. Indeed, industry most frequently are related to due process, equal protection, the right to be free from unreasonable searches and seizures, and invasion of privacy. Occasionally challenges regarding the Bill of Rights—for example, freedom of religion, freedom of speech, and the right to assemble peaceably—occur.

State Action

As a rule, the U.S. Constitution and state constitutions do not apply to private entities such as professional teams, athletic associations, private high schools or colleges, or private golf or health and fitness clubs. This is because, as stated earlier, the Constitution is a document where the "people" specifically define the role of the government, rather than the powers and duties of private companies. Nevertheless, in some cases, it can be argued that the private company or entity is so enmeshed with the public entity that the two are dependent upon each other. When a private entity meets this standard, it is called a **state actor** and the court may apply the Constitution to that private entity. For example, in *Brentwood Academy v. Tennessee Secondary School Athletic Association (TSSAA)* (2001), the U.S. Supreme Court found state action in the TSSAA's regulatory activity due to the pervasive entwinement of state school officials in the TSSAA's structure. The plaintiff, Brentwood Academy, is a private parochial high school member of the TSSAA.

The TSSAA found that Brentwood violated a rule prohibiting "undue influence" in recruiting athletes when it wrote to incoming students and their parents about spring football practice. The TSSAA placed Brentwood's athletic program on probation for 4 years, declared its football and boys' basketball teams ineligible to compete in playoffs for 2 years, and imposed a $3,000 fine. When the penalties were imposed, all the voting members of the board of control and legislative council were public school administrators. In *Brentwood Academy*, the Court found that the

TSSAA's private character was overshadowed by the pervasive entwinement of public institutions and public officials in its structure and activities. Factually, 84% of the TSSAA's members were public schools whose officials acted in their official capacity to provide interscholastic athletics to their students. Without the public school officials, who overwhelmingly determine and perform all but the TSSAA's purely ministerial acts, the TSSAA could not function. In addition, the TSSAA's staff participates in the state retirement system. To complement the entwinement from the bottom up, the state has provided entwinement from the top down: State board members sit *ex officio* on the TSSAA's governing bodies and association. Thus, the Court found constitutional standards applied to the TSSAA.

In a very important case for the NCAA, the U.S. Supreme Court declined to hold that the NCAA is a state actor. In *NCAA v. Tarkanian* (1988), the Court refused to find state action when the NCAA ordered the University of Nevada, Las Vegas (UNLV) to suspend its basketball coach, Jerry Tarkanian. The difference between the two cases is that the NCAA's policies were shaped not by UNLV alone, but by several hundred member institutions, many of them private and most of them having no connection with UNLV. In *Tarkanian*, the Court did, however, predict in dictum that state action could be found where there is public entwinement in the management or control of an entity whose member public schools are located in a single state (*Id.* at 193). (Dictum is an opinion of a judge expressed as a comment in a decision that is neither legally binding nor to be used as precedent in a future case.)

Due Process

Athletic associations adopt many rules and regulations that they enforce through their own administrative processes. If the athletic association is a state actor, its administrative process must also provide procedural **due process** as required by the Fifth and Fourteenth Amendments to the U.S. Constitution or an equivalent section of a state constitution. Procedural due process is the right to notice and a hearing before life, liberty, or property may be taken away. While no athletic association makes decisions to take away a life, some decisions affect liberty and property interests. Examples of liberty interests include the right to be free from stigma, to be free from damage to one's reputation, and to pursue one's livelihood. Property interests involve the taking away of anything of value. The U.S. Supreme Court has found property interests for teachers with tenure as well as in cases where the policies of an employer supported a claim of de facto tenure (*Perry v. Sindermann*, 1972). College scholarships have long been held to be property interests (*Gulf South Conference v. Boyd*, 1979). If a property interest exists, the plaintiff must be given an opportunity to be heard before an impartial hearing officer prior to the property being taken away by the government or state actor.

Equal Protection

The Equal Protection Clause of the Fourteenth Amendment guarantees that no person shall be discriminated against unless a constitutionally permissible reason for the discrimination exists. *Discrimination* occurs when two similarly situated individuals are treated differently on the basis of a status or classification. The Equal Protection Clause often applies in sport when there are allegations of discrimination on the basis of race, gender, or alienage in eligibility or employment decisions. The court employs three different standards of review for **equal protection** cases. The first, strict scrutiny, is the most stringent review a court can give. The second is the legitimate interest test, which is a mid-level review. The third is the rational basis test, which is the most lenient review a court can give.

Strict scrutiny applies when one discriminates on the basis of race, religion, or national origin. To withstand a constitutional challenge, a defendant—typically the government or a state actor—must convince the court it has a compelling need to violate a fundamental right or discriminate. This standard is the most challenging to meet, so defendants usually lose. For example, a recent Supreme Court case, *Fisher v University of Texas* (2016), applied strict scrutiny in a challenge to the admissions process. The Court ruled that the University of Texas must show a compelling reason why its affirmative action policies that consider the race of an applicant do not violate the Fourteenth Amendment's Equal Protection Clause. The university's affirmative action admissions system examined applicants in a holistic view, including race among a variety of factors. The Court held for the university and let stand an admissions policy that allows public universities to give limited consideration to race when admitting students.

The second standard of review applies to discrimination on the basis of gender. A defendant may discriminate on the basis of gender only if a **legitimate interest** for doing so exists. As a mid-level review from the courts, it is not as difficult a threshold as strict scrutiny, but is more stringent than the rational basis test. In high school and college athletics, courts have found two legitimate reasons for upholding the use of separate-gender teams: (1) to protect the health and safety of the athletes and (2) to avoid existing discrimination or make up for past discrimination.

However, a legitimate reason may not exist to have separate gender practices on the business side. For instance, in 1975, MLB Commissioner Bowie Kuhn enacted a rule that banned female reporters from baseball clubhouses. Despite the contrary wishes of Yankees players, Kuhn insisted that Melissa Ludtke, a female *Sports Illustrated* sportswriter covering the 1977 World Series, be banned from the Yankees' clubhouse (*Ludtke and Time, Inc. v. Kuhn*, 1978). Ludtke challenged the rule because it discriminated against her on the basis of her gender and kept her from pursuing her profession—a liberty protected by the Fourteenth Amendment's Equal Protection and Due Process clauses. The court found that MLB's expressed legitimate reason of protecting the privacy of the players and the family image of the game could not withstand judicial scrutiny when it allowed television cameras in clubhouses at the game's end to obtain interviews from scantily clad players.

The third standard of review applies to discrimination based on any other status or classification. Discriminatory actions have been challenged on the basis of economic or social background, sexual orientation, physical or mental disability, or athletic team membership. The court will allow the defendant's actions if it convinces the court there is a **rational basis** for the discriminatory rule. Rational basis standard cases are the easiest for defendants to win. For example, in *Jones v. West Virginia State Board of Education* (2005), the Supreme Court of Appeals of West Virginia held that prohibiting home-schooled children from participating in interscholastic athletics did not violate the equal protection clause of the West Virginia Constitution. The Court agreed with school officials that promoting academics over athletics and protecting the economic interests of the county school systems were two reasons that formed a rational basis for excluding (and thereby discriminating against) home-schooled children from participation in interscholastic athletics.

Unreasonable Search and Seizure

The Fourth Amendment provides that people have the right "to be secure in their persons, houses, papers and effects against **unreasonable searches and seizures**." The act of taking an athlete's urine or blood to test for doping may constitute a seizure and the testing may constitute a search within the meaning of the Fourth Amendment. Such a search may be considered reasonable by a court if the defendant can show a compelling need for it. The U.S. Supreme Court

has upheld drug testing of high school athletes on the grounds that schools have a compelling interest in deterring drug use by children to ensure their health and safety and to keep the school environment free from the disciplinary problems created by drug use (*Vernonia School District 47J v. Acton*, 1995). In 2002, the U.S. Supreme Court (in a narrow 5–4 decision) upheld the constitutionality of a random, mandatory suspicionless test of all students engaged in all competitive extracurricular activities because it was a reasonably effective means of addressing the school district's legitimate concerns in preventing, deterring, and detecting drug use (*Board of Education v. Earls*, 2002). Because the only disciplinary consequence of a positive test for illegal drugs was to limit participation in those activities, the Court allowed the school board to use the testing as a method of deterrence without waiting for a crisis to develop before imposing a testing policy.

The Supreme Court of Washington ruled that a random and suspicionless drug testing policy for student athletes violated the state of Washington's constitution and upheld the parents' appeal (*York v. Wahkiakum School Dist. No. 200*, 2008). The Court agreed with the parents' contention that such a policy violated Washington's state constitution, which provides "[n]o person shall be disturbed in his private affairs, or his home invaded without authority of law" (*Id.*). On the state level, several courts have also held that the NCAA drug testing program does not violate state constitutional rights (*Brennan v. Board of Trustees*, 1997; *Hill v. National Collegiate Athletic Association*, 1994).

Invasion of Privacy

The U.S. Constitution does not specifically provide a fundamental right to be free from **invasion of privacy**. However, the U.S. Supreme Court has implied that one exists based on the Fourth Amendment. To bring an action for invasion of privacy, a plaintiff must establish that the invasion is substantial and is in an area for which there is an expectation of privacy. In sports, this most often arises in challenges to drug testing programs. In *Vernonia School District 47J v. Acton* (1995), James Acton challenged the Vernonia School District's drug testing program on the basis of invasion of privacy. The Supreme Court found that school children had a reduced expectation of privacy when they entered school and that athletes had a lesser expectation of privacy, still. Because participating in athletics subjects an individual to a locker room environment, physical examinations, and the need for medical attention, this lesser expectation of privacy exists. Thus, drug testing of high school athletes was not deemed an invasion of privacy. Applying these concepts further, the Supreme Court in *Board of Education of Indep. School District No. 92 of Pottawatomie County v. Earls* (2002) stated specifically that student-athletes had a lesser expectation of privacy than students in other extracurricular activities, that the nature of the test by urinalysis was a negligible intrusion, and that the goal of preventing drug use in a nation where drug abuse is prevalent, even if there is no specific indication of a problem of drug use among athletes, passes constitutional muster.

It is uncertain if the *Vernonia* and *Earls* rulings apply to collegiate athletes. In the *Vernonia* opinion, Justice Antonin Scalia went to great lengths to explain that the high school students had a lower expectation of privacy because they were minors under the school's care while away from their parents and, therefore, the teachers had to enforce discipline in the school (*Vernonia School District 47J v. Acton*, 1995). College athletes, in contrast, are adults under far less supervision. Additionally, a little more than a year before the *Vernonia* decision, the U.S. Supreme Court refused to hear an appeal of the Supreme Court of Colorado's decision that found that drug testing of football players

at the University of Colorado was an invasion of privacy (*University of Colorado v. Derdeyn*, 1993). In *Derdeyn*, the Colorado court held that despite the University of Colorado's interest in protecting the health and welfare of student-athletes, and although student-athletes do consent to restrictions on their private lives by participating in collegiate athletics, those issues are not enough to justify the intrusion on privacy interests of the nature and extent involved in the random, suspicionless testing for drugs.

No constitutional challenge to drug testing in professional sport has been successful because as a general rule, professional sport leagues and teams are not state actors. Drug testing challenges in professional sport are most effectively made through the arbitration process set forth in the league's **collective bargaining agreement** (CBA). The CBA is the contract agreed to by the players association and the owners for all provisions related to hours, wages, and terms and conditions of employment. Drug testing is a term and condition of employment, so drug testing provisions, penalties, and systems of challenging the testing are set forth in the CBA. In leagues where there is no unionization, such as minor league baseball, the rules are set forth by the league and the process for appeal is to the league's commissioner.

Title IX of the Educational Amendments of 1972

Title IX is a section of the Educational Amendments of 1972, a comprehensive statute enacted to eliminate gender discrimination in educational institutions that receive federal funding; thus, it applies only to interscholastic and intercollegiate athletics, not to professional or Olympic/Paralympic sport. It states, in relevant part, that "No person in the United States shall, on the basis of sex, be excluded from participation in, be denied the benefits of, or be subjected to discrimination under any education program or activity receiving Federal financial assistance."

The U.S. Department of Education's Office of Civil Rights (OCR) establishes policies for applying Title IX to athletic participation. To decide whether a school or college is in compliance, the OCR focuses on three areas. First, the OCR assesses whether an institution's athletic scholarships are awarded on a substantially proportionate basis (male versus female). Second, the OCR assesses the degree to which a school or college has given equal treatment, benefits, and opportunities in specific athletic program areas. The OCR examines areas such as the provision of publicity, promotions, facilities, equipment, and supplies; the opportunity to benefit from quality coaching and support staff; and the scheduling of games and practices. Third, the OCR assesses the degree to which a school or college has equally and effectively accommodated the interests and abilities of male and female students.

Most Title IX cases have been brought under the third factor, but the OCR and potential plaintiffs have more recently begun examining the treatment of athletes. It became area of growing litigation after the U.S. Supreme Court ruled that Title IX did not preclude a plaintiff from receiving compensatory damages and attorneys' fees (*Franklin v. Gwinnett County Public Schools*, 1992). As a result, athletes and attorneys can better afford the cost of pursuing Title IX lawsuits.

The following decisions highlight various applications of Title IX. After seven men's and three women's sports at James Madison University (JMU) were cut in 2006 to comply with Title IX requirements, an action group (Equity in Athletics, Inc.) was formed by athletes, coaches, and fans to oppose the move. In *Equity in Athletics, Inc. v. The United States Department of Education* (2008), the plaintiff argued that the defendant university was discriminating against male athletes and, therefore, violating Title IX. The court took a "balance of hardship"

approach to its analysis and noted that students were unfettered in being able to transfer to other schools and would still keep their scholarship entitlements, while JMU would be significantly disadvantaged if it was forced to reconvene any or all sports. The court also denied the plaintiff's argument that equal opportunity should be determined by "expressed interest" rather than "actual participation."

The court applied the triple-pronged test of compliance in *Miller v. University of Cincinnati* (2008), in which the women's rowing team contended the program was inadequately facilitated in terms of resources. The sport was later eliminated in favor of women's lacrosse. The court found that the university was in compliance with Title IX, as 47.5% of the total student population was female and 48.9% of the school's student-athletes were female.

A more recent Title IX class action lawsuit, *Biediger v. Quinnipiac University* (2012), was brought by Quinnipiac University women's volleyball players and their coach Robin Sparks. In April 2009, Quinnipiac University announced the elimination of its women's volleyball program. The plaintiffs were granted an injunction to prevent the university from dropping the volleyball program (*Biediger v. Quinnipiac University*, 2009). Quinnipiac's plan was to eliminate volleyball and add competitive cheerleading. The plaintiffs argued that Quinnipiac was not in compliance with Title IX because the proportion of male to female students was 38.13% male and 61.87% female. The composition of male to female athletes was 37.73% male to 62.27% female according to the university. However, because the judge found competitive cheerleading was not a recognized NCAA sport, he found Quinnipiac to be out of compliance. The reasons the cheerleading team was not considered a competitive sport were varied: There was no off-campus recruiting, the season was inconsistent in terms of rules governing competition and the types and quality of opponents, the university did not treat it as a varsity team, and the postseason did not follow the structure of a competitive team. The judge noted that he did not mean to belittle the athletic endeavor of the athletes on the cheerleading team, but stated that at this point the sport was too disorganized and unstructured to be considered a competitive sport for purposes of Quinnipiac's compliance with Title IX (*Biediger v. Quinnipiac*, 2010). The Second Circuit upheld the district court's decision, also because the court discovered a disparity between the actual participation numbers of female roster spots on the women's teams. In some cases, women were counted more than once, making roster spots "illusory." Once a recalculation was done, 41 athletes were removed from the Quinnipiac calculations (30 cheerleaders and 11 track/cross-country runners counted twice), the participation rate changed to 58.25% female compared with an enrollment rate of 61.87% female. That 3.62% disparity was considered to be too great a differential, leading to the finding of a Title IX violation. The Second Circuit emphasized a 2% disparity would be acceptable but held that 3.62% was not (Dennie, 2012).

When applying Title IX to employment discrimination, courts rely on the standards set forth in Title VII, discussed later in this chapter (*Perdue v. City University of New York*, 1998; *Pitts v. University of Oklahoma*, 1994; *Stanley v. University of Southern California*, 1994).

Antitrust Law

A capitalist economy depends on competition (economic rivalry) between businesses, such that they are engaged in a contest for customers (Howell et al., 1987). To promote competition in the free market, Congress enacted the Sherman Antitrust Act of 1890. The Sherman Act's goal was to break up business trusts and monopolies and prohibit anticompetitive activity by businesses. It is the United States' primary **antitrust law** covering restraint of trade (Section 1)

and monopolies (Section 2). The penalty for antitrust violations is a tripling of the damage award. Because professional teams are worth hundreds of millions of dollars and athletes' salaries total millions of dollars, an anticompetitive practice that injures a competitor league, a team owner, or a player's ability to make use of a free market may create a crippling damage award. However, damage awards are seen only rarely in sports antitrust cases because most result in settlements.

Antitrust and Professional Sport

The application of antitrust laws to leagues has left an indelible mark on their structure and the nature of labor–management relations. Antitrust challenges have primarily occurred in professional sport, in which monopolization of the player, product, and geographic markets and restrictive policies are common. With only one viable major professional league for each sport, those leagues' domination of the market for each sport has been challenged by competitors as being a violation of the Sherman Act (*Federal Baseball Club of Baltimore v. National League of Professional Baseball Clubs*, 1922; *American Football League v. National Football League*, 1963; *Philadelphia World Hockey, Inc. v. Philadelphia Hockey Club, Inc.*, 1972; *United States Football League v. National Football League*, 1986). Through their restrictive policies, professional sports leagues strive to maintain competitive balance. Over time, many cases have been brought by players, owners, competitor leagues, prospective cities, and prospective owners challenging the restraints imposed upon them through league rules and policies.

The following cases highlight the more recent antitrust challenges in professional sport. In *American Needle v. National Football League* (2010), the U.S. Supreme Court reversed the Seventh Circuit Court of Appeals and ruled that NFL Properties (the NFL's licensing and merchandising arm) was not a **single entity** when promoting NFL football by licensing the teams' intellectual property. Relying on *Copperweld Corp. v. Independence Tube Corp.*, 467 U.S. 752, 773, n. 21, the Court reiterated that "'substance, not form, should determine whether a[n] . . . entity is capable of conspiring under section 1.' . . . The key is whether the alleged 'contract, combination, . . . or, conspiracy' is concerted action—that is whether it joins together separate decision makers." The Court found that each NFL team is a substantial, independently owned, and independently managed business, and that all teams' objectives are not shared in common. More specifically, the Court noted that NFL teams "compete with one another, not only on the playing field, but to attract fans, for gate receipts, and for contracts with managerial and playing personnel" (*Id*. at 9). The Court further explained that NFL teams do compete in the market for intellectual property, a fact directly relevant to the question of whether NFL Properties is a single entity. The Supreme Court remanded *American Needle* back to the district court for a trial consistent with its finding that NFL Properties was not a single entity. After a change in district court judges and a long discovery period, the *American Needle* case settled, five years after it was remanded to the trial court from the U.S. Supreme Court. Unfortunately, terms of the settlement were sealed and, without a trial, questions remain undecided over whether league-wide collective activities are anticompetitive. This ruling would have applied to league-wide broadcasting and Internet practices, as well (Edelman, 2015). After *American Needle*, it is unlikely that a traditionally created sport league will be considered a single entity and, therefore, immune from Section 1 of the Sherman Antitrust Act. The questions that remain are whether league-wide collective business practices are reasonable under the rule of reason and thus, if they survive antitrust scrutiny.

However, a Third Circuit Court of Appeals case upheld the jury's decision in *Deutscher Tennis Bund v. ATP Tour, Inc.* (2010), that the Association of Tennis Professionals (ATP) Tour did not violate antitrust law when it stripped the annual Hamburg event of its Masters Series designation and demoted it to "second-tier" status. The Third Circuit also upheld the jury's finding that the ATP Tour was a single entity immune from Section 1 liability.

Antitrust Exemptions

All unionized professional sport leagues are shielded from antitrust liability by the **labor exemption**, provided they negotiate collectively with the appropriate professional athletes' labor union. The U.S. Supreme Court has firmly established that during the term of a CBA, terms negotiated in that agreement are exempt from antitrust scrutiny. Provided the defendant proves the plaintiff is, was, or will be a party to the CBA; that the subject being challenged on antitrust grounds is a mandatory subject for bargaining (hours, wages, and other terms and conditions of employment); and that the CBA was achieved through *bona fide* arm's-length bargaining (bargaining that occurs freely, without one party having excessive power or control over the other); the defendant's actions will be exempt from antitrust (*McCourt v. California Sports, Inc.*, 1979; *Reynolds v. National Football League*, 1978; *Wood v. National Basketball Association*, 1987).

Curt Flood Act

All professional sport organizations except MLB are subject to antitrust laws. In 1922, the U.S. Supreme Court held that professional baseball was not subject to the Sherman Act (*Federal Baseball Club of Baltimore v. National League of Professional Baseball Clubs*, 1922). MLB's antitrust exemption survived two further Supreme Court challenges, and much of it remained intact despite the adoption of the Curt Flood Act (*Flood v. Kuhn*, 1972;

Toolson v. New York Yankees, 1953). The **Curt Flood Act** granted MLB players, but not minor leaguers, the legal right to sue their employers under the Sherman Act. It also confirmed that the exemption still applies to baseball's business areas, including the minor leagues; the minor league player reserve clause, the amateur draft; franchise expansion, location, or relocation; franchise ownership issues; marketing and sales of the entertainment product of baseball; and licensed properties. In 2017, the Ninth Circuit Court of Appeals upheld baseball's exemption from antitrust laws on the weight of Supreme Court precedent and the Curt Flood Act of 1998. Plaintiff minor leaguers in *Miranda v. Selig* claimed that MLB's antitrust exemption artificially depressed wages. The Ninth Circuit decided in favor of MLB, so it continues the practice of paying many minor league players less than a living wage.

This protection from antitrust liability sets MLB apart from other professional sport organizations, whose rules and practices are subject to antitrust scrutiny. In *Los Angeles Memorial Coliseum Commission v. National Football League* (1984), the Ninth Circuit Court of Appeals upheld a jury decision that the NFL's application of its franchise relocation rule was an unreasonable restraint of trade. The threat of prolonged litigation and a potentially large damage awards have allowed for more significant franchise movement in the NFL and NHL.

Labor Exemption

Collective bargaining provides an antitrust exemption called the labor exemption, which protects leagues from antitrust scrutiny during the term of and after a CBA has expired (*Bridgeman v. National Basketball Association*, 1987; *Brown v. Pro Football, Inc.*, 1996; *National Basketball Association v. Williams*, 1995; *Powell v. National Football League*, 1989). In *Brown v. Pro Football*, the U.S. Supreme Court noted that when a bargaining relationship exists between a league and a players association, labor policy favors limiting antitrust liability. The labor exemption eliminates the players association's threat to sue the owners on antitrust grounds provided collective bargaining is occurring. To maintain their negotiating leverage, players may opt to disclaim or to decertify their unions, thereby eliminating their bargaining relationship with management and gaining leverage at the bargaining table by threatening to bring antitrust suits—which carry the risk of triple damage awards. This strategy has been employed or threatened in recent negotiations in the NBA, NFL, and NHL. In a decertification, the players formally dissolve the union by using the same process with the National Labor Relations Board as when they create a union. By comparison, a disclaimer of interest is a quicker approach that allows the players to opt out of union representation. Once the players disclaim the union, they are instead represented by legal counsel. Without a formal union representing them, the players maintain the threat of antitrust litigation, providing leverage in labor negotiations.

Sports Broadcasting Act of 1961

Congress passed the Sports Broadcasting Act of 1961 to exempt sport leagues' national television deals from antitrust liability (15 U.S.C. §§ 1291–1294). This statute grants professional teams the right to pool their television rights as a league and increase their bargaining power when negotiating league-wide television packages without the threat of antitrust challenges. It also restricts leagues from defining geographic areas into which the pooled telecasts are broadcast and limits Friday and Saturday telecasts within a 75-mile radius of college and high school football. Practically speaking, this law allows, for example, the NFL to package its television deals to a limited number of national networks such as NBC, CBS, and ESPN.

Antitrust and College Athletics

Commercialization of college athletics has spawned antitrust challenges to NCAA rules by coaches, athletes, alumni, member institutions, and competitors (*Adidas America, Inc. v. National Collegiate Athletic Association*, 1999). Before subjecting NCAA rules and regulations to antitrust scrutiny, the court decides whether the rule regulates a commercial or noncommercial activity. To date, courts have found that eligibility rules are noncommercial (*Banks v. National Collegiate Athletic Association*, 1992; *McCormack v. National Collegiate Athletic Association*, 1988) and, therefore, not subject to antitrust law. However, rules such as those restricting coaches' earnings (*Law v. National Collegiate Athletic Association*, 1995) and limitations on NCAA members' television contracts (*National Collegiate Athletic Association v. Board of Regents of the University of Oklahoma and the University of Georgia Athletic Association*, 1982) have been deemed commercial and subject to antitrust laws.

Former University of California, Los Angeles (UCLA) men's basketball player Ed O'Bannon and 20 other plaintiffs recently alleged in *O'Bannon v. NCAA* that the NCAA's amateurism rules restrain trade and violate antitrust laws by not compensating athletes for their images, names, and likenesses. O'Bannon prevailed at the District Court level, and the NCAA appealed. The Ninth Circuit Court of Appeals affirmed the District Court ruling, in part, and upheld the portion of the ruling allowing NCAA members to give athletes scholarships up to the full cost of attendance for their education. However, the Ninth Circuit declared erroneous the District Court's remedy of having schools to pay athletes up to $5,000. Both parties appealed to the Supreme Court. It denied certiorari, letting the Ninth Circuit decision stand. At this point it is unclear if NCAA institutions will be required to compensate athletes for their names and likeness over and above the full cost of attendance. However, since the *O'Bannon* decision, some major college football and basketball programs have improved conditions for athletes by guaranteeing scholarships for four years and providing better food and luxurious locker room upgrades. These changes give an edge to the Power Five conferences due to the financial advantages those conferences have over smaller Division I conferences.

Labor and Employment Law

The sport industry is people intensive, so sport managers must have a working knowledge of both state and federal labor and employment laws. This chapter briefly discusses a few of the pertinent federal laws: the National Labor Relations Act, the Equal Pay Act of 1963, Title VII of the Civil Rights Act of 1964, the Age Discrimination in Employment Act, and the Americans with Disabilities Act. There are also many state employment laws, but a discussion of them is beyond the scope of this chapter.

The National Labor Relations Act

The **National Labor Relations Act** (NLRA), which applies to private employers, establishes the procedures for union certification and decertification and sets forth the rights and obligations of union and management. The law also created the **National Labor Relations Board** (NLRB), the federal agency that administers labor laws in the United States. The primary areas of the sport industry in which the NLRA applies are facility management and professional sport. Facility managers may employ various unionized employees, all with different CBAs. Currently, the five major professional sport leagues (MLB, Major League Soccer [MLS], NBA, NFL, and NHL), the Women's National Basketball Association (WNBA), the Arena Football League (AFL), the National Lacrosse League (NLL), and minor league hockey players in the ECHL (formerly the East Coast Hockey League), American Hockey League (AHL), and International Hockey League (IHL) are unionized. State labor laws, not the NLRA, apply to interscholastic coaches, often if they are members of a teachers' union. Staff members in college sports are often unionized under state law. College coaches are not unionized, except in Pennsylvania, where 400 coaches are members of the Association of Pennsylvania State College and University Faculty (APSCUF, 2013).

Whether student-athletes are employees for collective bargaining purposes was the subject of a recent NLRB decision. A regional director of the NLRB ruled that Northwestern University football players were employees under federal labor law, and had a right to unionize and negotiate better terms and conditions of employment at the bargaining table. However, in August 2015, the National Labor Relations Board declined to assert jurisdiction in the case because it would "not serve to promote stability in labor relations." This decline of jurisdiction by the NLRB ended the Northwestern football team's effort to unionize, but the employment status of college athletes will be litigated again in the future, as the top five athletic conferences (Atlantic Coast Conference [ACC], Big Ten, Big Twelve, Pac-12, and Southeastern Conference [SEC]) have incredible power because they bring in the lion's share of the revenue in college athletics. For instance, in 2012–2013, the 65 schools in those conferences generated 44% of the total revenues from college athletics. By comparison, the other 999 schools accounted for 56% of revenues (Plunkett, 2016). As a result, in late 2014, the NCAA granted the Power Five conferences some autonomy to vote on prospective changes to NCAA rules. Do not be surprised if payment to athletes and restrictions on agents and advisors are among the changes ahead. The question then becomes whether those changes also alter the status of the athletes to make them employees.

Labor relations in professional sport are unique for many reasons—notably, the individual bargaining power that professional athletes derive from their unique talent. This bargaining power creates leverage for athletes. To countermand this leverage, professional leagues have adopted restrictive practices to ensure the efficient management of their players (Masteralexis, 2017). Restrictive practices limit a player's ability to make money or move through the free market; they include the draft, salary cap or luxury tax, and restrictions on free agency. Such practices may violate antitrust laws (*Mackey v. National Football League*, 1976; *Smith v. Pro Football, Inc.*, 1978). As noted previously, practices that normally violate players' antitrust rights that are agreed to through the collective bargaining process may be free from antitrust liability through the labor exemption (*McCourt v. California Sports, Inc.*, 1979; *Zimmerman v. National Football League*, 1986). Therefore, it is in the leagues' best interests for players to form unions, and for these unions and team owners to negotiate restrictive practices through the collective bargaining process. This approach is unique to sport, because most management groups either prefer not to deal with unions or simply tolerate them. Generally, management in other industries tends to perceive that unions take power and control from them.

Players associations differ in important ways from the unions found in other industries. For one thing, job security is limited. The turnover rate for sport union members is much higher than that for other union members because athletes' careers are far shorter than those of employees in other industries. This rapid turnover forces players associations to constantly spread their message to new members. In spreading the message, the players associations also face the logistical challenges of being a bargaining unit with employees on different teams throughout the United States and Canada, not to mention employees from many different countries and cultures. Further, there is a great disparity between players' talent and their need for the union. A player such as LeBron James does not need the services of the union as much as a late-round draft pick or a recently released free agent trying to make his way back onto an NBA roster. When negotiating for the collective interests of the players, unions struggle to keep the superstars and the players on the bench equally satisfied. Without the solidarity of all players, a players association loses its strength (Masteralexis, 2017).

The Equal Pay Act

Enacted in 1963, the **Equal Pay Act** (EPA) prohibits an employer from paying one employee less than another on the basis of gender when the two are performing jobs of equal skill, effort, and responsibility and are working under similar conditions. The EPA only applies to sex-based discrimination on the basis of compensation. To qualify, the plaintiff and the comparable employee must be of opposite genders. For instance, the statute would not apply if a man coached a women's team and argued under the EPA that he should be paid a sum equal to the male coach of the men's team. Trivial differences between two jobs will not prevent them from being considered equal in terms of the EPA. Comparable worth is not an issue under the EPA.

Female coaches whose salaries are not equal to those of their male counterparts have filed EPA lawsuits. *Stanley v. University of Southern California* (1999) involved a complaint by the University of Southern California's women's basketball coach, Marianne Stanley, that she was not paid equally to the male basketball coach, George Raveling. In finding that their jobs were not equal, the court focused on the additional pressure to raise revenue and the responsibility it said Raveling had due to the fact that the men's team had a larger season

ticket base and a greater national presence. The court found such responsibility created more media pressure and a greater time investment in dealing with fans and the media (*Stanley v. University of Southern California*, 1999). Interestingly, the court never considered whether Stanley actually might have had more responsibility and pressure because she constantly labored to get a larger season ticket base and more media attention for her team. The court also focused attention on a comparison of Stanley's and Raveling's skills, qualifications, and work experience. Stanley had 17 years of coaching experience, whereas Raveling had 31 years of experience. Raveling had a background and prior work experience in marketing that Stanley did not have. Raveling had also worked as a television commentator, author, and actor. However, Stanley had done speaking engagements and had won four national championships while also leading her team to three other NCAA tournaments. Raveling had coached teams to the NCAA tournaments, but had never won a national championship. Despite this last comparative, the court found Raveling's skills and qualifications exceeded Stanley's and justified the pay difference.

If an employee proves the elements of an EPA violation, the four defenses available to the employer are that the disparity in pay is due to the presence of (1) a seniority system, (2) a merit system that is being followed in good faith, (3) a system measuring pay on the basis of quality or quantity of production, or (4) a factor other than gender.

Title VII of the Civil Rights Act of 1964

The Civil Rights Act of 1964 is a federal law prohibiting discrimination in many settings, including housing, education, and public accommodations. **Title VII** covers employers with 15 or more employees. Title VII, however, excludes Native American tribes and "bona fide membership clubs" (such as country clubs) from its definition of an employer. Title VII specifically prohibits any employment decision, practice, or policy that treats individuals unequally due to race, color, national origin, gender, or religion (*Wallace v. Texas Tech University*, 1996).

Although much of the U.S. civil rights movement focused on discrimination against African Americans, Title VII's definition of race is not that limited. It protects all classes of people from dissimilar treatment, including, but not limited to, Hispanics, Native Americans, and Asian Americans. The color focus under Title VII is on skin pigment or the physical characteristics of one's race. Regarding national origin, the court focuses on ancestry. Title VII does not prohibit employment discrimination solely based on a lack of U.S. citizenship; however, the lack of U.S. citizenship may not be used to disguise discrimination actually based on race or national origin. In other words, an employer may follow a policy of employing only U.S. citizens but may not give unequal treatment to different noncitizens based on their country of origin. Rules that require communication in "English only" are allowed only if the employer can prove the rule is a business necessity. This may bring to mind the Ladies Professional Golf Association's (LPGA) brief proposal for an English language rule for its players. While many cried foul under Title VII, the LPGA golfers are members, not employees. Nevertheless, under public pressure and criticism from its own members, the LPGA decided not to pursue this proposal (Associated Press, 2008).

As for gender, Title VII is self-explanatory, but it also includes sexual harassment (*Faragher v. Boca Raton*, 1998; *Ortiz-Del Valle v. National Basketball Association*, 1999). Title VII does not provide for remedies against discrimination on the basis of sexual orientation (*Rene v. MGM Grand Hotel*, 2002), although several states prohibit such discrimination under state law.

Title VII prohibits religious discrimination against all well-recognized faiths as well as those considered unorthodox, provided the court is convinced that the belief is sincere, genuinely held, and not simply adopted for an ulterior motive. Employers must make reasonable accommodations to religious practices and observances, unless they would place an undue hardship on the employers.

It is not illegal to discriminate based on religion, gender, or national origin if the classification is a **bona fide occupational qualification** (BFOQ). Race and color, however, are never BFOQs. The BFOQ must be reasonably necessary to the normal operation of the business. The BFOQ defense requires the employer to prove that members of the excluded class could not safely and effectively perform essential job duties, and the employer must present a factual basis for this belief. An example of a BFOQ might be as follows: An all-male boarding school makes it a requirement that resident directors in the school's dormitories also be male, justifying the requirement with such reasons as the comfort and security of the male students living in all-male dormitories and the school's desire to establish male role models in the school's social settings.

The Age Discrimination in Employment Act

Enacted in 1967, the **Age Discrimination in Employment Act** (ADEA) prohibits employment discrimination on the basis of age. Currently there is no age limit to protection, but the ADEA exempts several classes of workers, such as public safety personnel and certain top-level managers. It applies to employers that engage in commerce and hire more than 20 workers for 20 or more calendar weeks, as well as labor unions and state and federal governments. Proving discrimination under the ADEA is very similar to doing so under Title VII. The ADEA also contains a BFOQ exception that is almost identical to Title VII's. An employer can defend a claim by proving the decision was made due to reasonable factors other than age.

An example of how courts have applied the ADEA to age discrimination cases is *Moore v. University of Notre Dame* (1998). The plaintiff, Joseph Moore, the offensive line coach for Notre Dame, sued the school, alleging age discrimination. In ruling against Notre Dame, a jury found that the school did fire Moore because of his age, a violation of the ADEA. In choosing a suitable remedy, however, the district court refused to grant Moore's request for reinstatement to his former coaching position; reinstatement was not considered an appropriate remedy in this case because it would cause significant friction as well as disruption of the current football program (someone else was currently occupying Moore's position). Although reinstatement is the preferred remedy in ADEA cases, in this case the court granted Moore front pay, which represents the difference between earnings an employee would have received in his old employment and the earnings he can be expected to receive in his present and future employment (Wong, 2010).

The Americans with Disabilities Act

The **Americans with Disabilities Act** (ADA) protects employees with disabilities from discrimination at all stages of the employment relationship. An applicant or employee with a disability must be able to perform all the essential functions of a position to challenge discrimination in employment on the basis of disability. Therefore, an employer must assess the responsibilities required for a position and assess the individual's ability to perform the responsibilities. When interviewing, an employer cannot question an applicant about the specific nature of his or her disability or require medical records or exams as part of the screening process. An employer may, however, prepare a list of essential functions and ask if the applicant can perform those tasks. Although the ADA promotes the removal of barriers, it does not relieve employees with disabilities from carrying out the same job responsibilities as their able-bodied coworkers. If the individual can perform the job with or without a reasonable accommodation, the employer cannot refuse the employee based on disability. An employer must attempt to reasonably accommodate employees with disabilities unless doing so would cause undue hardship to the employer.

The most important ADA court decision related to sport management is *PGA Tour Inc. v. Martin* (2001). The case involved Title III, the public accommodation section, not the employment section. The reason was that competitors on the PGA Tour are not employees of the PGA Tour. The case involved Casey Martin, a golfer with a disability, Klippel–Trénaunay syndrome, that made it very painful and potentially dangerous to walk for long distances. He sued the PGA Tour, alleging that the failure to make a golf cart available to him and the failure to make its golf tournaments accessible to individuals with disabilities violated Title III of the ADA. In its defense, the PGA Tour argued that its walking-only rule was an essential element of professional golf on the PGA and Nike tours, and that waiving the rule would fundamentally alter the nature of the sport. The U.S. Supreme Court affirmed the Oregon District Court and Ninth Circuit Court of Appeals decision in Martin's favor, rejecting the PGA's argument that allowing Martin to use a golf cart would fundamentally alter the sport and finding that PGA golfers are not a protected class under Title III.

The Martin ruling clarified the application of the ADA to sport participation issues and has led to increased filings of ADA sport-related cases (*Kuketz v. MDC Fitness Corp.*, 2001). Recently, the Office of Civil Rights (2013) issued a clarifying letter (referred to as a "Dear Col-league Letter") stating that public elementary and secondary schools must provide extra-curricular athletic opportunities for disabled students under the Rehabilitation Act of 1973. Where a reasonable modification can be made to the sport, the students with disabilities will need to be mainstreamed or provided with an alternative opportunity for sport and physical education. An example is providing a visual cue simultaneous to the starting pistol for a hearing-impaired runner (OCR, 2013).

The ADA requires public assembly facili-ties, stadiums, theaters, and health and fitness centers to be barrier free. Sport managers work-ing in facilities that are open to the public must ensure that their facilities comply with the ADA regulations for such areas as entrances and exits, seating, walkways, parking, and locker room and bathroom facilities (*Access Now, Inc. v. South Florida Stadium Corp.*, 2001).

Intellectual Property Law

Intellectual property (IP) refers to creations of the mind. IP law governs the right to protect one's inventions, literary and artistic works, and symbols, names, images, and designs used in commerce. This area of law is very important to the commercial growth of sport (World Intellectual Property Organization [WIPO], 2013c). IP protection secures the economic value of sport through patents, trademarks, and broadcasting rights (WIPO, 2013a). A trademark is a distinctive sign or "mark" (one or a combination of words, names, numbers, sounds, shapes, vocal sounds, or symbols) used by a specific person or enterprise to help consumers identify and distinguish its goods or services because of its nature and quality, as indicated by its mark (WIPO, 2013b).

Trademarks can be strong, entitled to a wide scope of protection, or weak, entitled to limited protection in only a narrow field (Reed, 1989).

Strong trademarks are those that are completely distinguishable, such as Exxon, Polaroid, and Kleenex. Gus Macker (outdoor three-on-three basketball tournament) and Rucker Park Street Ball are good examples of fanciful, distinguish-able event names. On the other end of the spectrum are weak names, such as Musicfest, Food Fest, and Art Expo, which use common words in their ordinary meanings and would be difficult, although not impossible, to protect (Reed, 1989). Such names may be protected if they possess **secondary meaning**—that is, when the public distinguishes one product or event from another by the trademark. Reed (1989) uses *World's Fair* as an example. Although the words are common and used in their ordinary meaning, the trademark is descriptive due to the amount of advertising and public exposure it receives. Because there is only one World's Fair, use of this trademark by others without permission may lead consumers to confuse the secondary use with the original trademark.

The **Lanham Act**, which governs trademarks and service marks, gives protection to the owner of a name or logo, keeps others from sell-ing goods as the goods of the original source, and helps to protect against consumer confu-sion (Anderson, 2017). The law in this area is somewhat complex, and those sport managers involved with licensed products should rely on attorneys who are experts in trademark law to handle registering trademarks and pursuing claims against those who misappropriate them.

Some case examples may help to illustrate the diversity of IP issues. The University of South Carolina attempted to trademark the let-ters "S" and "C" that appeared in an interlocked design for use mainly on its baseball team's caps. The University of Southern California formally opposed this trademark application. In 2008, the U.S. Patent and Trademark Office found that confusion would likely occur if the mark was allowed and subsequently denied the application. In *Board of Supervisors for La. State Univ. v. Smack Apparel Co.* (2008), the plaintiff's argument that its university's purple and gold color scheme, when used in concert with specific information pertaining to the school on a T-shirt, even without the university's logo or other marks being present, infringed upon the trademark rights of the school, was upheld.

Another interesting case, *Callaway Golf Company v. Acushnet Company* (2008), involved a suit filed by Calloway against the parent company of Titleist, alleging that the Pro VI golf ball—the most popular golf ball on the PGA Tour at that time—infringed upon preexisting Callaway patents. The court's reasoning focused on a person of "ordinary skill" in the golf ball manufacturing industry and whether he or she could have created the Pro VI without Callaway's already patented material. Ultimately, the court decided that this would not have been the case and found in favor of Callaway.

Finally, the *Keller v. EA Sports* (2009) case was a companion case to *O'Bannon v. NCAA*. Keller's suit was based in the right of publicity; that is, Keller argued that EA Sports and the NCAA misappropriated his image and likeness for use in its NCAA football games. Keller settled out of court with EA Sports, but if Keller succeeded, college athletes would have won the right to be paid, which would violate current principles of amateurism.

The preceding discussion of legal concepts is not all inclusive. It should, however, serve as a place for a sport manager to begin to build a legal knowledge base to manage risk and limit liability.

Key Skills

Among the most important skills that a sport manager may acquire from the study of law is to identify a problem's issues before attempting to solve it. By practicing critical thinking and

problem solving, sport managers improve their logical and analytical reasoning skills, making it more likely that a sport manager facing a crisis will resolve it in a calm, logical, and thoughtful manner.

The analysis of case and statutory law will lead to more persuasive and clearer written and oral communication. The study of law involves studying the language used in cases and statutes and making arguments to apply that language to various situations. Practice in this area will help individuals develop the clearly stated written policies and procedures that are an important part of a sound risk management plan. Excellent communication also is a key to good leadership and good relations with staff, peer and superior administrators, the public, and clients. In addition, verbal communication skills can enhance negotiating skills, and sport managers negotiate on a daily basis, even if they do not realize it. Managers negotiate for everything they need, whether in a formal setting, such as negotiating with a television network to broadcast games, or more informally, such as negotiating with a staff member to cover a shift for a coworker. Finally, the study of law, particularly in areas such as negotiation and client interviewing, focuses on good listening skills. A successful sport manager should be prepared to invest time listening to staff and clients. A good listener

© EDHAR/Shutterstock, Inc.

will be a better judge of people and will know what it takes to motivate staff and to keep staff and clients satisfied.

Law and ethics are entwined. In setting parameters for acceptable conduct, the law establishes codes of ethical conduct. Studying law may not change a sport manager's behavior, because his or her personal values may already be instilled, but it may help sport managers to better establish codes of conduct in their workplaces. Sport law also may guide sport managers in how to best resolve disputes and violations of ethical codes without infringing on individual rights.

Putting Skills to Practice

A sport manager can effectively manage legal problems by understanding the law, specifically sport law. By knowing legal pitfalls, managers can avoid, prevent, or reduce many workplace problems. A well-written and well-administered risk management plan can help a sport manager avoid legal liability. The challenge for sport managers is to understand the legal implications, if any, of their decisions. Sport managers must determine

the answers to questions of legal liability, either alone or with the advice of in-house or outside counsel.

For example, a health and fitness club manager may be faced with the option of adding wall-climbing equipment at her club. The manager must make this decision based on consumer interest as well as on the financial benefits, costs, and potential legal liability. When contemplating legal liability, a club manager should consider all potential problems that may arise with the wall-climbing equipment. This analysis should involve creating a list of issues to consider. See **Box 5-1** for a list of considerations.

Although the list in Box 5-1 was compiled for a club manager, similar lists can be created for other program and policy decisions made by sport managers in other segments of the industry.

A second example reflects decisions to be made by sport managers at an association, institution, or organization considering the implementation of a drug testing program. **Box 5-2** is a list of important issues to consider (Wong, 2010).

Box 5-1 Issues to Consider When Purchasing and Installing Equipment for a Health and Fitness Club

- Who should be allowed to use this equipment?
- Should training be required before use?
- Who is qualified to train users? Which additional training may staff need to train users?
- Should participants be required to provide medical approval before use?
- Should participants be required to sign a waiver of liability?
- Should minors (and their parents) be required to sign a waiver of liability?
- What if someone refuses to sign a waiver of liability or alters it before signing?

- If used, how should a waiver of liability be drafted? Is it likely to hold up in court?
- Which types of signs or warnings should be posted on or near the equipment?
- What emergency procedures are in place if a participant is injured while using equipment?
- Should an individual who became injured while using the equipment be allowed to participate again? When and under which circumstances?

Box 5-2 Issues to Consider When Implementing a Drug Testing Program

- Before implementing a drug test, has the organization thoroughly discussed the reasons for implementing one? What are the goals and objectives that the drug test will accomplish?
- Is the drug testing policy clearly defined and in writing?
- Does the organization's drug testing policy conform to conference and association rules and regulations?
- Does the format and procedures for the test comply with state and federal law?
- Who will conduct the tests?
- Who will pay for the tests?
- Will the tests be random and mandatory or only for probable cause or reasonable suspicion?

- What constitutes probable cause or reasonable suspicion?
- How much notice should be given before testing begins?
- Which types of drugs (recreational and/or performance enhancing) will be tested for?
- How frequently will athletes be tested?
- What actions should be taken when an athlete tests positive?
- Will there be an appeal process for a positive test result?
- Is there a method for retesting positive results?
- What confidentiality and constitutional law issues does drug testing raise?
- Do the sanctions to be imposed adhere to federal and/or state law?

Sport managers considering drug testing professional athletes must ask many of the same questions, but they must also be cognizant of player rights negotiated through collective bargaining. The job of a professional sport team general manager once consisted of evaluating talent, drafting and signing amateur players, and making trades. Today a general manager has other responsibilities, often arising from complex provisions negotiated in the league's CBA or an individual player's contract, such as luxury taxes and salary caps, disciplinary measures, and arbitration processes. Further, given the global market for talent, there may be a need to understand international laws, plus global rules and regulations. As such, a general manager may find a law degree useful. Sport managers who can anticipate potential problems reduce risk. For example, a health club manager who allows only trained, healthy adults who have signed waivers of liability to participate in an activity has established parameters that

reduce the club's risk if people who meet the conditions then participate in a carefully and adequately supervised activity, with medical procedures in place. The sport manager has also eliminated risk by not allowing minors to participate.

A professional team's general manager may decide against acquiring a particular player if the potential future salary of the player, either through salary arbitration or leverage from free agency, will be too expensive. Alternatively, the general manager may reduce the risk of this expense by signing the player to a multiyear contract. In the NFL, the general manager can negotiate a "salary cap friendly" contract. For instance, the contract can be negotiated so that the cap impact is spread over the years, or structured so that the cap impact is greater or less in the early or late years of the contract. For example, a general manager whose team currently has room under the salary cap can structure a contract so that the salary cap impact is heaviest in the early years. This reduces the salary cap cost of the player in later years and gives the club more money and freedom to sign other players.

Current Issues

The impact of the law on sport organizations is more likely to increase, rather than decrease, in the future as sport business is becoming ever more complex and consequently more litigious. For instance, the 2011–2020 NFL CBA is a detailed 316-page document including several ancillary documents. The NCAA manual also is very detailed and complex. Due to restructuring in 1997–1998, the NCAA now publishes three manuals (one for each division). The 2017–2018 NCAA Division I manual is 428 pages and contains numerous provisions, rules, and regulations that require interpretation, resulting in more legal considerations by sport managers.

Olympic Games

In the Olympic sport industry, there are growing challenges related to rules and regulations imposed on participants. Sport managers working in the Olympic arena face legal challenges related to **ambush marketing**, the rights of individual athletes to market themselves, and the imposition of codes of conduct.

Ambush marketing occurs when an organization misappropriates the trademarks, logos, and goodwill of an event or organization (Reed, 1989). For most events of any significance, one brand will pay to become the exclusive and official sponsor of the event in a particular category or categories, and this exclusivity in turn creates a problem for one or more other brands. Often those other brands find ways to promote themselves in connection with the same event, without paying the sponsorship fee while managing not to break any laws. A company that has not paid to be a sponsor may engage in ambush marketing—and confuse the public—by indirectly associating itself with the events or organizations through buying commercial airtime during broadcasts or sponsoring individual athletes or teams at a fraction of the cost of official sponsorship. For example, although McDonald's is an official worldwide partner of the International Olympic Committee (IOC), its competitor Subway signed a marketing agreement with Olympic swimmer Michael Phelps. Subway ran ads with Phelps that, to consumers, suggested Subway was a sponsor of the Games. Based on those ads, in early 2010, the U.S. Olympic Committee (USOC) accused Subway of ambush marketing ahead of the Winter Olympic Games in Vancouver. Subway aired a commercial depicting Michael Phelps swimming toward Vancouver. The USOC said that by using Phelps, an Olympic gold medalist, and the words "Vancouver" and "winter" in its commercial, Subway was trying to falsely promote itself as a sponsor of the 2010 Winter Games (Gomez, 2010).

In anticipation of the London Olympics of 2012, the United Kingdom took the proactive approach of promulgating specific legislation aimed at preventing ambush marketing (Peachey, 2012). The legislation, known as the London Olympic Games and Paralympic Games Act of 2006, included the creation of a right known as the "London Olympics association right," which was designed to prevent false representations of sponsorships. It prevented the use of a combination of a list of words, including "games," "2012," "twenty-twelve," "two thousand and twelve" "gold," "silver," "bronze," "medals," "sponsor" and "summer."

While other legal issues beyond ambush marketing exist in the Olympic realm, such as possible unionization of Olympians, drug testing policies, and decisions about which sports are included in the Games, it exceeds the scope of this chapter to go into detail about them.

Collegiate Sport

On the collegiate level, challenges to NCAA amateurism rules and the conflict with the commercialism in Division I football and basketball dominate the current issues, along with eligibility violations. As noted earlier in the *O'Bannon* case, Division I football and basketball players are questioning NCAA rules that prohibit them from earning revenue from their playing talent and public image while they have remaining eligibility. Thus, problems will continue to arise regarding other such rules, including those restricting athletes' involvement with sport agents and athletes' abilities to market themselves. These issues are particularly salient in men's college basketball, where players face an opportunity cost in the millions of dollars if they stay in college and graduate with their respective class instead of turning pro.

Gender equity continues to present legal and financial challenges for athletic administrators at the high school and collegiate levels. In addition to participation rate issues, administrators need to be cognizant of how female coaches and administrators are treated in the athletic department. The California State University system provides an example of how costly litigation can be when this form of risk is not managed. In 2008 and 2009, this organization settled gender discrimination lawsuits totaling more than $17.5 million on behalf of the Fresno State University and San Diego State University athletics departments (Buzuvis, 2010).

The First Amendment of the U.S. Constitution states, in part, that "Congress shall make no law . . . abridging the freedom of speech, or of the press; or the right of the people peaceably to assemble." In recent times, there have been many instances of college athletes making statements on Twitter, Facebook, and other social media outlets that public and private colleges and universities find uncomfortable or objectionable. If these public institutions restrict the speech of their athletes, they run the risk of violating the First Amendment rights of students because they are public, government-funded institutions (Kimes, 2015).

Professional Sport

For years, the legal issues in professional team sport have focused on whether leagues could maintain labor peace. Currently, all of the professional leagues are in the midst of a period of relative labor peace. During the term covered by the CBA, the issues facing any league are related to administering that agreement, as well as disciplinary and drug testing challenges, plus addressing health and safety issues such as the impact of concussions.

Other legal issues include the implementation and administration of drug testing policies, particularly for individual athletes, and freedom of speech and expression for all athletes. The PGA Tour now has a drug testing policy. Men's and women's tennis and cyclists' tours do have testing, but challenges are waged regularly over their test procedures and test results. Private employers such as the Dallas Cowboys and San Francisco 49ers have more latitude in controlling the speech/expression of their players than governmental entities, as the First Amendment protects restrictions of speech by the government. Player protests, such as NFL quarterback Colin Kaepernick kneeling during the national anthem, are not protected by the First Amendment, and it is left up to the employer to decide whether to discipline the employee for such behavior. The NFL initially took the middle ground on this issue, stating that its players were encouraged, but not required, to stand during the playing of the national anthem. Private employers may choose to discipline employees such as Kaepernick (Sammin, 2016). As the 2017 NFL season went on and President Donald Trump took to Twitter to condemn players and fans put some pressure on owners, some teams took a stronger stand against the peaceful protests. As of this text's writing, Kaepernick (a free agent) remained unsigned by any NFL teams and had filed a grievance against the NFL, stating that teams colluded against him in violation of the CBA (Seifert, 2017).

Government Scrutiny

There has been a steady increase in governmental scrutiny and regulation of the sport industry. The Professional and Amateur Sports Protection Act (PASPA) bans betting on sporting events *except* in those states where such betting was legal at the time the law was approved, or in any state that legalized sports betting within a year of that date (American Sports Betting Coalition, 2018). In a landmark case being watched closely by other states, New Jersey has appealed, asking permission to offer wagering on professional and college sports. All four major professional leagues and the NCAA are against this extension of wagering (Buckstaff, 2014). The U.S. Supreme Court accepted certiorari and heard the arguments in December 2016, though no decision had been rendered as of this text's writing.

In recent years, online gambling websites such as Draft Kings and Fan Duel have exploded onto the U.S. sports betting scene. These entities are being regulated by states such as Massachusetts and New York, and their activities are being scrutinized (Woodard, 2016).

Summary

As the sport industry has evolved into a complex, multibillion-dollar global entity, the law has played an increasingly dominant role as sport professionals seek to carry out the management functions of sport organizations. When sport managers make decisions and disagreements arise, those working and participating in sport are relying more heavily on the legal system for resolutions of their disputes. Thus, knowledge of key aspects of sport law has become increasingly important to the sport manager's ability to manage risk and to know when to seek legal assistance to aid in decision making and dispute resolution.

Case Study 5-1

Can a High School Player Be Exempt from Transfer Rules Due to Homesickness?

Pat Sullivan was a standout football running back who rushed for more than 1,000 yards as a sophomore for Cold Spring High School in Massachusetts. Pat was also a fine pitcher, with a 90 mile-per-hour fastball. Big-time baseball programs such as the Universities of Arizona, Georgia, and Florida as well as Notre Dame offered him baseball scholarships, but he remained undecided about which university to attend.

After his sophomore year, Pat decided to enroll in a private high school in Connecticut to improve his grades through smaller classes while moving to a higher level of athletic competition. He transferred to a well-known athletic powerhouse prep school, the Revlon Acres School (RAS) about 100 miles from his home in Cold Spring. His junior year at RAS went well. As the starting running back for the varsity football team, he rushed for 1,150 yards and led the team in scoring. He also had a great varsity baseball season and was the top pitcher for RAS. Pat did well in school and lifted his GPA to 3.2 for his junior year. However,

(continues)

Can a High School Player Be Exempt from Transfer Rules Due to Homesickness? (*Continued*)

Pat became homesick and a year away from his family and friends proved to be hard on him. Due to his longing to be back home, Pat, with the permission of his parents, withdrew from RAS, moved back home, and re-enrolled at Cold Spring High for his senior year. Now, with the study skills he learned at RAS, he is confident that he will do well academically in his upcoming senior year. Thus, he feels his decision to go away for the year was well worth the costs.

The Cold Spring athletic director and head baseball coach, Craig Adopolos, is understandably thrilled that Pat has decided to move back and play football and baseball for his hometown school. However, his happiness abruptly ended when the Massachusetts Interscholastic Athletic Association (MIAA) sent Adopolos a letter informing him of MIAA Rule 57, which stated in relevant part:

> A student who transfers from any school to an MIAA member high school is ineligible to participate in any interscholastic athletic contest at any level for a period of one year in all sports in which that student participated at the varsity level or its equivalent during the one year period immediately preceding the transfer.

The letter to Adopolos stated that it was the MIAA Board of Commissioners' decision, which was reached without notice and a hearing to Pat or to Cold Spring High School, that Rule 57 prohibited Pat from competing in football and baseball for one year. MIAA rules also state that parties with an interest in the outcome should be given due process in hearings before the MIAA.

Pat, with the support of Cold Spring High School, appealed to the MIAA. Pat argued that the only reason he moved back home was homesickness; he was not recruited back to Cold Spring High School. The MIAA denied the appeal and ruled Pat ineligible for his senior year. To compound matters, every college that offered him a baseball scholarship has now withdrawn that offer.

Questions for Discussion

1. Pat is considering appealing the MIAA's decision to state court. Should he seek an injunction? Why or why not?

2. Which legal standards and analyses will the court use to decide this appeal?

3. Which arguments will Pat, Cold Spring High School, and the MIAA make to the court?

4. Which party will likely prevail and why?

Key Terms

administrative law, Age Discrimination in Employment Act, agency, agent, Americans with Disabilities Act, ambush marketing, antitrust law, bona fide occupational qualification, breach, capacity, collective bargaining agreement, consideration, constitutional law, contract, Curt Flood Act, defendant, disaffirm, due process, duty of care, Equal Pay Act, equal protection, fiduciary, fiduciary duty, gross negligence, independent contractor, injunction, intellectual property, invasion of privacy, judicial review, labor exemption, Lanham Act, legality, legitimate interest, mutual assent, National Labor Relations Act, National Labor Relations Board, negligence, plaintiff, principal, public policy, rational basis, release of liability, risk management, secondary meaning, single entity, sport law, state actor, statutes, strict scrutiny, Title VII, Title IX, tort, unreasonable searches and seizures, vicarious liability, waivers

References

Access Now, Inc. v. South Florida Stadium Corp., 161 F. Supp. 2d 1357 (S.D. Fla. 2001).

Adidas America, Inc. v. National Collegiate Athletic Association, 64 F. Supp. 2d 1097 (D. Kan. 1999).

Age Discrimination in Employment Act of 1990, 29 U.S.C. §§ 621–634 (West 1990).

American Football League v. National Football League, 323 F.2d 124 (4th Cir. 1963).

American Sports Betting Coalition. (2018). Sports betting FAQs. Retrieved from https://static1.squarespace.com/static /5696d0f14bf118aff8f1d23e/t/5a78eee0e4 966b21c8c8b482/1517874912595/HLG _ASBC_2_5_FAQ.pdf

American Needle v. National Football League, 130 S. Ct. 2201 (2010).

Americans with Disabilities Act of 1990, 42 U.S.C. §§ 151–169 (West 1990).

Ammon, R. (2017). Risk management process. In D. J. Cotten & J. T. Wolohan (Eds.), *Law for recreation and sport managers* (7th ed., pp. 274–282). Dubuque, IA: Kendall/Hunt Publishers.

Anderson, P. M. (2017). Principles of trademark law. In D. J. Cotten & J. T. Wolohan (Eds.), *Law for recreation and sport managers* (7th ed., pp. 602–612). Dubuque, IA: Kendall/Hunt Publishers.

Associated Press. (2008, September 5). LPGA backs down on English-only rule. Retrieved from http://www.golf.com/ap-news/lpga -backs-down-english-only-rule

Association of Pennsylvania State College and University Faculty. (2013). APSCUF members: Coaches. Retrieved from http://www.apscuf.org/members/coaches

Banks v. National Collegiate Athletic Association, 977 F.2d 1081 (7th Cir. 1992).

Biediger v. Quinnipiac University, 616 F. Supp. 2d 277 (D. Conn 2009).

Biediger v. Quinnipiac University, No. 3:09cv621 (SRU) (D. Ct. 2010). Retrieved from http://courtweb.pamd.uscourts.gov/ courtwebsearch/ctxc/KX330R32.pdf

Biediger v. Quinnipiac University, 691 F.3d 85 (2d Cir. 2012).

Black's law dictionary (5th ed.). (1979). St. Paul, MN: West Publishing Co.

Board of Education of Indep. School District No. 92 of Pottawatomie County v. Earls, 536 U.S. 822 (2002).

Board of Supervisors for La. State Univ. v. Smack Apparel Co., 550 F.3d 465 (5th Cir. 2008).

Brennan v. Board of Trustees for University of Louisiana Systems, 691 So.2d 324 (La. Ct. App. 1st Cir. 1997).

Brentwood Academy v. Tennessee Secondary School Athletic Association, 535 U.S. 971 (2001).

Bridgeman v. National Basketball Association, 675 F. Supp. 960 (D.N.J. 1987).

Brown, M. (2017, September 27). Where MLB ballparks stand on added safety netting, a week after a girl was hit by a ball. Retrieved from https://www.forbes .com/sites/maurybrown/2017/09/27/week -after-little-girl-hit-with-foul-ball-where -each-mlb-ballparks-are-on-added-safety -netting/#4b957d1a2b8a

Brown v. Pro Football, Inc., 518 U.S. 231 (1996).

Brown v. Woolf, 554 F. Supp. 1206 (S.D. Ind. 1983).

Buckstaff, C. (2014). "Covering the spread: An assessment of amateurism and vulnerability of student-athletes in an emerging culture of sports wagering," *Vanderbilt Journal of Entertainment & Technology Law*, 16(1), 133–168. Retrieved from http://www.jetlaw .org/wp-content/uploads/2014/01/Buckstaff _Final.pdf

Buse v. Vanguard Group of Investment Cos., No. 91-3560, 1996 U.S. Dist. LEXIS 19033 (E.D. Pa. 1996).

Buzuvis, E. (2010). "Sidelined: Title IX retaliation cases and women's leadership in college athletics," *Duke Journal of Gender Law & Policy*, 17(1) 1–45. Retrieved from https:// scholarship.law.duke.edu/cgi/viewcontent .cgi?article=1168&context=djglp

Callaway Golf Company v. Acushnet Company, 585 F. Supp. 2d 600 (D. Del. 2008).

Copperweld Corp. v. Independence Tube Corp., 467 U.S. 752, 773, n. 21.

Costa v. Boston Red Sox, 61 Mass. App. Ct. 299; 809 N.E.2d 1090; 2004 Mass. App. LEXIS 639 (2004).

Cotten, D. J. (2017). Waivers and releases. In D. J. Cotten & J. T. Wolohan (Eds.), *Law for recreation and sport managers* (7th ed., pp. 105–115). Dubuque, IA: Kendall/Hunt Publishers.

Crespin v. Albuquerque Baseball Club, LLC, 216 P.3d 827 (N.M. Ct. App. 2009).

Curt Flood Act, 15 U.S.C. § 27 (1998).

Dennie, C. (2012, August 14). *Biediger v. Quinnipiac University*: Second Circuit affirms and concludes cheerleading is not a sport (yet). Retrieved from http://www .bgsfirm.com/college-sports-law-blog /biediger-v-quinnipiac-university-second -circuit-affirms-and-concludes-cheerleading -is-not-a-sport-yet

Detroit Lions, Inc. and Sims v. Argovitz, 580 F. Supp. 542 (E.D. Mich. 1984).

Deutscher Tennis Bund et al. v. ATP Tour, Inc., 2010 WL 2541172 (C.A.3 (Del.).

Edelman, M. (2015, March 3). "American Needle settles antitrust suit with the NFL, preventing an inmortant sports law trial," *Forbes*. Retrieved from https://www.forbes .com/sites/marcedelman/2015/03/03 /american-needle-settles-antitrust-lawsuit -with-the-nfl-preventing-an-important -sports-law-trial/2/#21896c0673f4

Equal Pay Act of 1963, 29 U.S.C. § 206 (d)(1) (West 1990).

Equity in Athletics, Inc. v. The United States Department of Education, 291 Fed. Appx. 517 (2008).

Faragher v. Boca Raton, 524 U.S. 775 (1998).

Federal Baseball Club of Baltimore v. National League of Professional Baseball Clubs, et al., 259 U.S. 200 (1922).

Fisher v. University of Texas, 579 U. S.___; 136 S. Ct. 2198 (2016)

Flood v. Kuhn, 407 U.S. 258 (1972).

Franklin v. Gwinnett County Public Schools, 112 S. Ct. 1028 (1992).

Gomez, B. (2010, February 12). "USOC exec: Subway 'crossed the line' with Phelps ad," *The Gazette*. Retrieved from http://gazette.com/usoc-exec-subway -crossed-the-line-with-phelps-ad /article/94066

Griswold v. Connecticut, 381 U. S. 479 (1965)

Gulf South Conference v. Boyd, 369 So.2d 553 (Sup. Ct. Ala. 1979).

Hackbart v. Cincinnati Bengals, Inc., 601 F. 2d 516 (10th Cir. 1979).

Haworth, K. (1996, December 20). A cottage industry helps sports programs in trouble. *Chronicle of Higher Education*, p. A35.

Hendrickson v. Octagon, Inc., 225 F. Supp. 3d (N.D. Cal. 2016).

Hill v. National Collegiate Athletic Association, 865 P.2d 633 (Cal. 1994).

Hillard v. Black, 125 F. Supp. 2d 1071 (N.D. Fla. 2000).

Howell, R. A., Allison, J. R., & Henley, N. T. (1987). *The legal environment of business* (2nd ed.). New York, NY: Dryden Press.

Jones v. Childers, 18 F.3d 1899 (11th Cir. 1994).

Jones v. West Virginia State Board of Education, 622 S.E. 2d 289 (W.V. S.Ct. 2005).

Keller v. EA Sports, No. C 09-1967 CW (ND. Calif. 2009). Order re: motion to dismiss. *Scribd*. Retrieved from http:// www.scribd.com/doc/26624013/ Keller-v-NCAA-Order-re-Motion-to-Dismiss

Kimes, M. (2015, September 2) Social media bans may violate athletes' First Amendment rights. Retrieved from http://abcnews .go.com/Sports/social-media-bans-violate -college-athletes-amendment-rights /story?id=33482714

Kuketz v. MDC Fitness Corp., 2001 WL 993565 (Mass. Super. Ct. 2001).

Law v. National Collegiate Athletic Association, 902 F. Supp. 1394 (D. Kan. 1995).

London Olympic Games and Paralympic Games Act 2006. (United Kingdom), s. 33. Retrieved from http://www.opsi.gov.uk/acts/acts2006/pdf/ukpga_20060012_en.pdf

Los Angeles Memorial Coliseum Commission v. National Football League, 726 F.2d 1381 (1984).

Ludtke and Time, Inc. v. Kuhn, 461 F. Supp. 86 (S.D.N.Y. 1978).

Mackey v. National Football League, 543 F.2d 606 (8th Cir. 1976).

Mark v. Moser, 746 N.E.2d 410 (Ind. App. 2001).

Masteralexis, J. T., & Masteralexis, L. P. (2017). Judicial review. In D. J. Cotton & J. T. Wolohan (Eds.), *Law for recreation and sport managers* (7th ed., pp. 404–409). Dubuque, IA: Kendall/Hunt Publishers.

Masteralexis, L. P. (2017). Labor law: Professional sport applications. In D. J. Cotton & J. T. Wolohan (Eds.), *Law for recreation and sport managers* (7th ed., pp. 647–659). Dubuque, IA: Kendall/Hunt Publishers.

Matthews, W. (2018, Jan. 31). "All 30 M.L.B. teams will have extended netting next season," New York Times. Retrieved from https://www.nytimes.com/2018/01/31/sports/baseball/baseball-netting.html

McCormack v. National Collegiate Athletic Association, 845 F.2d 1338 (5th Cir. 1988).

McCourt v. California Sports, Inc., 600 F.2d 1193 (6th Cir. 1979).

Metropolitan Exhibition Co. v. Ewing, 42 F. 1989 (S.D.N.Y. 1890).

Metropolitan Exhibition Co. v. Ward, 9 N.Y.S. 779 (Sup. Ct. 1890).

Metropolitan Intercollegiate Basketball Association v. NCAA, 339 F. Supp. 2d 545 (S.D.N.Y. 2004).

Miller v. University of Cincinnati, 2007 WL 2783674 (S.D. Ohio 2008).

Mintz v. Mark Bartleson and Associates, Inc., 906 F.Supp.2d 1017 (C.D. Cal. 2012).

Miranda v. Selig, No. 15-16938 (9th Cir. 2017).

Moore v. University of Notre Dame, 22 F. Supp. 2d 896 (N.D. Ind. 1998).

National Basketball Association v. Williams, 43 F.3d 684 (2nd Cir. 1995).

National Collegiate Athletic Association v. Board of Regents of the University of Oklahoma and the University of Georgia Athletic Association, 468 U.S. 85 (1982).

National Collegiate Athletic Association v. Tarkanian, 488 U.S. 179, 193 (1988).

National Labor Relations Act, 29 U.S.C. §§ 151–69 (West 1990).

Noffke ex. rel Swenson v. Bakke, 760 N.W.2d 156 (Wis. 2009).

Northwestern University and CAPA, NLRB Case 13-RC-121359

O'Bannon v. NCAA, 7 F. Supp. 3d 955 (N.D. Cal. 2014).

O'Bannon v. NCAA, 802 F. 3d 1049 (9th Cir. 2015).

O'Bannon v. NCAA, Cert Denied No. 15-1167 & No. 15-1388 (2016).

Office of Civil Rights (OCR). (2013, January 25). Dear colleague letter. Retrieved from http://www2.ed.gov/about/offices/list/ocr/letters/colleague-201301-504.html

Oliver v. NCAA, 2009 Ohio 6587 (2009).

Ortiz-Del Valle v. National Basketball Association, 42 F. Supp. 2d 334 (S.D.N.Y. 1999).

Peachey, K. (2012, July 19). "Olympics: Tackling ambush marketing at London 2012," *BBC News*. Retrieved from http://www.bbc.com/news/business-18628635

Perdue v. City University of New York, 13 F. Supp. 2d 326 (E.D.N.Y. 1998).

Perry v. Sindermann, 408 U.S. 593 (1972).

PGA Tour Inc. v. Martin, 532 U.S. 661 (2001).

Philadelphia World Hockey, Inc. v. Philadelphia Hockey Club, Inc., 351 F. Supp. 462 (1972).

Pitts v. University of Oklahoma, No. Civ. 93-1341-A (W.D. Okla. 1994).

Plunkett, J. W. (2016). Major trends: NCAA are big revenue earners. In *Plunkett's sports industry research almanac 2017* (pp. 15–16). Houston, TX: Plunkett Research, Ltd.

Powell v. National Football League, 930 F.2d 1293 (8th Cir. 1989).

Reed, M. H. (1989). *IEG legal guide to sponsorship*. Chicago, IL: International Events Group.

Rene v. MGM Grand Hotel, Inc., No. 98-16924 (9th Cir. Sept. 24, 2002).

Reynolds v. National Football League, 584 F.2d 280 (8th Cir. 1978).

Rodgers v. Georgia Tech Athletic Association, 303 S.E.2d 467 (Ga. Ct. App. 1983).

Sammin, K. (2016, September 7). The First Amendment is a double-edged sword for Kaepernick and Rapinoe. Retrieved from http://thefederalist.com/2016/09/07 /first-amendment-double-edged-sword -kaepernick-rapinoe/

Seifert, K. (2017, October 16). Proving collusion by NFL owners will be tough for Kaepernick. Retrieved from http://www.espn.com/ blog/nflnation/post/_/id/252845/proving- collusion-by-nfl-owners-will-be-tough-for- colin-kaepernick

Shropshire, K. L., & Davis, T. (2003). *The business of sports agents*. Philadelphia, PA: University of Pennsylvania Press.

Smith v. Pro Football, Inc., 593 F.2d 1173 (D.C. Cir. 1978).

Sport Broadcasting Act, 15 U.S.C. §§ 1291–1294 (1961).

Stanley v. University of Southern California, 13 F.3d 1313 (1994).

Stanley v. University of Southern California, 178 F. 3d 1069 (9th Cir. 1999).

Staudohar, P. D. (1996). *Playing for dollars: Labor relations and the sports business*. Ithaca, NY: Cornell University Press.

Thurmond v. Prince William Professional Baseball Club, Inc., 574 S.E.2d 246 (Va. 2003).

Title IX of the Educational Amendments of 1972, 20 U.S.C. §§ 1681–88 (West 1990).

Toolson v. New York Yankees, 346 U.S. 356 (1953).

Total Economic Athletic Management of America, Inc. v. Pickens, 898 S.W.2d 98 (Mo. App. 1995).

Turner v. Mandalay Sports Entertainment, LLC. 180 P.3d 1172 (Nev. 2008).

Uniform Law Commission. (2017). Athlete Agents Act. Retrieved from http://www.uniformlaws. org/Committee.aspx?title=Athlete%20 Agents%20Act

United States Football League v. National Football League, 634 F. Supp. 1155 (S.D.N.Y. 1986).

University of Colorado v. Derdeyn, 863 P.2d 929 (1993).

Van der Smissen, B. (2007). Elements of negligence. In D. J. Cotten & J.T. Wolohan (Eds.), *Law for recreation and sport managers* (4th ed., pp. 36–45). Dubuque, IA: Kendall /Hunt Publishers.

Vernonia School District 47J v. Acton, 115 S. Ct. 2386 (1995).

Vick v. Wong et al., 263 F.R.D. 325 (U.S. Dist. 2009).

Wagenblast v. Odessa School District, 758 P.2d 968 (Wash. Sup. Ct. 1988).

Wallace v. Texas Tech University, 80 F.3d 1042 (5th Cir. 1996).

White v. NCAA, C.D. Cal. Case No. CV 06 0999 VBF.

Williams v. CWI, Inc., 777 F. Supp. 1006 (D.D.C. 1991).

Wong, G. M. (2010). *Essentials of sports law* (4th ed.). Westport, CT: Praeger Publishers.

Wood v. National Basketball Association, 809 F.2d 954 (2nd Cir. 1987).

Woodward, C. (2016, March 25). Mass. finalizes new rules for fantasy sports games, *Boston Globe*. Retrieved from https://www .bostonglobe.com/business/2016/03/25 /massachusetts-finalizes-new-rules-for -fantasy-sports-bans-college-games-players -under/POXUtUYBN2ITD2tqIRPs0O/story .html

World Intellectual Property Organization (WIPO). (2013a). What is intellectual property? Retrieved from http://www.wipo .int/about-ip/en

World Intellectual Property Organization (WIPO). (2013b). Sport and intellectual property. Retrieved from http://www.wipo .int/ip-sport/en/

World Intellectual Property Organization (WIPO). (2013c). Trademarks. Retrieved from http://www.wipo.int/trademarks/en/trademarks.html

Yasser, R., McCurdy, J., Goplerud, P., & Weston, M. (1999). *Sports law* (4th ed.). Cincinnati, OH: Anderson Publishing.

York v. Wahkiakum School Dist. No. 200, 163 Wash.2d 297 (Wash. 2008).

Zimmerman v. National Football League, 632 F. Supp. 398 (D.D.C. 1986).

Zinn v. Parrish, 644 F.2d 360 (7th Cir. 1981).

Chapter

6

Todd W. Crosset and
Mary A. Hums

Ethical Principles Applied to Sport Management

Learning Objectives

Upon completion of this chapter, students should be able to:

1. Understand the roles that ethics and morals play in guiding human behavior.

2. Appraise the importance of morality and ethics in the sport workplace.

3. Differentiate between moral and ethical dilemmas.

4. Analyze an ethical dilemma by using an ethical decision-making model.

5. Formulate a code of conduct for a sport organization.

6. Distinguish between *morality* and *legality*, and understand how a decision may be simultaneously legal and immoral.

7. Apply moral principles to the workplace through the incorporation of codes of conduct, self-examination, forums for moral discourse, and statements of consequences for ethical violations into organizational documents.

Introduction

Sport managers make tough decisions. Imagine for a moment that you had to decide what to do when the bomb attack took place at the 2013 Boston Marathon or how to respond to an over-reaching Muslim country travel ban that denies athletes entry to your country for international competition. In these cases, sport managers were faced with conflicting and equally compelling desires to care for those affected by the events and to get back to normal. How would you go about making those decisions? What would be your approach? Although these are extreme examples, sport managers frequently face decisions involving ethical dilemmas. What can help guide them with their decision making in complex situations?

Ethics is the systematic study of the values that guide our decision making. The process of making a correct and fair decision is called **ethical reasoning**. Ethical reasoning depends on our values or the values of the organizations for which we work. It reflects how we believe people should behave and how we want our world to operate. This chapter provides a framework to help future sport managers think critically and systematically about ethical issues. It discusses two types of ethical issues: ethical dilemmas and morality.

An **ethical dilemma** is a practical conflict involving more or less equally compelling values or social obligations (Solomon, 1992). When to resume play after a community or national tragedy is an example of an ethical dilemma. On the one hand, sport managers have an obligation to their teams, athletes, and leagues to put on events; on the other hand, they understand the public's need to grieve. Ethical dilemmas are solved when we articulate which commonly held values we admire most. In this case, the value of grieving and paying respects to those harmed by a tragedy will eventually give way to the desire to return to normal and

to resume play. An ethically astute manager will resume play at the appropriate time.

Ethical values should not be confused with personal preferences. **Ethical decision-making** affects other people in a way that personal preferences do not. Ethical dilemmas have social implications. As such, ethics requires decision makers to consider how their actions will affect different groups of people and individuals.

In recreational softball leagues, for example, teams are faced with the decision of whether to play only their best players or to play everyone. This decision is based on the relative value that team members place on winning versus the value they place on participation. The argument could be made that the primary purpose of a recreational softball league is for participants to play and have fun. Recreational leagues provide camaraderie and emphasize team spirit that grows out of cheering for one another, playing, and going out together after games. However, an equally compelling argument could be made for competition and winning, which are central to the enjoyment of sport—even on the recreational level. It can be argued that teams should field their best players to make competition more intense and victory more satisfying. Both outlooks make sense; hence, an ethical dilemma exists. In this softball league example, the decision makers have to put themselves in the shoes of both the bench warmers and the starters and consider how both will be affected. They also have to think about what type of values they want to emphasize through their teams.

Morality, like ethics, is concerned with the values that guide behavior, but it deals with a specific type of ethical issue. **Morals** are the fundamental baseline values that dictate appropriate behavior within a society (Solomon, 1992). The beliefs that stealing and murder are wrong, for example, are moral values in most societies. Morality is sometimes summarized as a list of those actions that people ought to do or refrain from doing. The concept of morality is discussed in further detail later in this chapter. For the moment, however, consider the case of the late Aaron Hernandez, formerly a player for the New England Patriots in the National Football League (NFL).

Hernandez was accused of murder in 2013. Killing people as a means of solving disputes is considered wrong in our society. If everyone in society resolved disputes in this manner, society would fall apart, making murder a moral issue. Hernandez's arrest, however, also created ethical issues for the Patriots organization. The main issue was whether the Patriots should release Hernandez immediately or wait for the court to decide his guilt or innocence before making a decision. Some of the related ethical questions were: Did the team have a responsibility to support an employee in difficult times, or would that support drag the organization down and alienate fans? How should the organization respond to consumers who had purchased an official Aaron Hernandez jersey and were now repulsed by the thought of wearing it? Did the team bear some responsibility for keeping the consumers happy given the special circumstances of Hernandez's fall from grace? There were no clear answers. Although the Patriots' choice of response would not undermine the functioning of society, it remained important because it would affirm the values of the team. The organization's responses to Hernandez's arrest were ethical decisions—namely, the decisions to release Hernandez immediately and to set aside one weekend for fans to exchange their Hernandez jerseys for the jersey of another current player.

Ethical Considerations

The world of sport has certainly seen its share of scandals of late, from Hernandez's murder charge to the sexual assault scandal involving Baylor University's football team. Whenever events such as these occur, sport managers need to respond in an ethical manner, making decisions that are guided by strong ethical principles. Meeting this lofty standard is not always easy to do, as these situations are complex and demanding, but sport managers need to respond to these challenges in a positive manner.

Sport managers face ethical dilemmas on a daily basis. Consider the following examples:

- Changing the start time of a contest to accommodate television programming, but at the expense of class time for college athletes.
- Encouraging the use of painkillers by injured athletes to enable them to "play hurt."
- Helping an athlete with a drug, alcohol, marital, or criminal problem.
- Using a team's limited resources to make stadiums accessible for people with disabilities.
- Relocating a professional team from a profitable site to another city that promises even more revenues to the team.
- Deciding between cutting a less visible, successful nonrevenue sport team or a highly visible football program when facing a budget crisis in a National Collegiate Athletic Association (NCAA) Division I athletic program.
- Working with athletes who use their platform to speak out on social issues.

How does a sport manager know when he or she is facing such a dilemma? What might be the warning signs that a sport manager is facing an ethical dilemma? Hunt (2011, para. 5) outlines some of these markers:

- If something about a situation makes a person feel *uncomfortable*, it is time to start digging and try to figure out what is bothering the person and why. There may well be an ethical issue at the root of the individual's discomfort.

- A clearer indication of an ethical problem is a *feeling of guilt*. If someone is feeling guilty, that person probably did something wrong—or is thinking about doing something he or she knows is wrong. The person should not deny this feeling, but rather should explore it and respond appropriately to it.
- *Stress* can be another indicator of an ethical dilemma. If an employee feels a lot of pressure or is losing sleep, those can be signs that the employee is putting off making a difficult, but necessary, choice. For the affected individual, it is time to take a closer look.
- *Anger* might also be a sign of an ethical problem. If an employee feels pressured to make a decision that makes the individual feel uncomfortable, he or she may be angry at the person or people who are the source of the pressure.
- *Embarrassment* is also a sign of possible misconduct—or the contemplation of misconduct. Would the employee be embarrassed to tell the boss, coworkers, friends, or family about what he or she is doing or thinking of doing? If so, there is a very good chance that the act is unethical and the employee should not do it. Why risk losing the respect of all these important people in the employee's life?
- If an employee is *afraid* of getting caught for what he or she is doing or thinking about doing, it is clear that the act is something the person should not be doing. The individual needs to pay attention to this feeling and stop before it is too late.

Few areas of sport management present more difficulty than ethical dilemmas. A sport manager's decision making is complicated because the outcomes of any decisions affect diverse groups of people (e.g., athletes, fans, the community, businesses, the media) whose interests are often in conflict. Plus, sport managers' decisions about ethical dilemmas are more publicly scrutinized than the decisions made by managers in other industries without high-profile employees (professional athletes) or without great media interest, especially in these days of omnipresent, fast-moving social media. At the same moment that managers are weighing decisions regarding the right thing to do, they are also considering financial costs, the effects on the team's and league's reputation, the law, and the impact on winning games.

If a sport manager does not approach ethical dilemmas systematically, the complexity of the issues and interests involved can easily overwhelm his or her judgment—especially when conflicting options seem to make equally good sense and are being argued emotionally by opposing parties. Ideally, ethical analysis should follow a systematic process of reasoning, rather than being a haphazard procedure where one guesses at the best solution (Cooke, 1991). Ethical decision making does not mean that the sport manager reacts solely based on his or her "gut" feeling. Instead, to solve an ethical dilemma, the decision maker tries to make a rational argument. He or she weighs the pros and cons of two or more seemingly valid choices that reflect equally cherished values. Ethical decision making is similar to the regular decision-making process in business situations in that there is a given structure to follow. A model suggested by Lipschutz (2011) outlines the following steps as means to facilitate the successful resolution of an ethical dilemma:

1. Awareness of all applicable codes, standards, laws, polices and personal values.

2. The ability to identify an ethical dilemma in a timely manner.

3. Application of a thorough and systematic decision-making process. The following steps outline a solid ethical decision-making template:

    a. Consult with colleagues and appropriate experts.

    b. Identify the ethical issues, including the values and duties that conflict.

    c. Identify the individuals, groups, and organizations that are likely to be affected by the ethical decision.

    d. Identify all possible courses of action and the participation involved in each; identify the possible benefits and risks with each option.

    e. Make the decision and document the decision-making process.

    f. Monitor, evaluate, and document the decision.

Although this may seem like a complicated process, remember that ethical decisions and dilemmas involve complicated problems, and that reasonable people often disagree over what is the "right decision." It is essential for sport managers to fully think through any ethical decisions they must make.

The 2010 NCAA Men's National Swimming and Diving Championships is one illustration of a successful resolution of an ethical dilemma. The Championships were scheduled for Thursday through Saturday, March 24–27. On Tuesday, 18 members of the Arizona, Texas, and Stanford teams fell ill. (About one-third of each squad became sick.) All three teams had traveled on the same flight into Columbus, Ohio, and had picked up a viral infection resulting in nausea, vomiting, and diarrhea. On Wednesday, the day prior to the start of the meet, the athletes were being treated at a local hospital. The teams affected were some of the best in the country and each had a chance to win a team trophy. The coaches of these teams

are very powerful within the world of swimming. Their athletes, weakened by the stomach bug, would not perform at their best until they could recover. An emergency coaches' meeting was called to discuss the situation. Should the meet proceed as scheduled or be delayed?

The NCAA Crisis Management Team led the effort to resolve the dilemma. Health experts from the Centers for Disease Control and Prevention and from The Ohio State University were consulted. Officials quickly realized that the first issue at hand was the health and safety of all athletes and spectators. The initial decision made by the NCAA Crisis Management Team was to have event managers take special precautions to keep the pool area sanitized as athletes (even the sick ones) were trying to prepare for the meet. Coaches of affected teams were asked to keep their athletes separated from other teams. Whatever the illness was, they did not want it spreading. But the question of what to do about the competition remained.

The NCAA Crisis Management Team prioritized health and safety and then considered the fairest option in light of the health priority. Officials did not want sick athletes on the deck or in the pool with other athletes until they were sure they were no longer contagious. Health experts recommended that the sick athletes not compete on Thursday. That meant either barring them from competition for one day or delaying the entire meet for one day.

Three options were considered. The first option was to start the meet on Thursday as scheduled and leave it up to the medical experts, coaches, and athletes to decide on a case-by-case basis which of the sick athletes could compete. Some coaches thought this was the right thing to do. They argued they had their athletes ready to go for Thursday. Delaying the meet was to their disadvantage. "Stick to the original plan," they argued. "Athletes get injured all the time. Let's swim and let the chips fall where they may." If there was a health risk, this contingent argued, affected athletes should not compete (similar to the rule that a player may not participate in a sport if he or she is bleeding). Healthy athletes should not be affected by the sick athletes. Delaying the meet, those opposed to this solution argued, imposed an unfair burden on the healthy teams. Further, these coaches argued, if a smaller number of athletes from weaker teams had become sick, the emergency meeting would never have been called. The fair thing to do was to treat every situation in a similar fashion. Many of the coaches who made this argument also knew they would gain a competitive advantage by starting the meet on time.

A second suggestion was to start the meet on Friday. This would ensure that the bug did not spread, and it also would give the affected athletes an additional day to recover. This, no doubt, was the primary concern of the Arizona, Texas, and Stanford teams. People who made this argument appealed to the notion of least harm. A one-day delay would not harm healthy athletes and teams as much as asking sick athletes not to compete or to compete in their weakened state on the first day.

Delaying the meet led to another dilemma: how to run the event if it started one day later. One suggestion was to run the Thursday and Friday events as timed finals on Friday, compressing the meet into two days. This choice ended the meet on Saturday and had the benefit of not disrupting team travel schedules. Another option was to push the entire meet back by one day and run it as intended, over three days, Friday through Sunday.

Most coaches thought running two-thirds of the meet as timed finals on Friday was too great of a modification and quickly rejected the idea of compressing the meet into two days. That left two options for the NCAA Crisis Management Team: start the meet on Thursday and make medical decisions on a case-by-case basis, or delay the meet by one day. In the end, the NCAA Crisis Management team decided the "fairest" way to proceed was to run the meet in full, beginning on Friday.

That decision seemed the most fair because it allowed all athletes who qualified to compete as intended and had the least disruptive impact on the outcome. Because such a large percentage of top athletes took ill, running the meet without them, even for a single day, would dramatically change the outcome of the championship. It was not clear if the athletes would still be contagious on Thursday. Barring the affected athletes put some teams at a disadvantage for a medical precaution that might not be necessary. However, allowing them to compete in a weakened state might cause medical problems and many of these athletes would not perform up to their capabilities. Pushing the meet back, the NCAA Crisis Management Team reasoned, was medically prudent and had the least adverse impact on the performances of the greatest number of athletes. While not a perfect solution, it meant that athletes would determine the outcome of the meet, rather than the coaches, officials, and medical staff.

Making ethical decisions is challenging. Managers in any industry need guidelines to help them make decisions and principles to help them assess themselves and their personal values. The Josephson Institute of Ethics (2016) provides an interesting framework for managers to use when making ethical decisions, based on what it calls the Six Pillars of Character. **Table 6-1** illustrates these Six Pillars and some of the subsets within each. Peter Carlisle, the agent for Olympic gold medal–winning swimmer Michael Phelps, refers to values as personal integrity. For Carlisle, integrity is like a keel on a ship. When the going gets tough and the correct choice is not clear, he advises, lean into the keel to help you steer the proper course.

Table 6-1 Josephson Institute of Ethics' Six Pillars of Character	
Pillar 1	Trustworthiness Includes honesty, integrity, reliability, and loyalty
Pillar 2	Respect Includes civility, courtesy, and decency; dignity and autonomy; and tolerance and acceptance
Pillar 3	Responsibility Includes accountability, pursuit of excellence, and self-restraint
Pillar 4	Fairness Includes process, impartiality, and equity
Pillar 5	Caring The "heart" of ethics
Pillar 6	Citizenship Includes civic virtues and duties

© 2007 Reprinted with permission of Josephson Institute. www.charactercounts.org

Codes of Conduct

The recent rash of corporate and government scandals in the United States illustrates the need to establish solid ethical climates within corporations. According to Sims (1992), an organization's ethical climate establishes the shared set of understandings that determine correct behavior and the manner in which ethical issues will be handled. One way to establish this climate is through codes of conduct or codes of ethics. According to Ingram (2017b, para. 2), "A **code of ethics** guides all managerial decisions, creating a common framework upon which all decisions are founded. This can help to create a cohesive understanding of the boundaries within an organization and the standards set for interacting with external stakeholders." A **code of conduct** explicitly outlines and explains the principles under which an organization or profession operates. The institutional/organizational values that should help managers and employees resolve ethical dilemmas are implicit in any code of conduct. These codes of conduct provide a roadmap for employees by helping them with strategic decision making,

day-to-day decisions, issues that may affect their company's reputation, and legal considerations (Ingram, 2017a).

Codes of conduct and codes of ethics are not twentieth-century inventions. In fact, they are as old as the earliest religious oral traditions and writings, such as the Torah and the Koran. Although the development of modern codes in the United States originated in the medical, accounting, and legal professions, these are not the only professional areas to have codes of ethics. The need to address ethical questions and encourage correct actions has led many professions to establish their own codes of conduct (Jordan, Greenwell, Geist, Pastore, & Mahony, 2004). Indeed, such codes are found in virtually every type of organization and corporation in the United States. Within the last decade, many corporations have hired ethics officers or created ethics boards to address ethical issues within organizations. Sport organizations such as the International Olympic Committee (IOC) and the International Paralympic Committee now have Ethics committees as well.

In the sport world, codes have been adopted or are being considered by a number of sport organizations. The U.S. Olympic Committee (USOC), the IOC, the National Intramural and Recreational Sports Association (NIRSA), the American Camping Association, and USA Hockey are just a few examples of sport organizations with codes of conduct or codes of ethics. Numerous youth sport programs, ranging from local organizations, such as the City of Huntington Park Youth Sports Program, to national groups, such as the American Youth Soccer Organization, have adopted codes of conduct as well, often creating separate codes for participants, coaches, and parents. Companies such as adidas and Nike created codes of conduct after years of dealing with backlash from consumers about improper and abusive work practices at their shoe manufacturing sites.

Codes of conduct are not unique to the sport industry in the United States. Australia's Geelong Cricket Association (2016) has a series of codes for junior cricket players, parents and spectators, senior players, and junior coaches. The Australian Sports Commission (2017) has its own series of codes of behaviors. England Basketball (2017) has an extensive set of codes for coaches, staff, institutions, players, match officials, club officials, parents/guardians/families, and spectators. Football Canada's (2014) codes of ethics and codes of conduct are grounded in respect for others, responsible action, integrity, and honoring sport.

Codes of conduct should be clear and straightforward. They need not be long or complex, and should encourage employees to understand the goals they are trying to accomplish instead of just outlining rules and punishments. If done well, codes of conduct can help create an ethical climate in an organization. Here are some basics for constructing or updating a useful code of conduct (DeLoitte, 2005, p. 2):

- The code language should be simple, concise, and readily understood by all employees.
- The code should not be legalistic—written as "thou shall not"—but rather state expected behaviors.

- The code should apply to all employees and be global in scope.
- The code should be written, reviewed, and edited by a multidisciplinary team to be reasonably confident that it is consistent with other corporate communications and policies, addresses relevant risk areas, has buy-in across the organization, and represents the organization's culture.
- The code should be revised and updated as appropriate.

An example of a code of conduct for a sport organization is given in **Figure 6-1**, which reproduces the International Health, Racquet and Sportsclub Association's (2010) Member Code of Conduct. As another example for comparison, the 53-page adidas Group (n.d.) code of conduct includes the following categories:

- Integrity in our business activities
  - Focus on consumers
  - Bribery and corruption
  - Gifts, travel, and entertainment
  - Dealing with suppliers
  - Conflicts of interest
  - Competition and antitrust
  - Improper market influence, marketing, and advertising
  - Insider trading
- Working relationships and workspaces
  - Treating each other with respect
  - Working in a safe environment
  - Product safety and quality
  - Privacy and data protection
- Our society and the environment
  - Government affairs
  - Corporate communications
  - Environmental requirements

The International Health, Racquet, & Sportsclub Association (IHRSA) is a non-profit trade association serving the athletic, racquet, and fitness industry worldwide. As an Associate Member of IHRSA, we consider it our mission to enhance the quality of life through physical fitness and sports. To this end, we endeavor to provide quality products and services. We further strive to instill in those we serve an understanding of the value of physical fitness to their lives.

In order to fulfill our mission, we pledge the following:

- That we produce quality products and services.
- That we deliver on our commitments.
- That we are an equal opportunity employer.
- That we will cooperate with our customers toward the continual expansion of the club and fitness industries.
- That we will utilize our benefits of IHRSA membership solely for the purposes and under the guidelines for which they were established.
- That we agree to conduct our business in a manner which commands the respect of those we serve.
- That customer satisfaction will be the determining factor in all our business dealings.

Figure 6-1 International Health, Racquet and Sportsclub Association Code of Conduct.

Courtesy of International Health, Racquet and Sportsclub Association, 2010.

Codes of conduct are not the be-all and end-all of organizational ethics. If codes of conduct are too long or too convoluted to easily understand, if they try to intimidate employees into acting morally, or if the organization does not demonstrate a commitment to them, codes of conduct may be at best unusable and at worst counterproductive. Further, if codes of ethics are too detailed, they can actually discourage moral reasoning. The NCAA "has become so rule dependent, so comprehensive, and so situation specific," sport ethicist Russell Gough argues, "that athletic administrators, coaches, and support staff are increasingly not required to make ethical judgments. A myopic emphasis on rule conformity has displaced a more circumspect emphasis on personal integrity and considered ethical judgment" (Gough, 1994, p. 5).

Morality

Not all ethical issues represent choices between equally compelling values. Some ethical dilemmas are about choosing between right and wrong—that is, two opposing choices. When the issue is about doing what is right, it is usually a moral issue. People tend to use the terms "morals" and "ethics" interchangeably, but morality actually relates to a specific type of ethical issue. As defined earlier, morals are the fundamental baseline values dictating appropriate behavior within a society (Solomon, 1992). A distinctive feature of moral values is their grounding in the practical affairs of social life, whereas other ethical decisions are based on broader abstract principles (DeSensi & Rosenberg, 1996).

In sport, an example of a moral principle is that all athletes give an honest effort whenever they compete. If athletes stopped trying to win, the essence of sport would be threatened. If you ask someone, "Why aren't athletes allowed to throw games [lose on purpose] in exchange for a nice paycheck from the highest

bidder?", that person is likely to say, "Because it is wrong." Pushed further, the person might say, "Because it would ruin sport." When Russia engaged in systematic doping programming with the country's Olympic and Paralympic athletes, those actions were wrong. It was not an ethical dilemma, because there was not an equally compelling value. Doping, which included tampering with drug samples in this case, is immoral. Similarly, it was immoral for Tommy Elrod, a disgruntled former football coach at Wake Forest University, to pass along part of the university's playbook to an old friend coaching for the University of Louisville in what became known as college football's "Wakey-Leaks" scandal.

Our social practices depend on people upholding certain baseline values. When people act morally—according to generally acceptable standards of behavior—they contribute to the maintenance and smooth functioning of society. In the management of sport, we trust people to behave in a moral fashion to ensure that sport is honest and fair. Shared morality cultivates trust between strangers and enables individuals and organizations to function within the world of sport.

Moral values are generally accepted so broadly within a community that they are considered self-evident and largely go unquestioned. Because people perceive moral values as basic and inalienable, it is often assumed these values are derived from a "higher order" or are common sense. If, for example, an athlete is asked why he or she strives to win, a common response would be "Because that's what sports are about." Managers will know they are dealing with a moral issue as opposed to an ethical dilemma if people justify their position with the simple response, "Because it is the right thing to do." If pushed, they might refer to a higher principle grounded in their religious convictions or their sense of good sporting conduct. Ethical decisions (e.g., the decision about whether to play everyone or only the best players) may be difficult to make and have serious implications for others, but they do not inherently ruin the game or an organization.

Consider the case of the University of Minnesota. During Joel Maturi's tenure as athletic director (2002–2012), he earned the nickname "Mr. Title IX." Maturi's approach to athletics was to support a broad array of teams—men's and women's, and non-revenue sports as well.

When Maturi was replaced by Norwood Teague in 2012, the athletic department culture changed. Under Teague, "major" men's sports gained higher stature. The shift in culture reflected a shift in which values were considered important by the department's leadership. A practical conflict became apparent with the new administration: Should the athletic department boost revenue sports in hopes of generating additional revenue, which might then be allocated to non-revenue sports, or should the athletic department support all teams in a more equitable fashion from the start? One can make a strong case for either side in this argument.

Another aspect of Teague's strategy was to bring in new coaches in basketball, even though the old coaches were well known and fairly successful. For example, Teague removed Tubby Smith as the head coach of men's basketball and replaced him with the younger Richard Pitino. Here we see the practical conflict between the value of respect for an older successful coach and the value of hope that an energetic young coach can bring. Again, the case can be made for either side, reflecting an ethical dilemma.

At the same time that he was remaking the University of Minnesota's athletic department, Teague struggled with moral failings. Three women complained that he sexually harassed and aggressively pursued them, cornering and touching them in inappropriate ways. Engaging in nonconsensual, inappropriate touching,

and sexual harassment is just wrong. Teague's behavior was repugnant, and no one would make a case for such behavior—sexual assault and harassment are immoral. Teague was removed from his position as Minnesota's athletic director in 2015.

Sometimes, moral values and ethical values can intersect. In this case, Teague's ethical choices to increase support for revenue sports—in particular, men's basketball and football—may have been influenced by his moral failings to treat all human beings (in this case, women) with dignity and full humanity.

Morality Versus the Law

Many moral values in a society are codified in laws. For example, theft is not only considered immoral, but also against the law. Occasionally, someone may justify distasteful behavior by saying, "It's not against the law, is it?" In sport, doping is one area where this happens. From time to time, performance-enhancing substances are developed or discovered that have not yet been banned. Taking these drugs may not be against the rules, but using them constitutes an immoral act because the drugs artificially enhance an athlete's performance, violating the principle of fair play. The "It's not against the rules" argument does not justify such behavior: Laws and morality are not the same.

Laws are created and enforced to maintain order and to help society function smoothly. Even so, at times immoral laws are instituted. For much of the twentieth century in the United States, laws in some states prohibited interracial competitive sports. Teams with both white and black players complied with these laws and at times left their black players at home (Adelson, 1999). The long history of legal segregation in this country was clearly immoral, yet it was protected by law.

Likewise, moral behavior cannot always be legislated, and people cannot be forced to act morally. For example, it is generally accepted that people should try to help others in need or distress, but laws cannot and do not require people to do so. If we see someone who is injured or the victim of a crime, our moral sensibility directs us to come to his or her aid, but in most cases laws do not punish us for failing to do so. Our moral sensibility creates a stronger obligation than the law. There may be cases where some individuals decide that the right thing to do is to break the law (i.e., civil disobedience). A classic example from sport involves the highly respected Muhammad Ali. When Ali was at the peak of his boxing career as an Olympic champion and world heavyweight title holder, he refused to report to be drafted into required military service during the Vietnam War based on his religious beliefs. He chose to risk going to jail and giving up his boxing career rather than violate his moral beliefs.

Sometimes people are able to comply with the letter of the law without achieving its spirit or its stated goals. For example, sport teams and events are increasingly adopting charity nonprofit status to gain tax advantages and beneficial bond ratings. They claim that a team or event is a fundraiser for a group in need, or that a new stadium will foster economic development. Meanwhile, they hire a private firm, often staffed by the same people who created the nonprofit organization, to manage the event. Any substantial revenue generation is eaten up by the private management firm and does not go to the group in need. This practice is legal, but it is certainly not moral.

Morality in the Workplace

Sound moral reasoning is the basis of a healthy sport organization. Some **moral principles**—cooperation, courage, perseverance, foresight, and wisdom, for example—are universal and recognized in all aspects of life. Other moral principles are tied to particular situations. For

example, a moral value such as competition is esteemed in business but not in family relations. Honesty is essential in scientific research, but in sport "faking out" an opponent is seen as an acceptable strategy and a way to gain advantage.

Academic discussions of morality often start with a discussion of **absolutism** versus **relativism**. Absolutism argues that moral precepts are universal—that is, they are applicable to all circumstances. Relativism argues that what is moral depends on the situation. Making moral decisions in the practical world of work falls somewhere in between these two extremes. We like to use the expression *situational absolutes* to describe this hybrid approach.

Moral rules prescribing "correct" behavior in one situation can generally be applied to similar situations within similar specific social contexts. For example, people believe it is always wrong for an elite athlete not to give his or her best honest effort. Similarly, it is wrong for a recreational athlete not to give an honest effort. In the workplace, regardless how large or small the monetary value of a contract, it is always wrong to violate a business agreement made voluntarily in good faith.

© Yuri Arcurs/Dreamstime.com

According to Jacobs (1992), there are two types of work: commercial and noncommercial. The moral rules guiding each type are distinct. Commercial moral rules have their roots in the rules of the marketplace and guide activities such as sales and marketing. Honesty is a linchpin of commercial trading. Honesty ensures fair trading practices and allows individuals to trust that they will receive agreed-upon goods or services. In commercial occupations, insider trading and deceiving customers are forms of dishonesty and are condemned.

Noncommercial moral values guide other occupations, such as accountants, police, and building inspectors. In sport, officials, league commissioners, athletes, and coaches most likely operate according to noncommercial principles. The most important value in noncommercial endeavors is loyalty. These occupations demand loyalty to an oath of office or professional standards to guard against "selling out." Here, loyalty overrides honesty. In these professions, it is sometimes acceptable to withhold information from others for the sake of the overall task (e.g., undercover police work, general managers' discussions of player personnel). Whereas innovation is admired in the commercial realm, tradition is admired in the noncommercial realm. If people holding these noncommercial positions violate moral precepts associated with loyalty, they will be accused of treason, selling out, or failure to uphold an oath.

Jacobs (1992) argues that our moral reasoning gets muddled when we do not understand which moral principles our job requires. Take, for example, the role of athlete. The moral order in which athletes operate is generally noncommercial. The expectation is that athletes should be loyal to their team, be obedient to and disciplined by the coach, and never compromise the integrity of the game. Within the limits imposed by the rules of the game, athletes are expected to try to win by any means available to them. In fact, many sport strategies depend on forms of deception. Feints and setting up opponents to believe you intend to do one thing when you plan to do another are fundamental

sport strategies. However, athletes are trusted not to cheat, gamble, or "sell out" the game. Conversely, if an equipment manager does not send purchase orders out in the marketplace for competitive bid but instead purchases goods from a loyal friend, he or she could create unnecessary departmental expenses and would be violating the principles of honesty and open competition in the commercial sphere.

Morality and Multiple Roles

Moral decisions are complicated by the fact that moral principles are often applied and valued differently in different social contexts. Decision making is made more difficult by the variety of roles each of us fills. One collection of moral rules does not necessarily apply to all situations, even within the same job.

Some jobs in sport do not actually reside completely within either the commercial or the noncommercial sphere. One example is the position of director of media relations for a college athletic department. To complete the tasks of this job, the director of media relations operates in both moral systems. At one point in the day, this person may be required to be absolutely honest (e.g., producing statistics for coaches and reporters) and at another time may exude loyalty to the point of stretching the truth (e.g., creating recruiting materials for a team). Professional athletes who demonstrate team loyalty throughout the season become commercially minded when renegotiating their contracts. Finally, recall the equipment manager. He or she has a job that is primarily driven by noncommercial precepts that include loyalty to the team, upholding traditions, and so on. But periodically—such as when purchasing new equipment—he or she enters the commercial sphere. At that point, noncommercial values are set aside and the manager embraces values that are admired within the commercial sphere. Although most jobs fall more or less into one moral order or the other (commercial or noncommercial), it is unrealistic to suggest that any occupation is completely commercial or completely noncommercial.

Consequently, the process of making a moral choice, of deciding what is right and wrong, involves understanding the parameters of acceptable behavior within the context of one's multiple roles in society. This does not mean, however, that people can arbitrarily choose which values will guide their behavior. Specific situations and roles in our society demand specific moral values.

Morality and Corruption

Among the biggest distinctions between moral decision making and other ethical decisions are the extensive ramifications of immoral choices. An immoral decision (e.g., to shave points) can ruin a whole enterprise. One of the most infamous immoral acts in sport occurred at the 1980 Boston Marathon when Rosie Ruiz fooled the world—momentarily at least. Ruiz was crowned the women's champion but actually had jumped out of the crowd and ran only the last half mile to cross the finish line first. Later it was revealed that her qualifying time from the New York City Marathon was a fraud, too. She broke from the race to ride the subway to the finish line. To this day, "pulling a Rosie Ruiz" means skipping out on part of an event, only to show up at the end to garner undeserved accolades.

Immoral behavior, such as cheating in sports, violates society's basic assumptions of right and wrong. There are clear-cut examples of immoral practices in sport such as Rosie Ruiz's subway run; the Black Sox scandal of 1919, in which players cooperated with organized gamblers to lose games in the World Series; and the recent Russian systematic state-sanctioned athlete doping situation. Immoral practices can also become institutionalized,

which leads to corruption. Corruption may start small, when just a few people act immorally, but can ultimately become a standard operating procedure.

In the world of work, corruption usually occurs when people hop from one set of moral precepts to another when it is inappropriate to do so. For example, the job of stock analysts requires honestly reporting the facts. When a stock analyst works for a large financial firm, there is supposed to be a "Chinese wall" (a reference to the Great Wall of China) between the analyst and the business side of the firm. During the boom years of the late 1990s, however, some companies that received poor reports from stock analysts would sometimes threaten to pull business from the investment banks for which those analysts worked. Under this pressure, the wall broke down. Stock analysts employed by investment banks felt pressured to give hyper-positive reports about certain companies to help drive up their stock prices. In these cases, the analysts became team players, stretching the truth to help their employer, which hoped to gain brokerage fees from investment deals. They sought to help their firm compete by setting aside their core job responsibility, which was the duty to provide clients with fair assessments of businesses.

Corruption might start when an employee takes a precept common to his or her profession and applies it in the wrong place. For example, military personnel take an oath to be loyal to their country. From a morals perspective, folks in the military have much in common with the medical profession, police, and accountants. All of these professionals take an oath attesting to their ethical standards. When an in-house accountant is convinced she needs to be loyal to the company she is auditing rather than staying loyal to the accounting profession, or when military officers in charge of procurement extend their tendency to be loyal to a buyer, immoral behavior is likely to result. In a nutshell, this is what happened in the infamous "Fat Leonard" Navy scandal.

Beginning in 2016, numerous U.S. Navy officers were accused of taking bribes from Leonard Glenn of Glenn Defense Marine Asia (GDMA). The officers provided information and steered work to defense contractors who had showered the officers with gifts. The gifts started small, such as a nice dinner out or a gift for a family member, which were perceived as generous tokens, but still appropriate. Through these gestures, "Fat Leonard" Glenn gained the loyalty of naval officers. Eventually, the gifts he provided escalated to include fancy hotel rooms, travel, and prostitutes. Naval personnel reciprocated by giving their own gifts to "Fat Leonard"—namely, information about ship movements, procurement needs, and military plans. In some cases, the officers even steered ships into ports controlled by GDMA to extract more revenue from corrupt docking systems in South Asia. With the help of these naval officers, GDMA had an advantage over other defense contractors. "Fat Leonard" took advantage of the military personnel's tendency to be loyal (to country and commanders) and extended that tradition of loyalty to himself and his company.

In both the financial analysis and military examples, "little lies" and "special favors" eventually became standard operating procedure. When immoral behavior is systemic, it is called *corruption*. At this writing, the "Fat Leonard" scandal has led to 13 guilty pleas, 20 indictments, censures of 4 admirals, and 200 military personnel under investigation.

When an organization's immoral actions become standard practice, moral reasoning becomes muddled and the rationale for moral behavior unclear. People justify immoral behavior by suggesting that "This is how things are done here" or "Others are doing the same thing," implying that they, too, must act

this way to maintain their competitiveness. Consider, for example, the doping scandals in Major League Baseball (MLB) and cycling. In both cases, the incidents and extent of performance-enhancing drug (PED) use initially may have been sporadic and small, but when regulators and officials turned a blind eye to the practice, the use of steroids and human growth hormone spread. Early adopters of these drugs justified their use in a variety of ways: to recover from injury, to be able to stay in the game, to help them recover from long workouts. Eventually some baseball players and cyclists were using PEDs just to keep up with the competition. Little by little, PED use spread, and when cheating became the norm, it no longer seemed so wrong.

Consider also the representation/agency business. Agents now pursue younger and younger athletes, and now there is an ongoing FBI investigation into this very topic. Even though some agents may be hesitant to engage in such behavior, many have come to believe they must follow suit to win clients. This same sort of muddled moral thinking can push college coaches to act immorally when recruiting athletes. When one coach offers certain inducements to a recruit, such as reduced rates on hotel rooms or merchandise, other coaches may feel compelled to offer similar favors out of fear of losing a potential star recruit.

Corruption spreads little by little through an organization or a sport. Once it becomes systemic, there is usually no way to fix the problem with in-house management tweaks. Systemic corruption needs to be exposed and the responsible parties held accountable. Exposure has serious consequences that usually extend far beyond the people who initiated the immoral behavior. The Lance Armstrong doping scandal, for example, had an impact on the Livestrong Foundation, cancer survivors, and the cyclist's primary sponsor, Nike. The exposure of the

University of Baylor football sexual assault scandal cost the football coach, the athletic director, and the president/chancellor of the university their jobs.

Moral Reasoning and the Changing Nature of Work

Contemporary society is characterized by innovation, which continually presents new ethical dilemmas. New technology makes shoes bouncier and swimsuits sleeker. Is it fair to wear these performance enhancers, especially when their costs may prohibit some people from ever being able to access the technology? Some therapies enhance performance. Is it fair for athletes who manage to get a medical exemption to compete against those who do not? In high school wrestling, sport managers are now struggling to resolve fairness and access issues for transgender athletes—another issue that has come to the fore only in recent years and is discussed in the case study at the end of this chapter.

It was once thought unsportsmanlike for coaches to send in plays from the sideline in football; instead, quarterbacks called the plays. Now coaches call in plays from booths high above the playing field, utilizing technological advances. In this case, the emergence of new communication technology changed our ideas about the role of the coach.

Or consider how computer technology forces us to think about privacy and intellectual property in new ways. Technology has made it much easier to spy on other teams. Teams have always tried to steal signs, but in the past, coaches did this with only the naked eye and notation. Knowing this, teams changed up their signs just enough to throw the other teams off. In 2007, Bill Belichick, head coach of the New England Patriots, was fined $500,00 for stealing the New York Jets' defensive signals with a video camera. In addition, the Patriots team was ordered to pay $250,000 and had to give up one draft pick. This may seem like a stiff penalty

for doing more efficiently what coaches have been trying to do for decades. Belichick's intent was to review the videotape to learn defensive signs or patterns of signs to decode the Jets' system and use the knowledge in the next game. The use of technology to steal signs pushed what some might argue is unethical behavior into an immoral act. Goodell's severe punishment reflects his understanding of the potential of new technologies to ruin the game. The practice of using technology to steal signs also took on a new menaing when Boston Red Sox team personnel used Apple watches in a scheme to steal signals from the New York Yankees.

Now consider MLB's punishment for the actions of a St. Louis Cardinals employee, Chris Correa. His punishment for being caught attempting to learn more about a competitor, the Houston Astros, was much more than a cease and desist order and a reprimand. For 2½ years, Correa engaged in computer espionage against the Astros. He accessed the Astros' internal database nearly 50 times and his actions provided the Cardinals with illegal competitive and economic advantages. As a result of his actions, St. Louis had to send Houston $2 million and give that team the Cardinals' first two draft picks of 2017. Correa was banned from baseball for life and sentenced to 46 months in a federal penitentiary.

As society changes, we periodically need to assess whether current practices are consistent with the values that underlie a just society or fair sport. Moral and ethical principles evolve over time. To make moral decisions in the sport industry and mete out appropriate punishments, managers must understand the responsibilities and duties of their jobs in the context of innovation. As discussed, people never hold only one position in society, so they cannot simply adopt one set of moral guidelines. Managers have to assess their responsibilities and choose virtues to help them do their jobs ethically and morally in changing times.

Key Skills

Although sport organizations tend to operate as single entities, sport managers must remember that all sport organizations are made up of individuals who have certain duties to perform. Each person brings something unique to the workplace, and each person's job requires certain moral behaviors. Each and every individual in a sport organization has the ability to make a difference within that sport organization. At the same time, the organization can shape the behavior of individuals. How, then, can sport managers attempt to establish a moral work climate?

Ensuring Morality in the Workplace

The complexity of competing interests in the sport industry makes moral and ethical dilemmas especially difficult to resolve. Sometimes athletes are simple participants in a sporting competition, whereas at other times they are businesspeople who have to reconcile endorsements or salaries relative to the game and their willingness to play. Rules designed to protect the integrity of sport operate uncomfortably alongside the business structure underwriting sport. Increasingly, managers, athletes, and coaches have to operate under commercial and noncommercial principles simultaneously, and it is easy for the distinction between the two to become blurred.

This complexity makes decision making more difficult—and more critical—for sport managers. There are ways, however, to simplify the decision-making process and ensure decisions are made as intelligently and conscientiously as possible. Organizations can help individuals make moral choices by promoting and supporting moral reasoning in four ways:

1. Establish clear standards of moral behavior (such as codes of conduct) and publicize them within the organization.

2. Encourage employees to periodically review their individual moral judgments through self-examination.

3. Provide support structures through which employees can consult one another during and after the decision-making process.

4. Make it clear that violations of codes of conduct will not be tolerated, and publicize a process for enforcing codes within the organization.

Self-Examination

One way to promote moral reasoning is to ask employees to think about hypothetical ethical dilemmas. This strategy assumes most people want to make the correct and moral decision. More people will do the right thing if they think about ethical behavior prior to making important decisions or if they think people in their organization care about their behavior. Self-examination is an effective tool to remind people of ethical actions and express institutional concern for ethical issues.

A self-examination does not have to be reviewed by management to be effective, nor is it necessary to take severe punitive measures against those who do poorly. The NCAA (2002), for example, requires all coaches involved in recruiting to take and pass a test of their knowledge of recruiting rules. It is not a difficult test, and most coaches pass it with little trouble. Coaches who fail the test can retake it until they pass. The test is not designed to keep immoral coaches from recruiting, but rather to remind coaches of "right" actions. The simple act of reviewing the rules reminds coaches of these right actions and reinforces the view that abiding by the rules matters.

According to Lederman (2016, paras. 1–2),

> More than a quarter of all Division I colleges, 43 percent of all universities that play in the high-profile Football Bowl Subdivision and more than half the members of the Power Five conferences committed major violations of National Collegiate Athletic

Association rules in the last decade, an *Inside Higher Ed* analysis shows. The NCAA's Division I Committee on Infractions issued findings of major violations in 114 cases during the 10-year period from January 2006 through December 2015.

It appears that self-examination may not be enough to make college coaches do the right thing, as they are constantly pressured to engage in questionable recruiting practices to remain competitive.

© Photodisc

Forum for Moral Discourse
Isolation contributes greatly to immoral behavior. Because morality is tied to social situations, communication is critical in deterring corruption and resolving ethical dilemmas.

Employees should be encouraged to get together to discuss where and how they face specific problems. These discussions can help employees understand they are not alone in making difficult choices and that their colleagues can provide significant insight, perspective, and help. This process takes the pressure off individuals and clarifies the issues at stake. It also brings employees together to resolve problems. Discussions of ethical or moral behavior can be incorporated into typical management systems, such as staff meetings or sales meetings. Decisions should not be reviewed only after they have been made; instead, employees should be encouraged to consult with one another and with their supervisors during the decision-making process. This helps them avoid making wrong choices, leaving out important parts of the decision, or becoming overwhelmed by the weight and complexity of issues.

Forums for discussion should not be confined to individual organizations. This is especially true for managers. Because management is often the smallest branch of an organization, there may not be an effective forum for the exchange of ideas. Annual conventions, executive education, or management training may be employed as forums for ethical discourse. Informal settings such as lunches among friends, confidential calls to colleagues with similar responsibilities, or casual conversations at a golf outing may also contribute to keeping the discussions alive.

Consequences
Finally, employees need to know there are consequences for immoral behavior. Even in the best organizations, some people will be motivated solely by self-interest. However, if people understand that corruption comes with certain risks, they become less likely to engage in immoral acts. Simply making consequences clearly understood can eliminate much poor judgment. People need to understand they will lose their jobs, customers, or eligibility if caught violating rules. By making

the consequences of immoral acts clear, organizations help promote ethical actions.

To be effective, discipline must meet two criteria: It must be meaningful and it must be enforceable. One complaint about rules that impose fines on professional athletes or professional team owners is that some of these individuals earn so much money that fines of even thousands of dollars are of little consequence to them. Furthermore, sometimes an athlete's team will pay the fine imposed on the athlete. Thus, fines have limited impact on behavior and are not meaningful in many cases. All the rules in the world will be ineffective if they are not enforceable, which is the second criterion of discipline. For example, prior to the 1980s, schools and coaches had little fear they would be punished by the NCAA because the NCAA enforcement staff was woefully inadequate to investigate charges of corruption (Mitchell, Crosset, & Barr, 1999).

Summary

Sport managers need to be aware of the importance of morality and ethics in the sport workplace. The decisions sport managers make on a daily basis affect many people, ranging from athletes to team owners to fans. Therefore, sport managers need to understand the far-reaching effects of their decisions and appreciate how management structures and personal values shape those decisions. Incorporating codes of ethics, self-examinations, forums for moral disclosure, and statements of consequences for ethical violations into organizational documents helps ensure that sport managers and employees make the "right" decisions.

Case Study 6-1

Ethical Dilemma: Fairness, Access, and Transgender Athletes

We like to think of sport as an inclusive institution. By and large, we believe that everyone should have access to sport. But sport also necessarily excludes. We have rules that are associated with the values of fairness and competitiveness that limit participation. For example, some recreational leagues limit the neighborhood or city from which a team can draw players because they want to prevent the recruitment of top players from other communities as a means to gain an advantage. The English Premiere League limits the number of teams in the first division, relegates the lowest-performing teams to a lesser division, and promotes the best performers from the second division in an effort to maintain a high level of competition.

Historically, dividing sport by sex has been a way that sport managers promoted fairness.

Boys, in general, are bigger and stronger than girls. Thus, it seems fair to have athletes compete in sex-segregated groupings. Another exclusionary structure used to promote fairness is designation of weight classes. In the sports of rowing, boxing, and wrestling, competitors are divided by weight, which limits the problem of bigger, stronger athletes competing against smaller, weaker athletes. The Paralympic Games uses a system known as classification, whereby athletes with similar types of disabilities compete against one another. For example, in track and field, athletes who use wheelchairs race against one another, while athletes who are visually impaired race against one another.

On occasion, fairness value bumps up against the value of access. In most states, when a sport is not offered for one sex, boys can join the girls'

(continues)

Ethical Dilemma: Fairness, Access, and Transgender Athletes (*Continued*)

team, and vice versa. Sometimes boys join girls' field hockey teams, and sometimes girls join boys' ice hockey teams.

High school wrestling is an interesting case. Not many states have enough interest in girls' wrestling to support teams or championships, so girls often join boys' teams. The National Wrestling Coaches Association (2016) reported that the number of girls participating in high school wrestling has increased from 804 in 1994 to 11,496 today. Indeed, girls appear so frequently in wrestling matches against boys that their participation in the sport is no longer news. In this sport, weight-class divisions mediate issues of fair competition. Weight classes may dissipate concerns about fairness because people understand all competitors will be competing against similarly sized athletes. Occasionally, girls exemplify excellence. Destiny Nunez, for example, won the 106-pound weight class title at the 5A Arkansas state meet in 2015. Nunez is the fifth girl to win a "boys" state high school championship in wrestling in the United States (Elliot, 2015).

In 2017, however, an interesting ethical dilemma arose in Texas high school wrestling. In August 2016, the Texas University Interscholastic League (UIL) enacted a rule that athletes are to compete either as male or female according to the sex registered on their birth certificate. While this rule can be intrepreted in a variety of ways, on some level it reflects this value of fairness and competition. We can also see this rule as part of a political/cultural backlash against transgender youth. Whatever the motivation of the superintendents of schools in Texas, the rule created an ethical dilemma for the UIL, the governing body for high school sport in the state, the very next season.

Mack Beggs, a 17-year-old transgender boy, would have preferred to wrestle against boys. He was more than a year into his female

to male transition when he qualified for the state championship. His testosterone therapy no doubt was enhancing Beggs' strength. Some argued it gave him an unfair advantage over the girls he wrestled against. Because Beggs had a medical reason for taking the testosterone therapy according to UIL rules, he was allowed to compete. The rules, however, barred him from competing in the boys' division, as his birth certificate listed Beggs as female. Beggs competed against girls in the 110-pound weight class, winning 56 straight matches and the state title for girls in 2017.

Despite strictly following the rule, Beggs' success was controversial. Some parents of other female wrestlers vocally objected to him wrestling girls. A few competitors forfeited matches rather than wrestle against Beggs. One parent even filed a lawsuit against the UIL.

Other sport organizations address the issue of transgender athletes differently than Texas's UIL. The NCAA, for example, allows athletes transitioning from female to male and taking testosterone to compete on men's teams but not women's teams. Collegiate cycling allows athletes to self-identify both their skill level and gender identity. The International Olympic Committee no longer requires reassignment surgery, but instead has deemed female-to-male athletes eligible to compete in men's competitions without restriction. Male-to-female athletes must show proof that their testosterone levels are below a designated cut-off level for at least one year before competing in women's competitions.

Questions for Discussion

1. What is the right thing to do? Should Beggs compete against boys or should he follow the rule of competing according to the sex recorded on his birth certificate? Does it really matter all that much because the athletes all weigh

110 pounds or less? If it does not matter, then what about a transgender boy swimmer or basketball player—would that be different?

2. Should the sport managers in the UIL have made an effort to seek an exemption for Beggs, or was their only responsibility to enforce the rules? Would it have been acceptable for the league to

switch Beggs from the girls division to the boys' division in mid-season once it became clear he had an advantage over the girls he was wrestling?

3. Should the UIL revisit its rule insisting that high schoolers compete according to the sex registered on their birth certificate regardless of their gender identity?

Key Terms

absolutism, code of conduct, code of ethics, ethical decision making, ethical dilemma, ethical reasoning, ethics, morality, moral principles, morals, relativism

References

Adelson, B. (1999). *Brushing back Jim Crow: The integration of minor league baseball in the American South.* Charlottesville, VA: University of Virginia Press.

adidas Group. (n.d.). Fair play: The adidas Group code of conduct. Retrieved from http://www.adidas-group.com/media/filer_public/f5/79/f5794aa8-514a-4463-8756-c1c496c124a0/coc_english_2016.pdf

Australian Sports Commission. (2017). Codes of behavior or conduct. Retrieved from http://www.ausport.gov.au/supporting/clubs/resource_library/managing_risks/codes_of_behaviour_or_conduct

Cooke, R. A. (1991). Danger signs of unethical behavior: How to determine if your firm is at ethical risk. *Journal of Business Ethics, 10,* 249–253.

DeLoitte. (2005). Suggested guidelines for writing a code of ethics/conduct. Retrieved from https://www2.deloitte.com/content/dam/Deloitte/il/Documents/risk/CCG/other_comittees/932__suggested_guidelines_writing_code_ethics_conduct0805.pdf

DeSensi, J. T., & Rosenberg, D. (1996). *Ethics in sport management.* Morgantown, WV: Fitness Information Technology.

Elliot, D. (2015, February 23). Arkansas crowns first female state wrestling champion. Retrieved from http://sports.yahoo.com/blogs/highschool-prep-rally/arkansas-crowns-first-female-state-wrestling-champion-193432201.html;_ylt=A0LEVkDyWs1YdjoA1oEnnIlQ;_ylu=X3oDMTEyb20wMHJ2BGNvbG8DYmYxBHBvcwMxBHZ0aWQDQjM0NDdfMQRzZWMDc3I-

England Basketball. (2017). Codes of ethics and conduct. Retrieved from https://www.basketballengland.co.uk/about-be/policies/code-of-ethics-and-conduct

Football Canada. (2014). Football Canada code of ethics and code of conduct. Retrieved from http://footballcanada.com/about/policies/code-of-ethics-and-code-of-conduct/

Geelong Cricket Association. (2016). Code of conduct. Retrieved from http://gca.vic.cricket.com.au/content.aspx?file=2105|24421j

Gough, R. (1994). NCAA policy's strangling effect on ethics. *For the Record, 5*(3), 3–5.

Hunt, H. (2011). Warning signs of ethical dilemmas. *Training Daily Adviser.* Retrieved from http://trainingdailyadvisor.blr.com/2012/07/warning-signs-of-ethical-dilemmas/

Ingram, D. (2017a). Advantages of a code of ethics in organizations. Retrieved from http://smallbusiness.chron.com/advantages-code-ethics-organizations-10802.html

Ingram, D. (2017b). Importance of creating a code of ethics for a business. Retrieved from http://smallbusiness.chron.com/importance-creating-code-ethics-business-3094.html

International Health, Racquet and Sports Club Association. (2010). IHRSA member code of conduct. Retrieved from http://www.ihrsa.org/about/member-code-of-conduct/

Jacobs, J. (1992). *Systems of survival: A dialogue on the moral foundations of commerce and politics*. New York, NY: Random House.

Jordan, J. S., Greenwell, T. C., Geist, A. L., Pastore, D., & Mahony, D. (2004). Coaches' perceptions of conference codes of ethics. *Physical Educator, 61*(3), 131–145.

Josephson Institute of Ethics. (2016). The six pillars of character. Retrieved from https://charactercounts.org/program-overview/six-pillars/

Lederma, D. (2016, January 11). The rule breakers. *Inside Higher Ed*. Retrieved from https://www.insidehighered.com/news/2016/01/11/96-division-i-colleges-violated-major-ncaa-rules-last-decade

Lipschutz, R. (2011, August 1). Ethics corner: Resolving ethical dilemmas. *NASW-IL News*. Retrieved from http://naswil.org/news/chapter-news/featured/ethics-corner-resolving-ethical-dilemmas/

Mitchell, R., Crosset, T., & Barr, C. (1999). Encouraging compliance without real power: Sport associations regulating teams. *Journal of Sport Management, 13*, 216–236.

National Wrestling Coaches Association. (2016). Women's wrestling facts and figures. Retrieved from http://www.nwcaonline.com/growing-wrestling/growing-womens-wrestling/womens-wrestling-facts-resources/

Sims, R. R. (1992). The challenge of ethical behavior in organizations. *Journal of Business Ethics, 11*, 505–513.

Solomon, R. C. (1992). *Above the bottom line: An introduction to business ethics*. Fort Worth, TX: Harcourt, Brace.

© Shutterstock, Inc./ Danilo_Vuletic

Part II

Amateur Sport Industry

Chapter

7

Dan Covell

High School and Youth Sport

Learning Objectives

Upon completion of this chapter, students should be able to:

1. Evaluate the importance of school and youth sports in contemporary American society.

2. Illustrate the need for well-trained professionals such as administrators, coaches, trainers, and officials in the school and youth sport segment.

3. Describe the historical development of school and youth programs in the United States from the mid-nineteenth century to the present.

4. Assess the role of local, state, and national governing bodies in school and youth sports.

5. Identify the various career opportunities available in the school and youth sports industry.

6. Apply basic management principles such as programmatic goal setting, performance evaluation, budgeting, and marketing to school and youth sports.

7. Assess the importance of ethics in school and youth sports, and describe how ethics apply to current issues such as coaches as predators, promoting gender equity, and providing participation opportunities for disabled athletes.

8. Examine the legal issues surrounding athlete eligibility in school and youth sports.

Introduction

Consider the following recent statistics:

- More than 3 million youth players are registered with U.S. soccer programs, an increase of 89% since 1990 (Johnson, 2015).
- Pop Warner Little Scholars (2016) provides youth football and cheer and dance programs in 42 states and several countries around the world for approximately 325,000 youths ranging in age from 5 to 16 years.
- More than 4.5 million young men and more than 3.2 million young women participated in high school athletics during the 2014–2015 school year (National Federation of State High School Associations [NFHS], 2015).
- More than 3 million coaches have been trained by the National Alliance for Youth Sports (NAYS, 2017), which also hosts orientation and training programs for parents and youth sports administrators.

Table 7-1 shows the most popular high school sports by participant, as compiled by the **National Federation of State High School Associations (NFHS)** (see the "Governing Bodies" section of this chapter) in 2015, and **Table 7-2** shows the participation totals over the previous three decades.

Table 7-2 Total Participants in High School Sports, 1971, 1986, 2002, and 2015

Year	Male	Female
1971	3,666,917	294,015
1986	3,344,275	1,807,121
2002	3,960,517	2,806,998
2015	4,519,312	3,287,735

Data from National Federation of State High School Associations. (2015). 2014–15 High School Athletics Participation Survey. Retrieved from http://www.nfhs.org/ParticipationStatics/PDF/2014-15_Participation_Survey_Results.pdf.

Participating in youth athletics has many benefits for youth, including promoting weight control, problem-solving skills, self-esteem, social competence, and academic achievement. Participation in youth sports can also lead to reduced rates of juvenile arrests, teen pregnancies, and school dropout (Taliaferro, 2010).

So what do all these facts and figures mean? The conclusion is that school and youth sports are perhaps the most influential sport programs in the United States today and directly reflect the importance that Americans place on involving youth in sport activities. Although professionals working in school and youth league sport do not garner the limelight and national prominence that sport management

Table 7-1 Top Five Boys' and Girls' High School Sports by Number of Participants, 2014–2015

Boys		Girls	
Sport	**Number of Participants**	**Sport**	**Number of Participants**
Football (11 man)	1,083,617	Track and field (outdoor)	478,726
Track and field (outdoor)	578,632	Volleyball	432,176
Basketball	541,479	Basketball	429,504
Baseball	586,567	Soccer	375,681
Soccer	432,569	Fast-pitch softball	364,103

Data from National Federation of State High School Associations. (2015). 2014–15 High School Athletics Participation Survey. Retrieved from http://www.nfhs.org/ParticipationStatics/PDF/2014-15_Participation_Survey_Results.pdf.

professionals do, working in this industry segment brings significant and important challenges and substantial personal rewards. A coach, official, or administrator at this level never lacks for responsibilities, and every day brings a fresh set of issues to tackle to ensure that the educational framework of youth athletics is maintained. To work in this segment is to make a difference in the lives of young people.

History

The recognition of the positive educational and developmental aspects of athletic participation is not a recent phenomenon. The history of youth athletic participation predates the signing of the Constitution and the formation of the United States. Native Americans played a game that French Jesuit priests called "lacrosse," because players used a stick that resembled a bishop's cross-shaped crosier. European settlers brought tennis, cricket, and several early versions of what would become baseball to America, and Africans brought to North America as slaves threw the javelin, boxed, and wrestled. Despite this long history of sport, formally organized athletic participation, particularly those programs run under the auspices of secondary educational institutions, did not emerge until the mid-nineteenth century (Swanson & Spears, 1995).

School Athletics in the Nineteenth Century

In 1838, educator Horace Mann noted that in an increasingly urbanized United States, outdoor recreation space was becoming scarce and children were at risk of physical deterioration. Urban populations were doubling every decade due to steady country-to-city migration as well as immigration from Europe. In response to the common popular appeal of baseball in the nineteenth century, schools and other agencies began to promote the sport as a solution to broad social problems such as ill health and juvenile delinquency (Seymour, 1990).

Private schools in the United States were the first to provide athletic participation opportunities. At many schools, activities were informal and organized by students, with little oversight from faculty or administrators. The Round Hill School in Northampton, Massachusetts, was the first institution known to have promoted the physical well-being of its students as part of its formal mission and curriculum. The school's founders appointed a German, Charles Beck, as the instructor of gymnastics, making him the first known physical education instructor in the United States. Many other early U.S. private schools followed the model of elite English boarding schools such as Eton, Harrow, and Rugby, where athletic programs were more formalized (although still managed by students) with the intention of promoting the ideal of "muscular Christianity," creating gentlemen who were morally and physically able to take on the challenges of modern life. Campus-based club teams focused on intramural-type play, which formed the early models of competition in the United States. In 1859, the Gunnery School in Washington, Connecticut, became the first school to feature games against outside competition in athletic programs that were actively encouraged and promoted by an administrator, school founder Frederick Gunn. Students who attended the school during Gunn's era were required to play baseball, and Gunn "encouraged and almost compelled every kind of rational exercise as part of his scheme of character-building" (Bundgaard, 2005, p. 74). In 1878, St. Paul's School in Concord, New Hampshire, hired the first full-time faculty member specifically to coach team sports, and in 1895, Phillips Exeter Academy, also in New Hampshire, appointed the first permanent faculty member as director of athletics (Bundgaard, 2005).

Courtesy of GH Welch, November 13, 1920, Library of Congress Prints and Photographs Division [LC-USZ62-127320]

Educators at established **public schools** were much slower to embrace the value of exercise and play compared to their private school counterparts. As at the collegiate level, students organized the games. Interscholastic athletics, much as with the collegiate system after which they were patterned, were seen by students as not only an outlet for physical activity, but also as a vehicle for developing communal ties with classmates and alumni.

The acceptance of University of Chicago educator John Dewey's theories encouraging games helped to hasten the incorporation of athletics into school curricula. The state of New York required every public school to include an adjacent playground; citywide school baseball tournaments were held in the 1890s in Boston and in Cook County, Illinois; and students from several Boston area public and private schools formed the Interscholastic Football Association in 1888 (Hardy, 2003; Wilson, 1994). Concurrently, statewide high school athletic associations in Illinois and Wisconsin were formed to coordinate interscholastic competition.

School Athletics in the Twentieth Century

During the first two decades of the twentieth century, youth athletics were popular vehicles through which newly formed secular government organizations sought to combat the proliferating ills of urban life. The social and political efforts of educators aligned with the **Progressive movement**, which touted athletics as a tool to prepare for the rigors of modern life and democracy and to assimilate immigrants into American culture. Progressives promoted child welfare by advocating for increased playground space, such as for the development of year-round play spaces in Los Angeles in 1904 and in Chicago's congested South Side in 1905. Progressives also promoted formalized public school athletics as an antidote to regimented physical education curricula based on the German tradition of body-building through repetitious exercise (Dyreson, 1989).

Emerging city, state, and parochial school athletic associations coordinated competitions in baseball, track, and rifle shooting and emphasized sportsmanship and academic integrity. As a result of the movement promoting athletics as a critical part of the educational experience, government-funded educational institutions eventually assumed the administration and provision of the vast majority of athletic participation opportunities for youth in the United States (Vincent, 1994).

In the period during and immediately following World War I (1914–1918), school sports for males were promoted as a source of physical training for the armed forces without directly encouraging militarism. Sport was also seen as a means to develop social skills such as cooperation and discipline, which were valued by an

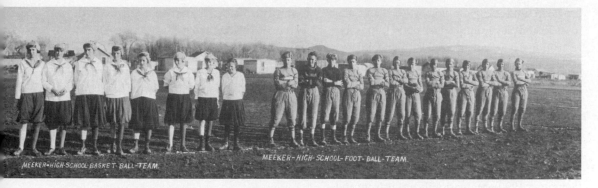

increasingly ethnically diverse and industrial society. Sport participation also boosted student retention and graduation rates. This was important, because in 1918 only one-third of grade school students entered high school and only one in nine graduated (O'Hanlon, 1982).

During this period, athletics became entrenched in schools, and educators took control of athletics from students. However, educators had voiced concerns about their abilities to administer and teach athletics since the 1890s. Individuals such as Dudley Sargent, James Naismith, and Amos Alonzo Stagg made significant contributions toward meeting the burgeoning instructional and curricular development needs. Although students initially organized most teams, by 1924 **state associations** managed high school athletics in all but three states.

Nonschool Youth Sport Organizations

Athletics promoted by **nonschool agencies** emerged in various locations in the United States nearly simultaneously. The most prominent private agency to promote youth athletics was the Young Men's Christian Association (YMCA). Protestant clergyman George Williams founded the YMCA in England in 1844, and the organization established itself in the United States in 1851 to attract urban youth to Christianity through athletics. By 1900, the YMCA had grown to include 250,000 members (this number would double by 1915) at 1,400 branches, with a national athletic league under the direction of Dr. Luther H. Gulick (Putney, 1993). The Young Women's Christian Association (YWCA), established concurrently with the YMCA, began offering calisthenics in its Boston branch in 1877 and opened a new gym there in 1884. By 1916, 65,000 women nationwide attended gym classes and 32,000 attended swimming classes sponsored by the YWCA (Cahn, 1994).

From the 1930s through the 1950s, YMCA branches were opened in suburban areas that allowed female members to join, as determined by local policies. Family memberships were made available in an effort to retain and attract members. In the 1960s, the organization's leadership faced the issue of whether to reestablish its Christian evangelical elements and drift away from promoting its athletic programs, even as the exercise-seeking membership grew to more than 5.5 million in 1969. The YMCA chose to emphasize individual values and growth, which dovetailed nicely with individual personal fitness goals (Putney, 1993).

The financial calamities of the Great Depression of the 1930s launched unprecedented government involvement in recreation. Private companies and businesses cut back on the athletic participation opportunities they had sponsored before the economic downturn, and government agencies were asked to fill the void. The Works Progress Administration (WPA) provided funds ($500 million by 1937) and labor for field and playground construction, and city recreation departments provided "schools" for athletic skill instruction and league coordination (Seymour, 1990).

Local government fostered participation as well. In 1931, 107 teams entered Cincinnati's boys' baseball tournament, and, in 1935, 75 teams of boys age 16 or younger played in a municipal baseball league in Oakland, California (Seymour, 1990). Many significant private and parochial youth sport organizations were also initiated during this period, including American Legion Junior Baseball in 1925, Pop Warner Football in 1929, the Catholic Youth Organization (basketball, boxing, and softball) in 1930, the Amateur Softball Association in 1933, and Little League Baseball in 1939.

Governance

The administration of school and youth sport is primarily a local affair, with most policy and procedural decisions made at the district, school, or youth-league level. However, local, state, and national **governing bodies** are organized to run championships, coordinate athlete eligibility, disseminate instructional information, and implement certain coaching and administrative certification programs. Governing bodies also create and maintain stated rules and guidelines and apply them to all affiliated athletic programs equitably and consistently.

© Rena Schild/Shutterstock, Inc.

National Federation of State High School Associations

The National Federation of State High School Associations, a nonprofit organization headquartered in Indianapolis, Indiana, serves as the national coordinator for high school sports as well as activities such as music, debate, theater, and student council. NFHS encompasses all 50 individual state high school athletics and activity associations as well as the District of Columbia and a number of affiliate members. It represents more than 11 million student participants in more than 18,500 high schools, as well as coaches, officials, and judges through the individual state, provincial, and territorial organizations. In addition to compiling national records in sports and national sport participation rates, NFHS coordinates certification for officials; issues playing rules for 17 boys' and girls' sports; prints 8 million publications annually, including officials' manuals and case books, magazines, supplemental books, and teaching aids; holds national conferences and competitions; and acts as an advocate and lobbying agent for school-based youth sports. NFHS also maintains a high school Hall of Fame (NFHS, 2016a).

The organizational structure of the NFHS comprises three components. The legislative body, the National Council, is made up of one representative from each member state, provincial, or territorial association. Each council member has one vote, and the council meets to conduct business twice each year. The administrative responsibilities are handled by the 12-member board of directors, who are elected by the National Council from the professional staffs of the member associations. Eight board members are elected to represent one of eight geographic regions, with the remaining four chosen on an at-large basis. The board of directors approves the annual budget, appoints an executive director, and establishes committees for conducting association business. In addition, NFHS has a paid administrative and professional staff, including the current executive director, Robert Gardner (NFHS, 2016b).

Other professional organizations and services offered by or affiliated with the NFHS include the following:

- NFHS Coaches Association
- NFHS Officials Association
- NFHS Music Association
- NFHS Speech, Debate, and Theatre Association

The National Interscholastic Athletic Administrators Association (NIAAA) operates as a non-NFHS affiliated professional association for high school athletic directors.

State Associations

The NFHS model is typically replicated at the state level by state associations. State associations, which are also nonprofit organizations, have a direct role in organizing state championships and competitions in athletics and activities and are the final authority in determining athlete eligibility. The scope of activities, size of full-time administrative and support staff, and number of schools represented vary from state to state and are proportionally related to that state's population.

The legislative business of state associations is administered in much the same manner as the NFHS, with several general meetings being held each year, which are attended by one voting representative from each member institution. Whereas championships and competitions are administered by the associations, committees consisting of coaches and administrators perform most of the actual duties associated with the events, including determining criteria for selection of event participants, event management, and the general rules pertaining to regular season competition.

National Youth League Organizations

National youth league organizations focus administrative efforts on promoting participation in a particular sport among children. The activities and duties of these organizations are illustrated by examining one such association, Little League Baseball, the best-known youth athletic organization in the United States. Oil clerk Carl Stotz founded Little League Baseball in 1939 as a three-team league in Williamsport, Pennsylvania. Stotz convinced three local businesses (Lycoming Dairy, Lundy Lumber, and a pretzel maker) to donate $30 each to purchase uniforms in exchange for team naming rights. The organization, initially for boys age 9–12 (girls were admitted in 1974 following a New Jersey state court order; soon thereafter Little League created a softball division), grew to 307 leagues by 1949, and 5,000 leagues by 1959. In 1961, the organization created a Senior division for 13- to 15-year-olds, and in 1967 a team from Japan was the first non-U.S. team to win the Little League World Series (Little League Baseball, 2016b). As of 2016, there were 2.4 million participants and 1.5 million adult volunteers in 6,500 Little League programs in nearly 90 countries. Twenty-one members of the National Baseball Hall of Fame in Cooperstown, New York, are former Little League participants, including Randy Johnson, Mike Piazza, Nolan Ryan, and Carl Yastrzemski (Little League Baseball, 2016c).

The Little League governance structure is organized on four levels: local, district, region, and international. Each league program is organized within a community that establishes its own boundaries from which it may register players. A board of directors guides each local league and is responsible for the league's day-to-day operations. Leagues may assess registration fees, which are used to purchase uniforms and equipment and maintain fields, but the organization states that "the fee cannot be a prerequisite for playing. The Little League philosophy does not

Courtesy of Mary Hufford, Archive of Folk Culture, Library of Congress [AFC 1999/008 CRF-MH-C101-13]

permit any eligible candidate to be turned away." Rules also require that every child plays in every game (Little League Baseball, 2016a, p. 1).

Ten to 20 teams in a given area usually form a district, and the district administrator organizes district tournaments. The district administrator reports to the regional director, of which there are five in the United States (located in California, Connecticut, Georgia, Indiana, and Texas) and four internationally (located in Canada, Japan, Poland, and Puerto Rico). All Little League operations are led by the president and chief executive officer (CEO), who report to a board of directors comprising eight district administrators elected to rotating terms by their colleagues at the periodic International Congress. The current Little League CEO is Stephen Keener. Today, the organization has 110 full-time employees worldwide. Its headquarters are near the city of Williamsport, on a 66-acre plot that contains six diamonds, practice facilities, housing, dining and recreation areas, Howard J. Lamade Stadium and Little League Volunteer Stadium (sites of the annual World Series in August), the John W. Lundy Conference Center, and the Peter J. McGovern Little League Museum (Little League Baseball, 2016a).

Career Opportunities

The employment opportunities in school and youth league sport are similar. What follows is a

brief listing of the roles critical to the operation of school and youth league sport, including major job functions and responsibilities.

School Athletic Director/League Director

Supervising a school athletic program or youth league includes responsibilities such as hiring, supervising, and evaluating coaches; coordinating nearly all facets of contest management, including the hiring and paying of officials and event staff; setting departmental/league training and disciplinary policies; determining departmental/league budgets; overseeing all associated fundraising; determining and verifying game scheduling and athlete eligibility; transmitting relevant publicity; and handling public relations. In addition, most school athletic directors do not have the luxury of devoting their whole working day to this job. Most must also coach, teach, perform other administrative roles, or do some combination of all three.

Youth league directors must sometimes perform their duties on a completely voluntary basis, without compensation or work release time. Compared to coaches, **school athletic directors** have less direct involvement with athletes and perform their duties less publicly, but these administrators by no means have a less important role in successfully managing an athletic program. Some of their major responsibilities and concerns are risk management, insurance, employment issues, sexual harassment, gender equity, and fundraising.

The job description for a school or youth league coach is quite demanding. **Coaches** face complex human resources management issues, deal with constant and extreme pressure to perform successfully, and work long and irregular hours for low (or no) pay. Significant knowledge of injuries and physical training, equipment, and bus-driving skills are highly recommended. High school coaches in most states are also required to pass certain certification requirements, many of which are delivered through the NFSH.

Because injuries inevitably occur in athletic activities, **trainers** and **physical therapists** are critical for school and youth sport operation. Most school districts and state associations require medical personnel and emergency medical transportation to be present at football games or other high-risk contact sports, although the dictates of youth leagues vary. Most schools and leagues do not have the personnel or financial resources to provide trainers or medical personnel (e.g., paramedics, certified athletic trainers, emergency medical technicians, physicians) for all contests, and such personnel are infrequently provided for practices.

Schools and leagues can contract with trainers from a local hospital, physical therapy center, or fitness club. This position can also be linked to an internal job, such as a classroom or physical education teacher, a school doctor or nurse, or an athletic administrator. Such programs benefit the school athletic program and can provide a student-trainer with an educational opportunity. Salaries for this position vary widely, depending on the employment status (part time or full time) and the other job responsibilities linked to the post.

Officials and Judges

Officials and **judges** are vital to the proper administration of school and youth athletics, and they share much of the public scrutiny associated with coaches and administrators. Officials are employed by schools and leagues but are considered independent contractors because the school or league has no supervisory capacity over officials. Depending on the locale, officials may require certification from national, state, and local sanctioning organizations to gain approval to work in interscholastic events. Most youth leagues rely on volunteers with such accreditation to officiate contests. Although

this aids in the logistical operations, the use of such nonprofessionalized personnel can leave a league liable for litigation based on the actions of these individuals. Officials possess a significant amount of control over game administration and supervision. In game situations, officials usually have the responsibility and authority to postpone and cancel games due to inclement and dangerous weather situations, and they are responsible for controlling rough and violent play. At this level, officials work on a part-time basis, because compensation is not sufficient to cover full-time employment. Officials are also responsible for submitting documentation of their income to the U.S. Internal Revenue Service (IRS) for tax purposes.

Employment opportunities also exist in national youth sport organizations such as the National Federation of State High School Associations (NFHS), the National Council of Youth Sports (NCYS), the National Alliance for Youth Sports (NYSCA), and various local and state youth sport organizations. Roles in functional areas such as program coordinators, event managers, directors of marketing, communication directors, and financial business managers perform important functions within these youth sport organizations. Sport management students interested in youth sports should pursue potential employment opportunities within these and other youth sport organizations.

Application of Key Principles

Management

Programmatic Goals

Critics of highly organized youth athletics often suggest that such activities create increased pressure to win and rob children of the opportunity to create and initiate their own play and competition. Professional physical educators and organizations such as the American Alliance for Health, Physical Education,

Recreation and Dance (AAHPERD) decried the "win at all costs" approach as early as the 1930s (Berryman, 1978). In 2013, AAHPERD changed its name to the Society of Health and Physical Educators (SHAPE), with its stated goals being to ensure physical education is available in K–12 schools and for sport coaches to develop youths to have the knowledge, skills, and confidence to enjoy a lifetime of healthful physical activity (SHAPE America, 2017). Today, these concerns continue to be addressed, with some of these efforts focusing on the health and safety of participants.

A recent issue that has garnered significant national attention is that of head injuries—not just in school and youth sport, but at all levels, especially in the sport of football. Concussions occur as a result of contact to the head, which leads to a series of changes in which the brain's nerve cells stop functioning as they should. It is commonly believed that concussions occur when a person's head (or helmet) makes contact with something, and the brain "bounces around in the skull like an egg yolk in a shell," leaving bruises on the brain's outer surface. Many scientists and medical experts, however, believe this is only part of the issue. The real damage from concussions, they claim, occurs deeper in the brain as a result of fibers pulling and twisting after impact. The better description is not of a yolk in a shell, but rather like vigorously shaking a plate of Jell-O, with the subsequent stretching and contorting of the gelatin approximating what happens to the wiring in the brain. As a result of implementation of technologies linked to mouthguards, the most damaging hits are no longer those that cause the head to snap back, but rather those that cause the head to move quickly side to side, or to twist from a glancing blow, because the brain's wiring runs left to right, not front to back. Scientists also believe that brain diseases like chronic traumatic encephalopathy (CTE) are caused not only by severe concussive hits, but also by the accumulation of more minor head blows (Borden, Grondahl, & Ward, 2017, p. SP5).

How have these and other serious medical realities affected organizational programmatic goals? Recently, Joey Blethen, the director of parks and recreation in Tega Cay, South Carolina (described as an upper-middle-class suburb of its northern neighbor Charlotte, North Carolina), opted to eliminate tackle football for participants age 7 to 12. Blethen portrayed himself as "the exact complete opposite of a person that you would think would make this decision," but was moved to act when he saw a report that in during the 2015 season, 11 high school football players died, four due to head trauma. "I asked myself . . . Could I live with myself if a participant in our football program were to become seriously injured, paralyzed or even worse?" (Kahler, 2016, p. 7).

As a result of Blethen's decisions, participants age 5 to 11 can play only flag football in Tega Cay, and participation in the sport has grown subsequently, from 195 players to 284 players in a single year. Tega Cay is not alone in this move. A recent survey conducted by USA Football (2016, p. 1)—a national governing body that describes its mission as promoting football through "innovative standards and best practices to advance coach and player development, participation and safety within the fun of the game and its inherent values"—notes that nationally flag football is the fastest-growing sport among children age 6 to 14, and other youth sport organizations cite significant growth in the football hotbeds of Florida, Michigan, Ohio, and Texas. One Tega Cay parent (who played football at Western Carolina University) put his 9-year-old son in flag football after a season in tackle football: "Even at that young age, the collisions are a lot harder than I thought they would be . . . [My son] was bummed about it, but at this age I just don't think hitting is necessary. As long as he learns the fundamentals of the game now, the tackling stuff is the easy part to learn" (Kahler, 2016, p. 8).

However, in the neighboring South Carolina towns of Fort Mill and Rock Hill (the home-town of National Football League [NFL] standout Jadeveon Clowney and 10 other NFL draftees), tackle football remains. Brown Simpson (a Clemson University football season ticket holder), director of Fort Mill Parks and Recreation, estimates that tackle football has been offered in Fort Mill for at least 50 years, and states that it will be continued to be offered for those age 7 to 12 (the town does offer flag football for younger children). Brown says Fort Mill is focusing on improving the game and making it as safe as possible, with the league and coaches participating in multiple trainings and certifications, much of it focusing on proper tackling to avoid head injuries. Simpson expects his league could grow by 75% or more with Tega Cay discontinuing tackle football. Many parents and families hear the concussion conversation, Simpson said, and choose what level of risk fits them. "I think they realize what they're sign-ing up for," he says, noting that concussions are not limited to tackle football. "Any type of sporting event, you always have that possibil-ity," Simpson asserts. "That's the name of the game" (Marks, 2016, p. 1). One Tega Cay mother agrees, stating: "We are being overly cautious. Life is going to happen" (Kahler, 2016, p. 8).

Performance Evaluation and Supervision

Given the physical demands and risks inherent in all school and youth sports, coaches are the principal supervisors of the athletic activities of their teams, and it is their responsibility to provide and ensure a reasonably safe environ-ment for all participants. A coach can ensure a safe environment by issuing the proper equipment, maintaining issued equipment, con-firming that all participants have had physical examinations and been found fit to participate, and maintaining the various necessary forms of documentation (confirmation of physical status, confirmation of eligibility, proof of insurance, parent permission to participate). In terms of the actual play of participants, coaches are responsible for organizing drills, ensuring that physical mismatches are mini-mized, maintaining safe practice and playing grounds, suspending practice or play during dangerous weather conditions, and monitoring locker rooms during the time preceding and following activities. In play situations, coaches must monitor activities to be sure that student-athletes are not performing in an improper and dangerous manner that might harm themselves and/or other participants.

Financial Concerns

Although school and youth sport organizations are nonprofit enterprises, this does not mean the associated programs are not concerned with controlling costs and maintaining bal-anced budgets. This issue has been particularly problematic since 2008, as the global economic recession has meant that many school and youth programs across the United States have severely curtailed athletic offerings in light of reduced funding from local and state sources. At the youth sport level, parents are primarily responsible for footing the bill for the expenses related to participation, as organizations such as Little League are not generally publicly funded. A 2016 study by the Aspen Institute, an organization that describes itself as "a nonpartisan forum for values-based leader-ship and the exchange of ideas," revealed that participation in most youth sports has steadily declined since 2008. Girls were less active than boys, but the strongest differentiator was family income. Only 1 in 5 children ages 6 to 12 from homes with a family income less then $25,000 participated in youth sport, while this increases to almost 50% of children participating from homes with a family income of more than $100,000 (Aspen Institute Project Play, 2016).

In a soccer fan forum sponsored by a Texas newspaper, parents and volunteers responded to a question about the socioeconomic divide. Several noted that time availability was a greater issue than funds: If a parent cannot leave work to shuttle a child to practice, his or her child will likely end participation in the sport. The forum noted that in northern Texas, families spend thousands of dollars to enroll children in club soccer programs. At Dallas-based Andromeda FC, the fee for the 2016–2017 season was $2,650 for soccer players age 11 to 19. The club allows parents to find sponsors, and anyone 14 or older—parents, siblings, or participants—can earn $10 per hour by working at games and tournaments. Even so, the cost issue can be very problematic. One club organizer notes that some parents "will roll up in a luxury car but not want to pay the full price. Other parents don't want to pay at all. And then there are parents who feel mistreated because they paid the full price while another family took advantage of the sponsor or volunteer options. It's a complicated business. You're dealing with kids, parents, egos, volunteers, nonprofits. At the end of the day, competitive soccer is not a right" (LaFreney, 2016, p. 1).

Marketing

Expanding the Relevance of Track and Field

The United States is only one of three countries in the world (along with Liberia and Myanmar) that does not use the metric system (or, more correctly stated, the International System of Units) to determine weights and measures. In the United States, weights are predominantly calibrated in ounces and pounds, distances in feet and miles, and liquid measures in quarts and gallons. This method is derived from the British imperial system, created in 1824, which evolved from thousands of local Anglo-Saxon, Celtic, and Roman units of measure dating back to the Middle Ages (1100–1450 CE) ("British Imperial System," 2011).

So why hasn't the United States followed the world and embraced the metric system? In the 1970s, American school children were introduced to the system and provided with meter (not yard) sticks to calculate sizes, and some road signs began showing distances in miles and meters, but many Americans fought the change at the time. While some definitively American sports such as baseball flirted with the metric system by putting outfield distance signs in both feet and meters, overall American metricization efforts had ended by 1982 (Longman, 2017). Nevertheless, one sport has embraced metric measurement: track and field (or, athletics, as it is known in the Olympic Games).

The Florida High School Athletic Association (FHSAA), the governing body for high school sports in the state, has opted to measure all field (i.e., throwing and jumping) events using metric measures in the outdoor season (most running events already employ metric measurements). This means, for example, if a male participant wants to beat the state record in the shot put (a throw of 65 feet 8¼ inches by Wesley Stockbarger of Punta Gorda in 2004), he will have to make a throw of approximately 19.90344 meters. One justification for the conversion is that because the metric system is more precise, fewer ties will result; supporters also argue that it will bring the state in line with the rest of the track and field universe. The director of FSHAA track and field opined that the state has the best track and field competitors in the country, and that "in light of that, it should be our position to lead. I take a lot of pride in breaking new ground and doing things that improve our sport." A coach at the Bolles School in Jacksonville agreed, noting, "I hope that 20 years from now, maybe Florida will be given credit . . . to unify the sport of track and field" (Longman, 2017, p. D3).

Much as in the 1970s, however, detractors abound. For example, the website letsrun.com carried the news about Florida's decision under the message board headline, "Let's make track even more unpopular," while another campaign labeled "Bring Back the Mile" advocates scrapping metric measurements for running events as well, eliminating the 1,600-meter run (four full laps around most tracks) for a return to the British mile (5,280 feet, or 1,609.344 meters). One supporter of the move says it will make the sport more popular because "There's not an American boy who has ever dreamed of breaking four minutes for the 1,600." While the NCAA may move to restore the mile at its outdoor championships, one former female NCAA champion miler discounts the move. "This isn't marketability, it's male nostalgia" (Longman, 2017, p. D3).

Expanding Participation Opportunities

Home-Schooled Students

Nearly 8 million students participate in athletic programs at National Federation of State High School Associations (NFSA) member schools, and there has been growing interest in developing participation opportunities for an even greater number of nontraditional youths, including home-schooled and special education students. Twenty-five states now allow the increasing number of home-schooled students to play sports at public schools with varying restrictions, according to the Home School Legal Defense Association (HSLDA), a self-described "nonprofit advocacy organization established to defend and advance the constitutional right of parents to direct the education of their children and to protect family freedoms," based in Virginia (HSLDA, 2017a, p. 1). Some states, such as Texas, do not specifically allow such participation, ceding the authority to local school districts; others, such as West Virginia, allow schools to prohibit home-schooled students from participation in public school

sport. In a recent example of statutes pertaining to this issue, the state of Wisconsin enacted a law (statute 118.133) that requires local school boards to permit home-schooled students to participate in sports and extracurricular activities on the same basis and to the same extent as public school students. Local school boards require a statement confirming that the student meets the board's requirements relating to age, and academic and disciplinary records (HSLDA, 2017b).

After the Wisconsin law passed, Wade Labecki, deputy director for the Wisconsin Interscholastic Athletics Association (WIAA), the state's athletics governing body, said if the law is interpreted to mean that home-schooled students have to play under the same rules as district students, they would have to be enrolled in a full load of classes, meet age requirements, and have clean discipline records. That is what most school boards require of players, because those are the requirements of the WIAA, he said. "We're trying to figure out what the best advice is for our member schools so there's not a conflict between WIAA rules and state law," Labecki said. However, a spokesperson for Wisconsin's Governor Scott Walker maintained the new law is quite clear, stating that it requires home-schooled students to meet the school board's requirements, and to provide accurate information verifying their eligibility upon request. This means the private home-school program—or more likely, the student's parent—would provide a written statement to the school board saying the child takes a full load of classes, for example. "The law explicitly states that they may not submit inaccurate information" to the school board, determined the spokesperson, but according to the law school boards may not question the accuracy of the statement, so verification is virtually impossible (Richards, 2015, p. 1).

The WIAA's Labecki maintains more clarity is necessary, because prior to the passage of the new law, for students to be eligible to participate in school athletics at a WIAA member school, the student had to be a full-time student at that school and adhere to the academic and athletic codes of conduct required by membership in the organization.

LGBT Athletic Participation

As noted earlier, youth and school-based athletic programs have been lauded and supported for providing numerous health and social benefits for participants, but certain youths have often felt that the structure and focus of these programs have meant that their participation has not been encouraged. Some research suggests that lesbian, gay, bisexual, and transgender (LGBT) students may not have access to the benefits of participating in school athletics because they may be less likely than their non-LGBT peers to attend physical education classes or play on a sports team. Data from the 2011 National School Climate Survey by the Gay, Lesbian, and Straight Education Network (GLSEN), self-described as "the leading national organization focused on ensuring safe schools for all students, regardless of sexual orientation or gender identity/ expression," describes LGBT students' experiences in school athletics, including the benefits of their involvement and the experienced barriers to participation. The survey sample group consisted of 8,584 LGBT students (grades 6 to 12) from all 50 states and the District of Columbia. More than half identified as gay or lesbian (61.3%), approximately half (49.6%) were female, and 8.3% identified as transgender. The greatest number of respondents were in grades 10 and 11 (GLSEN, 2013, p. 1).

The study noted that many LGBT students were targeted for bias-based harassment and assault in sports environments. More than one-fourth of LGBT student-athletes reported having been harassed or assaulted while playing on a school sports team because of their sexual orientation or gender expression. Additionally, many LGBT students reported that discrimination prevented them from participating in sports fully and safely, with some students indicating that LGBT students were either officially or informally disallowed from participating in certain school activities, including sports teams, often because the presence of an LGBT person was perceived to be "disruptive." Many also identified practices that particularly hindered transgender students' participation, such as requiring students to use gender-segregated locker rooms based on a student's sex assigned at birth. One male ninth-grader reported that he could not "join some sports because they say it's not appropriate for me. They also say that the other students on the team wouldn't want a gay student to play on the team and mess things up" (GLSEN, 2013, p. 3).

The report recommends that school athletics programs should incorporate policies and procedures for ensuring safe and affirming environments for LGBT athletes, such as prohibiting anti-LGBT name-calling or chants by spectators at games, providing professional development on LGBT issues for physical education teachers and coaches, and allowing students to participate on teams consistent with their gender identity (GLSEN, 2013, p. 4). Such actions would certainly help to allow all participants to access the benefits of youth and school-based athletics.

Ethics

Coaches as Predators

Many today are quite familiar with the sad and sickening case of decades of child sexual abuse perpetrated by Jerry Sandusky during and after his tenure as an assistant football coach at Penn State University. In 2012, a jury in a Pennsylvania state court found Sandusky guilty of repeatedly sexually assaulting 10 boys, all of whom came from disadvantaged homes and backgrounds. In addition, several members of the Penn State athletic and university administration, including university president Graham Spanier and longtime head football coach Joe Paterno, were fired for failing to report their knowledge of Sandusky's actions to law enforcement personnel (Drape, 2012).

Unfortunately, such incidents of sexual predation have not been restricted to the Penn State campus. Numerous examples exist in which youth league coaches acted similarly with male and female children. Experts note that youth coaches have close relationships with their child participants and periods of unsupervised access to them, and hold a position of trust and authority that can often keep children from reporting incidents to parents or other authority figures. "It's not new," says Dr. Sandra Kirby, a researcher who has examined such incidents, "but in sports it seems we are doomed to be shocked and appalled all over again" (Zinser, 2011, p. Y1). To support Kirby's point, across Pennsylvania at about the time the Sandusky allegations broke, Francis Murphy, athletic director and baseball and football coach at Archbishop Carroll High School in Radnor Township, was arrested and charged with seeking sexual favors from a former male student at the school in exchange for sneakers and other athletic gear. Murphy was taken into custody outside a local ice cream store, where he said he expected to meet the teen for sex. He later pleaded guilty to the charge, for which he faced up to 14 years in prison (Martin, 2011).

All sport organizations, but especially those managing school and youth sport programs, have been impacted by the Sandusky and other similar cases. In light of these incidents, legislators in more than a dozen states, including California, Pennsylvania, West Virginia,

and Washington, have introduced bills adding coaches and athletic directors to the list of "mandatory reporters" of suspected child abuse. Some bills would impose significant punishments for failing to fulfill these duties, including fines, felony charges, and potential prison time (McKinley, 2012). Background checks of coaches are also on the rise. The National Council of Youth Sports, an umbrella organization of 200 youth sport organizations, has recommended adding expanded and tightened criteria to such background checks (NCYS, 2012). Other national governing bodies have moved to set specific guidelines as well. In response to sexual molestation abuse allegations against former chief executive officer (CEO) and president Robert "Bobby" Dodd, the Amateur Athletic Union (AAU) announced mandatory background checks for the 50,000-plus coaches and volunteers in its programs. This organization, which lacks the oversight and enforcement of many national governing bodies and has struggled in the past to curb recruiting and athlete exploitation in sports such as boys' basketball, did not explain how the background checks would be conducted ("AAU to Announce," 2012).

Beyond these legal and procedural dictates, reaction to these incidents has caused more subtle changes in how coaches interact with participants. "I have become even more careful about being the initiator of hugs," admitted Dug Barker, a coach of a variety of youth sports in Louisville, Kentucky. "And I am very careful with words and phrases that can have double meanings." Other coaches are equally wary, including Karen Ronney, a professional tennis instructor in San Diego, California: "One potentially negative situation can destroy a career or life. Possibly my own." Such concerns may cause many able adults to forgo involvement in school and youth sport, but some managers discount such misgivings. Sally S. Johnson, executive director of NCYS, stated flatly: "I'm sure there's other people out there who want to coach." That might be true, but any meaningful background check system, like tests for performance-enhancing drugs, must protect against falsely accusing innocent parties. In the town of Mill Hall, near the Penn State campus, Little League coach Bill Garbrick agreed: "How it affects coaching Little League? It's certainly going to make it a little more difficult" (McKinley, 2012, p. 18).

Legal Issues

Student-Athlete Eligibility

The pursuit of wins and championships is part of the goals and objectives for many school and youth sport organizations. Sometimes the desire to win is so overwhelming that participants and managers accidentally misinterpret or willfully ignore eligibility rules to create competitive advantages for their programs. Such was the case in 2010, when Cheverus High School, a private Catholic all-boys secondary day school in Portland, Maine, won the state's Class A basketball title. Before this event, however, the Maine Principals' Association (MPA), the association that governs interscholastic sport in the state, had ruled that Cheverus's star player, Indiana Faithfull (his real name)—a transfer student from Australia whose father is American and claims his son is a U.S. citizen—had violated the MPA's "four seasons rule." The MPA ruled against Faithfull because he had participated in eight consecutive semesters, dating back from the beginning of his high school career in Sydney, Australia. After using three semesters of eligibility, Faithfull transferred to Cheverus in the fall of 2007 to begin his sophomore year, and the MPA ruled he had used his final semester of eligibility in the fall of 2009. Faithfull missed the last five games of the regular season after the school reported

the error (and did not contest the MPA's ruling), but he was allowed to participate in the postseason when a state judge granted a temporary injunction restraining the MPA from barring Faithfull from playing after his parents filed a lawsuit claiming their son had been the target of discrimination. Faithfull was reinstated only hours before the school's first-round playoff game and went on to score 23 points in the state final as Cheverus edged Edward Little High School of Auburn, 55–50. Faithfull was later named the state's outstanding boys' basketball player for 2010 (Chard, 2011; Jordan, 2011; Maxwell, 2010; Soloway, 2010, 2012). Cheverus coach Bob Browne, who has held coaching clinics in Australia and whose son Brett was the head coach of the 2012 Australian Olympic men's basketball team (and was named head coach of the National Basketball Association's [NBA's] Philadelphia 76ers in 2013), was unapologetic about the win, stating, "We went and played and the results are the results . . . We had a court order and our understanding is that you follow the court orders" (Chard, 2010, p. 2).

In May 2011, after reviewing the case at the request of the trial judge, the Maine Human Rights Commission voted not to support Faithfull's claim that the MPA discriminated against him based on his country of origin or that the MPA's actions were retaliatory because Faithfull sued the organization, sending the case back to the trial court. In spring 2012, the state judge lifted the temporary restraining order, finding in favor of the MPA. Cheverus and MPA officials were scheduled to meet on August 20, 2012, to resolve the issue, but the meeting was cancelled. Early in the proceedings, MPA Executive Director Richard Durost stated that Cheverus would forfeit the state title if the MPA won its case (Jordan, 2011; "MPA Meeting," 2012).

Cheverus did, indeed, forfeit the title when the MPA's Interscholastic Management Committee voted 11–0 in October 2012 to strip the Stags of their 2009–2010 Class A boys' basketball title. Cheverus also was stripped of its 2009–2010 Western Maine regional title. Edward Little High School did not garner the title as Durost had promised, because championships were not awarded to the teams that Cheverus beat in the regional and state finals. "We certainly would have liked to have settled this long ago," said the MPA's Durost, "but the court system does not move quickly" (Jordan, 2012, p. 1). Edward Little coach Mike Adams said the decision provides some closure for him and his players. "We've moved on. We've gotten past it," he said. "Nobody has called me up and offered me a Gold Ball [state championship trophy]." Adams said the majority of the players on that team do not want the title. If the offer ever came to him, he would decline it. "It still hurts to lose a game like that, and it still hurts and it will probably always hurt because we were so close," Adams added. "But for somebody to say, 'Here's a Gold Ball now,' I can't bring that moment back and bring the crowd back and say, 'Here's your crowd, here's your moment that you've worked so hard for so you can hold that ball over your head, hug your parents and jump around and have a good time'" (Whitehouse, 2012, p. 1).

After leaving Cheverus, Faithfull went on to play an additional season at St. Thomas More School in Connecticut, then enrolled to play at Wofford College, a National Collegiate Athletic Association (NCAA) Division I school located in Spartanburg, South Carolina. Faithfull lost a year of intercollegiate eligibility due to his extra year of high school participation, and after losing playing time his junior year at Wofford, he dropped out of school and returned to his native Australia (Shanesy, 2014).

It is reasonable that the MPA, on behalf of its member schools, pursued this case, given the fact that an increasing number of international students are entering Maine schools—especially those schools that are a unique public–private hybrid, with privately chartered high schools serving a local population much in the manner of a public school. At one such school, Foxcroft Academy in Dover–Foxcroft, more than 100 students, many from China, are now enrolled, paying tuition and living in dorms built by the school. This issue is all the more problematic because the MPA permits public schools, private schools, and the public–private hybrids to join and compete in state championship competitions it administers. This mixed membership means that a school like Cheverus can, in effect, draw students from around the world to compete against public schools that draw students from a specifically circumscribed and limited geographic area, leading to potential friction in terms of determining fairness in eligibility rules and procedures.

Summary

School and youth sport has evolved from its modest beginnings in New England private schools in the early 1800s to incorporate boys and girls of all ages in a multitude of sports and activities. These participation opportunities have expanded as administrators, coaches, and other associated personnel have developed the skills and expertise to deal with the challenges and issues that have accompanied this booming expansion. Although some contemporary issues complicate today's high school and youth sport landscape, the need and demand for well-run sport programs have never been greater. As long as there are boys and girls, the need for play and competition will exist, as will the need for well-trained professionals to ensure these needs will be met.

Case Study 7-1

The Football Conundrum at Cardinal Ruhle Academy

Derron Damone is the athletic director at Cardinal Ruhle Academy (CRA), a private Catholic high school of 350 boys, located in Akropolis, a fading industrial city of 75,000 people in northwest Ohio. CRA has a strict jacket-and-tie dress code, a traditional curriculum focusing on math and science (along with religious education), a 110-year-old classroom building that has seen better days, and a mix of students, many of whom are first-generation immigrants from Central America, Russia, and Somalia, and some of whom travel more than 2 hours per day on the city's transportation system to attend the school. Sixty-five percent of the school's students are ethnic minorities.

When he took the job, Damone had been charged by CRA's head, Monsignor Gennaro (Johnny) DiNapoli, to improve the school's profile and enrollment—which had been declining due to concerns about the dangerous neighborhood in which the school was located, and fallout from the clergy sex-abuse scandals that had rocked the U.S. Catholic church—by expanding its athletic programs, specifically boys' basketball. At that point, Damone learned the school was about to undertake a significant fundraising campaign (with a goal to raise $40 million) to refurbish its crumbling facilities. The creation of a nationally ranked boys' basketball team was going to be part of the public relations campaign to generate interest among alumni and prospective students. Initially the move to create a nationally prominent program had gone well. CRA had sent several players to top NCAA Division I men's basketball programs, and even had one player currently in the NBA, Jim Higgins, who played collegiate basketball for one year and then entered the NBA draft.

The long-serving and much-beloved DiNapoli died in 2012. His replacement, the much younger and less charismatic Walter McMullen, was well meaning but had been unable to connect with the alumni and other potential donors to meet the lofty $40 million goal. To help in this effort, McMullen pushed Damone to add a football program. While high school basketball has pockets of popularity in Ohio, high school football generates a far greater degree of buzz among the populace. Damone was wary of adding football, not because he disliked the sport (he was an average NCAA Division III player during his undergraduate days at DePauw University in Indiana), but primarily because of the cost of adding a program from scratch, which would mean securing equipment, supplies, uniforms, suitable practice and competition facilities, and, most importantly, good coaches.

On a gray October morning, as he waited in the drive-through line at McDonald's for his morning coffee, Damone's phone buzzed. It was a text message from his head football coach. The team's best player, Franklin Henry, had sustained a concussion in practice the previous day (his third of the season) and would miss the rest of the season. Henry was the fourth player to sustain a season-ending injury, and the team faced its final five games with a roster of only 24 healthy players. The team's record was a respectable 3–2, but was led by a handful of blue-chip players playing both ways (most of whom were on full scholarships), and very little depth beyond that. With Henry out, and the team's biggest game of the season the next night against perennial state power St. Ignacius of Cleveland (to be played at FirstEnergy Stadium, home of the Cleveland Browns), Damone feared that his team would not just be beaten, but physically overmatched and vulnerable to more injuries. Damone also knew that the team's expenses were more than triple the amount expected, leaving his annual budget nearly $400,000 in the red. He had hoped that the game in an NFL stadium would trigger interest from boosters, but tickets sales for the game were very, very light.

After picking up his coffee, Damone headed down the wet streets toward CRA. As he approached the school, he noted the sign touting the proposed school construction project, complete with an architectural drawing of the new structure, and a red, thermometer-like symbol depicting the amount of money raised to date. "Only $35,000 raised so far. And that number hasn't inched up in months," he thought. He then thought about other Catholic schools that had closed recently, including St. Anthony's of Jersey City, New Jersey, home to a boys basketball program that had produced dozens of college stars. As he pulled into the parking lot, he then thought about how much money the school had sunk into the nascent football program, and how much more it would take to make the program successful in generating revenue and visibility for the school. He parked the car, got out, and walked toward the aging building. "I don't think this is going to work," he thought. As he entered the building, he turned not left, toward his office outside the gym, but to the right, to the office of Father McMullen.

Questions for Discussion

1. Identify and explain how initiating a football program reflects a change in CRA's program goals and focus.

2. Identify and explain how the operation of the new football program is impacted by financial and other operational concerns related to youth and school-based sport.

3. Identify the governing bodies with which Damone must coordinate during the establishment of the football program, and explain how these bodies affect the operation of the program.

4. Identify with whom Damone should confer to determine whether to continue the operation of the football program, and explain the input he should solicit.

Resources

American Sport Education Program (ASEP)

Box 5076
Champaign, IL 61825-5076
800-747-5698; fax: 217-351-1549
http://www.asep.com

American Youth Soccer Organization (AYSO)

19750 S. Vermont Ave., Suite 200
Torrance, CA 90502
800-USA-AYSO
http://www.ayso.org

Little League Baseball and Softball

539 U.S. Route 15 Hwy
P.O. Box 3485
Williamsport, PA 17701
570-326-1921; fax: 570-326-1074
http://www.littleleague.org

National Alliance for Youth Sports, Inc.

2050 Vista Parkway
West Palm Beach, FL 33411
800-688-5437
https://www.nays.org

National Council of Youth Sports

7185 S.E. Seagate Lane
Stuart, FL 34997
772-781-1452
http://www.ncys.org

National Federation of State High School Associations (NFHS)

P.O. Box 690
Indianapolis, IN 46206
317-972-6900; fax: 317-822-5700
http://www.nhfs.org
Each state, Canadian province, and U.S. territory also has a high school athletic and activity association.

Pop Warner Little Scholars, Inc.
  586 Middletown Blvd., Suite C-100
  Langhorne, PA 19047
  215-752-2691; fax: 215-752-2879
  http://www.popwarner.com

SHAPE America
  1900 Association Drive
  Reston, VA 20191

800-213-7193
https://www.shapeamerica.org

YMCA of the USA
  101 N. Wacker Drive
  Chicago, IL 60606
  312-977-0031
  http://www.ymca.net

Key Terms

coaches, governing bodies, judges, National Federation of State High School Associations (NFHS), national youth league organizations, nonschool agencies, officials, physical therapists, private schools, Progressive movement, public schools, school athletic directors, state associations, trainers, youth league directors

References

AAU to announce screening policy. (2012, June 11). *USA Today*, p. 3C.

Aspen Institute Project Play. (2016). *State of play 2016: Trends and development*. Retrieved from https://statis1.squarespace.com /static/595ea7d6e58c62dce01d1625/t/5a58f43 90d929736142ad065/1515779136278 /StateofPlay_2016_FINAL.pdf

Berryman, J. W. (1978). From the cradle to the playing field: America's emphasis on highly organized competitive sports for preadolescent boys. *Journal of Sports History, 5*(1), 31–32.

Borden, S., Grondahl, M., & Ward, J. (2017, January 15). This is your brain after a football hit. *New York Times*, p. SP5.

British imperial system: Measurement system. (2011, March 1). *Encyclopaedia Britannica*. Retrieved from https://www.britannica.com /science/British-Imperial-System

Bundgaard, A. (2005). *Muscle and manliness: The rise of sport in American boarding schools*. Syracuse, NY: Syracuse University Press.

Cahn, S. K. (1994). *Coming on strong: Gender and sexuality in twentieth century women's sport*. New York, NY: Free Press.

Chard, T. (2010, March 4). Cheverus title forfeit is possible. *Portland (Maine) Press Herald*. Retrieved from https:// www.pressherald.com/2010/03/04 /cheverus-could-face-title-forfeit_2010-03-03/

Chard, T. (2011, January 28). Faithfull back in Maine for prep school tourney. *Portland (Maine) Press Herald*. Retrieved from https:// www.pressherald.com/2011/01/28 /faithfull-back-in-maine-for-prep-school -tourney_2011-01-28

Drape, J. (2012, June 22). Sandusky guilty of sexual abuse of 10 young boys. *New York Times*. Retrieved from https://www.nytimes .com/2012/06/23/sports /ncaafootball/ jerry-sandusky-convicted-of-sexually -abusing-boys.html

Dyreson, M. (1989). The emergence of consumer culture and the transformation of physical culture: American sport in the 1920s. *Journal of Sport History, 16*(5), 3.

Gay, Lesbian, and Straight Education Network (GLSEN). (2013) The experience of LGBT students in school athletics. Retrieved from https://www.glsen.org/sites/default/files /The%20Experiences%20of%20LGBT%20 Students%20in%20Athletics.pdf

Hardy, S. (2003). *How Boston played: Sport, recreation, and community, 1865–1915.* Knoxville, TN: University of Tennessee Press.

Home School Legal Defense Association (HSLDA). (2017a). About HSLDA. Retrieved from http://www.hslda.org/about/

Home School Legal Defense Association (HSLDA). (2017b). Public school access for homeschoolers: A legal summary: Wisconsin. Retrieved from https://www.hslda.org/laws /Equal_Access/Wisconsin_eq.asp

Johnson, A. (2015, May 27). Soccer by the numbers: A look at the game in the U.S. *NBC News*. Retrieved from http://www.nbcnews .com/storyline/fifa-corruption-scandal /soccer-numbers-look-game-u-s-n365601

Jordan, G. (2011, May 17). Indiana Faithfull case still in limbo. *Portland (Maine) Press Herald*. Retrieved from https:// www.pressherald.com/2011/05/17/ faithfull-case-still-in-limbo_2011-05-17/

Jordan, G. (2012, October 2). Cheverus stripped of 2010 basketball titles due to ineligible player. *Portland (Maine) Press Herald*. Retrieved from http://www.pressherald.com/news /MPA-vacates-Cheverus-basketball-titles -from-2009-10.html

Kahler, K. (2016, September 19). The town that doesn't tackle. *Sports Illustrated*, pp. 7-8.

Little League Baseball. (2016a). Structure of Little League Baseball and Softball. Retrieved from http://archive.littleleague.org/learn/about /structure.htm

Little League Baseball. (2016b). Timeline. Retrieved from http://archive.littleleague.org /Little_League_Big_Legacy/Timeline.htm

Little League Baseball. (2016c). Who we are. Retrieved from http://archive.littleleague.org /Little_League_Big_Legacy/About_Little _League/Who_We_Are.htm

Longman, J. (2017, January 21). Going the extra 1,609 meters, Florida extends metric use. *New York Times*, pp. D1, D3.

Martin, J. P. (2011, November 22). Former Archbishop Carroll AD pleads guilty to corrupting a minor. Philly.com. Retrieved from http://www.philly.com/philly/news /breaking/20111122_Former_Archbishop _Carroll_AD_pleads_guilty_to_corrupting _minor.html

Marks, J. (2016, May 27). Tega Cay out, Fort Mill in for tackle football. *Fort Mill (SC) Times*. Retrieved from http://www.heraldonline .com/news/local/community/fort-mill-times /article80310222.html.

Maxwell, T. (2010, June 11). Faithfull lawyer whistles a foul on MPA officials. *Portland (Maine) Press Herald*. Retrieved from https://www.pressherald.com/2010/06/11 /faithfull-lawyer-whistles-a-foul-on-mpa -officials_2010-06-11/

McKinley, J. (2012, April 15). After Penn State case, coaches face new scrutiny. *New York Times*, p. 18.

MPA meeting with Cheverus postponed. (2012, August 21). *Lewiston (Maine) Sun Journal*. Retrieved from http://www.sunjournal .com/news/local-sports/2012/08/21 /mpa-meeting-cheverus-postponed/1239318

National Alliance for Youth Sports (NAYS). (2017). NAYS coach training and membership. Retrieved from https://www .nays.org/coaches/

National Council of Youth Sports (NCYS). (2012). About NCYS. Retrieved from http://www .ncys.org/about/about.php

National Federation of State High School Associations (NFHS). (2015). 2014–15 high school athletics participation survey (2015). Retrieved from http://www.nfhs .org/ParticipationStatics/PDF/2014-15 _Participation_Survey_Results.pdf

National Federation of State High School Associations (NFHS). (2016a). About us. Retrieved from https://www.nfhs.org /who-we-are/aboutus.

National Federation of State High School Associations (NFHS). (2016b). Staff. Retrieved from https://www.nfhs.org /who-we-are/Staff

O'Hanlon, T. P. (1982). School sports as social training: The case of athletics and the crisis of World War I. *Journal of Sport History, 9*(1), 5.

Pop Warner Little Scholars, Inc. (2016). About us. Retrieved from http://www.popwarner.com/About_Us.htm

Putney, C. W. (1993). Going upscale: The YMCA and postwar America, 1950–1990. *Journal of Sport History, 20*(2), 151–166.

Richards, E. (2015, July 17). WIAA on home-schooled sports law: "It's just confusing." *Milwaukee (WI) Journal Sentinel*. Retrieved from http://archive.jsonline.com/news/education/wiaa-on-home-school-sports-law-its-just-confusing-b99539222z1-316145721.html

Seymour, H. (1990). *Baseball: The people's game.* New York, NY: Oxford University Press.

Shanesy, T. (2014, February 12). Indiana Faithfull, losing minutes, leaves Wofford basketball team. GoUpstate.com. Retrieved from http://campuscommuter.blogs.goupstate.com/19149/indiana-faithfull-losing-minutes-leaves-wofford-basketball-team/

SHAPE America. (2017). National Standards. Retrieved from https://www.shapeamerica.org/standards/

Soloway, S. (2010, February 27). Standing up when his son was told to sit. *Portland (Maine) Press Herald*. Retrieved from https://www.pressherald.com/2010/02/27/standing-up-when-his-son-was-told-to-sit/

Soloway, S. (2012, August 8). Discretion, for a Cheverus basketball title long past. *Portland (Maine) Press Herald*. Retrieved from http://www.press/standingherald.com/sports/discretion-for-a-title-long-past_2012-08-08.html

Swanson, R. A., & Spears, B. (1995). *Sport and physical education in the United States* (4th ed.). Dubuque, IA: Brown & Benchmark.

Taliaferro, L. A. (2010). Relationships between youth sport participation and selected health risk behaviors from 1999 to 2007. *Journal of School Health,* 399–410.

USA Football. (2016). Who we are. Retrieved from https://usafootball.com/about-usaf/

Vincent, T. (1994). *The rise of American sport: Mudville's revenge.* Lincoln, NE: University of Nebraska Press.

Whitehouse, R. (2012, October 1). MPA vacates Cheverus' 2010 Class A basketball title; EL still runner-up. *Lewiston (Maine) Sun Journal*. Retrieved from http://www.sunjournal.com/news/local-sports/2012/10/01/mpa-vacates-cheverus-2010-class-basketball-title-e/1258746

Wilson, J. (1994). *Playing by the rules: Sport, society, and the state.* Detroit, MI: Wayne State University Press.

Zinser, L. (2011, December 11). Opportunity and authority attract abusers to coaching. *New York Times*, pp. Y1, Y4.

Chapter 8

Carol A. Barr

Collegiate Sport

Learning Objectives

Upon completion of this chapter, students should be able to:

1. Assess the social and economic importance of modern intercollegiate athletics.

2. Describe the historical development of intercollegiate sport from 1852 to the present.

3. Evaluate the scope of the various governing bodies of intercollegiate athletics, such as the NCAA, NAIA, and NJCAA.

4. Appraise the unique characteristics of NCAA Division I, II, and III athletic programs as well as the differences between FBS and FCS football within Division I.

5. Diagram the organizational structure of the NCAA and understand how that structure may influence the organization's decision making.

6. Recognize the various career opportunities available in intercollegiate athletics and the skills required to succeed in each of them.

7. Debate current issues of importance in intercollegiate sport, such as the financial disparity in college athletics depending upon conference affiliation, the concept of paying student-athletes to participate, and hiring practices for minorities and women.

8. Assess the organizational, managerial, financial, and legal changes occurring in intercollegiate athletics; and the impact of crises and indiscretions such as academic fraud and inappropriate behavior by coaches.

Introduction

Intercollegiate athletics is a major segment of the sport industry. The number of student-athletes participating in intercollegiate athletics reached an all-time high of more than 600,000 in 2015–2016. The largest representation was the more than 486,000 student-athletes participating in all divisional levels of the National Collegiate Athletic Association (NCAA, 2016). This number was followed by 65,000 student-athletes participating in the National Association of Intercollegiate Athletics (NAIA, 2017), and more than 58,000 participating as part of the National Junior College Athletic Association (NJCAA, 2017).

Intercollegiate athletic contests are garnering increased television airtime as network and cable companies expand coverage of sporting events and athletic conferences create their own networks (e.g., Big Ten Network, SEC Network). College competitions are also attracting more attention from corporations seeking potential sponsorship opportunities. Television rights fees have increased dramatically. Sport sponsorship opportunities and coaches' compensation figures have escalated as well.

The business aspect of collegiate athletics has grown immensely as administrators and coaches at all levels have become more involved in budgeting, finding revenue sources, controlling expense items, and participating in fund development activities. Administrative aspects of collegiate athletics have changed as well. There are more rules and regulations to be followed in areas such as recruiting and academics. Public awareness and concern regarding issues such as sexual assault (i.e., Jerry Sandusky and Penn State University; Baylor University) and academic dishonesty/fraud (i.e., University of North Carolina) are higher than ever. These changes have led to an increase in the number of personnel and the specialization of positions in collegiate athletic departments. Although the number of athletic administrative jobs has increased across all divisions, jobs can still be hard to come by because the attraction of working in this segment of the sport industry continues to be high.

The global aspect of this sport industry segment has grown tremendously through the participation of international student-athletes. Coaches are more aware of international talent when recruiting. Athletic teams are taking overseas trips for practice and competitions at increasing rates. College athletic games are being shown internationally, and licensed merchandise can be found around the world. All levels and divisions of college sports must now grapple with the definitions surrounding amateurism and the rules in place for determining the eligibility of foreign-born student-athletes.

The evolution of collegiate athletics has also involved a proliferation of changes involving institutional membership in athletic conferences. These changes have significant financial implications, especially for the Bowl Championship Series (BCS) football conference affiliations and the College Football Playoff that was introduced in 2014–2015. But these changes have also led to historic team rivalries being dissolved. At least Ohio State and Michigan are still members of the Big Ten Conference (which currently has 14 members, not 10), and Williams and Amherst are still members of the New England Small College Athletic Conference (NESCAC). These topics will be explored later in the chapter, but first let's take a look at where it all started.

History

On August 3, 1852, at Lake Winnipesaukee in New Hampshire, a crew race between Harvard and Yale marked the very first intercollegiate athletic event in the United States (Dealy, 1990). What was unusual about this contest was that Harvard University is located in Cambridge, Massachusetts, and Yale University is located in New Haven, Connecticut, yet the crew race took place on a lake north of these two cities, in New Hampshire. Why? Because the first intercollegiate athletic contest was sponsored

Courtesy of George Grantham Bain Collection, 1915, Library of Congress [LC-USZ62-95947]

by the Boston, Concord, & Montreal Railroad Company, which wanted to host the race in New Hampshire so that both teams, their fans, and other spectators would have to ride the railroad to get to the event (Dealy, 1990). Thus, the first intercollegiate athletic contest involved sponsorship by a company external to sports that used the competition to enhance the company's business.

The next sport to hold intercollegiate competitions was baseball. The first collegiate baseball contest was held in 1859 between Amherst and Williams (Davenport, 1985), two of today's more athletically successful Division III institutions. In this game, Amherst defeated Williams by the lopsided score of 73–32 (Rader, 1990). On November 6, 1869, the first intercollegiate football game was held between Rutgers and Princeton (Davenport, 1985). This "football" contest was far different from the game of football known today. The competitors were allowed to kick and dribble the ball, similar to soccer, with Rutgers "outdribbling" its opponents and winning the game six goals to four (Rader, 1990).

The initial collegiate athletic contests taking place during the 1800s were student-run events. Students organized the practices and corresponded with their peers at other institutions to arrange competitions. There were no coaches or athletic administrators assisting them. The Ivy League schools became the "power" schools in athletic competition, and football became

the premier sport. Fierce rivalries developed, attracting numerous spectators. Thus, collegiate athletics evolved from games being played for student enjoyment and participation to fierce competitions involving bragging rights for individual institutions.

Colleges and universities soon realized that these intercollegiate competitions had grown in popularity and prestige and thus could bring increased publicity, student applications, and alumni donations. As the pressure to win increased, the students began to realize they needed external help. Thus, the first "coach" was hired in 1864 by the Yale crew team to help it win, especially against its archrival, Harvard University. This coach, William Wood, a physical therapist by trade, introduced a rigorous training program as well as a training table (Dealy, 1990). College and university administrators also began to take a closer look at intercollegiate athletics competitions. At the time, these competitive athletic activities were not well accepted by the educational sphere of the institution. With no governing organization and virtually nonexistent playing and eligibility rules, mayhem often resulted. Once again the students took charge, especially in football, forming the **Intercollegiate Football Association** in 1876. This association was made up of students from Harvard, Yale, Princeton, and Columbia who agreed on consistent playing and eligibility rules (Dealy, 1990).

The dangerous nature of football pushed faculty and administrators to get involved in governing intercollegiate athletics. In 1881, Princeton University became the first college to form a faculty athletics committee to review football (Dealy, 1990). The committee's choices were to either make football safer to play or to ban the sport all together. In 1887, Harvard's Board of Overseers instructed the Harvard Faculty Athletics Committee to ban football. Aided by many influential alumni, however, the Faculty Athletics Committee chose to keep the game intact (Dealy, 1990). In 1895, the **Intercollegiate Conference of Faculty Representatives**, better known as the **Big Ten Conference**, was formed to create student eligibility rules (Davenport, 1985). By the early 1900s, football on college campuses had become immensely popular, receiving a tremendous amount of attention from students, alumni, and collegiate administrators. Nevertheless, the number of injuries and deaths occurring in football continued to increase, and it was evident that more legislative action was needed.

In 1905 during a football game involving Union College and New York University, Harold Moore, a halfback for Union College, died of a cerebral hemorrhage after being crushed on a play. Moore was just one of 18 football players who died that year. An additional 149 serious injuries occurred (Yaeger, 1991). The chancellor of New York University, Henry Mitchell MacCracken, witnessed this incident and took it upon himself to do something about it. MacCracken sent a letter of invitation to presidents of other schools to join him for a meeting to discuss the reform or abolition of football. In December 1905, 13 presidents met and declared their intent to reform the sport. When this group met three weeks later, 62 colleges and universities sent representatives. This group formed the **Intercollegiate Athletic Association of the United States (IAAUS)** to formulate rules that would make football safer and more exciting to play. Seven years later, in 1912, this group took the name **National Collegiate Athletic Association (NCAA)** (Yaeger, 1991).

In the 1920s, college and university administrators began recognizing intercollegiate athletics as a part of higher education and placed athletics under the purview of the physical education department (Davenport, 1985). Coaches were given academic appointments within the physical education department, and schools began to provide institutional funding for athletics.

The **Carnegie Reports of 1929**, produced from research results obtained by the Carnegie Foundation after visiting 112 colleges and universities, painted a bleak picture of intercollegiate athletics, identifying many academic abuses, recruiting abuses, payments to student-athletes, and commercialization of athletics. One disturbing finding from this study was that although the NCAA "recommended against" both recruiting and subsidizing student-athletes, these practices were widespread among colleges and universities (Lawrence, 1987). The Carnegie Reports stated that the responsibility for control over collegiate athletics rested with the president of the college or university and with the faculty (Savage, 1929). The NCAA was pressured to change from an organization responsible for developing playing rules used in competitions to an organization that would oversee academic standards for student-athletes, monitor recruiting activities of coaches and administrators, and establish principles governing amateurism, thus alleviating the paying of student-athletes by alumni and booster groups (Lawrence, 1987).

Intercollegiate athletics experienced a number of peaks and valleys over the next 60 or so years as budgetary constraints during certain periods, such as the Great Depression and World War II, limited expenditures and growth among athletic departments and sport programs. In looking at the history of intercollegiate athletics, though, the major trends during these years were increased spectator appeal, commercialism, media coverage, alumni involvement, and funding. As these changes occurred, the majority of intercollegiate athletic departments moved from a unit within the physical education department to a recognized, funded independent department on campus.

Increased commercialism and the potential for monetary gain in collegiate athletics led to increased pressure on coaches to win. As a result, collegiate athletics experienced various problems with rule violations and academic abuses involving student-athletes. As these abuses increased, the public began to perceive that the integrity of higher education was being threatened. In 1989, pollster Louis Harris found that 78% of people in the United States thought collegiate athletics were out of hand. This same poll found that nearly two-thirds believed that state or federal legislation was needed to control college sports (Knight Foundation, 1993). In response, on October 19, 1989, the trustees of the Knight Foundation created the **Knight Commission**, directing it to propose a reform agenda for intercollegiate athletics (Knight Foundation, 1991). The Knight Commission was composed of university presidents, corporate executive officers and presidents, and a congressional representative. The reform agenda recommended by the Knight Commission, titled "Keeping Faith with the Student Athlete," focused on academic and fiscal integrity and called for presidential control in providing oversight of intercollegiate athletics. The Knight Commission's work and recommendations prompted the NCAA membership to pass numerous rules and regulations regarding recruiting activities, academic standards, and financial practices. Ten years later, the Knight Commission reviewed the progress made to that point and called for stronger commitment to academic standards in college sports. The most recent Knight Commission report, "Restoring the Balance: Dollars, Values, and the Future of College Sports," focused on athletics spending and the treatment of college athletes as students first and foremost (Knight Commission, 2010).

The debate continues over whether improvements have occurred within college athletics as a result of the Knight Commission reform movement and increased involvement of college presidents. Proponents of the NCAA and college athletics cite the skill development, increased health benefits, and positive social elements that participation in college athletics brings. Other athletic program supporters point to the entertainment value of games and the improved graduation rates of college athletes compared with the student body overall. Those critical of college athletics, though, cite the costs of fielding athletic teams (for the large majority of teams and schools), continual recruiting violations, academic abuses, concern over the health and safety of athletes in particular football and the attention surrounding concussions, and behavioral problems of athletes and coaches. These critics are concerned with the commercialization and exploitation of student-athletes as well. Ongoing discussions surrounding amateurism and rules and regulations regarding academic and financial integrity of college athletics will certainly continue as spectators and college administrators alike experience the evolution of this segment of the sport industry.

© Aspen Photo/Shutterstock, Inc.

Women in Intercollegiate Athletics

Initially, intercollegiate sport competitions were run by men, for men. Sports were viewed as male-oriented activities, and women's sport participation was relegated to physical education classes. Prevailing social attitudes mandated that women should not perspire and should not be physically active so as not to injure themselves. Women also had dress codes that limited the type of activities in which they could physically participate. Senda Berenson of Smith College introduced basketball to collegiate women in 1892, but she first made sure that appropriate modifications were made to the game developed by James Naismith to make it more suitable for women (Paul, 1993). According to Berenson, "the selfish display of a star by dribbling and playing the entire court, and roughhousing by snatching the ball could not be tolerated" (Hult, 1994, p. 86). The first women's intercollegiate sport contest was a basketball game between the University of California–Berkeley and Stanford University in 1896 (Hult, 1994).

The predominant theme of women's involvement in athletics was participation. Women physical educators, who controlled women's athletics from the 1890s to the 1920s, believed that all girls and women, and not just a few outstanding athletes, should experience the joy of sport. Playdays, or sportsdays, were the norm from the 1920s until the 1960s (Hult, 1994). By 1960, more positive attitudes toward women's competition in sport were set in motion. No governance organization for women similar to the NCAA's all-encompassing control over the men existed until the creation of the **Commission on Intercollegiate Athletics for Women (CIAW)** in 1966; it was the forerunner of the **Association for Intercollegiate Athletics for Women (AIAW)**, which was established in 1971 (Acosta & Carpenter, 1985).

The AIAW endorsed an alternative athletic model for women, emphasizing the educational needs of students and rejecting the commercialized men's model (Hult, 1994). The AIAW and NCAA soon became engaged in a power struggle over the governance of women's collegiate athletics. In 1981, the NCAA membership voted to add championships for women in Division I. By passing this legislation, the NCAA took its first step toward controlling women's collegiate athletics. The NCAA convinced women's athletic programs to vote to join the NCAA by offering to do the following (Hult, 1994):

- Subsidize team expenses for national championships.
- Not charge additional membership dues for the women's program.
- Allow women to use the same financial aid, eligibility, and recruitment rules as men.
- Provide more television coverage of women's championships.

Colleges and universities, provided with these incentives from the NCAA, began to switch from AIAW membership for their women's teams to full NCAA membership. The AIAW immediately experienced a 20% decrease in membership, a 32% drop in championship participation in all divisions, and a 48% drop in Division I championship participation.

In the fall of 1981, NBC notified the AIAW that it would not televise any AIAW championships and would not pay the monies due under its contract (a substantial percentage of the AIAW budget). Consequently, in 1982, the AIAW executive board voted to dissolve the association (Morrison, 1993). The AIAW filed a lawsuit against the NCAA (*Association for Intercollegiate Athletics for Women v. National Collegiate Athletic Association*, 1983), claiming that the NCAA had interfered with its commercial relationship with NBC and exhibited monopolistic practices in violation of antitrust laws. The court found that the AIAW could not support its monopoly claim, effectively ending the AIAW's existence.

Much has changed within women's college athletics since **Title IX** took effect in 1972. Since

1981, women's participation in NCAA collegiate athletics has increased from 74,239 to 211,886 student-athletes in 2015–2016 (NCAA, 2016). The 2017 NCAA Division I Women's Basketball National Championship between Mississippi State and South Carolina averaged a total live audience (TV plus streaming) of 3,886,000, a 3-year high (Volner, 2017). The popularity and importance of successful women's basketball programs is also reflected in the coaching salaries being provided, although coaches of women's teams continue to be paid much less than their counterparts on the men's side. According to *Forbes* magazine (2017), there are 31 men's basketball coaches making more than $1 million in annual salary—but just five women's basketball coaches who earn that much.

The growth in women's sports provides evidence that college athletics today is both a men's and a women's game and has come far from its birth in 1852. As the NCAA likes to remind viewers in a recent PSA, "Genders don't play sports, athletes do" (Lombardo, 2016, para. 5).

Organizational Structure and Governance

The NCAA

The primary rule-making body for college athletics in the United States is the NCAA. Other college athletic organizations include the **National Association of Intercollegiate Athletics (NAIA)**, which was founded in 1937 for small colleges and universities and has more than 250 members (NAIA, 2017), and the **National Junior College Athletic Association (NJCAA)**, which was founded in 1938 to promote and supervise a national program of junior college sports and activities and has more than 500 members (NJCAA, 2017).

The NCAA is a member-led organization with 1,123 colleges and universities, 98 voting athletics conferences, and 39 affiliated organizations (NCAA, 2017o). It is further divided into three divisions: **Division I**, consisting of 347 member institutions; **Division II**, hosting 309 member schools; and **Division III**, with 442 active institutions (these NCAA division classifications are defined later in this chapter) (NCAA, 2017n). Division I is further subdivided based on an institution's football classification. Institutions and their football programs are categorized as (1) the Football Bowl Subdivision (FBS), in which institutions are eligible to participate in bowl games; (2) the Football Championship Subdivision (FCS). which sponsors an NCAA-run football championship; or (3) Division I institutions, which do not sponsor a football team (NCAA, 2017m). Nearly 500,000 student-athletes participated on 19,500 teams involving 90 NCAA national championships in 24 sports (NCAA, 2017o). All collegiate athletics teams, conferences, coaches, administrators, and athletes participating in NCAA-sponsored sports must abide by the association's rules.

The basic purpose of the NCAA as dictated in its constitution is to "maintain intercollegiate athletics as an integral part of the educational program and the athlete as an integral part of the student body and, by so doing, retain a clear line of demarcation between intercollegiate athletics and professional sports" (NCAA, 2017a, p. 1). Important to this basic purpose are the cornerstones of the NCAA's philosophy—namely, that college athletics are amateur competitions and that athletics are an important component of the institutions' educational mission.

The NCAA is a membership-driven association, with more than 150 committees made up of members from NCAA institutions and conferences across all three divisions who consider issues that affect the NCAA (NCAA, 2017l). The NCAA Board of Governors, which includes representatives from each division as well as the NCAA president (nonvoting) and chairs of each divisional Council or Management Council (nonvoting), oversees the NCAA's Governance Structure. Each division has a governing body called either the Board of Directors (Division I) or the Presidents Council (Divisions II and III), as well as a Council (Division I) or a Management Council (Division II and III) made up of presidents, chancellors, athletic administrators, and faculty athletics representatives from member schools who meet and dictate policy and legislation within that division (**Figure 8-1**). In 2014, Division I restructured to expand the Division I Board of Directors to include 20 presidents, a student-athlete, faculty representative, athletics director, and female administrator. The Division I Council oversees day-to-day operations of the division and includes representatives from each conference plus two seats for student-athletes, two for faculty, and four for commissioners. The new restructuring in Division I also provides more flexibility to schools in the **Power 5 conferences** (Atlantic Coast, Big 12, Big Ten, Pac-12, and Southeastern Conferences) to change rules themselves in specific areas relative to their operations (NCAA, 2017k).

Under the unique governance structure of the NCAA, the member schools oversee legislation regarding the conduct of intercollegiate athletics. The NCAA holds an annual convention at which association-wide legislation and issues are discussed and voted upon. In addition, each division holds its own division-specific mini-convention or meeting. Member institutions and conferences vote on proposed legislation, thus dictating the rules they need to follow. The **NCAA National Office**, located in Indianapolis, Indiana, enforces the rules the membership passes, runs all NCAA championships, and manages programs that benefit the student-athletes (NCAA, 2017o).

Divisions I, II, and III

As described earlier, the NCAA is made up of three membership classifications, designated as Divisions I, II, or III. Each division creates its own rules, with some of

the more prominent differences occurring in the amount of athletic scholarships allowed, recruiting rules, and playing and practice seasons. The sport management student interested in pursuing a career in intercollegiate coaching or athletic administration should be knowledgeable about the differences in legislation and philosophies among the divisions so as to choose a career within the division best suited to his or her interests. Students should be aware that each institution has its own philosophy regarding the structure and governance of its athletic department. In addition, generalizations regarding divisions are not applicable to all institutions within that division. For example, some Division III institutions, although not offering any athletic scholarships, can be described as following a nationally competitive, revenue-producing philosophy that is more in line with a Division I philosophy. Some Division II schools may place one of their teams into Division I competition. For example, Division II Great Lakes Valley Conference Bellarmine University's men's lacrosse team competes in the Division I Southern Conference. The student should thoroughly research an athletic department to determine the philosophy that the school and administration embraces.

Division I member institutions, in general, support the philosophy of competitiveness, generating revenue through athletics, and national success. This philosophy is reflected in the following principles taken from the Division I Philosophy Statement (NCAA, 2017d):

- Strives in its athletics program for regional and national excellence and prominence.
- Recognizes the dual objective in its athletics program of serving both the university or college community (participants, student body, faculty and staff, alumni) and the general public (community, area, state, and nation).

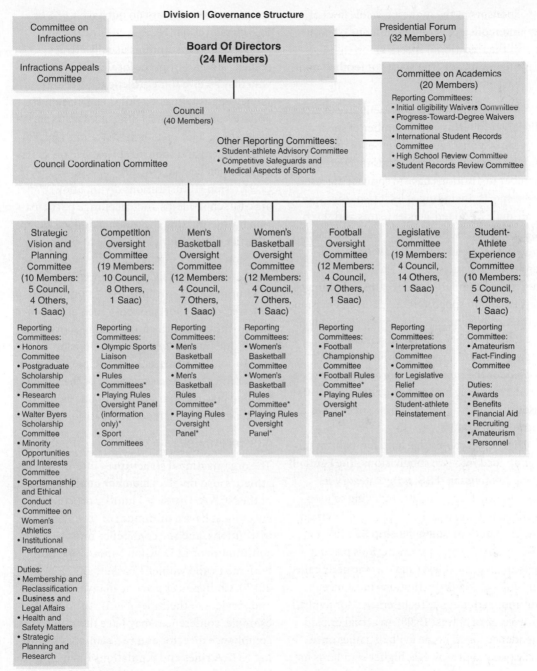

Figure 8-1 NCAA Governance Structure

- Sponsors at the highest feasible level of intercollegiate competition one or both of the traditional spectator-oriented, income-producing sports of football and basketball.

Division I athletic departments are usually larger in terms of the number of sport programs sponsored, the number of coaches, and the number of administrators. Division I member institutions have to sponsor at least seven sports, including at least two team sports, of all-male or mixed-gender teams and seven all-female teams, including at least two team sports; or six sports of all-male or mixed-gender teams, including at least two team sports, and eight all-female teams, including at least two team sports (NCAA, 2017e). Division I athletic departments also have larger budgets due to the number of athletic scholarships allowed and the larger operational budgets needed for the number of sport programs sponsored, recruiting budgets, and the salary costs associated with a higher number of coaches and administrators.

Division I schools that have football are further divided into two subdivisions. The **Football Bowl Subdivision (FBS)** is the category for the somewhat larger football-playing schools in Division I and was formerly called Division I-A. The **Football Championship Subdivision (FCS)** is the category for institutions playing football at the next level and was formerly called Division I-AA. FBS institutions must meet minimum attendance requirements for football (an average of at least 15,000 in actual or paid attendance for all home football games once every two years) as well as higher standards for sports sponsorship (16 teams rather than the minimum of 14 teams required of Division I members), whereas FCS institutions are not held to any attendance requirements and follow the minimum sports sponsorship rule for Division I. Division I institutions that do not

sponsor a football team do not have a FBS or FCS classification (NCAA, 2017f, 2017g).

Division II institutions usually attract student-athletes from the local or in-state area who may receive some athletic scholarship money but usually not a full ride. Division II athletics programs must offer at least 10 sports (at least 4 to 5 for men or mixed teams and 5 to 6 for women) and sponsor at least 2 team sports for each gender (NCAA, 2017h).

Division III institutions do not allow athletic scholarships and encourage participation by maximizing the number and variety of athletics opportunities available to students. Division III institutions must offer at least five sports for men and five sports for women (for institutions with enrollment of 1,000 students or fewer) or six sports for both men and women (for institutions with enrollment of more than 1,000 students) (NCAA, 2017i). Division III institutions emphasize the participant's experience, rather than the experience of the spectator, and place primary emphasis on regional in-season and conference competition.

Conferences

The organizational structure of intercollegiate athletics also involves **member conferences** of the NCAA. Division I multisport conferences must have a minimum of seven member institutions, and the conference must sponsor a minimum of 12 Division I sports, including both men's and women's basketball (NCAA, 2017j). Conferences provide many benefits and services to their member institutions. For example, conferences may have their own rules compliance director and run seminars regarding NCAA rules and regulations in an effort to better educate member schools' coaches and administrators. Conferences also have legislative power over their member institutions in the running of championship events and the formulation of **conference rules** and regulations. Note that although a conference rule can never be less restrictive than an NCAA rule, many conferences maintain additional rules that hold member institutions to stricter standards. For example, the Ivy League is a Division I NCAA member conference, but it prohibits its member institutions from providing athletic scholarships to student-athletes.

Conferences offer championships in sports sponsored by the member institutions within the conference. The conference member institutions vote on the conference guidelines to determine the organization of these conference championships. Conferences may also provide a revenue-sharing program to their member institutions in which revenue realized by the conference through NCAA distributions, TV contracts, or participation in football bowl games is shared among all member institutions. The increase in TV contracts with conferences over the years has contributed substantially to the revenue-sharing plans within conferences, but of even greater significance has been the emergence of conferences owning their own television networks. The Southeastern Conference (SEC) is the most valuable college athletic conference, bringing in $639 million in revenue during fiscal year 2016. The bulk of this revenue came from TV and radio rights deals, primarily the success of the conference's own SEC Network. When shared with member schools through the conference revenue-sharing program, SEC institutions received payouts ranging from $49.1 million (University of Georgia) to $39.1 million (Alabama and Mississippi) (Berkowitz, 2017).

Conference realignment is an issue that reemerges periodically, affecting the landscape of college athletics. Some of the reasons that a school might want to join a conference or change conference affiliation—in particular, within Division I—are (1) exposure from television contracts with existing conferences and participation in the football playoff or bowl games, (2) potential for more revenue from television and corporate sponsorships

through conference revenue sharing, (3) the difficulty that independent schools experience in scheduling games and generating revenue, and (4) the ability of a conference to hold a championship game in football, which can generate millions of dollars in revenue for the conference schools. One of the first major conference realignments, which took place in 1994, involved the movement of nine institutions and led to the demise of the 80-year-old Southwest Conference (Mott, 1994; "Western Athletic Conference," 1994). In 2003–2004, 18 institutions changed conference affiliations, involving the Big East, Atlantic Coast Conference (ACC), Conference USA, Atlantic 10, Mid-American, Western Athletic, and Sun Belt conferences (C-USA, 2016; Lee, 2003). In 2010, four large institutions changed conferences: Nebraska moved from the Big 12 to the Big Ten, Colorado shifted from the Big 12 to the Pac-10, Utah went from the Mountain West to the Pac-10, and Boise State departed the Western Athletic Conference (WAC) and joined the Mountain West Conference. A similar result occurred with the Big East conference in 2011–2012, when Syracuse, Pitt, and Notre Dame (all sports but football) indicated their intent to leave the Big East Conference for the ACC, West Virginia decided to join the Big 12, Maryland and Rutgers accepted invitations to join the Big Ten, and Louisville accepted an invitation to join the ACC (Lessner, 2013). The remaining seven institutions (known as the "Catholic 7"—Marquette, Georgetown, Villanova, St. John's, Seton Hall, Providence, and DePaul) formed a new conference but retained the Big East name. This had the effect of dissolving the Big East football conference status. The new basketball-focused Big East conference added Butler and Xavier from the Atlantic 10 and Creighton from the Missouri Valley conference and commenced operations on July 1, 2013 (Darcy, 2013). The remaining football-playing schools joined with several other schools to form a new conference called the American Athletic Conference (Gatto, 2013). Since 2014, realignment has slowed down considerably, with not much expected to change until 2023, when TV contracts with three of the Power 5 conferences expire (Rittenberg, 2017).

Conference realignment is not unique to Division I. Within Division III, the newly formed American Collegiate Athletic Association—consisting of Alfred State, SUNY Canton, Finlandia, Mills, Pine Manor, Maine-Presque Isle and Valley Forge—received approval from the NCAA Division III Membership Committee to begin operations on September 1, 2017. This allows the conference to be eligible for automatic bids to NCAA Division III championships in sports that all schools offer (D3sports, 2017). Conference realignment is discussed further in the "Current Issues" section of this chapter.

© Photodisc

Career Opportunities

For many decades, a person wanting a career in intercollegiate athletics started as an athlete, then became a coach, and then an athletic administrator. It was a very closed system. College athletic administrators selected people they knew to coach teams and then move into administrative positions. Much has changed since the original simple apprentice system used in college athletics. Today, athletic administrators are required to understand the financial,

managerial, and legal complexities that are a part of college athletics.

Coaches and Athletic Directors

Differences exist among the divisions in terms of coaching and administrative duties and responsibilities. When moving from the smaller Division III institutions to the larger Division I institutions, the responsibilities and profiles of coaches within these athletic departments change. At the smaller Division III institutions, the coaches are usually part time or, if full time, they serve as coach to multiple sport programs. These coaches may also hold an academic appointment within a department, have an administrative appointment, or teach activities classes. The Division III coach's budget, on average, is smaller than that of a Division I coach because most competition is regional and recruiting is less extensive. Athletic scholarships are not allowed in Division III. Division III athletic directors may sometimes also coach or hold an academic appointment. Division III athletic directors (ADs) usually have a staff of assistant or associate athletic directors providing administrative oversight of media relations, development, finances, human resources, compliance, and academic support among others.

Athletic department budgets at the Division I, and especially FBS, level are in the tens and often hundreds of millions of dollars. It is common at this level to find coaches and assistant coaches employed full time coaching one sport program. Athletic scholarships are allowed, increasing the importance of recruiting, travel, and other activities geared toward signing blue-chip athletes. Individual sport program budgets are larger, providing more resources for recruiting and competitive travel opportunities. The athletic director usually attends public relations and fundraising events, participates in negotiating television contracts, and looks out for the interests of the athletic department in the development of institutional policies and financial affairs. Managing the athletic department at a university in one of the more prominent athletic conferences (e.g., Power 5) requires a skill set comparable to that of running a major corporation. At the same time, it is important for the athletic director to understand the culture of a college campus and the role that college athletics plays on the campus. Division I athletic departments also employ a large number of associate and assistant athletic directors with specialized responsibilities.

Assistant or Associate Athletic Director Areas of Responsibility

Reporting to the athletic director are assistant and associate athletic director positions functioning in specialized areas, such as business manager, media relations director, social media coordinator, ticket sales manager, fund development coordinator, director of marketing, sport programs administrator, facilities and events coordinator, academic affairs director, or compliance coordinator. Depending on a student's interest, various educational coursework will be helpful in preparing for a position in these areas. For example, business courses will prepare students for positions working within the business aspect of an athletic department, communications courses will prepare students for a position working with public relations and the media (including social media), educational counseling coursework is beneficial for positions within academic affairs, and a legal background will be helpful to administrators overseeing the compliance area.

Areas of growth where increased attention is being directed within collegiate athletic departments are **student-athlete services**, **health and wellness**, and **social media**. Student-athlete services addresses the academic concerns and welfare of student-athletes, overseeing such areas as academic advising, tutoring, and counseling. The health and wellness focus of student-athletes has grown in importance as training regimes

and nutrition have become more complex and concern regarding injuries—including concussions in football, women's soccer, and other sports—has increased. Student-athlete mental health has also become an area of emerging importance. The use of social media as a way of marketing, branding, and communicating with prospective and current fans has exploded, with athletic departments looking more and more to hire employees in this role.

Two other positions important to the collegiate athletic department are the **senior woman administrator (SWA)** and the **faculty athletics representative (FAR)**. The SWA is the highest-ranking female administrator involved in the management of an NCAA member institution's intercollegiate athletics program (NCAA, 2017b). The FAR is a member of an institution's faculty or administrative staff who is designated by the institution's president or chancellor to represent the institution and its faculty in the institution's relationships with the NCAA and the school's member conference (NCAA, 2017c).

Conference/NCAA or Other Association Opportunities

Opportunities for students interested in a career in college athletics exist within the NCAA member conferences as well as within the NCAA itself. Administrative and management activities at the conference level now mirror the specialization of positions and expanded activities taking place within the campus athletic department. The size of athletic conference staffs has increased over the years, with conference administrators being hired to oversee growth areas such as conference championships, television negotiations, marketing activities, social media, and compliance services.

The NCAA, as well as other college athletic governing bodies such as the NJCAA and NAIA, employs numerous staff members. Students may be interested in pursuing a career in college athletics at the NCAA, NJCAA, or NAIA national office level.

No matter which level or area of student interest you choose to pursue, always keep one factor in mind: A job in college athletics is hard to come by because many people are trying to break into this segment of the sport industry. Therefore, students should set themselves apart from other applicants for the position to get noticed and hired. The way to do this is to prepare yourself academically by taking appropriate coursework and excelling in the classroom. Volunteer or help out in any way possible with the athletic department at your institution to gain valuable experience to include on your resumé. Network and get to know people working in the industry because it is an industry that relies on who you know and word-of-mouth during the hiring process. Make sure you complete an internship, ideally in the intercollegiate athletics setting. An internship gives you a valuable first step into the industry, where you then have the ability to prove yourself so that you can be hired into that first job.

Current Issues

Current issues affecting collegiate athletics abound and are constantly changing. Coaches and athletic administrators must be aware of the many different financial, legal, managerial, and ethical impacts of these issues.

Finances: The Revenue and Expense Explosion

The financial "arms race" in college athletics has long been a topic of conversation, with concern about this issue being expressed in the original 1991 Knight Foundation Commission report, which called for presidential control of intercollegiate athletics to ensure academic and fiscal integrity (Knight Foundation, 1991). This conversation has continued to escalate with recent highly priced television contracts, conferences forming their own television networks, and the recently established FBS football playoff system in place. The Power 5 conferences (ACC, Big Ten, Pac-12, Big 12, and SEC) pulled in a record $6 billion in revenues in 2015–2016, nearly $4 billion more than all other schools combined (Lavigne, 2016). This makes it difficult for institutions in the Group of 5 (the remaining athletic conferences in the Division I BCS—Conference USA, American Athletic, Mid-American, Mountain West, and Sun Belt), whose revenues come mostly from student fees and university subsidies, to compete. In the spring of 2016, the University of Idaho decided to leave the FBS, citing finances as one of the driving factors (Lavigne, 2016).

Institutions that do not belong to a conference with a strong revenue-sharing model need to be cautious about the amount of student fees and institutional subsidies that are used to support their athletic department operations. Although the University of Georgia does not need to worry about this issue based on the $40 million it receives through the SEC revenue-sharing model, the University of Georgia Board of Regents enacted a rule that limits how much money can be spent on athletics from student fees and tuition (Lavigne, 2016).

Many argue that this division between the "haves" and the "have-nots" is not good for college sports, and calls into question whether college athletics is truly "amateur sport." This leads to the next current issue to be discussed—whether college athletes involved in revenue-producing activities deserve to be compensated.

Pay-for-Play Debate and the Unionization of College Athletes

The debate about whether college athletes should be paid is not a new one. Ever since television contract rights fees began skyrocketing (both in football and in basketball) and colleges became able to fill their football stadiums with up to 100,000 or more spectators, many have argued that the source of this revenue—the student-athletes themselves—should be compensated.

Ed O'Bannon, a former basketball player at University of California, Los Angeles (UCLA), filed suit in 2009 alleging that the NCAA, Electronic Arts (EA) Sports, and the Collegiate Licensing Co. were in violation of antitrust laws. His lawsuit sought compensation for the use of players' likenesses in EA Sports/NCAA-licensed video games (Hinnen, 2013). In 2015, a $60 million settlement was approved in the class-action lawsuit, with EA Sports responsible for $40 million of the payout and the NCAA responsible for $20 million. Under the settlement, football and basketball players from the period 2003–2014 who appeared in the NCAA and EA video games were entitled to compensation up to a maximum claim of $7,200 (Passary, 2015).

In 2014, a district court judge ruled that colleges must reward men's basketball and football players up to $5,000 per year while they are in school for the use of their names, images, and likenesses, with payments to be made after they graduate (McCann, 2016). The U.S. Court of Appeals for the Ninth Circuit upheld this decision in 2015, although the same court rejected the more substantial remedies sought, including student-athletes receiving compensation through licensing agreements and other arrangements related to broadcasts and other commercial products. Instead, the Ninth Circuit reasoned that by increasing the amount of athletic scholarship aid to cover the full cost of attendance, including transportation and miscellaneous expenses (which was done at the 2015 NCAA Convention), the NCAA cures the antitrust harm caused by its otherwise unlawful amateurism rules (McCann, 2016).

In 2016, the U.S. Supreme Court refused to hear petitions by both O'Bannon and the NCAA to review the case, thereby leaving in place the 2015 decision by the appeals court (McCann, 2016). This debate will surely continue as the NCAA, college athletic departments, college athletes, and the general public weigh in on whether college athletes should be paid.

College athletes have also been pursuing the right to unionize as a means to provide them with more protection surrounding "working" conditions and benefits. Former Northwestern University quarterback Kain Colter was one student-athlete advocating for better working conditions for the Northwestern football team (Baker, 2017). In March 2014, a regional National Labor Relations Board (NLRB) director ruled that Northwestern players could unionize, but that decision was subsequently overturned by the national board in 2015 (Baker, 2017).

In February 2017, the NLRB general counsel stated that FBS football players at private universities are employees under the National Labor Relations Act and, therefore, are entitled to protection from unfair labor practices (Solomon, 2017). Although this opinion by the NLRB general counsel is not a ruling by the full board, it could open the door for future labor complaints on behalf of football players at the 17 FBS private universities. It is important to note the NLRB governs only private employers and their employees; it does not have any power over public universities (Solomon, 2017).

Coach Jerry Sandusky and Penn State

On November 5, 2011, former football assistant coach at Penn State Jerry Sandusky was arraigned on 40 criminal counts involving sexual abuse of minors. A month later he was arrested on additional child rape charges as more alleged victims came forward. Some of the incidents involved Sandusky showering with the boys and performing sexual acts in the football locker room facility at Penn State ("Jerry Sandusky Trial," 2012). As the history of Jerry Sandusky's prior behavior and even previous complaints and investigations came to light, questions were raised as to who at Penn State knew what was going on and why Sandusky was not stopped. Shortly after Sandusky's arraignment, Athletic Director Tim Curley and Senior

Vice President for Finance and Business Gary Schultz stepped down from their positions, and President Graham Spanier and football coach Joe Paterno were fired by the Penn State trustees ("Joe Paterno, Graham Spanier Removed," 2011). Spanier, Curley, and Schultz were found guilty of failing to alert authorities and sentenced to jail time and house arrest ("Jerry Sandusky Case," 2017). Joe Paterno died in January 2012, so we do not know whether he would have been indicted as well (Wetzel, 2012).

The NCAA's involvement in this case was based on the NCAA Constitution and Bylaws principles and what is expected of member institutions, administrators, and coaches. While the case was being investigated for criminal prosecution of Jerry Sandusky, Penn State hired an independent investigator, former FBI Director Louis Freeh, to perform its own investigation. The NCAA enforcement staff were not involved in the NCAA investigation. Instead, Penn State agreed to accept the findings of the Freeh report for NCAA violations determination and sanctions. Based on Freeh's report and its findings, the NCAA concluded that a significant lack of institutional control and a failure of institutional integrity led to a culture in which the football program was held in such high esteem that there was an imbalance of power, perpetuating an unhealthy culture. The NCAA fined Penn State $60 million (the approximate average of 1 year's gross revenue from the Penn State football program); handed down a 4-year ban on postseason play, a 4-year reduction in athletic scholarships, and 5 years of probation; and ordered all wins of the Penn State football team from 1998–2011 vacated. The changes in the team's wins and losses were also reflected in Coach Joe Paterno's career coaching record (NCAA, 2012).

The Sandusky case was a travesty and a tragedy for Penn State, but the case and NCAA involvement also had implications for all of college athletics. Coaches' behavior, the culture of athletics and football programs, and the responsibility of coaches, the athletic director and administrators, and the president and others in leadership positions on a college campus are all under the microscope. This case also demonstrated the ability of the NCAA to hand down punitive measures for individual personal conduct when an institution's athletic leadership and athletic culture are called into question.

Hiring Practices for Minorities and Women

Minority hiring has long been an issue of concern and debate within collegiate athletics. In 1993–1994, the NCAA's Minority Opportunity and Interests Committee found that African Americans accounted for fewer than 10% of athletic directors and 8% of head coaches, and when predominantly African American institutions were eliminated from the study, the results dropped to 4% representation in both categories (Wieberg, 1994). The University of Central Florida Institute for Diversity and Ethics in Sport releases an annual Race and Gender Report Card that assesses the diversity and demographics of college athletics. In 2016, college sports earned a "C+" for racial hiring and a "C" for gender hiring. Opportunities for coaches of color remain a concern, with 86.1% of Division I, 88.1% of Division II, and 91.7% of Division III men's coaches being white. For women's teams, white coaches held 84.5% of Division I, 87.5% of Division II, and 91.6% of Division III positions. The Race and Gender Report Card results indicated that 12% of FBS head coaches and 20.8% of Division I men's basketball coaches were African American. The results for women's basketball teams were even worse, with African Americans accounting for only 16.8% of coaches. More than 60% of all women's sports teams are coached by men. Athletic directors were overwhelming white: 87.6% in Division I, 89.4% in Division II, and 93.6% in Division III. Women also represented only 9.8% of Division I athletic director positions (Reed, 2017). This issue continues to demand—appropriately so—the attention of college athletic directors in the hiring of coaches and of institutional presidents in the hiring of athletic directors.

Summary

Sport management students and future athletic department employees need to be aware that intercollegiate athletics, as a major segment of the sport industry, is experiencing numerous organizational, managerial, financial, and legal issues. The NCAA, first organized in 1905, has undergone organizational changes throughout its history to accommodate the needs of its member institutions. Knowing the NCAA organizational structure is important because it provides information about the power and communication structures within the organization. The NCAA has also undergone major reform over the years in its academic rules, legislative and enforcement division, and its membership structure. These changes will surely continue as the world of college athletics evolves.

It is also important for students to know the differences that exist among the various divisions within the NCAA membership structure. These differences involve the allowance of athletic scholarships, budget and funding opportunities, and competitive philosophies. Distinct differences exist among divisions, and even among schools within a particular division. Students, future collegiate athletic administrators, and coaches must become informed of

these differences if they hope to select the career within a school or NCAA membership division that best fits their interests and philosophies.

In pursuing an administrative job within collegiate athletics, the sport management student should be aware of and work on developing skills that current athletic directors have identified as important. These skills include marketing expertise, strong public speaking and writing skills, creative and problem-solving abilities, the ability to manage complex financial issues, and the ability to manage and work with parents, students, faculty, alumni, booster groups, and sponsors. Appropriate coursework and preparation in these areas can better prepare the student interested in a career in collegiate athletic administration.

Probably the most important quality a coach or administrator needs to possess is being informed and knowledgeable about issues currently affecting this sport industry segment. Recently, these include coaches' behavior and the school's athletic culture (e.g., Sandusky and Penn State), the management of revenues and expenses and potential revenue opportunities through television and corporate sponsorship, the pay-for-play debate, health and wellness of student-athletes, academic improprieties involving student-athletes, and hiring practices for minorities and women. Staying on top of these and other issues affecting college athletics is important for all coaches, administrators, and people involved in the governance and operation of this sport industry segment.

The Role of an Athletic Director

Rebecca Jones has thoroughly enjoyed her job as athletic director at a Division I FCS institution. She has always enjoyed the day-to-day activities of managing

a $35 million athletic budget, overseeing 25 sport programs (well beyond the minimum 14 needed for NCAA Division I membership), and interacting with

(continues)

The Role of an Athletic Director (*Continued*)

the 15 assistant and associate athletic directors. But when she came into work one spring Monday morning, she knew some very difficult days were ahead of her that would test her managerial, financial, and communication skills. At the lacrosse game on Saturday, the chancellor cornered Rebecca to let her know of an emergency meeting the state legislators had held the previous day. The governor was forwarding, with the legislators' endorsement, a budget that called for a 10% reduction in the university's budget starting July 1. The chancellor, in turn, told Rebecca that she would need to reduce the $35 million athletic budget by 10% (or $3.5 million). The chancellor also told her that he would like to discuss more revenue-generating opportunities, and wanted to hear her thoughts about how the athletic department could offset the budget reduction in state/institutional subsidies with more revenue generation on its own.

Word spread quickly of this impending budget cut, and there in her office early on this spring morning were three head coaches (men's soccer, men's swimming, and women's volleyball). Rebecca has always employed an open-door philosophy, encouraging any coach, student-athlete, student, or faculty member at the university to stop by and talk to her whenever he or she had a question or concern. Rebecca could tell by the faces of these three coaches that they were worried that their sport programs, and their jobs, would be eliminated as part of the budget reduction.

Rebecca invited the coaches into her office and began to listen to what they had to say. The men's soccer coach was concerned that his was a low-profile sport and, therefore, might be considered expendable. The men's swimming coach was concerned that even though his team had been modestly successful over the years, the pool was in drastic need of repair—an expense the university could not afford—which he felt made the men's swimming program a target for elimination. The women's volleyball coach was concerned because of the high cost of volleyball (a fully funded sport at

the university), with a huge potential savings possible by cutting just this one sport program. Also, volleyball was not a popular sport in the region, so it was not drawing a lot of fan support.

As Rebecca was talking to the coaches, her administrative assistant interrupted to tell her that the local newspapers had been calling for a comment and that a local television station was camped outside the basketball arena interviewing coaches as they came to work. The administrative assistant overheard one of the questions being asked by the reporter: "Should the Division FCS football program, which has been running a deficit of between $1.3 million and $2.2 million per year over the past couple of years, be dropped completely or go non-scholarship?" Rebecca knew she had two initial concerns: one of an immediate nature, dealing with the media, and the second of a communication nature, regarding the coaches and administrators within the department. The chancellor asked her to submit a preliminary report in 2 weeks, so she had a little bit of time to address the bigger issue: What to do?

Questions for Discussion

1. Put yourself in Rebecca's position. What is the first thing that you should do with regard to the media? With the coaches and other athletic department administrators?

2. Which types of information and data does Rebecca need to collect to make a decision on how to handle cutting $3.5 million from the athletic department's budget?

3. If you were Rebecca, would you involve anyone in the decision-making process or make the decision by yourself? If involving other people, who would they be, and why would they be an important part of the process?

4. Which types of communication need to take place, and how would you go about communicating this information?

5. What are some potential solutions in terms of budget reduction? What are the possible ramifications surrounding these solutions?

6. If you choose to eliminate sport programs, which criteria would you use to determine which teams are eliminated?

7. What ideas come to mind in terms of revenue-generation opportunities? Where should Rebecca look to explore other avenues for revenue generation beyond ticket sales and the modest television contracts in place for men's football and basketball? Who should she involve in these discussions?

Resources

National Association for Intercollegiate Athletics (NAIA)

> 1200 Grand Boulevard
> Kansas City, MO 64106
> 816-595-8000
> http://www.naia.org

National Association of Collegiate Directors of Athletics (NACDA)

> 24651 Detroit Road
> Westlake, OH 44145
> 440-892-4000
> http://www.nacda.com

National Collegiate Athletic Association (NCAA)

> 700 W. Washington Street
> P.O. Box 6222
> Indianapolis, IN 46206-6222
> 317-917-6222
> http://www.ncaa.org

National Junior College Athletic Association (NJCAA)

> 1631 Mesa Avenue
> Colorado Springs, CO 80906
> 719-590-9788
> http://www.njcaa.org

Women Leaders in College Sports

> 2024 Main Street, #1W
> Kansas City, MO 64108
> 816-389-8200
> http://www.womenleadersincollegesports.org

Women's Sports Foundation

> 247 West 30th Street
> Suite 7R
> New York, NY 10001
> 646-845-0273
> http://www.womenssportsfoundation.org

Key Terms

Association for Intercollegiate Athletics for Women (AIAW), Big Ten Conference, Carnegie Reports of 1929, Commission on Intercollegiate Athletics for Women (CIAW), conference realignment, conference rules, Division I, Division II, Division III, faculty athletics representative (FAR), Football Bowl Subdivision (FBS), Football Championship Subdivision (FCS), health and wellness, Intercollegiate Athletic Association of the United States (IAAUS), Intercollegiate Conference of Faculty Representatives, Intercollegiate Football Association, Knight Commission, member conferences, National Association of Intercollegiate Athletics (NAIA), National Collegiate Athletic Association (NCAA), National Junior College Athletic Association (NJCAA), NCAA National Office, Power 5 conferences, senior women's administrator (SWA), social media, student-athlete services, Title IX

References

Acosta, R. V., & Carpenter, L. J. (1985). Women in sport. In D. Chu, J. O. Segrave, & B. J. Becker (Eds.), *Sport and higher education* (pp. 313–325). Champaign, IL: Human Kinetics.

Association for Intercollegiate Athletics for Women v. National Collegiate Athletic Association. 558 F. Supp. 487 (D.D.C. 1983).

Baker, G. (2017, February 13). College athletes hoping to unionize receive big boost from National Labor Relations Board. *The Seattle Times.* Retrieved from http://www.seattletimes.com/sports/college/college-athletes-hoping-to-unionize-received-big-boost-from-national-labor-relations-board/

Berkowitz, S. (2017, February 2). Some SEC schools received $40M-plus in 2016 fiscal year. *USA Today.com.* Retrieved from https://www.usatoday.com/story/sports/ncaaf/sec/2017/02/02/sec-tax-return-639-million-in-revenues-2016-fiscal-year/97400990/

C-USA. (2016). Conference USA. Retrieved from http://www.conferenceusa.com/sports/2016/7/1/ot-about-c-usa-html.aspx?

D3sports. (2017, February 17). New Division III conference approved. Retrieved from http://www.d3sports.com/notables/2017/02/new-d3-conference-approved

Darcy, K. (2013, March 20). New Big East adds Butler, 2 others. *ESPNNewYork.com.* Retrieved from http://espn.go.com/mens-college-basketball/story/_/id/9074722/new=big-east-adds-butler-bulldogs-creighton-bluejays-xavier-muskateers

Davenport, J. (1985). From crew to commercialism: The paradox of sport in higher education. In D. Chu, J. O. Segrave, & B. J. Becker (Eds.), *Sport and higher education* (pp. 5–16). Champaign, IL: Human Kinetics.

Dealy, F. X. (1990). *Win at any cost.* New York, NY: Carol Publishing Group.

Forbes. (2017). Highest paid college basketball coaches. Retrieved from https://www.forbes.com/pictures/eddf45gedg/highest-paid-college-basketball-coaches/#448971ead2e9

Gatto, T. (2013, April 3). Conference realignment: Big East becomes American Athletic Conference. *Sporting News.* Retrieved from http://www.sportingnews.com/ncaa-football/story/2013-04-03/conference-realignment-big-east-american-athletic-conference-catholic-7

Hinnen, J. (2013, April 1). USC AD Haden: Schools should "prepare" for O'Bannon suit loss. *CBSSports.com.* Retrieved from http://www.cbssports.com/college-football/news/usc-ad-haden-schools-should-prepare-for-obannon-suit-loss/

Hult, J. S. (1994). The story of women's athletics: Manipulating a dream 1890–1985. In D. M. Costa & S. R. Guthrie (Eds.), *Women and sport: Interdisciplinary perspectives* (pp. 83–106). Champaign, IL: Human Kinetics.

Jerry Sandusky case: Three ex-Penn State officials get jail terms. (2017, June 2). *NBCnews.com.* Retrieved from http://www.nbcnews.com/news/us-news/jerry-sandusky-case-three-ex-penn-state-officials-get-jail-n767676

Jerry Sandusky trial: All you need to know about allegations, how case unfolded. (2012, June 11). *CNN.com.* Retrieved from http://news.blogs.cnn.com/2012/06/11/jerry-sandusky-trial-all-you-need-to-know-about-allegations-how-case-unraveled/comment-page-2/

Joe Paterno, Graham Spanier removed. (2011, November 10). *ESPN.com.* Retrieved from http://espn.go.com/college-football/story/_/id/7214380/jow-paterno-president-graham-spanier-penn-state

Knight Commission on Intercollegiate Athletics. (2010, June). Restoring the balance: Dollars, values and the future of college sports. Retrieved from http://knightcommission.org/resources/press-room/933-restoring-the-balance

Knight Foundation Commission on Intercollegiate Athletics. (1991, March). *Keeping faith with the student-athlete.* Charlotte, NC: Knight Foundation.

Knight Foundation Commission on Intercollegiate Athletics. (1993, March).

A new beginning for a new century. Charlotte, NC: Knight Foundation.

Lavigne, P. (2016, September 6). Rich get richer in college sports as poorer schools struggle to keep up. *ESPN.com.* Retrieved from http://www.espn.com/espn/otl/story/_/id/17447429/power-5-conference-schools-made-6-billion-last-year-gap-haves-nots-grows

Lawrence, P. R. (1987). *Unsportsmanlike conduct.* New York, NY: Praeger Publishers.

Lee, J. (2003, December 8–14). Who pays, who profits in realignment? *SportsBusiness Journal,* pp. 25–33.

Lessner, Z. (2013, January 31). College basketball: How conference realignment killed the Big East. *Bleacher Report.* Retrieved from http://bleacherreport.com/articles/1509548-college-basketball-conference-realignment-led-to-the-dissolving-of-the-big-east

Lombardo, K. (2016, September 15). Watch: Ogwumike sisters and other female athletes are done with empowerment ads. Retrieved from http://www.excellesports.com/news/watch-ncaa-commercial-ogwumike/

McCann, M. (2016, October 3). In denying O'Bannon case, Supreme Court leaves future of amateurism in limbo. *SI.com.* Retrieved from https://www.si.com/college-basketball/2016/10/03/ed-obannon-ncaa-lawsuit-supreme-court

Morrison, L. L. (1993). The AIAW: Governance by women for women. In G. L. Cohen (Ed.), *Women in sport: Issues and controversies* (pp. 59–66). Newbury Park, CA: Sage Publications.

Mott, R. D. (1994, March 2). Big Eight growth brings a new look to Division I-A. *The NCAA News,* p. 1.

National Association of Intercollegiate Athletics (NAIA). (2017). About the NAIA. Retrieved from http://www.naia.org/ViewArticle.dbml?DB_OEM_ID=27900&ATCLID=205323019

National Collegiate Athletic Association (NCAA). (2012, July 23). Binding consent decree imposed by the National Collegiate Athletic Association and accepted by the Pennsylvania State University. Retrieved from http://s3.amazonaws.com/ncaa/files/20120723/21207236PDF.pdf

National Collegiate Athletic Association (NCAA). (2016, October). *2015–16 NCAA sports sponsorship and participation rates report.* Retrieved from http://www.ncaa.org/about/resources/research/sports-sponsorship-and-participation-research

National Collegiate Athletic Association (NCAA). (2017a). Article 1.3.1: Basic purpose. In *2016–17 NCAA Division I manual.* Indianapolis, IN: Author, p. 1.

National Collegiate Athletic Association (NCAA). (2017b). Article 4.02.4.1: Institutional senior woman administrator. In *2016–17 NCAA Division I manual.* Indianapolis, IN: Author, p. 12.

National Collegiate Athletic Association (NCAA). (2017c). Article 4.02.2: Faculty athletics representative. In *2016–17 NCAA Division I manual.* Indianapolis, IN: Author, p. 12.

National Collegiate Athletic Association (NCAA). (2017d). Article 20.9.2: Division I philosophy statement. In *2016–17 NCAA Division I manual.* Indianapolis, IN: Author, p. 339.

National Collegiate Athletic Association (NCAA). (2017e). Article 20.9.6: Sports sponsorship. In *2016–17 NCAA Division I manual.* Indianapolis, IN: Author, p. 341.

National Collegiate Athletic Association (NCAA). (2017f). Article 20.9.9: Football bowl subdivision requirements. In *2016–17 NCAA Division I manual.* Indianapolis, IN: Author, p. 344.

National Collegiate Athletic Association (NCAA). (2017g). Article 20.9.10: Football championship subdivision requirements. In *2016–17 NCAA Division I manual.* Indianapolis, IN: Author, p. 346.

National Collegiate Athletic Association (NCAA). (2017h). Article 20.10.3: Sports sponsorship.

In *2016–17 NCAA Division II manual*. Indianapolis, IN: Author, p. 300.

National Collegiate Athletic Association (NCAA). (2017i). Article 20.11.3: Sports sponsorship. In *2016–17 NCAA Division III manual*. Indianapolis, IN: Author, p. 192.

National Collegiate Athletic Association (NCAA). (2017j). Article 20.02.5 Multisport conference. In *2016–17 NCAA Division I manual*. Indianapolis, IN: Author, p. 329.

National Collegiate Athletic Association (NCAA). (2017k). Division I committees. Retrieved from http://www.ncaa.org/governance/committees?division=d1

National Collegiate Athletic Association (NCAA). (2017l). NCAA committees. Retrieved from http://www.ncaa.org/governance/committees

National Collegiate Athletic Association (NCAA). (2017m). NCAA Division I. Retrieved from http://www.ncaa.org/about?division=d1

National Collegiate Athletic Association (NCAA). (2017n). Our three divisions. Retrieved from http://www.ncaa.org/about/resources/media-center/ncaa-101/our-three-divisions

National Collegiate Athletic Association (NCAA). (2017o). What is the NCAA? Retrieved from http://www.ncaa.org/about/resources/media-center/ncaa-101/what-ncaa

National Junior College Athletic Association (NJCAA). (2017). About the NJCAA: Sponsors & partners. Retrieved from http://www.njcaa.org/about/sponsorships/official_sponsors_-_partnership

Passary, A. (2015, July 20). Court approves $60 million settlement for video game class action lawsuit again NCAA, Electronic Arts. *Techtimes.com*. Retrieved from http://www.techtimes.com/articles/69995/20150720/court-approves-60-million-settlement-for-video-game-class-action-lawsuit-against-ncaa-electronic-arts.htm

Paul, J. (1993). Heroines: Paving the way. In G. L. Cohen (Ed.), *Women in sport: Issues and controversies* (pp. 27–37). Newbury Park, CA: Sage Publications.

Rader, B. G. (1990). *American sports* (2nd ed.). Englewood Cliffs, NJ: Prentice Hall.

Reed, S. (2017, April 6). Racial, gender hiring decline in college sports in 2016. *Seattletimes.com*. Retrieved from http://www.seattletimes.com/sports/racial-gender-hiring-decline-in-college-sports-in-2016/

Rittenberg, A. (2017, June 27). Save the date: All eyes on 2023 for conference realignment. *ESPN.com*. Retrieved from http://www.espn.com/college-football/story/_/id/19743196/why-2023-next-big-date-conference-shuffling

Savage, H. J. (1929). *American college athletics*. New York, NY: Carnegie Foundation.

Solomon, J. (2017, February 2). NLRB counsel: Football players at private FBS schools are employees. *CBSSports.com*. Retrieved from http://www.cbssports.com/college-football/news/nlrb-counsel-football-players-at-private-fbs-schools-are-employees/

Volner, D. (2017, April 4). More than 3.8 million viewers for the NCAA women's basketball national championship; three-game NCAA Women's Final Four up nearly 20%. *ESPN MediaZone*. Retrieved from http://espnmediazone.com/us/press-releases/2017/04/3-8-million-viewers-ncaa-womens-basketball-national-championship-three-game-ncaa-womens-final-four-nearly-20/

Western Athletic Conference to become biggest in I-A. (1994, April 27). *NCAA News*, p. 3.

Wetzel, D. (2012, November 1). Indictment of ex-Penn State president reveals disturbing details of how PSU dealt with Sandusky. *Yahoo Sports*. Retrieved from http://sports.yahoo.com/news/ncaaf--indictment-of-ex-penn-state-president-reveals-disturbing-details-of-how-officials-dealt-with-jerry-sandusky01191010.html

Wieberg, S. (1994, August 18). Study faults colleges on minority hiring. *USA Today*, p. 1C.

Yaeger, D. (1991). *Undue process: The NCAA's injustice for all*. Champaign, IL: Sagamore Publishing.

Chapter

9

Mary A. Hums and
Per Svensson

International Sport

Learning Objectives

Upon completion of this chapter, students should be able to:

1. Discuss the concept of globalization in the sport industry.

2. Understand the basics of the club system and promotion/relegation.

3. Describe the basic organizational structures of the Olympic Movement.

4. Describe the basic organizational structures of the Paralympic Movement.

5. Compare international sport systems to North American ones.

6. Develop an awareness and appreciation of sport for development and peace.

7. Identify the numerous career opportunities in international sport.

8. Consider some of the current issues facing sport managers in the international sport industry.

Introduction

Thomas Mueller and Die Mannschaft. Lionel Messi and FC Barcelona. Formula One's Lewis Hamilton. eSports' Jun Ty Yang. Usain Bolt of Jamaica. South Korean skater Kim Yuna. How many of these athletes do you recognize? In North America, so much attention is placed on the traditional "Big Four"—Major League Baseball (MLB), the National Basketball Association (NBA), the National Football League (NFL), and the National Hockey League (NHL)—that people sometimes overlook the amazing athletes and sports in other countries on other continents.

The goal of this chapter is to introduce you to sport beyond North America—the athletes, the events, and the organizations. You will be amazed to learn some of the similarities and differences between North American sport and the rest of the world. We hope that learning about the global sport industry will help raise your interest in traveling to other countries (to watch a Finnish baseball game called *pesapallo* or Malaysia's *sepak takraw*), learning about new cultures (seeing a haka dance before a rugby match or the etiquette of sumo wrestling), and even sampling new food at a ballpark (how about trying some udon noodles or grilled squid at a baseball game?) somewhere thousands of miles from where you are sitting now.

Globalization

Advances in technology and transportation have enabled sport managers and individuals from around the world to exchange ideas, values, services, and products. This has altered where and how sports are played. For example, did you know American football is played in 71 countries, including Austria, Germany, Japan, Kuwait, Nigeria, and New Zealand, or that cricket is played in 105 countries, including Afghanistan, Australia, Canada, England, India, Rwanda, and Panama? **Globalization** of

sport is also found with smaller sport communities. For example, bandy–a winter sport that combines elements of ice hockey, soccer, and field hockey–was historically played only in Europe (Finland, Russia, and Sweden all have professional leagues), but recent Bandy World Championships have included teams from the United States, Mongolia, Somalia, Japan, Kyrgyzstan, and China.

© Lance Bellers/Shutterstock, Inc.

Professional sport teams and leagues are organizing increasing numbers of events in new geographic locations. As a result, these teams and leagues are expanding their international presence. Manchester United and FC Barcelona are not only two of the most successful soccer teams in the world, but both have also established themselves as global sport brands with millions of supporters worldwide. Similarly, the NBA operates offices in Hong Kong, Manila, Toronto, Beijing, Shanghai, Taipei, London, Madrid, Mumbai, Mexico City, Rio de Janeiro, and Johannesburg to grow the game of basketball.

Although globalization has allowed sports to transcend borders, it is also critical to be mindful of some of the thorny issues associated with globalization, including workers' rights in the sporting goods industry, cross-border player migration, the power of global sport media, and the impact of sport on the environment (Thibault, 2009). No matter where they work, sport managers need to develop an appreciation for local traditions, norms, and values to ensure the inclusion of local stakeholders in all decision making.

Club System

The sport system in the United States is built around a strong tradition of interscholastic sport teams operated by local schools. In many other countries, however, the sport system is structured quite differently. Countries such as Belgium, Canada, Germany, France, and Sweden enjoy a strong tradition of community sport clubs. Those clubs are typically operated as independent nonprofit and voluntary organizations that serve their local communities. Let's examine one of these countries to get a better idea of the central role of the sport **club system** in these societies.

In Sweden, 9 of out of 10 youth belong to a sport club at some point during their childhood. Sweden has a population of fewer than 10 million people, yet more than 3 million are active members of the country's more than 20,000 sport clubs (Riksidrottsförbundet, 2017). This makes sport the largest popular movement in Sweden, as in many other countries. In contrast to the school sport system, the club system allows for people to stay engaged in sport across their lifespan. Most of these sport clubs have teams participating in a variety of leagues across different age groups. All of these leagues (ranging from youth to professional levels) typically rely on what is known as the promotion and relegation system.

Promotion and Relegation

A major difference between sport in the United States and other countries is the use of the **promotion/relegation** system in leagues. As Li, MacIntosh, and Bravo (2012) explain:

> Promotion and relegation works by having a multitiered system of connected sport leagues in which teams

are exchanged from one league to the next based on performance. That is, teams finishing at the bottom of a higher league will be relegated to a league one tier down, and teams finishing at the top of a lower league will be promoted to the league in the next tier up. (para. 1)

Typically, this means the movement of the bottom two or three teams from one league down to the lower league, and the elevation of the top two or three teams in a lower league to the next league a level up. Here is an example from a hypothetical league setup. Let's say at the end of the 2017–2018 season, the final standings looked like this:

A League	B League
Anderlecht	Lierse
Cercle B	Lokeren
Charleroi	Mechelen
FC Brugge	Waregem
Genk	OH Leuven
Gent	Oostende
Kortrijk	S Liege

Using promotion and relegation, at the start of the 2018–2019 season, the league membership would look like this:

A League	B League
Anderlecht	Gent
Cercle B	Kortrjk
Charleroi	Mechelen
FC Brugge	Waregem
Genk	OH Leuven
Lierse	Oostende
Lokeren	S Liege

As you can see, the bottom teams from the A League were relegated to the B League, while the top teams in the B League were promoted to the A League. This system allows for leagues to have different member teams each season, and motivates teams at the bottom of the standings to keep playing hard to avoid relegation. This approach differs from U.S. leagues, where league membership rarely changes and teams at the bottom of the standings may see an advantage to finishing at the bottom because of the opportunity to have a high draft pick the following season.

Now that we have established some basics about structure of sport internationally, we provide a brief overview of the largest multi-sport event in the world—the Olympic Games.

Olympic Movement

When we think of the **Olympic Movement**, the images that come to mind are those of the athletes of the world gathered together to compete for medals and national pride. We think first of the elite-level competitors like Usain Bolt, Katie Ledecky, and Simone Biles, or the U.S. men's and women's basketball teams. These are the memorable images broadcast on TV or via the Internet. But there is much more to the Olympic Movement than the celebrations of sport that take place every four years in the summer or the winter. The stated goal of the Olympic Movement is to "contribute to building a peaceful and better world by educating youth through sport practiced without discrimination of any kind, in a spirit of friendship, solidarity and fair play" (International Olympic Committee [IOC], 2017d, para. 3). Indeed, the Olympic Movement is about much more than just world-famous celebrity athletes. These athletes had to get their start somewhere, competing from an early age against thousands of other athletes beginning at the grassroots levels. For purposes of this chapter, however, our focus will be on the primary Olympic governing structures where sport managers may find themselves employed. Other areas in this text will deal with recreational-level sport opportunities open to people at various levels of ability.

The Olympic Movement consists of three main constituents—the **International Olympic Committee (IOC)**, the International Sports Federations (IFs), and the National Olympic Committees (NOCs) (IOC, 2017d). As the IOC is the supreme governing body for the Olympic Movement, our discussion begins here.

International Olympic Committee

The IOC was established in 1894 by Pierre de Coubertin, who, along with the United Kingdom's William Penney Brooks, revitalized the modern Olympic Movement. The IOC is a nonprofit, non-governmental organization (NGO) headquartered in Lausanne, Switzerland, though the Swiss government does not directly govern the IOC. The governing document for the IOC, known as the Olympic Charter, codifies the fundamental principles, rules, and bylaws of the IOC.

The IOC is governed by a General Assembly, which is the regularly scheduled business meeting of the people who are the IOC members. The two most important decisions the General Assembly makes are (1) which city/country will host future Olympic and Paralympic Games and

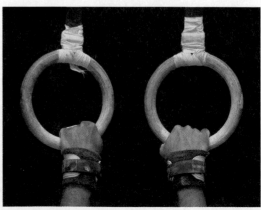

© Photodisc

(2) which sports will be competed in at future Olympic Games. The IOC members are people (as opposed to, say, the National Collegiate Athletic Association [NCAA], where the members are universities or conferences) "who are representatives of the IOC in their respective countries, and not their country's delegate within the IOC" (IOC, 2017b, para. 1). This is an important distinction from other sport organizations.

National Olympic Committees

According to the IOC, "the mission of the National Olympic Committees (NOCs) is to develop, promote and protect the Olympic Movement in their respective countries" (IOC, 2017c, para. 1). The NOCs are also responsible for choosing the city from their respective countries that may want to bid to host the Olympic and Paralympic Games. While multiple cities may place bids to host, each country can put forward only one city for the IOC to consider. For example, when deciding whether to host the 2016 Games, the U.S. Olympic Committee (USOC) chose Chicago over New York and Los Angeles because the United States could include only one city in its bid.

NOCs also have the responsibility to select and send teams and competitors to be a part of the Games. NOCs develop athletes and support high-performance sport programs in their respective countries, while also training sport administrators. Examples of NOCs include the USOC, the Canadian Olympic Committee (COC), the Japanese Olympic Committee (JOC), and the German Olympic Sports Confederation (Deutscher Olympischer Sportbund [DOSB]).

Organizing Committees for the Olympic Games

Once a city is officially awarded the Olympic and Paralympic Games, it must spring into action to get the planning process up and running. This organization, which acts as the event management corporation for an Olympic and Paralympic Games, is formally called the Organizing Committee for the Olympic Games (OCOG), and informally referred to as the local organizing committee. If you ever get the chance to work as a paid staff member or a volunteer at an Olympic and Paralympic Games, you will likely work for an OCOG. Examples of OCOGS include Rio2016, Tokyo2020, and Beijing2022.

© Herbert Kratky/Shutterstock, Inc.

International Sports Federations

The IFs are in charge of the technical aspects of their respective sports on the international level. They have regulatory power and make the rules for their respective sports. IFs are officially recognized by the IOC and administer their sports on the international level.

> The IFs have the responsibility and duty to manage and to monitor the everyday running of the world's various sports disciplines, including for those on the programme, the practical organisation of events during the Games. The IFs must also supervise the development of athletes practising these sports at every level. Each IF governs its sport at world level and ensures its promotion and development. They monitor the everyday administration of their sports and guarantee the

regular organisation of competitions as well as respect for the rules of fair play. (IOC, 2017a, para. 3)

Every sport competed in at the Olympic Games is overseen by an IOC-recognized IF. Every sport that has an IOC-recognized IF, however, is not necessarily part of the competition at the Olympic Games. Examples of these sports include bowling, orienteering, and American football, which are recognized by the IOC but are not contested at the Olympic Games.

You will undoubtedly recognize certain IFs such as FIFA, the IF for soccer, but there is actually a quite lengthy list of IFs and their respective sports. A comprehensive list of the International Federations, including their website information, is provided in **Table 9-1**.

To carry out their business year-round and tend to common issues and trends, the IFs band together into associations. These associations are the Association of Summer Olympic International Federations (ASOIF), the Association of International Olympic Winter Sports Federations (AIOWF), and the Association of IOC Recognised International Sports Federations (ARISF).

National Governing Bodies

The national governing bodies (NGBs) of sport promote their sport at all levels from grassroots to elite in a given country. In the United States, they include organizations such as USA Basketball, USA Softball, and the U.S. Field Hockey Association. In Canada, some NGBs are Hockey Canada and Canada Basketball.

Table 9-1 International Sport Federations (Recognized Olympic Sports)		
Sport	**International Federation**	**Website**
Aquatics	Fédération Internationale de Natation (FINA)	http://www.fina.org
Archery	World Archery Federation (WAF)	http://www.worldarchery.org
Athletics	International Association of Athletics Federation (IAAF)	http://www.iaaf.org
Badminton	Badminton World Federation (BWF)	http://www.bwfbadminton.org
Baseball*	World Baseball Softball Confederation (WBSC)	http://www.wbsc.org
Basketball	Fédération Internationale de Basketball (FIBA)	http://www.fiba.com
Biathlon	International Biathlon Union (IBU)	http://www.biathlonworld.com
Bobsleigh	International Bobsleigh and Skeleton Federation (IBSF)	http://www.ibsf.org
Boxing	Association Internationale de Boxe Amateur (AIBA)	http://www.aiba.org
Canoe/kayak	International Canoe Federation (ICF)	http://www.canoeicf.com
Curling	World Curling Federation (WCF)	http://www.worldcurling.org
Cycling	Union Cycliste Internationale (UCI)	http://www.uci.org
Equestrian	Fédération Équestre Internationale (FEI)	http://www.horsesport.org
Fencing	Fédération Internationale d'Escrime (FIE)	http://www.fie.org
Football	Fédération Internationale de Football Association (FIFA)	http://www.fifa.com

(continues)

Table 9-1 International Sport Federations (Recognized Olympic Sports) (*Continued*)

Sport	International Federation	Website
Golf	International Golf Federation (IGF)	http://www.igfgolf.org
Gymnastics	Fédération Internationale de Gymnastique (FIG)	http://www.fig-gymnastics.com
Handball	International Handball Federation (IHF)	http://www.ihf.info
Hockey	Fédération Internationale de Hockey sur Gazon (FIH)	http://www.fih.ch
Ice Hockey	International Ice Hockey Federation (IIHF)	http://www.iihf.com
Judo	International Judo Federation (IJF)	http://www.ijf.org
Karate*	International Traditional Karate Federation (ITKF)	http://www.itkf.org
Luge	Fédération Internationale de Luge de Course (FIL)	http://www.fil-luge.org
Modern pentathlon	Union Internationale de Pentathlon Moderne (UIPM)	http://www.uipmworld.org
Rowing	Fédération Internationale des Sociétés d'Aviron (FISA)	http://www.worldrowing.com
Rugby	World Rugby (WR)	http://www.worldrugby.org
Sailing	World Sailing (WS)	http://www.sailing.org
Shooting	International Shooting Sport Federation (ISSF)	http://www.issf-sports.org
Skateboarding*	International Skateboarding Federation (ISF)	http://www.international skateboardingfederation.org
Skating	International Skating Union (ISU)	http://www.isu.org
Skiing	Fédération Internationale de Ski (FIS)	http://www.fis-ski.com
Swimming and diving	Fédération Internationale de Natation (FINA)	http://www.fina.org
Softball*	World Baseball Softball Confederation (WBSC)	http://www.wbsc.org
Sport climbing*	International Federation of Sport Climbing (IFSC)	http://www.ifsc-climbing.org
Surfing*	International Surfing Association (ISA)	http://www.isasurf.org
Table tennis	International Table Tennis Federation (ITTF)	http://www.ittf.com
Taekwondo	World Taekwondo Federation (WTF)	http://www.worldtaekwondo federation.net
Tennis	International Tennis Federation (ITF)	http://www.itftennis.com
Triathlon	International Triathlon Union (ITU)	http://www.triathlon.org
Volleyball	Fédération Internationale de Volleyball (FIVB)	http://www.fivb.org
Weightlifting	International Weightlifting Federation (IWF)	http://www.iwf.net
Wrestling	Fédération Internationale des Luttes Associées (FILA)	http://www.unitedworld wrestling.org

* Denotes a newly added sport for the 2020 Summer Olympics.
Data from http://www.olympic.org/uk/sports/index_uk.asp (2017), http://www.wbsc.org, http://www.itkf.org, http://www.internationalskateboarding federation.org, http://www.ifsc-climbing.org, http://www.isasurf.org

NGBs are also typically involved in selecting the athletes and coaches to represent a country in international competition. These selection processes differ by sport. Some sports, such as baseball or hockey, must make decisions about athlete eligibility when the Olympic Games take place during a regularly scheduled season. In North America, this particularly affects MLB or NHL players. The NHL did not allow its players to compete in the 2018 Winter Olympic Games in South Korea. In contrast, the WNBA, whose season coincides with the Summer Olympic Games, allows its players to represent their home countries and no league games are played during the Olympic competition time. NGBs will weigh in on these types of discussions to help determine a workable solution for the sport and the athletes. In line with the sport's IF, NGBs ensure the growth and development of a given sport in a country.

As mentioned earlier, the Olympic Movement is about more than elite athletes. It also provides support for grassroots- and community-level sport and physical activity. The next section discusses how the IOC accomplishes this through the Sport and Active Society Commission.

Sport and Active Society Commission

Formerly known as the Sport for All Commission, the IOC's Sport and Active Society Commission serves to advise the IOC president, executive board, and members on the role of sport in creating a more active society. The commission has three primary responsibilities. First, it facilitates collaboration among organizations working to improve accessibility to sport as a human right. Second, it provides support in the development and inclusion of relevant activities, which promote an active lifestyle while implementing the Olympic Agenda. Last, it seeks to engage a broad range of stakeholders in leveraging the Olympic Games and major sport events for increased physical activity and community involvement in host cities. As part of this role, the IOC is not only involved in advocating for the role of sport in promoting social change, but has also developed toolkits for sport leaders and educators around the world to implement in their communities.

Paralympic Movement

The Paralympic Games, where the world's elite athletes with physical disabilities compete, represent one of the world's largest sporting extravaganzas. In 2016, 4,328 athletes from 159 countries plus a team of Independent Paralympic Athletes competed at the Rio Paralympic Games (International Paralympic Committee [IPC], n.d.c). In 2012 in London, 4,237 athletes from 164 countries competed (IPC, n.d.b). A wide variety of athletes with disabilities compete in the Paralympic Games, including amputees, athletes who use wheelchairs, athletes with visual impairments, dwarfs, athletes with cerebral palsy, athletes with spinal cord injuries, and a limited number of athletes with intellectual disabilities. Introduced in Rome in 1960, the Summer Paralympic Games have been held every Olympic year since then. The Winter Paralympic competition began in 1976 in Sweden (Hums & MacLean, 2018). The 2010 Vancouver Paralympic Games featured 502 athletes from 42 countries (IPC, n.d.e), and the 2014 Winter Paralympic Games in Sochi included 547 athletes from 45 countries (IPC, n.d.d). Ever since 1988 in Seoul, South Korea, the Paralympic Games have immediately followed the competition dates of the Olympic Games and shared common facilities.

It is important to note that the Olympic Movement and **Paralympic Movement** are governed by separate sport organizations. The IOC does not oversee the **International Paralympic Committee (IPC)**, and the IPC does not oversee the IOC. Rather, they are partners working together year-round, but particularly at Games time, when they work together to stage the month-long celebration of sport that includes both the 16 days of the Olympic Games and the 10 days of the Paralympic Games. The Paralympic Games commence two weeks after the Olympic flame is extinguished, with competitions taking place in the same cities and the same venues as the Olympic Games.

Organizers of the Paralympic Games face the same major challenge as do organizers of the Olympic Games: raising money to cover operating costs. With the Paralympic Games increasing in size and scope, the Games must generate revenues from corporate sponsorships, licensing agreements, and ticket sales. The IPC currently has six designated worldwide partners—VISA, Toyota, Otto Bock, Samsung, Panasonic, and Atos. Other levels of sponsorship include international partners (Allianz and BP), official suppliers (DB Schenker and 361°), and government partners (the German Ministry of the Interior, the Regional Government of North Rhine-Wesfalia, and the City of Bonn). The Agitos Foundation provides an additional source of revenue. According to the IPC, the Agitos Foundation works (IPC, n.d.a, paras. 3–4):

> . . . on a global basis to attract funding—philanthropic donations and grants—as well as a wide range of non-financial strategic support. Our key focus is to distribute these resources and expertise to the parts of the world where they are most needed. We do this by designing and delivering a number of core programmes that address common worldwide issues. This includes making grants available to the IPC membership.

As mentioned earlier, the Paralympic Games are not governed by the IOC, and thus do not share in the millions of dollars generated by the Olympic Movement. Instead, the Paralympic Games are governed by the IPC, which is headquartered in Bonn, Germany.

The Paralympic Movement does, however, have an organizational structure similar to that of the Olympic Movement. The IPC oversees National Paralympic Committees (NPCs). In May 2001, U.S. Paralympics became a division of the USOC. This structure is not the case in other countries, which usually have an independently operating NPC. In addition, the IPC recognizes 15 independent International Sport Federations and acts as the International Sport Federation for an additional 10 sports. Since the 2004 Athens Summer Games, management of the Olympic and Paralympic Games has been overseen by the host city's OCOG. For example, in 2016 the local organizing committee for the Olympic Games, Rio2016, was responsible for staging both the Olympic and Paralympic Summer Games. The same was true for PyeongChang, South Korea, for the 2018 Winter Paralympic Games (PyeongChang2018), and it will be true for Tokyo, Japan, in 2020 for the Summer Games as well. As it stands now, the Paralympic Games are included as a required element of a candidate city's bid proposal to host the Olympic Games.

While the Olympic and Paralympic Games are seen as the flagship events in international sport, they are not the only examples. Professional sport leagues, teams, and events also showcase sport on the international stage.

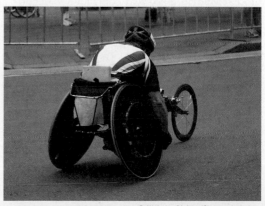

© Nicholas Rjabow/Shutterstock, Inc.

Professional Sport

Earlier in the chapter, you learned of the international reach and popularity of several new sports (e.g., bandy, cricket) and how they continue to grow through the globalization of sport. We have discussed the strong tradition of sport in local communities through the sport club system. It is also important to develop a better understanding of the scope of the largest international professional sport—football (i.e., soccer). Football is actively played and followed by billions of people across the globe, and its finances will soon be measured in trillions rather than billions of dollars or euros. The top five leagues worldwide include the English Premier League, Spanish La Liga, German Bundesliga, Italian Serie A, and French Lique 1. Many people may not realize the financial magnitude of these professional football leagues.

Unlike North American professional leagues, where players are acquired through drafts and traded between teams, football clubs instead buy and sell the rights to players. These transactions include **transfer fees** that can generate a great deal of revenue for an organization. For example, Real Madrid paid a transfer fee to Manchester United in excess of $130 million to acquire Cristiano Ronaldo in 2009. The club acquiring a player must then negotiate a contract with that individual player. In the case of Real Madrid, a six-year contract was negotiated with Ronaldo with a reported annual value of around $35 million. In 2016, Ronaldo and Real Madrid negotiated a new five-year contract worth more than $56 million per year.

These financial figures raise questions about how professional football clubs can afford these types of expenses. In 2015–2016, the top 20 football clubs in Europe combined to generated almost $8 billion in total revenues from match day, broadcast, and commercial sources (Boor, Green, Hanson, & Winn, 2017). These figures exclude the player transfer fees previously discussed. The average European football club generates commercial (43%) and broadcast (38%) revenues, followed by 18% from match-day revenues (Boor et al., 2017). Manchester United, Real Madrid, and FC Barcelona are the world's three top revenue-generating clubs.

Another important trend in international professional sport is the emergence of eSports. Traditional sport venues, including Madison Square Garden and the Staples Center in Los Angeles, have begun hosting sold-out eSports events. Revenues associated with eSports have grown from $194 million in 2014 to $463 million in 2016 (Newzoo, 2016). By 2019, industry experts expect that the eSports will generate revenues in excess of $1 billion. These revenue streams attracted the attention of not only sport facilities, but also sport media. ESPN now has a dedicated eSports platform and traditional TV networks around the world are broadcasting increasing numbers of live events.

Traditional professional sport teams have also entered the eSports market. For example, Paris Saint-Germain, one of the world's top revenue-generating football clubs, recently revealed the creation of a competitive gaming team. Its eSports team wears the same logo, colors, and apparel as the more well-known football team (PSG eSports, 2017). Several other professional sport organizations have similarly created eSports divisions to connect with younger generations and further build their global brands. Examples include Ajax (Netherlands), AS Roma (Italy), F.C. Copenhagen (Denmark), Manchester City (England), Milwaukee Bucks (United States), Philadelphia 76ers (United States), and Valencia (Spain). In a similar move, the NBA is creating an eSports league, in which NBA franchises will support and operate eSports teams (Fischer & Lombardo, 2017).

So far we have focused on international sport on the largest scale. But around the world children kick soccer balls on playgrounds and in villages, sport provides **refugees** displaced by wars and conflicts with a small sense of normalcy, and everyday people participate in sport because in many ways that participation improves their lives. This type of activity often falls under the umbrella of sport for development and peace.

Sport for Development and Peace

For years, the United Nations has used annual themes to bring attention to issues that its members believe the world needs to recognize. One of these years, 2005, was identified as the International Year of Sport and Physical Education. The UN-themed year stimulated growth in the number of organizations using sport as a tool to promote positive social change (Schulenkorf, in press). This area of international sport is referred to as sport for development and peace (SDP). More recently, the United Nations designated April 6 as the International Day for Sport for Development and Peace. As a result, a broad range of stakeholders including governments, grassroots community organizations, international sport federations, and for-profit corporations are increasingly involved in SDP (Giulianotti, Hognestad, & Spaaij, 2016). These SDP initiatives are found across low-, middle-, and high-income countries.

Before we discuss SDP in more detail, it is important to define sport, development, and peace. Sport is at the core of what we do, but it can be difficult to define. The United Nations Inter-Agency Task Force on Sport for Development and Peace suggests sport in the context of SDP refers to "all forms of physical activity that contribute to physical fitness, mental well-being and social interaction. These include: play; recreation; organized, casual or competitive sport; and indigenous sports or games" (United Nations, 2005, p. 2). Development is

also difficult to define, but important to address in order to better understand SDP. In its Declaration of Right to Development, the United Nations (1986) defined development as follows:

> [A] comprehensive economic, social, cultural and political process, which aims at the constant improvement of the well-being of the entire population and of all individuals on the basis of their active, free and meaningful participation in development and the fair distribution of benefits there from. (para. 2)

Peace is another term with a broad range of definitions. In the context of SDP, peace is primarily focused on conflict resolution and facilitating multicultural understanding. Even so, as highlighted in the challenges of defining these terms, SDP describes a broad range of programs and organizations using sport as a tool to promote positive social change. For example, Spirit of Soccer delivers landmine risk education through soccer in areas affected by conflict in Eastern Europe, the Middle East, and Asia. Waves for Change utilizes surfing to engage youth in HIV/AIDS awareness and education in South Africa. Street League uses football and dance to deliver career development training to address youth unemployment in the United Kingdom. In general, SDP programs can be divided into several categories based on their primary purposes: peace-building; post-disaster response; empowerment of girls and women; sport for persons with disabilities; and health, education, economic development, and career development. Questions may arise to whether these programs work in addressing social issues. Is there a template for sport managers to follow for success?

Whether outcomes of these SDP initiatives are positive or negative depends on many context-specific factors (e.g., Coalter, 2013). Sport managers need to critically reflect on the design of SDP programs and their funding partnerships to minimize potential unintended consequences. Many smaller SDP organizations are dependent on external funders—a relationship that is problematic because it can create a cycle of dependence whereby local program managers are hesitant to discuss unintended outcomes for fear of losing program support (Harris & Adams, 2016). A paradigm shift is needed among SDP stakeholders to embrace shared learning and working together to co-create innovative new ways in which SDP can contribute to address social issues. This requires more balanced decision making and an openness to learning from previous experiences.

Sport is not a magical solution to the world's social issues, but it may play a small role in a broader, more holistic approach geared toward addressing these issues and developing positive lasting change (Sugden, 2010). As Hartmann (2012) has suggested, "sport is best understood as a tool for development and social intervention whose influence depends upon the ends toward which it is directed, how it is implemented, and the context in which it is deployed" (p. 84). Transformational change requires inclusive decision making whereby program participants and local community leaders are actively involved in developing creative solutions to local problems (Hartmann & Kwauk, 2011; Spaaij & Jeanes, 2013). Therefore, sport managers should develop strategic short- and long-term plans for how their organizations will empower local communities to adapt and manage SDP programs over time (Schulenkorf, 2012).

Sport 4 Socialisation International (S4S) provides an example of how a SDP program can be structured. S4S was founded by Isabel De Vugt in 2007 to promote social inclusion of children with disabilities and their families in Zimbabwe. Approximately 80% of people with disabilities live in low- and middle-income countries and are often denied fundamental human rights and opportunities to education, health care, employment, and sport. S4S uses sport as a tool to empower youth with disabilities and their families. The organization also operates support groups, awareness programs, and advocacy efforts targeting families of youth with disabilities and local communities to promote sustainable social change and social inclusion of people with disabilities.

In summary, SDP is an emerging area of international sport whereby organizations and managers use sport as a platform to address social issues in communities worldwide. The number of organizations involved in this area has increased rapidly during the last decade, with a broad range of programs becoming available. Sport managers need to be aware of the importance of program structure, promoting local ownership, and the nature of funding partnerships for long-term sustainability of SDP organizations.

Career Opportunities

The sport management industry continues to evolve internationally, and potential job opportunities exist within a broad range of organizations in the private, public, and nonprofit sectors. International career opportunities in sport management vary between regions and countries. The following discussion highlights *some* of these potential opportunities and provides examples of organizations and events from countries around the world. It is important, however, to recognize the myriad and diverse opportunities in international sport. Anyone interested in pursuing an international career should conduct additional research on specific regions and segments of the sport industry to develop a better understanding of future opportunities.

Sport Agencies

The number of agencies specializing in sport continues to grow as the sport industry evolves. These specialized agencies provide services related to sport marketing, media, event operations, facility management, sales, licensing, athlete management, sponsorship activation, organizational management consulting, and more. Multidimensional agencies such as Lagardère Sports—employing more than 1,600 people—provide customized solutions to clients by leveraging expertise in core sport management areas across a broad range of sports, ranging from Formula 1 and rugby to cricket and team handball.

The emerging role of technology in sport has also resulted in agencies such as Finnish-based Uplause providing interactive crowd games for large sport teams and events worldwide to engage spectators through innovative technology. An example is No Goal, in which an animation of a soccer player getting ready to attempt a penalty kick appears on the stadium screens. Fans are encouraged to make noise: The more noise they make, the better chance the soccer player in the animation has of making a successful penalty kick rather than having his kick result in a "no goal." Typically, the games are associated with a sponsor, which garners brand recognition from the fans through this relationship. Uplause works with a broad range of clients across 20 countries around the world. These types of agencies need passionate and knowledgeable managers to organize and lead partnerships with professional sport teams and major event organizers.

Professional Sport Leagues and Clubs

Professional sport leagues also provide potential career opportunities in international sport. These positions require a detailed understanding of the sport, the organization, and the local culture and business environment. Many of the world's top sport leagues are in football (soccer) due to this sport's global popularity—for example, Bundesliga (Germany), Premier League (England), La Liga

(Spain), Serie A (Italy), Ligue 1 (France), Serie A (Brazil), and Liga MX (Mexico). Opportunities in other international sports include the Australian Football League (Australia), Nippon Professional Baseball (Japan), National Rugby League (Australia), and Super Rugby (Australia, New Zealand, and South Africa). Similar to the major professional leagues in North America, the largest professional sport clubs competing in these leagues have front-office staff members who specialize in marketing, communication, legal issues, accounting, finance, operations, facility management, community engagement, licensing, and crowd management. In a new twist, these organizations are also looking for individuals with a creative mindset and clear understanding of the eSports movement.

Similar to how employers in many English-speaking countries are increasingly looking for job candidates with bilingual or multilingual skills due to the globalization of sport, job opportunities require prospective employees to at least be fluent in the local language.

Sport Mega-Events and International Sport Competitions

Large-scale sport events are organized by local organizing committees (LOCs). The Olympic and Paralympic Games are the most well recognized, but other international sport events such as the Commonwealth Games or the Rugby World Cup provide similar career opportunities. Sport managers are often hired years ahead of time due to the logistical demands of large-scale sporting events. Thus, it is important to stay current on the bidding process for sport-mega events to be familiar with future sites and potential job opportunities. A useful website for this purpose is insidethegames.biz, which provides information about events many years in advance or while an event is taking place. Upcoming major international sport events include the 2018 Commonwealth Games in Gold Coast City, Australia; the 2019

Asian Games in Hanoi, Vietnam; and the 2020 Summer Olympic and Paralympic Games in Tokyo, Japan. These events involve between 6,000 and 10,000 athletes. Those interested in pursuing a career with international sport competitions should also consider working with sport agencies specializing in event management, as services are often outsourced to these organizations.

International Sport Federations

As noted earlier, international federations serve as the governing bodies for their respective sports. These organizations develop uniform rules, oversee and provide support to regional and national governing bodies, and promote their given sport. IFs also organize international competitions and world championship events. International football (soccer) provides opportunities for those interested in sport event management with the FIFA World Cups in Russia (2018) and Qatar (2022). Other sport-specific events range from the FEI World Equestrian Games, which are held every 4 years (2018 United States), to biannual events, such as the FINA World Championships (2019 South Korea; 2021 Japan; 2023 Qatar). SportAccord—an umbrella organization for IFs—is a useful source for anyone interested in learning more about sport governing bodies.

National Sport Confederations

A national sport confederation is an umbrella organization for all national sport federations and is responsible for a nation's elite and amateur sports. Its role includes representing and advocating for its members in national and international matters. The broad range of responsibilities of these organizations requires staff members with expertise in many different areas. For example, the Swedish Sport Confederation has departments dedicated to communication, marketing, legal issues, political affairs, finance, sport development (elite, youth, and recreation), anti-doping, and education. Similar to professional sport leagues and clubs, working for national sport confederations often requires knowledge of the local language.

Sport for Development and Peace

The growth of organizations using sport to promote social change provides a broad range of potential job opportunities. These career opportunities are primarily with nonprofit organizations operating grassroots SDP programs (e.g., Fight for Peace, Play International, Futbol Más, Street League, Sport 4 Socialisation, Right to Play). Fundraising and monitoring/evaluating program success are two of the biggest challenges facing SDP organizations. Strong analytical and critical-thinking skills are important attributes for employees, as a greater emphasis is being put on the strategic management of SDP organizations. Other potential career opportunities exist with funding agencies such as Comic Relief or the Laureus Sport for Good Foundation. The International Platform for Sport and Development (sportanddev.org, 2013) is a valuable resource for the latest job and internship opportunities in this area of international sport.

Sporting Goods

Globalization of sport is also found in the sporting goods industry. Sporting goods companies such as Nike, adidas, and Puma provide career opportunities in many areas, including sales, marketing, and environmental sustainability. For example, Li-Ning—one of the largest sporting goods companies in China—is aggressively expanding across international boundaries. Since 2012, Li-Ning has had an endorsement contract with the NBA Miami Heat's Dwayne Wade. The World Federation of Sporting Goods Industry (WFSGI) is a valuable resource for those interested in learning more about potential international career opportunities in the sporting goods industry. The WFSGI website provides a comprehensive list of its members.

Sporting goods companies are also increasingly involved in SDP. For example, Nike created Sport for Social Change networks in South America, Africa, and Europe to promote collaboration among SDP organizations. These initiatives need to be managed by professional staff to balance the diverse needs of each member organization.

Corporate Sponsors

Prospective sport management professionals sometimes overlook career opportunities with corporate sponsors because these organizations do not directly operate sporting events or services. Sport-specific positions, however, have emerged within many of these organizations as a result of the growth in sport sponsorships. Corporations often employ full-time staff members with marketing and sales expertise to manage and activate their sport-related sponsorships. For example, Jaguar Land Rover is the presenting sponsor for the Invictus Games. The corporation has dedicated staff who manage relationships and activate the firm's sponsorships through additional programs and on-site activities.

The IOC's **TOP** (The Olympic Partners) sponsor program provides a wealth of useful examples in this sector. Think about when you are watching the Olympic Games—which ads do you see? Of course, you may readily recall McDonald's, Coca-Cola, and VISA. These companies are considered official worldwide sponsors of the IOC and pay to own the exclusive rights in designated product categories. McDonald's is the official retail food services of the IOC, Coca-Cola is the official non-alcoholic beverage, and VISA is the official consumer payment system. To secure one of these exclusive sponsorship categories, these companies paid approximately 100 million euros (a little more than $110 million) for the 2013–2016 Olympic time frame (ISPO, 2016).

Organizing Committees for the Olympic Games

Jobs become available with the Organizing Committees for the Olympic Games from the time the committee is formed (approximately 6 years prior to the Games). However, the 3 years before the Games are a crucial time for recruiting the right staff to work at the Olympic and Paralympic Games. The available jobs can be related to any of the aspects needed to organize the Games, including administration, hospitality, international relations, language services, logistics, protocol, technology, transportation, and ticketing. Usually jobs with OCOGs are temporary, lasting until the Games are over. However, some people work for one organizing committee after another because they have become experts in a specific area and enjoy living in a variety of different settings. The most appealing part of working for an Organizing Committee is the unique experience it offers. The drawback is that such work is temporary and usually does not provide an opportunity to grow inside the organization. Most of the time, an employee is hired to perform a specific task without room for advancement.

National Olympic Committees

Many different job opportunities exist within a National Olympic Committee (NOC). Depending on its size, an NOC can have anywhere from zero to 100 or more employees. In the United States, the USOC is a large organization, employing approximately 375 people. This number can fluctuate during Olympic/Paralympic Games years. In the case of the USOC, many employees are hired via internships. The USOC offers a formal internship program, soliciting applications and conducting interviews prior to hiring interns. Job opportunities at the USOC vary, but include positions in athlete development, broadcasting, coaching, corporate sponsorship, fundraising, government relations, grants, human resources, international games preparation, international relations and protocol, legal aspects, licensing, management information systems, marketing, national events and conferences, public information and media relations, sports medicine, sports science, sports for people with disabilities, and training centers. In addition, working with an NOC may be helpful in securing a position with one of the many NGBs within each country's sport movement. Again, the number of opportunities will vary greatly from country to country and from sport to sport. If you are a student with an interest in working in international sport, we highly recommend you consider applying to the USOC internship program.

International Paralympic Committee

Similar to the IOC, the IPC offers employment opportunities for sport managers, including interns. Sport managers interested in working for the IPC should contact its office in Bonn, Germany, directly for additional information. Just as with the IOC, language fluency is necessary.

Current Issues

Choice of Host City for the Olympic and Paralympic Games

Hosting an Olympic and Paralympic Games was once seen as a badge of honor for the host city and country. Recently, however, fewer cities have expressed interest for various reasons (Zimbalist, 2015), most notably the negative economic impact and political fallout of the Games (Somin, 2017, paras. 5–9):

> An Olympic host city has to plan, pay for and construct massive sporting venues and infrastructure projects. . . . with little discernible economic benefit . . . host governments for the Olympics and the World Cup often resort to such

cruel tactics as forcibly displacing large numbers of people in order to make way for sports facilities . . . large-scale international sports events are also often used as propaganda showcases by authoritarian host governments. . . . That just adds political insult to economic injury.

The recent bidding contest for the 2022 Winter Olympic and Paralympic Games opened with interest from Almaty, Kazakhstan; Beijing, China; Krakow, Poland; and Stockholm, Sweden. Krakow and Stockholm withdrew their bids before Beijing was ultimately awarded the event. The 2024 Summer Olympic and Paralympic Games originally featured five cities in the running—Budapest, Hungary; Hamburg, Germany; Los Angeles, United States; Paris, France; and Rome, Italy. The USOC replaced Boston with Los Angeles as public support waned for the historic Massachusetts city. Later, Hamburg, Rome, and Budapest would drop out, leaving a two-horse race between Los Angeles and Paris.

In an attempt to make the bidding process more of an invitation, in 2013 the IOC released the document titled Agenda 2020. Meant to serve as a strategic roadmap for the future of the Olympic Movement, some of the key elements of Agenda 2020 include the following (IOC, 2013, para. 2):

- Changes to the candidature procedure, with a new philosophy to invite potential candidate cities to present a project that fits their sporting, economic, social and environmental long-term planning needs.
- Reducing costs for bidding, by decreasing the number of presentations that are allowed and providing a significant financial contribution from the IOC.
- Move from a sport-based to an event-based program.

Time will tell whether the strategies presented in this document will ignite interest in future cities entering the bidding process. At present, the Games are at a bit of a crossroads owing to their escalating costs and questionable legacies. While the allure of hosting the world's premier multisport event remains, the choice of future locations will most certainly continue to generate great debate.

Sport and Human Rights

When people in the United States think of human rights, they often think of rights such as freedom of speech or freedom from government-controlled religion. In reality, human rights are much broader than that definition. Amnesty International (2017) defines **human rights**, which are basic rights and freedoms all people are entitled to, by explaining that:

> Human rights include civil and political rights, such as the right to life, liberty and freedom of expression; and social, cultural and economic rights including the right to participate in culture, the right to food, and the right to work and receive an education. Human rights are protected and upheld by international and national laws and treaties (para. 2).

You might be wondering right now why a discussion of human rights appears in a text on sport management. There are actually two ways to frame the relationship between sport and human rights: (1) sport as a human right and (2) using sport to promote human rights (Wolff & Hums, 2014). Sport organizations such as the IOC recognize sport as a human right. The Olympic Charter states, "The practice of sport is a human right" (IOC, 2015, p. 13), and people should have the opportunity to be active in sport in an environment that is free from discrimination. In 2017, the IOC added a human rights clause to its Host City Contract (Etchells, 2017, paras. 11–12):

Host cities have an obligation to "protect and respect human rights and ensure any violation of human rights is remedied in a manner consistent with international agreements, laws and regulations applicable in the host country." It goes onto say that this should be done "in a manner consistent with all internationally recognised human rights standards and principles, including the United Nations Guiding Principles on Business and Human Rights, applicable in the host country."

Sport can also be used to promote human rights, as when athletes speak out on behalf of justice and social causes. Here one can harken back to the likes of the iconic Muhammad Ali, or more recently to NFL quarterback Colin Kaepernick and his choice to kneel during the national anthem in protest of the unfair treatment of African Americans in the United States, or the work of Hudson Taylor's Athlete Ally organization that promotes fair treatment of the LGBTQ community. Brave athletes champion the cause of human rights both on and off the field of play, and brave sport managers support them.

Refugee Athletes

Recent world events have forced people to move from their home countries to avoid wars and conflict. According to the most recent figures released in 2016 by the United Nations High Commissioner on Refugees (UNCHR), 65.3 million people are refugees, a number that surpasses even the number of displaced persons following World War II (McKirdy, 2016; UNHCR, 2016). Life as a refugee involves a constant state of flux and disarray, often laced with violence and fear, as people realize they have no home country to which to return and no known new country as a destination.

In the midst of such uncertainty, it is pivotal that when refugees do settle in a new location, something can be brought into their lives to offer a bit of familiarity, comfort, and a sense of connection. According to sportanddev.org (2013), sport offers five primary ways to rehabilitate refugees: (1) dealing with trauma, (2) improving conditions in refugee camps, (3) integrating with other groups or members of the host communities, (4) building skills for employability, and (5) providing an alternative to destructive behavior.

Refugee status is particularly difficult for children. Sport can serve as a vehicle to assist children during this traumatic time and help raise self-esteem. According to the UNHCR (2017, paras. 2–3):

> Sports programmes can help counteract psychosocial problems and environmental and health issues as well as stress and loneliness. They contribute to physical fitness, mental well-being and social integration by providing a safe forum in which a child can develop physically, emotionally and mentally.
>
> . . . sport can act as a vehicle for learning. This is extremely important for refugee girls, who may be deprived of other avenues for growth because of cultural beliefs or time-consuming chores.

A number of sport organizations have stepped up to help refugees around the world. Bayern Munich, for example, has donated $1.1 million to charitable organizations that work with refugees (McGowan, 2015). Other football clubs have made donations or taken public actions to show support for refugees, including Scottish champions Celtic, as well as FC Augsburg and Borussia Dortmund of Bundesliga (Whaling & Flanagan, 2015). Numerous sports people have spoken out against the Muslim-country travel ban issued by the United States, including the NBA's Luol Deng, Greg Popovich, and Steve Kerr, and soccer stars Megan Rapinoe and Alex Morgan.

The International Olympic Committee established a Refugee Olympic Team that competed for the first time at the 2016 Summer Olympic Games in Rio. This squad consisted of 10 athletes who marched in opening ceremonies under the Olympic flag—five competitors in field and track, two swimmers, two competitors in judo, and one marathoner (BBC, 2016). The IPC did this as well: In Rio, the Independent Paralympic Athletes Team included one swimmer and one discus thrower. One thing is for certain: Until worldwide political climates and aggressions change, there is no end in sight for multitudes of refugees in need of basic human dignity. People in sport can take the lead here.

Player Migration

The increased globalization of sport has resulted in **player migration**—that is, the migration of athletes across borders, predominately from low- and middle-income countries to high-income countries in Asia, Europe, and North America (Poli, 2010). For example, Major League Baseball clubs operate their own athlete academies throughout the Caribbean, while the world's top football clubs have similar academies across Africa. In addition, thousands of other nonsanctioned academies have also emerged where youth are recruited through lofty promises about the opportunity to become high-profile superstar athletes. Unfortunately, these academies often demand large sums of money from families, and people working with those academies may require athletes to sign contracts ensuring they will receive a large portion of any future player contracts (McDougall, 2008). These academies often even require children to drop out of school to only focus on a given sport.

There are exceptions where professional sport teams operate certified academies with not only sport training, but also rigorous educational programs. Unfortunately, many others exploit young athletes and illegally traffic them to high-income countries in hopes of making money from their athletic ability (Poli, 2010). Those athletes who do not succeed in securing a professional contract are often abandoned in a foreign country. Addressing issues associated with this type of exploitation of youth is critical for the sport management community (Thibault, 2009).

Summary

As this chapter illustrates, the term "international sport" encompasses a wide variety of sport activities, including elite-level Olympic/Paralympic sport, professional sport, and grassroots sport and physical activity that can be directed at solving social issues. As international sport becomes more professionalized, more opportunities will open up for sport managers who are willing to take their business acumen

to a different country and different culture. Job opportunities abound for those who want to broaden their horizons and work in an international business environment. The true measure of success in business today is the ability to respect and work with people of different cultures. The international sport environment allows one to be a part of the most global of industries—the sport industry. It has often been said that sport is a universal language. One needs to do no more than work an Olympic or Paralympic Games, a Premier League match, or a Formula One race to understand this power of sport.

One last piece of career advice: Learn a second language. Job applicants who can do so have a definite advantage over those who limit themselves to one language. No one language runs the world—the more you can interact with others in a native language, the more opportunities will be open to you. So get your first passport, or renew your current passport, and get on the road to an exciting career in international sport!

Case Study 9-1

The Future of Sport for Development and Peace

In the early 2000s, Kofi Annan, the United Nations Secretary General, created the UN Office on Sport for Development and Peace (UNOSDP). At the same time, he appointed the former president of Switzerland, Adolf Ogi, as the Special Adviser on Sport for Development and Peace. This formal recognition by the United Nations of sport as a tool for promoting positive social change is seen by many as the primary reason for the international growth of the SDP field during the past 15 years.

At the time of the 2016 Beyond Sport Summit (an international gathering of SDP leaders from around the world), thousands of SDP organizations

were operating SDP programs across more than 140 countries. Yet on May 4, 2017, the current United Nations Secretary General, António Guterres, suddenly announced the closure of the UNOSDP. This has raised concerns among practitioners about the immediate future of the SDP field since the UNOSDP was seen to provide a sense of legitimacy for this aspect of the international sport community.

Marc Probst, Executive Director of the Swiss Academy for Development, which operates the International Platform on Sport and Development, recognized the significance of recent events and

(continues)

The Future of Sport for Development and Peace (*Continued*)

the need for a new solution to maintain the international momentum and support for the SDP field. Sport has been recognized to serve an important role in achieving the United Nations' Sustainable Development Goals—a set of shared goals developed by world leaders from 194 countries. Probst was determined to do everything possible to maintain the involvement of stakeholders from sport because he believed it is critical for sport leaders to go above and beyond to help address local social issues and use the power of sport to transform society.

Thinking about this situation, Probst started asking himself many questions, including "How will I convince a diverse group of sport leaders to focus on the greater good and make SDP a priority?", "How do we make sure that local communities and program participants have a voice in shaping the future of SDP?", and "Which types of organizations need to be involved to ensure equality in the global leadership of SDP?"

Questions for Discussion

1. How could Probst maintain the global awareness and interest in SDP?

2. What could Probst do to ensure that the voices of local community leaders and SDP program participants are included in the global leadership of SDP?

3. Which sport industry stakeholders should Probst approach to help provide financial support for a global leadership council for SDP?

4. Which role(s) could different sport industry stakeholders (leagues, governing bodies, community sport organizations, charitable sport organizations, sponsors, ministries of sport) play in the support and development of the SDP field?

5. How could Probst utilize new technologies and the globalization of sport to create a successful global leadership council for SDP?

Other Questions for Discussion

1. Promotion and relegation are commonly used in leagues around the world, but not in North America. Do you think promotion and relegation could work in any of the North American leagues, including MLB, MLS, the NBA, the NFL, or the NHL? Why or why not? What would be the benefits of using that system? The barriers?

2. The global refugee crisis will be continuing for many years to come. As sport managers, we have an ethical obligation to help refugees who come to our countries. Which steps could an NCAA college athletic department take to help refugees settle into their new homes? What could

local recreation programs such as a YMCA do?

3. The International Paralympic Committee currently has six worldwide partners—VISA, Toyota, Otto Bock, Samsung, Panasonic, and Atos. If you were working for the marketing department of the IPC, which additional sponsors might you reach out to that might be a good match as a new worldwide partner? Why?

4. Jersey sponsorships have long played a central role in generating revenues for the world's leading professional soccer clubs, but are used only on game jerseys in the WNBA and MLS in North America. The NBA recently became the first of the

"Big Four" professional leagues in North America to launch a pilot program allowing for jersey sponsorships on NBA jerseys. Why have NFL, MLB, and NHL teams not pursued jersey sponsorships? Which teams and sponsors do you believe would be a good match for jersey sponsorships in the United States? Why?

5. eSports is projected to grow exponentially over the next few years and is increasingly attracting major sport organizations to this emerging market segment. What do leaders of professional sport teams need to do to successfully integrate eSports with

their regular sport team(s) and events? How would you manage the potential generational differences in how fans perceive eSports?

6. The international sport industry offers a broad range of career opportunities across different areas of specialization. If you were the hiring manager for an international sport organization (e.g., a sport event agency), which skills, abilities, and experiences would you prioritize? How can this information help you prepare yourself for a potential sport management career outside of North America?

Key Terms

club system, globalization, human rights, International Olympic Committee (IOC), International Paralympic Committee (IPC), Olympic Movement, Paralympic Movement, player migration, promotion/relegation, refugees, TOP program, transfer fees

References

Amnesty International. (2017). Human rights basics. Retrieved from http://www.amnestyusa.org/research/human-rights-basics

BBC. (2016, August 21). Rio Olympics 2016: Refugee athletes competed as "equal human beings." Retrieved from http://www.bbc.com/sport/olympics/37037273

Boor, S. Green, M., Hanson, C., & Winn, C. (2017). The Deloitte football money league. Retrieved from https://www2.deloitte.com/global/en/pages/consumer-business/articles/deloitte-football-money-league.html

Coalter, F. (2013). "There is loads of relationships here": Developing a programme theory for sport-for-change programmes. *International Review for the Sociology of Sport*, *48*(5), 594–612.

Etchells, D. (2017). IOC adds human rights clause to Host City Contract. Retrieved from

http://www.insidethegames.biz/articles/1047571/ioc-adds-human-rights-clause-to-host-city-contract

Fischer, B., & Lombardo, J. (2017, February 9), NBA, Take-Two Interactive set to launch e-sports league around "NBA2k" game. *SportsBusinessDaily, 23*(104). Retrieved from https://www.sportsbusinessdaily.com/Daily/Issues/2017/02/09

Giulianotti, R., Hognestad, H., & Spaaij, R. (2016). Sport for development and peace: Power, politics, and patronage. *Journal of Global Sport Management*, *1*(3-4), 1–13.

Harris, K., & Adams, A. (2016). Power and discourse in the politics of evidence in sport for development. *Sport Management Review*, *19*(2), 97–106.

Hartmann, D. (2012). Rethinking community-based crime prevention through sports. In R. J. Schinke & S. J. Hanrahan (Eds.), *Sport for development, peace, and social justice* (pp. 73–88). Morgantown, WV: Fitness Information Technology.

Hartmann, D., & Kwauk, C. (2011). Sport and development: An overview, critique, and reconstruction. *Journal of Sport and Social Issues, 35*(3), 284–305.

Hums, M. A., & MacLean, J.C. (2018). *Governance and policy in sport organizations* (4th ed.). New York, NY: Routledge.

International Olympic Committee (IOC). (2013). Olympic Agenda 2020. Retrieved from https://www.olympic.org/olympic -agenda-2020

International Olympic Committee (IOC). (2015). *Olympic charter.* Lausanne, Switzerland: Author.

International Olympic Committee (IOC). (2017a.). International sports federations. Retrieved from https://www.olympic.org /ioc-governance-international-sports -federations

International Olympic Committee (IOC). (2017b). Members. Retrieved from https://www .olympic.org/ioc-members-list

International Olympic Committee (IOC). (2017c). National Olympic Committees (NOCs). Retrieved from https://www.olympic.org /ioc-governance-national-olympic-committees

International Olympic Committee (IOC). (2017d). The organisation. Retrieved from https:// www.olympic.org/about-ioc-institution

International Paralympic Committee (IPC). (n.d.a). About us. Retrieved from https:// www.paralympic.org/agitos-foundation /about-us

International Paralympic Committee (IPC). (n.d.b). London 2016. Retrieved from https:// www.paralympic.org/london-2012

International Paralympic Committee (IPC). (n.d.c). Rio 2016. Retrieved from https:// www.paralympic.org/rio-2016

International Paralympic Committee (IPC). (n.d.d). Sochi 2014. Retrieved from https:// www.paralympic.org/sochi-2014

International Paralympic Committee (IPC). (n.d.e). Vancouver. Retrieved from https:// www.paralympic.org/vancouver-2010

ISPO. (2016, July 29). Sponsors at the Olympics: The multi-billion dollar business of the IOC. Retrieved from http://www.ispo.com/en /markets/id_78544462/2-billion-what-the -sponsors-are-paying-at-the-olympics.html

Li, M., MacIntosh, E., & Bravo, G. (2012). *International sport management.* Champaign, IL: Human Kinetics

McDougall, D. (2008, January 6). The scandal of Africa's trafficked players. Retrieved from https://www.theguardian.com/football/2008 /jan/06/newsstory.sport4

McGowan, T. (2015, September 3). Bayern Munich donate $1.1 million to help refugees. Retrieved from http://edition .cnn.com/2015/09/03/football/refugees -bayern-munich-borussia-dortmund-syria /index.html

McKirdy, E. (2016.) UNHCR report: More displaced now than after WWII. Retrieved from http://www.cnn.com/2016/06/20/world /unhcr-displaced-peoples-report/

Newzoo. (2016). Global esports market report. Retrieved from https://newzoo.com/insights /markets/esports/

Poli, R. (2010). Understanding globalization through football: The new international division of labour, migratory channels and transnational trade circuits. *International Review for the Sociology of Sport, 45*(4), 491–506.

PSG eSports. (2017). News. Retrieved from https:// psg-esports.com/home/

Riksidrottsförbundet. (2017). Idrotten i siffror. Retrieved from http://www.rf.se/globalassets /riksidrottsforbundet/dokument/statistik /idrotten_i_siffror_rf_2016.pdf

Schulenkorf, N. (2012). Sustainable community development through sport and events: A conceptual framework for Sport-for-Development projects. *Sport Management Review, 15*(1), 1–12.

Schulenkorf, N. (In press). Managing sport-for-development: Reflections and outlook. *Sport Management Review*.

Somin, I. (2017). Why cities are increasingly reluctant to host the Olympics. *Washington Post*. Retrieved from https://www .washingtonpost.com/news/volokh -conspiracy/wp/2017/02/23/why-cities -are-increasingly-reluctant-to-host-the -olympics/?utm_term=.21aaff4fbda0

Spaaij, R., & Jeanes, R. (2013). Education for social change? A Freirean critique of sport for development and peace. *Physical Education and Sport Pedagogy, 18*(4), 442–457.

sportanddev.org. (2013). Five ways sport can help rehabilitate refugees. Retrieved from https:// www.sportanddev.org/en/article/news/five -ways-sport-can-help-rehabilitate-refugees

Sugden, J. (2010). Critical left-realism and sport interventions in divided societies. *International Review for the Sociology of Sport, 45*(3), 258–272.

Thibault, L. (2009). Globalization of sport: An inconvenient truth. *Journal of Sport Management, 23*(1), 1–20.

United Nations. (1986). Resolution 41/128: Declaration on the Right to Development. Adopted at the 97th Plenary Meeting of the General Assembly. Retrieved from http:// www.un.org/documents/ga/res/41/a41r128 .htm

United Nations. (2005). Sport as a tool for development and peace: Towards achieving the United Nations millennium development goals. Retrieved from http://www.un.org /sport2005/resources/task_force.pdf

United Nations High Commissioner on Refugees (UNHCR). (2016). Figures at a glance. Retrieved from http://www.unhcr.org/en-us /figures-at-a-glance.html

United Nations High Commissioner on Refugees (UNHCR). (2017). Teaming up to give refugees a sporting chance. Retrieved from http://www.unhcr.org/en-us/sport -partnerships.html

Whaling, J., & Flanagan, A. (2015). How football clubs and fans have reacted to the refugee crisis—and what you can do to help. *The Mirror*. Retrieved from http://www.mirror .co.uk/sport/football/news/how-football -clubs-fans-reacted-6384019

Wolff, E. A., & Hums, M. A. (2014). More than a game: The nexus of sport and human rights. Retrieved from http://www .humanrightsfirst.org/blog/more-game -nexus-sport-and-human-rights

Zimbalist, A. (2015). *Circus Maximus: The economic gamble behind hosting the Olympics and the World Cup*. Washington, DC: Brookings Institute.

© Shutterstock, Inc./ Danilo_Vuletic

Part III

Professional Sport Industry

Chapter

10

Lisa P. Masteralexis and
James T. Masteralexis

Professional Sport

Learning Objectives

Upon completion of this chapter, students should be able to:

1. Compare and contrast the league structure and philosophy of the five major North American professional team sport leagues: NFL, MLB, NBA, NHL, and MLS.

2. Identify the primary sources of revenues for professional sport organizations: gate receipts, media rights fees, licensed product sales, and stadium revenues.

3. Describe the history of professional sport leagues in the United States, and explain how the leagues organized themselves using a system of self-governance rather than a corporate governance model.

4. Appraise the ownership rules of each league, and understand basic concepts such as franchise rights, territorial rights, and revenue sharing.

5. Analyze the role of the league commissioner in team sport and individual sport.

6. Distinguish the operational and philosophical differences between individual professional sports and team sports.

7. Examine the role that labor relations have played in the development and relative welfare of owners and players in North American professional sport leagues.

8. Describe the legal issues that are an important part of the professional sport industry, particularly contract, antitrust, labor, and intellectual property law.

9. Identify the various career opportunities available in professional sport and the key managerial skills needed for success.

10. Debate current issues in professional sport such as salary caps; racial diversity among players, coaches, and administrators; globalization; concussion litigation; drug testing; and analytics.

Introduction

The professional sport industry creates events and exhibitions in which athletes compete individually or on teams and are paid for their performance. The events and exhibitions are live, include a paying audience, and are sponsored by a professional league or tour. The professional sport industry is a major international business, grossing billions of dollars each year. Although leagues and events derive revenues from **gate receipts** (ticket sales) and **premium seating** (personal seat licenses, luxury suites, club seating) sales, the bulk of their revenues come from the sale of media rights. Professional sport has moved into new markets with the Internet and increased demand for television sports programming. Through the drafting of more international players by North American sport leagues and increased social media opportunities, professional sport has sought new international markets. The international sale of professional sport teams' licensed products (e.g., apparel, videos, books, memorabilia) and the worldwide availability of online services add to the industry's international growth.

North America is home to five preeminent professional leagues: Major League Baseball (MLB), the National Basketball Association (NBA), the National Football League (NFL), the National Hockey League (NHL), and Major League Soccer (MLS). As of 2017, those five leagues included 145 franchises. Each year new leagues, such as the Arena Football League (AFL), Major League Lacrosse (MLL), the National Lacrosse League (NLL), the Women's NBA (WNBA), and the National Women's Soccer League (NWSL), emerge. Some survive; others do not. The minor leagues in baseball, basketball, soccer, and hockey are far too numerous to list here. **Table 10-1** gives a breakdown of the number of major and minor league professional sport franchises operating in North America as of 2017. Numerous

professional leagues also operate throughout South America, Europe, the Middle East, Asia, Australia, and Africa in the sports of rugby and rugby union, cricket, baseball, basketball, Australian Rules and American football, soccer, hockey, and volleyball.

Professional athletes in leagues are salaried employees whose bargaining power and ability to negotiate salaries vary. In some cases, athletes are unionized, enabling them to negotiate collectively for better wages, benefits, and conditions of employment. In other cases, professional players may have little bargaining power. For instance, in the (MLB-affiliated) baseball minor leagues, unless the player has prior major league experience, the player has little leverage to negotiate. Minor league baseball salaries are relatively uniform across the league, and for many players wages fall below what would be considered a living wage. For example, a typical player's salary in the A-level league starts at $1,100 per month during the season plus a small amount of per diem money for meals incurred when on the road ($25 per day). Assuming that in an average week, half of the team's games are played at home and half at away venues, a player works (travel, practice, games, and community/ fan relations) approximately 60 hours. Players generally have 1 to 2 days off per month. At the lower levels of baseball, this is hardly a living wage. Players with some level of major league experience earn higher monthly wages ($10,000 to $15,000 per month in season and nothing out of season).

By comparison, minor league hockey players in the American Hockey League (AHL) and the ECHL (formerly the East Coast Hockey League) have far more favorable conditions because the leagues are subject to antitrust laws and the players are unionized. Through their collective bargaining agreements, the minimum salary in the AHL for 2016–2017 was $45,000 (but $32,500 for players on loan to the AHL from

Table 10-1 Number of Professional Sport Teams in North America, 2017

Sport	League	Number of Teams
Baseball	Major league (MLB) Minor league affiliates Minor league independents	30 232 53 (includes Mexican League)
Men's basketball	Major league (NBA) Minor leagues (G-League)	30 26
Women's basketball	Major league (WNBA)	12
Men's football	Major league (NFL)	32
Men's ice hockey	Major league (NHL) Minor leagues	31 76
Women's ice hockey	Major league (NWHL)	4
Men's soccer	Major league outdoor (MLS) Minor leagues (NASL, USL Pro)	22 41
Women's soccer	Major league outdoor (NWSL)	10
Men's lacrosse	Outdoor (MLL) Indoor (NLL)	9 9
Tennis	World Team Tennis	6
NASCAR	Sprint Cup (renamed Monster Energy NASCAR Cup in 2018) Nationwide Cup (renamed Xfinity Cup in 2018) Camping World Trucks Cup	20 full-time; 11 part-time 21 full-time; 11 part-time 18 full-time; 10 part-time

lesser leagues) with $74 day per diem (Professional Hockey Players' Association [PHPA], 2010). The ECHL has a minimum weekly salary due to its frequent player movement. The 2016–2017 weekly minimum fell between $400 and $500 (depending on the player's experience level), and the daily per diem was $42 per day (PHPA, 2013). However, teams were also held to a weekly salary floor of $9,500. If a team did not spend a minimum of $9,500 weekly on player salaries, the difference was paid by the club in equal allotments to all players on its roster. In sum, the AHL and ECHL through unionization have achieved very different working conditions for hockey's minor leaguers than those available for baseball's minor leaguers.

Countless professional sports events are also staged around the world in individual sports,

including action sports, boxing, fencing, figure skating, golf, tennis, racquetball, running, and track and field. Individual sports are generally organized around a tour, such as the NASCAR (National Association of Sports Car Auto Racing Sprint Cup Series), the Professional Golfers Association (PGA) Tour, and the Ladies Professional Golf Association (LPGA) Tour. An athlete on a professional tour earns prize money, and a top (seeded) player considered a "draw" might earn an appearance fee. Athletes on some tours are also required to play in professional–amateur pair events the day before the tournament. For some tours, like the LPGA, the pro-ams are the lifeblood of the sport, because they are a place where players cater to their sponsors, and players may be disqualified for failing to participate or for showing up late

(Crouse, 2010). Sponsorship provides income and the products necessary for individual athletes to compete (e.g., golf clubs, tennis racquets, and shoes). The value of sponsorship to athletes is easily apparent with just a quick look at a NASCAR vehicle or the apparel worn by a tennis player such as Serena Williams. A tour stops at various sites for events and exhibitions that are usually sponsored by one named corporation (the title sponsor) and a number of other sponsors. Some tours also have television, cable, and/or radio contracts.

Tours or exhibitions have also been created for athletes by sport agencies in sports such as tennis, golf, and figure skating. These events serve many purposes, such as generating revenue for the athletes and their agencies as well as satisfying fan interest. For instance, the 2014 "Smucker's Stars on Ice" annual tour began shortly after the Sochi Olympic Games and featured many medalists and competitors hoping to capitalize on their Olympic achievements and name recognition. Sochi Olympic ice dancing gold medalists Meryl Davis and Charlie White competed on the television program *Dancing with the Stars*. Television and cable networks have also created exhibitions for programming purposes in action sports (ESPN's X Games and NBC's Dew Tour), golf (ABC's Skins Game), and other sports (ESPN's Outdoor Games). These tours and exhibitions generate income for athletes, sport management firms, and the broadcasting industry primarily from sponsorship, media, and ticket sales. Occasionally, some of the income generated from these events is donated to charity.

History

Professional Sport Leagues

In 1869, the first professional team, baseball's Cincinnati Red Stockings, paid players to barnstorm the United States. The 10-player team's payroll totaled $9,300. At the time, the average annual salary in the United States was $170, so the average player's salary of $930 shows that as early as 1869 a professional athlete's income exceeded an average worker's wages (Jennings, 1989).

In 1876, North America's first professional sport league, baseball's National League, was organized (Jennings, 1989). Among the principles from the National League's constitution and bylaws that continue as models for professional sports today are limits on franchise movement, club territorial rights, and a mechanism for expulsion of a club. Interestingly, these rules also allowed a player to contract with a club for his future services (Berry, Gould, & Staudohar, 1986). It did not take long—just 3 years—for owners to change that rule.

Following the National League's lead, other professional leagues have organized themselves into a system of **self-governance**, as opposed to a **corporate governance model** (Lentze, 1995). Under a corporate governance model, owners act as the board of directors, and the **commissioner** acts as the chief executive officer (CEO). Although it might appear that leagues have adopted a corporate governance model, Lentze (1995) argues that the commissioner's power over the owners does not place the commissioner under the direct supervision and control of the owners in the same manner that a CEO is under the direct supervision and control of a corporate board. This distinction is made because the commissioner in a professional sport possesses decision-making power, disciplinary power, and dispute resolution authority (Lentze, 1995). The commissioner's role is discussed in greater detail later in this chapter.

In view of the fiscal challenges facing a new sport league, MLS was structured as a limited liability company, with owners initially investing $50 million in the league as a single entity to avoid financial and antitrust liability (Garber, 2004). Other leagues—the WNBA, AFL, MLL, and NLL, to name a few—have followed this trend to establish themselves as single entities to avoid antitrust liability and to create centralized fiscal control. The legal definition of a single entity is governed by substance, not form. In other words, to determine whether a league operates as a single entity, and thus is not subject to Section 1 Sherman Antitrust Act liability, one must evaluate whether the league joins together separate economic factors that would be actual or potential competitors (*American Needle v. NFL*, 2010).

Soon after MLS was established, the **single-entity structure** was scrutinized in a lawsuit. The structure withstood an antitrust challenge from MLS players, who argued that it was a sham created for the purpose of restraining competition and depressing player salaries (*Fraser v. Major League Soccer*, 2002). Although the First Circuit Court of Appeals disagreed with the players' allegations, it did not conclusively find that MLS was a single entity, instead construing it as a hybrid that settled somewhere between a traditional sports league and a single company (*Fraser v. Major League Soccer*, 2002). As a strategy, the MLS players chose not to unionize because doing so and negotiating a collective bargaining agreement would allow the league access to the labor exemption defense in an antitrust suit. After losing the lawsuit, the players established the Major League Soccer Players Union (MLSPU). Interestingly, while the WNBA maintained a similar structure, its players chose to unionize rather than pursue an antitrust challenge. Shortly after the union negotiated its second collective bargaining agreement with the league, the WNBA abandoned the single-entity league structure in favor of a traditional team ownership model. In 2010, the U.S. Supreme Court ruled that traditionally structured leagues with separate owners having individual control of their teams are not single entities for antitrust purposes (*American Needle v. NFL*, 2010).

Franchise Ownership

Historically, sport team ownership was a hobby for the wealthy, with many teams being family owned "mom and pop" businesses. While no longer operated as "mom and pop" businesses, family ownership continues. The owners of NFL clubs are listed in **Table 10-2**. For these owners, the investment is not simply a hobby, but a profitable business venture and status symbol. In the NFL, family or individual ownership is still the

Table 10-2 NFL Ownership

NFL Team	Ownership	Year Ownership Began
Arizona Cardinals	Bidwell family	1972
Atlanta Falcons	Arthur Blank	2004
Baltimore Ravens	Steven Bisciotti, Jr.	2004
Buffalo Bills	Terry and Kim Pegula	2014
Carolina Panthers	Jerry Richardson*	1993
Chicago Bears	McCaskey (Halas) family*	1983
Cincinnati Bengals	Mike Brown*	1991
Cleveland Browns	Jimmy Haslam	2012
Dallas Cowboys	Jerry Jones	1989
Denver Broncos	Pat Bowlen	1984

(continues)

Table 10-2 NFL Ownership (*Continued*)

NFL Team	Ownership	Year Ownership Began
Detroit Lions	Martha Ford	2014
Green Bay Packers	Publicly owned	1923
Houston Texans	Bob McNair*	1999
Indianapolis Colts	James Irsay	1997
Jacksonville Jaguars	Shahid Kahn	2012
Kansas City Chiefs	Hunt Family	1960*
Miami Dolphins	Steven M. Ross	2008
Minnesota Vikings	Zygi Wilf/Wilf family	2005
New England Patriots	Bob Kraft/Kraft family	1994
New Orleans Saints	Tom Benson	1985
New York Giants	Mara* family and Tisch family	1925, 1991
New York Jets	Robert Wood "Woody" Johnson	2000
Oakland Raiders	Carol and Mark Davis	2011
Philadelphia Eagles	Jeffrey Lurie	1994
Pittsburgh Steelers	Rooney family*	1933
Los Angeles Chargers	Spanos family	1984
San Francisco 49ers	Jed York	2009
Seattle Seahawks	Paul Allen	1997
Los Angeles Rams	Stan Kroenke	2010
Tampa Bay Buccaneers	Glazer family	1995
Tennessee Titans	Amy Adams Strunk	2015
Washington Redskins	Daniel Snyder	1999

* Denotes original owner or descendant of original owner.
Data from http://www.nfl.com and team websites.

norm, but the focus of these owners is on running the team like a business rather than a hobby.

Family or individual ownership is successful in the NFL because there is far more revenue sharing in this league than in the other professional leagues. Teams in other leagues with less revenue sharing are more dependent on groups of potential owners coming together to fund the purchase and operations of a team. That system

of "haves" and "have nots," however, has been under fire as more of the newer owners who have paid hundreds of millions of dollars for their teams are seeking to maximize their local revenues to make a return on their investments (Foldesy, 2004). Jerry Jones, who paid $140 million for the Dallas Cowboys, began the challenge to this system by entering into marketing deals through his stadium, some of which ambushed the league's exclusive deals and led to a legal battle with the NFL (*National Football League Properties, Inc. v. Dallas Cowboys Football Club, Ltd.*, 1996). A chasm between owners exists in the NFL because some owners have paid as much as $600 million (Steve Bisciotti, Baltimore Ravens), $700 million (Bob McNair, Houston Texans), and $800 million (Daniel Snyder, Washington Redskins) to purchase their teams, whereas others have inherited their franchises and have no acquisition costs to recover (Brown family, Cincinnati Bengals; Halas–McCaskey family, Chicago Bears; Mara family, New York Giants; Rooney family, Pittsburgh Steelers). Although a vote in 2004 extended for 15 years the NFL's Trust, which owns all team logos and trademarks, oversees and administers the league properties rights, and distributes revenues for those rights to each club, a growing number of owners are clamoring for more local control over the potential marketing revenues from using team logos, trademarks, and sponsorships. While not the sole factor in determining that the NFL was not a single entity for purposes of licensing, the battle for local control of licensing revenues undermined the NFL's argument that it was a single entity with licensed properties controlled at the league level in *American Needle v. NFL* (2010). Evidence was presented that showed the Dallas Cowboys, Miami Dolphins, and Oakland Raiders had different arrangements for their licensed properties than the other teams in the NFL, undermining the argument that the league was a single entity.

Ownership Rules

Not just anyone can become a sports franchise owner. It takes a great deal of money, of course—but even with the financial capacity and desire to purchase a team, ownership can be evasive. Permission to own a sports franchise must be granted by a league's ownership committee. Each league imposes restrictions on ownership, including a limit on the number of franchise rights granted and restrictions on franchise location. **Franchise rights**, which comprise the privileges afforded to owners, are granted with ownership. They include **territorial rights**, which limit a competitor franchise from moving into another team's territory without league permission and providing compensation to the rightsholder, as well as **revenue sharing**, which gives a team a portion of various league-wide revenues (e.g., expansion fees, national television revenues, gate receipts, and licensing revenues). Owners also receive the right to serve on ownership committees. Ownership committees exist for such areas as rules (competition/rules of play), franchise ownership, finance, labor relations/negotiations, television, and expansion. Ownership committees make decisions and set policies for implementation by the commissioner's office.

Leagues may also impose eligibility criteria for franchise ownership. For instance, MLB has no formal ownership criteria, but it does have key characteristics it looks for when granting ownership rights, such as substantial financial resources, a commitment to the local area of the franchise, a commitment to baseball, local government support, and an ownership structure that does not conflict with MLB's interests (Friedman & Much, 1997).

The NFL has the strictest ownership rules. It is the only league to prohibit **corporate ownership** of its franchises, which it has done since 1970. The NFL has made one exception to its rule for the San Francisco 49ers. In 1986, then-owner Eddie DeBartolo, Jr., transferred ownership of the team to the Edward J. DeBartolo Co., a shopping mall development corporation. Although the NFL fined DeBartolo $500,000 in 1990, it let the corporate ownership remain (Friedman & Much, 1997). The team is currently operated by DeBartolo's nephew, Jed York. The NFL also bans **public ownership** with one exception—the Green Bay Packers, which were publicly owned prior to the creation of the 1970 rule and thus were exempted from it.

Until March 1997, the NFL strictly banned **cross-ownership**—that is, ownership of more than one sport franchise (Friedman & Much, 1997). The NFL then softened, but reaffirmed, its rule on cross-ownership to allow Wayne Huizenga, then-majority owner of MLB's Florida Marlins and the NHL's Florida Panthers, to purchase the Miami Dolphins, and Paul Allen, majority owner of the NBA's Portland Trailblazers, to purchase the Seattle Seahawks. The new rule allows an NFL owner to own other sports franchises in the same market or own an NFL franchise in one market and another franchise in another market, provided that market has no NFL team (Friedman & Much, 1997). This change also paved the way for NFL owners to become investors in multiple MLS teams. The Kansas City Chief's Lamar Hunt became an investor-operator of the Kansas City Wizards, Dallas Burn, and Columbus Crew. The New England Patriots' Bob Kraft became investor-operator of the New England Revolution and the now-defunct San Jose Earthquakes. Paul Allen became the investor-operator of the Seattle Sounders. Although the clubs are in NFL markets, soccer club ownership does not violate the rule because investors in MLS invest in the league as a single entity, not in individual teams. The investors then operate the club locally and retain a percentage of local revenue.

The Commissioner

The role of the commissioner in professional sport leagues has evolved over time. Until 1921, a three-member board, the National Commission, governed professional baseball. In September 1920, an indictment was issued charging eight Chicago White Sox players with attempting to fix World Series games, an incident commonly known as the Black Sox scandal (*Finley v. Kuhn*, 1978). To squelch public discontent, baseball owners appointed Judge Kennesaw Mountain Landis as the first professional sport league commissioner in November 1920. Landis was signed to a 7-year contract and received an annual salary of $50,000 (Graffis, 1975). Landis agreed to take the position on the condition that he was granted exclusive authority to act in the best interests of baseball; in his first act, he issued lifetime bans to the eight "Black Sox" players for their involvement in the scandal. In his first decade in office, Landis banned 11 additional players, suspended Babe Ruth, and thwarted attempts to change the game by introducing marketing strategies or opening baseball to black players (Helyar, 1994).

In North American professional sport leagues, the leagues' constitution and bylaws set forth their commissioners' powers. In specific leagues, players associations have used collective bargaining to limit the commissioner's powers by negotiating for grievance arbitration provisions that invoke a neutral arbitrator and for procedures to govern disputes between the league or club and a player. As a general rule, courts will push cases back to arbitration. In recent years, some players, such as Tom Brady, have unsuccessfully challenged the broad sweeping power of the NFL commissioner in a court of law. The reason for the loss to the players is not that arbitration is a better forum, but rather that the NFL's constitution has given a great deal of power to the commissioner, which is unchecked by the collective bargaining agreement. It is a power that owner Jerry Jones of the Dallas Cowboys is promising to limit through changes in the NFL's constitution. Specifically, Jones hopes to limit the power the commissioner has over player discipline and on that and the business side of the game, wrestle some of the power back to the billionaire owners, the commissioner's employers (Robinson, 2017).

Players view the commissioner as an employee of the owners and believe that he or she will usually rule in the owners' favor for fear of damaging his or her standing with them. For example, many people cite former MLB Commissioner Fay Vincent's intervention in the lockout of 1990—a step Vincent took because of his belief that it was in the best interest of baseball and the best interest of the fans—as the beginning of the end of his term as commissioner.

Team owners have tried court challenges to limit the power of the commissioner. Three cases have upheld the baseball commissioner's right to act within the best interests of the game, provided that the commissioner follows league rules and policies when levying sanctions. In *Milwaukee American Association v. Landis* (1931), Commissioner Landis's disapproval of an assignment of a player contract from the major league St. Louis Browns to a minor league Milwaukee team was upheld. In *Atlanta National League Baseball Club, Inc. v. Kuhn* (1977), the court upheld Commissioner Bowie Kuhn's suspension of owner Ted Turner for tampering with player contracts, but found that the commissioner's removal of the Braves' first-round draft choice exceeded his authority because the MLB rules did not allow for such a penalty. In *Finley v. Kuhn* (1978), the court upheld Commissioner Kuhn's disapproval of the Oakland A's sales of Vida Blue to the New York Yankees and of Rollie Fingers and Joe Rudi to the Boston Red Sox for $1.5 million and $2 million, respectively, as being against the best interests of baseball. *Finley v. Kuhn* (1978) is particularly interesting when viewed against some recent moves made by team management to liquidate talent and shed high salaries—for example, the Miami Marlins trading Giancarlo Stanton and other players—that have gone unchecked by the current MLB commissioner.

To this day, commissioners maintain some of the original authority granted by baseball, particularly the authority to investigate and impose penalties when individuals involved with the sport are suspected of acting against the best interests of the game. The commissioner generally relies on this clause to penalize players or owners who gamble, use drugs, or engage in behavior that might tarnish the league's image. The commissioner no longer has the power to hear disputes regarding player compensation, except in MLS, where compensation is determined at the league level by the commissioner's staff. Because MLS is a single entity, compensation and personnel decisions are made centrally. Commissioners continue to possess discretionary powers in the following areas:

- Approval of player contracts.
- Resolution of disputes between players and clubs.
- Resolution of disputes between clubs.
- Resolution of disputes between players or clubs and the league.
- Disciplinary matters involving owners, clubs, players, and other personnel.
- Rule-making authority (Yasser, McCurdy, Goplerud, & Weston, 2003, p. 381).

Commissioners in other sports were modeled after baseball's commissioner, although not all embraced the role of disciplinarian as did Landis. Modern sport commissioners are as concerned with marketing as they are with discipline. For example, in the 1960s Pete Rozelle took the NFL to new levels of stability with his revenue-sharing plans. Rozelle introduced NFL Properties, an NFL division that markets property rights for the entire NFL instead of allowing each team to market its own property rights. This idea was consistent with the **"league think"** philosophy he introduced to the NFL. With league think, Rozelle preached that owners needed to think about what was best for the NFL as a whole, as opposed to what was best for their individual franchises (Helyar, 1994).

Labor Relations

John Montgomery Ward, a Hall of Fame infielder/pitcher and lawyer, established the Brotherhood of Professional Baseball Players as the first players association in 1885 (Staudohar, 1996). Although the Brotherhood had chapters on all teams (Staudohar, 1996), it became the first of four failed labor-organizing attempts. Ward fought the reserve system, salary caps of between $1,500 and $2,500 per team (depending on the team's classification), and the practice of selling players without the players' receiving a share of the profits (Jennings, 1989). Under the reserve system, players were bound perpetually to their teams, so owners could retain player rights and depress players' salaries.

When owners ignored Ward's attempts to negotiate, 200 players organized a revolt, which led to the organization of the Players League, a rival league that attracted investors and was run like a corporation, with players sharing in the profits. The Players League attracted players by offering 3-year contracts under which the salary could be increased but not decreased. The Players League folded after its first year, but only after the National League spent nearly $4 million to bankrupt it and after the media turned on the Brotherhood. Most players returned to their National League teams, and collective player actions were nonexistent for about 10 years (Jennings, 1989).

In the six decades following the Players League, three organizing attempts were unsuccessful largely due to the owners' ability to defeat the labor movement or the players' own sense that they did not belong to a union. Players were somewhat naive in their thinking and viewed their associations more as fraternal organizations than as trade unions (Cruise & Griffiths, 1991). Cruise and Griffiths noted that NHL players started their own players organizations to acquire information and improve working conditions, but feared that if they positioned themselves as a trade union their relationship with the owners would be so adversarial it would damage their sport.

Formed in 1952, the Major League Baseball Players Association (MLBPA) was initially dominated by management, with negotiations being limited to pensions and insurance (Staudohar, 1996). However, in 1966, things changed when Marvin Miller, an executive director with a trade union background, took over. Miller's great success is attributed to, among other things, organizing players by convincing all players that each of them (regardless of star status) was essential to game revenues and by bargaining for provisions that affected most players (e.g., minimum salary, per diem, pensions, insurance, salary and grievance arbitration) (Miller, 1991).

Miller also convinced the players to develop a group promotional campaign in an effort to raise funds for the players association. Players authorized the association to enter into a group licensing program with Coca-Cola in 1966, which provided $60,000 in licensing fees. Miller also encouraged the players to hold out with Topps Trading Card Company. By holding out, the players association doubled the fees for trading cards from $125 to $250 per player; they contributed a percentage of the royalties from the cards to the union (8% on sales up to $4 million and 10% thereafter). Twenty-five years later, the players association brought in approximately $57 million in licensing fees and $50 million in trading card royalties from five card companies (Miller, 1991).

The National Basketball Players Association (NBPA) was established in 1954, but it took 10 years for the NBA to recognize it as the players' exclusive labor union. In 1964, the average annual salary was $8,000 and there was no minimum salary. Players did not receive pensions, per diems, or healthcare benefits. The 1964 All-Star team, led by union leaders and future hall of famers Bob Cousy, Tommy Heinsohn, and Oscar Robertson, threatened not to play in the NBA's first televised all-star game, resulting in a players association victory when the NBA capitulated to its demands for recognition (NBPA, 2010).

NHL players first attempted to unionize in 1957, when Ted Lindsay, Doug Harvey, Bill Gadsby, Fernie Flaman, Gus Mortson, and Jimmy Thomson sought to protect the average hockey player and establish a strong pension plan. They received authorization from every NHL player but one. After the owners publicly humiliated players, fed false salary information to the press, and traded or demoted players (including Lindsay) in retaliation for their involvement with the union, the NHL finally broke the players association. Many average players feared for what might happen to them, if the NHL owners had no problem humiliating, threatening, trading, and/or releasing superstars such as Lindsay for their involvement in the players association (Cruise & Griffiths, 1991).

The Professional Hockey Players Association (PHPA), established in 1967, is the oldest union for minor league players. It has represented minor league hockey players in the AHL and ECHL. More recently, newer leagues' unions were created as divisions of more established unions. For example, the Women's National Basketball Players Association (WNBPA) became part of the NBPA in 1998, and the Arena Football League Players Union (AFLPU) became part of the AFL-CIO labor federation in 2014 (Jamieson, 2014).

In sum, labor relations did not play a major role in professional sports until the late 1960s, but has become a more dominant force in recent times. By the early 1970s, the professional sport industry had begun its transformation to a more traditional business model. Growing fan interest and increased revenues from television and sponsorship transformed leagues into lucrative business enterprises that lured additional wealthy business owners looking for tax shelters and ego boosters. New leagues and expansion provided more playing opportunities and thus more bargaining power to the players. The increased bargaining power and financial rewards led players to turn increasingly to agents and players associations (Staudohar, 1996). Players associations, once "weak or nonexistent, became a countervailing power to the owners' exclusive interests" (Staudohar, 1996, p. 4).

Under labor law, once players have unionized, professional sport league management cannot make unilateral changes to hours, wages, or terms and conditions of employment. These items are mandatory subjects for bargaining and must be negotiated between the league and the players association. The contract that results from these negotiations is called a **collective bargaining agreement (CBA)**. Collective bargaining in professional sports is far messier than in other industries. Players are impatient in negotiating provisions in the CBA. They have short careers and need to earn as much as possible in a short period of time, so their priorities tend to be the wage provisions; therefore, more is financially at stake for both sides. The owners seek cost containment through restrictions on free agency, salary caps, and other wage restrictions, whereas players seek payment and player movement through a free market.

Strikes and lockouts are also far more disruptive in professional sport than in other industries, because players possess unique talents and cannot be replaced. Thus, a strike or lockout effectively shuts the business down. A good example of the difference can be seen in the nationwide United Parcel Service (UPS) strike of 1997. Although the strike severely disrupted UPS's service, it did not completely shut down the company's business because managers could deliver packages and hire replacement workers. In contrast, it would be very difficult to find a replacement for a Mike Trout, Lebron James, Tom Brady, or Sidney Crosby. Fans will not pay to see unknown players on the field, and television networks and sponsors would pull their financial support from the league. In the 1995 MLB strike, the owners' attempt to use replacement players failed. The one time that replacement players did make an impact was during the NFL strike of 1987, which occurred shortly after the United States Football League (USFL) disbanded. The owners were able to break the strike by using replacement players from the available labor pool of marquee, unemployed, talented USFL players.

The NFL owners began a **lockout** (management not allowing the employees to work) of the referees after contract negotiations failed prior to the 2012 season; the season began with the league using replacement referees. The three weeks of replacement referees had players, coaches, and even fans outraged over missed and incorrect calls. Perhaps the most infuriating call was made at the conclusion of the Seattle Seahawks versus the Green Bay Packers Monday Night Football game on September 24, 2012. The replacement referees incorrectly awarded Golden Tate of the Seahawks a touchdown after he and Packers defensive back M. D. Jennings both got their hands on the ball in the end zone. Although the league office confirmed that the simultaneous catch rule supported the ruling that possession was to be awarded to the offense, and the play confirmed as a touchdown following a video review, the replacement referees missed a blatant offensive pass interference call prior to the ball reaching the two players' hands. Had this call have been made, the game would have ended on that play as a 12–7 win

for the Packers. Instead, the touchdown ruling as time expired resulted in 14–12 Seahawks victory. Just 48 hours later, the league and its officials managed to reach a tentative 8-year agreement and the lockout was temporarily lifted in time for referees to officiate the Thursday Night Football game. The deal was officially ratified later that week, sending regular referees back to work that Sunday.

When the collective bargaining process reaches an **impasse** (a breakdown in negotiations), the players can opt to strike (workers refuse to work) or the owners can opt to "lock out" the players to spur the process along. Over the three-decade history of labor relations in professional sports, there have been numerous strikes (involving the MLB, NFL, and NHL) and lockouts (involving the MLB, NBA, NFL, and NHL). It is unique to sport that often prior to negotiating to an impasse, owners will announce an inevitable lockout or players will announce a strike. In other industries, the lockout or strike is an economic weapon of last resort after bargaining to an impasse.

Another aspect unique to professional sport is the leagues' interest in players unionizing. In other industries, management prefers workplaces to be free from unions. In contrast, in professional sport, with a union in place, the league can negotiate with the players associations for acceptance of restrictive practices through the collective bargaining process. Under antitrust law, any restrictive practices that primarily injure union members and that are negotiated in a collective bargaining agreement are exempt from antitrust laws. All of the restrictive practices in professional sport included in the collective bargaining agreement—the draft, salary cap, restrictions on free agency, and the like—are therefore immune from antitrust lawsuits, saving the owners millions of dollars in potential antitrust damages.

Individual Professional Sports

Individual professional sports generally exist around a tour of events, meets, or matches. This chapter discusses the history of just one professional tour, the PGA Tour, as a case study of the different structures that are possible and the challenges facing individual sport governance and tours.

The first U.S. Open was held in 1895, but the PGA was not born until January 1916, when a New York department store magnate called together golf professionals and amateur golfers to create a national organization to promote the game and to improve the golf professional's vocation ("History of the PGA Tour," 1997). Its constitution, bylaws, and rules were modeled after those of the British PGA and were completed in April 1916 (Graffis, 1975). The PGA's objectives were as follows:

- To promote interest in the game of golf.
- To elevate the standards of the golf professional's vocation.
- To protect the mutual interests of PGA members.
- To hold meetings and tournaments for the benefit of members.
- To establish a Benevolent Relief Fund for PGA members.
- To accomplish any other objective determined by the PGA ("History of the American PGA," 1997).

During the PGA's formative years (1916–1930), much of its energy was focused on developing rules of play, establishing policies, cleaning up jurisdictional problems with manufacturers and the U.S. Golf Association, standardizing golf equipment, and learning its own administrative needs. In 1921, the PGA hired an administrative assistant and began a search for a commissioner. Unlike MLB, the PGA was not looking for a disciplinarian, but rather for an individual with strong administrative capabilities to conduct its daily operations. Nine years later, the PGA hired Chicago lawyer and four-time president of the Western Golf Association Albert R. Gates as commissioner for a salary of $20,000. Gates' guiding principle in making decisions was to ask the question, "What good will it do golf?" (Graffis, 1975).

The practice of charging spectators began at fundraisers by top male and female golfers to benefit the Red Cross during World War I. The PGA later adopted the practice for its tournaments to raise money for the PGA's Benevolent Fund. Soon golfer Walter Hagen began to charge for his performances (Graffis, 1975). Today, each PGA Tour event is linked to a charity. In 2016, the PGA Tour raised $166 million for charitable causes and, to date, the PGA Tour has contributed more than $2.46 billion to charity (PGA Tour Charities, 2017).

© Duard van der Westhuizen/Shutterstock, Inc.

When the PGA was founded, there was no distinction between club and touring professionals. Tournaments remained small and manageable until television began paying for golf programming. The influence of television made golf more of a business than a game. In the early to mid-1960s, a number of factors created a growing tension between the PGA tournament professionals and country club professionals, because the two groups' interests clashed. Questions were raised concerning the mission of the PGA. Was it to operate PGA Business Schools for local club professionals, who were primarily given the task of promoting interest in golf and golf-related products locally? Or was it to work with professionals coming through the Qualifying School (Q-School) for the PGA Tour circuit?

At annual meetings held from 1961 to 1966, the PGA became a house divided over control and power. Tour professionals claimed they had the support of a majority of golf's sponsors and threatened to leave the PGA to form a new association and tour. At the 1966 meeting, the PGA identified two different constituencies in professional golf: (1) the club professionals who served the amateur players and (2) the showcase professionals who provided the entertainment for golf's spectators (Graffis, 1975). Two years later, the PGA tournament players broke away to form a Tournament Players Division, which in 1975 was renamed the PGA Tour ("History of the American PGA," 1997). The PGA Tour, headquartered in Palm Beach Gardens, Florida, operates five tours: the PGA Tour, the Champions (Senior) Tour, PGA Tour Canada, PGA Tour Latinoamérica, and the Web.com Tour (PGA Tour, 2014). Television revenues and corporate sponsorship have greatly increased the purses for players on the PGA Tour ("History of the PGA Tour," 1997), and events are scheduled year-round. Purses (or winnings) for PGA Tour events range from $3 to $12 million per tournament. The purses for the Championship Tour events range from $760,000 to $4 million (PGA Tour, 2014), Web.com tour purses are $550,000 to $1 million (PGA Tour, 2014), tour purses for the PGA Tour Canada, also called the Mackenzie Tour, range from $120,000 to $200,000 (PGA Tour Canada, 2014), and tour purses for PGA Tour Latinoamérica range from $40,000 to $175,000 (PGA Tour Latinoámerica, 2014). Purses are paid for by the title sponsor and the PGA Tour (PGA Tour, 2018). The PGA Tour makes the majority of its revenues from television contracts (Antolini, 2014).

For six decades, players had to qualify annually for the PGA Tour through a grueling qualifying tournament known as Q-School, unless they earned an exemption by winning a tournament or one of the four majors. After the 2012 Q-School, the top 25 finishers no longer move to the PGA Tour, but instead go to the developmental Web.com Tour (Ferguson, n.d.). Players now qualify based on their prior year's performance on the PGA Tour or by moving up through the ranks on the Web.com Tour. The change was made as a result of the PGA Tour studying data on the comparative performance of players coming off the developmental tour versus the Q-School from 1990–2012. The data showed that the developmental tour better prepared players for the competitive challenges in playing on the PGA Tour, including the toll that travel takes on players. By making the developmental tour the primary path to the PGA Tour, there will be better branding between the two tours, plus more excitement for the Web.com Tour (Ferguson, n.d.).

Tours in the various individual sports have their own rules and regulations. In tennis, the 50 top-ranked players are required to submit their tournament schedules for the following year to their respective governing bodies by the conclusion of the U.S. Open "so decisions can be made on designations and fields can be balanced to meet the commitments the WTA and ATP have made to their tournaments" (Feinstein, 1992, p. 392). Throughout Wimbledon and the U.S. Open, players' agents and tournament directors negotiate appearance fees and set schedules for the top-ranked players' upcoming seasons, while the other players are left to make decisions about whether to return to the tour the following year.

Key Concepts

League Revenues

Leagues obtain their revenues from national television and radio contracts, league-wide licensing, and league-wide sponsorship programs. Leagues do not receive revenues from local broadcasting, gate receipts, preferred seating sales, or any of the stadium revenues. All those forms of revenues go to the teams, and disparities in local markets have caused competitive balance problems among teams. These problems are most pronounced in MLB, which has the least amount of national revenue sharing and no salary caps. However, MLB does have a **competitive balance tax**, which taxes teams that exceed a preset threshold on team salary spending for a given year. In 2018, the threshold was $197 million. Teams whose payrolls exceed the threshold will be taxed on each dollar above $197 million with a tax rate that increases based on the number of previous consecutive years that a team has qualified for the tax. In an attempt to avoid the tax for 2018, some MLB teams chose not to sign free agents, but rather adopted a rebuilding strategy (modeled after the Houston Astros). Because so many teams had adopted such a strategy, resulting in free agent players remaining unsigned, there was talk by agents and the union of collusion among team owners as this text was being written.

Franchise Values and Revenue Generation

In all leagues but the NFL, today's franchise costs make family or single ownership a challenge. Most franchise owners need to diversify their investments to protect against the financial risk of franchise ownership. Many owners purchase teams as a primary business investment, whereas others purchase them as an ancillary business. Still others are fulfilling a dream with a number of co-owners. Due to rising franchise fees, expansion fees, player salaries, and the leveling off of television revenues, there is too much at risk for one owner unless the person has diverse pools of money to cover a team's operating costs. For instance, when the Boston Red Sox and New England Sports Network (NESN) were sold for $660 million, more than 20 individuals made up the ownership group led by John Henry (Bodley, 2002). In 2012, the Los Angeles Dodgers were sold for a record $2 billion to Magic Johnson and the Guggenheim Partners (Solomon, 2012).

Currently, franchise values for major league clubs are in the hundreds of millions of dollars. Much and Gotto (1997) note that the two most important factors in determining a franchise's value are the degree of revenue sharing and the stability of the league's labor situation. Revenue sharing is a factor in creating competitive balance among the teams in the league. The NFL shares virtually all national revenues. Since it does not share stadium revenues, teams have used their leverage to negotiate favorable lease agreements that provide the teams with revenues from luxury boxes, personal seat licenses, club seating, and other revenues generated by the facility, including facility sponsorship (signage and naming rights), concessions, and parking.

As part of the race for these revenues, a strategy called **franchise free agency** emerged in the 1990s. Under this strategy, team owners threaten to move their teams if their demands for new stadiums, renovations to existing stadiums, or better lease agreements are not met. In other sports, such as hockey and basketball, teams have moved after being lured with better facilities and local deals by their suitors. As a result, in the NHL there is now a very strict franchise relocation policy with numerous factors that must be satisfied before a team can move, including evidence of a lack of fan support over three seasons prior to the request to move. Baseball has fewer relocations due to its exemption from antitrust regulations, which enables MLB to restrict team relocation. Without antitrust liability, owners interested in moving do not have the leverage to threaten a treble-damage antitrust suit in response to a no vote on a relocation request. At the same time, this exemption from antitrust regulations has allowed MLB teams leverage over their home cities, from which they can demand stadium renovations at their current sites (knowing the cities cannot sue on antitrust grounds, either).

Today, like never before, sport managers are hard at work to maximize revenue streams. A case study of the strategy of the Boston Red Sox to maximize the revenue potential in every inch of Fenway Park while adding to the fans' Fenway experience illustrates the various measures they have implemented. Since taking over the Red Sox in 2002, the management team has turned Jersey Street into a fan-friendly concourse to market the club and sell more concessions and licensed products. Because demand exceeds supply for tickets, the club has built additional seating in box seats near the dugout, on top of the Green Monster section of the park, and on the rooftop and in front of the grandstand. After adding the seats, the Red Sox discovered "dead space" used for media parking and laundry. Those functions were moved off-site to create more concourse space for revenue-generating opportunities, plus an improved

fan experience, as there is now less congestion around the concourse and restrooms (Fenway Park Improvements). To fill its schedule over the year, Fenway Park is also used for events other than baseball. In the summer, when the Red Sox are on the road, it hosts concerts by major stars such as Bruce Springsteen, Zac Brown Band, Foo Fighters, Lady Gaga, Sheryl Crow, and Billy Joel. The venue also hosts outdoor events such as international soccer matches, college football, and outdoor ice hockey games ranging from the NHL's Outdoor Classic to collegiate games and local high school rivalries. All of these events help the Red Sox maximize their profits.

Outside of Fenway Park, the Red Sox have created other innovations in an attempt to garner more revenues. One marketing innovation was to show games live at stadium-style movie theaters in select locations throughout New England. This movie theater experience came complete with vendors. The team has worked to stretch its market by hosting "state" (e.g., Vermont, New Hampshire, Maine, Rhode Island) days at Fenway Park and taking the Sox players and World Series Trophies on tour throughout New England. The team has spent years pitching itself as New England's team and the past decade battling the New York Yankees for territory in the state of Connecticut.

Another marketing innovation involves the Fenway Sports Group (FSG), which works from the built-in Red Sox Nation fan base. FSG is a venture of New England Sports Ventures (NESV), the holding company that also owns and operates the Red Sox, Fenway Park, and NESN (FSG, 2010a). FSG is a sport agency created with the twin goals to diversify the interests of the parent company and to drive more revenues into the venture. Its pioneers were Red Sox staff moonlighting at FSG (Donnelly & Leccese, 2007). In addition to working with the Red Sox, FSG represents sport properties such as Boston College, MLB

© Beelde Photography/Shutterstock, Inc.

Advanced Media, Liverpool Football Club, and the Lebron James brand. Additionally, it engages in corporate consulting and event business for clients such as Stop and Shop, Dunkin Donuts, Cumberland Farms, and Gulf Oil (FSG, 2010b). It also is entrepreneurial, operating FSG sport-related properties such as the Salem (Virginia) Red Sox (minor league baseball team), Fanfoto (a fan-centric sports photography business), Red Sox Destinations (travel agency), and Roush Fenway Racing (NASCAR) (FSG, 2018). As part of its quest to maximize revenues, FSG has a goal of leveraging the audience of 12 million Red Sox fans for crossover marketing, while reaching beyond that with new properties, new ventures, and ultimately new revenue streams.

One issue affecting franchise values is unique to MLB—namely, the large-market to small-market dichotomy created by the disparity in local broadcast revenues. MLB does not share local broadcast revenues. As a consequence, a team in a large media market, such as the New York Yankees, derives far more broadcast revenues than does a small-market team,

such as the Kansas City Royals. This disparity results in an unfair advantage for large-market teams in terms of operating revenue and franchise valuation. Due to this disparity, small-market teams, such as the Pittsburgh Pirates, are constantly building from their farm systems and often losing franchise players to the free market because they lack sufficient revenues to meet players' salary demands.

To meet the challenge of competitively operating a small-market club, teams such as the Oakland A's, under the leadership of General Manager Billy Beane, are focusing on efficiency and a new value system now termed *moneyball* (after the book by that name). In a nutshell, the concept is to win games with a small budget. Put simply, this system involves focusing on less commonly used statistics, drafting wisely, and drafting players who are "signable" in an effort to take away some of the uncertainty of drafting and developing players. According to Lewis (2003), Beane did not create the theories, but rather effectively collected and used the ideas of the baseball statistical wizard Bill James and those of some of today's best baseball writers and websites. Despite much vocal opposition from the establishment in the baseball fraternity (long-time general managers, scouts, and baseball writers), a significant number of general managers have since adopted many of these theories in building their own teams. In fact, James is a consultant to the Boston Red Sox and has led the team to use more quantitative analysis of player performance and evaluation alongside its traditional qualitative observations of players (Neyer, 2002). Only time will tell if these theories, which seek to create greater certainty in cost containment and player development, will pan out. One thing is certain, though: The *Moneyball* book (Lewis, 2003) has inspired employees and fans alike in other professional sports to try out new statistical theories. In this way, it has brought more innovative management to all professional sport organizations and in the process created a few new jobs for individuals focused on using statistics to bolster decisions on player development, investment, and acquisition.

Labor stability contributes to enhanced franchise value. A long-term CBA creates cost stability for teams. The combination of strong leadership from commissioners, shared revenue, and cost stability has enabled a league like the NFL to market what is arguably the strongest brand in North American professional sports. A quality product and the knowledge of long-term labor peace (and thus a lack of interruption in games) translate into media revenues in the billions.

Legal Issues

Almost all areas of law are relevant to the professional sport industry, but those most prevalent are contracts, antitrust, labor, and intellectual property (trademark and licensing). Historically, many high-profile cases have developed either when players and owners (current and prospective) have challenged league rules or when rival leagues have tried to compete against the dominant established league that possesses market power.

Over time many contract issues have been resolved, and all team-sport athletes now sign a standard player contract particular to each league. This does not mean that contract disputes are eliminated. Occasionally there will be cases in which the commissioner refuses to approve a player's contract if it violates a league rule or policy. For instance, sometimes player contracts contain provisions that the commissioner perceives as trying to circumvent the salary cap. The team and player may either renegotiate the contract or challenge the commissioner's finding. A good example is the rejection of the New Jersey Devils' 17-year contract with star left winger Ilya Kovalchuk. The NHL rejected the 17-year, $102 million deal, which would have been the longest contract in its history. The NHL's rejection of the contract was upheld by an arbitrator who found many problems with the contract, particularly the significant frontloading of salary and the length, which would have had Kovalchuk playing until he was 44 (Hughes, 2010). The Devils and Kovalchuk then submitted a new 15-year, $100 million contract, which the NHL approved. In the process, the NHL allegedly issued the NHLPA an ultimatum on long-term deals, conditioning them on changing the salary cap hit for contracts that end with the player older than 40 years of age and a new formula that counts the five highest years of salary in long-term (over 5-year) deals carrying additional weight in the cap calculation (Bamford, 2010). Such a change in the salary cap during the term of the CBA is unusual and shows the depth of the commitment by the NHL to the cap and actions it perceives will harm competitive balance.

In a global market, contract disputes also arise over which team retains the rights to a particular player who is attempting to move from one league to another. Such disputes may lead to legal battles between teams and players of different countries. To avoid these types of disputes, North American leagues and those abroad are continually evaluating their player transfer agreements.

Antitrust law is another area where disputes arise. Antitrust laws regulate anticompetitive business practices. MLB is exempt from antitrust laws. All professional sport leagues adopt restrictive practices to provide financial stability and competitive balance between their teams. The game would not be appealing to fans if the same teams dominated the league year after year because they had the money to consistently purchase the best players. Similarly, fans and front office staff would not like to see their teams change player personnel year after year. It is the nature of sport that teams must be built and that players and coaches must develop strong working relationships. However, restrictive practices such as drafts, reserve systems, salary caps, free agent restrictions, and free agent compensation developed for competitive balance may have ripple effects, such as depressing salaries or keeping competitor leagues from signing marquee players. In turn, players and rival leagues have used antitrust laws to challenge such practices as anticompetitive, arguing that they restrain trade or monopolize the market for professional team sports. Additionally, in the past decade, some owners have sued their own leagues on antitrust grounds to challenge restrictive practices. Antitrust laws carry with them a treble damages provision; thus, if a league loses an antitrust case and the court triples the amount of damages, the league could effectively pay millions or billions in damages.

Race and Gender in the Professional Sport Industry

In his book *In Black and White: Race and Sport in America*, Shropshire (1996) stresses that integration of more diverse employees into management positions will not happen without a concerted effort by owners, commissioners, and those in positions of power. He suggests that to combat racism in professional sport, there must be recognition of what "both America and sport in reality look and act like" as well as what both "should look and act like in that ideal moment in the future [when racism is eliminated]" (Shropshire, 1996, p. 144). Between these two phases is an intermediate period of transition. During that transition, the black community's youth must alter its focus away from athletic success as being a substitute for other forms of success. In addition, athletes must take a stronger united stand against racism. Moreover, league-wide action evidencing a commitment to address diversity is needed. An example is the **Rooney Rule** in the NFL. Named for Steelers owner Dan Rooney, the rule requires NFL teams with coaching openings to interview minority coaches as part of the search process. As **Table 10-3** shows, the NFL now has 19% minority coaches. The final step is a combination of continued civil rights political action coupled with legal action to combat racism through lawsuits and government intervention by such organizations as the Department of Justice and the Equal Employment Opportunity Commission.

Critics have argued that because there is great racial diversity among athletes on the field, more people of color should be represented in management positions. By the year 2004, the four major leagues had marked their fiftieth anniversaries of integration. In 2003, the NBA and MLB achieved major milestones by welcoming minority owners African American Bob Johnson and Mexican American Arte Moreno to the Charlotte Bobcats and Los Angeles Angels, respectively. In 2009, Lapchick and colleagues reported that for the first time in the 20-year history of the Racial and Gender Report Card's publication, each of the five major leagues received a grade of "A" for hiring people of color. All leagues showed increases for women in management positions, so it appears some positive movement forward is occurring. For current data on racial and gender representation by league, see Table 10-3 and **Table 10-4**.

Table 10-3 Racial Diversity in Professional Sports (Percentage) as of 2017–18 Reports

Segment	NBA	NFL	MLB	MLS	WNBA
Player	80.9	72.6	42.53	53.8	85.4
League office	35.1	28.4	33.8	36.7	51.2
Head coach	30	25	13.3	18.2	41.7
Assistant coach	45.4	31.3	45.9	25.9	54
CEO	6.9	0	0	3.2	13
Principal	10	18.8	13.3	18.2	27.2
Vice president	19.5	10.8	13.9	8	12.1
Senior administrator	23.4	18.2	20	11.4	23.8
Professional administrator	32.6	27.3	20	21.1	26.7

Data from Lapchick, R., The Institute for Diversity and Ethics in Sport, TIDES Making Waves of Change. Retrieved from http://www.tidesport.org
/reports.html (2018, May 21)
NBA: Lapchick, R., Balasundaram, B, The 2017 Racial and Gender Report Card: National Basketball Association, (June 29, 2017). Retrieved from http://
nebula.wsimg.com/74491b38503915f2f148062ff076e698?AccessKeyId=DAC3A56D8FB782449D2A&disposition=0&alloworigin=1
NFL: Richard Lapchick, R. Marfatia, S., The 2017 Racial and Gender Report Card: National Football League (2017, October 18). Retrieved from http://
nebula.wsimg.com/1a7f83c14af6a516176740244d8afc46?AccessKeyId=DAC3A56D8FB782449D2A&disposition=0&alloworigin=1
MLB: Lapchick, R., Neelands, B., Estrella, B., Rainey. P., and Zachary Gerhart, Z., The 2018 Racial and Gender Report Card: Major League Baseball
(2018, April 12). Retrieved from http://nebula.wsimg.com/2b20e1bb7ea3fad9f45263b846342d04?AccessKeyId=DAC3A56D8FB782449D2A&disposition
=0&alloworigin=1
MLS: Lapchick, R., Bello-Malabu, A., The 2017 Racial and Gender Report Card: Major League Soccer (2017, December 14, 2017). Retrieved from http://
nebula.wsimg.com/23638f0dcb6c7e85b810948ea02aefd6?AccessKeyId=DAC3A56D8FB782449D2A&disposition=0&alloworigin=1
WNBA: Lapchick, R., Taylor-Chase, T., The 2017 Women's National Basketball Association Racial and Gender Report Card (2017, November 15).
Retrieved from http://nebula.wsimg.com/b247da4018e6fd6d55ecef0570ddd376?AccessKeyId=DAC3A56D8FB782449D2A&disposition=0&alloworigin=1

Career Opportunities

Commissioner

The roles and responsibilities of a league commissioner were detailed earlier in this chapter. A wide variety of skills are required to be an effective commissioner. They include an understanding of the sport and the various league documents (league constitution, bylaws, rules and regulations, standard player contract, and CBA); negotiating skills; diplomacy; the ability to work well with a variety of people; an ability to delegate; a good public image; an ability to handle pressure, crises, and the media; an ability to make sound decisions; and, in general, a vision for the league. These are not skills that are easily taught. For the most part, they evolve over time through a combination of education and life experience.

Other League Office Personnel

Each league has an office staff working in a wide variety of positions. Although the number of positions in league offices varies, most leagues have literally hundreds of employees in a range of areas, from the commissioner's staff to the legal department to properties and marketing divisions to entertainment to communications to research and development. For instance, departments in the NBA's Commissioner's Office include administration, broadcasting, corporate affairs, editorial, finance, legal, operations, player programs, public relations, security, and special events (**Figure 10-1**). Departments in the NBA Properties Division include business development, finance, international offices, legal, licensing, marketing,

Table 10-4 Gender Diversity in Professional Sports (Percentage) as of 2017–18 Reports

Segment	NBA	NFL	MLB	MLS	WNBA
Player	0	0	0	0	100
League office	38.8	35.4	31.8	39	54
Head coach	0	0	0	0	50
Assistant coach	0	0	0.3	0	61.5
CEO	0	0	0	0	31.3
Principal	0	0	0	0	54.5
Vice president	24.2	20	18.5	22.1	29.5
Senior administrator	29.3	20	27.7	26.2	27.7
Professional administrator	40	35.9	27.7	32.4	41.2

Data from Lapchick, R., The Institute for Diversity and Ethics in Sport, TIDES Making Waves of Change. Retrieved from <http://www.tidesport.org/reports.html (2018>, May 21).
NBA: Lapchick, R., Balasundaram, B, The 2017 Racial and Gender Report Card: National Basketball Association, (June 29, 2017). Retrieved from http://nebula.wsimg.com/74491b38503915f2f148062ff076e698?AccessKeyId=DAC3A56D8FB782449D2A&disposition=0&alloworigin=1
NFL: Richard Lapchick, R. Marfatia, S., The 2017 Racial and Gender Report Card: National Football League (2017, October 18). Retrieved from http://nebula.wsimg.com/1a7f83c14af6a516176740244d8afc46?AccessKeyId=DAC3A56D8FB782449D2A&disposition=0&alloworigin=1
MLB: Lapchick, R., Neelands, B., Estrella, B., Rainey. P., and Zachary Gerhart, Z., The 2018 Racial and Gender Report Card: Major League Baseball (2018, April 12). Retrieved from http://nebula.wsimg.com/2b20e1bb7ea3fad9f45263b846342d04?AccessKeyId=DAC3A56D8FB782449D2A&disposition=0&alloworigin=1
MLS: Lapchick, R., Bello-Malabu, A., The 2017 Racial and Gender Report Card: Major League Soccer (2017, December 14, 2017). Retrieved from http://nebula.wsimg.com/23638f0dcb6c7e85b810948ea02aefd6?AccessKeyId=DAC3A56D8FB782449D2A&disposition=0&alloworigin=1
WNBA: Lapchick, R., Taylor-Chase, T., The 2017 Women's National Basketball Association Racial and Gender Report Card (2017, November 15). Retrieved from http://nebula.wsimg.com/b247da4018e6fd6d55ecef0570ddd376?AccessKeyId=DAC3A56D8FB782449D2A&disposition=0&alloworigin=1

media and sponsor programs, and team services. Departments in NBA Entertainment include administration, accounting, legal, licensing, operations, photography, production, and programming. Thus, a wide variety of opportunities in league offices are available for individuals with degrees in sport management and business and for those who couple their initial degrees with a graduate degree in a field such as law, sport management, or business administration. Skills necessary for working in a league office vary with the position, yet a few universal skills include having a working knowledge of the sport, the teams in the league, and the professional sport industry in general; good customer relations skills; and a willingness to work long hours (especially during the season and postseason).

Team General Manager

A team general manager is in charge of all player personnel decisions, including overseeing the scouting and drafting of players, signing free agents, trading players, and negotiating contracts with players and their agents. The general manager must understand the sport and be able to assess talent. He or she must also possess a working knowledge of all league documents (constitution, bylaws, rules and regulations, CBA, standard player contract).

A career path for a general manager has traditionally been to move into the position from the playing or coaching ranks. As the position has become more complex, individuals with graduate degrees in sport management, business administration, law, or a combination

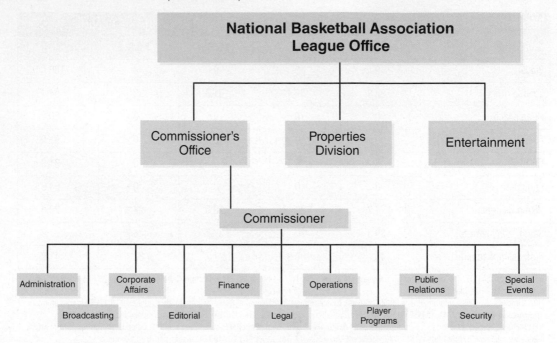

Figure 10-1 NBA League Office/Team Front Office Flowcharts

of these have become desirable employees. Some teams will have a general manager who has risen from the playing or coaching ranks, and then hire one or more assistant general managers to deal with complex contract negotiations and to decipher league rules and policies, such as salary caps, as well as to interpret and develop statistical models that have become commonplace in the moneyball era.

Other Team Front Office Personnel

Like league office staffs, team front offices offer a wide variety of positions. In the past decade, the number of positions and specialization of jobs has increased greatly. When the first edition of this text was published, the Miami Heat front office staff provided a glimpse of the variety of positions available. At that time the team possessed 40 full-time employees, 4 partners, and 4 limited partners (Miami Heat, 1993–1994). Compare that to a current Miami Heat directory (**Figure 10-2**) and the Philadelphia 76ers, whose website listed

200 front office employees in 2017. The employees included the following positions: an ownership group; a president; a chief operating officer; an executive vice president; 2 senior vice presidents; a vice president; a director of player personnel; a sales staff of 56 (including director and managers); a customer service staff of 6 (including directors and managers); a marketing and promotions staff of 3; a game operations staff of 6; a communications staff of 6 (includes community relations and public relations); and numerous other employees, such as coaches, scouts, broadcasters, accountants, and administrative assistants throughout the basketball and business operations (NBA, 2010a). It is noteworthy that the basketball operations staff is considerably smaller than the business operations side. The business side drives the revenue into the operation and, therefore, there tend to be more opportunities for employment on that side of the "house."

Front office entry-level positions tend to be in the sales, marketing, community relations,

Executive Office

**Managing General Partner President of Basketball Operations General Manager
President of Business Operations**

Executive Vice Presidents: Chief Marketing Officer, HEAT Group
Enterprises, Sales, General Manager, Chief Financial Officer, General Council

Vice Presidents

Senior VP of Basketball Operation Senior VP/Chief Information Officer

Vice Presidents: Sports Media Relations, Arena Bookings and
Marketing, Marketing Division, Operations, Assistant General
Manager, Finance, Corporate Partnerships, Ticket Operations
and Services, Human Resources, Player Personnel

Basketball Operations

Senior Director of Team Security

Directors: Sports Media Relations, College/International
Scouting, Team Services, Team Security, Pro/Minor League
Scouting

Other: NBA Scout, Scout, Assistant Director of Sport
Media Relations, Sport Media Relations Assistant,
Business Media Relations Assistant, Scouting and
Information Coordinator

Figure 10-2 Miami Heat Front Office Directory Chart

Data from http://www.nba.com/heat/contact/directory_list.html (December, 2006).

and media/public relations departments. Salaries are typically low, because many people would love to work for a professional team; therefore, supply always exceeds demand. Salaries are often higher in the sales department because employees earn a base salary plus commissions for ticket, corporate, or group sales productivity. As with league office positions, skills necessary for working in a front office are knowledge of the sport and the professional sport industry, good customer relations abilities, and a willingness to work long hours (particularly during the season and postseason). As for educational requirements, a sport management degree and, depending on the position, possibly an advanced degree, such as a JD or an MBA, are appropriate for someone looking to break into a front office position.

Tour Personnel

Tours such as the PGA Tour and the Association of Tennis Professionals (ATP) Tour employ many sport managers. The Dew Tour, which debuted in June 2005, consists of five major multisport events with a cumulative points system, a $2.5 million competitive purse (the largest in action sports), and an additional $1 million bonus pool based on participants' year-end standings. As with league sports, the positions vary from commissioner to marketer to special events coordinator.

For example, in 2017 the ATP Tour held 62 tournaments in 31 countries and was organized into three main offices: Player Council, Board of Directors, and Tournament Council. Each office is led by an executive and has a number of staff positions available.

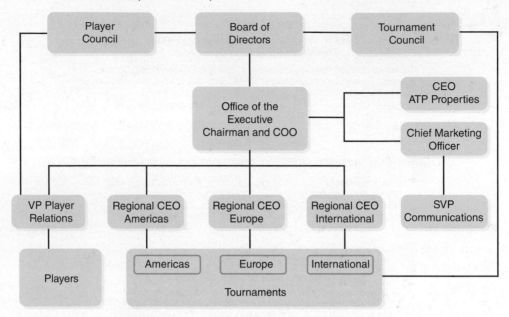

Figure 10-3 Executive Organizational Chart

The ATP has offices located in several countries, including Monaco, Australia, the United Kingdom (London), and the United States (Florida). An executive organizational chart is shown in **Figure 10-3**.

As with league sports, the positions vary from commissioner to marketer to special events coordinator. Much of the event management work for the actual site operations for the tour is, however, often left to an outside sports agency. Tours and sites contract with event marketing and management agencies to take care of all of the details of putting on the event at a particular country club or other event location.

Agents

Almost all team and individual athletes in the professional sport industry have sport agents representing them and coordinating their business and financial affairs. In addition, a growing number of professional coaches rely on sport agents.

Current Issues

Salary Caps

In an effort to contain player personnel costs, salary caps continue to be the rage in professional sport. They are used in the AFL, NBA, NFL, NHL, MLS, WNBA, ECHL, and NLL. Salary caps are intended to create parity among teams by capping how much a team can spend on its players' salaries. Salary caps are adjusted annually for changes in revenue.

To impose a salary cap in a league in which a union exists, owners must negotiate with the players (because the cap impacts wages). In the negotiation process, the union will inevitably negotiate for some exceptions to the salary cap. These exceptions have in reality created loopholes for creative general managers and agents representing players. For instance, in the NFL, signing bonuses are applied to the cap by prorating them across the life of the contract. Another problem with the caps is that they routinely force teams to cut established players or renegotiate their contracts to make room under the cap to sign another player. A third problem is that the caps provide a team with spending minimums, so low-revenue teams are prevented from cutting their payrolls to stay competitive (Fatsis, 1997). In the WNBA, the combination of a tight salary cap and a minimum salary scale negatively impacts veterans, whose minimum salaries are higher based upon years of service. Thus, in the case of a talented veteran competing for a spot against an equally talented rookie, the club may choose the rookie because the athlete takes up less room under the cap (Bergen, 2004).

Globalization

All major leagues are drafting and signing players from other nations and moving into those countries with their marketing efforts. MLB has an office in Tokyo to oversee its efforts in Japan, Taiwan, and China, and the league has been playing one game to open the season in Japan for the past few years. The NFL no longer operates NFL Europe, but has begun playing several regular season games in Europe. The NBA has expanded its footprint throughout the globe with probably the most international movement of all the North American leagues. Currently the NBA hosts 18 international NBA websites in addition to its main North American site (NBA, 2010b). Following the NFL and MLB, the NBA has also moved away from playing exhibition games in Europe, instead scheduling regular season games there each season (NBA, 2010c).

An interesting case study exists in examining NBA China and NBA India. NBA International is following its game plan in China to move into the Indian market. To grow its market in China, the NBA spent two decades building courts, teaching youth the game, and hosting promotions. Now more than 300 million people in China play basketball. The league notes that 89% of Chinese people age 15 to 54 are aware of the NBA brand, and NBA.com/China averages 2 million unique users each month. Games are shown in China on 51 outlets, drawing 1.6 billion viewers in 2008–2009 (34% more than in 2006–2007). China is now the NBA's biggest foreign market for its branded merchandise. Outside investors—including Disney/ESPN, Bank of China Group, Legend Holdings, China Merchant Group, and the Li Ka-shing Foundation—bought 11% of NBA China in January 2008 for $2.3 billion, with a goal of launching a professional league (Van Riper & Karmali, 2009). However, NBA China had a setback when AEG Facilities pulled out of its plan to build and/or operate NBA arenas in Beijing, Shanghai, and Guangzhou.

NBA International began bringing NBA stars to India in 2006. Since November 2008, the NBA has been staging youth tournaments in Mumbai, New Delhi, and Bangalore. NBA games on ESPN in India reach 120 million homes, nearly one-third of the country. That said, becoming the second most popular sport in India (behind cricket) will be a challenging goal, because India has not fielded an Olympic basketball team since 1980 (Van Riper & Karmali, 2009).

Journalists credit the global interest in the NBA to the 1992 Dream Team (Crowe, 2004), but it is also a product of the NBA's strategy of integrating international stars into its teams. To continue its global expansion, many NBA teams have drafted and signed players from other nations. NBA official rosters in the 2017–2018 season included 101 players from 37 different countries or U.S. territories, such as Puerto Rico and the Virgin Islands. Fans of these players represent new revenue sources for the NBA. Foreign markets generate as much as 20% of the $2.6 billion the NBA earns in television revenue, and they provide approximately 20% of merchandise sales (Crowe, 2004). In 2010, the NBA Finals were broadcast in 215 countries and in 49 languages (NBA, 2010b).

The international interest may also stem from overtures made by former Commissioner David Stern indicating that the NBA is looking to move into Europe and Asia. These overtures have encouraged AEG Facilities to build NBA-style arenas in London, Berlin, and China (Sandomir, 2008). These facilities allowed the NBA to consider many options, ranging from exhibitions to games to permanent "NBA-branded leagues" (Sandomir, 2008). As mentioned earlier in this section, the NBA held its first regular season game in Europe during the 2010–2011 season (NBA, 2010c).

Concussion Litigation

Among the most hotly debated current issues in professional sport is how professional leagues have managed concussions and how they will address player safety in the future. Retired NFL and NHL players have filed suit against both of these leagues. The retired players and their families allege that they have developed chronic traumatic encephalopathy (CTE) and other brain diseases, such as Alzheimer's disease and dementia, due to head trauma they received while playing professional football and ice hockey.

The NFL has settled concussion cases for players who retired prior to July 7, 2014. The settlement sets aside up to $1 billion for CTE injuries (NFL Concussion Settlement, 2017).

The NHL players' lawsuit involves 75 plaintiffs and has the complicating matter of the role of fighting in causing the head trauma. Tied to the issue of whether head trauma that occurs to players while playing the sport of hockey is the question of whether fighting causes more head trauma, and thus more brain

damage, *and* whether by having fighting as part of the professional game the NHL is condoning these injuries. The NHL Commissioner, Gary Bettman, has denied that a link exists between concussions and CTE; as a result, the NHL's response to concussions has been widely compared the cigarette industry's responses after the discovery of a potential link between smoking and cancer (Kugler, 2016; Macur, 2017). Bettman's position is that science has not discovered a definitive link. This position is one that may align with the NHL's defense in the pending litigation involving former players, but it is not popular, especially when compared to the NFL's decisions to settle its lawsuit and donate to research on brain trauma and the NFL (Armor, 2017).

Drug Testing and Human Growth Hormone

Another current issue that will need to be addressed is human growth hormone (HGH) testing in professional sport. The four major leagues have adopted drug testing policies that include the penalties noted in **Table 10-5**. The question will be how the leagues manage testing and punishment for use of HGH, which remains unresolved.

In MLB, the commissioner's power to suspend a player based on evidence gathered by means other than a drug or HGH test was at issue in the Alex Rodriguez arbitration case in 2013. MLB obtained documents from an antiaging clinic, then used information from those documents to suspend Rodriguez for 211 games under a provision in the CBA. The arbitrator reduced the commissioner's penalty to 160 games.

Analytics

Professional sport is becoming more and more dependent on analytics. The moneyball era ushered in the use of analytics such as

Table 10-5 Disciplinary Penalties for Performance-Enhancing Drug Use in the MLB, NBA, NFL, and NHL

	MLB	NBA	NFL	NHL
First offense	80-game suspension	20-game suspension and mandatory attendance in NBA SPED's program	Up to a 6-game suspension without pay	20-game suspension without pay and mandatory referral to SABH program for evaluation and possible treatment
Second offense	162-game suspension	45-game suspension and mandatory reentrance into NBA SPED's program	10-game suspension without pay	60-game suspension without pay and mandatory referral to SABH program for evaluation and possible treatment
Third offense	Lifetime ban	Dismissal and disqualification from NBA	At least a 2-year suspension without pay	Lifetime ban with possible discretionary reinstatement after 2 years pending application
Fourth offense				

Abbreviations: SABH (Substance Abuse and Behavioral Health program); SPED (steroid or performance-enhancing drug program)
Data from MLB (http://mlb.nbcsports.com/2014/03/28/mlb-mlbpa-announce-stronger-testing-harsher-penalties-for-peds/), NBA (https://www.nba.com/media/CBA101_9.12.pdf), NFL (http://www.espn.com/nfl/story/_/id/11542076/nfl-union-ok-new-performance-enhancing-drug-policy-human-growth-hormone-testing), NHL (http://www.latimes.com/sports/kings/la-sp-with-nhl-drug-policy-20150929-story.html)

sabermetrics in baseball player development; **sabermetrics** is the empirical study of baseball. Analytics has since moved from baseball into other sports—especially to basketball, where it is used to analyze all play on the court (Goldsberry, 2014), but also to football and hockey.

The technology known as Statcast records and tracks different sources and types of information to help explain how a player performs. In baseball, Statcast can measure the exit velocity or speed of a ball coming off of a player's bat. It also measures the spin rate of a ball thrown by a pitcher. Likewise, it measures the first step of an outfielder's route to a fly ball and determines if he took an efficient route to the ball's landing spot, the speed in miles per hour he ran to the ball, and the time and distance he took to get there. Statcast is a new

and comprehensive way to literally measure the performance of a baseball player (Bastien, 2016).

Beyond the use of analytics in player evaluation, player development, and team operations, teams have started to use analytics on the business side, in marketing, market research, customer relationship management, and other aspects of decision making. Leagues such as the NBA and MLS have league-level analytics departments that analyze data on the teams. The league departments then send their staff out to work with clubs as "consultants" to assist the team to do better.

Technology

MLB Advanced Media is the digital technology company of Major League Baseball. It has been an innovator in live streaming media, providing unique Statcast analysis of player performance as well as creating digital platforms for other entities such as the NHL and HBO Now (Rosen, 2015; Popper, 2015). MLB Advanced Media has created $7–8 million in revenues for each of the 30 MLB teams and is an expanding source of revenues for the league (Brown, 2017).

Another innovative use of technology in sports is the incorporation of wearable technology into the clothing and pads of players so as to track their performance, health, and technique (Maqbool, 2017). The wearable technology known as biometric trackers can track anything from sleep patterns and behaviors to sweat production, stress and fatigue, heart rate, skin temperature, and pulse rate, among other things (Venook, 2017). Professional teams in MLB, the NFL, the NHL, and the NBA are currently using some means of tracking and collecting data on players for health-related purposes and to bring more "big data" into their management decision making. Obviously, such use of biometric tracking and health and performance data tracking bring with it privacy concerns for the players, as well as concerns over whether those data will be used against players in contract negotiations. In fact, the NBA has limits in its collective bargaining agreement over the number of tracking devices that can be used in the league as well as a prohibition on the data being used against a player in contract negotiations. The agreement sets forth a $250,000 fine for a team's violation of the provision (Venook, 2017). It will be interesting to see the future of player performance and health tracking, as wearable technology is just making its entrance into professional sports, with more innovations and adoptions sure to come.

Summary

The professional sport industry involves the sale of the entertainment value of sport events and exhibitions. Revenues are generated primarily through media rights fees, licensed product sales, gate receipts, and stadium revenues. The leagues and tours face a number of challenges, including keeping fans satisfied in light of their perceptions regarding the "highly paid athlete." Directly related to this is finding a means for achieving labor stability in the leagues while developing methods of obtaining and retaining a fan base that is representative of society as ticket prices continue to skyrocket. The dominant major professional leagues (MLB, MLS, NBA, NFL, and NHL) also face challenges for market share from new upstart leagues (e.g., Major League Lacrosse), women's sports, expansion in the minor leagues, and the growing professionalization of collegiate sport.

The professional sport industry is entering an exciting period. Innovations in technology are making professional sport more global, particularly as leagues look for unsaturated markets and new revenue streams. This exciting environment, coupled with the perception of the glamour of working for a team or league, attracts many job seekers to professional sports. Thus, the competition for entry-level positions is fierce and salaries tend to be lower than in other segments of the industry. Those who are persistent, are willing to take on an internship or two, and are committed to keeping abreast of this fast-paced segment will be rewarded. Professional sports are constantly changing and facing new challenges. The sport manager who can adapt to change and resolve problems, and who possesses a vision for the professional sport industry in the twenty-first century, will find success in this field.

Case Study 10-1

Is the NFL's Conduct Policy Working?

In response to the murder charges levied against Baltimore Ravens linebacker Ray Lewis, the NFL owners established a personal conduct policy in 2000. Former Commissioner Paul Tagliabue used it to issue short suspensions. From January 2006 through April 2007, more than 50 players were arrested (Bell, 2007). In 2007, the NFL invoked its "integrity of the game" powers to lengthen the suspensions a commissioner could levy and even allowed for indefinite suspensions if the player's actions involved violent or criminal behavior that undermined the NFL's integrity, eroded public confidence, or resulted in tragic consequences to the perpetrator and/or victim (NFL Personal Conduct Policy, 2016).

In 2016, the NFL came up with its current policy. It emphasizes that: "**Everyone** who is part of the league must refrain from 'conduct detrimental to the integrity of and public confidence in' the NFL. This includes owners, coaches, players, other team employees, game officials, and employees of the league office, NFL Films, NFL Network, or any other NFL business. Conduct by anyone in the league that is illegal, violent, dangerous, or irresponsible puts innocent victims at risk, damages the reputation of others in the game, and undercuts public respect and support for the NFL. We must endeavor at all times to be people of high character; we must show respect for others inside and outside our workplace; and we must strive to conduct ourselves in ways that favorably reflect on ourselves, our teams, the communities we represent, and the NFL" (NFL Personal Conduct Policy, 2016).

To that end, the NFL established the following policy.

Expectations and Standards of Conduct

It is not enough simply to avoid being found guilty of a crime. We are all held to a higher standard and must conduct ourselves in a way that is responsible, promotes the values of the NFL, and is lawful.

If you are convicted of a crime or subject to a disposition of a criminal proceeding, you are subject to discipline. But even if your conduct does not result in a criminal conviction, if the league finds that you have engaged in any of the following conduct, you will be subject to discipline. Prohibited conduct includes but is not limited to the following:

- Actual or threatened physical violence against another person, including dating violence, domestic violence, child abuse, and other forms of family violence
- Assault and/or battery, including sexual assault or other sex offenses
- Violent or threatening behavior toward another employee or a third party in any workplace setting
- Stalking, harassment, or similar forms of intimidation
- Illegal possession of a gun or other weapon (such as explosives, toxic substances, and the like), or possession of a gun or other weapon in any workplace setting
- Illegal possession, use, or distribution of alcohol or drugs
- Possession, use, or distribution of steroids or other performance-enhancing substances
- Crimes involving cruelty to animals as defined by state or federal law
- Crimes of dishonesty such as blackmail, extortion, fraud, money laundering, or racketeering

(continues)

Is the NFL's Conduct Policy Working? (*Continued*)

- Theft-related crimes such as burglary, robbery, or larceny
- Disorderly conduct
- Crimes against law enforcement, such as obstruction, resisting arrest, or harming a police officer or other law enforcement officer
- Conduct that poses a genuine danger to the safety and well-being of another person
- Conduct that undermines or puts at risk the integrity of the NFL, NFL clubs, or NFL personnel (National Football League, 2014)

The policy was imposed unilaterally by the League.

Questions for Discussion

1. Once a players association (union) is in existence, any changes in the workplace that involve mandatory subjects for bargaining may not be unilaterally implemented by the league (management) but must be negotiated with the players. Mandatory subjects for bargaining are hours, wages, and terms and conditions of employment. Should this new conduct policy have been negotiated with the NFLPA through collective bargaining?

2. Commissioners have long held power to make decisions to maintain the integrity of the game. Historically, the "integrity of the game" decisions have involved gambling, drug use, on-field bad behavior, and bad behavior toward fans. Does this conduct policy fit within the integrity of the game provision? Does regulating off-field behavior go too far? Because the commissioner can act simply when someone in the organization is arrested, how do we reconcile it with the concept of "innocent until proven guilty"?

3. What will be some of the challenges in enforcing the policy? How will the league impose fairness?

4. As a manager, which strategies would you adopt to avoid having this policy invoked against members of your team (players and staff)?

5. Using Google, examine the news over a 3-year period to determine whether the NFL policy is working. Has it been applied to team and league management and coaches as well as players? As a fan, does the behavior of players on and off the field influence your decision to follow the NFL? Do you think it would affect the decisions of sponsors to be associated with the NFL?

6. Recently Ray Rice, Adrian Peterson, Tom Brady, and Ezekiel Elliot were suspended by the NFL. Did the NFL succeed in upholding these suspensions in arbitration and in court? Were the decisions fair? Did the decisions to suspend these players enhance or hurt the leagues image. Does the commissioner of the NFL have too much power in these cases, or is this type of authority necessary to police the actions of athletes and employees in the league?

Resources

Professional Sport Leagues

American Hockey League (AHL)
One Monarch Place, Suite 2400
Springfield, MA 01144
413-781-2030
www.theahl.com

ECHL
116 Village Boulevard, Suite 230
Princeton, NJ 08540
609-452-0770
www.echl.com

Major League Baseball (MLB)
> 245 Park Avenue, 31st Floor
> New York, NY 10022
> 212-339-7800
> www.mlb.com

Major League Soccer (MLS)
> 420 Fifth Avenue, 7th Floor
> New York, NY 10017
> 212-450-1200
> www.mlssoccer.com

Minor League Baseball (MiLB)
> 9550 Street North
> St. Petersburg, FL 33716
> 727-822-6937
> www.milb.com

National Basketball Association (NBA)
> Olympic Tower
> 645 Fifth Avenue
> New York, NY 10022
> 212-407-8000
> www.nba.com

National Football League (NFL)
> 345 Park Avenue
> New York, NY 10154
> 212-758-1500
> www.nfl.com

National Hockey League (NHL)
> 1185 Avenue of the Americas
> New York, NY 10036
> 212-789-2000
> www.nhl.com

National Professional Fastpitch (NPF)
> 3350 Hobson Pike
> Hermitage, TN 37076
> 615-324-7861
> http://profastpitch.com

National Women's Soccer League (NWSL)
> 1556 S. Michigan Avenue, Floor 2
> Chicago, IL 60605
> 312-808-1300
> www.nwslsoccer.com

Women's National Basketball Association (WNBA)
> 645 Fifth Avenue
> New York, NY 10022
> 212-688-9622
> www.wnba.com

Professional Sport Tours

Association of Tennis Professionals (ATP) Tour
> 200 ATP Boulevard
> Ponte Vedra Beach, FL 32082
> 904-285-8000
> www.atpworldtour.com

Dew Tour
> 2052 Corte Del Nogal, Suite 100
> Carlsbad, CA 92011
> www.dewtour.com/snow/

Indy Racing League (IRL)
> 4565 W. 16th Street
> Indianapolis, IN 46222
> 317-492-6526
> www.indycar.com

Ladies Professional Golf Association (LPGA)
> 100 International Golf Drive
> Daytona Beach, FL 32124
> 386-274-6200
> www.lpga.com

National Association for Stock Car Auto Racing Inc. (NASCAR)
> 1801 W. International Speedway Boulevard
> Daytona Beach, FL 32114
> 386-253-0611
> www.nascar.com

Professional Golfers' Association (PGA) Tour
> Champions Tour
> PGA Tour Latinoámerica
> PGA Tour Canada
> Web.com Tour

112 PGA Tour Boulevard
Ponte Vedra, FL 32082
904-285-3700
www.pgatour.com

Women's Tennis Association (WTA) Tour

100 2nd Avenue South, Suite 1100-S
St. Petersburg, FL 33701
727-895-5000
www.wtatennis.com

X Games/ESPN

ESPN Events
ESPN Plaza
Bristol, CT 06010
xgames.espn.com

Players Associations

Canadian Football League Players' Association (CFLPA)

6205 B Airport Road, Suite 208
Mississauga, Ontario, Canada L4V 1E3
800-616-6865
www.cflpa.com

Major League Baseball Players Association (MLBPA)

12 E. 49th Street, 24th Floor
New York, NY 10017
212-826-0808
www.mlbplayers.com

National Basketball Players Association (NBPA)

1133 Avenue of the Americas
New York, NY 10036
212-655-0880
www.nbpa.com

National Football League Players Association (NFLPA)

1133 20th Street, NW, Suite 500
Washington, DC 20036
202-572-7500
https://www.nflpa.org

National Hockey League Players Association (NHLPA)

10 Bay Street, Suite 1200
Toronto, Ontario, Canada M5J 2N8
416-408-4040
www.nhlpa.com

Professional Hockey Players' Association (PHPA)

3964 Portage Rd.
Niagara Falls, Ontario, Canada L2J 2K9
289-296-4567
www.phpa.com

Women's National Basketball Players Association (WNBPA)

1133 Avenue of the Americas, 5th Floor
New York, NY 10036
212-655-0880
https://wnbpa.org

Key Terms

collective bargaining agreement (CBA), commissioner, competitive balance tax, corporate governance model, corporate ownership, cross-ownership, franchise free agency, franchise rights, gate receipts, impasse, "league think," lockout, premium seating, public ownership, revenue sharing, Rooney Rule, sabermetrics, self-governance, single-entity structure, territorial rights

References

American Needle v. NFL, 130 S.Ct. 2201 (2010).

Antolini, M. (2014, February 11). *Presentation on the golf industry*. Mark H. McCormack Department of Sport Management, Isenberg School of Management, University of Massachusetts–Amherst, MA.

Armor, N. (2017, January 25). Skeptical of CTE link, NHL won't fund concussion research. *USA Today*. Retrieved from https://www .usatoday.com/story/sports/nhl/2017/01/25 /nhl-concussions-research-funding -nhlpa-gary-bettman-lack-of-support /97046568/

Atlanta National League Baseball Club, Inc. v. Kuhn, 432 F. Supp. 1213 (N.D. Ga. 1977).

Bamford, T. (2010, September 2). Ilya Kovalchuk Chaos: NHL Gives Players Association Ultimatum. Retrieved from http:// bleacherreport.com/articles/448720 -kovalchuk-chaos-nhl-gives-players -association-ultimatum

Bastien, J. (2016, January 3) , Statcast ushers in new era of player evaluation. Retrieved from http://wap.mlb.com/cle/news/article/2016010 3160362724/?locale=es_CO

Bell, J. (2007, April 11). Conduct unbecoming: NFL sets new standards with suspensions. *USA Today*. Retrieved from http://www .usatoday.com/sports/football/nfl/2007-04 -10-pacman-henry-suspensions_N.htm

Bergen, M. (2004, May 7). Salary issues scuttle WNBA veterans' chances. *Seattle Post-Intelligencer*. Retrieved from http://www .seattlepi.com/wnba/172352_storm07.html

Berry, R. C., Gould, W. B., & Staudohar, P. D. (1986). *Labor relations in professional sports*. Dover, MA: Auburn House.

Bodley, H. (2002, January 16). Baseball owners approve sale of Red Sox to Henry. *USA Today*. Retrieved from http://www.usatoday.com /sports/baseball/redsox/2002-01-16-sale-ag .htm

Brown, M. (2014, July 7). The biggest media company you have never heard of. *Forbes*. Retrieved from https://www.forbes.com /sites/maurybrown/2014/07/07/the-biggest -media-company-youve-never-heard-of/3 /#2d116808638f

Crouse, K. (2010, April 1). Absences worsen LPGA's headache. *New York Times*. Retrieved from http:// www.nytimes.com/2010/04/02 /sports/golf/02wgolf.html

Crowe, J. (2004, June 15). Outside influence. *Los Angeles Times*. Retrieved from http://articles. latimes.com/2004/jun/15/sports/sp-nba15

Cruise, D., & Griffiths, A. (1991). *Net worth*. Toronto, Canada: Viking Penguin Group.

Donnelly, G., & Leccese, M. (2007, April 23). Q&A: Dee leads Red Sox parent's drive to diversify. Retrieved from http://boston.bizjournals .com/boston/stories/2007/04/23/story9.html

Fatsis, S. (1997, June 25). Is battle looming over salary caps? *The Wall Street Journal*, p. B9.

Feinstein, J. (1992). *Hard courts*. New York, NY: Villard Books.

Fenway Park Improvements. (2018). Official Site of the Boston Red Sox. Retrieved from http://boston.redsox.mlb.com/bos/history /improvements_intro.jsp

Fenway Sports Group (FSG). (2018). About us: Who we are. Retrieved from http://www .fenwaysportsgroup.com

Ferguson, D. (n.d.). PGA Tour makes sweeping changes to Q-School, season schedule, and more. Retrieved from http://www.pga.com /news/pga-tour/pga-tour-makes-sweeping -changes-q-school-season-schedule-and- more

Finley v. Kuhn, 569 F.2d 527 (7th Cir. 1978).

Foldesy, J. (2004, June 17). NFL owners fear death of golden goose. *Washington Times*. Retrieved from http://www.washingtontimes.com /sports/20040617-120824-5896r.htm

Fraser v. Major League Soccer, 284 F.3d 47 (1st Cir. 2002).

Friedman, A., & Much, P. J. (1997). *1997 Inside the ownership of professional sports teams*. Chicago, IL: Team Marketing Report.

Garber, D. (2004). Major League Soccer: Establishing the world's sport in a new America. In *Inside the minds: The business of sports* (pp. 109–129). Boston, MA: Aspatore Books.

Goldsberry, K. (2014, February 6). Databall. *Grantland.* Retrieved from http://grantland.com/features/expected-value-possession-nba-analytics/

Graffis, H. B. (1975). *The PGA: The official history of the Professional Golfers' Association of America.* New York, NY: Crowell.

Helyar, J. (1994). *Lords of the realm.* New York, NY: Villard Books.

History of the American PGA. (1997). Retrieved from http://worldgolf.com/wglibrary/history/ampgahis.html

History of the PGA Tour. (1997). Retrieved from http://www.worldgolf.com/wglibrary/history/tourhist.html

Hughes, T. (2010). The full document: Richard Bloch's ruling in the Ilya Kovalchuk arbitration case. *SB Nation.* Retrieved from http://www.sbnation.com/2010/8/10/1614815/arbitration-ruling-ilya-kovalchuk-full-document

Jamieson, D. (2014). Arena Football Players Union Joins AFL-CIO as League Expands to China, https://www.huffingtonpost.com/2014/05/13/arena-football-players-union_n_5317671.html

Jennings, K. (1989). *Balls and strikes: The money game in professional baseball.* Greenwich, CT: Praeger.

Kugler, J. (2016, June 29). The NHL and cigarette companies have something dangerously in common. *Time.* Retrieved from http://time.com/4385311/hockey-concussions-bettman-blumenthal

Lapchick, R. The Institute for Diversity and Ethics in Sport, TIDES Making Waves of Change. Retrieved from http://www.tidesport.org/reports.html

Lapchick, R., & Balasundaram, B. (2017, June 29). The 2017 racial and gender report card: National Basketball Association. Retrieved from http://nebula.wsimg.com/74491b38503915f2f148062ff076e698?AccessKeyId=DAC3A56D8FB782449D2A&disposition=0&alloworigin=1

Lapchick, R., & Bello-Malabu, A. (2017, December 14, 2017). The 2017 Racial and Gender Report Card: Major League Soccer. Retrieved from http://nebula.wsimg.com/23638f0dcb6c7e85b810948ea02aefd6?AccessKeyId=DAC3A56D8FB782449D2A&disposition=0&alloworigin=1

Lapchick, R., & Marfatia, S. (2017, October 18). The 2017 racial and gender report card: National Football League. Retrieved from http://nebula.wsimg.com/1a7f83c14af6a516176740244d8afc46?AccessKeyId=DAC3A56D8FB782449D2A&disposition=0&alloworigin=1

Lapchick, R., & Taylor-Chase, T. (2017, November 15). The 2017 Women's National Basketball Association Racial and Gender Report Card. Retrieved from http://nebula.wsimg.com/b247da4018e6fd6d55ecef0570ddd376?AccessKeyId=DAC3A56D8FB782449D2A&disposition=0&alloworigin=1

Lapchick, R., Neelands, B., Estrella, B., Rainey. P., & Gerhart, Z. The 2018 Racial and Gender Report Card: Major League Baseball (2018, April 12). Retrieved from http://nebula.wsimg.com/2b20e1bb7ea3fad9f45263b846342d04?AccessKeyId=DAC3A56D8FB782449D2A&disposition=0&alloworigin=1

Lentze, G. (1995). The legal concept of professional sports leagues: The commissioner and an alternative approach from a corporate perspective. *Marquette Sports Law Journal, 6,* 65–94.

Lewis, M. (2003). *Moneyball: The art of winning an unfair game.* New York, NY: W. W. Norton.

Macur, J. (2017, February 8). The N.H.L.'s problem with science. Retrieved from https://www.nytimes.com/2017/02/08/sports/hockey/nhl-chronic-traumatic-encephalopathy-cte-juliet-macur.html

Maqbool, K., (2016, April 30). 7 pro sports wearables used by major teams and leagues. Retrieved from http://www.sportswearable .net/7-professional-sports-wearables-used -by-major-teams-and-leagues/

Miami Heat. (1993–1994). *Miami Heat media guide*. Miami, FL: Author.

Miller, M. (1991). *A whole different ballgame*. New York, NY: Birch Lane.

Milwaukee American Association v. Landis, 49 F.2d 298 (D.C. Ill. 1931).

Much, P. J., & Gotto, R. M. (1997). Franchise valuation overview. In A. Friedman & P. J. Much (Eds.), *1997 inside the ownership of professional sports teams* (pp. 6–7). Chicago, IL: Team Marketing Report.

National Basketball Association (NBA). (2010a). Philadelphia 76ers: Front office directory. Retrieved from http://www.nba.com/sixers /front_office/index.html

National Basketball Association (NBA). (2010b). Global sites. Retrieved from http://www.nba .com/global/map/

National Basketball Association (NBA). (2010c). NBA to stage first-ever regular season games in Europe. Retrieved from http://www.nba .com/global/europe_games_100809 .html

National Basketball Players Association (NBPA). (2010). About the NBPA. Retrieved from http://www.nbpa.com

National Football League (NFL). (2016). Personal conduct policy. Retrieved from https://static.nfl.com/static/content/public /photo/2017/08/11/0ap3000000828506.pdf

National Football League Properties, Inc. v. Dallas Cowboys Football Club, Ltd., 922 F. Supp. 849 (S.D.N.Y. 1996).

Neyer, R. (2002, November 5). Red Sox hire James in advisory capacity. *ESPN.com*. Retrieved from http://espn.go.com/mlb/s/2002/1105 /1456563.html

NFL Concussion Settlement. (2017). Retrieved from https://www.nflconcussionsettlement .com/Home.aspx

PGA Tour Canada. (2014). Tournament schedules. Retrieved from https://www.pgatour.com /canada/en_us/tournaments/schedule .html

PGA Tour Charities. (2017, January 25) PGA Tour generates record amounts for charity. Retrieved from https://www.pgatour.com /news/2017/01/25/pga-tour-166-million -charity-2016.html

PGA Tour, Inc. (2018). Tournament schedules. Retrieved from http://www.pgatour.com /tournaments/schedule.2018.html

PGA Tour Latinoamérica. (2014). NEC Series Latinoamérica tournament schedules. Retrieved from https://www.pgatour.com/la /en/tournaments/schedule.html

Popper, B. (2015, August 4). The changeup: How baseball's tech team built the future of television. *The Verge*. Retrieved from https://www.theverge .com/2015/8/4/9090897/mlb-bam-live -streaming-internet-tv-nhl-hbo-now-espn

Professional Hockey Players' Association (PHPA). (2013). ECHL-PHPA collective bargaining agreement. Retrieved from http://www.phpa .com/site/agreements#Salary Floor

Professional Hockey Players' Association (PHPA). (2018). AHL-PHPA collective bargaining agreement. Retrieved from https://www .phpa.com/site/agreements#Per%20Diem

Robinson, C. (2017, December 13). Jerry Jones won his fight with NFL Commish Roger Goodell. Retrieved from https://sports.yahoo.com /jerry-jones-won-fight-nfl-commish-roger -goodell-045522023.html

Rosen, D. (2015, August 4). NHL, Major League Baseball Advanced Media form transformative digital-rights partnership. Retrieved from https://www.nhl.com /news/nhl-major-league-baseball -advanced-media-form-transformative -digital-rights-partnership/c-776246

Sandomir, R. (2008, October 11). NBA and Partner to Help Build 12 Arenas in China. Retrieved from https://www.nytimes.com/2008/10/12 /sports/basketball/12arena.html

Shropshire, K. (1996). *In black and white: Race and sports in America*. New York, NY: New York University Press.

Solomon, B. (2012, March 29). $2 billion dollar Dodgers sale tops list of most expensive sports teams purchases ever. *Forbes*. Retrieved from https://www.forbes.com/sites /briansolomon/2012/03/29/2-billion -dodgers-sale-tops-list-of-most-expensive -sports-team-purchases-ever/#39b097f34206

Staudohar, P. M. (1996). *Playing for dollars: Labor relations and the sports business*. Ithaca, NY: ILR Press.

Van Riper, T., & Karmali, N. (2009, June 22). The NBA's next frontier. Retrieved from http:// www.forbes.com/global/2009/0622/china -india-adidas-nba-next-frontier.html

Venook, J. (2017, April 10). The Upcoming Privacy Battle Over Wearables in the NBA. Retrieved from https://www .theatlantic.com/business/archive/2017/04 /biometric-tracking-sports/522222/

Yasser, R., McCurdy, J., Goplerud, P., & Weston, M. A. (2003). *Sports law: Cases and materials* (5th ed.). Cincinnati, OH: Anderson.

Chapter

11

Lisa P. Masteralexis

Sports Agency

Learning Objectives

Upon completion of this chapter, students should be able to:

1. Describe the reasons why the sports agency industry has grown so rapidly over the past several decades.

2. Discuss the history of the sports agency industry and identify some of the key personalities who defined the industry, such as Mark McCormack, Donald Dell, and Scott Boras.

3. Compare and contrast the representation of team-sport athletes, individual-sport athletes, coaches, and management professionals.

4. Identify the differences involved in representing athletes in different sports.

5. Distinguish between the various types of sports agency organizations, such as freestanding sport management firms, law practice-only

firms, sport management firms affiliated with a law firm, and superagencies.

6. Explain the various fee structures that sports agencies utilize.

7. Identify the career opportunities available in the sports agency industry, and know the skills and education needed to succeed in each of them.

8. Analyze the responsibilities of a sports agent.

9. Discuss the unethical behavior that may occur in the sports agency business and its root causes.

10. Describe some of the methods that governing bodies, players associations, leagues, and government have utilized to regulate the activities of sports agents.

Introduction

This chapter focuses on the field of sports agency, examining how athlete management and marketing firms operate. Many sports agency firms that began by representing athletes have evolved to also include sports marketing and event management segments. They continue to evolve today as the sports agency business innovates.

A quick examination of International Management Group (IMG), one of the very first sports agencies, illustrates this evolution. IMG was launched in 1960 when its founder and sports agency industry innovator **Mark H. McCormack** began representing iconic golfer Arnold Palmer. He soon added Gary Player and Jack Nicklaus to his list of clients, before moving into tennis with Rod Laver in 1968 (IMG, 2004). In more than 40 years of leading IMG, McCormack transformed the company into the leader in managing golfers as well as "running tournaments all over the world in both golf and tennis, even controlling the computer that assigns worldwide rankings to golfers" (Feinstein, 1992, p. 131). IMG is in the business of representing talent across many platforms (modeling, music, sports), plus it owns and runs events for its talent, and produces, distributes, and markets television programming of those events as well as others. Shortly after McCormack's death in 2003, IMG's website posted a letter from its new co-CEOs describing the company as "[t]he world's largest athlete representation firm [that], through its broadcast division, TWI, is both the world's largest independent producer of televised sports programming and distributor of sports television rights" (Johnston & Kain, 2004). The letter also noted the diversity of IMG's areas of business, which Johnston and Kain (2004) attempted to pull together with the term "multi-faceted sports and lifestyle businesses."

Table 11-1 shows IMG's areas of business in 2004 under Johnston and Kain's leadership prior to the firm's sale to Ted Forstmann and Forstmann, Little. It compares the divisions before and after Forstmann's streamlining of the organization and its cost structure by eliminating any services that were not vertically integrated throughout the company, such as the representation of team-sport athletes, artists, and celebrities. Agents of team-sport athletes moved on to competitors, while Forstmann's IMG invested in new areas of business, such as IMG College, and joint ventures in the emerging markets of India, Brazil, China, and Turkey (IMG, 2014). As you'll learn in this chapter, team-sport athlete representation has higher costs and lesser financial rewards. Forstmann expanded IMG's focus to a more global one, acquiring only new companies that complemented IMG's strengths. These moves again positioned IMG as an innovator in the field.

At the time of its sale to William Morris Endeavor (WME) and Silver Lake Partners for $2.3 billion (Plunkett, 2017), IMG had a staff of 3,500 employees in 30 countries (IMG, 2014). The company had 12 identified areas of expertise, plus 4 joint ventures in emerging markets, for a total of 16 divisions (down from 26 divisions a decade earlier) (IMG, 2014). Compare the 2004 and 2014 versions of IMG in Table 11-1.

Today WME/IMG have been combined under the aegis of Endeavor, which positions itself as a global leader in entertainment, sport, and fashion; each of these branches include multiple areas of expertise (six to nine in each segment) (WME/IMG, 2017b). The acquisition of IMG spawned a sports practice. The new entity WME/IMG has even moved into owning and operating its own sports leagues such as the ELeague (an eSports joint venture with Turner Sports), the Ultimate Fighting Championship (UFC), and Professional Bull Riders (PBR), and is a partner in the Turkish Airlines Euroleague (WME/IMG, 2017a). Adding IMG puts WME in a space to better compete with Creative

Table 11-1 IMG's Areas of Business, 2004 and 2014

Areas of Business at Time of Sale to Ted Forstmann (2004)	Areas of Business at Time of Sale to William Morris Endeavor (2014)
IMG Golf	IMG Golf
IMG Tennis	IMG Tennis
IMG Broadcasting	IMG Media
IMG Licensing	IMG Licensing
IMG Consulting	IMG Consulting
IMG Football (American)	IMG College
IMG Academies	IMG Academy
IMG Action Sports	IMG Art + Commerce
IMG Special Projects	IMG Events and Federations
IMG Literary	IMG Performance
IMG Speakers	IMG Clients
IMG Hockey	IMG Joint Ventures (IMG Reliance, IMX, IMG Dogus)
IMG Rugby	
IMG Coaches	
IMG Stadium and Arena Group	
IMG Baseball	
IMG European Football	
IMG Figure Skating	
IMG Fashion	
IMG Winter Sports	
IMG Research	
IMG Creative	
IMG Artists	
IMG Olympics	
IMG Cricket	
IMG Golf Course Services	

Artists Agency (CAA) and its sports division, which has become CAA's most valuable division (J. A. Miller, 2016).

A question for all of you future sports agency entrepreneurs: How would a start-up agency compete with such a behemoth? It is a logical question to ask at a time when many agency firms are operating in an environment of mergers and acquisitions. In the past two decades, the sports agency business has seen

SFX Sports come and go. Built through the acquisition of more than 20 different sports and entertainment firms, SFX Sports was later sold to Clear Channel and spun off to Live Nation. Many of the original agents whose firms were bought by SFX (such as Arn Tellem, the Hendricks brothers, and David Falk) bought back their firms to make a fresh start after SFX Sports became lost within the entertainment giant Live Nation.

Other agencies that sought vertical integration in the sports and entertainment media and marketing businesses, such as Octagon, have outlasted SFX. Octagon is the sports arm of Interpublic Group, a large advertising and marketing communications agency developed through similar acquisitions of established sports agencies. Octagon boasts more than 800 employees in 50 offices across 22 countries on 6 continents (Octagon, 2017). It now manages more than 13,000 events annually, up from 3,200 events in 2007 (Octagon, 2017). It also represents approximately 800 professional athletes and celebrities in music and entertainment in its personalities division (Octagon, 2017). On its marketing research side, rather than target marketing its typical demographic segments (race, gender, ethnicity, etc.), it now focuses on mindset and culture to better connect consumer passion to brands (Octagon, 2018).

Still other firms—namely, Creative Artists Agency (CAA Sports) and Wasserman (formerly Wasserman Media Group [WMG])—are trying to dominate and shape the industry segment created by IMG. In 2006, CAA Sports evolved as a division of Creative Artists Agency, a dynamic and innovative entertainment agency. To the surprise of the firm's entertainment leaders, CAA Sports is now not just its most profitable division (J. A. Miller, 2016), but the most valuable sports agency in the world (Belzer, 2017c).

The concept of developing a sports agency business through growth and acquisitions will be discussed in greater detail later in this chapter. The aspects of the firms that involve event management, media, and marketing are left to those specific chapters. This chapter primarily focuses on representatives of athletes and coaches—the people we commonly refer to as sports agents.

The term **sports agent** is difficult to define. As Ruxin (2004) points out, this term covers a broad range of relationships with an athlete, including friend, lawyer, teacher, or coach. In some aspects, a sports agent is similar to a talent agent in the entertainment industry, in that both serve as personal managers who find the best outlet for the client's talent (Ruxin, 2004). When an agent acts as a representative of an athlete or coach, the law of agency imposes certain fiduciary duties on the agent.

Many people hold themselves out as sports agents. The exact number of sports agents is difficult to pinpoint, but one thing is certain: Barriers to entry are high, because the client pool is limited. Far more people claim to be agents than there are clients to be represented, leading some would-be agents to resort to unethical behavior in an effort to break into the field. This type of malfeasance has led players associations and some federations to certify or register agents.

To give you a sense of the ratios of clients to agents, consider that the four major North American leagues employ slightly more than 4,300 professional athletes. According to Belzer (2017c), 3,600 of those athletes are represented by the top 40 largest sports agencies in the world. Further, according to Belzer, the five largest conglomerates represent more than one-third of all professional athletes globally. Digging into the available numbers of agents, more than 1,900 agents are registered or certified with players associations and/or international federations (Pugh, 2014a, 2014b). Of those, the more than 300 agents certified by the Major League Baseball Players Association (MLBPA, 2017) represent the 1,200 players on a 40-man roster in Major League Baseball (MLB). There are 200 certified agents in the National Hockey League (NHL) (National Hockey League Players Association [NHLPA], 2017). In basketball, the International Basketball Federation (FIBA, 2017) has certified 612 agents globally, with 367 agents also certified by the National Basketball Association Players Association (NBPA, 2017). The National Football League Players Association (NFLPA, 2017) lists 832 agents.

At the global level, the Fédération Internationale de Football Association (FIFA) does not regulate agents, but relies on member associations to do so. When FIFA was deregulated in 2015, there were 6,861 registered soccer agents worldwide, including 160 in the United States, 13 in Mexico, and 44 in Canada (FIFA, 2015). In South America, Brazil (245) and Argentina (219) far outpace other countries in the number of agents registered. Europe has the most agents per continent, with England (451), France (226), and Germany (470) standing out. Italy, however, accounts for the largest number of agents not just for any country in Europe, but in the world—1,060 registered agents (FIFA, 2015).

The Canadian Football League (CFL) is yet another market that agents and their players explore. Currently, the CFL Players Association (CFLPA, 2017) lists 138 registered agents on its site, many of whom also are also registered with the National Football League Players Association (NFLPA). This number is down from the 159 that were registered in 2014 (Masteralexis, 2015).

Examining those numbers, it is easy to see how Shropshire and Davis (2003) estimated that fewer than 100 NBA agents have clients, and only 50% of registered NFL agents actually represent a client in the NFL (Levin, 2007). Many agents have no clients or work part-time to supplement their incomes through other professions, such as law, marketing, accounting, or financial planning. The fact that some athletes have more than one person representing their interests may contribute slightly to the large number of agents. One agent may be retained for contract negotiations; another employed for marketing, public relations, and media work; and yet another for financial advising. In any case, the number of sports agents clearly exceeds the number of potential clients, creating an environment ripe for unscrupulous conduct. Ironically, those who resort to unethical conduct during the recruiting process often do not end up with the clients whom they were pursuing. This chapter discusses in detail the field's challenges to entry and clarifies the role of the sports agent and agency firms in the sport industry and in the lives of the athletes they represent.

In such a competitive market, agents look for other areas in which they might land clients. Representing coaches and executives in professional sports and big-time Division I college programs is a growing area. Another growth area in the United States is in soccer, due to this sport's global popularity and the expansion of Major League Soccer (MLS). Still other representation opportunities exist for Olympic athletes, female professional athletes, and niche sports. It is still an open question as to whether eSports athletes will seek representation. On the one hand, eSports is a growing segment of the industry; on the other hand, eSports athletes may be products of a rebel culture who are not ready to work with establishment agents.

History

The growth of the agency business in recent years has been strong. But how did the agency profession become the entity that it is today? Taking a look back at its historical roots will shed some interesting light on that question.

Theater promoter C. C. "Cash and Carry" Pyle is known as the first sports agent. In 1925, Pyle negotiated a deal with George Halas's Chicago Bears for Red Grange to earn $3,000 per game and an additional $300,000 in endorsement and movie rights (Berry, Gould, & Staudohar, 1986). A few years later, New York Yankee George Herman "Babe" Ruth allegedly consulted sports cartoonist Christy Walsh to serve as his financial advisor during the Great Depression (Neff, 1987).

Until the 1970s, it was extremely rare for team-sport athletes to have agents, because teams refused to deal with them. Some athletes even found that having an agent was detrimental to their contract negotiations. One often-told story

involves a Green Bay Packers player, Jim Ringo. In 1964, Ringo brought his financial advisor to help him negotiate his contract with legendary coach and general manager Vince Lombardi. Lombardi immediately excused himself for a minute. When Lombardi returned, he told the agent he was negotiating with the wrong team, because he had just traded Ringo to Philadelphia (Hofmann & Greenberg, 1989). Interestingly, although this story is *not* true, Vince Lombardi publicly encouraged telling of this tale in the hopes that it would dissuade players from hiring agents or becoming difficult in contract negotiations. Privately, Lombardi stated, "Hell, no, the trade didn't take place in 5 minutes. That's no way to general-manage a football team" ("Sports Legend Revealed," 2011, para. 11).

The inability to negotiate on what the play-rs believed was a level playing field led the dgers' star pitchers Sandy Koufax and Don ale to hire Hollywood agent Bill Hayes present them in 1965. Hayes orchestrated

Koufax's and Drysdale's joint holdout, in which they each demanded a 3-year, $1 million contract, up from the $85,000 and $80,000, respectively, the Dodgers had paid them the season before (Helyar, 1994). The idea of a joint holdout, the amount of money the two demanded, and the prospect of other players trying the tactic outraged the Dodgers. Hayes lined up an exhibition tour for Koufax and Drysdale in Japan and threatened to get Drysdale a movie contract. Although the two had immense talent, the players still had little bargaining power because MLB rules did not allow them to negotiate with other major league teams. As a result, Koufax and Drysdale ended up settling for $125,000 and $115,000, respectively (Helyar, 1994). Those sums were significantly less money than they had sought, but more than they would have received had they bargained individually and without an agent.

Few team-sport athletes had agents until the late 1960s. In that era, even those with agents used them more as advisors than as agents. In 1967, Bob Woolf counseled Detroit Tigers pitcher Earl Wilson. Wilson went to the front office of the Tigers alone while Woolf stayed in Wilson's apartment. Whenever Wilson had a question, he excused himself from the room and called Woolf for more advice (Woolf, 1976). Despite the fact that the door to representation in team sports began to open in 1970, when the MLBPA negotiated for a player's right to be represented by an agent, it did not fully open until free agency was won in 1976 through the Messersmith–McNally arbitration decision.

Players in individual sports such as golf and tennis have relied on agents for a much longer time. C. C. Pyle also made his mark in professional tennis when, in 1926, he guaranteed French tennis star Suzanne Lenglen $50,000 to tour the United States (Berry et al., 1986). At the time people were startled by the sum, but by the end of the tour Pyle had helped popularize professional tennis, and all involved earned a handsome share of the revenues it generated (Berry et al., 1986). Mark H. McCormack, founder of IMG and one of the first agents to represent individual athletes, pioneered the sports marketing industry. A college golfer at William & Mary, McCormack became "famous for launching the modern sports-marketing business when he packaged and marketed Arnold Palmer, endorsement king of the pre–Michael Jordan era" (Katz, 1994, p. 231). Although golfers such as Bobby Jones and Walter Hagen pitched products such as cigarettes and liquor long before Palmer came along, McCormack and Palmer took a different approach to sport marketing, because Palmer told McCormack he would not endorse a product he did not like or use. In a brilliant move, McCormack did not tie Palmer's endorsements to his success on the golf course, but rather to his traits, such as his character, endurance, reliability, and integrity (Palmer, 2017).

This formula worked well. At the time of his death in 2016, Arnold Palmer was ranked second to Tiger Woods as the most wealthy golfer despite the fact that he stopped golfing in 2006 and had not won a tournament in more than 25 years. Palmer was a successful entrepreneur who founded the Golf Channel, and designed and owned golf courses, such as Orlando's Bay Hill. He garnered numerous endorsements and licensing opportunities, two areas where he generated much of his income with products such as the Arnold Palmer Iced Tea line with Arizona Teas (Worldwide golf, 2017).

At his death, Palmer had earned $875 million over his lifetime, putting him third on the all-time earnings list behind Tiger Woods and Michael Jordan. Adjusted for inflation, Palmer's lifetime earnings were $1.3 billion, only $3.6 million of which came from tournament winnings (Badenhausen, 2016). The reason Palmer continued to earn so much annually was due to his long-standing popularity and the resulting licensing fees, endorsement deals, and incredible thirst from customers for the Arizona Ice Tea drink that bears his name (Palmer, 2017; Rovell, 2013). Palmer's success over 60 years stands as a testament to Palmer's traits, his business sense, and the work done by his agency, IMG, to turn him into a corporate enterprise. Palmer truly was the first athlete to become a brand, through his Arnold Palmer Enterprises. The partnership of Palmer and McCormack created a model followed by other top athletes, such as Serena Williams, Maria Sharapova, Gary Player, Jack Nicklaus, LeBron James, Tiger Woods, and Michael Jordan.

Beyond his innovative work with Palmer, McCormack developed opportunities for revenue streams for individual athletes by branching into marketing the events in which they would compete. From there he developed TWI, a broadcast division that has been the largest independent producer of televised sports programming and distributor of sports television rights (IMG, 2003). McCormack's innovations created the model of today's multiservice sports agency—a business model that is employed in many facets of the sport industry, from representation to events to media development and corporate consulting, licensing, and other ventures.

As the sports agency industry has evolved, agencies have innovated to diversify their sport business interests beyond athlete representation. From the start, CAA Sports' model was to build from CAA's expertise in representation and superior client relations, then move into multiple aspects of the sport business, including consulting in many facets of the industry for sports properties, products, and now even ownership (J. A. Miller, 2016). WME/IMG has moved in similar directions—historically expanding into events, media, and consulting, plus more recently getting into league ownership.

Growth of the Sports Agency Business

By the late 1970s, most segments of the sport industry had acknowledged the role that agents had come to play in professional sports. According to Sobel (1990), five factors accounted for the growth of the sports agency business: the evolution of players associations, the reserve system, players' need for financial advice, the development of competing leagues, and an increase in the number of product endorsement opportunities.

Evolution of Players Associations

In the late 1960s and early 1970s, the players associations opened the doors of teams' front offices to sports agents. In negotiations for its second collective bargaining agreement, the MLBPA received a written guarantee that the players would have a right to use an agent in contract negotiations with management (Lowenfish, 1991). In its negotiations with MLB's Management Council, the MLBPA also achieved the right to labor grievance

arbitration. Labor grievance arbitration is a system that allows both players and management to settle work-related conflicts in a hearing before a neutral arbitrator. Players achieved free agency through an arbitration award in 1975.

Achieving free agency enabled agents to negotiate better contracts for players. Players associations opened the door for the agents to have more power, and together they collaborate with and monitor agents through negotiations and arbitrations because both represent the players' interests. The difference between the two is that the union represents the collective interests of all players, whereas an agent represents the individual interests of a particular player. As such, the union negotiates a collective bargaining agreement for all players in the league and the agent negotiates a **standard or uniform player contract** for the player he or she represents. Through collective bargaining, players associations establish salary and benefit minimums; in turn, agents try to negotiate salaries and benefits above and beyond those minimums for the athletes they represent. This dual system is unique to the sport and entertainment businesses—in most labor relationships, the union represents all employees. Players associations support agents by sharing a great deal of information to help them in contract negotiations, such as specific salary and contract terms, as well as by providing guidance in salary and labor arbitrations.

The Reserve System

Until the mid-1970s, MLB players were bound perpetually to their teams by the **reserve system**. Each league used a restrictive system to limit the movement of players and curtail a free and open market so that the owners could retain the rights to players and depress salaries. Baseball's reserve system—the first developed—consisted of the reserve clause and the reserve list. The **reserve clause** in the players' standard contracts gave teams the option to renew players for the following season. Each contract contained a reserve clause, such that a player's relationship with the team could be renewed season after season at the team's option. The **reserve list** was sent to each team in the league. League rules entitled each team to place its reserved players on a list, and the teams had a "gentlemen's agreement" not to offer contracts to any players reserved on a team's list. This two-part system kept players bound to their teams, depressing their salaries and their bargaining leverage.

In 1976, the Messersmith–McNally arbitration toppled the reserve system. In turn, free agency descended on baseball, and agents such as Jerry Kapstein (who represented 60 baseball players) elevated salaries by holding auctions for talented athletes (Helyar, 1994). Kapstein played to the owners' lust for talent by driving them into bidding wars for his free agents (Schwarz, 1996). As salaries increased, so, too, did the players' demand for agents.

Athletes' Need for Financial Planning

As athletes' salaries increased, tax planning (Sobel, 1990), financial planning (Grossman, 2002), and other forms of business advice became vital to a player's financial success. Agents help athletes negotiate more favorable contract clauses for increased income, tax breaks, and post-career income. According to Shropshire (1990), an agent also provides a level of parity in negotiations with the athlete and the team, event, or sponsor. Sports team and event management personnel have a great deal of experience negotiating many contracts each year, whereas an athlete may have just one opportunity to negotiate and, therefore, should hire an agent with the necessary negotiating experience to level the playing field (Shropshire, 1990). This is particularly important when complex systems such as salary caps and the luxury tax are involved. Most athletes likely have not seen the terms in a player contract before,

let alone a collective bargaining agreement. Without an agent's help, an athlete might be at a severe disadvantage in not understanding the terms in the proposed contract, and may also be uninformed on the practices in the industry that will employ the athlete.

Agents allow athletes to focus their attention on performing in their sport while acting as a shield to outside distractions. The shield is the transparent bubble that agents build around their clients to protect them from distractions such as tax and insurance forms, payment of bills, travel arrangements, the media, and the emotional challenges of being a professional athlete (Schwarz, 1996). Further, as Grossman (2002) notes, an athlete's long-term financial success requires the conversion of current income into longer-term financial resources. The dynamics are such that an athlete's career earnings debut at a rate far exceeding those of his or her peers in other industries. Often an athlete may be transformed from relative poverty to wealth almost overnight, but may lack the wisdom and maturity to control spending and save for the future. Grossman (2002) suggests that an athlete's financial team should consist of an accountant or tax advisor, business attorney, banker, investment advisor, insurance professional, and estate attorney. These individuals are separate from the agent representing the athlete's interest in contract negotiations or marketing.

Development of Competing Leagues

During the 1960s, 1970s, and 1980s, the development of competing leagues furthered the growth of the sports agency business (Sobel, 1990). The American Football League (AFL, 1960–1966), the American Basketball Association (ABA, 1967–1976), the World Hockey Association (WHA, 1972–1978), and the United States Football League (USFL, 1982–1986) offered higher salaries to induce marquee players to join the leagues, and these offers provided leverage during contract negotiations. As players jumped to competing leagues, their salaries increased; correspondingly, owners increased the salaries of players whom they were trying to retain. Agents often played a crucial role in locating interested teams in new leagues, sifting through players' offers, and negotiating new contracts. As sport has become more of a global phenomenon over the past three decades and athletes have moved into a worldwide market, agents with an understanding of leagues and teams on a global scale and with international contacts are critical to athletes capitalizing on playing opportunities in countries outside the United States.

Growth of Product Endorsement Opportunities

As professional sport grew into a nationally televised business and its entertainment value increased, so, too, did opportunities for athletes to increase their income through product endorsements (Sobel, 1990). Martin Blackman pioneered the negotiation of endorsement contracts for athletes with his deals for retired athletes to star in Miller Lite's television commercial series (Shropshire, 1990). Today, sports marketing experts create and market an athlete's brand to bring in endorsement revenue. Social media can play a critical role in athlete branding as well, and may call for assistance from professionals with communications expertise.

The lines between sport and entertainment continue to blur, and agents play an important role in parlaying athletes' success from the playing field to entertainment and celebrity. Some athletes have appeared on television shows, and still others have recorded music professionally. Professional athletes have also moved into the popular reality television genre. Former NFL stars Emmitt Smith and Jerry Rice, former NBA star Clyde Drexler, boxers Laila Ali and Evander Holyfield, auto racer Helio Castroneves, and

Olympians Apolo Anton Ohno, Kristi Yamaguchi, Meryl Davis, and Charlie White have all appeared on *Dancing with the Stars*. A number of former sports stars appeared on *Celebrity Apprentice* (e.g., Scott Hamilton, Jenny Finch, Dennis Rodman), putting them back into the spotlight and playing to their competitive fire. Shaquille O'Neal hosted a show called *Shaq Vs.* in which he challenged other star athletes and entertainers to competitions in their expertise, harkening back to popular shows from the late 1970s and 1980s, such as ABC's *Wide World of Sports Superstars* and *Battle of the Network Stars*, that featured athletes and entertainers competing. The latter two were joint productions between IMG's television production arm and ABC Sports, once again demonstrating IMG agents' branding of the athlete as celebrity and the integration of sports and entertainment.

Still other athletes get into entrepreneurial ventures such as golf course design, product development, theme restaurants, sports bars, and music clubs. The sports agent often carries out the business transactions required to establish these ventures.

Evolution of Sports Agencies

In the late 1990s, "uberagencies" were spawned by SFX founder Robert F. X. Sillerman's attempted corporate acquisition revolution. At the time, Sillerman's two companies, the Marquee Group and SFX Entertainment, were international leaders in marketing, concert promotion, and live entertainment production. Sillerman moved into the sporting world by buying up sports agencies, spending $150 million in just 18 months. As the line between sports and entertainment blurred, Sillerman believed SFX Sports Group could provide athletes with one-stop shopping for marketing and negotiation. The intention was for SFX Sports to use its resources to achieve vertical integration (Wertheim, 2001). Interpublic's sport marketing division Octagon also jumped into the fray, pursuing multiple acquisitions of smaller agencies to keep up with SFX Group and IMG, which was already the model of vertical integration that Sillerman sought to achieve.

SFX was brought down by internal strife. Sillerman did not effectively plan for the reality that the newly acquire agencies, which were once fiercely competitive, would have to work together in a cooperative manner when brought under the same financial umbrella. What ensued were numerous power struggles. The sale of SFX in August 2000 to Clear Channel made Sillerman $4.4 billion, but weakened SFX, because sports accounted for less than 10% of SFX's business, and SFX was less than 10% of Clear Channel's core business (Wertheim, 2001).

As SFX Sports disintegrated and many began to think the era of agency mergers and acquisitions was over, along came Wasserman and CAA Sports. Wasserman grabbed Arn Tellem's baseball and basketball agency, which he had bought back from SFX (Hamilton, 2002), plus more than one dozen other agencies, consulting groups, and digital media services over the 15 years since its founding in 2002 (Schoenfield, 2017). Meanwhile, in 2006, the Hollywood entertainment powerhouse Creative Artists Agency ventured into the sports business. The plan from the beginning was to create a sports division with athlete representation being a piece, called by one principal "the Trojan Horse." The plan, however, was to build something beyond a traditional athlete representation agency. That said, CAA Sports acquired IMG's baseball, football, and hockey divisions, as leaders of those divisions had key clauses in their contracts allowing them to leave IMG when IMG's president announced his departure in 2006 (J. A. Miller, 2016). CAA also acquired SFX's football division and Leon Rose's basketball division, which represents LeBron James (Mullen, 2006, 2007a). CAA has continued to pick off other IMG executives, and their clients have followed them to CAA Sports (Futterman, 2010a; Mullen, 2010b). In 2010, IMG settled its lawsuit against former coaches' agent Matthew Baldwin over his defection to CAA Sports and an alleged attempt to steal its coaching representation business (Futterman, 2010b; Mullen, 2010a). Incidentally, CAA dismissed Baldwin prior to his settlement with IMG (Futterman, 2010b).

These aggressive moves to merge and acquire agencies caught many observers by surprise, because this approach seemed to fail in the SFX experiment. However, according to Randy Vataha, president of Boston-based Game Plan, "If it was a complete failure the first time, it wouldn't be happening now. . . . The agent world is extremely entrepreneurial" (Mullen, 2006). Companies such as the old SFX Entertainment and the former Assante Corporation—which also bought a number of top sports agencies about a decade ago, only to dissolve the business a few years later—saw a big opportunity initially. "But once the dust cleared, they had to manage all these mavericks," Vataha said. "I think the people doing this now think they have learned from the mistakes of the earlier deals" (Mullen, 2006). Some industry experts, including agents and others who have talked to CAA President Richard Lovett, who is leading the sports agency acquisition charge, note that CAA may avoid some of the pitfalls of the past because, after all, talent representation is CAA's core business (CAA represents such entertainment stars as Tom Cruise, George Clooney, Eva Longoria, Meryl Streep, and Steven Spielberg). Additionally, CAA's leadership realized it must diversify to be successful, so it brings in the bulk of its revenue in other ventures such as representing sport properties. The culture of CAA was built on innovation and a focus on client relationships—a culture that translated well to sports (J. A. Miller, 2016). The plan has succeeded, as within a decade CAA became the top agency.

Tellem, who was one of the agents whose services were acquired by the old SFX Entertainment and is now the head of athlete management for Wasserman, knows about the mistakes of the past firsthand. "Our plan is not to do a roll-up of sports agencies. I have been there and that is a recipe for disaster," said Tellem. SFX's aggregation of sports agencies "was done as a way of building up a company of critical mass and then selling it," according to Tellem (Mullen & Broughton, 2008, p. 1). Tellem added that he decided to join Wasserman because the company's owner, Casey Wasserman, is committed to building something that lasts and because the company's core business is sports.

In December 2013, the sports agency world saw yet another acquisition, when entertainment talent agency William Morris Endeavor and Silver Lake Partners purchased IMG for $2.3 billion. The combination of WME and IMG will pose a challenge for would-be competitors when it comes to talent recruitment and acquisition. This acquisition by WME will bring together the sports and entertainment worlds, strikingly similar (at least on paper) to the plans followed by CAA Sports and Roc Nation, Jay-Z's new sports representation venture (Ozanian, 2013).

A further challenge that SFX faced was an issue noted by Donald Dell, sports agency pioneer and founder of ProServ: "We had 15 companies bought in 2½ years, . . . [so, w]e had 15 egomaniacs, all strutting around telling everyone what to do, and nothing happened" (Mullen & Broughton, 2008, p. 1). Finally, as noted by AEG president and CEO Tim Leiweke, another difference between SFX and CAA Sports is that the latter has aligned with a sports medicine and performance institute to help athletes get drafted in higher positions or signed to teams (Mullen & Broughton, 2008). As the agency business has evolved, athletes have come to expect that agents will pick up much of the cost of training for them. WME/IMG, for example, operates IMG Academy, a multisport

training academy in Florida. In 2007, one football agent suggested that the NFL Combine preparation runs at least $1,000 per week for training, plus housing, a stipend, a car, and food for the athlete. Thus, an agent may invest nearly $20,000 in preparing one player for the Combine (Kuliga, 2007). Creating alliances or partnerships with training facilities and car dealerships is one method of limiting these kinds of costs or even deriving some revenues from the relationships for sports agencies.

A key difference between firms that represent individual athletes and those that primarily represent team-sport athletes is that the firms doing individual representation are intimately involved in all aspects of the sport, from running the sports' tournaments to televising them. Such involvement can create a conflict of interest. As Brennan (1996) points out, athletes often decide that the conflict created when their agent becomes their employer is not as trying as the conflict created when their training and traveling bills come due and they have generated no income from their sport.

Top-level Olympic and Paralympic athletes have increasingly found that they, too, have a greater need for sports agents to connect them to corporate brands and find post-Games opportunities to earn revenue off their performances. From a marketing standpoint, these athletes have a six-week window of intense interest in them. Within that window and based on their performances, agents must find opportunities. At the Summer Games, the Olympians in the most demand are those in the sports of swimming, women's gymnastics, and track and field (D. Miller, 2016). In the Winter Olympic Games, athletes involved in skiing and figure skating rise to the top.

Octagon's Peter Carlisle created a niche in representation of Olympians, starting with Winter Olympic snowboarders and skiers and then moving into the Summer Games with swimmer Michael Phelps. Carlisle's work with

Phelps resembles the partnership of McCormack and Palmer. Like Palmer, Phelps was clear in what his marketing goal was. Phelps wanted to bring swimming into the mainstream—for instance, to get it on ESPN's *Sports Center*. Carlisle worked to create marketing opportunities that would bring Phelps and his sport into the mainstream. Phelps, the United States' most decorated Olympian, continues to keep the sport and himself on that global stage through such activities as his VISA sponsorship relationship and his development of the Michael Phelps Swim School, both of which emphasize his community work in swimming (Carlisle, 2012).

After the Rio 2016 Sumer Olympic Games, gymnastics gold medalist Simone Biles came away with $2 million in endorsements, but few others did as well (Peltz, 2016). Some, like swimmer Katie Ledecky, faced National Collegiate Athletic Association (NCAA) rules that limited their ability to cash in on Olympic fame; others are quickly forgotten as sports fans looked ahead to the annual return of the NFL and college football (Peltz, 2016).

Representing Individual Athletes

Representing the individual athlete differs significantly from representing the team-sport athlete. Much of what the individual athlete earns is dependent on consistent performance in events, appearance fees from events, and the ability to build a brand and market his or her image. An agent representing an individual athlete often travels with the athlete, tending to daily distractions so the athlete can stay focused on winning. For instance, as tennis star Ivan Lendl's agent for 7 years, Jerry Solomon of ProServ spent nearly 24 hours a day, 7 days a week, traveling and representing Lendl. As one can imagine, such commitment takes a toll on one's social and personal life, but often is necessary to retain the client. When Solomon eventually pulled away from this relationship with Lendl, Lendl resented it and moved from ProServ to IMG (Feinstein, 1992). An agent of an individual-sport athlete is often more involved in managing the individual player's career, much like business managers hired by entertainers.

Management tasks include booking exhibitions and special competitions to supplement the athlete's winnings from tour events as well as managing training, travel, lodging, and the athlete's personal life. For the team-sport athlete, the team takes care of most of these details. However, competition in acquiring and retaining clients is causing agents to offer more services to team-sport athletes as well, intensifying the 24/7 nature of the business for all agents. Some agents take a more active role in their athletes' training regimens by providing access to trainers and coaches (Helyar, 1997), or even signing an alliance with their Olympic appearances (Brennan, 1996). For example, as figure skating's popularity has increased, so has the amount of money flowing into the sport, legitimately creating an increased need for agents. Like other national governing bodies, the U.S. Figure Skating Association expects stars to be out participating in promotions, interviews, tours, and various competitions, and as a result these young athletes are now hiring agents to promote them and protect them from the "blast furnace media" (Brennan, 1996, p. 126). Families often struggle financially to enable a child to pursue the Olympic dream, but now, with the help of an agent, an Olympic athlete may earn some money to help defray at least a portion of his or her training and traveling expenses (Brennan, 1996).

Marketing is critical for individual-sport athletes, who are dependent on sponsorship contracts to provide them with products and equipment and to earn income for travel and training costs. There is great emphasis on branding athletes. Although branding is the current buzzword, innovative sport marketing agencies such as IMG have been doing it (just not labeling it as such) for years. For instance, in a 2004 interview with *BusinessWeek*, Arnold Palmer described how, even in the 1960s, IMG was thinking about the development of the Arnold Palmer brand. Palmer explained that he posed a question to his IMG agent about how a very intense commercial shoot could be replicated when he was old, and the agent responded, "We will have established you as a business, and you personally will not be so important" (Brady, 2004). This answer was given long before "branding" was a focus in the marketing world. Indeed, Mark McCormack's identification of Palmer's marketing appeal and his ability to manage Palmer's off-course ventures led to Palmer's continued success (Hack, 2008). Despite not having a major tour victory since 1973, Palmer was the second highest-paid retired athlete in 2013, earning $40 million in that year (Badenhausen, 2014). The Arnold Palmer name was licensed in a way that his brand continued to reap benefits for him and his heirs. For instance, the Arizona Ice Tea drinks that bear his name bring in 25% of the company's $200 million in revenues, and in Asia IMG continues to manage 50 Palmer licensees and 400 stores bear his name (Badenhausen, 2014).

Building a brand out of an athlete does not work for every athlete. The athlete must be good enough at the sport to command interest. Mark McCormack created brands for those clients who had talent, but also a marketing presence away from the field, court, or ice (Hack, 2008).

Challenges do exist in athlete branding. For instance, if advertisements and products are not a good fit with the athlete's personality or do not work to raise an athlete's image, they can work against the athlete. A good example of this dilemma was former 7-foot, 6-inch Chinese Houston Rocket star Yao Ming, who was criticized for not maintaining better control of his image outside of China. Ming did advertisements that furthered cultural stereotypes (VISA check cards) and positioned him as freakishly tall (Apple Computer), rather than as a premier athlete.

To change this perception, some marketers, such as branding expert Wendy Newman, advocate an approach called *person-centered branding*. Using this strategy, an authentic brand is created based on who the person is, focusing on the person's identity to establish an enduring brand, as opposed to capitalizing for the short term on an athlete's game or performance and contriving an image to fit a product or brand. The first strategy promises to last a lifetime, whereas the second will likely fade away with the end of the athlete's playing career (Newman, 2007).

Another challenge that arises from athlete branding is that it is tied so strongly to the public's perception of one individual's personality and reputation. If an athlete experiences damage to their reputation, such as those we've seen with Michael Phelps (marijuana use), Kobe Bryant (sexual assault charges), or Tiger Woods (marital problems and injuries), the challenge is whether the damage to the athlete might extend to the company's reputation. Another concern is if the athlete's performance does not live up to the hype or if their athletic career suffers, will the corporate brand also suffer. Another question, is whether the company should stick with the athlete in the hopes of a rebound or whether the athlete's image can rebound at all. Using Tiger Woods as an example, in his first round of challenges with the accusations of extramarital affairs, his sponsors stepped away from him, however, in his second round of challenges involving driving under the influence of painkillers, his endorsement companies have stayed supportive due to Tiger's brand strength and by adopting the sentiment that people have the capacity to forgive and forget (Schonbrun, 2018).

Representing Coaches and Management Professionals

A handful of sports agents represent professional and collegiate coaches. The growing income of coaches is one reason for their entrance into this segment. The top 10 NCAA men's college basketball coaches contracts fall in the range of $2 million to $7 million, with Mike Krzyzewski of Duke leading the group with a 2013 salary of $7,233,976, up $2,534,406 from 2012 (Berkowitz, Upton, Dougherty, & Durkin, 2013a). Compensation for NCAA college football coaches has increased substantially, with the top 10 2017 salaries ranging from Texas A & M's Kevin Sumlin's $5 million (*USA Today*, 2017) to number 1 Alabama football coach Nick Saban's $11.132 million (*USA Today*, 2017b). The salaries of the 10 highest-paid college basketball coaches range from $2.65 million for Virginia Tech's Buzz Williams (number 10) to $7.1 million for Kentucky's John Caliperi (*USA Today*, 2017a). By comparison, in the professional coaching ranks in 2017, the top 10 salaries in the NFL were in the range of $6 million at the low end to the more than $8 million earned by Seattle Seahawks coach Pete Carroll (Oregon Live, 2017). The top 10 coaching salaries in the NBA range from the San Antonio Spurs' Gregg Poppovich's $11 million to the $5.5 million earned by the Orlando Magic's Fran Vogel (Other League, 2017a). By comparison, the top five MLB managers earn $3 million to $5 million annually (Berman, 2017). In the NHL, the top five reported head coaching salaries fall in the range of $2.75 million to $6.25 million per year (Other League, 2017b). Agents can earn a respectable commission off coaches' salaries, and these clients often come with fewer problems and headaches due to their age and life experience. Coaching contract commissions are also set by the market, as there is no union regulation of the fees.

A second reason for coaches to hire agents is the increased job movement and added pressures on them to succeed (Greenberg, 1993). The increased complexities of the position of head or assistant coach may make having an agent to rely on for advice and counsel almost a necessity. One agent credited with growing the salaries of NFL coaches, Bob LaMonte, views the modern-day coach as a CEO. He therefore prepares the coach to be a CEO while at the same time negotiating CEO-like pay from club owners (Wertheim, 2004). For these same reasons, management professionals, such as general managers in professional sports, are turning to sports agents and attorneys to assist in their contract negotiations with clubs. The "Career Opportunities" section later in this chapter discusses specific details of coaching contract negotiations.

Sports Agency Firms

There is no blueprint for structuring a sports agency firm. In small firms, an agent works alone or with a small group of employees, and work may be outsourced to other professionals. In larger firms, the agent may be part of an international conglomerate representing many athletes in a broad range of sports and working on many aspects of an athlete's career. Often these divisions will have a big-name agent as the head of the division, with a number of subordinate agents working to make the operation run smoothly.

In a presentation before the American Bar Association's Forum Committee on the Entertainment and Sports Industries, law professor Robert A. Berry posited that there are three models for the sports agency business (Berry, 1990). The first and most popular model is the **freestanding sport management firm**. Here the business is established as a full-service firm providing a wide range of services to the athlete. Although each sport management firm may not perform all services discussed in the "Career Opportunities" section, it is likely that a firm performs several of them, including contract negotiations, marketing, and financial planning (Berry, 1990). These freestanding sport management firms have evolved to: represent athletes only, such as the Scott Boras Corporation (baseball) and Newport Sports Management (hockey), combine athlete representation, event management, and industry consulting, such as WME/IMG, Octagon, CAA Sports, and Wasserman, all of which have numerous divisions across many sports and events or be part of a venture, such as Fenway Sports Management that acts as an agent for its ventures subsidiaries as well as for unaffiliated clients.

According to Shropshire (1990), a freestanding sport management firm's main benefits are two-fold: (1) The athlete is presumably able to receive the best service without having to shop around for many experts and (2) the agent retains all aspects of the athlete's business. The firm benefits because the athlete usually pays fees for any services provided beyond the contract negotiation. Fees are discussed in greater detail later in this chapter.

Berry (1990) identifies a second type of firm as a **law practice only**. In this type of firm, "lawyer sports representatives often participate as principals in a sports management firm, but opt to include this as just one aspect of their law practice" (p. 4). In such a practice, the lawyer performs many legal tasks for the athlete, such as contract negotiation, legal representation in arbitration or other proceedings, legal counseling, dispute resolution, and preparing tax forms. Often the lawyers do not undertake financial management, marketing, or investing of the athlete's money. A sports lawyer may, however, oversee the retention of other needed professionals to advise the athlete and protect him or her from incompetent service (Berry, 1990). Lon Babby, formerly a partner at the Washington, D.C., law firm of Williams & Connolly, was known for charging clients an hourly rate and represented NBA stars Grant Hill and Tim Duncan as well as WNBA stars Alana Beard and Tamika Catchings. This practice was first popularized by Babby before he became the president of basketball operations for the Phoenix Suns. Babby also introduced the hourly rate to baseball representation. Williams & Connolly

continues the practice of hourly representation as part of the firm's services.

The third type of firm identified by Berry (1990) is the **sport management firm affiliated with a law firm**. Many sports lawyers who represent athletes worked within a law practice, but as their business grew they recognized the advantages of offering additional services to the athlete. Some have abolished their law practices in favor of becoming freestanding sport management firms, but others have retained a law practice and created a sport management subsidiary within the practice to provide those services not traditionally offered by lawyers. A trend in the past 20 years has been for law firms to create an affiliate relationship, whereby the law firm remains its own entity but creates a working relationship with a freestanding sport management firm, with each party providing services the other does not offer (Berry, 1990).

Small firms find greater success by representing athletes in one sport and focusing on one or two services for the athletes or coaches. Such firms generally outsource tax planning and preparation, financial investing, public relations, and, more recently, physical and psychological career preparation. Large firms employ professionals from many disciplines to provide services ranging from negotiating contracts to marketing the athlete's image to financial planning and developing outside business interests (Ruxin, 2004). Most agencies fall somewhere in between these two extremes, although the large multifaceted firm with offices worldwide is becoming an increasingly dominant force in the athlete representation market (Ruxin, 2004).

The different types of firms are market driven. Some athletes prefer association with a large firm, whereas others prefer the individual attention of a small firm. Those who choose the large firms often do so for the following reasons: (1) A large firm provides one-stop shopping by employing many skilled professionals to take care of all services; (2) a large firm may have a more established history, reputation, and industry contacts; (3) many athletes prefer representation by firms representing other star players (it is similar to being on the same team); and (4) some athletes believe that having an agent who represents many players helps their own bargaining position. For instance, some athletes choose an agency such as Octagon on the assumption that the sheer number of athletes it represents (approximately 800) must translate into contacts with a large number of general managers, events, and/or product companies, and an even larger number of marketing opportunities. Still others may choose to go with an agent due to the perceived or real influence that person has on the industry. For example, over the past 30 years **Scott Boras** has built an agency in baseball that some have argued influences the entire baseball industry. He has revolutionized the approach to player–team negotiations by relying on a deep understanding of the game and the business of baseball that enables him to wield baseball statistics, tough negotiating tactics, knowledge of the rules, and a free-market philosophy to change the market for players (Anderson, 2007; Pierce, 2007). In fact, it has been argued that Boras's player signings and deals with the owner of the team (to the chagrin of the club's general manager) influenced the ability of the Detroit Tigers to make it into the 2006 World Series (Kepner, 2006). Athletes have been known to choose Boras on the basis of this reputation (Pierce, 2007), knowing they have limited opportunities to get their full value in the market. Other athletes might prefer to be one of the few individuals represented by a person with whom they build a bond or whom they trust, rather than becoming one of a stable of clients at a large firm. Those athletes may opt to have many individuals work one-on-one with them for different aspects of their career, such as contract negotiations, marketing, financial planning, public relations, and career and post career planning.

Athletes who choose small firms often do so because of the attention they receive from such a firm. At large firms, the attention of the more established agents often goes to their superstar clients. Those professional athletes on the bottom of the priority list may be assigned an assistant to deal with or may have trouble getting telephone calls returned. Even established athletes may have difficulty with the large firms. For example, golfers Greg Norman and Nick Price moved away from the large IMG and formed their own management companies to focus solely on their own needs because they found that calls to IMG often took a couple of days to be answered—not because IMG was irresponsible, but because it had so many clients to service. Both golfers also thought it more cost-effective to hire their own staff than to pay IMG's 20% to 25% commissions on business deals (Feinstein, 1995). Interestingly, Greg Norman returned to IMG as a client and has since switched to CAA Sports.

Fees Charged by Sports Agents

Fees charged by agents are market driven, though they may also be limited by players association regulations. Fees are usually based on one of four methods: flat fee, percentage of compensation, hourly rate, or a combination of an hourly rate with a percentage of compensation cap (McAleenan, 2002). The first method, the flat fee arrangement, requires an athlete to pay the agent an agreed-upon amount of money before the agent acts for the athlete (McAleenan, 2002).

The second method, percentage of compensation, is by far the most popular arrangement. Although it is criticized as being inflated, agent Leigh Steinberg defends it. Steinberg "dismisses those who bill by the hour as 'egg-timer agents' and argues that such a fee structure militates against an important aspect of the agenting: developing a personal relationship with clients"

(Neff, 1987, p. 83). The fee often covers not just the negotiation, but all of the work related to the provisions of the contract over its term.

A drawback to the percentage formula is that the agent is not guaranteed to receive his or her expected percentage, in that an agent is paid as the athlete earns the money. For instance, the NFLPA limits the agent's fee to 1.5% to 3% of the contract, and in the NFL there is no such thing as a guaranteed contract (Heitner, 2016). An agent may negotiate a contract, but if the athlete is cut during training camp, the team owes the player nothing more than a signing or reporting bonus (if that was in the contract). Despite the time invested, the agent may never see the full fee from the contract he or she negotiated.

Another example of the riskiness of this approach can be found in baseball, where agent regulations limit an agent from earning any income from an athlete in the minor leagues. An agent may charge a fee for negotiating a signing bonus when a player is drafted, but the regulations prohibit an agent from receiving a percentage fee until the athlete has exceeded the league minimum salary (usually in the player's second season in the majors). While representing players in the minor leagues, an agent incurs a number of expenses, among them equipment, travel, and communication expenses, plus costs associated with negotiating trading card and in-kind product deals. In fact, because of the way the sporting goods industry has evolved, the agent actually supplies the products (e.g., gloves, cleats, bats, and apparel) that a minor leaguer needs to succeed out of his or her own budget. Until an agent lands a top-round client, the agent is often left paying dues and investing a great deal of time, energy, and personal money into clients who may not provide a financial return. To make matters worse, some established agents make it their practice to market themselves to players only once those players are legitimate prospects or after the players are called up to the major leagues. As a result, players may leave their agent from the minors for a more established one once they reach the majors, never having paid a cent to the agent who invested in them in the minors.

There are also numerous examples of agents in the NFL losing clients between the time of the draft and the actual signing of the contract. Recruiting by competitors does not stop simply because someone is drafted. In such a case, if there was a signed representation contract, the agent may pursue an arbitration case against the athlete for payment of services rendered and perhaps file a lawsuit against the other agent for tortious interference with a contractual or advantageous business relationship.

The third agent-payment method, the hourly rate, is often not used for the reasons stated previously by Leigh Steinberg. For a high-round draft pick or a superstar free agent, however, McAleenan (2002) suggests that an hourly rate will provide the lowest fee. For example, assume the agent charges $450 per hour and works 40 hours negotiating a 3-year, $1 million compensation package. Working with a 4% fee structure, the agent would receive $40,000; by comparison, working under an hourly rate, the agent would receive only $18,000 (McAleenan, 2002). What this example fails to recognize, though, are the numerous hours spent on the telephone with the athlete in career counseling or working out details of the contract with the team or athlete, which does not usually occur with, for example, a corporate client. The relationship between athlete and agent is such that for most athletes, it would probably sour the relationship to turn on the clock every time an athlete called to ask his or her agent a question or tell the agent about the previous night's game. The relationship between the athlete and the agent is as much a personal one as a business one.

The fourth method, the hourly rate with a compensation cap, addresses the athlete's concern that the agent may pad the billable hours and inflate the fee. This option provides an hourly rate, the total of which will not exceed a certain percentage of the athlete's compensation, called the percentage cap (McAleenan, 2002).

A key component of the MLBPA, NFLPA, NHLPA, and NBPA regulations governing agents is limits on agent fees. Players associations have set ceilings for agents' fees at between 1.5% and 6% of the athlete's compensation. The fierce competition for clients has driven the average fees down closer to 2% to 3%, although well-established agents still charge the maximum percentages (Burwell, 1996). The NFLPA and NBPA have set maximum fees. The NBPA's regulation sets the maximum fee an agent can charge for negotiating a minimum salary at $2,000, or 4% for those contracts above the minimum. The NFLPA has a similar measure that limits an agent's fee to between 1.5% and 3% of the player's compensation based on the player's contract and status/designation (i.e., free agent, franchise, transition player).

The MLBPA and NHLPA do not limit the fee charged by an agent. However, the MLBPA does not allow an agent to charge a fee unless the agent negotiates a contract above the minimum salary, which was $545,000 in 2018. Then, the MLBPA recommends an agent charge a fee based only on the amount that exceeds the minimum. For example, if a baseball player's salary was $600,000 in 2018, the union urges the agent to charge his or her percentage on $55,000 (the amount of value that the agent actually added to the minimum contract). Therefore, if the agent's fee was 5%, it would mean the agent would earn $2,750. Because that amount is so low, agents often take 5% of the total contract. Another stipulation is that the agent's fee cannot bring the athlete's compensation below the minimum player salary. In addition, an agent can be paid only as the athlete is paid, and can be paid a percentage of any bonus included in the contract only if the athlete actually earns the bonus.

Other aspects of player association regulations are discussed later in the chapter.

These fee limitations apply only to the fees the agents can charge for negotiating the athlete's contract. In an attempt to undercut their competition, occasionally some agents will charge the same fee percentage for negotiating the athlete's marketing deals as for negotiating the player's contract. That is definitely not the norm, as marketing fees charged by agents generally range between 15% and 33%. Although this is a much higher rate than the team contract negotiation compensation, a great deal of work goes into creating an athlete's image in the media and then selling that image to marketers at companies to create a positive fit for the athlete and the product. Imagine being the agent responsible for marketing athletes in the midst of scandals, such as Tiger Woods, Lance Armstrong, or Alex Rodriguez. High-profile scandals force agents to devote a great deal of time and energy to crisis management at the time of the incident and then to resurrecting images and convincing corporations to invest in endorsement opportunities with athletes whose images come with some baggage. Beyond the marketing fees, agents may also charge for other services rendered, such as tax planning, financial planning, and investment advising.

For athletes in other sports and for coaches, there are no regulations regarding fees, so the fees may be higher. The athlete or coach and the agent negotiate these fees individually, so the fee will depend on market factors and bargaining power. In tennis, for example, the standard fee players pay agents when they first become professionals is 10% of their prize money and 20% to 25% of all other revenues, whereas stars have their prize money fee waived and off-court fees cut to 10% or less (Feinstein, 1992). For example, when Ivan Lendl was a ProServ client, his contract provided for a flat fee of $25,000 and 7.5% of all earnings (Greenberg, 1993).

Career Opportunities

A sports agency is a business and, as with any other business, a range of opportunities exist for employees. As many sports agencies have evolved, they have hired employees similar to those in mainstream consulting businesses. These employees include individuals with expertise in marketing, management, finance, accounting, operations, and the like. They may be working to keep the agency business afloat or they may be working as consultants to the agency's clients. A quick look at job listings for one of the larger agencies on its website includes openings for accountants, a finance executive, account executives (sales/marketing), production assistants (broadcasting), communications specialists, event specialists, and more. Some agencies, such as WME-IMG and CAA, have new employees start in the mailroom so that they will literally work their way up through divisions, learning the firm from the bottom up.

Sports Event Manager

Some sport management firms control the rights to sporting events and hire **sports event managers** to run these events. Event managers generally have no involvement with the representation of professional athletes. Event managers must be very detail oriented, organized, and able to work in an environment that can be stressful at times.

Sports Marketing Representative/ Account Executive

The **sports marketing representative** or **account executive** coordinates all of the marketing and sponsorship activities for sport properties. Sport properties include sporting events run by the agency firm and the athletes the agency represents. A sports marketing representative's responsibilities may include conducting market research, selling sponsorships for an event, promoting an event and the

athletes participating in it, and making calls to find endorsement opportunities for athletes who are clients of the firm. As sports agencies face greater competition in the market, more firms are focusing their energies on marketing activities and even consulting in marketing because marketing activities generate significant new revenue streams with no restrictions on the fees charged for them.

Sports Account Executive

An account executive for a sports agency will be involved with the agency's corporate clients by servicing their needs and leading sales and marketing efforts. The position may involve revenue generation, consulting activities, and customer management.

Sports Agent

Sports agents often refer to themselves as athlete representatives or sports lawyers. To some, the term *sports agent* has a negative connotation. Not all sports agents are lawyers. While they need not be lawyers, most are required by the players associations to hold a bachelor's degree.

Functions of sports agents vary widely. Some agents perform just one function, whereas others may have a number of employees performing these functions for clients. The ability to offer a broad range of services depends on an agent's education, skills, and training, and the amount of time he or she can devote to these tasks. The amount of time spent per athlete is also dependent on the number of athletes the agent represents and their needs at the time. The number of agents or employees in the firm and the variety of skills each has to offer will influence the ability to offer many services. The eight essential functions performed by sports agents are as follows:

- Negotiating and administering the athlete's or coach's contract.
- Marketing.

- Negotiating the athlete's or coach's marketing and endorsement contracts.
- Financial planning.
- Career and post-career planning.
- Dispute resolution.
- Legal counseling.
- Personal care.

These eight functions are discussed individually in the following sections.

Negotiating and Administering the Contract

The Athlete's Contract

Contract negotiation varies depending on whether the agent is negotiating a contract for an individual athlete to participate in an exhibition or event or negotiating a team-sport contract. When negotiating a contract for an individual athlete, the agent must be familiar with the sport and the rules, regulations, and common practices of its governing body. When negotiating a contract for a team-sport athlete, the agent must understand the value of the player's service, be knowledgeable about the sport, and know the collective bargaining agreement, the standard or uniform player contract, and other league documents.

Some examples of negotiable terms for team-sport athletes include the following:

- Bonuses (signing, reporting to training camp, attendance, incentives).
- Deferred income (income paid after the player has retired from the sport).
- Guaranteed income (income guaranteed to be paid to the player even if he or she has retired).
- A college scholarship plan (available for MLB players leaving college early).
- Roster spots (generally not available, but positions on the 40-man roster in baseball are negotiable).

Although it might appear that with standard player contracts and many contractual limitations, such as restrictions on rookie contracts, anyone could negotiate an athlete's contract, such a thought loses sight of everything involved in contract negotiations. For instance, a player's value should drive the negotiating process, and a great deal of preparation goes into knowing and maximizing the player's value. Agents today are relying more on analytics and bringing metrics into negotiations. Like their team counterparts, some agency firms hire statisticians and analysts to prepare for salary arbitrations and contract negotiations. Understanding how an athlete's value and the team's needs create leverage on one side or the other is also a key to preparation. It is important to assess the role that salary caps or the luxury tax as well as team finances will play in the contract negotiation. Negotiations differ based on where an athlete falls in the span of his or her career, because rookie versus veteran contract negotiations differ greatly. Such a discussion exceeds the scope of this chapter, but please do give the differences in the types and context of negotiations some thought.

After negotiating the contract, the agent's work continues. Agents must administer the contract, which involves ensuring that the parties comply with their contractual promises. If promises are not kept, the agent may become involved in conversations, negotiations, and ultimately dispute resolution between the player and the club. The agent may have to resolve unanticipated situations through informal channels, such as partial or full contract renegotiation, or through formal ones, such as alternative dispute resolution systems or the courts. As the representative of the player and the negotiator of the contract, when problems arise, it is the agent's responsibility to represent the athlete's interests.

The Coach's Contract

Due to the lack of job security for coaches in the Division I college and professional ranks, it has become increasingly important for coaches to have well-drafted contracts and a representative available to administer the deal (Greenberg, 1993). When negotiating a contract for a college coach, an agent must be familiar with the sport, NCAA and conference rules, any applicable state open records laws, and common concerns of collegiate athletic directors and university presidents (Greenberg, 1993). It has also become standard practice that coaches' contracts contain a clause restricting coaches from seeking endorsements outside of university apparel contracts without consent from the university.

When negotiating a contract for a professional coach, an agent must understand the league's constitution and bylaws, as well as the coaching and management environment of a particular team or league. There is no uniform coaching contract, so there may be more flexibility in negotiable terms.

Examples of negotiable terms in coaches' contracts include the following (Greenberg, 1993):

- Duties and responsibilities.
- Term of employment and tenure.
- Compensation clauses (guaranteed, outside/supplemental, endorsement, and deferred income; bonuses; moving expenses; retirement; and fringe benefits).
- Termination clause.
- Buyout/release of contractual obligations by either side.
- Support of the team by athletic program or ownership.
- Support staff (assistant coaches, other personnel).
- Confidentiality (to the extent allowable under law, the promise to keep terms confidential).
- Arbitration of disputes.

In the past decade, representing coaches has become far more lucrative for agents, particularly for those representing Division I college football and basketball coaches and NBA coaches. Agents have played an important role in negotiating for coaches to serve in dual roles as general managers or team presidents. Such clauses give the coach more power in player personnel decisions and presumably more control over the athletes and the direction in which the team is headed in achieving its goals. This trend is a direct reaction to athletes' apparent loss of respect for their coaches and the athletes' temptation to remove the coach due to athletes' leverage and financial clout with the team (Boeck, 1997). It is also a reaction to the coaches having to take the brunt of the blame for a losing season. Long-term multimillion-dollar deals for coaches influence the dynamics in the locker rooms and on the basketball courts (Boeck, 1997).

Higher salaries paid to coaches reflect the greater importance now placed on the role of head coach as leader. In most sports, games are far more complicated and strategic than in years past owing to greater reliance on statistics, video, scouting, and the like (CBS News, 2004). The head coach must manage a fluid team whose roster changes frequently due to salary caps, free agency, and the occasional disciplinary problem. The head coach must also deal with 24/7 traditional media and social media in ways unheard of decades earlier.

Marketing the Athlete

The sports agent should develop a plan in which each endorsement creates an image consistent with the athlete's or coach's ambitions and long-range goals (Lester, 2002). At the same time, the agent must keep in mind that the client's career and public persona may be short-lived, and thus "every opportunity should be assessed according to its potential to maximize the [client's] earnings and exposure during and after his or her active playing [or coaching] career" (Lester, 2002, p. 27-2). The sports agent must also be familiar with restrictions that may limit an athlete's or coach's marketing opportunities. Restrictions include limitations on compensation set by the NCAA, national governing bodies, professional sports regulations, group licensing programs, and rules prohibiting the endorsement of alcohol or tobacco products (Lester, 2002).

Group licensing programs are very popular among professional sports unions, where a major share of the players association's funding often comes from trading card deals or marketing arms, such as the NFLPA's Players, Inc. Under these group licensing programs, the players pool their bargaining power and licensing resources in exchange for a prorated (proportionate) share of any surplus income. Such a scheme allows licensees one-stop shopping for multiplayer promotions. The definition of a group varies by league. The numbers of players necessary in group licensing programs are as follows: at least 6 for the NFLPA, at least 3 for MLBPA, at least 6 for NBPA, and 5 to 10 for the NHLPA (Lester, 2002).

Most athletes agree to participate in these programs. Some notable exceptions in the past were Michael Jordan (NBA), Barry Bonds and Alex Rodriguez (MLB), and LaVar Arrington (NFL). Keeping in mind that agents do not receive compensation from group licensing programs, the movement away from group licensing by superstars may provide additional revenues for agents.

Agents usually seek product endorsements (goods necessary for the athlete to play the sport such as equipment) before nonproduct endorsements because they are easier to obtain (Lester, 2002). Before targeting potential endorsements, the agent should assess the athlete's marketability. The assessment should include the athlete's desire for endorsements, willingness to make appearances, likes and dislikes of products, and strengths and weaknesses (Lester, 2002). To determine an athlete's marketability, an agent must be sure that the athlete has a positive image, a clean reputation, and on- and off-the-field achievements (Lester, 2002). An agent must also consider the level of appeal of the athlete—that is, whether he or she will be successful at a local,

regional, national, or international level and with a brand that has the same level of reach (Lester, 2002).

The agent should also conduct a market assessment. Some agents have well-developed networks of contacts with sports product and nonproduct endorsement companies. For those who do not, the agent should choose a product the athlete would align well with, identify that product's manufacturers, and determine whether they invest in athlete endorsements (Lester, 2002). To determine the products an athlete will align with, the agent should consider the athlete's reputation, personality, and image and make a match with a product line that fits with the athlete's characteristics.

Marketing an athlete or coach may include creating or polishing a public image for that person. To assist with image building, some agents are beginning to hire "sports-media coaches" to train athletes or coaches for meeting the press and public. Sports-media coaches offer training sessions that mix lectures, mock interviews, question-and-answer sessions, and videotapes of other athletes or coaches to critique (Dunkel, 1997). For instance, former NBA player Jerry Stackhouse's media coach, Andrea Kirby, began his session with an exercise in which he wrote down a list of his personal positive qualities (Thurow, 1996). Stackhouse's list included "friendly, caring, talkative, athletic, well-dressed . . . good son, good family person, a leader, warm, respectful, generous" (Thurow, 1996, p. A4). Kirby copied the list and told Stackhouse to carry it with him and review it every time he faced fans, the media, or commercial cameras so that he would consistently portray the image he had of himself. Beyond the media coaching, Stackhouse's training included taking a few college drama courses, practicing speaking with a smoother cadence, and shaving his mustache (Thurow, 1996).

This sort of image building supports the standard sport marketing practice for athletes—that is, brand building. As branding for athletes becomes more sophisticated, sport marketers are taking new approaches to it. For instance, Wendy Newman is a personal branding coach and has created Person-Centered Branding, which she claims endures because it is not contrived or based on temporary factors, but rather authenticates who the athlete is as a person. Newman's system has been embraced by the Ladies Professional Golf Association (LPGA), which hired her to work with elite golfers to develop personal narratives and individual brands (Dell, 2007). Table 11-2 identifies the differences in Newman's system versus traditional branding.

Another solution to the challenge of branding, called BrandMatch, is championed by the firm Sports Identity. The goal with BrandMatch is to create a profile of the athlete to find out who he or she is, then to use that unique image to strategically market the athlete based on where he or she is professionally and personally. Once that task is accomplished, the sports marketers match the athlete with brands that will create opportunities and experiences for both the athlete and the company that are meaningful

promotional experiences. This practice differs from that of some sport marketers who will just "dial for dollars," calling any and every company just to deliver an endorsement opportunity for the athlete, without paying attention to the long-term value or relationship between the athlete and the company. It also differs from the traditional Q score. The difference is that with the Q score, it will be the same for the athlete with every company, but with BrandMatch, a different score comes up for the same athlete with different companies or opportunities for marketing (Schakenbach, 2012).

© Yuri Arcurs/Shutterstock, Inc.

Table 11-2 Traditional Versus Person-Centered Branding	
Traditional Branding	**Person-Centered Branding**
Outside-in	Inside-out
Brand with shelf life; burns out	Brand built for endurance
Strategy dictates image	Identity dictates strategy
Short-term revenues; fad	Long-term revenues; consumer/brand loyalty
Starts with athlete's performance	Starts with athlete's life
Only as good as the last win	Sustains image regardless of performance
Starts with desired image of who/what athlete is being told to be	Starts with the identity of who athlete is
Revenues first; then happiness and fulfillment	Happiness and fulfillment first; then revenues
Brands athlete	Brands person
Athlete trying to be something	Being who athlete is
Contrived	Authentic
Endurance = sport, tenure, performance	Endurance = sustainable brand personality
Temporary	Permanent

Courtesy of Wendy Newman, MA, Founder and Developer, Person-Centered Branding.®

Finally, the agent should determine the athlete's market value. Many factors influence an athlete's market value, including the athlete's skill and success in sport, the athlete's individual characteristics (image, charisma, physical appearance, and personality), how badly the organization wants the athlete, and any negative factors (crimes, drug use, public scandal) (Lester, 2002).

Negotiating the Athlete's or Coach's Marketing and Endorsement Contracts

Due to salary caps and rookie wage scales, an agent's ability to supplement a team salary with lucrative endorsement contracts has gained greater importance in athlete representation (Thurow, 1996). Economically, agents fare far better in the amounts of compensation they can command from marketing work. As far as the specifics of marketing deals go, the agent must first know any limitations the sport places on an athlete's ability to endorse products. For instance, all major professional sport leagues prohibit the use of team names and logos in endorsements, and most professional sport leagues ban the endorsement of alcoholic beverages and tobacco products (Lester, 2002). Agents representing athletes in individual sports, such as golf, tennis, racquetball, figure skating, and auto racing, should examine the rules and regulations of each sport. Restrictions vary from the simple requirement of the PGA Tour that endorsements be "in good taste" to the specific rules in tennis and racquetball that limit the number and size of patches displayed on players' clothing and equipment bags (Lester, 2002).

Negotiation of endorsement deals can provide a lucrative supplement to Division I coaches' income. University athletic departments, however, have begun to examine coaches' outside endorsement deals and to negotiate contracts with athletic shoe, apparel, and equipment companies that benefit the entire athletic department. NCAA rules also require that the university's chancellor or president approve coaches' endorsement deals. To get a sense of

how much money is at issue, the top 10 Division I NCAA football coaches' outside pay falls in the range of $31,000 to $300,000 (Berkowitz, Upton, Dougherty, & Durking, 2013b). For the top 10 men's Division I NCAA basketball coaches, the range of outside pay is $38,000 to $895,000 (Berkowitz et al., 2013a). Outside pay is defined as self-reported athletics-related income outside of what the institution pays the coach (Berkowitz et al., 2013b).

When negotiating an endorsement contract, an agent should be certain to maintain the client's exclusive rights and control over his or her image and other endorsements. The agent must also be familiar with the terms typically negotiable in athlete endorsement contracts. After reviewing numerous endorsement contracts, the following list emerges:

- Grant of rights regarding the distribution, marketing, advertising, promotion and sale of products.
- Grant of rights regarding the design, development, creation, manufacture, production, distribution, marketing, advertising, promotion, and sale of licensed products in all channels of trade.
- Exclusivity.
- Compensation, including bonuses for sales or bonuses for awards achieved in sport. May also include compensation for:
  - Appearances.
  - Commercials (print, television, other media).
- In-kind products. May include in-kind products for the athlete's family. May include a clause barring the sale, loan, or trade of in-kind products.
- Athlete's agreement to maintain the value of the endorsement. This clause may include:
  - The need for the athlete's visible use and endorsement of the product(s) in the contract.

- A morals clause in which the athlete acknowledges the role that his or her actions or behavior plays in the value of the relationship.
- The athlete's agreement to stay in good physical condition.
- The athlete's agreement not to break rules or regulations of the sport.
- The athlete's agreement not to promote alcohol or tobacco.
- Terminations, including reasons for termination such as not complying with exclusivity, no longer being an athlete of a certain status (i.e., major leaguer versus minor leaguer), morals clause violation, or damaging statements against the product. The termination clause may also include the terms of termination.
- Liquidated damages.
- Rights of first refusal and renegotiation terms.
- Confidentiality.
- Indemnities.
- Governing laws.
- Dispute resolution. This is often an agreement to pursue mediation and arbitration, as opposed to pursing a suit a court of law.

Financial Planning

Financial planning covers a wide range of activities, such as banking and cash flow management, tax planning, investment advising, estate planning, and risk management (Grossman, 2002). Many lawsuits concerning sports agents' incompetence, fraud, and breaches of fiduciary duties involve financial planning and investing. Many sports agents have made mistakes because of the complex nature of the financial affairs of athletes. Sports agents often attempt to take on this function without proper skills and training, which can lead to allegations of incompetence and negligence. In addition, a less scrupulous agent may be enticed by access to the athlete's money.

Allegations of agents "double dipping" into athletes' funds, investing money into businesses from which the agent derives benefit, and outright embezzlement of an athlete's money are all too common. This unethical behavior is discussed in greater detail later in the chapter.

An athlete earning a multimillion-dollar salary should adopt a budget (Willette & Waggoner, 1996). Without a budget, athletes who earn sudden wealth face risks (Waggoner, 1996), one of which is rushing into what may be an ill-advised investment. Athletes often receive many unsolicited prospectuses and requests for investments, and many have lost money in failed business ventures. Thus, financial planners often advise athletes to see a written business plan and have the plan analyzed by a professional before investing—and even if an investment seems to be worthy, planners should advise an athlete to commit no more than 5% to 20% of his or her portfolio to it (Willette & Waggoner, 1996). The second risk is making a radical lifestyle change. NBA agent Curtis Polk shares this example: For a client earning $10 million per year, he gives the athlete a budget of $1 million per year and invests $4 million, leaving the remaining $5 million for local, state, and federal taxes (Willette & Waggoner, 1996). The third risk is guilt, which often leads athletes to make bad loans to family and friends or to hire them as an entourage. To overcome guilt, advisors suggest that athletes raise money for charities (Waggoner, 1996).

Athletes should be aware of companies reaching out to them with predraft lines of credit. One such company, Datatex Sports Management, a division of Huntleigh Securities in St. Louis, uses its own in-house football analysts to calculate predraft lines of credit for potential draft picks. Obviously, problems arise for athletes who do not end up drafted. Southern Mississippi offensive lineman Torrin Tucker and New York City high school guard Lenny Cooke were given predraft lines of credit and neither was drafted. For Cooke, taking the line of credit also eliminated his ability to play for the University of Louisville because it violated NCAA rules for two reasons: He arranged it through a sports agency firm, Immortal Sports, and the line of credit through CSI Capital Management was based on Cooke's future earnings potential. CSI Capital Management's Chairman Leland Faust and a runner for agents, Ernest Downing, Jr., argue that lines of credit are now so common that athletes request them before hiring the agent (Farry, 2003).

Finally, insurance plays a key role in an athlete's financial planning. Star athletes usually invest in disability insurance plans to protect themselves during and after their playing career. In contract negotiations with a professional team, an agent may negotiate for the team to cover the cost of this policy. Many insurance companies, though, will insure an athlete only after that athlete is likely to achieve a certain level of income.

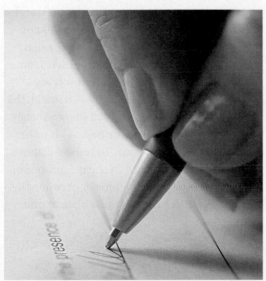

© LiquidLibrary

Career and Post-Career Planning

An agent must help an athlete with the transition to a professional career, and again with the transition into retirement. The average career length varies by sport, but generally is less than five years. Thus, the agent must maximize the athlete's earning potential during and after his or her playing career. An agent must also "insure" the athlete's future earnings by building and protecting the athlete's image against damage, such as overexposure. In addition, an agent must balance the need to capitalize on opportunities while doing what is best personally and professionally for the athlete.

The 1994 Olympic figure skating silver medalist Nancy Kerrigan provides an example of these dangers. Kerrigan had a reputation for being nervous and painfully inarticulate (Longman, 1994). On January 6, 1994, she was attacked and clubbed on the knee by a competitor's bodyguard in a conspiracy. When attacked, her screams were characterized as whiney. She was criticized for her response, even though she was the victim. In the next seven weeks, Kerrigan was named to the U.S. national team. She recovered from the injuries sustained in the attack, won an Olympic silver medal, and was overheard criticizing the gold medalist. Already an athlete with an inaccurate media portrayal as an "ice princess," her comments exposed her flaws. Kerrigan should have been given a rest. Instead, her agent swept her away from the Olympic Games prior to the closing ceremonies to participate in a parade at Disney World for her $2 million sponsor. During the parade, Kerrigan complained that it was dumb and corny and that she didn't want to be there (Lowitt, 1999). She moved on to hosting *Saturday Night Live* and more. Saying yes to every opportunity, especially those not suited to her personality, created pressure for Kerrigan and subjected her to criticism for verbal missteps made while exhausted and under stress. According to Hersch (1994), Kerrigan was unprepared and uncomfortable with celebrity, but did nothing to respond to her missteps, which led to an image meltdown. Hersh noted, "[H]er agent and companion Jerry Solomon. . . . made her fabulously wealthy, but at what cost?" (1994, para. 10). Although it is important to capitalize on opportunities in the short window that opens up after the Olympic Games, an agent must balance the athlete's long-term interests against the prospect of short-term earnings.

Career planning may also involve the agent investing time, energy, and money into a player's career while the player is training in the minor leagues or for events, exhibitions, or the Olympic or Paralympic Games. More and more athletes have come to expect that agents will cover the costs of products, some training and coaching costs, and even travel. Many factors have caused this expectation, among them the unrealistic costs of training, collegiate programs and minor leagues that do not supply athletes with a living wage, entitled athletes who expect a certain level of treatment due to their status, and a competitive industry in which those trying to recruit clients throw many inducements their way. Further, product companies have taken note of this trend, and until a player makes it into the major leagues, in lieu of giving in-kind products, the manufacturers and suppliers have created agent accounts to purchase products for athletes. Often such investment is required when the agent is trying to break into the business, creating a financial barrier to entry. This investment represents a great risk for agents and they may reap little financial reward if the athlete does not achieve his or her goals or leaves for a competitor agent.

Agents may also help establish sports camps, training academies, or charitable organizations under the athlete's name. Running sports camps or academies and charitable organizations does many positive things for the athlete. Camps or academies provide additional income, and possibly a career after playing. Charities create goodwill for the athlete; give the athlete contact with his or her community; give something back to children, communities, or a worthy cause; provide a useful outlet for the athlete's energy and time in the off-season; and may provide a tax break.

During the career transition out of sport, the agent must address the potential for a financial crisis (Grossman, 2002). Proper financial planning that includes income investment, insurance coverage, and contracting for deferred income can avert a disaster. Beyond the financial aspects, the athlete needs a sense of purpose. Participation in sport has defined many athletes' lives and self-images, and agents can be helpful in preparing athletes for the psychological difficulties that may accompany retirement. By exploring career and business opportunities for the athlete inside and outside the sport industry, such as in broadcasting, the agent can help the athlete make a more successful transition.

Dispute Resolution

It is the agent's responsibility to resolve disputes the athlete or coach may have with his or her league, team, teammates, fans, referees or umpires, media, endorsement companies, and the like. Baseball agent Dennis Gilbert likens the role of the agent to a "shield," stating that it is the agent's task to protect the athlete from the headaches that go along with resolving disputes (Schwarz, 1996). Acting as a shield, the agent allows the athlete or coach to focus solely on playing or coaching to the best of his or her ability without distractions. To resolve disputes, the sports agent may need to engage in labor or commercial arbitration forums or occasionally in court or, better yet, help the athlete to find expert counsel.

Legal Counseling

If the sports agent is a lawyer, the agent may provide legal counseling. Legal counseling includes contract negotiation, legal representation in court, arbitration or sport-related administrative proceedings, estate planning, and the preparation of tax and insurance forms. However, the nature of the legal work may dictate that a lawyer specializing in a particular area is better suited to provide the actual legal services. For instance, a sports agent may be very confident in providing negotiation and contract advice on any matter in his or her client's life, yet that same agent will not likely be the best lawyer to handle the client's high-profile divorce proceedings.

Personal Care

The tasks required of the sports agent under the personal care function include such responsibilities as assisting when an athlete is traded, arranging transportation, finding and furnishing a house or apartment for the season or training camps, purchasing cars, and helping the athlete's family and friends.

Key Skills Required of Sports Agents

Although there are no established educational standards for becoming an agent, some unions are now requiring a bachelor's degree. Some agents may be lawyers, certified public accountants, investment advisors, financial planners, or former players. With the various services athletes demand of agents and in light of competition in the field, a professional degree is practically a necessity.

Primarily, the sports agent must have a good working knowledge of the sport industry, particularly the specific sport in which he or she practices. This knowledge should include an understanding of the economic picture of the sport industry, the inner workings of the industry, the sport the athlete plays, the types of data analytics and metrics used to assess talent, and documents used in the industry (e.g., contracts, policies, rules and regulations, constitutions and bylaws, and collective bargaining agreements), along with a great network of contacts in the sport and its support industries. Although the skills needed by sports agents vary depending on the services provided, all agents must possess good listening and counseling skills. The agent works for the athlete and must invest time in getting to know the athlete on a personal level. This builds trust and a stronger relationship between the two. Agents must make decisions according to the athlete's desires and goals. The agent should act only after consulting the athlete and must always act in the athlete's best interest.

Excellent verbal and written communication skills are also essential because the agent represents the athlete in many forums. Many of the agent's functions require polished negotiation skills. An agent must also be loyal to the athlete and strong enough to shield the athlete from the media and even from his or her own club's front-office staff. Professional athletes, like entertainers, find their lives scrutinized by the press and social media. The agent must help the athlete adjust to the pressure that accompanies fame and counsel the athlete to properly deal with the media. When the athlete has to negotiate a contract or go into arbitration against his or her team, the relationship is adversarial. This is not always the best situation for professional athletes, for whom psychology plays a key role in their on-field success. The agent must shelter the athlete from the derogatory statements made about him or her in those forums, because those types of statements can often damage the athlete's confidence.

Current Issues

Unethical Behavior

In the five decades since sports agents became prevalent, the sports agency field has endured a great deal of criticism. The public often perceives the behavior of those in the profession as excessively unethical. While many ethical agents run their businesses professionally, a number of high-profile cases of unethical and illegal behavior have tainted the image of the profession as a whole. Sports agency is an industry that attracts people seeking quick and easy money, glamour, and the spotlight. It is a risky business, clients are scarce, and barriers to entry high. These factors combine to bring elements of corruption to the profession. According to Sobel (1990), the major types of misbehavior include (1) income mismanagement, (2) incompetence, (3) conflicts of interest, (4) excessive fees, and (5) overly aggressive client recruitment. Of these five problems, **income mismanagement** is probably the most devastating to the athlete. Because the agent is often dealing with the income of a multimillion-dollar athlete, the losses can be great, and it is unlikely the athlete will be able to reclaim the money from the agent or earn back the amount lost. Although many reported cases stem from incompetence, others begin with incompetence and deteriorate to fraud or embezzlement (Sobel, 1990).

A good example is the case of agent Tank Black, who was sentenced to 5 years in prison for swindling millions of dollars from the NFL players he represented. Black was sentenced to more than 6 years in jail for laundering $1.1 million for a drug ring in Detroit (Voyles, 2011). Abusing his clients' trust, he was accused of stealing $12 million to $15 million from them by encouraging them to put their money in bogus investments and pyramid schemes (Wertheim, 2000, Voyles, 2011). The Tank Black saga has made the NFLPA more vigilant in its efforts to regulate agents. As a result of this unscrupulous agent's actions, in 2003 the NFLPA created the first registration system for financial advisors who work with NFL players. Black was eventually cleared of stealing clients' money, but was guilty of perjury and paying college athletes to sign with his firm (Black, 2012).

Agents have at times performed their responsibilities negligently because of sheer incompetence. As the industry has become more complex, some agents have run into problems because they are incapable of figuring out their clients' worth, working with the complex documents necessary to effectively negotiate contracts, or carrying out tasks they promise athletes they are capable of doing. Competition in the industry may compound the losses associated with incompetence, because agents may make promises they cannot keep for fear of losing a client or may exaggerate their abilities when trying to land a client. In short, they over-promise and under-deliver. If they are not, for example, trained as lawyers or do not have experience in arbitration, they may be more likely to settle a case to avoid having to proceed to the actual arbitration. Due to fear of losing a client to a competitor, many are afraid to outsource a labor or salary arbitration case.

Conflicts of interest raise serious questions about the fiduciary duty of loyalty required under agency law. A conflict of interest occurs when the agent's own interest may be furthered more or rather than the athlete's (principal's) interest. Keep in mind what you learned in the chapter on legal issues in sport: An agent works for an athlete and possesses a fiduciary duty to put the athlete's interest first. It is clear, though, that in business settings there are bound to be conflicts of interest. If the agent fully discloses the conflict and allows the athlete to direct the agent, or in some cases suggests that the athlete hire a neutral party to see the athlete through the conflict, the agent will not have breached his or her fiduciary duties.

Conflicts of interest in the sports agency business are quite common. Conflicts may arise for agency firms that represent athletes as well as the events in which the athletes are competing. Those firms have a fiduciary duty to fully reveal the extent of the conflict of interest and to allow the athlete to bring in a neutral party to negotiate with that particular event. Some, such as Jerry Solomon, argue that these companies operate as diverse entities (athlete representation versus event management), such that the two groups have built invisible walls between them to prevent this kind of conflict from arising (Feinstein, 1992; Solomon, 1995). Another type of conflict may arise when an agent is representing two players on the same team or two players who may be vying for the same position on a team. Clearly, in these situations, there may be a tendency for the agent to give greater attention to the athlete who will better serve the agent's own interest (make the agent more money). Another source of conflicts is dual representation—for example, when an agent represents both a coach and a player or represents a player and is also the head of the union. The NBPA and NHLPA prohibit representation of both a coach and a player, but this practice is allowed in the NFL and MLB. The days of representation by an agent who also leads the union in the major leagues are now past, but there is always potential for it to happen again in the future because agents could become very powerful and convince their clients to vote them into the role.

The complaint of charging excessive fees occurs when agents charge fees that do not fairly represent their time, effort, and skills. To an extent, this complaint has been addressed by the players association regulations mentioned earlier and by competition in the market. Competition for clients has forced some agents to reduce their fees to attract clients. Although the fees have dropped for the negotiation of team-sport contracts, many agents continue to charge what may be considered excessive fees in the marketing area or charge the athlete for every service the agent performs, even when the athlete believes that all services are provided in the original fee charged for the contract negotiation. In the past, confusion arose because some agents did not use written representation agreements. Players associations in team sports now require agents to use standard-form representation agreements that clearly establish fees and contractual promises; however, in individual sports or emerging leagues there are no such requirements.

Charges of misuse of an athlete's money may also be more problematic when an agent controls the athlete's bank accounts and has power

of attorney for the athlete. There have been cases of agents who had access to an athlete's money and paid themselves amounts unbeknownst to the athletes.

Overly aggressive client recruitment is a problem that has plagued collegiate athletics. First, it can wreak havoc with NCAA rules because an athlete loses his or her eligibility if he or she signs with a sports agent or accepts anything of value from a sports agent. In fact, in 2008, collegiate pitcher Andy Oliver was ruled ineligible for simply engaging advisors who contacted a MLB team on his behalf after Oliver was drafted in 2006. In the intense competition for clients, many agents have resorted to underhanded tactics such as paying athletes to encourage them to sign with agents early. The difficulty in becoming an agent or obtaining clients has led some to offer inducements to woo athletes. For example, World Sports Entertainment (WSE), an athlete representation firm operated by entertainment agent Norby Walters and partner Lloyd Bloom, spent approximately $800,000 to induce athletes to sign representation agreements with them before their NCAA eligibility expired. Walters argued that what he did broke no laws (just NCAA rules) and was a common practice in the music industry, where entertainers often receive financial advances from their agents (Mortensen, 1991).

Athletes are also to blame, because some encourage this type of activity from the agent, believing that their skills and talent should enable them to make this money for signing. For instance, when football player Ron Harmon signed with WSE as a junior at the University of Iowa, the FBI investigation discovered he ran up expenses of more than $54,000 in cash, plane tickets, concert tickets, and other entertainment. Clearly, Harmon was taking advantage of the situation for his own interests and was not using the money, as other athletes did, for bills and family expenses (Mortensen, 1991). When ex NFL super agent Tank Black was a college coach, he was offered $50,000 to deliver athletes to agents. As a result, he left college coaching to become a sports agent (Black, 2012). In 2012, Black spoke to the National Association of Collegiate Directors of Athletics and said today that amount is $250,000 or more (Black, 2012).

Second, overly aggressive client recruitment has created a very ugly side to the sports agency industry. Most agents can tell stories about the dirty recruiting that goes on in the industry as competitors vie for clients. This behavior mirrors the recruiting scandals prevalent in big-time college athletics. Many veteran agents claim the unethical recruiting has reached epidemic proportions that will have a lasting negative effect on the industry (Mullen, 2004). In addition to the promises of prohibited inducements, among the noted lasting negative impacts from unethical recruiting are the following: (1) Representatives are spending more time on retaining clients, so it cuts back on their time to develop new business opportunities for current clients; (2) recruiters are targeting teenagers in the sports of basketball, baseball, and hockey, making promises that may not come to fruition; and (3) in an effort to compete with the large conglomerates, smaller agencies are promising late-round picks marketing guarantees in the six-figure range that will be difficult to deliver (Mullen, 2004).

Such recruiting became so intense among baseball players that the MLBPA and its Executive Board (made up of active players) examined how to curb the behavior. As a result, the MLBPA put new agent regulations into effect on October 1, 2010 (MLBPA, 2010). The 48 pages of regulations are so sweeping in their changes that all certified agents had to reapply for certification and those who were operating as recruiters or handlers for the players also had to apply for certification. That requirement signals that the union plans to more seriously monitor contact between players and competitor agents. In addition, agents must inform the MLBPA if they speak to a player whom they do not represent, or intend to do so, or travel to meet a player whom they do not represent [MLBPA, §5(A)(11), 2010]. Often, agents attempt to lure players away from their current agent when they become eligible for free agency or salary arbitration because that is when a player will receive a significant increase in compensation and, therefore, the agent will receive a fee increase. The new regulations prevent a player at this stage in his career from changing agents "unless they first consult with the MLBPA" [MLBPA, §6(L), 2010]. This consultation requirement is an attempt by the MLBPA to monitor the recruitment of its members and an attempt to limit overly aggressive recruitment by agents seeking clients. Thus, these regulations limit players' freedom to switch agents at whim, because any player facing salary arbitration or free agency must consult with the union before switching agents during those critical periods of his career (Clifton & Toppel, 2010).

The final two areas of significant change in the regulations involve the areas of restrictive covenants and the use of arbitration to settle disputes among the MLBPA's player-agent group. Historically, the union's position has focused on the player's choice of agent being a priority over supporting an agency's restrictive covenant (a promise in a contract that works against the interests of the grantor) against an agent who has left the firm and taken the player. These new regulations permit employers to utilize "reasonable" restrictive covenants in agent employment agreements. The determination of the reasonableness of each covenant will be made on a case-by-case analysis. Lastly, the union is requiring all disputes involving agents to be resolved through arbitration rather than litigation (Clifton & Toppel, 2010).

The NFLPA has been the most active in disciplining agents. One of the challenges that players associations face in going after agents is that it is difficult to find proof unless athletes are willing to testify against agents. In addition, pursuing these cases takes a great deal of energy and personnel away from the main mission of the union. Even so, the NFLPA is continuing to take the lead in this area. Beginning in 2004, it required all registered agents to also list their runners with the NFLPA so it can keep better tabs on the individuals who recruit clients for agents. This step was another first in the regulation of the agency industry, and it will be interesting to see if the other unions follow the NFLPA's lead. More recently, in 2014, the NFLPA began requiring agents to file with them any and all additional agreements for other services they provide clients beyond the standard player representation agreements that they are already required to have on file with the players' union. In addition, the NFLPA upped their disciplinary suspensions from six months for a first offense to a year, plus instituted a rule that three suspensions lead to a permanent ban (Red & O'Keefe, 2014). Another step that some regulatory groups, such as the NFLPA, are taking is to require sports agents to have professional liability insurance.

Regulation of Sports Agents

Sports agents navigate a maze of conduct governing regulations set forth by college governing bodies and university athletic departments, professional athletes' unions, state ethics boards, boards of bar overseers, state legislatures, and the federal government (Sobel, 2002). Of these many forms of regulation, NCAA and other college/university regulations carry the least weight with agents. Because agents are not NCAA members, the NCAA cannot enforce its rules against them. Instead, NCAA agent regulations are intended for the athletes and member institutions to stop athletes from having contact with agents.

NCAA bylaws permit student athletes to retain the service of an attorney or an outside consultant, provided that this personal representative does not consult with professional teams. In *Oliver v. NCAA* (2009), pitcher Andy Oliver was ruled ineligible by the NCAA for violating this bylaw. The Ohio state district court upheld Oliver's argument that the NCAA's ruling was against public policy and affected an attorney–client relationship, with the court adding that the bylaw was "capricious . . . [and] . . . arbitrary." Oliver settled with the NCAA prior to appeal, thus limiting the precedential value of the case. In a similar case that followed the *Oliver* decision, a baseball player from University of Kentucky was deemed ineligible after he had relied on an agent to (unsuccessfully) sign him to a contract with the Toronto Blue Jays.

Agents representing MLB, NFL, NBA, NHL, and CFL athletes are regulated by players associations. MLS had adopted the FIFA agent regulations, but FIFA deregulated agents in 2015, deferring regulation to national associations. FIFA, instead, regulates intermediaries and bans third-party organizations that serve as intermediaries and those that purchase the rights to soccer players.

Application fees to become registered or certified by players associations are as follows:

- MLBPA: $2,000 annual fee.
- NBPA: $100 application fee plus $1,250 for the first year. In successive years, the fee is pro-rated based on the number of clients represented, with fewer than 10 players costing $2,500, 10–19 players costing $5,000, and more than 20 players costing $7,500 in annual dues.
- NFLPA: $2,500 application fee plus $1,200 annually if representing fewer than 10 players; $1,700 for more than 10 players.
- NHLPA: $1,500 annual fee.

To become registered sports agents, candidates must take written exams administered by the unions. They must submit uniform athlete–agent representation agreements that set forth the terms of the relationship and contain clauses mandating the arbitration of disputes between players and their agents. The uniform agreement is renewable annually by the player, but the player is free to end it at any time to go to another agent. This puts the players associations on notice about who is representing the athlete and allows the agent access to union assistance with salary information, dispute resolution, and the like.

Currently, 43 states have some form of athlete–agent regulation. The National Conference of Commissioners, with prodding and backing from the NCAA and the Sports Lawyers Association, created a uniform agent registration law, called the Uniform Athlete Agent Act (UAAA), that can be adopted by all states. Forty states, plus the District of Columbia and the Virgin Islands, have adopted this legislation. In addition, three states have their own statutes on athlete–agent relationships that predate the UAAA.

After many attempts at passing federal legislation governing sports agents, the Sports Agent Responsibility and Trust Act (SPARTA) was enacted in 2004. This act prohibits some conduct by sports agents when they sign contracts with student athletes and makes it unlawful for an agent to give false or misleading information or promises or give anything of value to an athlete to induce them into signing an agency contract. This behavior is designated as unfair and deceptive acts or practices to be regulated by the Federal Trade Commission (FTC, 2017). SPARTA prohibits agents from directly or indirectly recruiting or soliciting a student to enter into an agency contract by providing false or misleading information, making false promises, or providing anything of value to amateur athletes or their families. It also prohibits agents from entering into an oral or written agency contract with a student without providing a required disclosure document both to the student-athlete and to the athlete's academic institution. Finally, SPARTA

prohibits the act of predating or postdating an agency contract (SPARTA, Sec. 3, 2004). Each violation of SPARTA is deemed an unfair or deceptive act or practice under the Federal Trade Commission Act (FTCA) (SPARTA, Sec. 4, 2004). Further, SPARTA authorizes civil actions by the FTC, state attorneys general, and educational institutions against violators. It supplements, but does not preclude, other actions against agents taken under other federal or state laws (SPARTA, Sec. 5, 2004).

With the enactment of this law, the maze of legislation regulating sports agents has become even more unwieldy. The goal of the law is to protect student-athletes from deceptive practices and keep them eligible to play NCAA sports. Senator John McCain noted that SPARTA serves as a federal backstop for the ongoing efforts by the NCAA, college coaches, university presidents, and athletic directors to support state-level legislation (Associated Press, 2004). The UAAA legislation requires that sports agents be registered with the states in which they operate and provide uniform state laws addressing their conduct and practices.

One challenge for agents is that the law is decidedly one-sided. Only the agents are regulated, while the athletes are perceived as playing no role in the practice of providing inducements to athletes to sign with agents. In fact, stories abound of athletes and families of athletes literally "selling" their services to the highest bidder among the myriad of agents competing to sign a high-round pick to an agency agreement. If little or no penalty is assessed against the athlete, it will be interesting to see if the federal law actually deters the unethical recruitment of athletes. To date, legal action under UAAA and SPARTA has been scarce.

Finally, athletes and others abused by agents can seek recourse under tort, criminal, agency, and consumer protection laws. More agents are resorting to the courts when they are wronged, filing lawsuits for unfair competition, tortious interference with contract, libel, and slander (Mullen, 2004). The willingness to resort to the courts may be a result of the large amounts of money involved and the fact that in a legal proceeding witnesses can be subpoenaed, making witness testimony potentially more easily obtainable than in a complaint filed with a players association.

Summary

The field of sports agency can be exciting. Landing a first-round draft pick and negotiating a playing contract or creating an image and negotiating major marketing deals for a Wimbledon champion can bring an incredible thrill for an agent. Servicing clients' needs introduces agents to the world of these elite athletes. As a result, it is a highly competitive business. Those seeking an entry-level position face an uphill battle, because there are tremendous barriers to entry, first of which is the fierce competition for the small number of potential clients. Recruiting a client is just part of the struggle, because keeping the client in this competitive market is an equally competitive battle. Furthermore, it is estimated that more than 80% of athletes are represented by approximately 20% of agents. Many agents work part-time supplementing their income through other professions, such as law, marketing, or financial planning. Nevertheless, a handful of large, dominant multiservice firms engaged in athlete representation and event management may provide a good launching point to break into the field. On the representation side, few entry-level positions at these firms are in client recruitment. In reality, employment exists if the entry-level agent can deliver a client. With the trend toward mergers and acquisitions, many entry-level positions seem to be limited to those who have a few clients already in hand. This competitive environment may lead new agents to act in an overly aggressive manner while recruiting clients.

Case Study 11-1

King Sport Management

King Sport Management (KSM) is a sports agency firm based in Chicago that has been in business for 5 years. KSM is owned and operated by law school graduate Jake King. KSM suddenly arrived on the sports agency scene as the company having one of the largest stables of clients in baseball behind the Scott Boras Corporation and ACES, which had been in business for many more years. As the owner of DiamondTalent, Inc. (DTI), an agency in business built ethically for more than a decade, Nate Santana was bewildered about how an agency with so little experience in the industry grew so quickly. Soon that would change. DTI represented 30 players, 25 of whom were in the minors and

5 who were on major league rosters. Two of the players on the 40-man roster were still in the minor leagues at the AAA level.

One day Nate received a call from Mark Carlson, a top prospect in AA, telling him that he had just met with an agent from KSM. The agent told Carlson that he could get him a Topps trading card deal worth $10,000, and suggested that if Nate couldn't deliver that kind of money, then he must not know what he was doing in the trading card business. Nate knows that Topps is the exclusive baseball card licensee of Minor League Baseball ("MiLB") and that the MiLB license provides Topps the right to include every player who is playing in

(continues)

King Sport Management (*Continued*)

the minors. Minor league players are not compensated for inclusion in these products, so Nate told Mark that he doubted KSM could arrange such a deal. Nate told Mark to ask KSM to show him a trading card contract with those figures on it. Mark said, "I really don't care where the money comes from, because at this point I could really use the $10,000. If you can't find a similar deal, I may have to leave. Besides, KSM has been to visit my dad, and the KSM representative and my dad wait for me after every game with a KSM contract to sign. I think they have given my father some money to cover some of his bills, and I can't let my own father down." Two weeks later, Nate received a standard form letter terminating their business relationship postmarked from Chicago, even though the prospect was playing for a team on the West Coast.

The next day Nate called one of his clients, Terrell Sharpe, to talk about the client's outing the day before. Sharpe was an all-star high school athlete in Florida and a top pitching prospect for the Tampa Bay Rays. Sharpe struggled the first few years in baseball, but had suddenly begun winning and had just been moved from A-ball to AA. When Nate reached Sharpe, he was on the golf course with his roommate and some agents. Sharpe told Nate about the brand-new golf clubs he had just purchased at the club's pro shop. Sharpe told Nate that he really didn't feel like talking about yesterday's outing and, because he had just purchased a MacBook Pro, Nate should email him at IMSharpe@gmail.com so he could get back to his golf game. Nate hung up the phone and thought, "On a minor league salary, where would Terrell get the money for golf clubs and a laptop?" Nate knew that Terrence barely had enough money to get by, because he came from a poor background and had given his signing bonus to his grandmother, who had raised him. Nate had a terrible feeling that he was going to lose Terrell to KSM. Nate sent a few emails and text messages to Terrell, but received no response. A week later,

Nate received the same form letter in the mail from Terrence that he had received from Mark. It, too, was postmarked from Chicago.

Two months later, Nate was visiting Josh Bartley, a catcher and a 40-man roster player for the Atlanta Braves. Josh told Nate that he knew he was great defensively and if he could just hit more homeruns, he was told he would make the major league roster the next year. Josh believed that if he could use steroids and bulk up, he could make that goal. Josh asked Nate to help him obtain steroids. Nate told Josh that there were many reasons he should not use steroids, top among them being his own health and the violation of baseball's rules. Nate assured Josh that the best way to better his hitting ability was to work with a hitting coach, both on the club and during the off-season. Nate told Josh that he would happily invest in a hitting coach and nutritionist for Josh to work with in the off-season. Nate also suggested some books for Josh to read on hitting. Josh said that he was convinced steroids were the answer to his hitting problems. Nate ended the evening worried about Josh.

Three days later, Nate received a call from Josh's dad. Ken began the conversation in a surprising way: "So I understand you won't help my son bulk up. . . ."

Shocked, Nate took a moment to respond. "Excuse me, is this Ken Bartley, Josh's dad?"

"Yes, Nate, you know it's me. I thought you were on our side. Here to help Josh make it to the 'bigs,' and now you won't get him steroids or HGH [human growth hormone]."

Nate said, "Ken, you are aware of the health risks to your son and the fact that baseball conducts tests for steroid and HGH use. . . ."

Ken said, "Sure, I know, I know. But Josh just needs it to get to the majors, then he'll stop. Short-term use should not be that big a deal. I don't understand your reasoning. I thought you were

King Sport Management (*Continued*)

here to help us. Isn't that what you said when you recruited Josh as a client?"

Nate said, "I did say that. Yet, none of us know the real risks of steroid or HGH use. Besides, using steroids and HGH violates the rules of baseball. And steroids are illegal substances. As a lawyer, I'm not going to lose my license trying to acquire steroids for your son—end of story! I told Josh I'd happily invest in a hitting coach for him in the off-season. In my professional judgment, that is his best way to the majors. Don't you remember the suspension of Alex Rodriguez for HGH use? MLB is serious about cheating."

At that point, Ken ended the conversation by saying, "Nate, we like your service, but you're making a big mistake. If you want to compete with the big dogs, sometimes you have to bend the rules. A guy like A-Rod may have been out a year, but think of all the money he's made in the process. Money for himself and his agent. Out of all those players who have been suspended, most have earned more money than they'd have made without using these substances. And besides, no penalties have come to their agents. So, I'd suggest you find an anti-aging clinic to help you get what these guys need to make it. You'll make more money and these guys will live their dreams."

Nate immediately called Josh. Josh told him that if Nate wouldn't find him performance enhancers, he'd find an agent who would. A month later, Nate received a letter from Josh, postmarked from Chicago, terminating their contractual relationship.

As the baseball season was nearing an end, Nate couldn't help but worry about his business. He had lost three of his top prospects to KSM, and two of his better clients were off to the Arizona Fall League, long known as a place where clients are ripe for the picking by unscrupulous agents. One of his clients, Chad Kelley, was like a son to Nate, and

Nate had a heart-to-heart talk with him before he left about the types of inducements Chad should expect to receive while in Arizona. Chad left by saying, "Nate, you should know by now, you have nothing to worry about."

A few weeks later Nate flew to Arizona to see Chad. With a smile on his face, Chad said, "Have I got a story for you!" Chad went on to explain that he had relented about going to dinner with a KSM runner only after the runner had asked him to dinner numerous times. Chad figured that after that much badgering, he deserved a free steak! At dinner the runner offered him money to leave Nate for KSM. Chad said, "I have all the money I need." Then the runner offered a car. Chad said, "I have a nice car and don't need another." Then the runner coyly offered a prostitute. Chad said, "I'm engaged and am not interested." The runner said, "Then why are we having dinner?" Chad said, "You tell me—you're the one who made the invitation." So the runner went on to tell Chad that at the beginning of the year KSM hired 10 runners under a 1-year contract and gave them a list of prospects to recruit. The two runners who recruited the most clients from that prospect list would then be hired into full-time positions. Nate thought he had heard it all.

As he arrived home from the trip, he opened up his *SportsBusiness Journal* to see a special edition on sports agents. There staring up at him was a picture of Jake King smiling with the headline, "KSM Principal Lobbies for New Ethical Standards to Govern Agents." Nate angrily thought, "Sure, now that he's broken the rules and built his business by stealing our clients, he wants to be the guy leading a cleanup of the industry."

Questions for Discussion

1. Should Nate contact the MLBPA to pursue a claim against KSM? What about the state

(*continues*)

King Sport Management (*Continued*)

of Illinois (which has an agent regulation statute)? What about the Illinois State Bar Association?

2. Should Nate engage in legal action against KSM for unfair competition or tortious interference with contractual or advantageous business relations? Should Nate consider legal action against the players who have left him for KSM?

3. Should Nate contact the police, the Chicago U.S. attorney's office, or the state or federal legislators about the steroid allegation against KSM?

4. Do you think the actions taken by Jake King to build KSM are the norm in the industry? What would be your response if Jake King were to tell you that to compete in this industry, you must give the athletes what they want or someone else will?

5. What do you think about the athletes and their decisions? What is their role and responsibility in the sports agency business?

6. If you were a partner to Nate, what would be your strategy going forward to retain current clients and to recruit new ones?

Resources

Professional Associations

American Bar Association Forum Committee on the Entertainment & Sport Industries
321 N. Clark Street
Chicago, IL 60654
312-988-5000
http://www.americanbar.org/groups
/entertainment_sports.html

Sports Lawyers Association
11130 Sunrise Valley Drive, Suite 350
Reston, VA 20191
703-437-4377
http://www.sportslaw.org

Agency Firms

ACES
188 Montague Street, 6th Floor
Brooklyn, NY 11201
718-237-2900
https://acesincbaseball.com/

BDA Sports
700 Ygnacio Valley Road, Suite 330
Walnut Creek, CA 94596
925-279-1040
http://www.bdasports.com

Beverly Hills Sports Council
1666 20th Street, Suite 200
Santa Monica, CA 90404
310-858-1872
http://bhscouncil.com

CAA Sports
2000 Avenue of the Stars
Los Angeles, CA 90067
424-288-2000
http://www.sports.caa.com

Career Sports and Entertainment
150 Interstate North Parkway, SE
Atlanta, GA 30339
770-955-1300
http://www.groupcse.com

Excel Sports Management
1700 Broadway, 9th Floor
New York, NY 10019
646-454-5900
http://www.excelsm.com/

Gestifute
Avenida da Boavista, Nr. 1837
Floor 17, Offices 17.1-17.4
4100-133 Porto
Portugal
351-22-608-4455

IMG

U.S. Headquarters
Endeavor
11 Madison Avenue
New York, NY 10010
212-586-5100
Multiple headquarters and offices in the
United States and throughout the world:
http://img.com/offices/

Lagardere Sports and Entertainment

4th Floor Cardinal Place
80 Victoria Street
London, SW1E 5JL
United Kingdom
https://lagardere-se.com/

Newport Sports Management, Inc.

201 City Centre Drive, Suite 400
Mississauga, ON L5B 2T4, Canada
905-275-2800
http://www.thehockeyagency.com

Octagon Worldwide

290 Harbor Drive
Stamford, CT 06902
203-354-7400
http://www.octagon.com

Priority Sports and Entertainment

325 N. LaSalle, Suite 650
Chicago, IL 60654
312-664-7700
http://www.prioritysports.biz

PSR, Inc.

1220 Plumas Street
Reno, NV 89509
775-828-1864
http://www.psr-inc.net

Roc Nation

1411 Broadway, 38th floor
New York, NY 10018
212-292-8500
http://rocnation.com/sports/

Scott Boras Corporation

18 Corporate Plaza Dr.
Newport Beach, CA 92660
949-833-1818
http://www.borascorp.com

The Legacy Agency (TLA USA)

1500 Broadway, 25th Floor
New York, NY 10036
212-645-2141
http://tlaworldwide.com/

Wasserman (formerly Wasserman Media Group [WMG])

10900 Wilshire Boulevard, Suite 2200
Los Angeles, CA 90024
310-407-0200
http://www.teamwass.com

For a more definitive list of sports agencies, go to: http://www.sportsagentblog.com /agencies/agencies-by-alphabetical-order/

Key Terms

account executive, Scott Boras, conflicts of interest, freestanding sport management firm, income mismanagement, law practice only, Mark H. McCormack, overly aggressive client recruitment, reserve clause, reserve list, reserve system, sport management firm affiliated with a law firm, sports agent, sports event managers, sports marketing representative, standard or uniform player contract

References

Anderson, J. (2007, May 22). The Boras factor. *LA Weekly*. Retrieved from http://www.laweekly .com/2007-05-24/news/the-boras-factor/

Associated Press. (2004, September 10). Legislation aims to protect student athletes. Retrieved from http://sports.espn.go.com /espn/news/story?id=1878699

Badenhausen, K. (2014, February 27). The highest paid retired athletes. *Forbes*. Retrieved from http://www.forbes.com/sites/kurtbadenhausen/2014/02/27/the-highest-paid-retired-athletes/

Badenhausen, K. (2016, September 26). How Arnold Palmer earned $875 million during legendary career in golf. *Forbes*. Retrieved from https://www.forbes.com/sites/kurtbadenhausen/2016/09/26/arnold-palmer-earned-875-million-during-legendary-career-in-golf/#11ed3d573e53

Belzer, J. (2017, September 25). The world's most valuable sports agencies 2017. *Forbes*. Retrieved from https://www.forbes.com/sites/jasonbelzer/2017/09/25/the-worlds-most-valuable-sports-agencies-2017/#358813c65eaf

Berkowitz, S., Upton, J., Dougherty, S., & Durkin, E. (2013a). NCAAB college coach salaries. *USA Today*. Retrieved from http://www.usatoday.com/sports/college/salaries/ncaab/coach/

Berkowitz, S., Upton, J., Dougherty, S., & Durkin, E. (2013b). NCAAF college coach salaries. *USA Today*. Retrieved from http://www.usatoday.com/sports/college/salaries/

Berman, N. (2017). The five highest paid MLB coaches heading into 2017. Retrieved from http://moneyinc.com/five-highest-paid-mlb-coaches-heading-2017/

Berry, R. C. (1990). Representation of the professional athlete. In American Bar Association Forum on the Entertainment and Sports Industries (Ed.), *The law of sports: Doing business in the sports industries* (pp. 1–6). Chicago, IL: ABA Publishing.

Berry, R. C., Gould, W. B., & Staudohar, P. D. (1986). *Labor relations in professional sports*. Dover, MA: Auburn House Publishing.

Black, T. (2012, May 4). "An inside look at the agent business." Panel discussion at annual National Association of Collegiate Directors of Athletics. Retrieved from https://www.youtube.com/watch?v=qG5OByiTPbY

Boeck, G. (1997, September 25). Cooper cashes in for NBA coaches: Agent snags rewarding deals. *USA Today*, pp. C1–C2.

Brady, D. (2004, July 12). Arnold Palmer: With IMG from the start. *BusinessWeek Online*. Retrieved from https://www.bloomberg.com/news/articles/2004-07-11/online-extra-arnold-palmer-with-img-from-the-start

Brennan, C. (1996). *Inside edge: A revealing journey into the secret world of figure skating*. New York, NY: Doubleday.

Burwell, B. (1996, June 28). David Falk: The most powerful man in the NBA? *USA Today*, pp. C1–C2.

Canadian Football League Players Association (CFLPA). (2014). Players agents. Retrieved from https://cflpa.com/advisors/

Carlisle, P. (2012, November 27). *Marketing an Olympic icon: Behind the business of a global sports superstar*. Lecture at University of Massachusetts, Amherst.

CBS News. (2004, December 26). The secret of their NFL success. Retrieved from http://www.cbsnews.com/stories/2004/09/16/60minutes/main643894.shtml

Clifton, G., & Toppel, J. (2010, September 24). MLBPA issues new sweeping regulations governing agents. Retrieved from http://www.hackneypublications.com/sla/archive/001133.php

Dell, K. (2007, Apr. 26). New driver at the LPGA. *Time*. Retrieved from http://www.time.com/time/magazine/article/0,9171,1615197-1,00.html

Dunkel, T. (1997, March). Out of the mouths of jocks. *Sky*, 97–103.

Farry, T. (2003, August 28). Bank(rupting) on the future. Retrieved from http://sports.espn.go.com/espn/print?id=1605207&type=story

Federal Trade Commission (2018). Sports agent responsibility and trust act. Retrieved from https://www.ftc.gov/enforcement/statutes/sports-agent-responsibility-trust-act

Federation International de Football Association (FIFA). (2015). About FIFA: Player agents list. Retrieved from http://www.fifa.com/aboutfifa/organisation/footballgovernance/playeragents/list.html

Feinstein, J. (1992). *Hard courts*. New York, NY: Villard Books.

Feinstein, J. (1995). *A good walk spoiled: Days and nights on the PGA tour*. Boston, MA: Little, Brown.

FIBA. (2017). FIBA certified agents. Retrieved at http://www.fiba.basketball/find-basketball-agent

Futterman, M. (2010a, May 7). Talent agencies cry foul, lawsuits fly. *Wall Street Journal*. Retrieved from https://www.wsj.com/articles/SB10001424052748703686304575228314238507620

Futterman, M. (2010b, September 15). Agent drops suit to end IMG-CAA spat. Retrieved from https://www.wsj.com/articles/SB100014240527487037435045754942911654797 92

Greenberg, M. J. (1993). *Sports law practice*. Charlottesville, VA: Michie Company.

Grossman, J. W. (2002). Financial planning for the professional athlete. In G. A. Uberstine (Ed.), *Law of professional and amateur sports* (pp. 3-4–3-11). St. Paul, MN: West Group.

Hack, D. (2008, December 15). McCormack and Palmer changed world of sports and business forever. Retrieved from http://www.golf.com/tour-and-news/mccormack-and-palmer-changed-world-sports-and-business-forever#ixzz37AUp0uI3

Hamilton, S. (2002, February 26). Wasserman acquires OnSport. *Golfweek*. Retrieved from http://golfweek.com/2002/02/26/wasserman-acquires-onsport/

Heitner, D. (2016, September 20). Why NFL agents are furious with new regulations. Retrieved from https://www.inc.com/darren-heitner/why-nfl-agents-are-furious-with-new-regulations.html

Helyar, J. (1994). *Lords of the realm*. New York, NY: Villard Books.

Helyar, J. (1997, June 25). Net gains? A Providence guard leaves college early, hoping for NBA gold. *Wall Street Journal*, pp. A1, A8.

Hersch, P. (1994, December 11). Commentary: Kerrigan's off-ice spins create "image meltdown." *The Seattle Times*. Retrieved from http://community.seattletimes.nwsource.com/archive/?date=19941211&slug=1946743

Hofmann, D., & Greenberg, M. J. (1989). *Sport$ biz*. Champaign, IL: Leisure Press.

IMG. (2003). IMG chairman's letter. Retrieved from http://www.imgworld.com/chairmansletter/default.htm

IMG. (2004). IMG history. Retrieved from http://www.imgworld.com/history/

IMG. (2014). About us. Retrieved from http://img.com/about-us.aspx

Johnston, A. J., & Kain, R. D. (2004). CEO message. Retrieved from https://web.archive.org/web/20041204181151/http://www.imgworld.com:80/message/default.sps?itype=4440&icustompageid=9195

Katz, D. (1994). *Just do it: The Nike spirit in the corporate world*. New York, NY: Random House.

Kepner, T. (2006, October 21). Baseball; The Boras bunch. *New York Times*. Retrieved from http://select.nytimes.com/search/restricted/article?res=F20815F93D5B0C728EDDA90994DE404482

Kuliga, K. (2007, April 4). Interview as part of the "Someone to be Proud of Series." University of Massachusetts Club, Boston, MA.

Lester, P. (2002). Marketing the athlete: Endorsement contracts. In G. A. Uberstine (Ed.), *Law of professional and amateur sports* (pp. 27-2–27-39). St. Paul, MN: West Group.

Levin, M. (2007, February 12). Telephone conversation with Director of Salary Cap and Agent Administration of NFLPA.

Longman, J. (1994, February 6). Focus on sports: The whole world is watching. *New York Times*. Retrieved from http://www.nytimes.com/1994/02/06/sports/focus-on-sports-the-whole-world-is-watching.html?pagewanted=print&src=pm

Lowenfish, L. (1991). *The imperfect diamond* (rev. ed.). New York, NY: Da Capo Press.

Lowitt, B. (1999, November 29). Harding, Kerrigan are linked forever by skating incident. *The St. Petersburg Times*. Retrieved from http://www.sptimes.com/News/112999/Sports/Harding__Kerrigan_are.shtml

Major League Baseball Players Association (MLBPA). (2010). MLBPA agent regulations. Retrieved from http://reg.mlbpaagent.org

Major League Baseball Players Association (MLBPA). (2017). Frequently asked questions. Retrieved from https://www.mlbpa.org/faq.aspx

McAleenan, G. (2002). Agent–player representation agreements. In G. A. Uberstine (Ed.), *Law of professional and amateur sports* (pp. 2-10–2-12). St. Paul, MN: West Group.

Miller, D. (2016, August 19). How talent agencies help athletes who "transcend sports" cash in on Olympic heroism. *L.A. Times*. Retrieved at http://www.latimes.com/entertainment/envelope/cotown/la-et-ct-olympics-rio-talent-agencies-20160816-snap-story.html

Miller, J. A. (2016). *Powerhouse: The untold story of Hollywood's Creative Artists Agency.* New York, NY: Harper Collins.

Mortensen, C. (1991). *Playing for keeps: How one man kept the mob from sinking its hooks into pro football.* New York, NY: Simon & Schuster.

Mullen, L. (2004, April 19–25). Dirty dealings spark debate. *Street & Smith's SportsBusiness Journal*, pp. 23–27.

Mullen, L. (2006, October 16–22). New players emerge in athlete rep business: Ranking the agencies. *Street & Smith's SportsBusiness Journal*, p. 26.

Mullen, L. (2007a, January 15). LeBron's agent close to CAA deal. *Street & Smith's SportsBusiness Journal*, p. 1.

Mullen, L. (2007b, January 8). Two agents exit Octagon for WMG. *Street & Smith's SportsBusiness Journal*, p. 5.

Mullen, L. (2010a, May 17). Bear with them: CAA Sports signs to represent Jack Nicklaus. *Street & Smith's SportsBusiness Journal*, p. 14.

Mullen, L. (2010b, May 17). Lawsuits may affect big-name sports agencies. *Street & Smith's SportsBusiness Journal*, p. 1.

Mullen, L., & Broughton, D. (2008, August 25). Survey puts CAA tops in player salaries. *Street & Smith's SportsBusiness Journal*, p. 1.

National Basketball Players Association (NBPA). (2017). Certified agent directory. Retrieved from https://nbpa.com/agents/directory/view/all/

National Football League Players Association (NFLPA). (2017). Agents. Retrieved from https://www.nflpa.com/agents/agentsearch?company=&firstName=&lastName=&city=&state=&zip=&h=true&sort=

National Hockey League Players Association (NHLPA). (2017). Certified agents. Retrieved from https://www.nhlpa.com/the-pa/certified-agents?range=A-B

Neff, C. (1987, October 19). Den of vipers. *Sports Illustrated*, pp. 74–104.

Newman, W. (2007). Person-centered branding: Coaching to create an authentic brand. Retrieved from http://www.personcenteredbranding.com

Octagon. (2017). About us. Retrieved from http://www.octagon.com/about

Octagon. (2018). Mindset and culture. Retrieved from http://www.octagon.com/brands/mindset-culture

Oliver v. NCAA, 2009 Ohio 6587 (2009).

Oregon Live. (2018, January 11). Who are the highest paid coaches in the NFL? Retrieved from http://www.oregonlive.com/nfl/index.ssf/2018/01/10_highest_paid_nfl_coaches.html

Oregon Live (2018, Jan. 10). Who are the highest paid NFL coaches? Retrieved from http://www.oregonlive.com/nfl/index.ssf/2018/01/10_highest_paid_nfl_coaches.html

Other League. (2017a). NBA head coaching contracts. Retrieved from http://www.otherleague.com/contracts/nba-head-coach-contracts-salaries/

Ozanian, M. (2013, December 18). IMG sold for $2.3 billion to William Morris Endeavor and Silver Lake Partners. *Forbes*. Retrieved from http://www.forbes.com/sites/mikeozanian/2013/12/18/img-sold-for-2-3-billion-to

-william-morris-endeavor-and-silver-lake
-partners/

Arnold Palmer Group (2017). Arnold Palmer: A life well played. Retrieved from http://www.arnoldpalmer.com

Peltz, J. F. (2016, August 19). Most Olympic athletes won't be able to cash in on their glory. *L.A. Times*. Retrieved at http://www.latimes.com/business/la-fi-olympics-endorsements-20160819-snap-story.html

Pierce, C. (2007, April 1). Why Scott Boras is the best (and worst) thing to happen to baseball. Retrieved from http://www.boston.com/news/globe/magazine/articles/2007/04/01/why_scott_boras_is_the_best_and_worst_thing_to_happen_to_baseball/

Plunkett, J. W. (2017). "Sports agents become indispensable." *Plunkett's Sports Industry Almanac 2017*. Houston, TX: Plunkett Research, Ltd.

Pugh, J. (2014a, August 8). Interview with Greg Bouris, Director of Communications, MLBPA.

Pugh, J. (2014b, August 13). Interview with Carl Francis, Director of Communications, NFLPA.

Red, C. , & O'Keefe. (2014, June 9). NFL players association cracks down on agents in wake of DeSean Jackson, Drew Rosenhaus lawsuit. *New York Daily News*.

Retrieved from http://www.nydailynews.com/sports/football/nflpa-cracks-agents-wake-jackson-rosenhaus-suit-article-1.1823067

Rovell, D. (2013, March 21). Arnold Palmer: The man, the drink, and the legend. Retrieved from http://abcnews.go.com/WNT/video/arnold-palmer-man-drink-legend-18786235

Ruxin, R. (2004). *An athlete's guide to agents* (4th ed.). Sudbury, MA: Jones and Bartlett.

Schakenbach, J. (2012, Nov. 13). "BrandMatch touts new way to find celebrity endorsers." Retrieved from https://www.bizjournals.com/boston/blog/mass-high-tech/2012/11/brandmatch-touts-new-way-to-find-celebrity.html

Schoenfeld, B. (2017, May 5). *Wasserman's world*. Retrieved from https://www.sportsbusinessdaily.com/Journal/Issues/2017/05/08/People-and-Pop-Culture/Wasserman.aspx

Schonbrun, Z. (2018, March 31). Tiger Woods is back. Will sponsors buy in? *The New York Times*. Retrieved from https://www.nytimes.com/2018/03/31/business/tiger-woods-advertising.html?ribbon-ad-idx=4&rref=business&module=Ribbon&version=context&region=Header&action=click&contentCollection=Business%20Day&pgtype=article

Schwarz, A. (1996, March 4–17). Agents: What's the deal? *Baseball America*, pp. 14–19.

Shropshire, K. (1990). *Agents of opportunity*. Philadelphia, PA: University of Pennsylvania Press.

Shropshire, K. L., & Davis, T. (2003). *The business of sports agents*. Philadelphia, PA: University of Pennsylvania Press.

Sobel, L. (1990). The regulation of player agents and lawyers. In G. A. Uberstine (Ed.), *Law of professional and amateur sports* (pp. 1-1–1-107). Deerfield, IL: Clark, Boardman, and Callaghan.

Sobel, L. (2002). The regulation of player agents and lawyers. In G. A. Uberstine (Ed.), *The law of professional and amateur sports* (pp. 1-1–1-6). St. Paul, MN: West Group.

Solomon, J. (1995, April 26). Guest lecture: Professional sports and the law class. University of Massachusetts, Amherst. Sports Agent Responsibility and Trust Act (SPARTA), Pub. L. No. 108-304 (2004)(enacted).

SportsBusiness Journal (2017, May 8). Casy Wasserman timeline. Retrieved from https://www.sportsbusinessdaily.com/Journal/Issues/2017/05/08/People-and-Pop-Culture/CW-timeline.aspx

Sports legend revealed: Did Vince Lombardi trade a player five minutes after learning the player hired an agent? (2011, February 8). *L.A. Times*. Retrieved from http://latimesblogs

.latimes.com/sports_blog/2011/02/sports-legend-revealed-did-vince-lombardi-trade-a-player-five-minutes-after-learning-the-player-hire.html

Thurow, R. (1996, February 9). The 76ers are lowly, but Jerry Stackhouse scores big in marketing. *Wall Street Journal*, pp. A1, A4.

USA Today. (2017a). NCAAB tournament coaches salaries. Retrieved from http://sports.usatoday.com/ncaa/salaries/mens-basketball/coach/

USA Today. (2017b). 2017 NCAAF coaches salaries. Retrieved from http://sports.usatoday.com/ncaa/salaries/

Voyles, K. (2011, Aug.15). "Ex-sports agent William "Tank" Black set to return to prison." Retrieved from http://www.gainesville.com/news/20110815/ex-sports-agent-william-tank-black-set-to-return-to-prison

Waggoner, J. (1996, July 12). Walk, don't run, after a windfall. *USA Today*, p. 5B.

Wertheim, L. J. (2000, May 29). Web of deceit: Smooth talking agent Tank Black allegedly ensnared nearly two dozen NFL and NBA players, including Vince Carter, in a mind-boggling series of scams and defrauded them of some $15 million." *Sports Illustrated*. Retrieved from https://www.si.com/vault/2000/05/29/281480/web-of-deceit-smooth-talking-agent-tank-black-allegedly-ensnared-nearly-two-dozen-nfl-and-nba-players-including-vince-carter-in-a-mind-boggling-series-of-scams-and-defrauded-them-of-some-15-million

Wertheim, L. J. (2001, November 5). SFX needs an Rx. *Sports Illustrated*. Retrieved from https://www.si.com/vault/2001/11/05/313370/sfx-needs-an-rx-sfx-sports-was-supposed-to-be-the-ultimate-in-players-reps-but-its-struggling

Wertheim, L. J. (2004, May 3). The matchmaker: Agent Bob LaMonte represents NFL coaches on the rise. *Sports Illustrated*. Retrieved from http://www.psr-inc.net/docs/TheMatchmaker-SportsIllustrated_050304.pdf

Willette, A., & Waggoner, J. (1996, July 12). Rich can't afford to dismiss budget: Even superstars need financial coaching. *USA Today*, p. 5B.

WME/IMG. (2017a, August 16). Expertise: League development. Retrieved from http://www.endeavorco.com/expertise/league/

WME/IMG. (2017b, August 16). Our story. Retrieved from http://www.endeavorco.com/story/sports/

Woolf, B. (1976). *Behind closed doors*. New York, NY: New American Library.

Worldwide golf. (2017, November 4). The ten richest golfers of all time. Retrieved from http://worldwide.golf/feature/top-10-richest-golfers-time/

© Shutterstock, Inc. / Danilo_Vuletic

Part IV

Sport Industry Support Segments

Chapter

12

Lisa P. Masteralexis

Facility Management

Learning Objectives

Upon completion of this chapter, students should be able to:

1. Describe the history of sport facilities, with an emphasis on the recent trend toward single-purpose stadiums and arenas.

2. Categorize the various types of public assembly facilities, such as arenas, stadiums, convention centers, university venues, metropolitan facilities, and local/civic venues.

3. Identify the types of events that may be held at public assembly facilities.

4. Distinguish between public and private financing of sport facilities, and discuss the advantages and disadvantages of each.

5. Analyze the arguments for and against government subsidization of public assembly facilities.

6. Understand the importance of the relationship between facility ownership and management staff.

7. Describe the basics of marketing and promoting events.

8. Identify the sources of revenues and expenses of sport facilities.

9. Appraise the career opportunities available in the sport facility management segment, and identify the skills needed to succeed in each.

10. Analyze some of the current issues in the public assembly facility industry, including enhanced security, sustainability, access for persons with disabilities, and universal design.

Introduction

People congregate in large groups for a number of reasons. Public assembly facilities must be big enough to accommodate the large numbers of people who want to be entertained at a sport or entertainment event or who meet together for social or business purposes. The facilities designed and built to accommodate these large groups of people include arenas, stadiums, convention centers, theaters, performing arts facilities, racetracks, and amphitheaters. Arenas and stadiums are the primary venues for professional and amateur sport events. Although convention centers and theaters are not designed primarily to host sport events, they are utilized and marketed for this function. The growth in the popularity of sports such as volleyball and mixed martial arts (MMA) has created a new market for these venues because they offer the large, unobstructed space that is vital for successful functions. Additionally, convention centers host sport-related conventions, such as sporting goods expositions, recreation and boat shows, and league meetings.

In this chapter, the discussion of public assembly facilities considers arenas, stadiums, convention centers, and theaters. Management principles are similar for all types of these facilities, and their managers are eligible for membership in the **International Association of Venue Managers (IAVM)**, the professional trade association for this field. Facility managers provide the public with a safe, enjoyable experience while providing a cost-effective and efficient means for the venue owner. This chapter focuses on significant areas in facility management to identify the structure and reasons why facilities are managed in certain ways.

History

Public assembly facilities have existed since ancient times. In fact, the word **stadium** is derived from the ancient Greek *stade*, a site for early Olympic-style athletic competition, such as the early Olympic Games first held in Olympia, Greece. Many of today's famous facilities bear the names of ancient and medieval facilities (e.g., Forum, Coliseum, Globe Theater). Throughout recorded history, people have gathered to witness sporting competitions and live theater at their era's version of public assembly facilities. From a sport management perspective, today's version of public assembly facilities evolved during the late nineteenth and early twentieth centuries in the United States, coinciding with the development of professional and intercollegiate athletics.

Early stadiums saw professional baseball and football teams sharing the same facilities. There was once a time when both the Chicago Cubs and the Chicago Bears called Wrigley Field their home! Professional hockey moved to arenas first, followed by basketball, which hockey owners used to fill dark days when the hockey teams did not play.

The Modern Era of Stadium and Arena Construction

Basketball and hockey, as tenants of one arena, are much more compatible in terms of building design and sightlines than are baseball and football. Stadium quirks and fan annoyance factors were never as critical in developing arenas capable of hosting both indoor sports as they were in stadiums attempting to host both outdoor sports. Still, it is clearly advantageous for sport facility owners (whether indoor or outdoor) to have two prime sport tenants. The baseball-only stadiums that had served their owners and fans for more than 40 years became obsolete during the 1960s. Some were too small, and most lacked modern amenities such as wide seats, leg room, easy access to concession stands, and artificial turf. Several new stadiums were built during the 1960s and 1970s, although not by the team owners.

Team owners at that time were beginning to learn a lesson they would use to their advantage in the future: They could save a great deal of money by having their host city build their stadium, rather than building it themselves. Cities, driven by the civic pride that "big league" status endows, built shiny new facilities to keep their teams as enthusiastic about their hometowns as were the civic leaders. It made sense for the cities to build facilities with both their football and baseball tenants in mind, because more activity justified the public investment. The result was the emergence of "cookie-cutter stadiums," such as Veterans Stadium in Philadelphia, Three Rivers Stadium in Pittsburgh, and Riverfront Stadium in Cincinnati. They were new, they were modern, they had artificial turf (so field maintenance was easy), and they all looked alike. Arena construction boomed during this era, too. Civic centers and civic arenas sprang up in a number of major and secondary markets as cities competed for major and minor league sport teams by building suitable facilities. This period also marked the dawn of the touring concert industry, and concerts became an extremely lucrative addition to a facility's schedule. City leaders generally believed that a publicly built stadium with both baseball and football tenants or a publicly built arena with both basketball and hockey tenants, along with the concert and family show tours, was a good investment. Such facilities contributed to the city's quality of life by providing sports and entertainment for the citizens and spin-off benefits for the local economy.

Eventually, team owners, and many of their fans, decided that multipurpose facilities were not quite good enough. Stadiums designed to be acceptable for both baseball and football ended up being desirable for neither. Thus, the trend over the past two decades has been to build single-purpose stadiums. This specialization has extended to facilities built solely for soccer teams, called **soccer-specific stadiums (SSS)**. SSS have become the legacy of soccer investor Lamar Hunt, late owner of the Columbus Crew, whose SSS in Columbus, Ohio, was the first venue of its size to be built in the United States and has fueled SSS growth. The Crew Stadium opened in 1999 and has become a model for all Major League Soccer (MLS) franchises. Now, SSS in MLS are the norm.

Financing these facilities has become an interesting dilemma, particularly given team owners' desire to use facility revenues to compete for free-agent players and boost their own profits. Some cities have constructed (or have promised to construct) facilities that will provide team owners with the design and revenue streams they need to be successful. Team owners have traditionally sought lucrative stadium leases that provide revenue from four sources: preferred seating (i.e., luxury suites, club seating, and personal seat licenses), parking, concessions, and stadium sponsorship (i.e., signage and naming rights) (Greenberg & Gray, 1993).

Technology in Stadiums

New technology has created additional revenue streams. For example, in the Dallas Cowboys' AT&T Stadium, there is an emphasis on second-screen viewing. According to Stephen Jones, son of Cowboys owner Jerry Jones, "This is about smartphones, iPads, computers and technology . . . we have targeted them from the get-go. This was not just about settling for a naming rights deal. . . . This is a bigger deal" (Jacobson, Robinson-Jacobs, & Moore, 2013). This idea was taken one step further in the brand-new Mercedes Benz Stadium, home of the Atlanta Falcons of the National Football League (NFL) and the Atlanta United FC of the MLS. This stadium includes the largest videoboard in the world, providing 63,000 square feet of coverage. The 360-degree board has been labeled the "halo board" and truly revolutionizes the ability for second-screen viewing inside the stadium (Moriarty, 2017).

On the West Coast, Levi's Stadium, home of the San Francisco 49ers, set the standard for the new era of high-tech stadiums. Based in the heart of Silicon Valley, a technology hub of its own, the 49ers wanted a stadium that appropriately reflected the area in which they reside and also offered fans a more pleasurable in-stadium experience. Incorporated in Levi's Stadium is more than "400 miles of cabling, 70 miles of which are just dedicated to connecting the 1,200 distributed antenna systems that serve the Wi-Fi routers that are placed to serve every 100 seats" of the nearly 69,000 seats in the stadium (Bajarin, 2014). The overall goal of implementing this level of technology is to provide fans with a platform to consume content even when live action is not occurring. Through the use of an app that was developed specifically for Levi's Stadium, fans are able to view content from any smartphone or tablet, just as if they were watching from home. The app also provides fans with information such as directions to an exact parking spot, directions to the individual's seat, estimated waiting times at the nearest restroom, and so much more.

Due to the geographical expectation for being a beacon of futuristic technology, it is likely that Levi's Stadium will remain at the forefront of the high-tech stadiums for the near future (Bajarin, 2014). Nonetheless, it should come as no surprise if other stadiums and arenas increase their attention to technology to get fans out of their homes and into those venues' seats.

Forces Behind Team Relocation

The lucrative revenue streams associated with emerging technology and innovative stadium designs have created an irresistible lure for team owners, leading to the emergence of franchise free agency. Some team owners have chosen to flee their traditional locations for greener pastures not because of small market sizes or limited prospects for growth, but because of more profitable facility deals. In fact, the facility in which a professional sport team plays has the most significant impact on its profitability and is often the primary consideration in choosing to remain or move to a new location.

Take, for example, the Los Angeles Rams, which made the move from St. Louis, Missouri, to the now-crowded NFL market of Los Angeles in 2016. The driving force behind this decision appears to be the state-of-the-art Los Angeles Stadium at Hollywood Park, which is set to open in 2020. The location offers an entertainment and retail experience unlike any other, and the truly unique design will allow for maximum use for events of all kinds on a year-round basis (Lago, 2018).

Another team in the process of relocating is the Oakland Raiders, which will be known as the Las Vegas Raiders in the near future. This team also has its sights set on a brand-new stadium that offers fans in attendance an experience like nothing they have seen before. One stand-out feature of the Raiders to-be stadium is the videoboard on the outside of the stadium, which will give tailgaters a view of the game. Innovations like this are providing reasons for fans to leave the comfort of their homes and to go out and experience sports the way that they are meant to be consumed, live and in person (Davis & Gaines, 2017).

Types of Public Assembly Facilities

Arenas

Arenas are indoor facilities that host sporting and entertainment events. They are usually built to accommodate one (or more) prime sport tenant(s) or to lure a prime tenant to the facility. Colleges and universities typically build an arena for their basketball teams and occasionally their hockey teams, as at the University of Notre Dame's Compton Family Ice Arena. These arenas may also be used for volleyball, such as the Bob Devaney Center at the University of Nebraska, and gymnastics, as well as for concerts and other touring shows. Intercollegiate facilities are financed by private donations, endowments, student fees, fundraising campaigns, and, in the case of public institutions, public grants or capital bonds.

Some National Basketball Association (NBA) and National Hockey League (NHL) teams have built their own arenas. In other cases, municipalities, state governments, or public authorities have built them. Sometimes the public owner manages its facility, and sometimes it contracts out for private management. The public or private manager then negotiates a lease with the prime sport tenant. If the arena is privately built, commercial lenders issue loans to the team, which pledges facility revenue streams as collateral. Public

financing typically involves issuing bonds that can be tied to direct or indirect facility revenue, but more often are a general obligation of the governmental entity.

Basketball and hockey teams can generally peacefully coexist in the same arena without either being forced into unacceptable compromises. Arenas also host indoor soccer leagues, arena football, concerts, ice shows, family shows, graduations, other civic events, and some types of conventions. Recent trends in facility construction include adjacent practice facilities for the primary tenants. The NHL's Columbus Blue Jackets and New Jersey Devils both have this arrangement. The Minnesota Timberwolves of the NBA and the Minnesota Lynx of the Women's National Basketball Association (WNBA) have their practice facility across the street from their home arena, and Mayo Clinic will open a sport medicine clinic on the site as well (NBA Media Ventures, 2014).

Stadiums

The ownership, financing, and management issues discussed in the arena section also apply to stadiums. Like their arena counterparts, stadium managers try to maximize bookings, but it is more difficult. First, far fewer nonsport events can play in stadiums, primarily because stadiums are significantly larger than other venues and most other events cannot attract stadium-sized crowds. The main nonsport events for stadiums are outdoor concerts given by performers who have the drawing power to fill a stadium. The large parking facilities that are adjacent to most stadiums have long been utilized for pregame tailgating. On nongame days, they are now being utilized and marketed to fairs, festivals, circuses, carnivals, outdoor marketplaces, and drive-and-buy car shows. They are also sometimes rented out for staging areas for new cars in transit to dealers or for parking for nearby events such as state fairs or major civic events such as the Kentucky Derby.

Convention Centers

Convention centers are almost always built and owned by a public entity. Convention centers are built to lure conventions and business meetings to a particular municipality. They are publicly financed because the rents and fees they charge do not always cover their costs. However, the municipality they serve benefits in other ways—namely, through the economic impact the conventions or business meetings have on the municipality. Organizations such as the International Association of Convention and Visitors Bureaus evaluate the economic impact of various events, considering spending that includes hotel, meal, entertainment, and related expenditures.

Convention centers are typically located near the downtown districts of large cities. The convention business is extremely competitive, and municipalities (and states) offer significant financial inducements to convention and meeting planners for the opportunity to host visitors. The conventioneers and meeting attendees stay in local hotels, eat in local restaurants, shop in local stores, and patronize local tourist attractions—and all of these activities support business and employment in the region. Conventioneers also are typically taxed, so the state and municipality receive indirect revenues from the events. The increased business, employment opportunities, and fiscal revenues justify the public entity's construction and continued subsidy of convention centers.

In addition to the nontraditional sporting events previously discussed, convention centers host a wide variety of events, such as volleyball and basketball tournaments; trade shows, such as car, boat, and home shows; corporate meetings; banquets; and similar functions.

University Venues

University venues consist of stadiums, arenas, and theaters that operate under different economic factors. The market for university and college venues is generally dictated by the student population. Universities and colleges have different geographic locations, but the general intent when selling tickets is to market to the student population; in turn, certain types of events will play better than others.

Theaters are often part of the college and university menu of facilities. A **theater** is a building or outdoor area (amphitheater) that has been designated for plays or other dramatic, comedic, and musical performances that occur on a stage. Often they also serve as a place for public or private gatherings such as convocations, graduations, and speaking engagements.

Universities tend to provide their venues with tenant teams as well as a certain amount of content through the educational and extracurricular activities of the university. Providing the university with the content that may be routed through the area can sometimes prove to be difficult based on the occupied dates scheduled for university programs.

Metropolitan Facilities

Metropolitan facilities are venues located in large cities such as Madison Square Garden in New York, the Wells Fargo complex in Philadelphia, and the Staples Center in Los Angeles. Venues such as these are generally referred to as a *must play* based on the size of the potential audience. The three venues just listed can present as many as 400 events a year if the scheduling allows for it. They often have multiple tenants, including NHL, NBA, WNBA, NBA Development League (NBA G-League), and arena football leagues. Typically the staffs operating these venues are larger based on the event load, whereas a smaller venue will generally run a more streamlined staff.

A must-play venue is popular with promoters for several reasons. Promoters with established routing have a variety of local staff, making tour travel less expensive and more efficient. Metropolitan venues often have larger capacities, allowing for greater ticket sales. Skilled labor in metropolitan venues is almost always unionized. In smaller venues, specific labor may be mandated to be contracted to the unions, but there is often a component that can be nonunion. The venues located within city limits utilize skilled labor from the union, but their expertise often costs more than hiring a private contractor. Venue managers often are required to use union labor because of contracts negotiated before the venue opened that were based on funding and economic impact studies.

Local/Civic Venues

Local/civic venues may have a smaller capacity and are located in towns or small cities. The CURE Insurance Arena in Trenton, New Jersey, and the Santander Arena in Reading, Pennsylvania, are examples of local or civic venues. They have a smaller surrounding population and seating capacity. The venues themselves are able to host large-scale events and concerts but tend to host smaller-capacity events due to artist costs. The venue manager needs to identify what works for a venue in the 5,000 to 10,000 seat range. Although the venue may have an NBA or NHL minor league affiliate (such as the Reading Royals in Reading) as a tenant, it is essential to host additional events to fill the calendar. Facility-operating teams have successfully held events that play to local groups, such as cheerleading competitions, political conventions, and church conferences. The civic venue has a niche that is based in the surrounding community, and the support the venue receives is critical to its success.

Types of Events

Many different types of events are possible. Some are mainstream, such as Disney On Ice, whereas others may be somewhat nontraditional, such as the X Games or Dew Tour. Venue managers should know about a wide variety of genres and be able to quickly assess the type of event that would have the biggest impact on the community and the venue. When looking at event types, the promoter and facility director must first consider the market to ensure the success of an event.

Family events, such as the Harlem Globetrotters show, are always popular. The well-known Harlem Globetrotters act encompasses comedy, athleticism, and pop culture. The Globetrotters travel throughout the world and are well received in every venue they play. Family events such as traveling circuses may not do as well, because some activist groups believe that the animals involved in such programs are being treated unethically. Venue managers and promoters need to take these kinds of market concerns into consideration prior to booking a routing event. The facility manager also has to be aware of the specifics of his or her market to provide the public with the desired event at the best time of the year to avoid undue competition with other events that may be occurring simultaneously.

The following subsections describe some event genres and how they operate.

Sport Events

Sports have seasons that allow events to be scheduled approximately 8 months out. Several venues will have primary tenant teams that play a home schedule and require certain dates contractually. For example, the primary tenants in Chicago's United Center are the NBA Bulls and the NHL Blackhawks. Facility managers walk a fine line when booking shows around team games because of playoffs. Should the tenant team make the playoffs, it will require that home days be available. A close eye needs to be kept on the booking calendar to make sure conflicts or double bookings do not occur. Nontenant **sport events** must be booked around the primary tenants. Examples of these types of sport events may include AAU basketball tournaments or high school all-star games.

Family Events

Family events are products geared toward the toddler through the "tween" markets. Often these are acts produced from television or movie programs that are run on mainstream television or in movie theaters. Sesame Street, Nickelodeon, and Disney are among the top names in the family genre. They produce the artists that children identify with.

When playing a venue, the show usually has a multiple-day run and generates large demands for food and beverages as well as merchandise sales. Booking can be challenging based on the amount of preparation the venue will need and how long of a run the show will have.

Ice programs will need ice specifically tailored to the artists and the performance. Preparation for changes to an ice sheet from hockey usage to ice show usage can take time and commitment from the operations team. Should the schedule be tight and a quick turnaround necessary, the venue manager may need to look at the event and try to find alternative dates that work.

Concerts

Concerts are booked, on average, 6 months before the performance date. Tours and routings are established, and the dates are promoted after an agreement is reached. When booking concerts, it is important to look at the potential ticket sales and the intended market. Size, age of the arena, and the building's technology capacity can dictate the types of performers who will appear. Booking Ed Sheeran, Chance the Rapper, or Taylor Swift, for example, would be possible only in the most state-of-the-art facility.

Timing also is critical when scheduling a concert. Consider university students, for example. Students have breaks throughout the year that generally include fall, winter, and spring breaks. It would not make sense to schedule a big-name performer that appeals to this demographic group when the students are on winter break. In addition, some schools are more of a commuter type and do not have a central location where students are housed in large numbers. These are all critical factors when looking at booking a venue with a show geared toward a student body.

Some cities have amphitheaters that host outdoor music events. These are particularly popular in the summer season when the evenings are warm and comfortable.

Trade Shows

Trade shows are mostly multiple-day events held annually in the same location. Trade shows work best in convention centers because hotel and exhibition space are specifically intended for that usage, but they can also play in stadiums and arenas that can be converted to accommodate the event. An example is the Phoenix Convention Center in Arizona, which hosts an annual expo for outdoor enthusiasts and fans of recreational vehicles. This venue utilizes its retractable roof and stadium field to fill dates, which gives the promoter the ability to expand the show into a larger, more unique space.

Religious Events

Religious events encompass mass worship. These events are generally booked as a rental with expenses guaranteed. The rental structure is preferred because religious organizations generally do not charge for tickets. Some groups, such as the Jehovah's Witnesses, can provide a good opportunity to utilize a venue when bookings for the facility are slow. Arenas have been able to schedule religious events in the summer to fill dates that would otherwise go vacant. Concerts and tours tend to play outdoor facilities in the summer, so religious events present a nice opportunity to make a small profit on days that would otherwise not be utilized.

Convocations

Convocations, graduations, and speaking engagements are great ways to get community involvement and interaction with the venue. Venue managers generally approach these types of events with the understanding that graduations happen in the spring and weather conditions may present certain challenges to hosting them outside. Another plus is the capacity of the venue and the graduates' ability to have additional tickets for friends and family. Graduations can be a busy time of year depending on the number of local schools hosting at the facility and the size of the class.

Seasonal Events

Seasonal events are defined as events that take place during a specific time frame. Summer tours are a perfect example of a seasonal event. In the past, large summer music tours were held mostly at outdoor theaters, but more recently stadiums are hosting large country music festivals and touring programs. One event that seems to mark the beginning of the summer for many concert goers is the appearance of Jimmy Buffet. Buffet's Margaritaville tour is one of the most heavily attended summer touring events. The shows are generally held at outdoor facilities so the fans can experience the music in an outdoor and relaxed fashion.

Other types of seasonal programming that the facility manager may consider are seasonal programs directed at holidays, such as the Radio City Music Hall Rockettes touring holiday program or the Trans-Siberian Orchestra. Both programs tour around the November–December holiday season and attract good attendance from families looking to get into the holiday spirit.

Facility Financing

Facility financing starts with the federal government, which allows state and local governments to issue tax-exempt bonds to help finance sport facilities. Tax exemption lowers interest on debt, thereby reducing the amount that cities and teams must pay for a stadium. Public assembly facilities can be financed in a variety of ways, but the specific financing decision is always preceded by a single fundamental question: Will the facility be financed publicly or privately? The answer depends on a number of factors, including the type of facility being constructed. Convention centers are almost always financed publicly because they are not intended to make money. These venues do not book events to make a profit for themselves; rather, they book events that maximize the impact on the local economy, particularly the hospitality industry. Because of their "public" focus, the public sector pays for them, often by initiating or raising taxes on the state or local hospitality industry (e.g., hotel room taxes, restaurant meal taxes, and rental car fees).

Arena and stadium financing is not as clear-cut, particularly when a major league professional sport team is a prime tenant. Professional sport teams are in business to make money—sometimes enormous amounts of money. Some argue that any for-profit enterprise should build its own facility where it conducts its business. At the same time, a number of studies have shown that sport facilities provide significant economic benefits to their host communities, and teams are undeniable sources of civic pride and community spirit. Attracting a sport team can provide a public relations boost to a city, too, particularly one attempting to prove it is "major league."

Controlling stadium revenue streams such as concessions, advertising, sponsorship, premium seating and suites, and seat licenses has become the primary means to the owners' ends. Single-purpose facilities designed to the specifications of a particular sport with one team as primary tenant are desirable to team owners because revenue streams do not have to be shared.

For the cities, states, stadium authorities, and other representatives of the public sector, these issues have become increasingly problematic. The public benefits justifying stadium construction remain, but costs continue to rise, particularly if two teams are looking for their own separate stadiums or arenas. Cities, in particular, face hard choices, because most have stable or declining tax revenues and increasing municipal government costs. Building public assembly facilities means that other services have to be neglected. In many locations, the question of publicly financing a stadium has been put to a vote.

Facility Financing Mechanisms

The facility arms race for college and professional sports continues to push forward with the construction of new arenas and stadiums across the country. The key question that arises is how these facilities are being funded and for how much. Over the past two decades, professional sport venues of the Big Four (MLB, NHL, NBA, and NFL) have cost approximately $37 billion, with 54% or $20 billion of this being funded through tax dollars (Crompton, 2014). This trend has continued, with the industry seeing the introduction of the first $1 billion stadiums, including MetLife Stadium, Yankee Stadium, AT&T Stadium, and Wembley Stadium.

A team or city has a variety of options for funding a new facility or financing a renovation. As previously stated, public financing has accounted for 54% of costs for professional facilities. These monies are obtained through bonds, hard taxes, or soft taxes.

A **bond** is defined as "an interest-bearing certificate issued by the government or corporation, promising to pay interest and to repay a sum of money" (Samuelson & Nordhaus, 1985, p. 828). A variety of bonds are available for facility financing. Tax-exempt bonds used by government entities are available in two types: general obligation and nonguaranteed. General obligation bonds are repaid with a portion of the general property taxes and require voter approval (Sawyer, 2006). Stadiums funded by these bonds include AT&T Stadium in Dallas, Texas; Time Warner Cable Arena in Charlotte, North Carolina; and the Tampa Bay Times Forum in Tampa, Florida (Kuriloff & Preston, 2012).

Another example of the use of tax-exempt bonds to build facilities can be found in Cleveland. Jacobs Field (MLB Indians) and Gund Arena (NBA Cavaliers) both opened in 1994 and saw great early success after opening. The new venues were also credited with sparking the revitalization of downtown Cleveland. Nevertheless, Gateway Development Corporation (GDC), which owns both venues, was not collecting enough money from the leases to pay on the debt service on the $120 million in bonds that helped finance the project (Burke, 1997). In turn, Cuyahoga County, the guarantor of the debt, was forced to cover the costs through its taxpayers (Burke, 1997).

Nonguaranteed bonds are sold on the basis of repayment from designated revenue sources (e.g., concessions, naming rights, parking revenues) (Sawyer, 2006). Although nonguaranteed bonds do not generally require voter approval, the interest rate is higher compared to general obligation bonds (Sawyer, 2006).

Another form of bond is a taxable bond issued by private entities. There are two forms of these bonds: private-placement bonds and asset-backed bonds. Both types are sold by the team, but private-placement bonds provide a lien on all future revenues generated by the team, whereas asset-backed bonds are secured through specific assets (Sawyer, 2006). For example, the Pepsi Center, home of the Denver Nuggets, Colorado Mammoth, and Colorado Avalanche, was financed through asset-backed bonds in the 1990s (CAA ICON/Pepsi Center).

Another bond option that has become popular is tax-increment financing (TIF). TIF is available in a specific square mileage of land around the facility (usually an urban area that has been identified for renewal or redevelopment) where the tax base is frozen and any additional taxes added are used to repay the TIF bonds (Sawyer, 2006). For example, the KFC Yum! Center is owned by the Louisville Arena Authority and is home of the University of Louisville men's and women's basketball teams and women's volleyball team; it is surrounded by a TIF district with a 6-square-mile radius.

The public can also help finance a new venue through additional taxes. Hard taxes include taxes on local income, real estate, personal property, and general sales. They often require voter approval because the burden of payment becomes that of the public (Sawyer, 2006). Soft taxes include added taxes to car rentals, taxis, hotels/motels, restaurants, "sin" (e.g., alcohol, tobacco, gambling), and players (additional tax imposed on visiting professional athletes) and affect a much smaller portion of taxpayers, making them easier to levy (Sawyer, 2006). The Minnesota Vikings football team helped fund its new stadium by imposing an additional tax on tobacco products (Bradley, 2013). Houston's Reliant Stadium was partially funded by a 2% tax on hotels and a 5% tax on car rentals (Plunkett, 2017).

Another option for financing a new facility is private funding. Many universities across the United States choose to go this route through their athletic development and fundraising departments. Ways to gain private funding for a facility project include selling naming rights, food and beverage rights, luxury suites and premium seating, advertising rights, and so on. The University of Maryland was able to pen a 25-year agreement with Comcast Cable for the naming rights to its basketball arena (Howard & Crompton, 2004). Private donors to university athletic departments also may provide funding and have their names placed on the new facilities. Recent examples include the University of Louisville's $18.5 million Dr. Mark and Cindy Lynn Stadium (soccer); Oklahoma State's Boone Pickens Stadium (football), which opened in 2009; and the University of Notre Dame's Compton Family Ice Arena, which began operations in 2011.

Many municipalities will not support additional taxes for stadium projects, so team owners have to seek private funding. A prime example of a team that successfully built an arena with limited tax support was the Utah Jazz. Team owner Larry H. Miller received minimal public financing support for the team's new home, and he ended up supporting the project with his own money (Jensen, 2000). As a result, he built a cost-efficient arena on land given to him by the state of Utah while taxpayers saw no new direct tax increases from this project (Jensen, 2000). The Palace at Auburn Hills, former home of the NBA's Detroit Pistons, which opened in 1988 as one of the first single-purpose venues, was funded wholly through private sources (Crompton, Howard, & Var, 2003). Incidentally, the Pistons have now moved back into downtown Detroit in the Little Caesars Arena, which they share with the Red Wings (NHL). The Arena is in close proximity to Ford Field, home of the Lions (NFL), and Comerica Park, home of the Tigers (MLB), and is located within the District Detroit development (discussed later in this chapter).

Oftentimes, opportunities are available to combine private and public funding to build a new facility. For example, the Minnesota Vikings' U.S. Bank Stadium was constructed using $348 million in Minnesota state funds, $150 million in Minneapolis city funds, and $550 million in funding from the Vikings. Of the $550 million, $220 million will come from the U.S. Bank naming rights over 20 years (Plunkett, 2017).

The desire for new facilities continues to grow, as teams, universities, and cities alike try to upgrade their status. Whether their venues are used as a recruiting tool for college athletes, a state-of-the-art destination for pro sport fans, or a visible sign of civic pride, sport facility managers will need to work creatively to find the best sources of revenues to meet this ongoing demand. This is especially challenging when the tenants in the facilities vie for as many revenue streams as they can maximize in and around the facility, putting pressure on the facility's management team to satisfy their demands while also driving revenues to the facility management company.

Why Cities Subsidize Sport Facilities

The economic rationale for cities to subsidize sport facilities comes from the expectation that sport facilities will improve the local economy in four ways. First, building a facility creates construction jobs. Second, people who attend games or work for the team generate new spending in the community, expanding local employment. Third, a team attracts tourists and companies to the host city, further increasing local spending and jobs. Finally, all this new spending has a "multiplier effect" as increased local income stimulates still more new spending and job creation (Noll & Zimbalist, 1997). Advocates argue that new stadiums spur so much economic growth that they are self-financing, in that subsidies are offset by revenues from ticket taxes, sales taxes on concessions and other spending outside the stadium, and property tax increases arising from the stadium's economic impact.

Unfortunately, these arguments contain poor economic reasoning that leads to overstatement of the benefits of stadiums. Economic growth takes place when a community's resources—people, capital investments, and natural resources such as land—become more productive. Building a stadium is good for the local economy only if a stadium is the most productive way to make capital investments and use an area's workers (Noll & Zimbalist, 1997). According to Reed (2014):

> Urban populations need to get past that "civic pride" foolishness and put their governments "in check." League-wide, 70% of the capital cost of NFL stadiums is being provided by taxpayers. Many governments also pay stadiums' ongoing costs, by providing power, sewer services, and other infrastructure improvements.

No recently built facility appears to have earned anything approaching a reasonable return on investment. In addition, no such facility has been self-financing in terms of its impact on net tax revenues (Noll & Zimbalist, 1997). According to Demause (2011), "Owners of teams in the 'big four' sports leagues . . . have reaped nearly $20 billion in taxpayer subsidies for new homes since 1990. And for just as long, fans, urban planners and economists have argued that building facilities for private sports teams is a massive waste of public money."

Prospects for cutting sport subsidies are not good. Although citizen opposition has had some success, without more effective intercity organizing or more active federal antitrust policy, cities will continue to compete against each other to attract or keep artificially scarce sport franchises. Given the profound penetration and popularity of sports in U.S. culture, it is hard to see an end to rising public subsidies of sport facilities. A great example of this is the relationship of the city of New York to its professional sport teams. Despite the current economic challenges, the city helped to subsidize the building of new stadiums for the Yankees and the Mets. Mayor Michael Bloomberg nixed the plan of his predecessor Rudy Giuliani to spend $800 million in city funds due to the recession. However, 3 years later, Bloomberg's own plan, while calling on the two teams to pay for the construction of their stadiums, provided for the city to build parks, parking garages, and transit stations near the stadiums at a cost of $485 million to the city and another $201 million to the state. These totals do not include an estimated $480 million in tax breaks to the teams, while the teams are also using city-owned land on a tax-free basis (Bagli, 2008).

According to Crompton (2014), the idea that sport facilities are catalysts for economic growth is only valid under certain conditions. These venues can serve as catalysts for retail, commercial, and residential properties if they are not built as isolated incidents. Crompton (2014, p. 9) explains that through the principle of cumulative attraction, cities that plan well create urban entertainment districts where there is a critical mass of unique properties to attract people to the city; thus, the sport facility as a catalyst is effective only if it is part of an integrated, coherent masterplan. Citing Rosentraub (2010), Crompton (2014) notes other factors needed for a sport facility to serve as an effective catalyst: The city investments are concentrated in a district or area, the catalysts offer unique experiences (sport facilities do), and they are located near convenient parking and/or public transportation.

Facility Ownership and Management Staff

The relationship between the owner of a facility and management is critical, with efficiency and profitability determined by the purpose of the building (Farmer, Mulrooney, & Ammon, 1996). Facility ownership generally falls into three categories: community or state, which may have a "plethora of regulations and procedures in place"; colleges, where "funding is based on continued student growth, gifts, and institutional subsidies"; and private facilities, whose motive is solely to make a profit (Farmer et al., 1996).

Responsibilities of the management staff include serving tenants' needs and providing a clean, safe, and comfortable environment for patrons. Various functions performed by the management team include security, cleanup, marketing and sales, scheduling and booking, operations, event promotions, and finance and box office operations.

Private Management Options

The growth of private management in the operation of public assembly facilities in the past decade is indicative of the pressure to achieve maximum operating results by municipal and private ownership entities. Private management offers expertise and resources not usually available to individual venue managers. Most private management companies have a network of facilities that create leverage in cultivating key event relationships and, in turn, event bookings. Additionally, these companies have dedicated corporate personnel who are available to provide oversight and assistance that otherwise would most likely have to come from other municipal departments. Other examples of the benefits of private management include increased operating efficiencies, purchasing leverage for supplies and maintenance items, and labor negotiation resources. Some of the larger private facility management companies include Global Spectrum, which manages facilities ranging from Philadelphia's Wells Fargo Center to the United Arab Emirates Zayad Sport City in Abu Dhabi, and AEG, which manages a wide array of facilities, ranging from the Barclay's Center in Brooklyn, New York, to the O2 Centers in London and Berlin, to the Brussels National Arena in Belgium.

Private management companies have also added many career options for individuals entering the venue management field. With a network of facilities, these companies may offer growth and advancement opportunities to their employees across a wide geographic area. Companies such as Global Spectrum have also widened their reach by acquiring PACIOLAN ticketing systems and Ovations Food Systems.

Facility Marketing
Marketing

Identifying the market and the specifics of the venue are critical to successfully marketing the facility and its events. Facility managers need to focus on several aspects of marketing, including marketing new facilities, securing anchor tenants, attracting events, and developing relationships (Fried, 2010). The facility manager needs to account for the location of the venue, the types of events that best fit the community and culture of the facility, and the means by which those events will be produced. Routing shows and artists are key elements to making a new or existing venue a sustainable option for the community and the facility's owners. Concerts generally confirm dates several months out, whereas family programs such as Disney On Ice, Sesame Street, and the Big Apple Circus book annual dates. These two types of events book in the manner that they do for several reasons. Annual events generally have a several-day run and provide groups such as schools, churches, Boy and Girl Scouts, and other clubs the ability to budget for the program. Concerts oftentimes rotate off the release of an artist's new music or an event that sparks public interest.

The information culture that has developed as a result of the Internet and social media outlets gives the facility manager the ability to access information much more quickly than in the past. These critical advances in technology also increase the demand for the manager to utilize his or her facility's calendar and team in the most efficient and effective manner. By using online tools, the manager can quickly react to inquiries for available dates and can establish a routing for a program or show.

The geographic location of a facility is a critical factor in the routing of artists and acts. *Saturated markets* are markets with several venues in a close proximity to one another. When booking programs, some facilities may have radius clauses prohibiting the same act from playing another venue within 50 miles. These types of clauses are very difficult to manage when defining a geographic market, because state lines often are crossed and in certain circumstances potential patrons will not travel across state lines to see a program. Markets tend to define themselves, but the venues can define the market and decide how and which types of programs to host.

Finally, the local economy will be the driving force behind ticket sales and ticket price points. Promoters need to earn a base amount to cover the artist guarantees and venue expenses depending on the way the deal is negotiated.

Promoting

Shows and events can be promoted in several different ways. The facility manager may have a series of rules or guidelines to use when negotiating a contract for an event or program for the facility. His or her task is to keep financial risks low and profit margins high. Deal structures can be negotiated between promoters and venue managers to share revenue streams and risk certain profits such as rent, facility fees, or parking revenues. A deal structure in which risk and revenues are shared is generally defined as a *co-promotional model*. Should the venue manager be prohibited from taking on risk in holding events, most likely he or she will operate under a rental agreement guaranteeing a specified rental amount, with the external costs being covered by the promoter. Co-promotional agreements can provide a greater profit, but they also carry the risk of loss should ticket sales not be favorable. The rental is a fixed cost for the venue but it relies on **ancillary revenue** to help increase the profit margin.

Generally, the majority of shows are brought to venues by professional promoters. Live Nation, AEG Live, and Feld Entertainment are three of the largest promoters in the world. Live Nation works with talent such as Bruno Mars, Jay Z, Katy Perry, and the Dave Matthews Band. Large promoters such as Feld own their products and tour them internationally or regionally. Feld's most recognizable program is Disney On Ice.

Venues often rely on the local convention and visitors bureau (CVB) to help push certain types of events. The CVB has better synergies with convention centers, but is able to work with most public facilities to promote a city and help to create commerce.

Facility Revenues and Expenses

The majority of facilities generate revenues from tickets, luxury suites and club seating, concessions, parking, sponsorships, and facility rentals. The primary expenses are mortgage and rent, maintenance and repairs, utilities, taxes, marketing and sales, personnel, and insurance (Ammon, Southall, & Nagel, 2010). This section highlights some of these areas.

Ticket sales generate the majority of revenues when promoting events. Venues can have ticket deals with ticketing agents, and artists and promoters can have deals that can be tied into the facility's contract with those artists and promoters.

Strategies to provide ticketing are developing quickly, and new profit centers are being realized daily. The most common ticketing profit center is the **ticket rebate**. The rebate is part of the surcharge that consumers must pay when they purchase a ticket to an event. This additional fee is structured based on the ticket price, and it is returned to the facility or venue as a result of the sale. Most ticketing contracts are awarded based on the size of the rebate and the number of points of sale available to the consumer. Ticketing to the public is more convenient now than it has ever been. Internet tickets or print-at-home tickets are frequently used, and now account for the majority of purchases.

Ticketing and event promotion can make or break a program. The promoter and the venue manager need to work together to ensure that tickets are priced reasonably. If the artist has packages for fan clubs or the venue holds a number of tickets for sponsors, these need to be accounted for prior to any tickets going on sale to the public. Certain groups mandate that fan club members get the first opportunity to buy tickets to the program. These groups are contacted by band representatives and are given codes to access a *presale* prior to the ticket sale to the general public. The code grants the buyer access to better seats in the facility and lower price points for the tickets. When the tickets go on sale to the general public, it is possible that the capacity of the program will be less than initially estimated based on the size of the fan group in that area.

When promoters are establishing ticket prices, they look at the guarantee from the artist, the venue expenses, and the capacity of the venue to find a price point for the program. Should one of these numbers be too little or too great, the promoter will need to decide how or if it makes sense to host a particular show or artist at a venue. This type of market knowledge makes the difference between venues that host successful programs and those that do not. An additional factor is the demographic to which the show is playing. Naturally, the audience for a family program is not necessarily same as the audience for a rock show. Ticket prices for the rock concert can be higher and the audience will have different event behavior that would affect how a facility would prepare for the show. Family events geared toward children will have lower ticket prices and security costs because of the nature of the events and the event culture.

Ancillary revenue is obtained through the sale of concessions, parking charges, ticket fees, and sponsorships. These fees are useful to the venues not only for their obvious income, but also because their profit margins allow venue managers to get creative with promoters when developing their deal structures.

Markets are becoming increasingly more saturated with venues hosting large-scale events. Facility managers are forced to constantly reevaluate the model they are using to fill the venue. One plan of action is to allow the promoters to share in profits from the ancillary revenues. Depending on the deal structure, all or only certain revenues can be included in the mix. Promoters are incentivized to bring larger acts to an area based on the potential revenue they will earn. Ticket sales are the first attempt at making a show profitable, but promoters have realized that significant opportunities exist beyond the standard ticket price. The bond fee or facility fee can be increased and rebated back to the promoter, or there can be a ticket rebate to the promoter based on the venue contract deal. Companies such as Ticketmaster, New Era, Eventim, and Ticket Pro all return a percentage based on the ticket price back to the facility as part of the program. Venues are incentivized to sell tickets because of the added fees that will return to the bottom line.

In the case of in-house promotion, some of the catering companies have joined forces with the venues to set aside a marketing fund. This **marketing fund** is a pool of money that is reserved from the profits of other shows. The concessionaire and the venue director each agree to a certain share of the percentage of sold goods, and they use the pool to help invest in future programs. The investment by both parties allows each to earn more money in the future.

One of the largest revenue drivers in venues today is the sale of alcohol. Alcohol sales are effective drivers of sponsorship dollars as well as being very popular at sporting and entertainment events. Alcohol sales have brought about changes in venues' structures, including sponsored areas, such as suites, as well as renovations for sport-themed bars and pubs. Alcohol and the culture that goes with selling it do open up the concessionaire to more liability, but experienced and trained venue operators should be well aware of the dangers that present themselves as well as prepare for the artists and acts that may pose a higher risk. Alcohol sales may be prohibited for intercollegiate athletic events such as basketball or football games depending on conference rules. The Southeastern Conference (SEC), for example, bans alcohol sales at events.

Sponsorship is also an important part of the equation. Naming rights are a particularly robust manner for driving revenues, typically generating millions of dollars per year for a facility. For example, the average annual value of Citi Group's sponsorship of Citi Field, home of the New York Mets, is approximately $400 million over 20 years. A 25-year deal at MetLife Stadium in New Jersey produces approximately $17 to $20 million annually, with an overall value estimated up to $625 million ("Top 10 Stadium," 2014).

In terms of expenses, a facility usually carries with it an obligation to pay a mortgage (just like one would have to do on a home) as a monthly fee. Facility managers must make sure these fees are managed appropriately, because revenues may ebb and flow during the year. These expenses are quite predictable, as are annual taxes and insurance; however, other expenses may not always be. Maintenance and repairs may take place on a regular schedule, but some items may not be predictable. For example, flooding from extreme snowmelt or damage from a natural disaster such as a tornado may result in higher than anticipated costs. Utilities also are somewhat predictable, but climate change and extreme weather conditions may affect the monthly bill as well. Personnel expenses can add up with the number and size of events. To put on one NFL home football game, a facility may require up to 1,000 workers, most of whom are part-time employees. Finally, facility managers need to spend money to make money; hence, a trade for in-kind services is always a bonus, but cash is always the preferred medium of payment. Sponsorship needs to be approved by the promoter and the act prior to its sale, but is a surefire means of event revenue generation. When applied correctly, the revenues from this source can be the deciding factor between breaking even and suffering a loss.

When looking at a calendar, a facility manager should always be trying to fill nonevent days with some type of function. Events that just break even are still good events to hold.

Career Opportunities

College graduates seeking career opportunities in the facility management industry will be pleasantly surprised at the wide variety of options available in arenas, convention centers, stadiums, and performing arts centers. No matter what their job title, facility managers need to master a set of managerial skills that the IAVM refers to as core competences (Russo, Esckilsen, & Stewart, 2009):

- Administration (people and organization).
- Sales and marketing (selling time and space and event activity).
- Fiscal management (financial performance).
- Facility services and operations (physical plant and event management).
- Leadership and management.

The career opportunity areas in facility management are shown in **Table 12-1** and discussed in the sections that follow.

Table 12-1 Career Opportunity Areas in Facility Management
Marketing
Public relations/communications
Event management
Booking
Operations
Advertising, signage, and sponsorship sales
Group ticket sales
Box office

Marketing Director

Being the **marketing director** for an arena, performing arts center, or other venue is one of the more exciting careers in facility management. It is a fast-paced, highly stressful, enormously challenging career track that can lead a successful individual all the way to the executive suite.

Facility marketing directors act primarily as in-house advertising agents for the various events booked into facilities. Buying media advertisements (e.g., TV, radio, print, billboards, Internet), coordinating promotions, working with social media, and designing marketing materials (e.g., TV commercials, brochures, flyers, newspaper advertisements, websites) are some of a marketing director's primary responsibilities. A typical day in the life of a facility marketing director may include creating a marketing plan and ad budget for Sesame Street Live, meeting with radio and TV sales staff to discuss cross promotions with McDonald's for the Harlem Globetrotters, and designing a print ad for Sunday's newspaper.

The most successful marketing directors are multiskilled performers who possess excellent people skills, sales ability, and written and oral communication skills. Most important, a successful marketing director possesses an almost uncanny ability to consistently earn profits for facilities or promoters. The quickest way to become a facility general manager or executive director is to showcase the talents and skills it takes to improve the bottom line. Moneymakers are few and far between, so proven producers will get noticed—and promoted.

Public Relations/Communications Director

A good **public relations (PR) or communications director** is essential for facilities as they deal with the media on a wide variety of issues. A talented PR or communications director can "spin" the news, good or bad, and position a facility in the best possible light. This is a very important skill to have when the media are banging on the door wanting to know why the arena's $2 million scoreboard just came crashing down on the ice, why attendance is down 20%, or why the box office is missing $25,000 and the director has just left for a long trip out of the country. One of the primary goals for a facility's PR department is to forge solid working relationships with TV and radio news directors, newspaper editors, and reporters so that when bad news hits, the media report a balanced story. Good rapport with local media helps a great deal when seeking publicity for positive stories, and at times it can mean the difference between receiving front-page coverage or being buried next to the obituaries.

A typical day in the life of a facility PR director may include coordinating a live TV broadcast from the arena with the local sport anchor to publicize that evening's basketball game, writing a press release announcing that tickets are going on sale that weekend for a Katy Perry concert, discussing an upcoming Twitter campaign to promote an event, and arranging a publicity stunt for Bert and Ernie to visit the local children's hospital while they are in town for an upcoming Sesame Street Live tour.

© Ken Inness/Shutterstock, Inc.

The most important attributes of a good PR director are a strong writing ability, a creative mind, and an ability to respond rationally while under pressure. Excellent training grounds for facility PR people are college and daily newspapers, TV stations, and internships in corporate PR departments.

Event Director

Events are the lifeblood for all types of facilities. Hundreds of events may be booked at a facility in the course of a year. With thousands of people in the venue at any given time, it is imperative that there be excellent crowd control and exceptional customer service at all times. The **event director** acts as the point person for the facility during each show. Supervising a full staff of ushers, police officers, firefighters, emergency medical technicians, and private concert security staff, the event director manages the show from start to finish.

The event director must be able to think and react quickly to any problems arising during the event and must be able to deal with show promoters, angry customers, lost children, intoxicated patrons, and other situations calmly but forcefully. He or she must handle all this pressure while thousands of guests are in their seats enjoying the show. Being in charge of the safety and satisfaction of so many people is an immense responsibility, and for this reason the event director's position is not for everyone.

A typical day in the life of an event director might begin as early as 8:00 a.m. with six tractor-trailer trucks pulling up to the facility to begin the load-in for a major concert.

The event director supervises and schedules traffic, parking, and security personnel to help ensure that the concert load-in runs as smoothly as possible. Later that day, he or she meets with the band road manager and reviews all security requirements for that evening's show. As the concert time draws near, the event director will meet with all ushers, police, and private security staff, giving instructions on how to handle that evening's event. During the concert, he or she will likely deal with customers, emergency situations, intoxicated patrons, and perhaps an altercation or two. By the end of the night, he or she will have been at the facility for 18 long hours.

Booking Director

Events in smaller facilities are booked by the general manager or executive director. In larger venues, however, there is usually a separate position devoted to booking events. This person works in tandem with the general manager or executive director to land as many events as possible. This is an exciting career path involving much time spent talking on the telephone to agents and promoters and attending conventions to solicit events.

A facility **booking director** can land events in several different ways. Most concerts and Broadway shows are booked by dealing directly with agents who represent the acts or by negotiating with promoters who rent the facility and deal directly with agents on their own. The booking director may choose to rent the facility to a promoter, to co-promote an event, or to purchase the show directly from an agent. There are advantages and disadvantages associated with all three methods. Renting the facility to a promoter is a risk-free way to increase the number of events; however, it limits the amount of income a building may receive from an event. For some events with limited income potential or risky track records (e.g., conventions, trade shows), this method is the smartest way to do business. For potentially highly lucrative events (e.g., concerts, family shows, Broadway shows), partnering with a promoter for a share of the profits or purchasing the event directly from an agent may be the more profitable strategy—albeit also the one with the greatest risk to lose money if the show is not successful.

A typical day in the life of a booking director might begin at 8:00 a.m. with telephone calls to local radio program directors gauging the current popularity of a specific concert act. At 10:00 a.m., the constant phone calls back and forth with Broadway agents in New York begin as the booking director tries to fill up next year's Broadway lineup for the performing arts center. Lunch with a local concert promoter cutting a rental deal for an upcoming show will be followed by telephone tag the rest of the day with other agents and promoters. Negotiating contracts and getting them out in the mail completes a typical facility booking director's day.

Operations Director

Facility operations departments are the heart and soul of this industry. The **operations director** supervises facility preparation for all types of events. He or she typically spends the lion's share of a facility's annual expense budget on labor, maintaining and repairing all equipment, and purchasing all the necessary supplies (e.g., toilet paper, cleaning materials) events require on a weekly basis.

Perhaps the most important part of an operations director's job is coordinating, scheduling, and supervising the numerous changeovers that constantly take place as one show moves in and another moves out. An operations director faces logistical problems daily because the facility may change over from hockey to basketball, then to a concert, and then to a Broadway show, all in one week. The job requires a mechanical knowledge of a facility's inner workings. A good operations director must be an expert on heating, ventilation, and air conditioning equipment; ice making; and structural issues, such as how many pounds of pressure can be rigged to the roof without it collapsing. An operations director must also possess superior people skills, because he or she is directly in charge of the majority of the facility's staff, including foremen, mechanics, laborers, stagehands, and the 50 to 500 part-time workers required to set up events and clean up after them.

A typical day in the life of an operations director likely begins early in the morning with a check of the previous night's changeover from basketball to hockey. Inspecting the overnight cleanup and the temperature and condition of the ice surface and discussing any problems with assistants will keep the operations director busy most of the morning. Then it will be time to plan ahead for next week when the circus rolls into town with 30 horses, 14 tigers, and other assorted animals and equipment. The circus will take over the entire facility and two square blocks in the downtown business district for 6 days. Meetings with circus managers and city officials to plan for the event, as well as scheduling, will complete the day for the person with his or her hand constantly on the pulse of the facility operation.

Advertising, Sponsorship, and Signage Salesperson

Advertising and sponsorship revenues represent a significant portion of a facility's annual revenues. Most facilities, depending on size, designate a staff person or an entire department to sell signage and event sponsorships to corporations. College graduates who perform well in high-pressure sales environments can make a substantial amount of money selling signage and sponsorships. This area offers good entry-level positions. Most facilities hire sales staff on a commission-only basis. Commissions

can range from 5% to 20% depending on the size of the deal.

Salespeople must possess excellent interpersonal and presentation skills. They also must be able to handle plenty of rejection on a daily basis. For every 100 telephone calls a salesperson makes to corporations, an average of only 5 or 10 will result in actual business. Sales is a numbers game, and only strong, thick-skinned personalities are successful in such an environment. Successful salespeople generate money for themselves and the facility—and that will be noticed at the executive level. It is common for good salespeople to ultimately end up in the general manager's or executive director's chair.

A typical day in the life of an aggressive signage and sponsorship salesperson will include at least 25 cold calls to corporate decision makers, 2 to 4 face-to-face sales presentations, and plenty of writing. A good salesperson must have strong writing skills because he or she must create outstanding sales proposals, follow up meetings with thank-you letters and to-do lists, and draft contracts once deals have been finalized.

Group Ticket Salesperson

Many college graduates begin their facility management careers in the group sales department. Entry-level opportunities are numerous because there is fairly high turnover. Group salespeople are primarily responsible for selling large blocks of tickets for various events to corporations, charity organizations, schools, Boy Scout and Girl Scout troops, and other parties. Group sales for certain types of shows (e.g., Sesame Street Live, Disney On Ice, the Harlem Globetrotters, professional sport teams) contribute significantly to an event's success. Similar to the successful signage and sponsorship staff person, a good group salesperson is tenacious and excels on the telephone and in face-to-face presentations. Usually paid on a commission basis (typically 10% to 15%), group sales is also a numbers game. However, renewal business is usually strong, and solid personal relationships with key decision makers at area corporations, agencies, and other organizations can result in excellent sales year after year. A good group salesperson is an important asset to a facility.

Box Office Director

This facility position is responsible for the sale of all tickets to events as well as the collection of all ticket revenues. The facility box office is typically the first impression patrons have of the venue, making good customer service critical. The **box office director** must be a patient, understanding individual with a great mind for numbers. He or she must also have good supervisory skills. Within most venues, the box office is usually the second largest department, after operations. Made up of a combination of full- and part-time help, the box office personnel must be completely trustworthy, because millions of dollars and thousands of credit card numbers flow through the department each year.

A typical day for a box office director begins at 9:00 a.m. On any given day, event tickets may be going on sale, and the telephones and lobby windows are generally extremely busy. Meetings with promoters to set up scaling of shows and filling ticket orders for advertisers and very important persons (VIPs) takes up a good portion of the day. Scheduling staff for all of the shows and daytime hours is also a time-consuming job. The box office director will be in his or her office for most of the day, but the real work begins when the event starts.

Dealing with customers who have lost their tickets, are unhappy with their seats, or have other concerns will occupy the box office director's time during the event. The box office will usually close halfway through the event so the staff can begin their paperwork. Counting all the money, preparing settlement documents for the promoter's review, and completing other tasks take up the rest of the evening. By the time all is said and done, the box office director will have worked 12 to 18 hours.

Current Issues

Security

The area of security was propelled to the highest level of importance for facility management after the terrorist attacks of September 11, 2001. Since then, a number of tragic attacks at athletic and entertainment venues continue to challenge facilities security. Bag checks, pat-downs, and metal detectors are now normal, regular functions in day-to-day operations. Large arenas and stadiums have placed barricades, posts, and fencing around the perimeters of facilities to create a "moat" effect to keep potential threats and terrorist activities away from crowds and buildings. Special attention is being given to the U.S. Homeland Security system of rating possible threats and to facility managers implementing procedures to safeguard patrons during events as well as the facility itself. Facility managers must evaluate every event for its security risk, taking into account the performer and crowd attendance profiles as well as the anticipated media coverage.

Large international events such as the Olympic Games have garnered worldwide attention because of security issues. Security costs for the Sydney Summer Games in 2000 were estimated at $176.9 million. These costs skyrocketed at the first post–September 11 Summer Games, held in Athens, Greece, in 2004, with organizers paying out approximately $1.5 billion for security (Epstein, 2011). The cost estimates for securing the 2020 Tokyo Olympics have doubled to $3 billion (Associated Press, 2016). A good example of how the costs have increased comes from reviewing the needs of the most recent Winter Games at PyeongChang. In addition to cyber-security costs of $1.2 million, plus $18.4 million in security screening, the PyeongChang Winter Games employed 5,000 South Korean military personnel, 13,000 police, and the Olympics also sought help from security staff from other nations. For instance, the United States contributed the expertise of 200 U.S. Security forces (Kiernan, 2018).

The best tool for crowd management is a **crowd management plan**. Such a plan encompasses categorizing the type of event; knowing the surrounding facilities and environment, team or school rivalries, threats of violence, and the crowd size and seating configuration; using security personnel and ushers; and having an emergency plan.

In November 2004, an on-court fight during a Detroit Pistons–Indianapolis Pacers NBA game ended up spilling into the stands, involving members of the attending crowd as well. In response, then NBA Commissioner David Stern stated that the NBA would set new security guidelines for its arenas, an area previously left to individual teams to control ("NBA to Set," 2004). Shortly thereafter, the NBA issued arena guidelines that included policies dealing with the deployment of security personnel, alcohol sales, and a new Fan Code of Conduct (NBA, 2005).

The National Center for Spectator Sports Safety and Security (NCS[4]) publishes an Intercollegiate Athletics Safety and Security Guide. The NCS[4] is located at the University of Mississippi. (NCS[4] Best Practices Guide). The NCS[4] approach to stadium and arena security is comprehensive. The NCS[4] combines nine topical areas as best practices for stadium security including: game day planning, crowd control, emergency action planning, routine non-game day operations, risk assessment, sports facilities

design, staff performance, security and safe aware culture, and technology use. (NCS[4] Best Practices Guide). Because more than 48 million spectators attend NCAA football games in a given season, the issue is one that needs to be addressed to create risk management plans, and provide for adequate training and emergency services (Associated Press, 2007). Rules are also in place to deter fans from rushing the court after a big win. The SEC rule against court storming reads, "For the safety of participants and spectators alike, at no time before, during or after a contest shall spectators be permitted to enter the competition area." A $50,000 fine can be assessed to a school on a first offense; a second offense could result in a $100,000 fine; and additional offenses can bring fines of up to $250,000 (Ching, 2015).

Sustainability

Public facilities such as convention centers, stadiums, and arenas consume large amounts of energy. As a result, the Green Sports Alliance (GSA) is working to promote green buildings, and to create a culture where teams and sport organizations "embrace renewable energy, healthy food, recycling, water efficiency, safer chemicals and other environmentally preferable practices." Almost 600 sports teams and facilities have joined the GSA in this effort (Green Sports Alliance).

The Olympic and Paralympic Games require extensive facility construction and can have an enormous environmental impact. The London 2012 Olympic Stadium set new standards for sustainability. The stadium used recycled materials, including an unused gas pipe from a North Sea oil project. Approximately 40% of the concrete used was made of recycled aggregate. The London Organising Committee of the Olympic and Paralympic Games (LOCOG) also saved energy by transporting materials to the site by boat or train. LOCOG analyzed the carbon footprint of the stadium and concluded that it had the lowest carbon footprint of any stadium ever built (International Olympic Committee [IOC], 2013). The London Games were billed as the greenest Games on record (Singh, 2012). Unfortunately, the same cannot be said for the 2014 Winter Olympic and Paralympic Games in Sochi, Russia, which were surrounded by reports of 1,500 unsanctioned waste dumps and encroachment into protected wildlife areas for construction of venues and transport (Luhn, 2014).

A gold standard today for facilities is **LEED certification**. LEED, which stands for Leadership in Energy and Environmental Design, helps facility operators identify green building design, construction, operation, and maintenance. LEED certification includes an examination of the following elements: sustainable site development, water savings, materials and atmosphere, energy efficiency, and indoor environmental quality (U.S. Green Building Council, 2014). Based on a point system, four levels of LEED certification are possible: platinum, gold, silver, and certified. MLB's Washington Nationals Park was the first major sport stadium to be silver certified. The San Francisco 49ers' new Levi's Stadium became the first NFL certified stadium when it opened in 2014. As of 2017, 30 North American professional sport facilities were LEED certified or in the midst of earning the certification, including the American Airlines Arena and Soldier Field, in addition to Nationals Park (JLL Staff Reporter, 2017). Colleges and universities are slowly following suit, with the University of North Texas opening the first major college football stadium that is LEED certified.

Sport Facilities as Part of Entertainment Districts

Many urban areas have lost their luster as residents move to the suburbs, but sport facilities are playing a key role in some urban redevelopment plans. Neighborhoods are emerging in which one or more sport facilities serve as anchors for redevelopment. Team owners also want to be part of the trend toward **entertainment districts**: Cities frequently balk at sharing costs of stadium construction, but having cities invest in surrounding the stadium with entertainment venues, hotels, retail, office space, and public transportation can help the team owners achieve greater long-term financial success (Baker, 2015). This model has trended upward in the wake of the success of Columbus, Ohio's Arena District, which likely built upon earlier models such as that employed in Baltimore, with Camden Yards and the Inner Harbor urban renewal plan. The Arena District in Columbus is a recreation destination made up of retail establishments, restaurants, and entertainment venues, coupled with the office, residential, and tourist markets necessary for successful urban redevelopment (Kirk, 2015). For sport- and entertainment-driven districts to emerge, they need critical mass of all of these segments to drive not only tourists to visit the area, but also local citizens to choose to live and work in the district.

To successfully lure real estate and sports and entertainment properties, municipalities will usually need to make some public investment and/or some infrastructure investment (Kirk, 2015). This model has fueled the successful $3.5 billion–plus L.A. Live neighborhood, which was started through investments by AEG, Wachovia Corporation, Azteca Corporation, and MacFarlane Partners, and by tax deferments provided by the city of Los Angeles. Many cities are looking to the L.A. Live model and it may work for some, but not all. An example is Glendale, Arizona, which was located too far from Scottsdale, Arizona, a city that is more affluent than Phoenix, to capitalize on this model (Baker, 2015).

While sport anchors are important properties, they are not critical to rejuvenating cities (Caulfield, 2017)—though they may be in some cases, depending on the plan for a particular city. For instance, with the new District Detroit, a 50-block sports and entertainment district, part of the draw is that the Lions, Tigers, Pistons, and Red Wings venues will be co-located in that district. There is also a movement afoot to attract an MLS team to the area. The goal is to revitalize Detroit as other entertainment, retail, and office venues plus residential and hotel space evolve in that district (Rische, 2016).

This trend has become so popular that it is hard to keep track of the number of cities adopting it. Cities large and small have embraced this approach—from Atlanta to Austin; Nashville to Omaha; Irving, Texas, to Sacramento; Louisville to Brooklyn; and Birmingham to Green Bay, Wisconsin, just to name a few. In Utica, New York—an even smaller city—the Utica Comets hockey team has proposed the U District, an entertainment district scaled to emulate the developments in Buffalo, New York, and Detroit, as well as the $2.5 billion L.A. Live and $4 billion Texas Live neighborhoods in Los Angeles and Irving, respectively (Utica Comets, 2017). In sum, this trend is being pushed not only by sport teams, but by sports and entertainment conglomerates such as AEG, real estate developers, architects, and municipalities alike, and is likely here to stay.

Access for Persons with Disabilities

On July 26, 1990, President George H. W. Bush signed into law the **Americans with Disabilities Act (ADA)**. The intent of the ADA is to prevent discrimination against qualified people with disabilities in employment, public services, transportation, public accommodations, and telecommunications services According to Pate and Waller (2012):

[T]he ADA was adopted to prevent discrimination against persons with physical disabilities. Accessibility problems continue to exist despite ADA regulations, and they may be brought to light at athletic events when individuals with physical disabilities experience accessibility problems. Therefore, it is essential that athletic facility managers be knowledgeable of the ADA regulations and accessibility to address the needs of individuals with physical disabilities who [are] attending sporting events. (p. 4)

The ADA defines a disability, with respect to an individual, as a "person who has a physical or mental impairment that substantially limits one or more major life activities" …, who has "a record of such an impairment", or who is "regarded as having such an impairment" (Americans with Disabilities Act, 42 USC § 12102). In 2011, the ADA was updated with a number of changes directly applicable to stadiums and arenas. For example, ADA guidelines about tickets and seating include the following (Clifton & Lynett, 2014).

Accessible Seating

Covered entities must comply with the following requirements:

- 500 to 5,000 seats: Six wheelchair spaces and companion seats plus one additional wheelchair space for each additional 150 seats (or fraction thereof) between 501 through 5,000.
- More than 5,000 seats: At least 36 wheelchair spaces and companion seats plus one additional wheelchair space for each 200 seats (or fraction thereof) over 5,000.
- Premium seating standards: Each luxury box, club box, and suite in an arena,

stadium or grandstand is required to be wheelchair accessible and to contain wheelchair and companion seating.
- Sightlines: Significant new technical requirements for providing lines of sight over seated and standing spectators.

Ticket Sales

Tickets for disabled seating must be available for purchase during the same hours, at the same stages, through the same methods of distribution, in the same types and numbers of ticketing sales outlets, and under the same terms and conditions as other tickets sold for the same event or series of events.

Other accessibility features involve concession areas, public telephones, restrooms, parking areas, drop-off and pick-up areas, entrances and exits, water coolers, visual alarms, and signs. Assisted-listening systems must also be provided when audible communications are integral to the use of the facility. The ADA requires that a facility make adaptations to ensure accessibility, but only to the extent that the reasonable accommodation does not cause an undue burden on the facility.

Universal Design

A new concept that extends the ADA and makes facilities more accessible for all people is **universal design**. A new arrival on the sport facility scene, the concept of universal design is best seen in places such as art galleries, museums, and airports. Facility design is essential for accessibility for all regardless of factors such as disability, age, or language spoken. The Institute for Human Centered Design (2014) in Boston suggests the following principles for universal design:

- *Equitable use:* The design does not disadvantage or stigmatize any group of users.
- *Flexibility in use:* The design accommodates a wide range of individual preferences and abilities.

- *Simple, intuitive use:* Use of the design is easy to understand, regardless of the user's experience, knowledge, language skills, or current concentration level.
- *Perceptible information:* The design communicates necessary information effectively to the user, regardless of the ambient conditions or the user's sensory abilities.
- *Tolerance for error:* The design minimizes hazards and the adverse consequences of accidental or unintended actions.
- *Low physical effort:* The design can be used efficiently and comfortably, and with a minimum of fatigue.
- *Size and space for approach and use:* Appropriate size and space are provided for approach, reach, manipulation, and use, regardless of the user's body size, posture, or mobility.

In the context of access to stadiums or arenas, these principles provide guidance for facility managers who wish to enhance the in-house experience for all customers. Universal design takes the ADA one step further and looks to enhance the total customer experience at a sport facility. Sport managers who incorporate universal design into their stadiums and arenas will be ahead of the curve in terms of the customer service experience they provide.

Summary

Public assembly facilities provide a site for people to congregate for entertainment, social, and business purposes. The many types of facilities range from stadiums and arenas to convention centers and theaters. The key challenges facing facilities are financing new facilities or renovations, retaining the revenues generated by the facility, preparing fully integrated security programs, retaining tenants, and addressing the ADA requirements. Facility management provides a career field that is fast-paced and exciting, though filled with long hours and, at times, pressure and stress.

Case Study 12-1

The Booking Process in a University Venue

The Mullins Center is a 10,000-seat multipurpose facility with an attached ice rink located on the campus of the University of Massachusetts in Amherst, Massachusetts. It is managed for the University of Massachusetts by Global Spectrum. As part of the management contract, the general manager for the Mullins Center is responsible for the booking of the main facility and the attached practice rink. The Mullins Center has three tenant teams: the university's men's hockey, women's basketball, and men's basketball teams.

The campus and surrounding five-college area are home to as many as 30,000 students from September to May. During that time frame, the Mullins Center is busy hosting athletic events and entertainment programs. To be successful, the general manager utilizes several different setups and capacities to provide the university and the community with entertaining programs. Concert seating capacities are set at 7,200, 8,500, or 9,000 seats. Seating capacity for comedy or theater programs is set at 1,700 to 3,500 seats. Basketball events have 9,400 seats, while hockey or ice show events have 8,400 seats.

Questions for Discussion

1. As the general manager of the Mullins Center, which specific genre of entertainment do you think would do well in this venue, taking into account the demographics, available time frames, and seating capacities?

2. Identify a group, act, team, or entertainer that will be touring with available dates to play the Mullins Center, and specify who will be acting as the promoter for the event.

3. Assume that the act will cost $75,000 and the venue will be rented for an all-inclusive package of $35,000. Provide ticket prices that will appeal to the target demographic market in a spreadsheet that reflects the total costs and the balance according to estimated ticket sales.

4. Explain the impact of ancillary revenues on the event, including the potential role that food and beverage revenues, ticket fees, and parking revenues will play when negotiating a deal with a promoter.

5. Provide an event recap and explain why you did or did not book this event at the Mullins Center, noting why it would have been successful or unsuccessful.

Resources

AEG Corporate Headquarters
  800 West Olympic Boulevard, Suite 305
  Los Angeles, CA 90015
  213-763-7700
  www.aegworldwide.com

Aramark Corporation
  1101 Market Street
  Philadelphia, PA 19107
  215-238-3000
  www.aramark.com

Delaware North
  40 Fountain Plaza
  Buffalo, NY 14202
  716-858-5000
  www.delawarenorth.com

European Association of Event Centers (EVVC)
  Eschersheimer Landstraße 23
  D-60322 Frankfurt am Main
  Germany
  49 (0) 69/915-096-98-0
  www.evvc.org

Information Display and Entertainment Association (IDEA)

2001 E, Lohmen Avenue, Suite 101-65
Las Cruces, NM 88001-3116
575-405-1977
www.ideaontheweb.org

International Association of Convention Centres (AIPC)

Marianne de Raay 1060
Brussels, Belgium
32-496-235327
www.aipc.org

International Association of Venue Managers (IAVM)

635 Fritz Drive, Suite 100
Coppell, TX 75019
972-906-7441
www.iavm.org

International Facility Management Association

800 Gessner Road, Suite 900
Houston, TX 77024-4257
(713) 623-4362
www.ifma.org

International Ticketing Association

5868 East 71st Street, Suite E 365
Indianapolis, IN 46220
212-629-4036
www.intix.org

Kroenke Sports Enterprises, LLC

1000 Chopper Circle
Denver, CO 80204
303-405-1100
www.pepsicenter.com

Live Nation Entertainment

9438 Civic Center Drive
Beverly Hills, CA 90210
(800) 653-8000
www.livenationentertainment.com/

Maple Leaf Sports & Entertainment, Ltd.

50 Bay Street, Suite 500
Toronto, ON M5J 2L2 Canada
416-815-5400
www.mlse.com

SMG

300 Conshohocken State Road, Suite 450
West Conshohocken, PA 19428
(610) 729-7900
www.smgworld.com

Spectra (Comcast Spectacor)

3601 South Broad Street
Philadelphia, PA 19148
215-389-9587
http://www.spectraexperiences.com/

Stadium Managers Association

525 SW 5th Street, Suite A
Des Moines, IA 50309
515-282-8192
www.stadiummanagers.org

Venue Management Association Limited

30-34 Gladstone Road, Suite 1
Highgate Hill
QLD 4101 Australia
61-0-7-3870-4777
www.vma.org.au

Key Terms

ancillary revenue, Americans with Disabilities Act (ADA), arenas, bond, booking director, box office director, concerts, convention centers, convocations, crowd management plan, entertainment district, event director, facility financing, family events, International Association of Venue Managers (IAVM), LEED certification, local/civic venues, marketing director, marketing fund, metropolitan facilities, operations director, public relations (PR) or communications director, religious events, seasonal events, soccer-specific stadium (SSS), sport events, stadium, theater, ticket rebate, trade shows, universal design, university venues

References

Americans with Disabilities Act, 42 USC § 12102. Retrieved from https://www.gpo.gov/fdsys/pkg/USCODE-2010-title42/pdf/USCODE-2010-title42-chap126-sec12102.pdf

Ammon, R. A., Southall, R. M., & Nagel, M. S. (2010). *Sport facility management* (2nd ed.). Morgantown, WV: Fitness Information Technology.

Associated Press. (2007, December 26). Stadium security a concern at colleges. *New York Times.* Retrieved from http://www.nytimes.com/2007/12/26/sports/ncaafootball/26stadiums.html

Associated Press. (2016, September 30). A look at rising costs for Tokyo 2020 Olympics. *USA Today.* Retrieved from https://www.usatoday.com/story/sports/olympics/2016/09/30/a-look-at-rising-costs-for-the-tokyo-2020-olympics/91312266/

Auerbach, N. (2013, February 7). The forecast for college basketball: Storming the court. *USA Today.* Retrieved from http://www.usatoday.com/story/sports/ncaab/2013/02/05/storming-rushing-the-court-college-basketball/1890851/

Bagli, C. (2008, November 4). As stadiums rise, so do costs to taxpayers. *New York Times.* Retrieved from http://www.nytimes.com/2008/11/05/nyregion/05stadiums.html?_r=1

Bajarin, T. (2014, August 18). Meet Levi's stadium, the most high tech sports venue yet. *Time.* Retrieved from http://time.com/3136272/levis-stadium-tech/

Baker, G. (2015, February 15) Team owners now want "entertainment districts." *Seattle Times.* Retrieved from https://www.seattletimes.com/sports/hockey/team-owners-now-want-entertainment-districts/

Bradley, B. (2013, August 21). Minnesota using tobacco tax to pay off debt on new Vikings stadium. Retrieved from http://nextcity.org/equityfactor/entry/minnesota-using-tobacco-tax-to-pay-off-debt-on-vikings-new-stadium

Burke, D. (1997). The Stop Tax-Exempt Arena Debt Issuance Act. *Journal of Legislation, 23*(1), 149–157.

CAA/Pepsi Center. (2018). Retrieved from https://www.caaicon.com/portfolio/pepsi-center

Caulfield, J. (2017, September 8). Urban heartbeat: Entertainment districts are rejuvenating cities and spurring economic growth. *Building Design and Construction.* Retrieved from https://www.bdcnetwork.com/urban-heartbeat-entertainment-districts-are-rejuvenating-cities-and-spurring-economic-growth

Ching, D. (2015, May 29). Fines could reach $250,000 for fans storming the competition area. *ESPN.com.* Retrieved from http://www.espn.com/college-football/story/_/id/12977211/sec-passes-tougher-fines-court-storming

Clifton, G. E., & Lynett, J. J. (2014). Top ten ADA regulatory changes. Retrieved from https://www.acc.com/legalresources/publications/topten/ADA-Title-III-Changes.cfm

Crompton, J. L. (2014). Proximate development: An alternative justification for public investment in major sport facilities. *Managing Leisure, 19*(4), 1–20.

Crompton, J. L., Howard, D. R., & Var, T. (2003). Financing major league facilities: Status, evolution, and conflicting forces. *Journal of Sport Management, 17*(2), 156–184.

Davis, S., & Gaines, C. (2017, March). Here is the gorgeous $2 billion stadium the Las Vegas Raiders are expected to call home. Retrieved from http://www.businessinsider.com/raiders-las-vegas-stadium-2017-3

Demause, N. (2011, August 5). The nation: Stop the subsidy-sucking sound. *NPR.* Retrieved from http://www.npr.org/2011/08/05/139018592/the-nation-stop-the-subsidy-sucking-sports-stadiums

Epstein, D. (2011, September 9). Olympic Games after 11 September: More expensive, less patriotic. *Sports Illustrated.* Retrieved from https://www.si.com/more-sports/2011/09/09/olympics-afterseptember11

Farmer, P., Mulrooney, A., & Ammon, R., Jr. (1996). *Sport facility planning and management*. Morgantown, WV: Fitness Information Technology.

Fried, G. (2010). *Managing sport facilities*. Champaign, IL: Human Kinetics.

Green Sports Alliance. (2018). Retrieved from http://greensportsalliance.org/about/

Greenberg, M. J., & Gray, J. T. (1993, April/May). The stadium game. *For the Record*, pp. 2–3.

Howard, D. R., & Crompton, J. L. (1995). *Financing sport*. Morgantown, WV: Fitness Information Technology.

Institute for Human Centered Design. (2014). Principles of universal design. Retrieved from https://humancentereddesign.org/index.php?q=universal-design/principles-universal-design

International Olympic Committee (IOC). (2013). Flexible and sustainable London's Olympic Stadium sets new standards. Retrieved from http://www.olympic.org/news/flexible-and-sustainable-london-s-olympic-stadium-sets-new-standards/170181

Jacobson, G., Robinson-Jacobs, K., & Moore, D. (2013). Cowboys–AT&T Stadium deal pioneers new revenue source for big-time sports. *Dallas Morning News*. Retrieved from http://www.dallasnews.com/business/headlines/20130725-cowboys-att-stadium-deal-pioneers-a-new-source-of-revenue-for-big-time-sports.ece

Jensen, S. A. (2000). Financing professional sports facilities with federal tax subsidies: Is it sound tax policy? *Marquette Sports Law Review, 10*(2), 425–460.

JLL Staff Reporter. (2017, September 27). Stadiums go for gold with green design. *JLL*. Retrieved from https://www.jllrealviews.com/trends/sustainability/stadiums-go-for-gold-with-green-design/

Kiernan, J. (2018, February 2). 2018 PyeongChang Winter Olympics Facts. Retrieved from https://wallethub.com/blog/olympics-facts/1819/

Kirk, P. (2015, April 29). Making sports-oriented mixed use work. *Urbanland*. Retrieved from https://urbanland.uli.org/planning-design/making-sports-oriented-mixed-use-work/

Kuriloff, A., & Preston, D. (2012, September 5). In stadium building spree, U.S. taxpayers lose $4 billion. *Bloomberg News*. Retrieved from http://www.bloomberg.com/news/2012-09-05/in-stadium-building-spree-u-s-taxpayers-lose-4-billion.html

Lago, K. (2018, January 11). L.A. Rams new stadium in Inglewood take shape. Retrieved from http://www.therams.com/news-and-events/article-1/Los-Angeles-Rams-New-Stadium-in-Inglewood-Begins-to-Take-Shape/5b0fde0e-89e2-4593-8c72-632793e28507

Luhn, A. (2014, January 22). The hidden environmental and human costs of the Sochi Olympics. *The Nation*. Retrieved from http://www.thenation.com/article/178051/hidden-environmental-and-human-costs-sochi-olympics#

Moriarty, M. (2017, December 2). The new Atlanta stadium's 7 wildest features from roof to field. *SB Nation*. Retrieved from https://www.sbnation.com/2017/8/26/16141026/new-atlanta-falcons-mercedes-benz-stadium-peach-bowl-sec-championship-playoff

National Basketball Association (NBA). (2005, February 17). NBA establishes revised arena guidelines for all NBA arenas. Retrieved from http://www.nba.com/news/arena_guidelines_050217.html

NBA Media Ventures. (2014). Timberwolves, Lynx to open new practice facility. Retrieved from http://www.nba.com/2014/news/02/04/timberwolves-practice-facility.ap/

NBA to Set New Security Guidelines. (2009, October 29). Voice of America. Retrieved from https://www.voanews.com/a/a-13-2004-12-01-voa26-67334187/271973.html

NCS4 Best Practices Guide. (2017, April 13). Retrieved from https://www.ncaa.org/sites/default/files/2017DIIISpo_NCS4Intercollegiate BestPractices_20171220.pdf

Noll, R. G., & Zimbalist, A. (1997). Build the stadium—Create the jobs! In R. G. Noll & A. Zimbalist (Eds.), *Sports, jobs, and taxes: The economic impact of sports teams and stadiums* (pp. 1–54). Washington, DC: Brookings Institution Press.

Pate, J. R, & Waller, S. N. (2012). Measuring athletic facility managers' knowledge of access and the Americans with Disabilities Act: A pilot study. *International Journal of Sport Management, Recreation, and Tourism. 9,* 1–22.

Plunkett, J. W. (2017). *Plunkett's sports industry almanac 2017.* Houston, TX: Plunkett Research.

Reed, W. (2014). Cities pressured to subsidize sports stadiums. *Atlanta Daily World.* Retrieved from http://atlantadailyworld.com/2014/01/01/cities-pressured-to-subsidize-sports-stadiums/

Rische, P. (2016, November 24). District Detroit: The most compact sports district in America is revitalizing downtown Detroit. *Forbes.* Retrieved from https://www.forbes.com/sites/prishe/2016/11/24/district-detroit-the-most-compact-sports-district-in-america-is-revitalizing-downtown-detroit/#e5adf76669a2

Rosentraub, M. S. (2010) *Major league winners: Using sports and cultural centers as tools for economic development.* Boca Raton, FL: CRC Press.

Russo, F. E., Esckilsen, L. A., & Stewart, R. J. (2009). *Public assembly facility management: Principles and practices* (2nd ed.). Coppell, TX: International Association of Assembly Managers.

Samuelson, P. A., & Nordhaus, W. D. (1985). *Economics.* New York, NY: McGraw-Hill.

Sawyer, T. (2006). Financing facilities 101. *Journal of Physical Education, Recreation & Dance, 77*(4), 23–28.

Singh, T. (2012, August 14). The London 2012 Summer Games were the greenest Olympics ever. *Inhabitat.* Retrieved from http://inhabitat.com/the-london-2012-summer-games-were-the-greenest-olympics-ever/

Top 10 stadium, arena naming rights deals. (2014). *San Francisco Business Times.* Retrieved from http://www.bizjournals.com/sanfrancisco/blog/2013/05/stadium-naming-rights-deals-49ers-levis.html?s=image_gallery

U.S. Green Building Council. (2014). About LEED. Retrieved from http://www.usgbc.org/articles/about-leed

Utica Comets (2017, June 28). The rise of sports and entertainment districts: The U District. Retrieved from http://www.uticacomets.com/news/detail/the-rise-of-sports-and-entertainment-districts

Chapter 13

Carol A. Barr

Event Management

© Shutterstock, Inc./ Danilo_Vuletic

Learning Objectives

Upon completion of this chapter, students should be able to:

1. Describe the emergence and history of the sport event management industry.

2. Identify the various roles of sport marketing and event management agencies, such as event development, event management, television production, sponsorship solicitation, hospitality services, grassroots programming, and market research.

3. Differentiate between full-service, specialized, and in-house sport marketing and event management agencies.

4. Analyze critical event management functions, including budgeting, risk management, operations, registration, volunteer management, and event marketing.

5. Recognize that when multiple agencies work together to produce a sporting event, coordination and cooperation between those agencies are critical to the event's success.

6. Identify the career opportunities available in the event management industry, and understand the skills necessary to succeed in each of them.

7. Critically evaluate current issues of interest in the field of event management, such as the heightened awareness of event security, the impact of social and political issues on sporting events, and the growth of niche and extreme sports.

Introduction

A local Young Men's Christian Association (YMCA) basketball game, the State Junior Amateur Golf Championship, and the Super Bowl are all examples of events that need to be managed. They all also share one common element: the need for educated and trained managers and marketers to ensure success. Further, the critical event management functions are quite similar, although different in scope, whether the event is small (e.g., a local 5K road race) or large (e.g., Major League Baseball's All-Star Game). For the purposes of this chapter, we define sport event management as all functions related to planning, implementing, and evaluating a sport event.

This chapter presents an overview of the event management segment of the sport industry. First, the historical evolution of event management is discussed. Then, because many large and small events are managed and marketed by sport marketing and event management agencies, the types and roles played by these unique sport organizations are explored. Successful event management requires the appropriate application of all the management functions, so this chapter reviews finance/budgeting, risk management, tournament operations, registration, volunteer management, and event marketing within the context of event management. The next section explores career opportunities in event management, including information on educational backgrounds appropriate for those in sport event management. Finally, current issues surrounding the management of events are discussed.

History

Although even the earliest documented sport event probably required management, it was not until the late 1800s that the focus turned to the professional aspects of managing sport events. A desire to increase profits was the catalyst for such an emphasis. Following his retirement as a professional baseball player in the 1870s, Albert Spalding organized tours throughout North America to promote baseball, with the ultimate aim of creating a larger market for his products. Spalding's tours were an early example of what were called **barnstorming tours**. Touring star athletes and teams around the country to promote a particular sport soon became an exercise in event management. George Halas, longtime owner of the Chicago Bears, used his star player, Red Grange, to increase the popularity of professional football in the early 1900s (Schaaf, 1995). Professional boxing also provided a platform for professional event management. With the stakes of boxing events reaching more than $1 million by the turn of the twentieth century, boxing event promoters were forced to attend to the business aspects of managing such events.

Just as the need for a business focus prompted the creation of the sport management discipline, so, too, profit motives spurred the introduction of professional event managers in the 1960s and 1970s. The growth of sport event management led to the emergence of multifaceted companies called sport marketing and event management agencies. A **sport marketing and event management agency** is defined as a business that acts on behalf of a sport property. A **sport property** can be a person (LeBron James), company (Under Armour), event (Super Bowl), team (Houston Astros), or place (Royal and Ancient Golf Club of St. Andrews).

Sport marketing and event management agencies were initially established to represent the legal and marketing interests of athletes. International Management Group (now known as IMG), for example, was founded in 1960 by Mark McCormack to locate endorsement opportunities for professional golfer Arnold Palmer. As the sport industry evolved, agencies expanded to incorporate a myriad of functions beyond representing athletes. For example, as IMG signed more athletes as clients, its business grew to include managing and promoting events in which those athletes competed. Agencies capitalized on the concurrent growth of and public's interest in televised sporting events to rapidly increase the revenues generated through events of all sizes. Agencies also started to create their own made-for-TV events (content creation) that they both owned and managed.

Today, hundreds of sport marketing and event management agencies are intricately involved with the creation and promotion of most sport events. A number of these agencies have also expanded beyond sporting events into other entertainment or charitable types of events, as IMG has done with its entertainment division. The sport event management industry has also developed its very own industry conference. TEAMS: Travel, Events, and Management in Sports is a conference and exposition held every year for the sports-event industry (TEAMS, 2017).

Sport Marketing and Event Management Agencies

Sport management companies and agencies involved in the sport event management space usually describe themselves as sport marketing and event management agencies. **Table 13-1** lists the various roles that sport marketing and event management agencies play. Although some agencies perform all of the functions on this list, many others specialize in just one or a few of these functions. The first two functions listed in Table 13-1, client representation and client marketing, refer to acting on behalf of a client who is usually an athlete. These functions will not be covered in this chapter, as we will focus on the event management side of the work these agencies perform.

Given the increased number of outlets for sport events, such as satellite and digital television and the Internet, a variety of events have

Table 13-1 Sport Marketing and Event Management Agencies' Roles
Client representation
Client marketing
Event development
Event management
Television production
Sponsorship solicitation
Hospitality services
Grassroots programs
Market research
Financial planning

been created to provide programming. The X Games, for example, are a direct result of the growth in sports television. ESPN created the X Games in the summer of 1995 to provide programming, and currently manages all X Games (summer and winter) in-house. (The term *in-house* refers to producing a product or service within the organization.) Alli Sports is a media, event, and branded content company that is a division of the NBC Sports Group. Its properties include the Dew Tour, the Lucas Oil Pro Motocross, the Red Bull Signature Series, and the World of Adventure Sports (Alli Sports, 2017). As can be seen in this list of Alli Sports properties ("Dew" Tour, "Lucas Oil" Pro Motocross, and "Red Bull" Signature Series), a majority of sport marketing and event management agencies solicit corporate sponsorships for the events they manage.

Although one result of the growth in televised sports has been the creation of new events, another impact has been increasing demand for television production and development work. Potential revenue streams from television have led to the creation of television production divisions within some of the larger agencies. IMG, which was acquired in 2014 by William Morris

Endeavor (WME) to form WME/IMG, is one of the largest independent producers and distributors of sports media (IMG, 2017b). WME/IMG changed its name to Endeavor after announcing the creation of a new holding company to take on the full portfolio of owned and operated brands formerly under the WME/IMG umbrella (Kroll, 2017).

© Eric Limon/Shutterstock, Inc.

Another function of sport marketing and event management agencies is to develop and market **grassroots programs**. These programs are created by organizations attempting to target individuals at the most basic level of involvement, sport participation. A number of professional sport leagues are involved in grassroots programming, including the National Football League (NFL) Punt, Pass, & Kick national skills competition; the NFL Flag Football league (NFL Flag, 2017); and the Urban Youth Academy program of Major League Baseball (MLB, 2017). LEJ Sports Group (2017) is a full-service marketing and event management agency that works with clients including professional sport leagues to develop and manage youth sports programs.

Sport organizations require market research to evaluate the success of events and initiatives. By implementing mail surveys, focus groups, on-site surveys, and sponsorship/economic impact surveys, sport marketing and event management agencies assist sport properties in documenting the relative success or failure of programs and pinpointing areas that need improvement. Market research is particularly crucial for corporations wanting to know the impact of their sponsorship activities. Turnkey Sports & Entertainment (2017) is a full-service market research organization that works with a number of sport properties and organizations, including professional and college athletic teams, sport arenas and facilities, sport media organizations, and corporations engaged in sport sponsorship activities.

Types of Sport Marketing and Event Management Agencies

Sport marketing and event management agencies vary widely in terms of their numbers of employees, revenue generation, scope of services provided, and types of target clients. Sport agencies can be categorized as full-service agencies, specialized agencies, or in-house agencies. These different types of agencies are briefly described in this section.

Full-Service Agencies

Full-service agencies perform the complete set of agency functions discussed in the previous section. Although a number of firms fall into this category, the largest are WME/IMG (now under the brand Endeavor) and Octagon. WME/IMG (2017a), for example, owns, manages or commercially represents more than

© Ryan McVay/Photodisc/Thinkstock

800 events across entertainment, sports, and fashion, and includes operating divisions for athlete representation and management, event management services, licensing, media, and global brand partnerships. The firm covers the entire gamut of sport event and athlete functions. WME/IMG's clients include athletes such as Cam Newton (football), Venus Williams (tennis), and Ian Poulter (golf). Octagon (2017), by contrast, has more than 800 employees globally in 50 offices across 22 countries.

Fenway Sports Management (FSM) provides another example of the services and portfolio that can be found within sport marketing and event management agencies. FSM is a global sports marketing firm that oversees sponsorship sales for Fenway Sports Group's sports portfolio, which includes the Boston Red Sox, Liverpool Football Club, New England Sports Network (NESN), and Roush Fenway Racing.

FSM also serves as the exclusive marketing agency for LeBron James through a partnership with LRMR, the marketing company James launched in 2006 (FSM, 2017b). In addition, FSM provides consulting services on how sports can be used as a platform for brands to realize their business goals. Through its Special Events Group, FSM (2017a) participates in creating, planning, and executing unique sports and entertainment events including Frozen Fenway, a two-week winter festival with outdoor hockey games, ice skating events. and sledding held at Boston's iconic Fenway Park.

Specialized Agencies

Specialized agencies limit either the scope of services performed or the type of clients serviced. For example, Redmandarin is a London-based sport marketing agency that focuses on advising corporations on how to maximize their involvement with sponsorship opportunities, and offers consultancy services to partners of the Olympic Games (Redmandarin, 2012).

In-House Agencies

Another trend (which will be discussed in detail later) is the formation within major corporations of separate departments or divisions dealing with event management, typically called **in-house agencies**. For example, MasterCard Worldwide has a department solely dedicated to identifying sponsorship opportunities, creating activation programs, and overseeing the implementation of the sponsorship. These in-house agencies exist to coordinate the sponsorship function across the various divisions of the company.

Critical Event Management Functions

Regardless of the size of the event or the responsible agency, nearly all events must attend to a variety of critical functions. These functions include the following:

- Finance/budgeting.
- Risk management.
- Tournament operations.
- Registration.
- Volunteer management.
- Event marketing.

The remainder of this section examines these six functions in depth and then discusses a comprehensive project management approach involving all of these areas.

Finance/Budgeting

The complexity of managing events, coupled with the need to constantly monitor financial conditions, places the budgeting and finance functions at the forefront of successful sport event management. **Budgeting** is the process of developing a written plan of revenues and expenses for a particular accounting cycle. For events, an *accounting cycle* is usually the time period necessary to plan, organize, and operate the upcoming event. This cycle can be as short as a month or, in the case of an organization such as the United States Olympic Committee (USOC), budgeting can attempt to predict revenues and expenses for the following 4-plus years of activity.

Although several different types of budgets and budgeting processes exist, two that are particularly important for sport events are zero-base budgeting and cash-flow budgeting. **Zero-base budgeting** requires a review of all activities and related costs of an event as if it were taking place for the first time. Previous budgets and actual revenues and expenses are ignored. All projected revenues and expenses have to be justified prior to becoming part of the overall budget. This type of budget process forces managers to view their event from a fresh perspective, never taking elements for granted and always searching for ways to become more efficient and effective.

Cash-flow budgeting refers to accounting for the receipt and timing of all sources and expenditures of cash. This type of budgeting informs the manager of the cash amount needed to pay expenses at predetermined times throughout the accounting cycle. Events often expend sizable amounts of cash during the planning and organizing phases, while only receiving cash just prior to the actual execution of the event. Planning carefully to avoid cash shortfalls is therefore critical.

Risk Management

According to Prairie and Garfield (2004), **risk management** is defined as "the function or process by which [an organization] identifies and manages the risks of liability that rise from its activities" (p. 13). Usually this refers to personal injury risk management, although the sport event manager should broaden this definition to also include financial loss, equipment or property damage, loss of goodwill (customers becoming unhappy based on their experience), and loss of market share, to name a few potential risks.

Thus, risk management is broader than just protecting one's organization from a lawsuit. It essentially encompasses protecting the organization from anything that could possibly go wrong and lead to a loss of revenue or customers.

A common tool used by events to reduce the potential for a lawsuit from a participant or volunteer is the *waiver and release of liability*. This form, which is signed by participants and volunteers, releases the venue and event organizers from a negligence action in case of accident or injury. If the participant is a minor, the signature of a parent is required. The validity of a waiver is determined by the law in each state. The best practice for event organizers to follow is to consult with an attorney to determine whether waivers are recognized in a particular state and, if so, which important phrases and descriptions of activities need to be included within the waiver. Event organizers must also recognize that a waiver or release of liability does not exonerate them from all responsibility and liability regarding the event.

Waivers and releases of liability can be used only to waive or release a defendant from negligence claims. Event organizers are still responsible for running an event in a responsible, safe manner or they may be found liable for any injuries or problems that may occur.

Another approach to handling risk factors associated with an event is to purchase insurance. Insurance can be purchased not only to cover safety concerns, but also to provide security to an event regarding potential financial losses as well as to cover buildings or other structures/contents involved in the event. For example, an outdoor event that collects sponsorship dollars and registration fees from participants in advance may need to refund a portion, if not all, of this revenue if the event is cancelled due to inclement weather. The event organizers, though, still incurred expenses in getting ready to host the event. Purchasing cancellation insurance can help to offset some of these expenses. Most venues require that the promoter, sponsor, or organizer of the event maintain a minimum level of insurance. The premiums for these types of insurance are based on the level of risk. Events that hold high-value contests, such as a "Hole in One Contest" for cash, will also need to secure a contest coverage insurance package to cover the risk that a contestant actually succeeds in making the hole in one shot.

Risk management and insurance are of primary importance to event organizers and should not be overlooked when running an event. Appropriate advance planning in these areas can help alleviate problems when the event actually takes place. In addition, event

© Lowe R. Llaguno/Shutterstock, Inc.

organizers should realize the importance of addressing risk management and insurance concerns surrounding an event to limit the legal liability of the event.

Tournament Operations

Tournament operations can be described as the nuts and bolts of an event. The tournament operations staff stage the event, meet facility and equipment needs, and provide any operational items for the event. Tournament operations can be divided into pre-event, actual event, and post-event activities.

Pre-event tournament operations require appropriate planning and information collection to ensure that all aspects and details surrounding the actual event are identified. Depending on the size and scope of the event, pre-event tournament operations planning may start 4 months prior to an event, as is common for local events such as bike races or basketball tournaments, or 8 to 10 years prior to an event, as is common with large events such as the Olympic and Paralympic Games. During the pre-event planning stages, it is important for the tournament operations staff to be clear as to the type of event being planned and the event's goals. This information is critical in determining how the tournament will be organized and run—components central to the responsibilities and concerns of the tournament operations staff.

Items that should be addressed in the pre-event planning stages include the following:

- Venue plan and layout.
- Equipment and facility needs.
- Schedule of activities.
- Sponsorship needs.
- Signage commitments and locations.
- Food and beverages.
- Merchandise sales.
- Media concerns.
- Promotional activities and needs.
- Transportation concerns.
- Housing of athletes.
- Staff communication.
- Personnel responsibilities.
- Lines of authority.
- Security issues.
- Americans with Disabilities Act requirements.
- Policies to address other legal concerns such as alcohol use.
- Crowd control.

This list is not all-inclusive, because the items handled by the tournament operations staff will vary depending on the type, goals, size, and scope of the event.

During the actual event, the tournament operations staff are responsible for ensuring that the event takes place as planned. This includes attending to the activities and needs relating to participants, sponsors, spectators, and media. To help in this area, many events utilize a script of activities. The **script** is a specific, detailed, minute-by-minute (or even second-by-second) schedule of activities throughout the day, including information on the tournament operations responsibilities for each activity. This script provides information relative to (1) the time of day and what is taking place, (2) the operational needs (equipment and setup) surrounding each activity, and (3) the event person(s) in charge of the various activities. During the actual event, the tournament operations staff implement the tournament script while also troubleshooting as needed. Advance preparation and planning can certainly assist in running an event, but the tournament operations staff must always be prepared to troubleshoot and be flexible and adaptable to change when an unforeseen problem arises.

The post-event stage consists of the activities surrounding the completion of an event. Areas covered during the post-event stage include the following:

- Tear-down of the venue.
- Storage of equipment and supplies.
- Trash pickup and disposal.
- Return of borrowed equipment, sponsorship signage, and other items.
- Final financial accounting regarding expenses relative to the operations portion of the event.
- Thank-you notes or appropriate forms of recognition to appropriate constituencies who assisted in the tournament operations area.

It is important for the tournament operations staff to realize that the completion of the actual event does not signal the end of their responsibilities. Numerous items such as those just listed still need to be addressed before the event is wrapped up.

Large sporting events usually outsource the operations of the event to a professional company, sometimes partnering with local organizations or community groups that handle portions of the event such as solicitation and scheduling of the volunteers working the event. For example, the PGA and Web.com Tours use the golf management company Global Golf Management (GGM) to oversee tournament operations for these events. GGM (2017) oversees the tournament operations for more than 40 golf events around the world.

Registration

Registering participants for an event is of the utmost importance, because this is the first time the event is interacting with and providing a service to the customers—that is, the participants. An efficient **registration system** is crucial for making a good first impression on the event's clientele. Appropriate advance planning and attention to information the participants need will help guide the development of a registration system that is appropriate for the event and convenient for participants.

In developing a registration system, event managers must consider the following items:

- Number of participants who will be registering.
- Information that needs to be collected from or disseminated to the participants (e.g., waiver forms, codes for sportsmanship conduct, inclement weather policy, event schedule).
- Registration fees that must be collected.
- Whether identification is needed (e.g., regarding age limitations).
- Whether information will be collected manually or via a computer system.
- Whether the event involves minors, who require the signature of a parent or guardian on a waiver form.

This list is not all-inclusive because the type of event will dictate the specific items that need to be covered during the registration process.

The registration process for numerous sporting events, large and small, has evolved to mostly online registration processes. Also, an increasing number of sport events are choosing to outsource their registration process instead of developing and servicing an online platform themselves. One of the more successful online registration and event and activity management companies is Active Network, which hosts Active.com, an online event search and registration website. Active Network (2017) works with more than 36,000 organizations worldwide.

Volunteer Management

The importance of volunteers to an event cannot be emphasized enough. Most events cannot be successfully executed without volunteers. This is a good opportunity for sport management students looking to gain experience. You should always be able to find an event in your area that is in need of a volunteer. Events from the smallest local bike race to those as large and complex as the Olympic and Paralympic Games rely on volunteer help.

Volunteer management staff supervise the volunteers involved with an event. **Volunteer management** can be divided into two areas: (1) working with event organizers and staff to determine the areas and quantity of volunteers needed and (2) soliciting, training, and managing the volunteers. Once again, advance planning and preparation are critical in determining how many volunteers are needed and in which capacities they will serve. The volunteer management staff must communicate with every division or area within an event to determine volunteer needs. Information must include the number of volunteers a particular area may need, qualifications of volunteers, and the type of work to be performed. This information is important when scheduling volunteers because the volunteer management staff would not want to assign a volunteer to work moving heavy equipment, for example, if the volunteer were not physically capable of doing so.

Once the volunteer management staff have calculated or estimated the number of and areas of work where volunteers are needed, the staff can make sure that recruitment efforts are appropriate to solicit that number of volunteers. Volunteer recruitment should begin well in advance of the event to ensure the appropriate number of volunteers are recruited.

After volunteer recruitment takes place, appropriate training sessions must be held. Training sessions typically include several components, starting with a general information session and progressing to more specialized direction on how to manage the specific responsibilities in each of the individual event departments. Items covered in the basic educational component training session may include how the volunteers should dress or obtain their volunteer uniforms, how they can obtain food and beverages during the event, and how the communication system will be used so they know whom to contact in case of a problem. In addition, all volunteers should be trained concerning risk management and the procedures they should follow in case of an injury or accident. Specific department training may include a description of volunteer duties, how to carry out these duties, when and where volunteers should check in, the name of their direct supervisor, and any other information specific to the volunteer work they will be performing.

Event organizers must also understand the importance of volunteers to the continual operation and success of an event. It is important for the volunteer management staff and event organizers to make sure certain things are done to keep the volunteers happy so they will keep coming back year after year. First, volunteers should not be scheduled into too many time slots so they do not become tired. The schedule should also include appropriate food and bathroom breaks. Second, volunteers need to be recognizable to participants and spectators. Uniforms can help the volunteers be more recognizable while increasing the professional perception of the event. Uniforms can also be color-coded to indicate the vounteers' area of responsibility. For example, medical staff may have a red shirt sleeve while operations staff might have a blue shirt sleeve. Additionally, uniforms help build goodwill with volunteers, in that they are the only ones able to wear the special volunteer uniform. Finally, volunteers need to be recognized for their assistance and contribution to the event. This can be done in a number of ways, including constant recognition during the event via daily newsletters and website announcements, holding a volunteer party after the event is over, and running volunteer raffles in which the volunteers have a chance to win prizes such as event merchandise or gift cards from local sponsors or receive some benefits in exchange for volunteering.

Event Marketing

Sport and special events cannot be successful without carefully planned **event marketing** programs. Event marketers must focus on nine areas:

- Sales of corporate sponsorship.
- Advertising efforts.
- Public relations and media activities including social media.
- Hospitality.
- Ticket sales.
- Broadcasting.
- Website development and management.
- Licensing/merchandising.
- Fundraising.

These nine areas are intricately linked. Efforts toward soliciting corporate sponsors will affect advertising strategies, and broadcasting agreements will influence ticket sales. Because these areas are so interrelated, the event marketer must employ an integrated marketing approach. **Integrated marketing** entails long-term strategic planning to manage functions in a consistent manner. For example, ticket sales strategies should be developed while considering the potential sales promotion efforts of sponsors. Similarly, ticket purchases and/or registration should be possible on the website. With these caveats in mind, each of the nine event marketing areas will now be explored.

Corporate Sponsorship

As mentioned earlier in this chapter, the number of sport events has grown significantly in recent years. With this growth, the competition for sponsors (and other marketing revenues such as ticket sales) has increased. At the same time, events have become increasingly reliant on sponsorship. This is true of small events as well as large events. The 15 biggest sponsorship deals in the world involving events and sports are presented in **Table 13-2**.

Typically, corporate sponsorships are either sold by the event (in-house) or by an outside sport marketing agency. Sport marketing agencies are hired by a sport property because the property does not have sufficient personnel or expertise in selling sponsorships. In the early 1980s, the International Olympic Committee (IOC) decided the Games were becoming too reliant on broadcasting fees for funding. In response, it decided to sell worldwide sponsorships for the Olympic Games. However, the IOC did not have the expertise or personnel to approach global companies asking for multimillion-dollar sponsorship commitments. Therefore, in 1983 the IOC turned to ISL Marketing, which raised $100 million for the 1988 Olympic Games (Simson & Jennings, 1992). In an effort to generate more revenue and garner more control over sponsorship sales, the IOC partnered with Chris Welton and Laurent Scharapan to form the sport marketing agency Meridian in 1997 (Woodward, 2003). Meridian was responsible for finding and servicing IOC sponsors. In 2003, the IOC brought its sponsorship effort completely in-house when it purchased the Meridian Agency. This move allows the IOC to earn more money from its

Table 13-2 Top 15 Biggest Sponsorship Deals of Sports and Events
1. Toyota signs $1.63 billion deal with the International Olympic Committee over 8 years, 2017–2024
2. AB InBev signs $1.4 billion deal with the National Football League (NFL) over 6 years, 2017–2022
3. Nike signs $1 billion deal with the National Basketball Association (NBA) over 8 years, 2017–2025
4. adidas signs $940 million deal with Bayern Munich over 15 years, 2015–2030
5. Verizon signs $400 million deal with the NBA over 3 years, 2015–2018
6. adidas signs $330 million deal with the Spanish Football Federation over 11 years, 2015–2026
7. Majestic Athletic signs $275 million deal with Major League Baseball (MLB) over 5 years, 2015–2019
8. Nike signs $250 million deal with the University of Texas over 15 years, 2017–2031
9. adidas signs $238.7 million deal with Juventus over 6 years, 2015–2021
10. US Bank signs $200 million deal with the Minnesota Vikings over 20 years, 2016–2035
11. Hyundai signs $200 million deal with the NFL over 4 years, 2015–2019
12. Shell signs $200 million deal with Ferrari over 5 years, 2016–2020
13. Charles Schwab signs $200 million deal with the PGA Tour over 20 years, 2015–2034
14. Sony signs $200 million deal with the Union of European Football Associations (UEFA) over 3 years, 2015–2018
15. Yokohama Tires signs deal with Chelsea Football Club worth at least $183 million over 5 years, 2015–2020

Reproduced from Glendinning, M. (2016, January 8). Sports sponsorship insider top 40 deals of 2015. *Sport Business.* Retrieved from http://www.sportbusiness.com/sponsorship-insider/sports-sponsorship-insider-top-40-deals-2015

sponsorship sales because it no longer has to pay fees to an outside agency (Woodward, 2003).

Advertising

Many events operate on very tight budgets. As a result, such events are not able to allocate significant expenditures for advertising through traditional forms of media. Although advertising expenditures often represent a very minor portion of an event's expenses, this does not mean that events do not expend energy devising alternative means of mass-media advertising. Events typically seek advertising through one of two means: (1) media sponsors or (2) attachment to corporate sponsor advertisements.

In addition to selling corporate sponsorships, nearly all successful events sell sponsorships to media outlets. Such sponsorships are often referred to as in-kind sponsorships. **In-kind sponsorships** rarely involve a cash exchange. Instead, an event provides the typical sponsorship benefits to a newspaper, magazine, radio station, or television station in exchange for a specified number of free advertising spots or space. Event promoters will also work with sponsors to promote their events through traditional forms of mass media. Most often, such advertising is geared toward promotions.

Public Relations

Because events are so constrained in their advertising budgets, generating free publicity is extremely important. Most important to attaining publicity is developing a good working relationship with the members of the media. Hospitality efforts can greatly assist in this endeavor and are discussed later in this section. In addition, regular communication with media outlets helps increase the publicity an event receives. However, because members of the media seek stories of interest to the masses, the event must be creative to ensure it receives media attention.

Social media can often be used through minimal effort to help generate free publicity

for an event. Various social media platforms, including Twitter, Snapchat, and Instagram, among others, can be used in a coordinated fashion to gain publicity or in an ad hoc fashion through volunteers' and participants' usage of social media.

Hospitality

Hospitality refers to providing a satisfying experience for all the event stakeholders, including participants, spectators, media, and sponsors. Most events occur on a regular basis, and providing good hospitality is one way of improving event loyalty. The sport manager should take strides to ensure that prominent event participants receive private housing, meals, changing areas, and warm-up space. If the participants are also celebrities, the sport manager must ensure that extra security is available to shield them from the public. If hospitality is not successfully implemented, the participants are less likely to return to the event. With respect to spectators, hospitality entails attempting to ensure that people attending the event have an enjoyable time. This includes clear signage directing participants, including those with disabilities, to their seats, restrooms, and concession stands. In addition, training all support staff personnel is imperative so that interpersonal interactions with event staff are always positive.

The event manager will often expend the most energy providing hospitality to members of the media, corporate sponsors, and other VIPs. Because the event manager is seeking positive publicity from the media, there should always be a separate, prime seating location for the media. In addition, members of the media are accustomed to having private meals and accessibility to a private room where they can complete their work.

Increased spending on corporate sponsorships has led to growing awareness and interest in hospitality services. Sport sponsors utilize hospitality for a variety of reasons, including the following:

- To reward and build relationships with current customers.
- To generate business from new customers.
- To reward employees for good performance.
- To reward suppliers for excellent sales.

For these reasons, hospitality has become one of the 10 most common functions of a sport marketing and event management agency (as presented in Table 13-1).

Ticket Sales

Sporting events rely on ticket sales to varying degrees. For larger events, such as college football games, ticket sales are a very important revenue stream. For example, the stadium at the University of Michigan is the largest venue for college football. With a seating capacity of more than 109,000, the stadium generates a significant amount of ticket revenue. However, for medium-sized and smaller events, ticket sales are a less effective way to generate revenues. Much of the ability to charge admission for these events depends on where the event is held and how easily the event manager can control entry to the event. For example, many professional golf tournaments experience difficulty generating revenues through ticket sales because it is hard to control entry to the course and because so many tickets are given away to corporate sponsors. In these cases, the event is more reliant on sponsorship or broadcasting revenues. Event managers, however, have discovered creative ways to increase revenues tied to ticket sales. In exchange for a higher monetary outlay, golf tournaments have begun offering preferred viewing lanes, whereby spectators receive premium seating in front of the typical gallery areas.

Advances in technology have also impacted the ticket sales area. A number of professional sport franchises have recently implemented Flash Seats, an electronic ticketing system in which spectators gain entrance to a sporting event via an encrypted code that can be placed on a personal form of identification such as a driver's license or credit card. This technology has aided in eliminating fraud and duplicate tickets and has decreased spectator no-show rates (Sutton, 2010).

Broadcasting

Radio and television broadcasts of an event add credibility to the event and provide increased exposure benefits to sponsors. A wide variety of broadcast outlets are available for sporting events:

- National television networks (e.g., ABC, NBC, CBS, Fox).
- National sports networks (e.g., ESPN, ESPN2, Fox Sports Net).
- National cable outlets (e.g., TNT, TBS, TNN, The Golf Channel).
- Local television stations.
- Regional sports networks (e.g., Big Ten Network, New England Sports Network).
- National radio (e.g., CBS, ESPN, XM/Sirius).
- Local radio stations.
- Websites and livestreaming (e.g., MLB livestreaming baseball games on Facebook).

Although the increased number of sport outlets has accelerated the demand for sport event programming, a sport property must still meet certain criteria to interest a radio or television broadcast outlet. In fact, only the most valuable sport properties, such as the Super Bowl, the Olympic Games, Wimbledon, the Masters, professional sports, and Division I college athletics, are able to secure direct rights fee payments from broadcasting affiliates. It is important to remember that television and radio stations are funded by advertising sales. Advertisers purchase advertising time during programs that will attract large viewing or listening audiences. Therefore, if a broadcast outlet does not believe an event will be attractive to a large audience, which in turn limits its ability to sell advertising time, then the outlet will not be willing to pay a rights fee to televise or broadcast an event.

Sport organizations and governing bodies have also pursued access to consumers by broadcasting games and highlights via popular video-sharing sites such as YouTube and social-networking sites such as Facebook and Twitter. A "tweet" that goes out while a sporting event is taking place can often drive consumers to turn on their televisions or computers and watch the event live.

Website Development and Management

Because access to the Internet is now widespread and the connection speeds associated with such access are no longer an issue, people are becoming more reliant on websites for information. For this reason, it is imperative that every event, no matter its size, has an online presence to promote important information about the event. Ideally, the website's uniform resource locator (URL) will be the name of the event or something very similar (for example, www.masters.com, https://tokyo2020.jp/en/, www.worldbaseballclassic.com). In terms of content, the website can include a wide variety of information. At the very least, it should include the basic details of when and where the event is occurring and how tickets can be purchased. If the event charges admission, it is sometimes easier for customers to purchase tickets through a website than by phone or at the event. The website can also be a source for the most up-to-date information about the event. For example, it can include news releases about the event, or it can provide real-time updates of event results. In the case of inclement weather during an outdoor event, the website can serve to inform participants and spectators about whether the event is actually occurring.

Licensing/Merchandising

The sale of **licensed merchandise**—that is, items that display an event's name or logo—is beneficial in a number of ways, including event advertising and brand recognition as well as a potential revenue source through sales generated. Popular events such as the Olympic Games and the Super Bowl generate significant demand for licensed merchandise. However, for smaller, less recognizable events, such as a high school football game or a 10K road race, the demand may not be as great; thus, less of a profit may be realized if sales do not come through.

Fundraising

When an event is classified as **not-for-profit**, another marketing tool is fundraising. Fundraising differs from sponsorship in that it does not offer advertising benefits associated with a donation. Most often, not-for-profit events center on raising money for some charitable enterprise, such as the Susan G. Komen Race for the Cure, which generates money for breast cancer research. The Komen Race for the Cure is the largest series of 5K runs/fitness walks in the world, with more than 1 million participants in more than 150 races across four continents (Susan G. Komen for the Cure, 2017a). Another successful event is the Tough Mudder. Created in 2010 by former members of the British Special Forces, these 10- to 12-mile events have grown exponentially, from three events held in the year the series was created to reaching tens of millions of people around the world through its events, brand, and television presence (Rath, 2017) and raising more than $10 million for charities in the process (Tough Mudder, 2017).

Cause-related marketing efforts by corporations are another instance in which fundraising may be appropriate. For example, the CVS Caremark Charity Classic is Rhode Island's largest charitable event. It hosts teams composed of one player each from the PGA Tour, LPGA Tour, and PGA Tour Champions players, who take part in a one-day, 18-hole competition. Since its inaugural event in 1999, the CVS Caremark

Charity Classic has raised more than $20 million for charities throughout Rhode Island and Southern New England (CVS Health Charity Classic, 2017). Similarly, since 1993, the V Foundation has awarded more than $170 million in cancer research grants nationwide from a combination of smaller events, such as local golf outings, and larger events, such as the Jimmy V Basketball Classic and the ESPY Awards (V Foundation, 2017). Sport teams and leagues also engage in their own charitable activities.

Project Management

Project management is an approach that has long been used in management and industry circles to organize and oversee all of the details and various aspects of a project from start to finish. The Project Management Institute, Inc. (PMI) defines **project management** as "the application of knowledge, skills, tools and techniques to a broad range of activities in order to meet the requirements of a particular project" (Project Insight, 2017, para. 1). This project management approach certainly makes sense in the planning and operations of an event, and can be implemented through the use of a Gantt chart. A **Gantt chart** shows the activities, tasks, and events that need to occur associated with an event displayed against time. Gantt charts can also utilize color coding to show which functional area (e.g., marketing, registration, volunteer management) is involved in each activity being charted. Historically Gantt charts were kept by hand, but today project management software is available to help organize and track various activities associated with an event from the pre-planning phase through post-event wrap-up (Gantt.com, 2017).

Career Opportunities

Event management offers a diverse array of career possibilities. Any event, from the local 3-on-3 basketball tournament to the Olympic and Paralympic Games, requires

event management expertise. As a result, the event management field represents one of the most fertile areas for career opportunities. To successfully run a sporting event, the event manager's day often begins before dawn and concludes late at night. In addition, because events are usually held on weekends, employment in event management often requires extensive travel and work over weekends. Thus, to be successful in event management, a person must be prepared to work long and typically inconvenient hours. Career opportunities in event management center on working with one of three types of organizations: sport management/marketing agencies, events, and charities.

Sport Marketing and Event Management Agencies

Because of the wide range of tasks carried out by these agencies, job responsibilities within such agencies vary. Typically, an entry-level position with a sport marketing and event management agency will require a person to implement programs on behalf of corporate clients. These programs can include any combination of the key event management functions already discussed. Although an entry-level person is usually not responsible for recruiting corporate clients, he or she is required to successfully manage events and programs created for specific sponsors. For example, an account manager might be responsible for supervising hospitality at an event or for ensuring that a corporation's signs are properly placed throughout an event site.

To move beyond an entry-level position within an agency, a person is usually required to accept more business development responsibilities. For example, most vice presidents of sport marketing and event management agencies are responsible for attracting new clients for the agency. This function is typically called **business development**.

Events

Although sport marketing and event management agencies can be involved with almost any sport event, many events have their own offices of full-time employees. This is most often true for events to which a corporation or sport marketing and event management agency does not own the rights. Instead, the rights to the event may be owned locally. In this case, the management team for the event would not be from an agency or corporation. Because most events are seasonal in nature, the full-time year-round staffs for such events are not very large; in some cases, the full-time staff for an event may be only one person.

Many charities view events as a way to increase revenues. Raising money and managing the events require staff. For example, the Komen Foundation is led by more than 100,000 breast cancer survivors and activists in more than 120 cities and communities (Susan G. Komen for the Cure, 2017b).

Key Skills

As this chapter has described, an event manager assumes a variety of responsibilities. To successfully execute these responsibilities, sport managers must have the necessary skills and experience. First, sport managers must possess the proper educational background. Students interested in event management should seek a sport management program or business school that will provide them with coursework in areas such as sport marketing, event management, sport management, business, and finance. Many events are created by one person and begin as a small business, so classes in entrepreneurship and accounting are also appropriate for the prospective event manager.

In terms of experience, an internship is almost always required prior to being hired for an entry-level position in event management. In many cases, sport marketing and event management agencies will turn to their most effective interns when seeking to fill full-time entry-level positions. Because agencies are charged with supporting corporate clients, new accounts often mean that agencies will need to hire additional personnel. Students must therefore put themselves in a position to be hired when new accounts are acquired.

It is never too early to begin working for events. A number of volunteer and paid opportunities exist in any university community: the athletic department, intramural department, community recreation programs, sports commissions, charity events, and so on. Nearly all of these activities can help improve a student's background in event management, making him or her more knowledgeable and marketable.

Current Issues

Event Security

After the terrorist attacks of September 11, 2001, the security presence at sporting events and facilities was heightened, including installation of metal detectors through which spectators needed to pass to get into the event, searches of purses for suspicious objects, and even a ban placed on backpacks and larger bags being brought into certain facilities. Event security has assumed an even higher level of importance and scrutiny after the bombing during the 2013 Boston Marathon, which claimed three lives and injured hundreds more, and the Paris attacks of 2015, which included suicide bombings outside the Stade de France stadium where a soccer match between France and Germany was being played.

Providing appropriate security to outdoor events is very difficult, especially for events that involve a large area with generally open public access, such as a marathon route. Events held within stadiums have also been subjected to increased scrutiny related to the security as well. Oftentimes event management companies or facility operators will hire a private security firm to provide security guards for the event/facility. However, these security guards are often low-paid, part-time employees with little to no training in security techniques. The U.S. Department of Homeland Security has been advising stadium officials for years and has conducted assessments to detect vulnerabilities in the security being provided. The National Center for Spectator Sports Safety and Security (NCS4) offers the Certified Sport Venue Staff (CSVS) certification for front line venue and event staff. The CSVS curriculum is designed to enhance safety and security efforts for sports and entertainment venues (NCS4, 2018). This is an area that will continue to receive increased attention from national, state, and local governments as additional training and licensing gaps are addressed and as the rigor of minimal event security expectations escalates.

Social and Political Concerns Impacting Hosting of Events

In 2016, the North Carolina legislature passed and the state's governor signed House Bill 2, referred to by many as the "bathroom bill," which required transgender people to use the bathrooms, changing rooms, and showers in state-run buildings that correspond to the sex on their birth certificate rather than their gender identity. Passage of this bill led to outrage and protests by many, including the withdrawal of tournament games hosted in the state by the National Collegiate Athletic Association (NCAA) and the National Basketball Association (NBA) All-Star game scheduled to be played in Charlotte (Jenkins & Trotta, 2017). The Atlantic Coast Conference (ACC), which includes University of North Carolina–Chapel Hill, Duke University, N.C. State University, and Wake Forest University, moved all of its 2016–2017 tournaments and championship events from the state (Walton, 2017). This law was repealed in March 2017, with the NCAA and ACC ending their boycotts as a result; the NBA also awarded the All-Star game to Charlotte in 2019. Although the original HB2 bill was repealed, there is still much debate in North Carolina and other states (Texas) surrounding this and other social political issues that may impact the hosting or running of sporting events in the future.

Niche and Extreme Sports

Octopush (underwater hockey), ultimate frisbee, quidditch, and chess boxing are considered by many to be **niche sports**. These kinds of unique sports appeal to distinct segments of the market, whether defined by age, such as the Millennial generation or Generation Z (the teenagers of today), or by socioeconomic class, as is seen with the appeal of sailing and polo to those with higher incomes. Some niche sports have also been identified as extreme sports—that is, high-octane, on-the-edge types of sporting events. One of the most popular extreme sports today seems to be Ultimate Fighting Championship Mixed Martial Arts (UFC MMA). Niche and extreme sports can be very valuable to an organization from a sponsorship perspective. Red Bull, for example, sees extreme sports as an opportunity to connect with young audiences and has been involved in sponsoring more than 500 extreme sports ("Red Bull's Success," 2017). Even small, local extreme or niche sporting events can find sponsorship opportunities.

New events have been spawned from the appealing nature of these sports to their respective demographic groups. The Dew Tour (2017) was established in 2005 and has since evolved into a winter (snow) and summer (skate) event schedule involving the world's best snowboarders, skiers, and skateboarders. The X Games, presented by ESPN, follow a similar Winter and Summer Games approach. Winter sports and their variations include snowboarding, boardercross, skiing, ski cross, slopestyle, snowmobiling, and snocross. The summer sports and their variations include skateboarding, BMX biking,

Case Study 13-1

Planning for a New Event

David Tompkins sat in his third-floor office contemplating the new challenge dropped in his lap by his employer, Excellent Events, Inc. David has been working for Excellent Events as Northeast Regional Director of 3-on-3 Basketball Operations for the past 4 years. David's job responsibilities involve overseeing all operational details and sponsorship properties of the 3-on-3 basketball tournaments run by Excellent Events.

This morning at a meeting with the company's CEO, David had been presented with a new challenge. Excellent Events wants to expand into the soccer market, hosting soccer tournaments throughout the Northeast region. Excellent Events has been in the 3-on-3 basketball tournament business for more than 10 years. The company has seen participation in these tournaments start to fall in recent years, so it is looking to introduce a new sporting event. After researching various potential events, such as beach volleyball and lacrosse, the company decided to go with soccer. It was up to David Tompkins to organize and run these soccer tournaments in his territory.

Raised in Minnesota, David had never played organized soccer while growing up. While working in the Northeast over the past 4 years, though, he had realized that soccer was a popular sport in the area. Just how popular, he wasn't sure, and he made a note on the notepad in front of him to find out. David also wasn't familiar with the rules of soccer, the equipment that would be needed, the different formats for soccer tournaments, the age classifications for playing divisions, risk management or liability concerns surrounding the sport of soccer, or even the types of youth soccer leagues and organizations that might already exist in the area. Again, his pen was busy scratching down ideas and thoughts on the pad of paper in front of him.

David was also well aware of the financial goals of Excellent Events. He realized that the financial success of the soccer events was contingent on a combination of team registration fees and corporate sponsorships. But he also knew that the demographics for soccer participants might differ from what he knew regarding participants and spectators for the 3-on-3 basketball tournaments. David also wanted to explore the possibility of the event giving back to the community, perhaps through a connection with a local charitable organization. Once again David made note of these thoughts.

David had never felt so challenged in his life. Although he considered himself a great event manager, he was not sure how much of his success at running 3-on-3 basketball tournaments would transfer to this new venture. However, one thing he had learned during his experience as an event manager was that attention to details sprinkled with creativity could carry an event manager far.

Questions for Discussion

1. David decided the first thing he needed to do was to research the sport of soccer in his area. Which types of information would you suggest that David research and collect?

2. Although David is well aware of the equipment and supplies necessary to run a 3-on-3 basketball tournament, he lacks familiarity with the sport of soccer. Depending on the age divisions of the participants, the equipment might vary (e.g., a smaller soccer ball and goal size might be used for younger age divisions that play on a smaller field). Provide a comprehensive list of all equipment required to successfully operate a soccer event.

3. Given the demographics and psychographics of soccer participants and spectators, which types of corporations should David target for sponsorship solicitation?

4. Which suggestions would you have for David in terms of a marketing strategy? How should David market these new tournaments?

motorcycling, rally car racing, and surfing (National Geographic, 2017).

The growth and popularity of niche and extreme sporting events targeting specific demographic cohorts will be maintained in the future. What will be interesting to follow, though, is which sports are able to secure the needed sponsorship, spectator interest (both in person and via network, streaming, and social media outlets) to be sustainable over time.

Summary

By virtue of the continued increase in the number and variety of sporting events, sport event management offers a wide array of career opportunities for young sport managers. Most of these opportunities exist within sport marketing and event management agencies—the entities that most often organize, manage, and market sport events. Due to the variety of event management functions, multiple agencies frequently work together on a sporting event. For example, a professional golf tournament may have one sport agency responsible for the operational aspects of the event and another agency responsible for the sponsorship sales, public relations, and hospitality for sponsors and VIPs. Yet another agency could be financially and legally responsible for the event and, therefore, be in charge of implementing budgeting and risk management practices. In some cases, one large agency will handle all of these aspects and perhaps even produce a television broadcast or live streaming of the event. Regardless of how these functions are delegated, each is crucial to the sporting event's success.

With the proliferation of made-for-TV events, opportunities for sport managers in event management will continue to grow. To enter the event management field, a student must have a strong background in sport management, marketing, entrepreneurship, finance, and accounting. The good news is that the student can begin immediately by seeking both volunteer and paid opportunities with sporting events on campus and in the local community.

Resources

16W Marketing, LLC
75 Union Avenue, 2nd Floor
Rutherford, NJ 07070
201-635-8000
http://www.16wmktg.com

Alli Sports
http://www.allisports.com/about

Bruno Event Team
100 Grandview Place, Suite 110
Birmingham, AL 35243
205-967-4745
http://www.brunoeventteam.com

ESP Properties
350 North Orleans Street, Suite 1200
Chicago, IL 60654
312-725-5100
http://www.sponsorship.com

Fenway Sports Management
82 Brookline Avenue
Boston, MA 02215
http://www.fenwaysportsmanagement.com

Fuse Integrated Marketing, Inc.
110 W Canal Street #101
Winooski, VT 05404
http://www.fusemarketing.com

Genesco Sports Enterprises
5944 Luther Lane
Dallas, TX 75225
214-826-6565
http://www.gsesports.com

GMR Marketing
5000 South Towne Drive
New Berlin, WI 53151
800-447-8560
https://gmrmarketing.com

IMG
U.S. Headquarters
1075 Peachtree Street NE 3300 & 3200
Atlanta, GA 30309
770-956-0520
http://www.img.com

LEJ Sports Group
4015 Wetherburn Way
LEJ Building
Norcross, GA 30092
770-641-7584
http://www.lejsports.com

Octagon Sports and Entertainment
290 Harbor Drive
Stamford, CT 06902
203-354-7400
http://www.octagon.com

Redmandarin
Somerset House, West Wing
Strand

London, UK
WC2R 1LA
+44 (0) 207 566 9410
http://www.redmandarin.com

Spectrum Sports Management
2058 N. Mills Avenue #454
Claremont, CA 91711
909-399-3553
http://spectrumsports.net

Turnkey Sports & Entertainment
http://turnkeyse.com

Wasserman Media Group
10960 Wilshire Boulevard
Suite 2200
Los Angeles, CA 90024
310-407-0200
http://www.teamwass.com

Key Terms

barnstorming tours, budgeting, business development, cash-flow budgeting, cause-related marketing efforts, event marketing, full-service agencies, Gantt chart, grassroots programs, hospitality, in-house agencies, in-kind sponsorships, integrated marketing, licensed merchandise, niche sports, not-for-profit, project management, registration system, risk management, script, specialized agency, sport marketing and event management agencies, sport property, tournament operations, volunteer management, zero-base budgeting

References

Active Network. (2017). Retrieved from http://www.activenetwork.com/

Alli Sports. (2017). About Alli Sports. Retrieved from http://www.allisports.com/about

CVS Health Charity Classic. (2017). Facts. Retrieved from http://www.cvshealthcharityclassic.com/facts.html

Dew Tour. (2017). About. Retrieved from http://www.dewtour.com/about/

Fenway Sports Management (FSM). (2017a). Portfolio. Retrieved from http://www.fenwaysportsmanagement.com/portfolio/#frozen-fenway

Fenway Sports Management (FSM). (2017b). What we do. Retrieved from http://www.fenwaysportsmanagement.com/what-we-do/

Gantt.com. (2017). Home page. Retrieved from http://www.gantt.com/

Glendinning, M. (2016, January 8). Sports sponsorship insider top 40 deals of 2015. *Sport Business*. Retrieved from http://www.sportbusiness.com/sponsorship-insider/sports-sponsorship-insider-top-40-deals-2015

Global Golf Management (GGM). (2017). A bit about us. Retrieved from http://globalgolfmanagement.com/about

IMG. (2017a). Expertise. Retrieved from http://www.img.com/expertise/

IMG. (2017b). Our story. Retrieved from http://www.img.com/story/

Jenkins, C., & Trotta, D. (2017, March 30). Seeking end to boycott, North Carolina rescinds transgender bathroom law. Reuters. Retrieved from http://www.reuters.com/article/us-north-carolina-lgbt/seeking-end-to-boycott-north-carolina-rescinds-transgender-bathroom-law-idUSKBN1711V4

Kroll, J. (2017, October 9). WME-IMG renames holding company Endeavor. Variety. Retrieved from http://variety.com/2017/biz/news/wme-img-endeavor-1202584304/

LEJ Sports Group. (2017). Home page. Retrieved from http://www.lejsports.com/Home/tabid/211/Default.aspx

Major League Baseball (MLB). (2017). Urban Youth Academy. Retrieved from http://mlb.mlb.com/community/uya.jsp

National Geographic. (2017). X Games. Retrieved from https://www.nationalgeographic.org/encyclopedia/x-games/

NCS4. (2018). Professional development. Retrieved from https://www.ncs4.com/professionaldevportal/certifications/csvs

NFL Flag. (2017). Home page. Retrieved from https://www.nflflag.com/home/index

Octagon. (2017). About us. Retrieved from http://www.octagon.com/about

Prairie, M., & Garfield, T. (2004). Preventive law for schools and colleges. San Diego, CA: School & College Law Press.

Project Insight. (2017). 5 basic phases of project management. Retrieved from http://www.projectinsight.net/project-management-basics/basic-project-management-phases

Rath, J. (2017, January 24). Tough Mudder is generating $100 million in revenue and is about to launch a TV show—here's how it began. Business Insider. Retrieved from http://www.businessinsider.com/how-tough-mudder-went-from-harvard-business-to-tv-show-on-sky-and-cbs-2017-1/#-1

Red Bull's success in sponsorship, marketing and branded content. (2017). Puzzle Sport. http://puzzlelondonsport.com/red-bulls-success-sponsorship/

Redmandarin. (2012). Olympic partner consultancy. Retrieved from http://www.redmandarin.com/redmandarin/services/olympic-partner-consultancy

Schaaf, P. (1995). Sports marketing: It's not just a game anymore. New York, NY: Prometheus Books.

Simson, V., & Jennings, A. (1992). Dishonored games: Corruption, money and greed at the Olympics. New York, NY: S.P.I. Books.

Susan G. Komen for the Cure. (2017a). About the race. Retrieved from https://ww5.komen.org/raceforthecure/#RFTC_AboutRace

Susan G. Komen for the Cure. (2017b). Our people and teams. Retrieved from http://ww5.komen.org/AboutUs/OurPeople.html

Sutton, W. A. (2010, May 10–16). Using technology to build ticket database can boost bottom line. Street & Smith's SportsBusiness Journal, p. 11.

TEAMS. (2017). About us. Retrieved from http://teamsconference.com/about/

Tough Mudder. (2017). Tough Mudder by the numbers. Retrieved from https://toughmudder.com/press-room/

Turnkey Sports & Entertainment. (2017). Retrieved from http://turnkeyse.com/

V Foundation. (2017). Our story. Retrieved from https://www.jimmyv.org/about/our-story/

Walton, B. (2017, March 4). Asheville spared amid NC sports boycott over HB2. Citizen-Times. Retrieved from https://www.citizen-times.com/story/news/local/2017/03/04/asheville-spared-amid-nc-sports-boycott-over-hb2/98493690/

Woodward, S. (2003, May 26). IOC does a 180, buys Meridian agency in move to take marketing in-house. Street & Smith's SportsBusiness Journal, p. 5.

Chapter 14

Stephen McKelvey

Sport Sales

© Shutterstock, Inc. / Danilo_Vuletic

Learning Objectives

Upon completion of this chapter, students should be able to:

1. Recognize that there are more entry-level job opportunities in sales than any other segment of the sport industry.

2. Evaluate the relative importance of the factors that influence the sport consumer's purchase decision: quality, quantity, time, and cost.

3. Apply the concept of customer relationship management to the sales process.

4. Identify traditional sales methods such as direct mail, telemarketing, and personal face-to-face selling; explain the advantages and disadvantages of each; and describe how industry trends have shaped each.

5. Discuss the growing impact of technology and digital and social media on the sales process.

6. Apply the techniques of benefit selling, up-selling, eduselling, and aftermarketing to the personal selling process.

7. Evaluate the key skills that make for a good salesperson.

8. Distinguish between the various items in a typical sport organization's sales inventory, including tickets, premium hospitality, TV/radio advertising, signage, naming rights, promotions, community programs, digital and social media assets, and sponsorships.

9. Recognize that regardless of your occupation, you will always be selling yourself and your ideas, so selling is an integral part of your career growth and success within the sport industry.

Introduction

Few, if any, avenues within the sport industry hold more job opportunities, particularly at the entry level, than sales. Chances are, many of you reading these words now are already sufficiently discouraged: Sales?! However, as you read on within this chapter, you will begin to realize three important things about sales. First, sales is the lifeblood of any sport organization. Whether it is season ticket packages, in-venue signage, advertising spots on the team's local radio broadcasts, print advertisements in the game-day magazine, online advertising, or multiyear sponsorship deals, the sales function accounts for the vast amount of revenues for any sport organization or team. Those who can learn to master the art and science of selling become invaluable, and often irreplaceable, assets to their organizations.

Second, sales can be fun! Contrary to popular notions, successful salespeople are not born; they are developed through training, experience, and enthusiasm. Sales involves interacting and communicating with other people—typically people who are predisposed to like and even admire your product or service. The successful salesperson wakes up each morning not bemoaning sales as a drudgery, but enthusiastic about the opportunity to help meet the wants and needs of his or her potential customers!

Third, regardless of your job in the industry, it will entail some element of sales. Baseball executive Mike Veeck, the son of the legendary founder of sport promotion, Bill Veeck, provides a quote that he attributes to "17,325 failed potential major-minor league executives": "Oh, I love marketing. But you won't catch me selling. It's just not something I do" (Irwin, Sutton, & McCarthy, 2008, p. ix). The point of Veeck's quote is that whether you are employed in the marketing department, the public relations department, or the operations department, you will always be selling—selling yourself and selling your ideas!

Regardless of the sport, organizations—from the major professional leagues and colleges/universities to sport broadcasting companies and teams at the lowest rungs of the minors—are being challenged daily to better utilize traditional sales methodologies, employ innovative sales tactics, create new inventory, and discover new ways of packaging their sales inventory to provide not only new revenues to the organization, but also longer-term value to their customers.

In today's world, consumers have more and more options for spending their discretionary entertainment dollars, and companies have more and more options for investing their advertising and sponsorship dollars. In this competitive environment, how do sport organizations use the sales process to attract and retain consumers? What do sport organizations have to sell? Which methodologies do they use to sell it? What does it take to be a successful salesperson in sport? In exploring the evolving world of sport sales, this chapter provides an introduction to the range of sales approaches and methodologies that sport organizations are embracing in the increasingly competitive sport marketplace. Among them is a shift in emphasis from product-oriented to consumer-oriented sales and recognition of the importance of building long-term relationships with customers. But first, it is important to understand how we arrived at this point.

History

As sport management as a discipline has become more sophisticated, so too, has the sales process within sport. What was once viewed as a form of "hucksterism"—one-size-fits-all ticket packages and short-term gimmicks to "put fannies in seats"—has evolved into a dynamic discipline. Historically, sport sales consisted of simple tactics such as handing out season ticket brochures or mailing out simple two-page proposals listing a range of advertising and sponsorship options that could be purchased by companies. As noted by Mullin, Hardy, and Sutton (2007), sport marketing, including the sales function, has historically fallen victim to an array of "marketing myopias," defined as "a lack of foresight in marketing ventures" (p. 12). However, today's leading-edge sales departments have adopted the following "truisms" with regard to the sales function:

- A winning team can certainly be a selling advantage; however, a sales staff needs to be trained and prepared to sell either a winning team *or* a losing team.
- The major emphasis should be on identifying and satisfying consumers' wants and needs instead of focusing simply on selling the sport organization's goods and services.
- A priority needs to be placed on the collection and effective use of customer data. This includes initiatives to seek to identify each and every consumer who attends the sport organization's events, an initiative made easier by the advent of digital (or paperless) ticketing. Digital ticketing serves several valuable functions for the sport organization, including helping to eliminate waste and fraud, as well as streamlining fan entry into stadiums. However, perhaps most important for the sales force, digital ticketing not only helps to identify each and every fan who attends the event, but also can create a wealth of data on consumer behavior and preferences (Fisher, 2012).
- Simply standing on street corners and handing out free tickets to a sporting event sends a distinct message to fans about the perceived quality of the product: *If it's free, it can't be worth all that much.* The strategic and controlled distribution of complimentary tickets can, however, have positive returns when, for instance, they are offered to sales prospects as a means of allowing them to "sample" the product. In another instance, although distributing blocks of "complimentary" tickets to charity groups is one exception to this "freebie" caveat, the most effective means of doing this is to secure a local business to underwrite the cost of these tickets and distribute them as part of a community goodwill initiative.
- Success begins with an organizational commitment to the disciplined hiring, ongoing training, motivating, and evaluating of each and every salesperson, premised on an understanding that the first line of interaction and communication between the sport organization and its potential customers is typically the entry-level salesperson making the initial phone calls and selling tickets at the ticket window. One example of this is Major League Soccer (MLS), which in 2010 launched the first-ever league-wide ticket sales training center in Minnesota (Mickle, 2010). The MLS National Sales Center provides a 45-day curriculum designed to train beginners in ticket sales in preparation for them to then join an MLS team and is a model that other sport leagues should consider implementing. Since its inception, the training center has placed more than 200 graduates with 22 different MLS teams (MLS National Sales Center, 2017).

The ever-increasing competition for consumers' discretionary dollars, the influx of professionally trained sport marketers, and the continued evolution of sport management and marketing as a scientific discipline have gradually eradicated many of the myopias associated with the sales discipline. This has resulted in a much higher level of sophistication and understanding of the sales process and its importance to the overall success of any sport organization. As you read on, you will hear more about how sport organizations are changing their attitudes toward sales as well as enhancing their ability to succeed in selling in an increasingly competitive environment through the use of new technologies and creative innovation.

Sales in the Sport Setting

Sales is the revenue-producing arm of a sport organization. It has been defined as "the process of moving goods and services from the hands of those who produce them into the hands of those who will benefit most from their use" (Mullin, Hardy, & Sutton, 2014, p. 183). Any discussion of sport sales might best begin with Mark McCormack, the industry-proclaimed "founder of sport marketing" who built IMG (formerly International Management Group) into one of the world's premier sport management conglomerates. McCormack (1996) explained that selling consists of four ingredients: (1) the process of identifying customers, (2) getting through to them, (3) increasing their awareness and interest in your product or service, and (4) persuading them to act on that interest.

As suggested by Honebein (1997), sales can also be viewed as "customer performance: When a customer purchases your product, he or she performs the act of buying" (p. 25). As Mullin, Hardy, and Sutton (2014) further elaborate, four main factors cause sport consumers to purchase (or not purchase) a sport organization's product or service:

- *Quality:* Teams' win–loss records are one obvious example of identifying the quality of the product or service and influencing consumers' purchase-behavior decisions.
- *Quantity:* An individual might wish to purchase only an eight-game ticket plan from a National Basketball Association (NBA)

team rather than a full-season ticket package, so the numbers (the units) in which the product is sold can become an influencing factor.

- *Time:* Family obligations, work schedules, and everyday life can dictate whether the consumer has the time to consume the product. For instance, to make a season ticket purchase worthwhile, the individual must have the time available to attend the majority, if not all, of the team's home games.
- *Cost:* Each year, *Team Marketing Report (TMR)*, an industry trade publication, publishes a Fan Cost Index (FCI). The FCI measures the cost of taking a family of four to a game for each of the major professional sport leagues; it includes not just the cost of tickets but also the other costs that consumers are likely to incur, including the average cost of parking, concessions, and souvenirs. For instance, the average cost of tickets for a family of four to attend a Major League Baseball (MLB) game in 2016 was $216, with the Boston Red Sox having the highest FCI ($360) and the Arizona DiamondBacks the lowest ($312) (Shea, 2016). Thus, the price of game tickets is just part of the equation that influences consumers' purchase decisions. In addition to direct out-of-pocket expenses, the concept of cost encompasses such aspects as payment options, value received for the purchase price, and the investment of time required to attend the event.

One element that distinguishes sport sales from the selling of other traditional consumer products or services such as cereal or mobile phone services is the presence of emotion (Mullin et al., 2007). The emotion inherent in sport adds a special excitement to the sales process. Think about it: Would you rather work the phones calling Boston residents to sell them a new credit card or to sell them Red Sox tickets?

Sales Strategies and Methods

Innovation in the sales process and methodologies within the sport industry have often lagged behind those in other service industries, due in part to the myopias described earlier in this chapter. However, in recent years, certain innovative sales methodologies have begun to be more widely utilized throughout the sport industry. Historically, sport organizations communicated with customers once it was time to "renew the order." With the increased competition for the loyalties of the sport consumer, organizations have recognized the need to expand and enrich their relationships with current and potential customers. This section provides an overview of the methodologies and terminology that have become the linchpins of the sales process in the sport industry today.

Two of the most critical determinants of success of a sales department are (1) the ability to accurately identify and understand the needs of potential and current customers and (2) the ability to maximize the generation of sales leads. One key to achieving these objectives is through the maintenance of a **customer relationship management (CRM)** system that enables the sport organization to build and utilize a database of demographic (e.g., age, gender, education level, occupation, and ethnicity) and psychographic (e.g., motivations, interests, and opinions) information, as well as past purchase behaviors, for existing and potential customers. CRM systems enable sales departments to more effectively and efficiently segment their various target markets. Most sport organizations use Microsoft Dynamics or SalesForce to manage their databases. In addition to sales reps logging information and tracking touch points with current and potential clients, teams can purchase data to fill in profiles, track purchase history, log benefits, track scan/usage rates, and connect contacts to show relationships between accounts. In addition, teams typically survey their season ticket holders twice a year to fill in missing information.

The evolution of data analytics has dramatically changed the landscape of sport sales over the past decade. One of the earliest data-capturing products designed for sport sales departments was Archtics, a Ticketmaster product enabling teams to consolidate their sales and marketing operations into a single operating suite. More recently, Veritix introduced a paperless ticketing product called Flash Seats that enables customers to enter the stadium or arena via an encrypted code that can be placed on a driver's license, credit card, or other form of identification. "What I have loved about this product . . . is the data-capture ability that enables the venue or the team to know the identity of every person in the building on any given night," said Bill Sutton, a leading sport industry sales expert. "The value of the data for future marketing and sales efforts along with cross-promotional opportunities is a significant revenue opportunity" (Sutton, 2010, p. 11). Today, teams excelling in sales at the highest professional levels complement their CRM and ticketing systems with third-party services such as SSB Central Intelligence and SAP, which pull additional data into the team's ecosystem.

Another relatively new technology is a program called Prospector, an online data enhancement platform designed by Turnkey Intelligence (Sutton, 2010). Licensed by more than 220 teams, colleges and live events, Prospector enables properties to easily manage all critical data processes—hygiene, de-duping, append purchasing, record completion, list buying, lead scoring, and more—in a single location. This platform is integrated with the industry's major ticketing platforms (Ticketmaster/Archtics, Tickets.com, Paciolan) and CRM systems (MSCRM, SalesForce.com), further simplifying its use: Data can flow from those systems to Prospector, and vice versa, with the click of a button.

Prospector's roots are in lead scoring—that is, using custom-built models to identify a lead's likelihood to purchase a particular ticket package from a particular team. Lead scoring is important because it increases sales efficiency: By identifying the best leads, and then calling them first (and spending more time and resources trying to close them), more money will come in the door more quickly. Prospector also offers comprehensive reporting functionality, which helps sales managers identify reps' strengths and weaknesses (for example, one rep may have higher close rates when selling to working parents; another may do better selling to people who are new to the area), and then assign leads based on that knowledge.

Sport organizations utilize their CRM systems to generate sales through three primary methods: direct mail, "inside sales" (which has increasingly replaced the old concept of "telemarketing"), and in-person face-to-face selling. **Direct (e)mail** communications are a staple within the sport sales business, and not surprisingly the bulk of these communications are now electronically delivered via email and smartphones. As suggested by Mullin, Hardy, and Sutton (2014), the major advantage of using direct mail campaigns is that they can be targeted to only those people the organization seeks to reach, thereby minimizing the expense of circulating a sales offer to individuals who would have little interest in it. Organizations often promote season tickets, partial season ticket plans, and single-game tickets through direct mail campaigns. Furthermore, because they can easily measure the effectiveness of direct mail, organizations can devise and test a variety of sales offers to better ensure the success of future direct mail initiatives. Of course, one potential drawback of the direct mail approach is that, unlike with phone calls and in-person face-to-face selling (discussed later in this section), direct mail solicitations typically do not provide an opportunity to verbally explain the sales offer, counteract objections, or answer questions. Thus, the organization must clearly communicate the sales offer so that it is easily understood by the recipient.

Although it has been a staple throughout the history of sport sales, the word "telemarketing" has today taken on the negative connotation of salespeople simply trained to call random people and read from a script while "dialing for dollars." The evolution of the sport sales process, coupled with the ever-increasing sophistication and accessibility of CRM systems, has completely changed the nature of **telemarketing** within sport organizations. Today, the model for selling full- and partial season ticket packages looks much different. The majority of teams, especially within the major professional sport leagues, engage in **inside sales**, which typically involves a 9- to 12-month sales training program that focuses on taking people with little or no sales experience and training them in professional development and sales strategies. These young sales professionals are trained to become effective listeners, and to best meet the specific needs of the customer. More and more teams, however, are realizing that the initial "introductory" phone call is merely the start of the sales process. Most teams train their sales representatives to use the phone only as a starting point to gather information about a prospect. To close the sale, they may meet in person with the prospect or, better yet, invite the prospect for an appointment at the arena or stadium (King, 2010). "People aren't going to make purchases over the phone anymore," predicts Diamondbacks CEO Derrick Hall. "They're not going to commit. We've got to get them here [to the stadium for a tour] and then we have success" (King, 2010, p. 1).

Personal selling consists of face-to-face, in-person selling and typically incorporates use of the sport organization's CRM system. Although personal selling can be more costly and time-consuming than direct mail and "inside sales" campaigns, the process of in-person selling can

© Monkey Business Images/Shutterstock, Inc.

to introduce a macro trend that is beginning to shape the sport ticket sales landscape: the **membership model**. More and more professional sport teams, as well as colleges and universities, have begun replacing their traditional season ticket plan with a "membership program." The purpose is two-fold: (1) to alter fans' perspective on the commitment they are making and (2) to provide benefits designed to engage fans on an year-round basis, so that season tickets are supplemented by other benefits such as experiential awards, exclusive merchandise, and, in some cases, even the ability to vote on franchise initiatives (Fisher, 2016). "Instead of a fan or company purchasing 41 or 81 games, they are purchasing something that feels more like a gym membership," said Michelle Price, a ticket sales executive with the Washington Nationals. "Your gym membership gives you access to the gym every day but you may only go three times per week. In sports, a membership gives you access to the seats, but also to other year-round benefits and 'once in a lifetime' experiences" (M. Price, email interview, April 15, 2017).

Benefit Selling

What should a sport organization do when the product or service package it is selling doesn't meet the specific wants or needs of a consumer? One approach, called **benefit selling**, "involves the promotion and creation of new benefits or the promotion and enhancement of existing benefits to offset existing perceptions or assumed negatives related to the sport product or service" (Irwin et al., 2008, p. 107). The first step in benefit selling is to understand which objections customers have to your product or service, and why. This information can be obtained through customer surveys and focus groups. Once benefits have been identified, they must be publicized and must be judged by the consumer to have worth or value.

The concept of the *flex book* is one example of benefit selling in action (Irwin et al., 2008).

be more precise, enabling sales executives to more closely target the most promising prospects and build personal relationships with those prospects. Personal selling is also essential for successfully selling higher-priced inventory such as luxury suites and sponsorship packages, because these items involve a greater financial investment by the prospective customer. It is rare, indeed, that a company would ever purchase a team sponsorship package over the phone!

As the race to obtain—and retain—the business and loyalties of both consumers and corporations has intensified over the past decade, successful sport organizations have adopted proactive sales approaches, or philosophies, that are premised on the concept of relationship marketing. These include benefit selling, up-selling, eduselling, and aftermarketing. Each of these concepts is introduced in the following section, but before doing so, it is important

This concept arose in response to the frequent objection by potential customers, when being pitched partial season ticket plans, that they were not able to commit to a certain number of games on specific dates well in advance of the season. Flex books (also called *fan flex plans*) contain undated coupons for a specified number of games that can be redeemed for any games of the customers' choosing (subject to seating availability). It is an example of creating a new benefit to offset existing perceptions or assumed negatives related to the sport product or service. Another increasingly popular example is *open houses*, in which teams allow potential consumers into their venues to get a feel for the "experience" and the benefits associated with it. Another benefit that teams have made a staple of their season ticket plans are online ticket exchange programs that help ensure that tickets are not wasted when a fan cannot make a particular game within her season ticket package.

Up-Selling

Successful sport organizations are never satisfied with simply renewing a customer at his or her current level of involvement. By effectively managing and maintaining their CRM system and by embracing the sales philosophies of relationship selling and aftermarketing, sales personnel should be well positioned to up-sell current customers. When it comes to tickets, the idea of **up-selling** corresponds to the "escalator concept," whereby sport organizations are continually striving to move customers up the escalator from purchasing single-game tickets to purchasing mini-ticket plans, and then to full-season ticket packages (Mullin et al., 2014). For those involved in sponsorship sales, the goal should always be to increase, over time, the company's involvement with the sport organization. Relationship selling and aftermarketing put the salesperson in an advantageous position when it comes time to renew and up-sell a client.

Eduselling

At this point, one thing should be clear to you, the reader and future sales executive: *The customer rules!* Product- or service-focused sales activities that emphasize the product (its benefits, quality, features, and reputation) or the sport organization itself have been replaced by the mantra of customer-focused selling that stresses the needs and requirements of the customer (Irwin et al., 2008). A salesperson engaged in customer-focused selling views himself or herself as a consultant to the prospective customers, helping to provide them with a *solution*, rather than simply trying to convince them to purchase a product or service they may not want or need.

Irwin and colleagues (2008) specifically describe the importance of eduselling in the context of selling corporate sponsorships; they define **eduselling** as "an instructive process that continually and systematically supplies information and assistance to the prospective sponsorship decision maker in order to enhance product knowledge, facilitate understanding of product benefits, and establish a sense of partnership between rights holder and buyer" (p. 175). Eduselling is more than just educating a customer before the sale, or providing short-term service after the sale. Rather, it is a continual process that involves the sales staff monitoring consumer utilization and satisfaction through regular communication. Through this monitoring process, the sport organization is able to ensure that the product or service is being utilized properly. By ensuring the product is being utilized properly and to its fullest extent, the sales staff is able to maximize customer satisfaction and ultimately the lifetime value of the client.

One way a salesperson engages in eduselling is by proactively assisting customers in developing ways to better utilize and leverage their investment with the organization. For instance, more and more teams are providing corporate season ticket holders with something as simple as an online planner that allows the company to more easily keep track of who has use of which tickets for which games. Other teams are providing a means for season ticket holders to seamlessly and electronically forward unused tickets to worthy local charities, through which the company can derive some goodwill. Tactics such as these are aimed at helping to make sure that the season tickets don't end up buried in a desk drawer, unused—a scenario that would make the season ticket renewal process quite difficult.

Furthermore, sport organizations committed to eduselling will themselves develop promotional ideas showing how their sponsors can utilize the team's game tickets and other merchandise to help generate new business opportunities and sales. Remaining in constant communication with customers, and displaying a vested interest in achieving customers' business goals, helps ensure that both parties, if they live up to their commitments, will benefit from the relationship in both the short term and the long term.

Aftermarketing

As competition for customers has intensified and the emphasis has shifted from acquiring customers to *retaining* them, the ability to provide consistent high-quality service has been recognized as a source of competitive advantage for sport organizations. **Aftermarketing**, defined by Vavra (1992) as "the process of providing continued satisfaction and reinforcement to individuals or organizations who are past or current customers" (p. 22), is a critical consideration because of the significant competition for the sport consumer's entertainment dollars. Think of "aftermarketing" as the academic term for **retention marketing**. That is, it has become critical for sport organizations to have an aggressive plan for retaining their market share of fans. From a practical business standpoint, aftermarketing serves to encourage an organization to view a season ticket holder not as a one-time $3,000 customer, but, based on a potential span of 10 years, as a

$30,000 client. Mullin and colleagues (2007) have referred to the concept of viewing customers as an organizational asset as "lifetime value" (LTV) (p. 309). Through this lens, every single season ticket holder becomes much more worthy of cherishing! "It's all about relationships," said Mullin. "If you didn't build the relationship with a sponsor or season-ticket holder or fan back when things were good, it's very hard to all of a sudden do it now" (King, 2010, p. 1).

Toward this end, it has become more the norm than the exception that teams have split their sales department into those responsible for selling new accounts and those responsible for "client retention." The latter typically consists of a staff of 5 to 12 representatives who are charged with retaining and growing relationships with existing accounts. These departments are filled with strong relationship sellers who are aggressive referral seekers, as opposed to the "hunters" who thrive on the adrenalin of ferreting out and tracking down entirely new clients.

Given the fact that it takes exponentially more money and human resources to get *new* customers onto the frequency escalator than it takes to retain current customers, successful sport sales organizations have also embraced the importance of customer service as a critical component of the sales process. The goal of providing exceedingly superior customer service should permeate the sales culture of a sport organization. A successful customer service program includes the following elements (the following list is adapted from a professional team sport organization):

- Personal calls by sales account reps to 50 season ticket holders per week.
- Emails to 50 season ticket holders per week.
- Personal notes to 25 season ticket holders per week.
- Direct-dial phone numbers and email addresses given to each season ticket holder for contacting his or her personal service representative.

- In-seat visits by sales account reps during home games.
- Maintenance of a customer sales and service booth in the arena that is staffed by sales and service team members.
- Invitations to attend "Fan Forums" with the team's general manager and its president.
- A handbook or manual sent to season ticket holders describing the goals and values of the team's sport product.
- A complimentary team magazine sent to season ticket holders and fans on the season ticket holder waiting list.
- Advance sale opportunities for season ticket holders for other nonsporting events held at the team's facility (e.g., concerts).
- Special events for season ticket holders (e.g., an opportunity for them to visit the team locker rooms or practice on the team's court and field).
- Automated phone calls from players and team front office personnel to season ticket holders identified in the team's database.
- A holiday card from the team with a redemption coupon for a gift, such as a team cap.

Beyond keeping current customers happy, this kind of comprehensive customer service program has the added benefit of spurring referrals of new customers.

Finally, teams should continually encourage feedback on customer satisfaction through regular customer surveys, online polls, monitoring of chat rooms, and focus groups. All comments and feedback should be logged on individual accounts in the CRM system to enable the sales staff to track patterns and uncover opportunities to improve service.

Ticket Sales and Social Media

Social media channels have become an increasingly effective tool for sport organizations to enhance their ticket sales revenues. Today, sales representatives routinely use both the team and their own personal social media accounts not only to connect and engage with current customers by sharing news, posting videos, and hosting contests, but also to prospect for new customers via platforms including Facebook, Twitter, and LinkedIn. The benefit of such social media–driven campaigns is that they enable sport organizations to keep their products readily accessible on a computer, smartphone, or iPad. The increasing reliance on social media in the sales process has also created many new entry-level sales positions for those who are particularly savvy in the use of social media.

Key Skills: What Makes a Good Salesperson?

It is the rare person who is truly "born to sell." It takes a certain degree of confidence to pick up the phone and cold-call strangers to interest them in purchasing season tickets or an Internet advertising package. If you are engaged in personal selling, it takes a certain degree of courage to knock on a company door, ask yourself in, and pitch a group sales or sponsorship package. More often than not, successful salespeople develop their skills through training, trial and error, and experience.

Mark McCormack (1984), a salesman who mastered his craft by selling clients such as Arnold Palmer, Jack Nicklaus, and Tiger Woods to corporate America, has stated:

> Effective selling is directly tied to timing, patience, and persistence—and to sensitivity to the situation and the person with whom you are dealing. An awareness of when you are imposing can be the most important asset a salesman can have. It also helps to believe in your product. When I feel that what I am selling is really right for someone, that it simply makes sense for this particular customer, I never feel I am imposing. I think that I am doing him a favor (p 92).

The following is a "Top 10 Rules for Successful Selling" list that incorporates McCormack's sage advice (McCormack, 1996) in addition to experience gleaned by this author during 15 years in the sport sales business:

1. *Laugh.* It never hurts to have a sense of humor. Remember, sport is entertainment!

2. *Use a commonsense fit.* Make sure that what you are selling makes sense for your prospective customer. Never try to shoehorn inventory down a prospect's throat.

3. *Wear Teflon.* The most successful salespeople believe that being told "no" is the *start* of the sales process; they don't take rejection personally, and they accept it as a challenge. (Beware, however, of rule 2!)

4. *Know the prospect.* There's an old adage: Knowledge is power. Undertake to know as much as you can about the sales prospect *before* making the initial sales call. If you're calling on an individual, does your CRM system show that he or she has attended games in the past? If you're pitching a local company for sponsorship, do you know if that company is currently sponsoring other sport properties? Is the person you're going to meet with a sport fan? Find out in advance (ask his or her assistant). Knowing that information, alone, can make the sales process easier.

5. *Pump up the volume.* Sales is a numbers business. As a rule of thumb, 10 phone calls to solicit a meeting may result in 1 actual sales call. For every 10 meetings, you might get 1 sales nibble. Sales is about volume—making a lot of calls and seeing a lot of people (see rule 3).

6. *Knock on old doors.* Don't abandon potential customers just because they turned you down the first time. Individual consumers' interests and financial circumstances change, as do companies' business strategies and personnel—and when they do, you don't want to be a stranger. Be polite, but persistent.

7. *Consult, don't sell.* Successful salespeople seek to learn potential customers' wants and needs, and then work with them to find solutions that are mutually beneficial. They let the sale come to them.

8. *Listen!* Perhaps the best skill a salesperson can develop is the art of listening. If you ask, prospective customers will always provide clues that open avenues toward an agreement, if not today, then somewhere down the road (see rule 6). Good listeners pick up on these clues.

9. *Have two kinds of belief.* Successful salespeople have an unwavering belief in what they are selling and in themselves.

10. *Ask for the order.* This sounds self-explanatory, but closing the sale is one of the toughest steps to successful selling. You will never know if a potential customer wants to buy your product until you ask!

Sales Inventory

Because sales is the lifeblood of a sport organization, for many people a position in sales is often the first step into the industry. **Sales inventory** is "the products available to the sales staff to market, promote and sell through [the] sales methodologies" discussed earlier (Mullin et al., 2014, p. 189). Sport organizations have a broad range of sales inventories, each of which entails different sales methodologies as well as levels of sales experience. The typical front office of a team sport organization includes sales management positions ranging from vice president to director to manager, overseeing the sale of a variety of sales inventory including season ticket sales, group sales, advertising sales (print, broadcast, and Internet), sponsorship sales, and luxury suite/premium seating sales. It is important to note, as we review the sales inventory of a typical sport organization in this section, that many of the inventory items discussed are often packaged together when being presented to a company (Mullin et al., 2014).

Tickets and Premium Inventory

People traditionally get their start in the industry in the ticket sales department, first staffing the ticket booth and then advancing up the sales ladder to group sales and partial- or full-season ticket plans. Mullin and colleagues (2014) describe the game ticket inventory as a "club sandwich" (p. 209) consisting, from the bottom up, of community promotional tickets, tickets bought through day-of-game "walk-up" sales, advance sales, group tickets, and partial plans, topped off by full-season tickets. The authors suggest the "recipe" in **Table 14-1** for a good-tasting and profitable "club sandwich" through which to maximize ticket sales revenue (Mullin et al., 2014, p. 209).

Although historically the "sizzle" in sport sales was in selling sponsorships and advertising, sport organizations have come to realize that the "steak" is in ticket sales. As the lifeblood of most franchises, sales from tickets and club seats make up more than half of a typical franchise's local revenue in all of the four major sport leagues, ranging as high as 80% for some teams (King, 2010). Bernie Mullin, former CEO of the NBA Atlanta Hawks and National Hockey League (NHL)

Thrashers and senior vice president of team marketing for the NBA, described how resources from teams were traditionally pumped into sponsorship sales and services, even though most of the teams' locally generated revenues were coming from ticket sales. This has since changed as teams have recognized the economic realities of ticket sales. Ticket sales have become a more sophisticated endeavor; in turn, by utilizing technology and other ticket sales strategies, teams have begun to do a much better job in the ticket sales arena.

Sport organizations' continued emphasis on customer accommodation and hospitality has expanded the sales inventory over the past decade to include club seats (with personal waiter service), luxury suites complete with catered food and beverage service, private seat licenses (PSLs), and VIP parking, among other perks.

Advertising Inventory

Advertising inventory includes both electronic and print inventory. Electronic advertising inventory includes television, radio, and team websites. Although most sport organizations still sell their local broadcast rights to media outlets (called *rightsholders*) in exchange for an annual rights fee, some teams have brought their television or radio rights, or both, in-house. Although in this latter situation the team bears the production costs of its broadcasts, it also has the opportunity to retain all of the advertising sales revenues. The New York Yankees provides an example of a team willing to bear this risk, having taken control of its television broadcasts through the creation of the YES Network and the hiring of its own in-house sales staff to sell the advertising inventory. Print inventory includes advertising in game programs, media guides, and newsletters as well as on ticket backs, ticket envelopes, scorecards/roster sheets, and other items.

Signage Inventory

Signage inventory has traditionally been limited to dasherboards, scoreboards, outfield signs,

Table 14-1 Recipe for Maximizing Ticket Sales Revenue	
Ingredient	**Percentage of Customers**
Season ticket equivalencies (full and partial plans)	50–65%
Advance ticket sales	15–25%
Group sales	10–25%
Day-of-game/walk-up sales	5%

Reproduced from Mullin, B., Hardy, S., & Sutton, W.A. (2014). *Sport marketing* (4th ed.). Champaign, IL: Human Kinetics.

and concourses. However, the quest for new revenue streams has expanded the signage sales opportunities to include the playing surface itself, the turnstiles, the marquees outside the venue, and most recently player jerseys, among other locations.

Naming Rights

Naming rights provide a sport organization with the opportunity to sell the title of its arena or stadium, the practice facility, or the team itself. The corporate naming of stadiums and arenas has resulted in a significant new revenue stream for sport organizations. Witness, for example, the Golden State Warriors' deal in early 2016 with financial services giant JPMorgan Chase. Experts pegged the 20-year deal at $10 million per

year, making it the largest naming rights deal ever (Badenhausen, 2016). Just to provide some historical perspective on the astronomical growth of the naming rights business, the first major stadium naming-rights deals occurred in 1973, when Buffalo-based Rich Products inked a deal to pay $37.5 million over 25 years for the stadium used by the Buffalo Bills (that lump sum equates to $1.5 million per year). Four decades later, corporate names blanket sport venues. Entering 2016, only 19 of 122 teams in the four major U.S. sport leagues played in a facility without a corporate name (Quick, can you name five of them?). The top 13 most valuable U.S.-based sport facility naming rights deals, as of 2016, can be found in **Table 14-2**. College sport venues have become the ripest source of newfound

Table 14-2 Biggest U.S. Venue Naming-Rights Deals (as of January 2016)

Stadium	Team	Sponsor	Sponsor pays each year ($ million)
Citi Field	New York Mets	Citigroup	20
AT&T Stadium	Dallas Cowboys	AT&T	19
MetLife Stadium	New York Jets/Giants	MetLife	18
Hard Rock Stadium (formerly Sun Life Stadium)	Miami Dolphins	Hard Rock International	13.9
Mercedes-Benz Stadium	Atlanta Falcons	Mercedes-Benz	11.5
U.S. Bank Stadium	Minnesota Vikings	U.S. Bank	11
Levi's Stadium	San Francisco 49ers	Levi's	11
NRG Stadium (formerly Reliant Stadium)	Houston Texans	NRG Energy	10
Barclays Center	Brooklyn Nets/NY Islanders	Barclays Banks	10
SunTrust Park	Atlanta Braves	SunTrust Bank	10
Mercedes-Benz Superdome	Saints	Mercedes-Benz	10
Philips Arena	Atlanta Hawks	Royal Philips Electronics	9.25
Gillette Stadium	New England Patriots	Gillette	8

Data from Steinmetz, K. (2016, Oct. 14). America's 20 biggest stadium-naming deals. Money Talks News. Retrieved from https://www.msn.com/en-us/sports/more-sports/america%F2%80%99s-20-biggest-stadium-naming-deals/ss-AAiXcvT#image=1

Table 14-3 College Stadium Naming Rights Deals, Ranked by Average Annual Value

Facility	School	Sponsor	Cost (Years); Average Annual Value	Expiration
L.A. Memorial Coliseum*	University of Southern California	United Airlines	$70 million (15 years); $4.7 million	2031
Alaska Airlines Field at Husky Stadium	University of Washington	Alaska Airlines	$41 million (10 years); $4.1 million	2025
Kroger Field	University of Kentucky	Kroger	$22.2 million (12 years); $1.85 million	2028
TDECU Stadium	University of Houston	Texas Dow Employees Credit Union	$15 million (10 years); $1.5 million	2024
TCF Bank Stadium	University of Minnesota	TCF National Bank	$35 million (25 years); $1.4 million	2034
Apogee Stadium	University of North Texas	Apogee	$20 million (20 years); $1.0 million	2030
Spectrum Stadium	University of Central Florida	Charter Communications	$15 million (15 years); $1.0 million	2022
TD Ameritrade Park Omaha†	College World Series	TD Ameritrade	$15 million (15 years); $1.0 million	2022
UFCU Disch-Falk Field†	University of Texas	University Federal Credit Union	$13.1 million (15 years); $873,333	2021
Albertsons Stadium	Boise State University	Albertsons	$12.5 million (15 years); $833,333	2029

* Name to be determined.
† Baseball stadium.

Reproduced from Smith, M. & Ourand, J. (May 22, 2017). United Airlines grabs Coliseum naming rights. *SportsBusiness Journal*, p. 4. Retrieved from https://www.sportsbusinessdaily.com/Journal/Issues/2017/05/22/Marketing-and-Sponsorship/United.aspx

revenues for athletic departments, as well as the firms that specialize in the sales of stadium and arena naming rights (e.g., Scout Sports & Entertainment, Shamrock Sports & Entertainment, The Gemini Group, and Van Wagner Sports & Entertainment). **Table 14-3** lists college stadium naming rights deals ranked by average annual value.

Digital and Social Media Inventory

Websites hosted by sport organizations represent attractive platforms for companies to advertise the products and/or services they sell. Banner ads, blogs, instant messaging applications, and pop-up ads are all common online inventory that sport organizations can sell. The high traffic that many sport websites attract makes this online inventory both valuable and important for a sport organization's bottom line. Often online inventory (e.g., banner ads, company links) is included as an important value add in a larger sponsorship deal. Social media platforms have also spawned new inventory for salespeople in the form of assets such as "takeovers" (whereby a company can pay to take control of a team's Twitter account for a day) and access to the sport organization's mobile app advertising inventory.

Promotions Inventory

Promotions inventory ranges from premium giveaway items and on-floor/on-field promotions to videoboard promotions and pregame or postgame entertainment. Popular examples include sponsored "T-shirts blasts," in which team-logoed T-shirts are shot up into the stands by a specially designed, handheld cannon, and the fan-favorite sponsored "Dot Races" that appear between innings on the videoboard. Among the most popular types of sponsored postgame entertainment are fireworks displays.

Community Programs

Community programs offer a wealth of inventory for sport organizations to sell to local organizations, including, but not limited to, school assemblies, camps and clinics, awards and banquets, kick-off luncheons, and golf tournaments.

Miscellaneous Inventory

What is included in "miscellaneous" inventory is often up to the ingenuity and resourcefulness of the sport organization. It can include fantasy camps, off-season cruises with players, ballpark and locker room tours, and road trips. Sport organizations have become increasingly creative in developing new inventory and, in turn, generating new revenue streams by selling companies the opportunity to associate themselves with the sport organization's sanctioned events. For instance, many teams now conduct off-season "fanfests" involving interactive games and exhibits, which provide an entirely new source of sponsorship and advertising inventory.

Another type of miscellaneous inventory that is rapidly evolving within North America's major professional sport leagues is the opportunity to sell advertising on player jerseys. While corporate patches on jerseys have long been a staple in international sport leagues, this practice has been slow to take hold in the United States. The Women's National Basketball Association (WNBA) and MLS have taken the lead within North American sport leagues in introducing jersey patches. In a groundbreaking deal in advance of the WNBA's 20th anniversary season, the league announced a marquee partnership deal with Verizon in which that company's logo will appear on 10 of the 12 teams' jerseys (Lombardo, 2016). Given the tremendous new revenue potential for sales of corporate jersey patches, the other major leagues have begun to follow suit. For instance, in 2016, the NBA announced that it would allow its individual teams to sell corporate logos on its game jerseys (Rovell, 2016). In May 2017, the Cleveland Cavaliers became the fifth NBA team (joining the Utah Jazz, Boston Celtics, Philadelphia 76ers, and Brooklyn Nets) to secure a jersey advertiser, inking a multiyear deal with Goodyear (Boone, 2017).

Sponsorships

Of all the inventory that a sport organization has available to sell, sponsorships often are the most involved and time consuming. Before even presenting a sponsorship proposal, the property must do extensive homework on the targeted company. Who is the decision maker? Who are its competitors? What have the company and its competitors done in the past in the area of sport sponsorship? Based on this research, who are the company's primary customers and how does the sport organization's property or event deliver this audience? Is the company on solid financial ground? (After all, you don't want to sign a sponsor that either cannot afford to properly leverage its sponsorship or that may be out of business in a year!) What are some top-line promotional ideas that can reinforce the company's marketing objectives or its company slogan? Why would the targeted company be a good fit for the sport organization, and why would the company believe this?

Sponsorship packages typically incorporate some, if not all, of the various inventory described previously. The sponsorship sales process requires a great deal of up-front research, creativity, sales acumen, and patience, for several reasons. First, sponsorship packages often entail a much larger emotional and financial commitment on the part of the potential customer. Second, because of the many inventory elements typically included in sponsorship packages, they often require input, review, and sign-off by a number of departments within the company, including advertising, sales, promotions, and public relations. Third, because the company will want to fully utilize and effectively leverage its sponsorship, the process of selling sponsorship packages must allow the company sufficient lead time, particularly if the company needs to plan retail promotions.

For instance, if a company were interested in sponsoring its local National Football League (NFL) team, which begins play in September, the deal would ideally have to be completed by the prior April (at the latest!) to allow the company sufficient lead time to develop and begin to implement its sales promotion and advertising campaign by the start of the season. In short, it is much easier for an individual to decide to purchase a ticket package than it is for a corporation to decide to invest in a sponsorship package.

In selling sponsorship packages, Mullin and colleagues (2014) have suggested the following sales process:

1. Schedule a meeting with the sponsorship decision maker. Remember, don't accept a "no" from someone who is not empowered to say "yes."

2. At the first meeting, listen 80% of the time and sell only when you have to. You are there to observe and learn. Where does the potential sponsor spend its marketing dollars right now? What is working? What

isn't working? Which other sport organizations or events does the company sponsor or support? What does the company like or dislike about these relationships?

3. Arrange a follow-up meeting for the presentation of your proposal before leaving this initial meeting (ideally, within 1 week).

4. Create a marketing partnership proposal. Give the potential sponsor a promotional program that can be proprietary to that company. Act more like a marketing partner than a salesperson.

5. Present the proposal as a "draft" that you will gladly modify to meet the company's needs. Custom-tailored proposals are much more likely to succeed than generic proposals.

6. Negotiate the final deal and get a signed agreement. Close the deal when you have the opportunity—ask for the order! Be sure that the final signed deal has agreed-upon deliverables, payment terms, and mutually agreed-upon timetables.

Summary

The steadily increasing competition for customers—both individuals and corporate—has sparked changes in the sales methodologies used within the sport industry. Today, smart sport organizations build and manage well-trained sales staffs that are committed to the philosophy of customer-focused, long-term relationship building. If you choose to begin your sport management career with a team sport organization, as so many people do, chances are you will find yourself situated somewhere within the organization's sales department. In addition to actual sales positions, an increasing number of sport organizations are looking for students with the strong analytical skills needed to manage and mine the organization's customer relationship management system. Finally, as sport organizations further split their sales function from their customer retention function, opportunities exist for students to begin their careers within customer retention departments.

No matter what your specific role within the sales department, there may be no better place to begin! Sales are the lifeblood of any sport organization, and regardless of your career path—from ticket sales to suite sales to sponsorship sales and perhaps into other disciplines within a sport organization—you will always be selling. The tools, the training, and the experience garnered from responsibilities such as "inside sales"—a sport industry form of "paying one's dues"—can pay big dividends as you move up in your career.

An article entitled "The Changing Environment of Selling and Sales Management," although not specific to the sport industry, illuminates many of the challenges salespeople face today (Jones, Brown, Zoltners, & Weitz, 2005). For instance, potential and current customers today have higher expectations of salespeople; among other things, they expect salespeople will have a better understanding of and concern for their needs, be it soliciting a small business for a season-ticket package or attempting to sell a major corporation a multiyear sponsorship package. As such, sport organizations and their sales staffs need to become increasingly adept at customer-focused selling. Additionally, sales managers and salespeople are required to have much higher levels of technological aptitude, including, but not limited to, the willingness to adapt to technological advances and the ability to utilize selling tools ranging from CRM software to social media.

When asked to comment on the concerns and trends within the sport sales industry, a panel of sport industry executives expressed the difficulty they experienced in determining pricing of their product, because the sport industry still revolves around fans' emotional responses, including the popularity of a team, its players, and its owners. Social media and the understanding of its importance to fans is another trend impacting sport organizations ("Industry Insider: Sales Panel," 2011). In addition, the consumption of the sport product has rapidly evolved to include digital ticketing and various other ways to purchase a ticket. Brent Stehlik, Executive Vice President and Chief Revenue Office for the Cleveland Browns, observed:

> Tickets have become a commodity like wheat or copper; think about the secondary ticketing market and how many outlets there are to purchase a ticket to the same event. It's changed dramatically in the last 3, 5, and 10 years, as there are dozens of places you can go to purchase a ticket. How we can keep the lifeblood of our business (ticket sales) strong in the future is of the utmost importance.

Sport organizations need to constantly be aware of these changes, and respond accordingly so as to stay current with how their sport product is consumed.

As discussed throughout this chapter, many factors are fueling new levels of complexity and sophistication within the realm of sport sales. The constantly changing competitive environment for sport sales of everything from online advertising to season tickets to sponsorship provides many skills-enhancing challenges for those who decide to begin their career in sport sales.

Case Study 14-1

The Outsourcing of College Ticket Sales Operations

For decades, colleges and universities have relied upon the expertise of consulting companies to handle the sales and management of their licensing, sponsorship, and broadcasting rights. Firms such as Collegiate Licensing Company (now a division within IMG College), Licensing Resource Group (now operated under the umbrella of Learfield Licensing Partners), and the former Host Communications (subsequently purchased by IMG) were among the first major players when colleges and universities began **outsourcing** those rights as early as the 1970s. Today, the landscape has narrowed, through mergers and acquisitions, to encompass just a handful of firms specializing in the sale of licensing, media (local television, radio, and print), and sponsorship rights, including WME-IMG (IMG College), CBS College Sports, ESPN College, and Learfield. Typically, the same firm will handle both the media and sponsorship sales for an institution, since the two are so closely intertwined.

Outsourcing agreements typically provide the collegiate institution with some combination of a guaranteed annual cash rights fee payment and a percentage of revenues above a certain monetary threshold. In exchange, the firm secures the exclusive rights to represent the institution in the sales of its media and sponsorship rights. The more the firm can sell, the more financial upside it can realize. This sort of partnership has historically been viewed as a win–win relationship for both parties. The primary reason these outsourcing arrangements work so well is that, unlike in professional sports, the focus of colleges and universities is primarily on the educational, student-athlete enhancement mission. As a result, most intercollegiate athletic departments lack the personnel, resources, expertise, and corporate connections needed to successfully engage in the sale and management of licensing, media, and sponsorship rights.

While outsourcing of licensing, media, and sponsorship rights has become the norm in college athletics, the outsourcing of ticket marketing and sales is a relatively new phenomenon. From an historical perspective, in 2009, Georgia Tech University hired the Aspire Group, a newly formed Atlanta-based firm, to handle ticket marketing and sales for the university's football and men's basketball programs. It was the first arrangement by a major university to entirely outsource its ticket sales operation. The publicity surrounding the deal, coupled with the rapid growth of the Aspire Group, ushered in a new trend in the collegiate marketplace. Shortly thereafter, IMG created a new division, called IMG Ticket Solutions, to compete with the Aspire Group.

The decision of a college or university to outsource its ticket sales, or alternatively to build an in-house sales force, is influenced by three major factors. First, among all Football Bowl Subdivision (FBS) schools, the top source of revenues continues to be ticket sales (Popp, 2014). Second, only an extremely small percentage of collegiate programs routinely sell out their venues, suggesting that ticket sales represent the greatest potential for revenue growth when compared to sponsorship or media rights fees (Popp, 2014). Finally, particularly within college football, attendance has been declining (Rishe, 2015).

Many of the same factors that led colleges and universities to outsource their licensing, media, and sponsorship rights prompted the latest new trend of outsourcing ticket marketing and sales. However, in the case of outsourced ticket marketing and sales, a few additional factors are driving this trend. Many universities, and especially public universities, have difficulty funding the significant number of new full-time positions that labor-intensive, proactive, outbound phone sales demand. Further, the payment of commissions and bonuses to sales staff and sales managers is frequently prohibited by public colleges and universities. Finally, the staffs of college and university athletic departments have their time spread very thinly across a multitude of sports (both ticketed and nonticketed), making it difficult to allocate the time and resources necessary to recruit, train, and daily manage a full-fledged ticket sales staff.

Although ticket sales outsourcing is a relatively new concept, by 2017 more than 60 NCAA Division I programs had decided to outsource their ticket sales efforts to one of the two major players, the Aspire Group or IMG Ticket Solutions. Ironically, the overall increased focus on the ticket sales function within college athletics has also resulted in no less than 30 NCAA Division I programs developing their own in-house ticket sales departments. **Table 14-4** shows the sales results of collegiate institutions in the season before deciding to outsource their football ticket sales or to bring sales in-house, and the season following this decision.

The advantages and disadvantages with the in-house approach are obvious. On the one hand, the university is able to exert more influence on the sales team, enjoy a greater amount of flexibility, and retain *all* of the revenues generated through ticket sales. On the other hand, in-house sales teams are generally not as well trained and lack many of the resources available to third parties whose sole purpose is to advance their clients' sales operations, often making it exceedingly difficult to sell tickets during unsuccessful seasons or for low-demand games. Additionally, the art of ticket selling has become increasingly data and technology driven. Today, advanced analytics such as consumer demand modeling and CRM systems allow sales managers to intelligently predict demand and sales personnel to better understand the individual customer. These CRM systems, as well as the hiring of analytics-savvy individuals to effectively utilize them, are expensive propositions and can often be beyond the financial wherewithal of many college athletic departments.

(continues)

The Outsourcing of College Ticket Sales Operations (*Continued*)

Table 14-4 Football Ticket Sales for Colleges and Universities Before and After Outsourcing or Bringing Sales In-House

School	In-House/Vendor	Percent Increase	Football Team Record Prior	Football Team Record After
Akron	IMG Ticket Solutions	36.67%	1–11	1–11
Bowling Green	Collegiate Consulting & Hands-On Sports	14.9%	2–10	5–7
Florida International	Aspire Group	39.41%	7–6	8–5
Florida State	In-house	13.98%	7–6	10–4
Georgia Tech	Aspire Group	23.09%	9–4	11–3
Kansas State	In-house	5.86%	6–6	7–6
Louisiana State	In-house	10.59%	11–2	13–1
Maryland	Aspire Group	25.96%	9–4	2–10
North Carolina State	IMG Ticket Solutions	8.19%	7–6	3–9
South Florida	IMG Ticket Solutions	14.36%	5–7	3–9
University of Texas at El Paso	IMG Ticket Solutions	30.97%	5–7	3–9
Western Michigan	Aspire Group	30.31%	6–6	7–6

Reproduced from Popp, N. (2014, December 8). Ticket sales in college athletics. *Athletics Administration*. pp. 26–31.

Questions for Discussion

1. The outsourcing of licensing, media, and sponsorship rights is a business-to-business (B2B) operation. Firms such as Learfield and IMG College endeavor to find local, regional, and national businesses to buy media advertising and sponsorships. Selling tickets is, in contrast, primarily a business-to-consumer (B2C) endeavor. Assume you are the athletic director for a midsize Division I university. What would you see as some fundamental differences in and challenges to these two sales approaches?

2. Assume the same situation. Which concerns might you have about an outside firm selling tickets for your university from a sales call center in another location, perhaps even another state?

3. Assume you are the athletic director for a major Division I football powerhouse. Would you recommend that your athletic department outsource its ticket operations? Why or why not? Which factors would influence your decision?

Resources

The Aspire Group
404-389-9100
www.theaspiregroupinc.com

Gemini Group
480-513-7100
www.geminisports.net

IMG College
540 North Trade Street
Winston-Salem, NC 27101
336-831-0700
www.imgcollege.com

Learfield Licensing Partners
Offices in Indiana, Michigan,
North Carolina, and Iowa
www.learfieldlicensing.com

Major League Soccer National Sales Center
www.mlssoccer.com/nationalsalescenter

Scout Sports & Entertainment
www.horizonmedia.com/content_and
_experience/scout_sports_and
_entertainment_marketing

Shamrock Sports & Entertainment
215 Commercial Street, #200
Portland, ME 04101
207-899-0490
www.shamrockse.com

Turnkey Sports & Entertainment
9 Tanner Street
Haddonfield, NJ 08033
www.turnkeyse.com

Van Wagner Sports & Entertainment
212-699-8400
www.vanwagner.com

WME/IMG
11 Madison Avenue
New York, NY 10010
www.wmeimg.com

Key Terms

aftermarketing, benefit selling, customer relationship management (CRM), direct (e)mail, eduselling, inside sales, membership model, naming rights, outsourcing, personal selling, retention marketing, sales inventory, telemarketing, up-selling

References

Badenhausen, K. (2016, January 28). Warriors, Chase Bank tie-up ranks among biggest stadium naming rights deals ever. Retrieved from https://www.forbes.com/sites /kurtbadenhausen/2016/01/28/warriors -chase-tie-up-joins-ranks-of-biggest-stadium -naming-rights-deals/#11cb575855c0

Boone, K. (2017, May 15). Goodyear reportedly signs multiyear deal to be on jersey of Cleveland Cavaliers. Retrieved from http:// www.cbssports.com/nba/news/goodyear -reportedly-signs-multiyear-deal-to-be -on-jersey-of-cleveland-cavaliers/

Fisher, E. (2012, March 19). MLB FanPass to make paperless ticketing push. *Street & Smith's SportsBusiness Journal*, p. 1.

Fisher, E. (2016, September 19). Ticketing's wide "open" approach to sales. *SportsBusiness Journal*, p. 1.

Honebein, P. (1997). *Strategies for effective customer education.* Lincolnwood, IL: NTC Business Books.

Industry insider: Sales panel. (2011). *Sport Marketing Quarterly, 20*(2), 69–74.

Irwin, R., Sutton, W. A., & McCarthy, L. (2008). *Sport promotion and sales management* (2nd ed.). Champaign, IL: Human Kinetics.

Jones, E., Brown, S., Zoltners, A., & Weitz, B. (2005). The changing environment of selling and sales management. *Journal of Personal Selling & Sales Management, 25*(2), 105–111.

King, B. (2010, March 15). Always be closing. *Street & Smith's SportsBusiness Journal*, p. 1.

Lombardo, J. (2016, March 14). Verizon stakes out space on WNBA jerseys. *SportsBusiness Journal*, p. 3.

McCormack, M. (1984). *What they don't teach you at Harvard Business School*. New York, NY: Bantam.

McCormack, M. (1996). *On selling*. West Hollywood, CA: Dove Books.

Mickle, T. (2010, May 24). MLS will be first league to run extensive ticket sales training. *Street & Smith's SportsBusiness Journal*, p. 5.

MLS National Sales Center. (2017). Retrieved from http://www.mlsnationalsalescenter.com/

Mullin, B., Hardy, S., & Sutton, W. A. (2007). *Sport marketing* (3rd ed.). Champaign, IL: Human Kinetics.

Mullin, B., Hardy, S., & Sutton, W. A. (2014). *Sport marketing* (4th ed.). Champaign, IL: Human Kinetics.

Popp, N. (2014, December 8). Ticket sales in college athletics. *Athletics Administration*, 26-31.

Rishe, P. (2015, December 22). Examining the decline in college football attendances: Do remedies exist? Retrieved from https://www.forbes.com/sites/prishe/2015/12/22/examining-the-decline-in-college-football-attendances-do-remedies-exist/#2943a3917df4

Rovell, D. (2016, April 15). NBA approves on-jersey advertising program. Retrieved from http://www.espn.com/nba/story/_/id/15210151/nba-jerseys-carry-advertisements-beginning-2017-18

Shea, B. (2016, April 7). Tigers in middle of pack for fan-cost friendlessness. Retrieved from http://www.crainsdetroit.com/article/20160407/NEWS/160409873/tigers-in-middle-of-pack-for-fan-cost-friendliness

Smith, M., & Ourand, J. (2017, May 22). United Airlines grabs Coliseum naming rights. *SportsBusiness Journal*, p. 4.

Sutton, B. (2010, May 10). Using technology to build ticket database can boost bottom line. *Street & Smith's SportsBusiness Journal*, p. 11.

Vavra, T. G. (1992). *Aftermarketing: How to keep customers for life through relationship marketing*. New York, NY: Irwin.

Chapter

15

Stephen McKelvey

Sport Sponsorship

Learning Objectives

Upon completion of this chapter, students should be able to:

1. Discuss the reasons for the rapid growth of the sport sponsorship segment over the past three decades.

2. Explain why companies are eager to engage in sport sponsorship and the benefits that can accrue to sponsors.

3. Describe the effects that the commercial success of the 1984 Los Angeles Olympics had on the sport sponsorship industry.

4. Evaluate the role of sales promotion in sponsorship programs, with particular emphasis on the increasing use of cross-promotion.

5. Identify the broad range of sponsorship platforms that are available, including governing body, team, athlete, media, facility, and event sponsorships.

6. Examine some of the major challenges companies face in seeking to evaluate the effectiveness and "return on investment" from sport sponsorships.

7. Discuss current issues in the sport sponsorship industry, including the emphasis of ethnic marketing through sport sponsorship; the potential for overcommercialization of sport; the emergence of eSports as a sponsorship platform; and the challenges posed by ambush marketing.

Introduction

The National Basketball Association (NBA) has always shown a willingness to test innovative marketing and sponsorship concepts with the NBA Development League (NBDL), popularly called the D-League. In 2017, the NBA again "pushed the envelope" by reaching an agreement with Gatorade to rebrand the D-League as the G-League. This overarching "entitlement sponsor" deal—an unprecedented step in the five major American professional sports leagues—places the Gatorade logo in the bottom right corner of the official NBDL logo. It might also come as no surprise that the NBA took such an innovative step, considering that the league has led all major American professional sports leagues in sponsorship revenue growth since 2015, with revenues climbing at an 8.1% rate ("Sponsorship Spending," 2016).

The most important aspect of this entitlement sponsorship deal are the benefits that Gatorade receives from the NBA. These include Gatorade logo exposure on game balls, team jerseys, on-court signage, and the vast majority of the developmental league's digital assets, as well as access to all players for promotional and marketing purposes (Lombardi, 2017a). In turn, the company will showcase its Gatorade Sports Science Institute by partnering with the NBDL on player nutrition and training programs, focusing on technologies related to Gatorade's testing, products, and equipment. This innovative sponsorship illustrates a major industry trend: the creation of fully integrated and "ownable" relationships that extend beyond simply increasing brand awareness and visibility. The greater focus of the arrangement is on the integration of the Gatorade brand into the NBDL's digital and social media content and the athletic performance metrics as a means of providing an authentic platform for Gatorade to test its innovations (Lombardi, 2017a).

With the newly minted G-League serving as a shining example, this chapter provides an introduction to the sponsorship segment of the sport industry. What is sport sponsorship all about? Which benefits do sport organizations provide to sponsors? What are the key elements of a sponsorship package? How do sponsors evaluate the effectiveness of their sponsorships? And, perhaps most importantly, what are the major trends that budding sport marketers need to recognize?

Sponsorship is one of the most prolific forms of sport marketing. It has been defined as "a cash and/or in-kind fee paid to a property . . . in return for access to the exploitable commercial potential associated with that property" (Ukman, 1995, p. 1). For the major professional sport leagues and associations, sponsorship fees can exceed $10 million per year per sponsor and are often structured as multiyear deals. Sponsorship provides a company with the right to associate with a sport property. A sponsorship agreement also gives the company the opportunity to leverage its affiliation with the sport property to achieve the company's own marketing objectives. Sponsorship is more integrated than other traditional marketing and advertising activities and typically entails a variety of marketing-mix elements designed to send messages to a targeted audience, including, but not limited to, advertising, sales promotion, grassroots event programs, public relations and publicity, cause-related marketing initiatives, and corporate hospitality. As a result of the evolving sophistication and data-driven dynamics of the industry, today the term "sponsorship" has, especially when applied to the major sport properties, been replaced by the term "strategic partnership"—nomenclature that acknowledges the emphasis on more fully "integrating" the relationship between the company and the sport property.

The challenges that confront sport sponsorship executives today, on both the properties and corporate sides, have become vastly more complex than in earlier times. On the sport properties side, key questions include the following (Sood, 2017):

- How can we use our reams of data to best demonstrate the value of our property to prospective sponsors in the face of increasing competition for sponsorship dollars?
- How can we more strategically and creatively integrate sponsors' products and services into our property?
- How can we "prove" that our sponsors are receiving a return on their investment and their objectives?

For companies engaged in sport sponsorship, today's trending questions include these (Sood, 2017):

- How can we use our sponsorship to engage with consumers in the most authentic and experiential way that adds value for them?
- Through our sponsorship, how can we make the consumers' interactions and experiences with our brand as relevant, timely and personalized as possible, particularly through the leveraging of digital and social platforms?
- How can we work with the sport property for our mutual benefit, in terms of both activation strategies and measurement?

A Brief History of Sport Sponsorship

Although we can trace some semblance of sport sponsorship back to the ancient Greek Olympics—local businesses paid charioteers to wear their colors—the increasing commercialization of sport has led to exponential growth in the area of sport sponsorship. Whereas $300 million was spent on sport sponsorship in 1980 (Mullin, Hardy, & Sutton, 2007), that number had grown to $16.3 billion by 2016 ("Sports Sponsorship," 2017). The number of

U.S. companies spending $15 million or more on sport sponsorship grew from 77 in 2010 to 122 in 2015 ("Sponsorship's Big Spenders," 2016). **Table 15-1** lists the top 20 sport sponsors in 2015.

Industry pundits have identified the 1984 Los Angeles Olympic Games as a watershed event in the evolution of sport sponsorship. The Los Angeles Olympic Organizing Committee, under the direction of its president,

Table 15-1 Top 20 U.S. Sport Sponsors, 2015

Amount	Company
$370–375 million	PepsiCo, Inc.
$360–365 million	Anheuser-Busch InBev
$275–280 million	Coca-Cola Co.
$260–265 million	Nike, Inc.
$200–205 million	AT&T, Inc.
$195–200 million	Toyota Motor Sales U.S.A., Inc.
$190–195 million	Adidas North America, Inc.
$155–160 million	Ford Motor Co.
$150–155 million	General Motors Co.
$145–150 million	Verizon Communications, Inc.
$125–130 million	MillerCoors LLC
$95–100 million	FedEx Corp.
$85–90 million	Microsoft Corp.
	The Procter & Gamble Co.
$80–85 million	Bank of America Corp.
	Citigroup, Inc.
	Hyundai Motor America
$75–80 million	Berkshire Hathaway, Inc.
$70–75 million	Sprint Corp.
$65–70 million	Allstate Corp.

Reproduced from Sponsorship's big spenders: IEG's top sponsor rankings (2016, September 19). *IEG Sponsorship Report*. Retrieved from http://www.sponsorship.com/IEGSR/2016/09/19/Sponsorship-s-Big-Spenders--IEG-s-Top-Sponsor-Rank.aspx

Peter Ueberroth, brought a new commercial mind-set to the L.A. Games in its effort to make its Games the first Olympic Games to ever turn a profit for the host city. Employing a "less is more" sales strategy, Ueberroth and his marketing team signed a limited number of companies to exclusive official sponsorship contracts, with fees ranging from $4 million to $15 million per company. AT&T alone paid $5 million to sponsor the first-ever cross-country Olympic torch relay. Fuji Photo Film USA paid $9 million to outbid goliath Kodak for the official sponsorship rights in the film and camera category in an effort to firmly entrench itself in America as a major player (Dentzer, 1984). The publicity surrounding this highly successful commercial venture not only resulted in Ueberroth being named *Time* magazine's "Man of the Year," but also ushered in a new era of sport sponsorship by demonstrating that companies could gain tremendous benefits from sponsorships.

Although the commercial success of the 1984 Los Angeles Olympics put a new spotlight on sport sponsorship, several other factors have contributed to the tremendous growth in sport sponsorship. One influence is the increased media interest in sport, both traditional and online, which has provided companies with a highly visible mechanism for promoting and activating their sponsorship involvements. This has assured sponsors that there is a better chance that their sponsorship will be publicized. Sponsorship is also being viewed as a way for companies to break through the clutter of traditional advertising. Through sponsorship, companies are able to derive numerous in-venue, in-broadcast, retail, and online promotion and publicity benefits that go far beyond the impact of a 30-second commercial spot in connecting with and influencing consumers. Especially in the age of technology, sports is one of the only areas of content that remains "DVR proof." While so-called appointment television programs have significantly decreased, sports still drive major live audiences due to fans' fear of "missing out" on a magical moment.

Further, companies have come to realize the impact that sponsorship has in reaching their target consumers through their lifestyles (Mullin, Hardy, & Sutton, 2014). Corporate marketing executives have found that linking their messages to leisure pursuits conveys their messages immediately, credibly, and to a captive audience. Targeted sponsorships also enable corporate marketers to reach specific segments, such as heavy users, shareholders, and investors, or specific groups that have similar demographic, psychographic, or geographic commonalities. For instance, the German sports apparel manufacturer Adidas understood this opportunity as well as anyone, and decided to partner directly with arguably world soccer's most recognizable superstar, Argentina's and FC Barcelona's Lionel Messi. The company's relationship with the four-time Ballon d'Or winner has enabled it to create an entire community, Team Messi, that revolves solely around the superstar, his skills and successes, and his partnership with Adidas. Team Messi has become the world's official Lionel Messi fan club, and it was created and is still organized by Adidas. Such global fan and customer engagement can hardly be matched by any other sports apparel company in the world, even Nike.

Last, but not least, the discipline of sport sponsorship has emerged as the decision-making process has been gradually transferred from the company's CEO to the company's team of marketing professionals. Historically, companies delved into a sponsorship program because the CEO wanted to; the CEO liked to golf, so he made sure his company became a sponsor of a Professional Golfers' Association (PGA) or Ladies Professional Golf Association (LPGA) tournament. Today, however, sport sponsorship involves in-depth consumer research, significant financial investment, and strategic planning. Buying decisions have become much more sophisticated and data driven, requiring sellers to provide compelling business reasons to the prospective sponsor (e.g., demographic and psychographic research demonstrating that the property will deliver the right target audience for the company) and requiring potential buyers to demonstrate to their CEO that a sponsorship program will meet the company's specific marketing and sales objectives in some measurable way. This outcome is commonly referred to as **return on investment (ROI)** or **return on objectives (ROO)**—topics that are more fully discussed in the "Evaluating Sport Sponsorships" section in this chapter.

The increased competition for the loyalties of sport consumers has also changed the priorities of sport properties in terms of the companies with which they choose to partner. Today, sport properties prefer not to partner with companies that simply purchase the sponsorship rights (thereby blocking out the category from their competitors) and then do little or nothing to utilize, or leverage, their sponsorship to the benefit of both the sponsor and the sport property itself. Thus, increasingly more sponsorship contracts are requiring that the sponsor commit financial resources in support of its sponsorship through promotion and advertising that thematically includes the sport property's imagery—a concept known as sponsorship **activation**. The oft-cited rule of thumb for activating a sponsorship is 3 to 1—that is, $3 in advertising/promotion support for every $1 spent in rights fees.

Concurrently, given the increased competition for corporate sponsorship dollars, prospective sponsors have gained leverage in negotiations. The age-old question applies in this area: Who needs whom more? Thus, companies have become more demanding of sport properties in terms of the marketing rights and benefits they are provided. For instance, among some of the perks provided, it is now commonplace for leagues and teams to allow their official sponsors to conduct sweepstakes that reward winners with aspirational opportunities, such as the chance to throw out first pitches at the World Series, drop the ceremonial puck at a Stanley Cup Playoff game, or participate in the ceremonial coin toss at a National Football League (NFL) game.

New themes and initiatives have also started to emerge in the sport sponsorship space over the past few years. One example has been the development and activation of sponsorships that support sustainability, called "green" initiatives. The National Association for Stock Car Auto Racing (NASCAR), for instance, has built a Green Partners program that today includes more than 20 companies, ranging from New Holland Agriculture and 3M to Coca-Cola and Sunoco. One of the fastest-growing sources of sponsorship revenues are social and digital media companies such as Facebook, Twitter, and Snapchat, whose partnerships with leagues and teams are increasingly incorporating broadcasting elements. For instance, Snapchat recently partnered with Formula 1 racing, representing Formula 1's first commercial partnership with a major digital platform (Roettgers, 2017). The partnership includes Snapchat covering Formula 1 races through its Our Stories feature, meaning that it will editorially curate Snaps generated by attendees.

From electric vehicle–charging companies and fruit growers' associations to casinos and social media platforms, the range of commercial entities seeking to engage in sport sponsorship continues to expand. If your sport organization or property can deliver the audience that these and other companies are seeking to target, there is a sponsorship possibility for those with creative minds and strong sales skills. Examples abound. In May 2017, the sporting world witnessed multiple needle-moving deals, including the Baltimore Orioles signing a sponsorship deal with a 111-year-old local company (Pompeian, Inc.), claiming to be America's first national brand of imported extra virgin olive oil (Lefton, 2017); the WNBA signing FanDuel as its first-ever "official one-day fantasy sports partner," allowing fans to compete against each other for unique game-day experiences (Lombardo, 2017b); and Tough Mudder, the international obstacle course series, signing Amazon as its "official online retailer" in a multifaceted partnership that includes the creation of an Amazon.com/Tough Mudder storefront to market training content, workout videos, and fitness guides (*BusinessWire*, 2017). In sum, there is no shortage of potential sponsorship deals waiting to be consummated!

Sales Promotion in Sport Sponsorship

Sponsorship programs are often built upon some type of promotional activity, generally referred to as sales promotion. **Sales promotion** is defined as "a variety of short-term, promotional activities that are designed to stimulate immediate product demand" (Shank, 2009, p. 312). Although aimed primarily at driving sales in the short term, typically over the course of a month or two, sponsors' sales promotion efforts may also be aimed at increasing brand awareness, broadening the sales distribution channels for their product or service, and getting new consumers to sample their product or service. A typical example of a sport-themed sales promotion is when a sponsoring company provides all fans with a free item featuring the company's logo (also known as a *premium item*) as they enter the arena. In addition to such in-venue activities, sales promotions are often implemented at the retail level (known as *in-store promotions*), such as an offer of a free game ticket when fans redeem a soft drink can at the box office. This section first discusses the implementation and benefits of in-venue promotions, and then describes in-store promotion tactics.

In-Venue Promotions

No other sport has utilized in-stadium promotion as widely as baseball. One major reason for this is that "putting fannies in seats" has traditionally been more of a priority in baseball than in the other major sports: Major League Baseball (MLB) teams have 81 home dates with thousands of seats to fill each game. At the opposite extreme, NFL teams have historically had little need to attract additional fans with "freebies" and giveaways because the majority of NFL teams sell out their stadiums for all home games. The trend across all sports, however, has been to increase the amount of "value-added" benefits that teams provide their paying customers, which has resulted in the growth of in-stadium promotions across the sport industry. In-stadium promotions run the gamut from traditional giveaway days, in which the sponsor underwrites the cost of a premium item in exchange for its logo on the item and advertising support that promotes the event, to themed-event days, such as nostalgia-driven "Turn Back the Clock Days," which are popular in MLB. Many teams have also created *continuity promotions*, which require fans to attend multiple games to obtain, for instance, each player card in a limited-edition trading card set, thereby building attendance frequency.

Sport organizations are constantly on the prowl for the hottest fad in giveaway items. For instance, back in the late 1980s and early 1990s, baseball teams gorged on the collectible trading card craze. Fans would line up hours before games to ensure that they received the hottest new trading card–themed giveaway item, ranging from Surf detergent–sponsored Topps Baseball Card books to Smokey the Bear–themed collectors sets and Upper Deck Heroes of Baseball card sheets. Beanie Babies emerged as hot items for giveaways in the late 1990s, and the bobblehead doll craze followed shortly thereafter. **Table 15-2** lists MLB's most

Table 15-2 MLB In-Stadium Giveaways, 2016		
Rank	**Category (Number of Teams)**	**Number of Dates**
1	Bobblehead (29)	148
2	T-shirt (27)	106
3	Headwear (28)	96
4	Wall hanging (27)	66
5	Backpack/bag (30)	58
6	Retail coupon (12)	39
7	Magnet schedule (25)	37
8 (tie)	Baseball gear (10)	35
8 (tie)	Jersey (18)	35
10	Figurine (19)	31

Reproduced from Broughton, D. (2016a, Nov. 21). Nod on: Bobbleheads top MLB promos again. *Sports Business Journal*, p. 11. Retrieved from http://www.sportsbusinessdaily.com/Journal/Issues/2016/11/21/Research-and-Ratings/MLB-promotions.aspx

Table 15-3 Top MLB In-Game Promotions/Events, 2016		
Rank	**Category (Number of Teams)**	**Number of Dates**
1	Concession discount (18)	229
2	Fireworks (24)	209
3	Ticket discount (13)	174
4	Autographs (7)	152
5	Run the bases (19)	147
6	Festival (18)	121
7	Theme night (26)	117
8	Family day (15)	97
9	Cultural celebration (19)	96
10	Team history tribute (26)	88

Reproduced from Broughton, D. (2016a, Nov. 21). Nod on: Bobbleheads top MLB promos again. *Sports Business Journal*, p. 11. Retrieved from http://www.sportsbusinessdaily.com/Journal/Issues/2016/11/21/Research-and-Ratings/MLB-promotions.aspx

successful promotional giveaway items during the 2016 season (Broughton, 2016a).

The success of an in-venue promotion varies widely based on a number of factors, including time of season (and teams' current win–loss records), the day of promotion (weeknight versus weekend), opponent, and perceived quality of the giveaway item or themed promotion event day. Contrary to what one might expect, teams generally build their promotional calendars to feature their most attractive giveaways or events on their more attractive dates (in terms of opponents and game times) because of the popular notion that a strong promotional giveaway or event typically attracts a larger *incremental* audience. For example, a perennially losing MLB team staging a fan appreciation day against an equally unattractive opponent on a midweek night might attract an incremental 1,000 fans. That same promotion versus an historically high-drawing opponent such as the Boston Red Sox or New York Yankees on a Saturday afternoon might draw an incremental 10,000 fans. **Table 15-3** shows a ranking of the most popular in-stadium promotions for MLB teams during the 2016 season (Broughton, 2016a).

In-Store Promotions

One of the primary reasons that companies secure sponsorships is to drive sales of their product or service. Not surprisingly, companies often leverage their sponsorships at the retail level: in stores where their product is sold or within their own retail stores. In-store promotion encompasses a wide variety of tactics to incentivize consumers and to communicate offers, including premiums, contests and sweepstakes, sampling, point-of-sale or point-of-purchase marketing, and couponing.

Premiums

Premiums are items offered for free or at a reduced price as an inducement to buy a product or service. Typical premiums include tangible items such as bobblehead dolls, T-shirts, and caps. In recent years, technology has expanded the range of premium offerings to include, for instance, a free-year subscription to MLB.TV for all T-Mobile customers as a way to further leverage T-Mobile's official sponsorship of MLB. One of the most popular tactics is offering a premium (think of it as a gift for purchasing) to consumers who redeem a certain number of proof-of-purchase seals (also known as UPCs) that are printed on the product itself. Premiums can also be delivered to consumers through in-pack or on-pack placement. For example, a cereal company might activate its NASCAR sponsorship by offering consumers a free mini-race car inside specially marked boxes.

Contests and Sweepstakes

Contests and sweepstakes are other popular sales tools used in sales promotion. **Contests** are competitions that award prizes based on contestants' skills, whereas **sweepstakes** are games of chance or luck. A sport team or company may require a purchase as a condition of consumers being entered into the contest (e.g., requiring contestants in a football accuracy throwing contest to enter by submitting proofs-of-purchase); however, contests typically appeal to a much smaller universe of potential customers than sweepstakes (where everyone has a *chance* to win). Companies and sport teams conducting sweepstakes may not require the purchase of a product or service for consumers to become eligible to win prizes (thus, the "No Purchase Necessary" notice that precedes all sweepstakes rules).

Sweepstakes typically offer trips to special sporting events, the opportunity for the winner to meet a celebrity athlete, or some other "aspirational" prize that would be difficult (if not impossible) for the winner to otherwise obtain. For example, Discover Card has leveraged its National Hockey League (NHL) sponsorship through its "Day with the Cup" sweepstakes,

allowing lucky winners the chance to spend the day with the coveted Stanley Cup. In another sweepstakes tied to driving credit card usage, Visa has conducted a sweepstakes offering the chance for consumers to win Super Bowl tickets for life. Sport teams and companies have also increasingly turned to an online sweepstakes entry process as a means of driving traffic to their websites. After all, it is easier to post a sweepstakes entry form on one's own website than to hope that the sweepstakes entry forms get appropriately displayed in retail stores.

Sampling

Sampling is one of the most effective sales promotion tools to induce consumers to try a product; it is most often used in the introduction of a new product. Companies typically use sampling to leverage their sport sponsorship by gaining access to a major sporting event, such as the MLB All-Star FanFest or a college bowl game, at which they can hand out product samples to the captive and targeted audience that attends such events. Sampling is not without its hard costs. Although the product samples may be free to consumers, bear in mind when planning a sampling campaign that it still costs money for the company to produce the samples and hire individuals (usually a professional sampling firm) to distribute them to the 70,000 consumers attending, for instance, MLB's All-Star FanFest.

Point-of-Sale or Point-of-Purchase Marketing

Point-of-sale or **point-of-purchase marketing**, interchangeably referred to in industry lingo as POS or POP, is used by marketers to attract consumers' attention to their product or service and their promotional campaign at the retail level. POS display materials can include end-aisle units (large cardboard displays that sit on the floor and are featured at the end of retail store aisles), "shelf-talkers" (cardboard displays that hang on aisle shelves), and banners that are designed to attract potential customers. The life-sized cardboard cutouts of star athletes that you see in grocery and footwear stores are examples of POS materials. Typically these display pieces hold brochures, coupons, or sweepstakes entry forms.

Couponing

Coupons are another popular sales promotion tool. They most often appear in print advertisements such as **freestanding inserts (FSIs)**, which are the coupon sections that appear each week in Sunday newspapers. Coupons may also be delivered to consumers on the product package itself, inserted into the product itself, direct mailed to consumers or, increasingly, distributed electronically and via mobile platforms. In-store promotions are also typically supported by coupons that appear in the participating retailers' circulars (the coupon magazines available for free in the store).

Although coupons have been found to induce short-term sales, one disadvantage is that the continual use of coupons can detract from the product's brand image in the mind of consumers. In addition, studies have shown that most coupon redemption is done by consumers who already use the product, thereby limiting the effectiveness of coupons in attracting new customers (Shank, 2009).

Putting It All Together

Kraft Foods is one of the world's largest sport sponsorship spenders. Kraft's "Taste of Victory" promotion, a multifaceted corporate-wide engagement, perfectly illustrates the implementation of the various sales promotion tactics discussed previously. The promotion, which was thematically tied to Kraft's celebration of its 100 years in business, leveraged the company's sponsorship of Dale Earnhardt's NASCAR race team and was supported by a multitude of Kraft brands, including Country Time Lemonade, Miracle Whip, A1 Steak Sauce, and Grey Poupon mustard. Titled "Get a Taste of Victory," the promotion was communicated via in-store POS end-aisle displays, advertisements and coupons in retailers' circulars, and a full-page FSI in the nation's Sunday newspapers. The FSI included a mail-in form enticing consumers to mail in two proofs-of-purchase from any featured Kraft products (plus $4.00 shipping and handling) to receive a "free" premium: a Kraft 100th anniversary die-cast race car (miniature die-cast cars are among the hottest collectibles in the auto-racing industry). The FSI also encouraged consumers to visit Kraftfoods.com to enter a sweepstakes to win the grand prize: a "street-legal" version of Kraft's 100th anniversary race car valued at $31,000. The POS displays served as a means to attract consumers to Kraft products while in the store, the premium offer of the die-cast racing car served as a means of driving incremental sales (particularly among the extremely loyal race fans), and the online sweepstakes served as a vehicle for collecting the names and addresses of Kraft customers (for future direct mailings). Finally, Kraft's purchase of advertisements and coupons in retailers' circular magazines served to ensure the retailers' in-store support of the promotion, in the form of providing Kraft with the most valuable "real estate" in any store: the end of aisles, where the bulk of impulse purchases take place. If this sounds like a creative form of blackmail, well, it is! It is how the game is played at the retail level.

© Beelde Photography/Shutterstock, Inc.

As college basketball's official snack sponsor, Cheez-It provides another example of a well-executed and comprehensive sports-related sweepstakes activation (Smith, 2016). Utilizing its status as an official sponsor, Cheez-It's "Munch Mania Sweepstakes" directly engaged consumers through an annual celebrity charity game, allowing them to vote for the celebrity they wanted to see on the team through social media or on the sweepstakes' website. In turn, voters were automatically entered into the sweepstakes and could win the grand price, a trip for two to the so-called Big Games in Houston and a chance to play a pick-up game with the stars. The sweepstakes also included 200 first-prize winners, who were given a $100 gift card toward official team merchandise. While not as comprehensively communicated as the Kraft Foods sweepstakes described earlier, Cheez-It's activation still included in-store displays, on-product advertisements, and, most importantly, digital advertisements, among other strategies.

To practice your research skills, find and study the Cheez-It sweepstakes online, and compare and contrast it with the Kraft Foods sweepstakes above. What differences do you see? Why do you think the two companies approached the activation differently?

The Importance of Cross-Promotion

As companies tackle the need to break through the clutter, drive sales, and better leverage their sport sponsorship investments, they often seek to expand the scope and impact of their sponsorships through **cross-promotion** with other companies or with other business units within the same company. This joining together of two or more companies to capitalize on a sponsorship is becoming increasingly popular and effective. Cross-promotion is viable in today's marketplace for a number of reasons, as suggested by Irwin, Sutton, and McCarthy (2008):

- Cross-promotions allow companies to share the total cost of the sponsorship and/or the promotional execution.
- They allow promotion of several product lines within the same company, often drawing from separate budgets, as illustrated in Kraft's "Taste of Victory" promotion.
- These arrangements enable companies to utilize existing business relationships.
- A weaker company can "piggyback" on the strength and position of a bigger company to gain an advantage over its competitors.
- Cross-promotions allow testing of a relationship when future opportunities are under consideration.
- They create a pass-through opportunity, typically involving grocery chains that agree to a sponsorship and pass some or all of the costs (and benefits) to product vendors in their stores.

As an example, Kroger sponsors a NASCAR team, but passes most of the sponsorship rights fees on to vendors such as Pepsi and Nabisco. In exchange, Kroger then agrees to feature Pepsi and Nabisco products in its stores.

The concept of pass-through rights is also extremely important in the credit card industry. For instance, a majority of the value of Visa's NFL, International Olympic Committee (IOC), and Fédération Internationale de Football Association (FIFA) sponsorships derive from the company's ability to "pass through" its official sponsorship rights to its clients (the banks). In this way, Visa uses its sponsorship assets to build unique programs (such as sweepstakes) with hundreds of client banks annually. Given that Visa does not sell its product or services directly to consumers, its sports sponsorships would be rather useless without the ability to "pass through" these rights to its clients.

Sponsors team with other sponsors to create more bang for their buck under the premise that two sponsors working together can gener-ate more interest and awareness among the targeted sport consumers. The "Got Milk?" campaign's leveraging of its NASCAR sponsor-ship through a cross-promotion with Kellogg's cereals illustrates the growing trend of spon-sorship activation involving what has been dubbed "peanut butter and jelly" (PB&J) part-ners (IEG, 2003b). FedEx's highly publicized promotion to deliver the newest edition of the Madden NFL video game to unsuspecting NFL fans (while levering social media via #FedEx-DeliversMadden) provided a terrific example of two league sponsors working in tandem to the benefit of both.

Another increasingly popular cross-promotion tactic involves *codependent partners*, referring to companies whose products or services are integral to each other—such as com-puter software and hardware manufacturers—teaming up to leverage a sport sponsorship (IEG, 2003a). For example, IBM, as a sponsor of the NBA, might offer a free NBA video game with the purchase of a new laptop.

Finally, cross-promotions can be staged between *customer-partners*, two discrete brands that stand alone but do so much business with each other that they are almost siblings (IEG, 2003b). For example, to better leverage its sponsorship of MLB, Pepsi incorporated one of its biggest national customers, Subway restau-rants, as a partner in an official All-Star Game balloting promotion. The involvement of both customer-partners not only greatly broadened the impact and awareness of MLB's All-Star balloting program nationwide, but also enabled Pepsi to pass through an invaluable marketing asset to one of its largest national customers, thereby strengthening its business relationship with Subway.

For the sport marketer, whether on the property side or the corporate side, it has become increasingly important to think outside the box as to how the official sponsors

within a specific league or team can join together to increase the overall effectiveness of their sponsorship investments. The offi-cial sponsors of the major professional sport leagues often look for creative ways to cross-promote their companies. **Tables 15-4** through **15-7** list the official sponsors for several of the major North American professional sport leagues; **Tables 15-8** provides a list of some of

Table 15-4 NHL Corporate Marketing Partners for 2016–2017	
Sponsor	**Category**
Anco	Automotives
Bridgestone	Tires
Constellation	Energy
Coors Light	Adult beverages
DraftKings	Daily fantasy sports
EA Sports	Electronic gaming
Enterprise	Rental cars
Gatorade	Sports and energy drinks
Honda	Automaker
Kraft Heinz	Food
Lays	Food
Las Vegas	Other
Molson Canadian	Adult beverages
PepsiCo	Soft drinks
PPG	Paint
Reebok	Sports apparel
SAP	Cloud software
Sheraton	Hotels
SiriusXM	Subscription-based Radio
Ticketmaster	Ticketing agency
Upper Deck	Trading cards

Data from NHL.com. Retrieved from, https://www.nhl.com/info/corporate-marketing-partners

Table 15-5 NBA Corporate Marketing Partners for 2016–2017

Brand	Category
2K Sports	Videogame software
Adidas	Apparel/footwear
American Express	Credit card
Anheuser-Busch InBev	Beer (alcohol, non-alcoholic malt beverage)
AutoTrader.com	Online auto retailer
BBVA Compass	Banking
Cisco	Information technology; networking solutions
ExxonMobil (Mobil 1)	Motor oil; fuel; lubricant
FanDuel	Daily fantasy sports
Foot Locker	Athletic retailer
Harman	Audio
Kaiser Permanente	Health care
Kia Motors	Automotive
Kumho Tire	Tire
Nike	Footwear
PepsiCo (Gatorade)	Sports drinks; nutrition
PepsiCo (Mountain Dew, Aquafina, Brisk, Doritos, Ruffles)	Soft drink; water; iced tea; salted snacks
Samsung	Handset; tablet; TV
SAP	Business analytic and intelligence software
Spalding	Basketballs; backboards
State Farm	Insurance
Taco Bell	Quick Service Restaurants (QSR)
Tissot	Timekeeper
Under Armour	Footwear
Verizon	Wireless service provider

Reproduced from Spons-O-Meter: NBA Rolls Into '16-17 Season With 25 League-Level Marketing Partners (2016, October 20). *SportsBusiness Daily.com*. Retrieved from http://www.sportsbusinessdaily.com/Daily/Issues/2016/10/26/NBA-Season-Preview/Sponsometer.aspx

the Worldwide IOC Olympic Partner Sponsors. Here's a challenge: Review the sponsors for each of these properties and see if you can develop a few effective cross-promotion opportunities for them. Would you classify them as PB&J promotions, codependent partner promotions, or customer-partner promotions?

Table 15-6 NFL Corporate Marketing Partners for 2016–2017

Sponsor	Category	Sponsor Since
Gatorade (PepsiCo)	Sports nutrition	1983
EA Sports	Video games	1993
Visa	Payment systems services	1995
Campbell's Soup	Soup	1998
FedEx	Package delivery services	2000
Frito-Lay (PepsiCo)	Salted snacks/popcorn/peanuts/dips/salsa	2000
Snickers/Skittles/M&M's (Mars Snackfoods)	Chocolate/non-chocolate confectionery	2002
Pepsi (PepsiCo)	Soft drinks	2002
Dairy Management Inc.	Dairy products (milk/yogurt/cheese)	2003
SiriusXM	Satellite radio	2004
Bridgestone	Automotive tires	2007
TicketMaster	TicketExchange	2008
Gillette/Head & Shoulders/Vicks/Old Spice (Procter & Gamble)	Health/beauty/household products brands	2009
Verizon	Wireless telecommunication service	2010
Barclays	Affinity card/rewards program	2010
Papa John's	Pizza	2010
Under Armour	Footwear/glove provider, Combine sponsor	2010
Castrol	Motor oil	2010
Anheuser-Busch	Beer	2011
USAA*	Insurance/military appreciation	2011
Bose	Home theater system, headsets, headphones	2011
Courtyard by Marriott	Hotel	2011
Xbox, Surface, Windows (Microsoft)**	Tablets, operating systems, game consoles, interactive video entertainment consoles	2011
Quaker Oats (PepsiCo)	Hot cereal, granola bars	2012
New Era	Hats	2012
Nike	On-field apparel, footwear, gloves	2012
Duracell (Procter & Gamble)	Batteries	2012
Tide (Procter & Gamble)	Household cleaning	2012

(continues)

Table 15-6 NFL Corporate Marketing Partners for 2016–2017 (*Continued*)

Sponsor	Category	Sponsor Since
McDonald's	Quick Service Restaurants (QSR)	2012
SAP	Business software solutions, cloud software solutions, business analytics software	2012
CoverGirl (Procter & Gamble)	Beauty	2013
Zebra Technologies	Real time location solutions, on-field player tracking	2014
TD Ameritrade	Investment services, wealth management	2014
Extreme Networks	Wi-Fi analytics, network solutions	2014
Nationwide Insurance*	Insurance	2014
Hyundai	Auto	2015
Dannon	Yogurt	2015
Ford	Truck partner	2016

* Nationwide and USAA have co-exclusivity in the auto/home/life insurance category.
** Deals for Surface and Windows were signed in 2013.
Reproduced from Spons-O-Meter: NFL Roster Of Partners For '16 Season Highlighted By Ford Entry (2016, Sept. 8). SportsBusiness Daily.com. Retrieved from http://www.sportsbusinessdaily.com/Daily/Issues/2016/09/08/NFL-Season-Preview/Sponsometer.aspx.

Table 15-7 MLB Corporate Marketing Partners for 2016

Sponsor (Brand)	Category Rights	Sponsor Since
Procter & Gamble (Gillette)	Men's, women's shaving and grooming products	1939
Anheuser-Busch (Budweiser)	Alcoholic, non-alcoholic malt beverages	1980
PepsiCo (Gatorade)	Sports/energy drink, isotonic beverage	1990
MasterCard	Credit card, payment system	1997
PepsiCo (Pepsi, Aquafina)	Non-alcoholic, non-milk-based beverage	1997
Nike	Athletic footwear, athletic eyewear	1998
Bank of America	Banking services and affinity card	2004
Taco Bell	Quick Service Restaurants (QSR) casual dining (postseason only)	2004
SiriusXM	Satellite radio	2005
General Motors (Chevrolet)	Foreign, domestic vehicle	2005
PepsiCo (Frito-Lay)	Salty snack	2006
Scotts	Lawn care	2010
EMC	Online data storage, data security	2012
T-Mobile	Wireless service, hardware, tablets	2013

Table 15-7 MLB Corporate Marketing Partners for 2016 (*Continued*)

Sponsor (Brand)	Category Rights	Sponsor Since
DraftKings	Daily fantasy baseball	2013
Church & Dwight (Arm & Hammer)	Laundry detergent, baking soda, dish cleaner	2014
Church & Dwight (OxiClean)	Air freshener, pet care, dental care, nasal care	2014
Amazon	Cloud storage provider	2015
Esurance	Car insurance	2015
Falken Tire	Tires	2015
The Hartford	Home and group benefits insurance	2015
Starwood (Sheraton)	Hotels, resorts	2015
Vixlet	Social platform	2015
Papa John's	Pizza	2016

Reproduced from Spons-O-Meter: MLB Boasts Official Sponsors For 23 Categories This Season (2016, April 4). *SportsBusiness Daily*. Retrieved from http://www.sportsbusinessdaily.com/Daily/Issues/2016/04/04/MLB-Season-Preview/MLB-sponsors.aspx

Table 15-8 IOC's The Olympic Partner (TOP) Program

Company	Category
Alibaba Group	Cloud services, e-commerce platform services
Atos	Information technology
Bridgestone	Tires, automotive vehicle services
Coca-Cola	Nonalcoholic beverages
DOW	Official chemistry company
General Electric	Energy generation systems; energy distribution systems; health care: diagnostic imaging, monitoring, and electronic medical records; technology; lighting fixtures and systems; aircraft engines; rail transportation; water treatment facilities and services; equipment and transportation management
Omega	Time pieces (watches, clocks, and official countdown clocks); timing systems/services; electronic timing, scoring, and scoreboards systems and services
Panasonic	Audio/TV/video equipment
Procter & Gamble	Personal care and household products
Samsung	Wireless communications equipment
Toyota	Vehicles, mobility services and mobility solutions
Visa	Consumer payment systems (e.g., credit cards)

Data from The Olympic Partner (TOP) Program (2017). International Olympic Committee. Retrieved July 8, 2017 from http://www.olympic.org/sponsors

Sponsorship Packages

In 2010, Bridgestone Tire signed a 5-year sponsorship deal with the NHL; it renewed that deal for another 5 years in 2015. Bridgestone's sponsorship of the NHL provides a good illustration of the benefits typically included in a league or team sponsorship package, as well as the types of commitments the sponsoring company makes to the sports organization. Benefits typically include the following assets and inventory:

- *Exclusivity* in one's product or service category. For example, Bridgestone became the only company the NHL could sign as a national sponsor in the tire category.
- *"Official" designations* that tie the sport to the sponsor's product or service category. For instance, Bridgestone became the "official tire of the NHL," the "official tire of the NHLPA," and the "official tire of the Hockey Hall of Fame." (Many sport organizations, embracing a relationship marketing mentality, today prefer the use of "official partner" designations.)
- *Rights* to utilize the sport organization's intellectual property in advertising and promotion campaigns. For Bridgestone, this includes the rights to use the NHL logo in promotional activities. (Typically, the major professional sport league sponsorship departments do not have the authority, via their agreement with their member teams, to grant national sponsors the right to utilize team logos on an individual team basis; such rights must be obtained directly from the desired team or teams.)
- *Title naming rights* for the "Bridgestone NHL Winter Classic," an annual regular-season outdoor hockey game typically played on or near New Year's Day.
- *In-stadium signage and promotional announcements* during NHL-controlled events such as the All-Star Game and the Stanley Cup Playoffs, often in the form of 30-second commercials and sponsor "thank you" messages via scoreboards, matrix boards, and public address (PA) announcements.
- *Access to tickets* for NHL-controlled events, including the All-Star Game and the Stanley Cup Playoffs.
- *Access to the use of* NHL player rights and images.
- *Rights to leverage* the NHL's social media and digital assets.
- Access to the NHL's video and photographic content.

In exchange for these benefits, Bridgestone, as is typical with most sport sponsorship contracts, made the following contractual commitments to the NHL:

- *A rights fee* in the form of a cash payment (typically spread out in periodic payments throughout the season).
- *A multiyear commitment* (most established sport properties insist on multiyear sponsorship deals to ensure stability for the league and a longer-term commitment by the sponsor; Bridgestone entered into a 5-year agreement with the NHL).
- *Advertising commitment* to spend a predetermined dollar amount on NHL-controlled media and/or with NHL's broadcast partners (i.e., NBC, CBC, and RDS).

Companies engaged in sport sponsorship use a wide variety of marketing elements, often collectively, to achieve their marketing objectives. The next section considers some possible sport sponsorship platforms.

Sport Sponsorship Platforms

A broad range of platforms are available through which a company can become involved in sport sponsorship. As suggested by Irwin and colleagues (2008), these platforms are often integrated to expand the depth and breadth of the sponsorship.

Governing Body Sponsorship

A governing body sponsorship entails securing the "official sponsor" status with a national or international sport league or governing association. Companies that play upon this platform tend to be larger, international companies due to the size of the financial investment required. Governing bodies range from the IOC, which grants companies the right to be an "official worldwide partner" of the Olympic Games, to the major professional sport leagues (e.g., MLB, NFL), to organizations such as the National Collegiate Athletic Association (NCAA) and Little League Baseball. Most of these sponsorships, while providing "official sponsor" status across the entire organization, do not necessarily grant "official sponsor" status to the individual teams within the organization. These rights must be secured separately from the individual teams.

Team Sponsorship

Team sponsorship is often a more appropriate platform for local or regional companies or companies with smaller marketing budgets. Such sponsorships typically include the right to be the "official sponsor" of the team, the opportunity to conduct in-venue promotions, and access to team tickets and hospitality. Most governing bodies allow for competitors of their sponsorship partners to sign sponsorship deals with the local teams. For instance, although Bank of America is the "Official Bank of the MLB," many MLB teams have sponsorship deals with local banks.

This loophole has served as an avenue for ambush marketing for some companies. Take, for example, the 2010 FIFA World Cup: Although Adidas was the "Official Licensee and Supplier of the FIFA World Cup," Nike was a sponsor (and jersey provider) of many national teams, including the United States, Brazil, and the Netherlands.

Athlete Sponsorship

Athlete sponsorship serves as a platform for companies to develop a sponsorship based on support of individual athletes (versus a team or a league). Such arrangements typically involve some type of endorsement of the sponsor's product or service. Athletes in individual sports, such as tennis and golf, tend to attract more sponsor interest because they are able to generate a greater number of visible, well-focused sponsor impressions on television. Among the most prolific current athlete endorsers is LeBron James, who in 2015 added to his robust portfolio of corporate deals by signing a lifetime contract with Nike that could eventually net him more than $1 billion (Badenhausen, 2017).

One of the services that companies use to help determine which athletes to sponsor is the Q-Score, compiled by New York City–based Marketing Evaluations/TvQ, a research firm that has been measuring the notoriety of athletes, actors, and entertainers for more than 40 years. The Q-Score uses a scale to measure celebrities' familiarity and appeal among the general public. A more comprehensive measure that has since been developed by Nielsen is the so-called N-Score, which uses the same measures as Q-Score plus an additional handful of components to determine the marketability of celebrities. Based on 2016 N-Score rankings, in order, the 10 highest-ranked athletes were Peyton Manning (who barely qualified at the time because he had just announced his retirement from professional football), Michael Phelps, Simone Biles, Serena Williams, LeBron James, Venus Williams, Eli Manning, Dale Earnhardt, Jr., Danica Patrick, and Tom Brady (Badenhausen, 2016).

Sponsoring an individual athlete can be riskier than sponsoring a league or team. Sport celebrities garner a great deal of attention and interest from the public, so the media are quick to report on any news involving the athlete. Unfortunately for sponsors, this news may involve the sport celebrity getting into some sort of trouble or breaking with the company on a very public issue. Given the prevalence of smartphone cameras and social media accounts in today's world, the issue of athlete misbehavior takes on even graver importance.

In an interesting twist, and also as a result of the power of social media, we are beginning to see the dynamics of this sponsorship relationship cut both ways. NBA and Golden State Warriors superstar Stephen Curry, for example, did not appreciate the endorsement given by Kevin Plank, CEO of Under Armour, to then presidential candidate Donald Trump (Williams, 2017). Curry, who had a sponsorship deal with Under Armour, voiced his concerns to the media, suggesting that he would not align himself with a company that accepts bigotry or racism—two issues directly related to Donald Trump, according to Curry. In turn, Under Armour received significant backlash over the comments of its CEO and had to assure Curry that his values were shared by the company.

Companies must carefully evaluate the risks associated with sponsoring an individual athlete prior to entering into any agreement, and nurture the relationship once an agreement is entered.

Media Sponsorship

Media sponsorship occurs most often in the form of broadcast sponsors—that is, companies that purchase advertising or programming during sport-related broadcasts. For several years, Home Depot has been the presenting sponsor of ESPN's *College GameDay* show, positioned as "College GameDay Built by the Home Depot" (a clever way to further entrench Home Depot's brand message in the minds of consumers). This media sponsorship includes commercial spots, on-site signage, and game tickets for hospitality and entertainment purposes. The sponsorship "helps Home Depot fortify its base of active, male, do-it-yourself customers," said a Home Depot marketing executive. "College football and home improvement projects are two things that people associate with the weekend, particularly Saturdays. This sponsorship allows Home Depot to strengthen that connection with our consumers" (Wilbert, 2003, p. 1D).

Often broadcast sponsors have no affiliation with the team or league being broadcast, a situation that can result in ambush marketing, whereby the broadcast sponsor seeks to convey to consumers some "official" relationship that does not actually exist. Although not illegal, one classic example was Wendy's advertising as an "official broadcast sponsor" of the Olympics, although McDonald's was the official sponsor of the Olympics in the fast-food category. Many sport organizations now either require their official sponsors to purchase advertising within their event broadcasts or, alternatively, provide them with a "right of first refusal" to purchase broadcast advertising time, with the intent of eliminating or curtailing such ambush marketing activity.

Facility Sponsorship

Facility sponsorship is one of the fastest-growing sponsorship platforms, most notably in the form of naming rights agreements. Over the past 20 years, almost every professional sport facility (and many collegiate athletic stadiums and arenas) has sold its naming rights to a company. For example, Citizens Bank signed a 25-year, $95 million naming rights deal that put its name on the Philadelphia Phillies' ballpark. As an example of platform integration, Citizens Bank was already an official sponsor of the team, and its naming rights deal also included a commitment to media sponsorship (i.e., advertising within Phillies television and radio broadcasts). Another example of platform integration is Red Bull's sponsorship of both the New York Red Bulls (a Major League Soccer [MLS] team) and Red Bull Arena (the facility where the team plays).

Facility sponsors typically sponsor the sport properties that play in the facility in some other capacity. Many sport organizations are further slicing and dicing areas within the facility to attract incremental sponsorship revenue beyond the naming rights deal. For instance, most stadiums now sell corporate sponsorship to specific entryways, concourse areas, luxury box levels, and even practice facilities. As an example, prior to the 2013 football season, the NFL's New York Giants signed Quest Diagnostics as the training facility sponsor, replacing a 4-year deal with Timex valued at more than $2 million per year (Vacchiano, 2013).

Event Sponsorship

Event sponsorship enables companies to tie directly into the event atmosphere over a relatively short time period, typically a few days or a weekend. Examples include sponsorship of triathlons and marathons, college football bowl games, extreme sports events such as the X Games, and professional golf tournaments, typically events that are locally based and annual.

A great example is the Abbott World Marathon series (Karp, 2014). This sponsorship has allowed Abbott Laboratories to attach its name to essentially every single popular and globally recognizable marathon event, including the Tokyo and Boston Marathons, providing immense benefits to the company in terms of exposure and engagement. Other companies have followed Abbott's example and entered agreements to have marathons named after them as well. Examples include the BMW Berlin Marathon and the Bank of America Chicago Marathon, both of which are run under the Abbott World Marathon umbrella.

Evaluating Sport Sponsorships

There is a saying: "It you can't measure it, you can't manage it." Companies that fail to set clear and measurable objectives before entering into a sport sponsorship program are more likely to meet with failure. Given the growing financial commitments necessary to sponsor and effectively activate sport sponsorship programs, the evaluation of sponsorships has become a necessary component of the sport sponsorship process. It is critical that sponsoring companies develop metrics to answer questions such as the following:

- Do consumers understand the sponsorship?
- Can consumers identify the sponsorship after being exposed to it?
- Has the sponsorship led to a meaningful connection with the target audience?
- How many media impressions has the sponsorship generated?
- Has the sponsorship driven increases in brand awareness, brand perception, and brand consideration (i.e., purchase intent)?
- Has the sponsorship led to quantifiable new business opportunities?

Measuring ROI from sport sponsorships poses several challenges for sponsors. First, there is no one exact formula for measuring ROI, forcing companies to establish their own internal criteria. Companies use a wide range of criteria to help determine whether their sport sponsorship is a valuable asset in achieving their marketing objectives: include internal feedback for sales departments; sales promotion bounceback measures; social media impressions, engagements, and percentage of social conversation; print media impressions; television and digital media impressions; primary consumer research; dealer/trade response; and syndicated consumer research. Second, it is difficult to precisely quantify the incremental sales directly attributable to a specific sponsorship program or the sponsorship's direct effects on consumers' awareness of the sponsoring company or brand.

The difficulties that arise with ROI measurements have called for a new way to evaluate not only sport sponsorships, but investments in general. As a result, return on objectives has been established by many businesses as a metric. The difference between ROI and ROO is the focus variable. Instead of emphasizing the revenues generated from an investment, or its costs, ROO focuses on the objectives sought to be met through the sponsorship. For instance, an objective might be to generate more positive attitudes toward the brand. This is not something that can necessarily be monetarily quantified (like the typical ROI measures), but rather would be determined through consumer surveys conducted before and after the sponsorship activity.

Consumer surveys are often deployed as a first step in measuring sponsorship effectiveness. For example, an annual survey regarding the sponsorship awareness of NFL fans conducted by Turnkey Intelligence (the research arm of Turnkey Sports & Entertainment) found that a mere 28% of all respondents correctly identified Verizon as the league's official wireless service provider. While that was a 3% increase over the previous year, it means that fewer than one-third of average NFL fans know that Verizon has invested enormous sums of money into an official sponsorship with the NFL (Broughton, 2016b). Surveys such as these provide sponsors with a general understanding of the level of awareness consumers have of their sponsorship alliances. It would be a faulty approach, however, to use survey research to conclude that Verizon's sponsorship of the NFL is not effective and valuable, given the many other objectives and metrics that Verizon would also want to consider.

Sponsorship evaluation has become a burgeoning business, and today many companies specialize in measuring sponsorship ROI. Research companies such as Performance Research, Nielsen Sports Marketing Service (also the parent company of Repucom), Turnkey Sports & Entertainment, and Sponsorship Research International (SRi) are among the firms that have emerged to provide professional services for evaluating, through quantitative and qualitative research instruments, the many components of a sponsor's involvement with a sport property.

Students with an aptitude for and interest in the research process may find career opportunities with market research companies that specialize in sport marketing and sponsorship, such as those listed in the "Resources" section at the end of this chapter.

Sponsorship Consulting Agencies

As you are probably well aware, there is much that makes the sport product, sport consumers, and, therefore, sport marketing unique. Recognizing the specialized skills needed to get the most out of their sponsorships, many companies engaged in sport sponsorship have chosen to outsource the negotiation, strategic development, and/or implementation of their sponsorship programs, leaving the nuances of sport marketing to the experts. Many companies rely on sponsorship consulting agencies because they do not possess the internal expertise, experience, industry connections, or resources to negotiate and implement sponsorship programs on their own. Instead, those tasked with selling sport property sponsorships may negotiate directly with the prospective sponsor's agency in pitching their sponsorship opportunities. In turn, career opportunities exist for trained sport marketers to apply their skills on the agency side. A list of some of the major agencies that specialize in the negotiation and implementation of sport sponsorships on behalf of their clients (the sponsoring companies) is provided in the "Resources" section of this chapter.

Issues in Sport Sponsorship

Multicultural Marketing Through Sport Sponsorship

The expanding markets consisting of ethnic consumers, coupled with the increasing globalization of sport, are compelling more corporations to direct a portion of their sport sponsorship spending to **multicultural marketing**. Likewise, sport organizations have begun to adopt strategies to more effectively target ethnic groups, particularly the Latino and Asian communities, who historically have represented only a small percentage of the sport spectator base in the United States.

Hispanics, in particular, are the fastest-growing ethnic population in the United States, with 40% of Hispanics being younger than the age of 21 (Pellerano, 2014). In terms of sport interest, 94% of Hispanic men consider themselves to be sport fans, with 56% falling into the avid fan category (Tagliani, 2015). At least 75% of Hispanics have purchased sport-related merchandise within the last 12 months, and Hispanic households spent more than $1.7 billion on participation fees and sport lessons in 2013 (Pellerano, 2014). These figures, which one can only assume will increase in line with the size of the Hispanic population, represent a huge opportunity not only for sport teams, but also for companies seeking to expand the reach of their sponsorships. For instance, many of the companies that sponsor MLS, such as Sierra Mist, Kraft, and Budweiser, have identified an interest in reaching the largely Hispanic audience that attends these games. Sport broadcasting also represents a growing opportunity for companies to "sponsor" programming in an effort to reach Hispanic viewers. For instance, in September 2016, ESPN launched *Nación ESPN*, which targets bilingual sport fans, on ESPN2; this group is a highly lucrative consumer audience whom advertisers are working

hard to reach. The show premiered with four big inaugural sponsors—Allstate, Toyota, Gillette, and Taco Bell (Villafane, 2016). *Sports Business Journal*'s Adam Stern (2014) has provided a very comprehensive report on how teams and companies are marketing to the Hispanic market, for those seeking further insights into this topic.

The influx of Asian athletes into major U.S. professional sport leagues (particularly soccer, basketball, and baseball) has also fueled the interest of companies in using sport sponsorship to target Asian communities. The arrival of Yao Ming to the NBA in 2002 has become a classic example of the impact that athletes and their fans can have on local corporations' ethnic marketing initiatives. Shortly after Ming signed with the Houston Rockets, Harbrew Imports of New York, marketers of Yanjing Beer, signed a multiyear sponsorship deal with Ming's team (shortly thereafter, the company also signed a sponsorship deal with the Los Angeles Clippers when that team signed Chinese player Wang Zhizhi). Ming's ability to resonate with Chinese consumers in both the United States and China quickly resulted in athlete sponsorship deals between Ming and companies that included Pepsi, Gatorade, Apple, and Visa. More recently, after Taiwanese American Jeremy Lin signed with the Houston Rockets, the team quickly signed five sponsorship deals with companies doing business in China (Gregory, 2012).

Sport marketers must be cognizant of key cultural differences among and between ethnic groups in terms of how sponsorship and its various tactics are communicated to and perceived by targeted ethnic groups (Cordova, 2009). For example, ethnic marketing cannot be, or be perceived as, a token effort by the company to reach out to a particular ethnic market. Sport marketers must also understand the difference between marketing to first-generation immigrants and those who, although identified as part of an ethnic group, are well indoctrinated into American culture. Armstrong (1998) has identified a number of strategies that sport organizations and corporations should employ when marketing to black consumers, including involving the black media, demonstrating concern and respect for the black community and causes salient to it through socially responsible cause-related marketing, and patronizing black vendors. Nevertheless, much research and work remains to be done on effectively reaching ethnic markets through sport sponsorship.

Innovation from Across the Pond

One such innovative sport sponsorship approach that appears increasingly intriguing to the major U.S. sport properties is the idea of jersey sponsorships. Such a sponsorship activation includes placing the name and/or logo of a corporation or brand, selected either by the team or by the league, or both, in a visible location on the jersey worn by the players. This type of sponsorship has been extremely prominent throughout European sports. The best soccer teams in the world, such as Bayern Munich, FC Barcelona, and Manchester United, all proudly present a sponsor on the front of their jerseys, as does literally every other professional soccer team throughout all of Europe's leagues.

MLS was the first of the major North American sport leagues to allow teams to sell jersey sponsorships. There was little public "push-back" with this decision, due mostly to the fact that soccer fans are accustomed to the reality of jersey sponsorships owing to its long-time prevalence in professional soccer leagues outside of North America. Driven by the need to generate new revenue streams, the WNBA's decision to sell jersey sponsorships also was met with little public or media outcry. The key question, though, is how mainstream sport fans and media might react to the wholesale emergence of jersey sponsorships within the four major professional leagues. Beginning with the 2017–2018 season, the NBA became the first of the four major American professional sport

leagues to blaze this path, allowing individual teams to sell jersey sponsorships (Mahoney, 2016). According to commissioner Adam Silver, jersey sponsorship was an inevitable next step in growing the NBA's business and adding another lucrative revenue stream (Mahoney, 2016). Which of the remaining three North American professional sport leagues will follow suit, and when, remains to be seen. In the meantime, ask yourself: How would you feel about seeing your favorite NHL, NFL or MLB players competing in a uniform emblazoned with the logo of a local business?

eSports: A Game-Changing Sponsorship Platform?

When you think of the best athletes in the world, those who earn millions of dollars each year through their athletic abilities, who do you think of? Probably players such as LeBron James, Aaron Rodgers, Lionel Messi, Rafael Nadal, or Jason Day, depending on which sport you follow most. You probably did not think of Chu Zeyu, the leader of the Wings Gaming team between 2015 and 2017. In 2016, Wings Gaming won the most prestigious eSports tournament in the world, The Internationals, also known as DOTA 2. The victory earned each one of the team's five members, including Chu Zeyu, more than $1.87 million. The total prize money at DOTA 2 in 2016 reached close to $21 million, roughly four times the total prize money available at the Australian Open, one of world tennis's most prestigious events (Lozano, 2016).

Over the past few years, eSports has enjoyed a growth rate rarely seen in the history of sports, and this trajectory is not expected to slow down for the foreseeable future, leading to an entirely new dimension for sport sponsorship. Before discussing sponsorships in eSports, however, it is important, and will certainly become vital in the future, for a sport marketer to understand the structure of the eSports industry and its tournaments. Currently, tournaments are organized by specific organizations such as the Electronic Sports League. Depending on the prestige of the event, teams either can join freely (i.e., ESL Open tournaments) or must first qualify through other tournaments (i.e., ESL Major and ESL Pro). Naturally, the better the tournament, the better the competition, and the higher the prize money. Other eSports leagues have also begun to emerge, such as the Activision Blizzard's Overwatch League, which features teams in cities including New York, Los Angeles, Shanghai, and Seoul (Fischer, 2017). Among the newest owners of an Overwatch League franchise is New England Patriots' owner Robert Kraft, suggesting the long-term viability of eSports (Fischer, 2017).

While the eSports industry is still young, its teams and tournaments have already become attractive entities for sponsorships. In fact, it was estimated that in 2016 alone, companies spent $325 million on advertising and sponsorships tied directly to eSports and its teams (Rovell, 2016). Coca-Cola, which annually spends approximately $300 million on sport sponsorships and is the third largest American sport sponsor, is the official sponsor of the League of Legends World Championships. Buffalo Wild Wings and Arby's both sponsor the ELeague and have secured naming rights for the *Counter-Strike*–focused competition. Both Geico and Red Bull have vested sponsorship interests in eSports nowadays, and the Philadelphia 76ers bought two eSports teams, Team Apex and Team Dignitas (Heitner, 2016). The NBA's Houston Rockets actually employ a Director of eSports (Wolf, 2016).

The massive engagement opportunities for big brands through eSports do not stop at simple sponsorships, however. Since 2015, Verizon has hosted one of the largest eSports tournaments in the United States, called the Epic Gaming Lounge Dallas 10K (Gaudiosi, 2015). Because eSports, its players, and its fans all rely on strong networks to even be possible, Verizon recognized this opportunity to showcase its vast network capabilities and the strength of its Fios high-speed networking product by providing everything that an eSports tournament needs to be organized, executed, and distributed. In addition, by live streaming the tournament on mobile devices, Verizon is able to connect with consumers nationwide. This partnership allows Verizon to have constant exposure during the eSports tournament both during and outside of the actual games. It is an opportunity that provides even more benefits in terms of exposure than a simple sponsorship (Gaudiosi, 2015).

Summary

Sport sponsorship has evolved into a billion-dollar industry that has grown increasingly competitive. The increase in the sheer number of sport organizations pursuing corporations' sponsorship dollars and the never-ending expansion of inventory—including everything from venue naming rights to turnstile signage to championship parades to social and digital media sites—has spurred a new level of data-driven sophistication in the sales, implementation, servicing, and evaluation of sport sponsorships. At the same time, there has been a tremendous increase in the number of companies and industry trade associations eager to engage in sport sponsorship. These companies, although today much more attuned to the benefits of sport sponsorship, continue to put increasing emphasis on the evaluation and measurement of their sport sponsorship involvements to ensure they receive an adequate return on their investments. Thus, there is a broad range of opportunities for individuals seeking careers in the area of sport sponsorship, including on the sport organization side, the corporate side, the sport marketing consulting agency side, and the sponsorship evaluation side.

The bright future for sport sponsorship is perhaps best summed up by Wasserman Media Group Executive Vice President Heidi Pellerano:

> This is an exciting time to be in sponsorships. The industry is expanding not only via the new mediums and opportunities . . . but also by the true globalization of sport. There is more competition on both sides as brands have access to more sponsorship opportunities, but also more brands are investing in sponsorships, looking to organically integrate [those brands] into the fan experience. This should,
>
> hopefully, lead to increased creativity not only in how deals are structured, but also in how they are brought to life. My hope . . . is that these changes will result in sponsorships going away and being replaced by true partnerships, where both properties and brands are creating value for each other to move their businesses forward. If that happens, we all win, not only because our industry flourishes, but also because as fans we will have tremendous access to the sports, athletes, and content we love, when, where, and how we want to consume it. (Sood, 2017)

Case Study 15-1

Shining a "Red Light" on Ambush Marketing

As with any global sport property, the International Olympic Committee (IOC) and each country's national governing body face a major challenge in seeking to protect the exclusive marketing rights of their official sponsors from "ambush marketing," a tactic in which companies use advertising and promotions in an attempt to *imply* a commercial association with the Olympics *without* having secured official sponsorship rights. The IOC had long taken to publicly calling these companies "parasites."

Such were the circumstances for the Canadian Olympic Committee (COC) as its members prepared for the Olympic Winter Games to be hosted in Sochi, Russia, in February 2014. As in many countries, Canada's Olympic movement is funded almost exclusively by the private sector through financial investments in the COC's official sponsorship program. Hence, one of the COC's chief concerns heading into the 2014 Winter Games was to protect the investments of those companies, which had paid more than $100 million to become official sponsors of the Canadian Olympic Team.

Beginning with the Vancouver 2010 Winter Games, the COC had made a conscious strategic decision to move away from the overly aggressive, heavy-handed enforcement mentality that had been utilized in previous Olympic Games. Instead, the COC emphasized education and relationship development, seeking to encourage cooperation from the Canadian business community in protecting the integrity of the COC's official sponsorship program. The focus on education versus enforcement was rooted in three key messages: (1) an understanding and appreciation that the COC is primarily funded by Canada's business community; (2) the importance of sponsorship funding in enhancing the medal-platform success of its athletes; and (3) fairness in business practices. Some might call it a strategy of "killing them with kindness."

Despite the COC's proactive efforts to educate the country's business community regarding its exclusive rights to Olympic logos, phrases, and imagery, the organization knew that some companies would undoubtedly try to capitalize on the goodwill associated with the Olympics generally,

Figure A
© Roberto Machado Noa/LightRocket/Getty Images.

Figure B
© Iurii Osadchi/Shutterstock, Inc.

and Canada's Olympic participation in particular. Days prior to the opening ceremonies of the Sochi Winter Games, Budweiser beer launched an advertising campaign titled "Let the Goals Begin." Budweiser was a direct competitor to the COC's official beer sponsor, Molson Canadian. Budweiser's campaign featured the brand's blimp (the "Red Zeppelin") flying over Canadian cities; the plan was for the blimp to light up in red every time Team Canada's men's or women's hockey team scored a goal (cleverly replicating how red lights go off behind the hockey nets when goals are tallied) **(Figure A)**.

One of Budweiser's television advertisements featured a fictional scene that took place in Russia, during which a group of fans watched Team Canada score a goal during a hockey game, followed by Budweiser's blimp lighting up in red. The advertisements were scheduled to air during Olympic Games telecasts. Although Molson was the COC's official beer sponsor and had right of first refusal to secure exclusivity in the actual Olympic Game telecasts throughout Canada, it instead elected to purchase a smaller, non-exclusive advertising

package—opening the opportunity for Budweiser to purchase advertising time as well.

In addition to launching its advertising campaign, Budweiser supported its Red Light promotion with an aggressive social media campaign. There were no Olympic marks or visuals being used in Budweiser's ads, and the ads did not convey any factually inaccurate messages. Budweiser's campaign was designed to continue its long-time association with the sport of hockey in Canada **(Figure B)**. Although the Red Zeppelin was used for promotion during the Olympics, a Budweiser spokesperson stressed that the brand would continue to use it for many months after the Winter Games, to capitalize on the NHL and Junior Hockey seasons. Budweiser had also made it a point to clarify to consumers that its promotion was not officially authorized by any sanctioning body, a legal tactic known as a "disclaimer." For instance, the fine print on Budweiser's marketing materials included acknowledgments that it was *not* an official sponsor of the 2014 Sochi Olympic Games, the Canadian Olympic Committee, Hockey Canada or the National Hockey League. The primary purpose of its disclaimer was to cure any potential consumer confusion as to Budweiser's "official" relationship with the various Olympic marks rights-holders.

One week later, the Winter Games in Sochi commenced. Over the course of the Games, the Budweiser blimp would light up in red a total of

(continues)

Shining a "Red Light" on Ambush Marketing (*Continued*)

34 times, as both the Canadian men's and women's ice hockey teams won coveted gold medals, with each team having a total of 17 goals.

Questions for Discussion

1. Do you believe that ambush marketing is ethical? Why or why not? In other words, do you think what Budweiser did is an acceptable marketing practice?

2. If you were the vice-president of marketing and sponsorship for Budweiser, what would be your arguments for engaging in this "Red Light" campaign?

3. Assume you are the chief marketing officer for the COC, and you and your lawyers have determined that there is not a strong enough legal basis to sue Budweiser to halt its ambush marketing campaign. How should the COC respond instead? Would you recommend the COC just ignore the campaign and hope that it will not resonate with Canadian consumers or overshadow the advertising and promotional campaign of official sponsor Molson Canadian? Or should the COC call a press conference and publicly decry Budweiser as an "ambush marketer" (popularly known as a "name and shame" campaign)?

Resources

Sport Research Firms (Corporate Headquarters)

Performance Research
25 Mill Street
Newport, RI 02840
www.performanceresearch.com

Sponsorship Research International (SRi)
57 Greens Farms Road
Westport, CT 06880
www.teamsri.com

Turnkey Sports & Entertainment
9 Tanner Street, Suite 8
Haddonfield, NJ 08033
www.turnkeyse.com

Sports Marketing and Promotion Agencies (Corporate Headquarters)

ARC Worldwide
35 W. Wacker Drive
Chicago, IL 60601
www.arcww.com

The Championship Group
1954 Airport Road, Suite 200
Atlanta, GA 30341
www.championshipgroup.com

Endeavor
11 Madison Avenue
New York, NY 10010
9601 Wilshire Boulevard
Beverly Hills, CA 90201
www.endeavorco.com

Fuse Marketing
110 W. Canal St #101
Winooski, VT 05404
www.fusemarketing.com

Genseco Sports Enterprises
1845 Woodall Rogers Freeway
Dallas, TX 75201
www.gsesports.com

GMR Marketing
5000 S. Towne Drive
New Berlin, WI 53151
www.gmrmarketing.com

IEG, LLC

    350 N. Orleans Street, Suite 1200

    Chicago, IL 60654

    www.sponsorship.com

Ion Marketing

    501 Seventh Avenue, Suite 1610

    New York, NY 10018

    www.ionmktggroup.com

Leaddog Marketing

    440 Ninth Avenue

    New York, NY 10001

    www.leaddogmarketing.com

MKTG (previously Team Epic)

    57 Greens Farms Road

    Westport CT 06880

    www.mktg.com

Momentum, Inc.

    250 Hudson Street, 2nd Floor

    New York, NY 10013

    www.momentumww.com

Octagon

    290 Harbor Drive

    Stamford, CT 06902

    www.octagon.com

The Strategic Agency

    177 Mott Street

    New York, NY 10012

    www.thestrategicagency.com

Wasserman

    10960 Wilshire Boulevard, Suite 2200

    Los Angeles, CA 90024

    http://www.teamwass.com

Key Terms

activation, contests, coupons, cross-promotion, free-standing inserts (FSIs), multicultural marketing, point-of-sale/point-of-purchase marketing, premiums, return on investment (ROI), return on objectives (ROO), sales promotion, sampling, sweepstakes

References

Armstrong, K. (1998). Ten strategies to employ when marketing sport to black consumers. *Sport Marketing Quarterly, 7*(3), 11–18.

Badenhausen, K. (2016, December 27). The 10 most marketable athletes in 2016. *Forbes*. Retrieved from https://www.forbes.com/sites /kurtbadenhausen/2016/12/27/the-10-most -marketable-athletes-of-2016/#1caff3a74fe7

Badenhausen, K. (2017, April 26). LeBron James walked away from $15 million in endorsement money from McDonald's for Blaze Pizza. *Forbes*. Retrieved from https://www.forbes .com/sites/kurtbadenhausen/2017/04/26 /lebron-james-walked-away-from-15 -million-in-endorsement-money-from -mcdonalds/#61a13a4c5b23

Broughton, D. (2016a, November 21). Nod on: Bobbleheads top MLB promos again. *SportsBusiness Journal*. Retrieved from http:// www.sportsbusinessdaily.com/Journal /Issues/2016/11/21/Research-and-Ratings /MLB-promotions.aspx?hl=MLB%20Game -Day%20Promotional%20Wrap-up%20&sc=1

Broughton, D. (2016b, March 14). Hyundai drives to the top among NFL sponsors. *SportsBusiness Journal*, p. 18.

BusinessWire. (2017, May 8). Tough Mudder teams up with Amazon to launch digital health, training and personal care resource. Retrieved from http://www.businesswire. com/news/home/20170508005774/en /Tough-Mudder-Teams-Amazon-Launch -Digital-Health

Cordova, T. (2009, April 27). Success begins with understanding the demo. *Street & Smith's SportsBusiness Journal*, p. 17.

Dentzer, S. (1984, August 20). What price prestige. *Newsweek*, p. 28.

Fischer, B. (2017, July 17). Kraft Sports buys a e-sports league franchise. *Boston Business Journal*. Retrieved from https://www .bizjournals.com/boston/news/2017/07/12 /kraft-sports-buys-an-e-sports-league -franchise.html

Gaudiosi, J. (2015, August 6). Here's why Verizon is breaking into eSports. *Fortune*. Retrieved from http://fortune.com/2015/08/06/verizon -esports/

Gregory, S. (2012, July 19). Can Jeremy Lin's appeal in China really help Houston's bottom line? *Time*. Retrieved from http:// keepingscore.blogs.time.com/2012/07/19 /can-jeremy-lins-appeal-in-china-really-help -houstons-bottom-line/

Heitner, D. (2016, September 26). Philadelphia 76ers buy into the business of esports. *Forbes*. Retrieved from https://www.forbes .com/sites/darrenheitner/2016/09/26 /philadelphia-76ers-buys-into-the-business -of-esports/#158f5b35105b

IEG, Inc. (2003a, February 10). Sponsorship is key ingredient for venerable Southern snack brand. *IEG Sponsorship Report*.

IEG, Inc. (2003b, February 10). Assertions. *IEG Sponsorship Report*.

Irwin, R., Sutton, W. A., & McCarthy, L. (2008). *Sport promotion and sales management* (2nd ed.). Champaign, IL: Human Kinetics.

Karp, G. (2014, October 10). Abbott to sponsor world marathon series. *Chicago Tribune*. Retrieved from http://www.chicagotribune .com/business/chi-abbott-to-sponsor-world -marathon-series-20141010-story.html

Lefton, T. (2017, May 1). At $30M a year, will AT&T mobilize for Inglewood stadium? *SportsBusiness Journal*, p. 10.

Lombardo, J. (2017a, February 20). Gatorade's NBA D-League deal seen as boon for research and development as much as brand marketing. *SportsBusiness Journal*, p. 5.

Lombardo, J. (2017b, May 11). FanDuel signs deal to become WNBA's daily fantasy partner. *SportsBusiness Daily*. Retrieved from https:// www.sportsbusinessdaily.com/Daily /Morning-Buzz/2017/05/11/WNBA.aspx

Lozano, K. (2016, August 14). Wings Gaming are the international 2016 champions. *ESports Inquirer*. Retrieved from http://esports .inquirer.net/16246/wings-gaming -international-2016-champions

Mahoney, D. (2016, April 15). NBA to begin selling jersey sponsorships in 2017–2018. Retrieved from http://www.nba.com/2016 /news/04/15/nba-to-begin-selling-jersey -sponsorships-in-2017-18.ap/

Mullin, B., Hardy, S., & Sutton, W. A. (2007). *Sport marketing* (3rd ed.). Champaign, IL: Human Kinetics.

Mullin, B., Hardy, S., & Sutton, W. A. (2014). *Sport marketing* (4th ed.). Champaign, IL: Human Kinetics.

Pellerano, H. (2014). View from the field: Heidi Pellerano. *Sports Marketing Quarterly, 23*, 123–124.

Roettgers, J. (2017, July 13). Snapchat teams up with Formula 1 for Grand Prix stories. *Variety*. Retrieved from http://variety .com/2017/digital/news/snapchat-formula-1 -grand-prix-1202494623/

Rovell, D. (2016, March 242). Estimate: Brands will spend $325 million on esports in 2016. *ESPN.com*. Retrieved from http://www .espn.com/esports/story/_/id/15060795 /brands-spend-325-million-esports-2016

Shank, M. (2009). *Sports marketing* (4th ed.). Upper Saddle River, NJ: Prentice Hall.

Smith, M. (2016, January 5). Cheez-It launches promotion around Final Four called "Munch Mania." *SportsBusiness Journal*, p. 5.

Sood, A. (2017, January 9). 30 sponsorship executives discuss opportunities and trends headed into 2017. *The Sponsorship Space*. Retrieved from https://www

.thesponsorshipspace.com/single
-post/2017/01/12/30-Partnership-Executives
-Discuss-Expected-2017-Trends

Sponsorship's big spenders: IEG's top sponsor
rankings (2016, September 19). *IEG
Sponsorship Report*. Retrieved from http://
www.sponsorship.com/IEGSR/2016/09/19
/Sponsorship-s-Big-Spenders--IEG-s-Top
-Sponsor-Rank.aspx

Sponsorship spending on the NBA totals
$799 million in 2015–2016 season (2016,
May 1). *IEG Sponsorship Report*. Retrieved
from http://www.sponsorship.com
/IEGSR/2016/05/31/Sponsorship-Spending
-On-The-NBA-Totals-$799-Millio.aspx

Sports sponsorship: Statistics & facts. (2017).
Statista. Retrieved from https://www.statista
.com/topics/1382/sports-sponsorship/

Stern, A. (2014, June 16). In the trenches of
Hispanic marketing. *SportsBusiness
Daily*. Retrieved from https://www
.sportsbusinessdaily.com/Journal/Issues
/2014/06/16/In-Depth/Marketers.aspx

Tagliani, H. (2015, April 3). Hispanics and sports:
How to make a big business play. *Orlando
Business Journal*. Retrieved from https://
www.bizjournals.com/orlando/blog/2015/04
/hispanics-and-sports-how-to-make-a-big
-business.html

Ukman, L. (1995). *The IEG's complete guide to
sponsorship: Everything you need to know
about sports, arts, events, entertainment and
cause marketing*. Chicago, IL: International
Events Group.

Vacchiano, R. (2013, July 30). The "Quest" begins
at the Meadowlands. *New York Daily News*.
Retrieved from http://www.nydailynews
.com/blogs/giants/2013/07/the-quest-begins
-at-the-meadowlands-0

Villafane, V. (2016, October 4). ESPN targets
Hispanic audience for growth. *Forbes*.
Retrieved from https://www.forbes.com
/sites/veronicavillafane/2016/10/04/espn
-targets-hispanic-audience-for-growth
/#b3c7cb06ea93

Wilbert, T. (2003, June 24). Home Depot to
sponsor ESPN college pregame show. *Atlanta
Constitution*, p. 1D.

Williams, J. (2017, February 8). Stephen Curry
takes issue with Under Armour leader on
Trump. *New York Times*. Retrieved from
https://www.nytimes.com/2017/02/08/sports
/basketball/stephen-curry-under-armour
-donald-trump-warriors.html?_r=0

Wolf, J. (2016, December 1). Houston Rockets
dive into gaming, hire director of esports.
ESPN.com. Retrieved from http://www.espn
.com/esports/story/_/id/18180082/2017-nba
-houston-rockets-hire-former-archon-ceo
-director-esports

Chapter 16

William Norton

Sport Analytics

Learning Objectives

Upon completion of this chapter, students should be to:

1. Clearly communicate the definition and goals of sport analytics.

2. Conceptualize the theoretical framework of sport analytics and its corresponding components: data management, analytic models, and information systems.

3. Analyze the inter-related nature of analytics and technologically enabled data collection, communicating how connected data sources are shaping how the sport industry utilizes fan and consumer data inputs.

4. Identify key analytics applications in disciplines such as sport finance, economics, facility and event management, marketing, and contract negotiations.

5. Communicate the manner in which analytics is closely linked to business objectives and a process-driven skill set, guided by continuous improvement and constant refinement of data, organizational goals, and measurement techniques.

6. Identify key stakeholders and current industry segments fueling growth in analytics.

7. Identify core skills necessary to pursue a career in analytics.

Introduction

"Numbers tell great stories," says Steve Ballmer, former Microsoft CEO and current owner of the NBA's Los Angeles Clippers (Freakonomics, 2017). "The numbers tell the story that can direct action, and help put things in context." While the rise of big data and the use of the term "analytics" has increased dramatically since the turn of the century, using numbers to direct action and improve results, as Ballmer notes, is nothing new. Managers in many fields have long relied upon data collection, organization, and analysis to create a more complete picture of their business challenges and craft the best path forward. What has undeniably changed in recent years, however, is the size of available data sets, the speed with which managers can organize those data sets, and the computing power that exists to translate that data into actionable insights. As the creation and consumption of data continue to grow by leaps and bounds, managers in sports are being driven to gather the tools and personnel necessary to keep pace and create competitive advantages through the use of analytics. Data expert Bernard Marr notes that "the basic idea behind the phrase 'big data' is that everything we do in our lives . . . soon will leave a digital trace (or data), which can be used and analyzed" (Harrison & Bukstein, 2017, p. 2). As fans young and old flock to stadiums, interact with teams on social media, purchase team apparel online, and memorialize their association with sports through digital means, the need for a sound understanding of analytics has never been greater.

While many hear the term "sport analytics" and think of Billy Beane's "moneyball" Oakland Athletics—and the subsequent Michael Lewis book and adapted movie starring Brad Pitt—it is critically important to realize that the sport analytics industry is not limited to the realm of scouting, player development, and on-field improvement. If anything, the functions of a baseball or basketball operations group borrow heavily from other departments that utilize analytics techniques in day-to-day operations, such as marketing, sales, and information technology. Thus, it is instructive to think of sport analytics as a subset or category within the broader analytics industry that applies to virtually every business sector in today's marketplace. We can divide the subset of sport analytics further, into two idea camps: **business analytics**, which is applied to strategic initiatives such as ticket pricing, customer relationship management, social media marketing, or facility financing; and **player-performance analytics**, which is applied to the more commonly discussed areas of scouting, player development, and the statistical analysis of in-game strategy.

The definition of **sport analytics** is useful to understand, as it uncovers both the processes and goals of analytics endeavors: "the management of structured historical data, the application of predictive analytic models that utilize that data, and the use of information systems to inform decision makers and enable them to help their organizations in gaining a competitive advantage" (Alamar, p. 4, 2013). This definition underscores the three basic components of a sport analytics program, as applied to teams, leagues, and a variety of sports industry stakeholders: **data management**, **predictive models**, and **information systems** (Alamar, 2013). These three components should work as one, forming an integrated system that organizes and processes relevant data, utilizes that data in some novel way, and then displays or visualizes the information to key decision makers. All three components are critically important. As applied to the sport business industry, analytics programs provide managers with novel insight while also saving them time by providing relevant information in an accessible and actionable manner, thereby reducing the time spent by key decision makers on gathering and organizing data (Alamar, 2013).

One can immediately see how having leaders in place who understand and embrace the power and usefulness of data-driven insights in the organization's day-to-day operations is the linchpin to this entire process. Managers who are skeptical of data—or even worse, blind to data due to a lack of proper processes in place—are missing out on a key competitive advantage in today's sports marketplace. These "old guard" managers are depicted in *Moneyball* as the front office personnel in Major League Baseball (MLB) who refused to conceptualize a different scouting and evaluation mind-set, one steeped in the statistical analysis of the value of a run to baseball teams. Beholden to the value of a player as determined by the "eye test" provided to them from scouts and former players, teams overpaid drastically for individual performance outcomes that did not directly contribute to on-field wins. Oakland general manager Billy Beane's quantitatively driven approach exposed a crisis in leadership, one that sent ripples throughout the league and eventually launched a revolution throughout sports. In particular, it led to a dramatic increase in the resources that teams were willing to allocate to realize the competitive advantages from player-performance analytics.

Discussing the definition of sport analytics makes it very clear that there is a meaningful difference between sport statistics and performance-based **metrics**, such as earned run average (ERA), wins above replacement (WAR), and defense-adjusted value over average (DVOA, used in the National Football League [NFL]), and analytics. A metric is a standard of measurement, whereas analytics is a continual process defined by integrating the aforementioned three components to improve organizational efficiency and effectiveness. As statistical circumstances change, such as the spot for a point after touchdown (PAT) in the NFL

shifting from the 2-yard line to the 15-yard line in 2015, or the capacity of the Oakland Raiders football stadium changing with the team's move from the San Francisco Bay Area to Las Vegas in 2019, managers must constantly evolve their analytical techniques in search of more valid and reliable conclusions. In-game strategy under the old PAT rules, or tiered ticket pricing packages in the old Oakland–Alameda County Coliseum, may no longer provide managers with optimal results under the new circumstances in which they do business. Analytics-based projects in the realm of business or player performance, therefore, must constantly evolve and recalibrate based on their desired output, to avoid becoming stagnant and creating misleading results.

In this sense, it is instructive to think of analytics as a *process-driven* discipline. Anytime a decision maker must evaluate how useful data analysis is, a discussion of uncertainty will take place. Simply put, decisions based on unreliable or limited data will carry inherently more uncertainty, or risk, than decisions based on data with greater depth, historical precedent, and clarity. A decision steeped in data analytics will rarely give managers an output that is 100% predictive, but neither will it produce an output that is 0% predictive. The answer will likely lie somewhere in between these two extremes, in the middle ground. To decipher how useful a given analytics output is and how much confidence the work merits, we can ask five simple questions to guide the process (Alamar, 2013):

1. What was the thought process that led to the analysis?

2. What is the context of the result?

3. How much uncertainty is in the analysis?

4. How does the result inform the decision-making process?

5. How can we further reduce the uncertainty?

Through this continual process of intuitive questioning, managers can identify holes in the analysis that require greater amounts, or more accurate forms, of data. They can also carefully recalibrate the focus of the project to reduce the uncertainty and variance inherent in the data collection. This step-by-step questioning of assumptions is key and core to analytics as a process, as the five-question model outlined here is an exercise in reducing *noise* within our analysis. What does this mean? Nate Silver, a popular modern statistical analyst and political forecaster who created the quantitatively driven analytics website *FiveThirtyEight.com*, offers a perspective on thinking in terms of probabilities in the work that we do, and shortening the gap between what we know, and what we think we know: "The signal is the truth. The noise is what distracts us from the truth" (Silver, 2012, p. 17).

Just because two variables have a statistical relationship, or **correlation**, to each other—like, say, higher attendance at a Tuesday afternoon Chicago Cubs game in late April than on a Tuesday afternoon in early September—it does not mean that the month of the game has any reliable effect on attendance. The April game may have had higher attendance because of weather, team performance, opponent, promotional activity, or the fact that the September game fell around Labor Day weekend, when Chicago-area consumers travel. In other words, the month may just be noise surrounding the analysis of in-season stadium attendance. This speaks to the commonly cited maxim, "causation doesn't imply correlation," which cautions us to not let relationships between variables that could be simple coincidence—the noise—be mistaken as the signal, or truth. The five-question process described here addresses this hazard in data analytics and minimizes the likelihood of misguided analytics conclusions.

This process of careful examination, and reexamination, is important to industry

stakeholders and research firms that have staked their reputation on concise analysis and accurate forecasting. The Society for American Baseball Research (SABR) is largely credited with pioneering advanced statistical analysis in the game of baseball and is the source of the term "sabermetrics." This term refers to the empirical analysis of baseball, primarily the analysis of in-game activity, and in large part evolved out of the work of Bill James. In the 1960s, James began publishing his annual *Baseball Abstract*, which was full of groundbreaking, novel insights about how the industry could better measure performance. James spoke at the 2017 SABR Analytics Conference, where he shared his thoughts on the proper use of data in an age in which data have never been more accessible, and the use of data has never been more encouraged by industry practitioners:

> Analysis does not start with data. Analysis starts with a *question*, like "Does clutch hitting actually exist?" or "Does the pitcher actually control the number of hits he gives up as a percentage of balls in play?" If you can find a question that is up in the clouds, and you can connect the data to the question that is up in the clouds, that's analysis. If you start with data and go wherever that data leads you, that's just farting around with statistics. (James, 2017)

This idea ties nicely to Silver's insight about the confusion that often exists between the inherent "noise" tied up in following data wherever it may take us, versus the concerted effort to use analytics as a tool to create novel insight and quicker, more efficient decision-making processes. Wherever one works in sports, fighting to find the most meaningful questions—who are our most valuable fans from a revenue perspective, what is the optimal price for a Tuesday night Yankees game on a chilly night in New York, or what is the best way to capture social media engagement from Duke University basketball fans—is the beginning of creating true value from analytics endeavors.

History of Sport Analytics

The arc of analytics as we know it today is following a parallel path to the rise of computer science and machine-based programming. As computing power increased exponentially in the mid-twenty-first century, the three components of sport analytics defined earlier—data management, predictive models, and information systems—became more refined, capable of more complex and sophisticated methods of data-based learning. IBM and other technology leaders drove innovation through the computer revolution of the 1960s, developing tools that would later contribute to competitive advantages in virtually every segment of sport analytics: ticketing, sales, scouting and development, corporate sponsorship, customer relationship management, finance, event management, and more.

The phrase **business intelligence** became commonplace and synonymous with the analytics industry after 1988 and the Multiway Data Analysis Consortium, wherein it evolved as a more relatable term to describe projects rich in data storage, analysis, and operations (Better Buys, 2014). From 1956 to 2015, there was a 1 trillion-fold increase in computing performance, which is almost impossible to fathom but provides context as to the historical arc of what, say, a sport organization could do with fan data in the 1950s compared to what it can do today (Experts Exchange, 2017).

Much of the discussion about the historical foundations of sport analytics revolves around player-performance analysis in the game of baseball, given its history in America and the fact that each discrete pitcher-versus-hitter event represents a probabilistic outcome that can be quantified in a unique way. In the late 1850s, Henry Chadwick created the baseball box score, giving fans and journalists a way to follow the game numerically and keep track of player performance (SABR, 2008). Data collection and the importance placed on specific outcomes, such as the home run as Babe Ruth ascended to greatness in the early 1900s, evolved as the economics of the sporting industry developed. The 1950s and early 1960s ushered in the development of more nuanced accounts of advanced strategy used in sport, such as George Lindsey's analysis of lineup adjustments and defensive strategy, or Earnshaw Cook's 1964 book *Percentage Baseball* (Lindsey, 1959). These research endeavors advanced the conversation around in-game strategy, and began to chip away at the decades-old conventional wisdom of trusting instinct over numbers.

The aforementioned *Baseball Abstract* by Bill James, however, altered the trajectory of player-performance analytics. Beyond the detailed, thought-provoking work James conducted in an effort to confront conventional wisdom and reveal a more mathematically sound way to play the game, his writings inspired a generation of readers who would go on to shape the analytics industry. John Dewan was one of those readers. In the 1984 *Baseball Abstract*, James proposed an idea that would revolutionize the game and spawn the birth of, among other things, the fantasy gaming industry we see thriving as a multibillion-dollar enterprise today: *Project Scoresheet*. What James was proposing was a grassroots endeavor to collect and catalogue detailed levels of data on every single MLB game, and enter that data into a computer database. James knew it all had to start with a more candid and honest look at data, which, to that point in time, were neither centralized nor properly analyzed. With followers like Dewan on board, James believed, "there is no need for the next generation of fans to be as ignorant as we are" (Sawchik, 2015).

Project Scoresheet created robust data that fans, media entities, and teams could use to unearth new and revolutionary insights about player performance. But beyond this one endeavor, James's energy for truth through analytics inspired men like Dewan to start their own projects built on the passion they had for uncovering truth through analytics. In 1987, Dewan invested in, and became the president of, a company called STATS, now an industry leader in cutting-edge statistical analysis; he later founded Baseball Info Solution (Sawchik, 2015), a leading commercial provider of statistical information for teams, publications, and online services.

With baseball fueling the growth and acceptance of advanced analytics in sport decision making, other sports began to take notice. As the industry grew steadily through the 1990s and early 2000s, hundreds of companies like the ones Dewan formed began to sprout up in search of ways to provide teams, leagues, and managers with the newest technological and data-driven tools.

At the league level, managers also began to invest in technology capable of growing the game. MLB's *PITCHf/x* software was installed in every MLB stadium starting in 2006 (Fangraphs, 2010). Capable of using an algorithm to track the velocity, movement, release point, spin, and pitch location for every pitch thrown via mounted cameras in each stadium, *PITCHf/x* changed the way fans, media, and front office personnel could analyze player performance. It was, in a way, the modern-day equivalent of James's *Project Scoresheet*, executed at the much more detailed level of a singular pitch and available in real time through digital means.

The National Basketball Association (NBA) and many European soccer leagues followed a similar path, working with the aforementioned STATS and its *SportVu* optical tracking software, a six-camera computerized program installed in arenas that collected data at a rate of 25 times per second. If sound data analysis starts with the *question*, then having expansive data sets to help address those questions naturally follows next. As the pace of technological innovation has increased and the investment in analytics platforms has grown, so, too, have the tools available for stakeholders across the industry.

Now, let's turn our attention to sport analytics practices in context, examining several ways stakeholders in the industry are implementing analytical methods in their work.

Applied Analytics Topics in Sport

This section profiles relevant analytics areas of the sport management industry today, focusing on several examples of how data analytics is being applied to provide competitive advantages to sport business stakeholders.

Marketing

Strategic marketing initiatives have always hinged on an organization's ability to understand its target consumer, and position products according to the functional and emotional needs of that consumer. Nike, Gatorade, Madison Square Garden, and the Golden State Warriors, while vastly different enterprises in terms of capabilities, goals, and staffing, all have similar goals when it comes to collecting market research and data-driven insights, and then using those insights to target high-value consumers and inform marketing strategy. The data being used can be as general as market demographics, or it can drill down with greater specificity to understand individual buying habits, sensitivity to pricing, and sentiment toward particular events or brand campaigns.

Growth in available consumer data has increased on a parallel path with the increase of tracking technology in the market. The smartphone, mobile purchasing platforms such as PayPal, and various geo-tracking technologies have opened up new pathways for viewing consumer behavior data; this, in turn, allows marketers to analyze and filter those data to unlock strategies that target consumers along their path to purchase. Have you ever walked past the souvenir store in your favorite ballpark, and been served an automated message through the ballpark application for 20% off the jersey of your favorite player? Or maybe after the purchase of a multi-game ticket package for five games in August, you have been served a direct email from the team promoting the promotional giveaways for those five specific games, and a digital coupon for 50% off sunscreen from the team's sunscreen sponsor. After all, it will be hot in August!

Some of these communications can feel overly intrusive, but as digital capabilities in the sport industry continue to grow and consumers shift more of their interactive experiences to mobile platforms, key stakeholders will continue to try to utilize the data available to them to offer value, grow revenue, and increase affinity for their products. Specifically, given the "event-based" nature of sports programming, the industry has witnessed the rise of **proximity marketing** as a key part of the marketing mix. Proximity marketing is a form of location-based advertising powered through data-based profiles, where communication with a consumer is timely, relevant, and personal. It is tech driven and targeted, providing key decision makers with teams, leagues, brands, and stadiums new ways to interact with different types of consumers and personalize the sports experience. True personalization can come only with data collection and better understanding of a typical customer—for example, a hypothetical person named Joe Smith, a 25-year-old engineer, who has come to 5 to 10 games each year for more than 5 years, prefers bleacher seats to lower grandstand seats, buys hot dogs and water primarily, and is a part of the team's fan loyalty program. This personal profile is created through data traces such as credit card purchases, email registrations, and membership accounts, all opted into by the user and then strategically filtered and analyzed by the organization.

This kind of personalized, one-to-one understanding of fan preferences is supported and maintained by analytics platforms such as team apps and proximity marketing technologies such as **beacons**. Beacons have been implemented in 93% of MLB stadiums, 75% of NFL stadiums, 53% of NBA arenas, and 47% of National Hockey League (NHL) arenas to date (Unacast, 2016). These small, portable devices are positioned in key locations (e.g., the fan shop, stadium entrance, and 300-level seating sections) and serve up a contextual communication relevant to each particular location. Gone are the days of managers simply hoping a family of four comes to the stadium and automatically knows about the interactive new display on the stadium concourse, the customized new jersey and hat offerings in the team store, or the wildly appetizing new barbeque cuisine added to six concessionaire stands throughout the arena. Gathering data on fan preferences, locations, and past behaviors enables managers to segment their customers, and then retarget specific customers with customized offers, loyalty campaigns, seat upgrades, and event navigation features. Beacons represent one of a number of proximity marketing delivery platforms being utilized today, as marketers look to strike a balance between keeping the sporting experience authentic and fun, while serving up added value to the fan and increasing revenue and loyalty to the organization.

Similar mobile-enhanced, data-driven experiences will continue to define the sporting experience across a range of various sport marketing touch points: in-stadium, in-store, in-app, direct email, and especially on social media, where user behavior and sentiment at the one-to-one level can not only be tracked, but actually encouraged through user-generated engagement promoted by the nature of social media. The creation of experiences that encourage a mutually beneficial data exchange, followed by the careful management and analysis of centralized, standardized data, will continue to be the fuel that drives the sport marketing world of personalization that we see today.

Management

You need look no further than the newly designed Mercedes Benz Stadium—home to the NFL's Atlanta Falcons, Major League Soccer's (MLS's) Atlanta United FC, and other marquee college sports games and top-tier music events— for an example of how analytics will continue to pace the maturation and growth of the sport business industry. According to an announcement made in early 2016, IBM's Smarter Stadium Network (SSN) technologies will partner with AMB Sports & Entertainment to power the stadium and create a fully digitized fan experience driven by the power of data. While IBM is certainly not a sport-centric company, it has expanded its applications to the sport industry. In the case of Mercedes Benz Stadium, IBM is leveraging the power of mobility to create a "highly contextual, more personalized game day experience for fans, all through the integration of analytics, mobile, social, security and cloud technologies" (Atlanta Falcons, 2015). The average event attendee no longer sits back in the seat and passively consumes what is presented to him or her. This has become abundantly clear to facility and event management agencies, which have a vested interest in presenting engagement opportunities through the convergence of physical and digital experiences delivered through the context of sports.

Data lie at the center of this exchange, with a **back-end** partner like IBM supplying hardware, software, and information technology services capable of powering the experience and housing data for future analysis, and a **front-end**

platform like a team app or league website delivering the benefits of a more connected sport experience. Back-end tools usually consist of a server, an application, and a database. These power the data management functions of a given project. What a user interacts with and ultimately communicates through is referred to as the front-end. A website is a good example of a front-end platform, while the server and database storing your credit card information and checkout preferences remain out of sight on the back-end. Thus, in Atlanta, the consumer-facing benefits available to attendees of events held at Mercedes Benz Stadium will be communicated and delivered through the sports property serving as the front-end provider (the Falcons or United FC), rather than through IBM.

Of course, not all data-driven insights need to come from IBM, or from other digitally powered endeavors. Mercedes Benz Stadium will also offer the lowest food and beverage prices in all of team sports in 2017, largely because of quantitative analysis of a simple fan survey that examined the primary drivers of fan experience (*Sports Illustrated*, 2016). Here, the role of analytics in stadium and event management can be viewed through two applications.

First, surveying represents a common data collection method in sport market research. The management and communication of key survey findings to senior decision makers through a clear and concise information system may provide novel insights, such as the recommendation to dramatically lower food and beverage prices based on negative customer sentiment. This research process is steeped in the understanding that data will inform more accurate decision making.

Second, utilizing analytics can be seen in the process, or approach, taken to arrive at this pricing strategy. Managers may have conducted research to examine discretionary income in the greater Atlanta area, and examined average prices for other substitute entertainment expenditures such as a city fair or music concert. Compiling and visualizing these data help to inform the decision as to which pricing range is appropriate on the basis of quantifiable market data, instead of depending on raw guesswork. The stadium ownership group likely believes they will make up for the lost revenue on $2 sodas and $3 pizzas through increased purchase volume (the 670 concession points in the stadium represent a 65% increase over purchase points in the now-extinct Georgia Dome), or a willingness from event attendees to spend more on tickets, merchandise, or parking given the bargain they received on food and beverage. Regardless of whether the price drop was made with larger goals in mind, this decision was motivated by a careful consideration of data and the use of analytics.

Finance

Financial managers in the sport industry use analytics on a daily basis, whether they are carefully structuring player contracts in accordance with their league's salary cap policy, calculating the projected cost of new stadium enhancements, or assessing the risk of future investment options for their organization. Finance departments in sport are typically not as large as other industry segments, especially considering the market valuation that most teams, leagues, and brands hold. For example, the NFL's Baltimore Ravens, valued in September 2016 by *Forbes* at $2.3 billion, list just six principal finance employees on the team's website. While quite lean, this group will implement analytics processes across a range of integral tasks for the organization. If we lean on the three-pronged definition of sport analytics outlined earlier in the chapter, we can examine the ways managers in sport finance roles would utilize this framework. In the brief outline that follows, we will use the example of salary cap and player compensation management for illustrative purposes.

Data Management

The process starts with managing the data available to you, and cleaning those data appropriately. This cleaning process consists of three steps: (1) **data standardization**, where all information and data are organized in a common format with a standard set of definitions; (2) **data centralization**, where all organizational data are stored in a central location; and finally (3) **data integration**, where data are merged to maximize value to the organization (Alamar, 2013). In the salary cap and player compensation example, this process would consist of gathering historical data on the performance, health, and personal information of the player in question, and standardizing all of those inputs in accordance with league-wide compensation models. The data would then be centralized in a location accessible to key decision makers, and integrated with other data inputs, such as the existing compensation for players on the roster, and luxury tax implications associated with going over certain salary cap thresholds.

Predictive Models

Much of the finance industry revolves around assessing risk, and recommending appropriate future actions that lessen the risk exposure experienced by the organization. In this area, **predictive analytics**—which uses statistical models and forecasting techniques to understand the future and answer the question, "What could happen?"—is particularly useful. By comparison, **descriptive analytics** uses data aggregation and data mining to provide insight into the past and shed light on what has happened (Halo, 2016).

In our example, let's assume our hypothetical manager works in baseball and that our player in question is a former high school draft pick who has emerged as a star in his third year with the team. To sign this player as a draftee, the team had to pay a $1.25 million signing bonus—which has been well worth it, given the player's performance to date. Since that signing date, the player has been paid at a bargain to the organization, close to the league minimum for his position. Now, however, a decision must be made: Is it financially prudent to offer the player a long-term contract and lock up his services for an extended period, or should the team let him shop for a new home in free agency?

The organization has an idea of what it would like to pay the player, but more data are needed. Here, a predictive model is put in place that aggregates the historical performance of players with similar profiles over time, calculates the opportunity cost of losing the player and having to replace his value in free agency, and examines common success metrics such as wins above replacement to assess the player's fair market value. An algorithm is also used to calculate the impact of the player on ancillary revenue streams—not just wins and losses—by examining the player's impact on attendance, merchandise, and sponsorship (this will be more difficult given the "noise" surrounding these data).

Lastly, once the fair market value of the player is determined, the finance team may carefully analyze inflation and interest rates during the life of the contract, to understand how organizational income will change over time. The team may also structure the deal to backload much of the salary toward the end of the contract; this strategy is often used by managers in sport finance as a way to lessen the impact on current cash flows. A dollar today is worth more than a dollar seven years from now, because the team can invest and earn interest on the dollar it has today. Thus, backloading the compensation lessens the present-day impact of the contract financially to the team and utilizes the financial concept of time value of money. In this way, the predictive model

employed by the finance team uses a variety of data-based inputs to create a holistic forecast of what the player is worth and, in turn, what the initial team offer should be.

Information System

Hours of research, statistics, and discussions have been spent in hopes of creating a financial strategy for this particular player that (1) mitigates the risk to the organization and (2) provides novel insights to the ultimate decision maker in an efficient and effective manner. But visualizing and presenting the recommendation in a clear and strategic format is as important as the analytical rigor that went into the process. One cannot simply hand a manager an Excel spreadsheet full of data and expect clear, concise decisions to be made in a business setting. Data-driven storytelling is a key skill set of managers in sport analytics, and in this example the power of the financial insight lies in how it will be visualized using graphs, charts, colors, and other visual aids, utilizing information systems as such scorecards, dashboards, and automated systems.

The financial insight in our hypothetical example is that our star player should be paid a given salary in a specifically structured manner, based on historical precedent, personal performance metrics, team and league cap constraints, revenue considerations, and the time value of money. As you can see, that is a lot of information and insight to communicate; thus, careful consideration must be given to which information is most relevant, how it should be prioritized, and what the overarching organizational goals are. Seeing that analytics is just one component of a broader interconnected business strategy, the financial management of player compensation must adhere to the business goals of the team, and be presented as such.

This is just one example outlining how analytics may be applied to the field of team finance in sport. Other applications are seen in the management of stadium financing projects, risk assessment across key organizational assets such as practice facilities, and profit and loss forecasting in the realm of ticket operations.

Economics

Ticket pricing in sports is inherently based on supply and demand, which ties directly to the field of economics. Sport management has seen an increase in employees joining the industry with economics backgrounds in recent years, in part because of how clearly new digital tools portray market demand and consumer behavior. This is especially true with ticket pricing. The rise of secondary ticket platforms such as StubHub and Seat Geek have given sport stakeholders a vast amount of data to work with as they customize ticket offerings and seek to capture all revenues available to the organization. This evolution, in turn, has led to vastly more sophisticated pricing models, and an influx of ticketing techniques targeted at meeting organization goals, whether that be maximizing game revenue or maximizing game attendance.

Analytics techniques are used in pricing tickets, specifically with two different approaches seen today: **variable ticket pricing** and **dynamic ticket pricing**. Variable ticket pricing is the concept of tiered pricing: Not every game is created equal, so why should the prices always be equal? A Tuesday night game at Fenway Park in April pitting the Boston Red Sox against the Tampa Bay Rays will attract a vastly different level of market demand than a Saturday afternoon matinee against the New York Yankees in August. Thus, teams variably price their games and create tiers, or groups, of similarly priced inventory. This does not always mean the price goes up; in fact, oftentimes teams will lower prices on historically low-attended events to try to increase demand and fill seats. Look at a team's ticket pricing today

and you will notice "premium," "value," "weekday saver," and other terms assigned to groups of games and their assigned prices, so consumers can understand what level of investment the inventory carries.

Dynamic ticket pricing takes into account the cost of a game on the secondary market—like StubHub—in the lead-up to a single game. Hypothetical demand for an event may be understood by the event organizer in the preseason, but as we get closer to game time and actual demand becomes clearer, analytical adjustments can be made to pricing to maximize revenue or attendance. In this way, the price is dynamic, in that it shifts constantly. A $85 ticket in the lower concourse may adjust to $65, or $115, depending on how market demand is fluctuating in real time. These transactions take place quickly on digital platforms, which allows teams to capture data and create real-time demand curves based on actual market behavior, and then model future games accordingly. If the Red Sox managers have five years of historical data on April weekday games, complete with average weather temperatures, team records, and concession sales data, they can optimize their business objectives through the use of data analytics and ticketing models.

Major League Baseball has seen the greatest use of dynamic ticket pricing across all of its member clubs, given that variation of demand from game to game is greatest across its 162-game season. MLB has, therefore, sought to differentiate through the use of supply and demand models in tune with each of its franchise markets. With many teams utilizing this economically sound ticket approach and adjusting prices five or six times before sale, in-market data showed that in 2012 that teams were able to raise full-price attendance by 15% and total ticket revenue by 30% (*The Economist*, 2012). This is yet another example of how data unlock key insights that can drive better decision making in sports.

Law

Contract negotiations as it applies to sport law provides yet another example of how data analytics is used in today's sports world. "Player value" is constantly debated within a sport-crazed culture, but when sport agents and team representatives sit down to assign the term (number of years) and dollar figure to a contract, any subjective opinion takes a back seat to objectively sound data and the ability to tell a story about relative value using quantitative analysis. One of the more commonly talked-about figures in sport agency is Scott Boras, the famous (or infamous, depending on how you view the state of baseball compensation today) MLB agent who has represented players such as Alex Rodriguez and Bryce Harper. A lawyer by trade, Boras has earned a reputation for earning his clients exorbitant contracts, through intelligent negotiating and an in-depth knowledge of both the market for premier talent and MLB's collective bargaining agreement and salary cap.

Boras always works with an information edge, approaching contractual negotiations with thick binders consisting of in-depth analysis, player comparisons, and performance-driven arguments in favor of the bottom-line figure he believes his client deserves. These reams of data are fueled by Boras's embracing of analytics as a strategic tool to accomplish business results: They are built from a $7 million computer system operated by numerous staffers, including engineers and computer programmers from prestigious scientific universities (*Grantland*, 2015). Profiles are built from the ground up for clients, with a careful understanding of market demand and which traits are most sought after in the market. Another manager of the baseball division of a major athlete representation agency, commenting on negotiations following a sub-par statistical season, reports that his team used "complex analysis

to recreate the player's statistical profile in order to more accurately demonstrate his future potential. This convinced two teams to enter the process that had not previously been engaged, resulting in more options for a client" (*Grantland*, 2015).

Whatever the figure a player seeks in contract negotiations, the days of simply making a subjective argument regarding attitude, community impact, and team-first marketability are gone. This is not to say that a player's "soft skills," or personality, do not matter in contractual negotiations, because they very often do. Nevertheless, objective, mathematically sound performance metrics on positional value, durability, key metrics of success such as wins above replacement, and defensive acuity are now critically important tools to accomplishing success in negotiations. In the final offer arbitration system utilized by MLB, the richness of one's data can oftentimes make a difference equating to millions of dollars for the player. For the most part, the power in this relationship lies with the team, which has more data and greater levels of insight into player performance than most representation agencies. Boras Corporation and other agency stakeholders have made strategic investments in analytics to reshape that balance of power and unlock a competitive advantage through advanced analytics to better serve their client bases.

Skill Sets and Career Opportunities

Many sports fans have likely heard of the term "five-tool player," which refers to the five traditional scouting grades assigned to baseball players: hitting for power, hitting for average, base running skills and speed, throwing ability, and fielding ability. A five-tool player is a star who grades out well in all five categories, and a similar rubric has been utilized to assess prospective analytics professionals' ability to add value to the industry. The **five-tool analytics**

profile consists of an individual's ability to do the following (King, 2015):

1. Ask the right questions that get at the problem, or objective, the organization wants solved.

2. Collect the correct data—clean, complete, and representative.

3. Understand statistics sufficiently to model the data properly.

4. Interpret the data, sorting out what is likely meaningful from what is not.

5. Communicate findings in a way that a given audience can understand and act on.

As you can see, the three-pronged definition of sport analytics folds nicely into this five-tool analysis: Data management (question 2), predictive models (question 3), and information systems (questions 4 and 5) are integral to understanding the value one can offer the sport analytics industry. Just as in baseball, it is difficult to find a true five-tool analytics player. Those individuals who are best at collecting and modeling data sometimes struggle to communicate and visualize those data to key decision makers. Others may be able to ask the right questions amidst a cluttered landscape, identify a key challenge to the organization that requires data-driven insights, and articulate findings in a clear, manageable manner, yet struggle with the statistical analysis necessary to create a metric or measurement of success. Specializing in even two or three of these five tools will allow prospective applicants to attract interest in the analytics industry. It's also important to be able to blend soft skills (questions 1 and 5) and hard skills (questions 2–4), so as to bring a variety of capabilities to the table and be flexible enough to work within and across different organizational departments (marketing *and* information technology departments, for example).

As an understanding of analytics becomes more prevalent for organizations across the sport industry, greater emphasis is certainly being placed on academic coursework that stresses quantitative rigor and mathematical techniques. Concentrations such as computer science, information technology, statistics, data science, computer systems engineering, and economics are all becoming more commonplace among applicants to the sport industry. While sports serve as the overarching context for many jobs in the field of analytics, the day-to-day details of the work itself involve proficiency with mathematics, statistics, machine learning, programming, database design, and data visualization.

Specifically, linear algebra, probabilities, and statistics are all fundamental courses that will help one understand the quantitative techniques driving analytics projects. R, Python, C/C++, and SQL are all types of programming and database languages that will differentiate applicants from their peers in an interview or job application process. It is not necessary to know all of these computer languages, but to implement sport analytics projects in a timely and organized manner, organizations most assuredly need coders and database technicians who can operate with large amounts of data in a streamlined way.

The types of organizations one can work for within sport analytics, and the pathway into those organizations, vary. All sectors of the industry—from teams, to leagues, agencies, associations, stadium management firms, and third-party vendors—hire frequently for business analytics roles often tied to revenue-generating projects. The sport analytics market, in terms of size, is forecast to expand from $123.7 million in 2016 to $616.7 million by 2021, with a growth rate of nearly 38% (*Markets and Markets*, 2017). The increased demand from management for real-time access to insights that can be transformed into revenues represents a huge opportunity for the sport analytics market, which in turn creates hiring opportunities.

There are typically three structural ways that sport analytics will be implemented into the day to day processes of an organization. The first is a centralized structure known as **analytics center of excellence (ACE)**, in which all analytics personnel are grouped together fulfilling tasks across multiple departments (Alamar, 2013). The second is a **decentralized structure**, in which individual analytics employees are embedded into each department to help address the needs, of, say, the coaching, scouting, and front office groups separately. The third is a **hybrid structure**, in which the first two approaches are blended to maximize the benefits of each. These structural considerations are noteworthy as one examines companies of interest and their management approach to grouping, and implementing, analytics workflows.

It is helpful to think of the sport analytics ecosystem in terms of two groups: analytics **vendors** and analytics **end users**. Vendors provide solutions and services to the end users for different application areas. Today's vendors consist of companies you may or may not have heard of—IBM, SAP, SAS, STATS, and Opta, to name just a few. These technology and data providers create proprietary tools, systems, and models that provide end users with a competitive advantage in a given business area. Companies such as STATS, Baseball Info Solutions, Sportvision, and Catapult Sports differentiate themselves based on applications that offer novel insights unavailable to end users due to the investment needed in terms of time, technology, and critical thinking.

Some vendors to watch and keep note of are listed in **Table 16-1**, along with specific details about the competitive advantage they offer the market through analytics initiatives.

Table 16-1 Notable Analytics Vendors		
Vendor	**Description**	**End-User Application**
STATS, LLC	A sports data, technology, statistics, and content company providing content to media platforms, broadcasters, leagues, teams, fantasy providers, brands, and players.	Provides *SportVu* product to multiple European soccer clubs; it consists of a camera system and tracking algorithm that extracts and processes tracking data for players and the ball.
Baseball Info Solutions (BIS)	A specialized collector, interpreter, and distributor of baseball statistics to sports teams, agents, media, fantasy services, and game companies.	BIS provides multiple MLB teams with defensive shift data, used for advance scouting and player development.
WHOOP	A performance-enhancing wearable technology company aimed at optimizing human performance through biometric and training analytics.	Partnership with NFL Players Association to use WHOOP Strap 2.0, which will provide athletes with access to, and the ability to earn money off of, their health data.
Sportvision	A leader in sports broadcasting technology and an innovator of sports and entertainment products for fans, media companies, and marketers.	Partnership with MLB and its media partners to create "K-Zone" live pitch tracking visualization on screen, allowing fans and broadcasters to track the strike zone and umpire performance in real time.
TrackMan	Technology company that develops, manufactures, and sells 3D ball-flight measurement equipment used in different sports.	TrackMan technology is used in golf broadcasts on every major network. More than 150 Professional Golfers' Association (PGA) Tour players rely on it to fine-tune their game.
Catapult Sports	A wearable technology company that creates scientifically validated analytics on athlete performance for teams, players, and managers.	Catapult and University of Oregon are collaborating to measure athlete training and rehabilitation metrics, to increase performance and health.

All information is publicly available on the company websites. The information presented here is not a complete description of company services or an endorsement of said services.

End users are more recognizable to the average sports consumer, and adoption within this group is expanding rapidly. We can examine several sectors of the industry to more clearly see which leading players constitute the end users of analytics solutions.

Leagues

Leagues, such as the NBA's TMBO arm (Team Operations & Business Operations), hire employees predominantly along the business analytics track; for example, they often hire former team executives or those with experience in the management consulting and financial investment industry. MLB Advanced Media (MLBAM) is another league-affiliated company that specializes in digital strategy, interactive technology, and advanced analytical thinking within the sport industry. MLBAM manages not only all things digital for Major League Baseball, but also owns the rights to manage digital assets and/or streaming capabilities for the National Hockey League, March Madness, and WWE's Wrestlemania, among others (*Forbes*, 2014). Operating primarily as digital tech company, MLBAM is built on the skills of analytics personnel managing data tied to sports consumption behavior, fan preferences, and digital media activity.

Teams

The typical team in the United States will utilize analytics across a variety of business units. In terms of player-performance analytics, sports teams hire statistical analysts, coders, and data scientists to manage matters such as salary cap finances, scouting and player development, and predictive forecasting, with baseball and basketball leading the way in terms of the number of positions available. Football, hockey, and soccer teams lag behind on player-performance analytics, largely due to the complexity of the game play and a lack of reliability in data collection.

Kraft Analytics Group (KAGR) is a technology company focused on data management, advanced analytics, and strategic marketing in the sport and entertainment industry. If you recognize the name, it is because the company stems from Kraft Sports Group, a subsidiary of the Kraft family, who own the New England Patriots and New England Revolution. As the importance placed on data analytics expands, more teams will likely create "analytics arms" within their organizations, which function as stand-alone companies mining for insights and competitive advantages across a range of business concentrations.

Media and Research Companies

As more data regarding games, athletes, performance statistics, and venues become available, media and news distributors will directly benefit from this trend. Visually enhancing the product presented to consumers viewing at home, reading online, or streaming on their tablet creates additional engagement with the sport product and, therefore, additional opportunities to expand content offerings and generate advertising and sponsorship revenues. Major broadcast and media partners have begun embracing the analytically inclined viewer, implementing technology and statistics-focused resources available to them so as to amplify the experience for the viewer. As you watch the next major broadcast of your favorite sports team, pay close attention to the ways in which statistics, player/ball tracking, and game play data are visualized and implemented into the production of the broadcast.

A host of performance analytics websites, research platforms, and think tanks have also emerged in the industry. Companies such as SportDesk Media, Fangraphs, Baseball Prospectus, Society for American Baseball Research (SABR), NBA Savant, Football Outsiders, and Pro Football Focus, to name a few, have emerged as leading providers of analytics insight into the games and sports we love. The free and widely accessible use of these data has created a new generation of sport fans, armed with more accurate data on their favorite players and teams, and a more nuanced view into how performance is tracked, compared, and rewarded within a given sport. These platforms represent immense growth opportunities for those interested in the detailed creation of content that is backed by analytical insight.

Current Issues

The preceding section on skills and career opportunities in sport analytics reveals a new and emerging field of **wearable analytics**, which provides cutting-edge data and performance insights based on the biometric activity of the user. As the technology to acquire real-time data about everyday athletes became more sophisticated with the rise of health trackers in the market, such as Fitbit, stakeholders across the sport industry took notice. Many of the top apparel and sport lifestyle brands such as Adidas, Nike, and Under Armour began crafting direct-to-consumer wearable products that would empower daily exercise regimens with customized workouts, detailed performance history, and tracking capabilities. For sport brands, wearable technology not only serves as a revenue-generating product category, but also offers direct engagement with and data collection from current buyers. Given the value being offered from the brand to the consumer—essentially a computer worn on the wrist, which helps the user improve performance and craft a more purposeful, insightful exercise routine—the opportunity to gather personalized data and valuable market research is wide-ranging in this field.

For an industry segment that is not even a decade old, it has not taken long for wearable technology to attract the interest of sport stakeholders. The insights being gathered on the consumer side of the market can just as easily be capitalized on the professional side, especially in the realm of player health and asset management. Teams at both the professional and amateur levels have moved away from the performance metrics of the past, such as how much weight a player can lift or how many repetitions of a given workout the athlete can perform, and have started thinking more strategically about recovery, optimal practice and travel times, and injury prevention. The financial savings available to teams that can, for example, keep their best players healthy even just 5% more per season is substantial, when one considers the annual impact of player costs.

Wearables implemented by companies such as Catapult Sports provide instantaneous power, acceleration, and speed metrics, as well as mid-workout reviewing capabilities for constant improvement. This specific technology is placed within the back of a basketball jersey, and supplies **inertial movement analysis** (IMA) (YouTube, 2016). The data are collected, tracked, and then fed to a back-end computer dashboard, where the data can be sorted, filtered, and analyzed by managers in search of performance insights.

The adage "You can't manage what you can't measure" has been embraced by the leading companies within this innovative new industry segment, one that seemingly holds promising value in terms of uncovering areas of athlete performance previously thought to be unquantifiable, such as sleep efficiency and micro-muscle recovery. The platforms tied to wearable technology assist teams, players, and coaches across a range of analytically driven outputs, from scheduling optimal practice times, to understanding the lift of a jump shot or the burst of a player's first step, to creating a baseline benchmark for an athlete's hydration level when she wakes up in the morning. Organizations have begun to create positions such as "director of sports performance" and "vice-president of wearable tech performance" to develop internal competency with this emerging technology.

While certain college programs have instituted wearable tech on an in-game basis, professional leagues have primarily utilized these tools in practice, carefully monitoring the market and the types of insights available before approving the technology for official game use. Starting in 2017, however, MLB approved players to use WHOOP's suite of performance wearables, marking one of the first league-wide wearables deals. The *WHOOP Day Strain*, for example, allows players to quantify and analyze strain on the body across the entirety of the day—a marked improvement over, say, analyzing pitch counts or miles run on the treadmill (WHOOP, 2017). Strain is measured on a 0–21 scale, providing a more sophisticated examination of health, performance, and recovery. Also, as noted earlier, the *WHOOP Strap 2.0* is being utilized in football by the NFL Players Association, to unlock the value of personal performance profiles.

The wearables revolution is shaping the future of how fans, consumers, and managers analyze performance. To date, though, leagues have been somewhat tepid about the widespread implementation of in-game biometric tracking data. Some NFL teams use jersey chips in practice to gather player data, while the NIIL has just recently started experimenting with motion-based tracking technology. The NBA has seen hundreds of its players, coaches, and on-court managers embrace the influx of performance data; behind the scenes, however, a battle for control over personal data is taking place. Much of the tension revolves around the use of highly specific performance data in contract negotiations, and the degree to which an increase in the data available could impact player compensation in the labor market.

The NBA Players Association, for example, is wary of widespread adoption of technologies to collect biometric data, and such data are protected via the league's collective bargaining agreement (CBA) between the players union and the league ownership group. The current CBA addresses wearables, stipulating that the devices are prohibited in games, while practice use is voluntary on a team-by-team basis and limited in terms of brands acceptable for use. Transparency is key here, as any team requesting a player to wear a tracking device must submit an explanation of which specific use the data are being collected for and how those data may be used in the future. This explanation is given to the player as well as a six-person panel made up of equal representation for the union and the league (*The Atlantic*, 2017). Perhaps most vital to the issue at hand, the CBA also assesses financial penalties to teams that use player performance data collected in practice for leverage in contractual negotiations, drawing a bright line between the collection of data to enhance in-game strategic insights and use of data for player comparisons across performance attributes. Considering the hundreds of millions of dollars teams invest in players, it is easy to see how critical a distinction this is, and how important industry developments surrounding the analysis and legal protections inherent in the use of wearable technology will continue to be.

Major League Baseball has recently experienced an epidemic of "Tommy John surgeries," wherein players replace the ulnar-collateral ligament of their throwing elbow due to damage sustained by the violent nature of throwing a baseball at high velocity. The number of these surgical procedures has reached historical highs in the last five years. While many in the industry would likely applaud innovative technology that would allow players, scouts, and front office personnel to more acutely understand the strain placed on throwing arms over time, and to determine which specific actions cause the most damage to the ligament, one can foresee the challenges that exist in uncovering those data. Come contract time, do players really want a "strength scale" or "Tommy John likelihood" score being placed on their money maker? Therein lies the delicate balance between optimizing athlete performance and protecting labor market leverage in the sports industry of the future.

Summary

While quantitative analysis has been present in the sport industry for decades, a dramatic increase in computing power and tech-enabled data collection has led to sharp growth in the investments that sport organizations are dedicating toward analytics resources. Analytics is a three-pronged, process-driven endeavor carefully aligned with an organization's business objectives, which can be reasonably applied to a wide array of industry sectors and implemented

as part of player development, marketing, sales, finance/economics, or technology initiatives.

Individuals seeking employment in the sport industry can differentiate themselves by cultivating an understanding of the value delivered through data analytics, and acquiring specific skills and techniques that are valued by employers searching for data-driven competitive advantages. Practicing analytics takes on various forms, from asking the right questions, to improving one's mathematical and statistical skills, to understanding programming languages and computer software, to fine-tuning data visualization and communication techniques critical to maximizing the use of data in key decision making. A variety of league, team, media, and technology-centric business units are sprouting up in response to the clear evolution toward digitization in all segments of sport business. This evolution will create growth opportunities and innovative new analytics strategies for managers in the industry and should be monitored carefully.

Case Study 16-1

Proximity Marketing

As improvements in the at-home viewing experience and second-screen platforms like Twitter have generated fan interest over time, teams in every sport face the challenge of creating game experiences that measure up to modern expectations for interactivity, convenience, and engagement. This applies to managers across the industry, as game attendance fuels many of the primary revenue centers for teams, venues, and event management properties. Thinking strategically about how game attendance can generate engagement data, which will then be used intelligently to inform future strategies for continuous improvement, is front and center on the mind of managers in the industry today.

Table 16-A outlines a relevant, timely example of the use of proximity marketing within a major

U.S. sport arena. In this case, an NBA team was able to accomplish its marketing goals and increase its revenues through data collection and event customization, managed through in-app communications on the front-end, and a comprehensive view of event guests' behavior on the back-end. Using proximity marketing technologies such as beacons, Wi-Fi, and near-field communication (NFC; allows electronic devices to talk to each other when within a certain distance), the team was able to track guest behavior and monitor activity such as bathroom traffic, concessions demand, and seat upgrade experiences. Through improved services communicated to guests in-app, the team was able to collect data and make alterations in real time to the entire venue enterprise system. These data

Table 16-A	NBA Franchise Partners with App Analytics Platform to Increase Fan Offerings and Grow Revenue
Analytics use	• NBA team app powered by back-end analytics platform captures fan behavior associated with real-time notifications, geo-targeted messages, and Wi-Fi–enabled services to enhance the event experience and grow revenue
Marketing goals	• Increase offerings in-app to enhance fan experience, beyond simple content • Sell more tickets • Increase season ticket holder renewal rate
Proximity marketing messaging in-app	• Ticket packages at lower price points offered through in-app marketplace • Seat assignments made once the user is 1 mile from arena, instead of after entry • Real-time, geo-targeted updates on merchandise sales and exclusive offers, food and beverage offerings, line wait times, and sponsor activities
Results	• 30% app adoption (5% industry standard) • Team generated $500,000 in marketing and advertising revenue in-app, based on increased downloads and fan usage • $1 million increase in ticket sales attributable to app-enabled ticket package communications • Data collected on fan behavior to improve services for next season

Unacast Proximity Solution Providers. (2016). *Proxbook industry report.*
Data from Unacast. (2016, February). Proximity Marketing in Sports & Events: The Proxbook Report: The State of the Proximity Industry. Retrieved from www.proxbook.com

provided insights into communications relevant to specific consumer groups based on their location, as well as real-time data on food, beverage, and merchandise demand. User traffic in-app also allowed the team to sell advertising revenue on the app, communicating products and services relevant to the consumer group in-stadium.

Questions for Discussion

1. Choose a sport organization, event, and consumer target, and sketch out a one-page proposal for implementing an analytics project specific to that event that would deliver value to the organization. Which data will you collect, and why? How will you collect the data? What value—financial or otherwise—does the data hold for the organization in question?

2. Which component of the three-pronged analytics framework discussed in the chapter does user-generated content, such as in-app behavior, apply most directly to?

3. In your opinion, does proximity marketing within the event/facility management sector of the industry provide greater insight as descriptive analytics or predictive analytics, or both? Provide a rational for your answer.

Students may reference reports on sport marketing via proximity technology and data analytics here: https://www.proximity.directory/reports/.

Resources

Print References

Harrison, K., & Bukstein, S. (2017). *Sport business analytics: using data to increase revenue and improve operational efficiency.* Boca Raton, FL: CRC Press.

Troilo, M., Bouchet, A., Urban, T. L., & Sutton, W. A. (2016). Perception, reality, and the adoption of business analytics: Evidence from North American professional sport organizations. *Omega,* 59(Part A), 72–83.

Organizations

STATS, LLC

203 North LaSalle Street, Suite 2200
Chicago, IL 60601
847-534-8022
www.stats.com

Baseball Info Solutions (BIS)

41 S. 2nd Street
Coplay, PA 18037
610-261-2370
www.baseballinfosolutions.com

Society of American Baseball Research (SABR)

Cronkite School at Arizona State University
555 N. Central Avenue, #416
Phoenix, AZ 85004
602-496-1460
www.sabr.org

WHOOP

1325 Boylston Street, Suite 401
Boston, MA 02215
617-670-1074
www.whoop.com

MLB Advanced Media (MLBAM)

75 9th Avenue
New York, NY 10011
212-485-3444
www.mlbam.com

Catapult Sports

8755 W Higgins Road, Suite 1000
Chicago, IL 60631
312-762-5332
www.catapultsports.com

IBM Sports

IBM Corporation
1 New Orchard Road
Armonk, NY 10504
914-499-1900
www.ibm.com/sports

Sportvision, Inc. (SMT)

6657 Kaiser Drive
Fremont, CA 94555
510-736-2925
www.sportvision.com

STRIVR Labs

Menlo Park, CA
www.strivrlabs.com

Baseball Prospectus

858-256-6716
www.baseballprospectus.com

Fangraphs

Arlington, VA
www.fangraphs.com

FiveThirtyEight

147 Columbus Avenue, 4th Floor
New York, NY 10023
www.fivethirtyeight.com

Key Terms

analytics center of excellence (ACE), back-end, beacons, business analytics, business intelligence, correlation, data centralization, data integration, data management, data standardization, decentralized structure, descriptive analytics, dynamic ticket pricing, end users, five-tool analytics profile, front-end, hybrid structure, inertial movement analysis, information systems, metrics, player-performance analytics, predictive analytics, predictive models, proximity marketing, sport analytics, variable ticket pricing, vendors, wearable analytics

References

Alamar, B. (2013). *Sports analytics: a guide for coaches, managers, and other decision makers.* New York, NY: Columbia University Press.

Atlanta Falcons. (2015). New stadium to feature IBM technology. Retrieved from http://www.atlantafalcons.com/news/article-1/New-Stadium-to-Feature-IBM-Technology/06a78fdd-e660-45a0-afa4-d8e8117d9956

The Atlantic. (2017). The upcoming privacy battle over wearables in the NBA. Retrieved from https://www.theatlantic.com/business/archive/2017/04/biometric-tracking-sports/522222/

Better Buys. (2014). History of business intelligence. Retrieved from https://www.betterbuys.com/bi/history-of-business-intelligence/

The Economist. (2012). The price is right: dynamic pricing is the latest advance in sports' statistical revolution. Retrieved from http://www.economist.com/blogs/gametheory/2012/01/sports-ticketing

Experts Exchange. (2017). Processing power compared. Retrieved from http://pages.experts-exchange.com/processing-power-compared/

Fangraphs. (2010). What is PITCHF/x? Retrieved from http://www.fangraphs.com/library/misc/pitch-fx/

Forbes. (2014, July 7). Sports money: the biggest media company you've never heard of. Retrieved from https://www.forbes.com/sites/maurybrown/2014/07/07/the-biggest-media-company-youve-never-heard-of/#4a0a99cf1cef

Forbes. (2016). Sports money: 2016 NFL valuations. Retrieved from https://www.forbes.com/teams/baltimore-ravens/

Freakonomics: Hoopers! Hoopers! Hoopers! [WNYC Studios audio blog interview]. (2017, May 17).

Grantland. (2015). Boras's binders: what baseball's in-house analytics revolution means for MLB agents' edge. Retrieved from http://grantland.com/the-triangle/2015-mlb-agents-shifting-analytics-edge-scott-boras-caa/

Halo. (2016). Descriptive, predictive, and prescriptive analytics explained. Retrieved from https://halobi.com/2016/07/descriptive-predictive-and-prescriptive-analytics-explained/

Harrison, K., & Bukstein, S. (2017). *Sport business analytics: using data to increase revenue and improve operational efficiency.* Boca Raton, FL: CRC Press.

James, B. (2017, March). *Are we doing the best work we are capable of doing?* Presentation at the 2017 SABR Analytics Conference, Phoenix, AZ.

King, B. (2015, October 12–18). Analyze this! *Sports Business Journal*, p. 1.

Lindsey, G. (1959). Statistical data useful for the operation of a baseball team. *Operations Research, 7*(2), 197–207.

Markets and Markets. (2017). Sports analytics market worth USD 616.7 million by 2021. https://www.marketsandmarkets.com/PressReleases/sports-analytics.asp

Sawchik, T. (2015). *Big data baseball: math, miracles, and the end of a 20-year losing streak.* New York, NY: Flatiron Books.

Silver, N. (2012). *The signal and the noise: why so many predictions fail—but some don't.* New York, NY: Penguin Press.

Society for American Baseball Research (SABR). (2008). Henry Chadwick. Retrieved from https://sabr.org/bioproj/person/436e570c

Sports Illustrated. (2016). Hot dogs for $2! New Falcons stadium to offer affordable concessions. Retrieved from https://www.si.com/nfl/2016/05/16/new-atlanta-falcons-stadium-food-concessions-cheap

Unacast Proximity Solution Providers. (2016). *Proxbook: proximity marketing in sports & events: the state of the proximity industry Q2 2016.*

WHOOP. (2017, February 27). Cumulative day strain as a tool for ballplayers in spring training. Retrieved from https://thelocker .whoop.com/2017/02/27/cumulative-day -strain-as-a-tool-for-ballplayers-in-spring -training/

YouTube. (2016). Inside Marquette basketball sports performance. Retrieved from https://www.youtube.com/watch?v =fqzTqGxaP2E

© Shutterstock, Inc. / Danilo_Vuletic

Chapter 17

Jim Noel

Sport Broadcasting

Learning Objectives

Upon completion of this chapter, students should be able to:

1. Discuss broadcasting as an advertising medium, whose very existence depends on the ability of the provider to produce advertising fees in excess of the fees that are paid to the rightsholders.

2. Trace the history of sport broadcasting from telegraph to radio, television, and cable television, through Internet streaming, and explain how the industry has been shaped by technological change.

3. Identify the key personalities, programming, and organizations that have influenced the sport broadcast industry such as Roone Arledge, Pete Rozelle, *ABC's Wide World of Sports*, *Monday Night Football*, and ESPN.

4. Explain how rights fees for sporting events are valued and how those rights fees are distributed by the rightsholder.

5. Describe the way in which the broadcast of sporting events are produced.

6. Explain how ratings are determined and how they affect the value of advertising time during a specific sporting event.

7. Differentiate between the various methods of sport broadcast distribution, such as broadcast networks, syndication, cable networks, digital networks, and pay-per-view.

8. Describe how American sport organizations are expanding their broadcast presence in foreign markets while their international counterparts are doing the same in the United States.

9. Debate some of the current issues of interest in the sport broadcast industry, such as the potential market bubble for rights fees, the bundling of cable channels, the emergence of "cord-cutters," the widespread use of mobile devices, and the trend of audience fragmentation.

10. Identify the career opportunities available in the sport broadcast industry and the skills needed to succeed in each of them.

Introduction

The coverage of sport by electronic media—television, radio, and digital technology—has grown into one of the biggest and most powerful forces in the business of sport. Today, fans can watch events unfold around the world as they happen, no matter where or when. The images and sounds of every major event—and many not-so-major ones—flash into our homes instantaneously, and we have come to expect the instant replays, dazzling computerized graphics, and expert commentary that accompany the events. When Usain Bolt won the Olympic 100-meter dash at the 2012 London Olympics, his performance was witnessed not only by 80,000 fans in Olympic Stadium, but also by a global television audience of an estimated 2 billion people. Thanks to advanced technology, fans saw not just the race and Bolt's triumphant victory lap in high-definition video, but multiple replays using slow motion, multiple camera angles, and extreme close-up images. Even the fans who witnessed the race in person were treated to replays on the large video boards in the stadium.

Along with changing the way fans follow sport, electronic media profoundly impact the economics of the sport industry. Television and related media pay billions of dollars for the rights to transmit coverage of various events to their audiences. **Rights fees** are a major source of revenue for sport leagues and organizations, and the volume of this revenue has exploded in recent years. Sport **rightsholders** rely on the rights fees they receive from broadcasters. In turn, sport programming makes money for broadcasters through the advertising contained in the programs and the distribution fees received from cable and direct-broadcast satellite companies.

In these ways, the sport industry and the broadcast media business are allied in a **symbiotic relationship**. It is a relationship that produces valuable, compelling programming content that has become an essential element of the worldwide sport industry.

History of Sport Broadcasting

The telegraph was the first electronic communications medium used for transmission of information about sport events. Samuel F. B. Morse created the first commercial telegraph service in 1844, a 40-mile circuit between Washington, D.C., and Baltimore. It sent messages along a wire by opening and closing an electrical circuit in a series of dots and dashes representing letters and numbers, which then were transcribed into text and hand delivered to recipients (Head, Sterling, & Schofield, 1994). The service quickly grew into the nation's first transcontinental electronic communications system. By the early twentieth century, many newspapers had their own telegraph machines, which allowed them to provide play-by-play reports of important sport events as they happened. Public interest in the 1915 World Series between the Boston Red Sox and Philadelphia Phillies was so great that 10,000 people gathered in Times Square in New York City to watch a 50-foot-high mechanical scoreboard and baseball diamond depicting every play of the game, based on telegraph reports received in the *New York Times* newsroom (Fullerton, 1915).

The telephone was first demonstrated to the public in 1876 by Alexander Graham Bell, who used a microphone to transmit sound along wires (Head et al., 1994). Long-distance telephone service was relatively expensive for several decades thereafter, however, so the telephone was not a commercially viable means of transmitting game reports directly to consumers. However, phone lines became an important means of connecting radio and television stations, enabling the formation of nationwide networks.

In the late nineteenth century, experimentation with the transmission of wireless sound waves led to the development of radio. By the time that World War I broke out in 1914, the wireless (radio) was a standard method of communication for business, government, and the military. Ironically, one feature of radio was initially regarded as a drawback to commercial applications of the technology: Once a message was transmitted, anyone within range who had a receiver tuned to the proper frequency could hear it. Why would anyone want to send a message through the air that thousands, perhaps millions, of people could listen to? The answer came from a Westinghouse Electric Company executive named Harry Davis, whose company had a warehouse full of World War I surplus radio receivers. Perhaps, he reasoned, if a wireless station broadly transmitted entertainment and news programs every day on a fixed radio frequency—hence the term **broadcasting**—people would buy his receivers, tune into the specific frequency, and listen.

The first commercial radio broadcast occurred on November 2, 1920, when a radio station set up in a Westinghouse plant in Pittsburgh, Pennsylvania, with the "call letters" KDKA broadcast the returns of the 1920 U.S. presidential election. After the election of Warren G. Harding was duly reported, KDKA began broadcasting entertainment and news programming. Less than 6 months later, on April 11, 1921, KDKA broadcast the first live sport program, a boxing match between Johnny Dugan and Johnny Ray, and the first play-by-play coverage of a Major League Baseball (MLB) game (the Pittsburgh Pirates versus the Philadelphia Phillies) on August 5, 1921 (KDKA, 2010). The radio boom of the 1920s soon began, and it took the United States (and much of the rest of the world) by storm (Barnouw, 1966–1970).

The early radio industry was based on a business model that still underpins over-the-air electronic media: Stations produce programs and transmit them on specific channels of

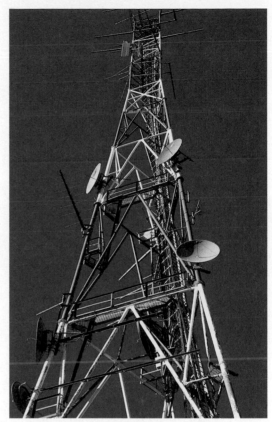

© AbleStock

the electromagnetic spectrum (because the airwaves are public property, the spectrum is regulated by the federal government), funded by advertisements sold by the stations and interspersed in the programs, and received by people having devices capable of converting the electronic signal into usable form.

The radio business grew dramatically during the 1920s. National broadcasts became feasible by linking individual stations via telephone wires to create **networks** that allowed multiple stations to broadcast the same program. This enabled the first nationwide sport broadcast in 1926—a heavyweight championship boxing match between Jack Dempsey and Gene Tunney. Within 2 years, Dempsey's promoter, Tex Rickard, began demanding rights fees from broadcasters for the privilege of covering

Dempsey's bouts (Dunning, 1998). The first national radio broadcast of a college football game, by the then-fledgling NBC network, was the Rose Bowl on New Year's Day, 1927, between the University of Alabama and Stanford University. This event also demonstrated the early power of national media coverage as a recruiting tool: A young Arkansas farm boy named Paul Bryant, who had not yet earned his nickname "Bear," said that listening to that game was how he first learned of the University of Alabama, where he eventually went to play football and then meet his destiny as an iconic coach (Schexnayder, 2009).

Radio's ability to reach a national audience also created national advertising opportunities. In 1926, the Royal Typewriter Company became the first national sport-related programming **sponsor**, by paying the now charmingly modest sum of $35,000 for exclusive sponsorship rights to the Dempsey–Tunney fight broadcast (Evensen, 1996).

Although the World Series was broadcast as early as 1923, Major League Baseball, the self-proclaimed "national pastime," did not immediately embrace the new technology. Owners initially were concerned that free game broadcasts would make fans less likely to buy tickets to games. Throughout the 1930s, the three powerful New York teams—the Yankees, Giants, and Dodgers—banned all broadcasters (from the away teams as well as home teams) from their ballparks (Smith, 1995).

Nevertheless, the trend of more extensive coverage gained momentum. In 1933, a controlling interest in the Cincinnati Reds was sold to Powel Crosley, who both manufactured radios and owned two radio stations, including the powerful WLW, which Crosley converted into the Reds' flagship station (Ohio History Central, n.d.). In 1935, MLB Commissioner Kenesaw Mountain Landis reached an agreement for exclusive national radio coverage of the World Series (Todayinsports.com, n.d.).

Essential legal protection for the sport broadcasting business model was provided by two important decisions in the late 1930s. In *Twentieth Century Sporting Club, Inc. v. Transradio Press Service, Inc.* (1937), a New York state court enforced an exclusive contract for play-by-play coverage of a boxing match. The following year, in *Pittsburgh Athletic Co. v. KQV Broadcasting Co.* (1938), a federal court in Pittsburgh ruled that the home team controls all commercial **broadcasting rights** to a sport event. The rationale for this landmark decision was that the team owner or event organizer, who invests in establishing the organization, training and paying the players, renting (or owning) a stadium or other venue, providing amenities to spectators, and engaging in the other activities required to conduct a sport competition, also has the legal right to control access to the venue by broadcasters and otherwise to commercially exploit the distribution of accounts and descriptions of the event. This holding remains a core principle in the sport industry to this day.

As important as the *Pittsburgh Athletic* legal case was in 1938, an even more important business milestone occurred that year—the first television sets were sold in the United States (Early Television Museum, n.d.). As had been the case with radio, the first telecasts were local in nature, and they included various sport events as well as news coverage and entertainment programming. In 1941, television was still in its infancy—but then the commercial television industry was put on hold during World War II. Production of radio and television equipment for consumers was banned during the war (Early Television Museum, n.d.). Radio remained the primary electronic medium for news, entertainment, and sports during World War II.

That situation changed dramatically when the war ended in 1945. At that time, fewer than one-half of 1% of U.S. homes had a television set. Fifteen years later, that proportion had grown to 86% (TVhistory.tv, 2001–2013). By 1960, the **Federal Communications Commission (FCC)** had licensed five times more commercial TV stations (515) than there had been in 1950 (96).

In the 1940s and 1950s, television's business model mirrored that of radio. Individual stations transmitted signals on government-regulated frequencies for viewing by receiving sets. Individual stations were owned by a variety of local and national interests, and were licensed and regulated by the FCC (Stephens, n.d.). Advertising revenue was the sole meaningful source of income for stations and networks (Meyers, 2011). Network telecasting became possible in the early 1950s with the completion of an infrastructure of coaxial cable and microwave relays (Early Television Museum, n.d.). Videotape playback technology was not perfected until 1956 (Ampex, n.d.), meaning that all of the value in the coverage of an event was vested in the live telecast.

With only three national television networks, most programming was intended to appeal to the broadest possible audience. During evening **primetime** hours, when the most people were at home, almost all network programming was entertainment in nature—comedies, dramas, movies, and variety shows (Classic Television Database, n.d.). Sport programs appeared mostly on weekend afternoons, when fewer people were watching television (Keller, 1982). However, sport audiences have always been predominantly male. This **demographic** subset was an efficient way for advertisers of male-oriented products to target the audience most likely to be purchasers (MacDonald, 2009).

Inexorably during the 1950s, television replaced radio as the nation's primary mass medium. By 1960, television was generating twice as much advertising revenue as radio (Oracle Education Foundation, n.d.). Sport programming followed the migration of

entertainment and news programming from radio to TV (MacDonald, 2009).

Television grew explosively in the 1950s, but the industry truly came of age in the 1960s. Technology improved the quality of the product. After wrangling throughout the 1950s among the FCC, networks, and equipment manufacturers, color television went mainstream in the early 1960s (Television Obscurities, 2005, 2013). The first use of videotaped "instant replay" in a sport telecast came during the 1963 Army–Navy game on CBS (Gelston, 2008). "Solid state" transistor-based cameras and zoom lenses enhanced picture quality and mobility, making for increasingly compelling video images. The first Telstar communications satellite, allowing the transmission of live transcontinental programming, was launched in 1962 (Howell, 2013).

Network newscasts expanded from 15 to 30 minutes in 1963 (IMDB, n.d.b). Variety shows such as *The Ed Sullivan Show* hosted then-controversial new performers such as the Beatles, whose 1964 American tour and the phenomenon of "Beatlemania" were major news events (Rauscher, n.d.).

This convergence of cultural forces and technology included sport, led by an upstart network. In 1960, ABC was still the weakest of the three domestic television networks. Its structure as a national network was not finalized until 1954, well after CBS and NBC had become entrenched (MacDonald, 2009). But three events occurred in the early 1960s that profoundly changed both ABC and sport television.

First, ABC purchased Sports Programs, Inc., an independent sport and production company, that became ABC Sports (Carter, 2002). The network named 29-year-old **Roone Arledge** as producer of its new weekly college football telecasts. In his new role, Arledge implemented a revolutionary vision of "taking sports fans to the game," including close-up shots of cheerleaders, the school bands, and the crowd and sideline images of players and coaches, instead of the traditional style of showing only play-by-play action (Meserole, 2002). Second, ABC acquired rights to the new American Football League (AFL), which began operating in 1960 (Loup, 2001). The AFL immediately became popular owing to its wide-open, high-scoring style of play, and it gave ABC its first coverage of a major professional sport. Third, an innovative anthology series, *ABC's Wide World of Sports*, debuted in 1961. Each program opened with the famous greeting, "Spanning the globe to bring you the constant variety of sport—the thrill of victory, and the agony of defeat." But the next line of the introduction, although less well known, was more instructive about the essence of the programming: "the human drama of athletic competition." It was "up close and personal" stories of athletes, punctuated by compelling images that conveyed emotions as well as action, that personified Arledge's style of blending sport action with entertainment and pageantry.

Wide World of Sports covered everything from major events such as the Indianapolis 500 (which did not permit free live television coverage until 1986) and the FA Cup Soccer Finals to inane spectacles such as barrel jumping and cliff diving. It also provided riveting coverage of two politically charged track meets between the United States and the Soviet Union at the height of the Cold War (Shannon, 2010).

The most important athlete to appear on *Wide World of Sports* was undoubtedly Muhammad Ali. No one personified the "modern" athlete more than Ali. He started the decade as Cassius Clay, a boxer who won a gold medal for the United States at the 1960 Olympics, but soon became the most controversial athlete in the world. He broke the mold of the stereotypical humble athlete by brashly predicting that he would become heavyweight champion. When he backed up that boast, he changed his name to Muhammad Ali, converted to Islam, and eventually refused to be enlisted into the U.S. Army. And it was on *Wide World of Sports*, hosted by Howard Cosell—himself a groundbreaking figure—where Ali received his most celebrated coverage (Kindred, 2006).

Cosell called the action during Ali's first six defenses of his heavyweight championship on *Wide World of Sports*. When Ali was stripped of his title for refusing to be drafted at the height of the Vietnam War, Cosell conducted numerous interviews with Ali and provided highly opinionated commentary about the controversy, which continued until 1971 when the U.S. Supreme Court overturned Ali's criminal conviction for draft evasion.

By 1960, the National Football League (NFL) was becoming a major force in the sport world. Its 1958 championship game, in which the Baltimore Colts defeated the New York Giants in sudden-death overtime, was already being called the greatest football game ever played (Maule, 1959). Although MLB was still regarded as America's "national pastime," the NFL became the nation's first truly national sport league in 1946 when the Cleveland Rams moved to Los Angeles (Pro Football Hall of Fame, n.d.), 12 years before the Dodgers and Giants became MLB's first teams on the West Coast (History.com, n.d.). In 1950, the Rams became the first team to televise all of its home and away games (NFL, n.d.). The team also hired a young public relations executive, **Pete Rozelle**, as its general manager in 1957. Three years later, Rozelle was elected NFL commissioner and his media-savvy leadership transformed the league and the American sport landscape (Carter, n.d.).

Rozelle's first act as commissioner was to move the NFL headquarters to New York City, home to all of the television networks and major advertising agencies. He then convinced the league's owners to pool their television rights and equally share all television rights fees ("Economy in NFL History," n.d.).

Revenue-sharing had a seismic impact on the league. It meant that the New York Giants, located in the largest media market in the country, received the same amount of national television revenue as the Green Bay Packers, which played in the 70th-largest market. This arrangement promoted competitive balance among all teams, instead of large-market teams being able to dominate the NFL by having disproportionate financial resources. This, in turn, produced consistently close, exciting games, which made for a better television product. An unofficial slogan of the league was "On any given Sunday, any NFL team could beat any other team in the league." As the first U.S. professional sport league to have meaningful revenue-sharing, the NFL proved the importance of this economic structure. In the 1960s, the Green Bay Packers, playing in the smallest market of any pro sport team in the country, were the best team in the NFL, winning five championships and the first two Super Bowls.

With the NFL's new business model in place, Rozelle then secured league-wide television agreements with CBS for the regular season and with NBC for the NFL Championship Game. When a federal court held that these contracts violated antitrust law, Rozelle lobbied for and secured passage of the Sports Broadcasting Act of 1961, which provided an antitrust exemption for pooled media rights agreements by professional sport leagues (Davis, 2008).

In 1964, the fledgling AFL left ABC and signed a lucrative 5-year agreement with the more established NBC. "After I signed that contract," said AFL Commissioner Joe Foss, "people stopped asking me if we were going to make it. Everyone knew we were" (Gruver, 1997, p. 125). The following year, the AFL and NFL merged into one league (NFL, n.d.). The first Super Bowl was played on January 15, 1967, and was televised by both CBS and NBC (NFL, n.d.). By the mid-1960s, the NFL had surpassed MLB as the most popular sport in the nation (Florio, 2009).

In 1968, the popularity of the NFL was demonstrated when NBC cut away from its New York Jets–Oakland Raiders game telecast to show the movie *Heidi* at its regularly scheduled time of 7:00 p.m. in the Eastern Time Zone. The resulting protest by football fans became a national news story (Davis, 2008). It also demonstrated that professional football fans wanted to watch their favorite sport at times other than Sunday afternoons.

Two years later, *Monday Night Football* became the first sport programming series in primetime. Arledge produced the games for ABC, using the same human-interest production techniques he pioneered on *Wide World of Sports*, and he included the bombastic Cosell on the announcing team. The series not only was a ratings success, but also became a cultural phenomenon—as much as 40% of the audience were women (*ABC Sports Online*, 2003).

Television also played an important role in the growth of public interest in the Olympic Games during the 1960s. The Cold War rivalry between the United States and the Soviet Union translated into a sport-related propaganda war between the two countries and their allies, all watched by a television audience that was worldwide in scope due to the proliferation of telecommunications satellites. By 1968, ABC had turned itself into "The Network of the Olympics" (Chad & Reid, 1998). The Games involved ongoing controversies related to amateurism, political demonstrations, on-field issues, and, in 1972, tragedy with the massacre of Israeli athletes by Arab terrorists in Munich, Germany. ABC turned all of it into compelling television (Guthrie, 2012).

The success of *Monday Night Football* prompted increased television coverage of sport at times traditionally reserved for entertainment programming. The final game of the National Collegiate Athletic Association (NCAA) men's basketball championship was first televised on Monday night in 1973.

MLB began staging World Series games in primetime in 1971.

Throughout the 1970s, virtually all major sports received coverage on network television. Professional Golfers' Association (PGA) Tour golf tournaments became weekly fixtures. The National Basketball Association (NBA) received regular national coverage, although the league's ratings were so low that playoff games were regularly shown on tape-delay. The first live flag-to-flag coverage of the Daytona 500 occurred in 1979. College football was a Saturday-afternoon staple in the fall. A new college basketball conference, the Big East, was formed in 1979 to take advantage of the large concentration of **television markets** in the Northeast.

Television occasionally was responsible for blurring the lines between sport and entertainment. "The Battle of the Sexes" was a tongue-in-cheek, made-for-TV extravaganza between Billie Jean King and Bobby Riggs in 1973. Riggs, who had won the 1939 Wimbledon men's singles championship, claimed that he could still beat King at a time when she was one of the top female tennis players in the world. The two played an exhibition match in the Houston Astrodome, in which after Riggs was carted by a team of models onto the court in a rickshaw, and King was borne in Cleopatra-style by a team of muscular men. A worldwide television audience of nearly 50 million people watched King win in straight sets (Wertheim, 2012). Other made-for-TV shows, such as *The Superstars*, which debuted in 1973 and featured famous athletes competing against each other in a variety of sports other than the ones in which they were professionals, prompted the creation of a new word—**trashsports**, referring to entertainment that purported to be sport but had no real sporting significance.

As secure as the over-air network business model seemed to be in the early 1970s, with the vast majority of television programming being delivered and received by free over-air signals, profound changes in the television industry soon began to occur.

HBO became the first network to continuously deliver its signal via telecommunications satellite when it telecast the "Thrilla in Manilla" boxing match between Ali and Joe Frazier in 1975 (Forsyth, 2002). In 1977, Ted Turner transformed a low-powered independent television station in Atlanta into a "superstation" by beaming its signal nationwide via satellite. In 1979, another cable network opened for business, based on the then-unimaginable notion that people would watch sports 24 hours a day—ESPN (Miller & Shales, 2011).

Cable television services had been available since the 1940s, when an appliance store owner in rural Pennsylvania got frustrated because the lack of clear broadcast signals meant that he could not sell TV sets. His solution was to build a master antenna on a nearby mountain and connect it by a cable to his showroom. When his customers saw a clear picture, they not only bought TVs, but also paid fees for access to the **master antenna**. In the 1970s, the cable industry expanded to urban areas, offering enhanced picture quality plus access to additional networks other than the three networks and local independent stations (Eisenmann, 2000).

The growth of cable **penetration** of American households increased steadily in the 1980s (Grant & Meadows, 2013). By the end of the decade, nearly 60% of all U.S. homes were wired for cable, and there were 79 new cable networks distributing programming (NCTA, n.d.). In the early 1990s, DIRECTV launched a competitive technology to cable, delivering programming to homes via **direct broadcast satellites (DBS)** (DIRECTV, n.d.).

The proliferation of networks had a major impact on sports, especially on the professional team sports that played games on a nearly daily basis—baseball, basketball, and hockey.

Previously, their television coverage was limited either to over-the-air network stations willing to occasionally preempt network programming or independent stations having no network affiliations. Suddenly, there were new competitors for game-coverage rights, which increased rights fees to the clubs and increased the number of games on TV.

The willingness of consumers to pay for sport programming on cable was demonstrated in 1987, when ESPN signed its first agreement with the NFL. The only way the then-fledgling ESPN could afford the rights fee charged by the NFL was to levy a surcharge on its subscriber fees, which cable operators willingly paid—and passed along to their subscribers (Miller & Shales, 2011).

By the mid-1980s, ESPN was emerging as a sport television force. It covered college football and basketball, the NBA, and the National Hockey League (NHL) and was the first network to extensively cover NASCAR. It provided the first "early round" coverage of professional golf tournaments simply by hiring the crews already on site to produce weekend coverage on the traditional over-air networks. ESPN also covered events that had never been televised before, such as the NFL draft. In addition, it shrewdly associated itself with big events for which it was not a rightsholder, such as by sending its *College GameDay* pregame show to the sites of major college football games being covered by broadcast networks.

ESPN's *SportsCenter* program revolutionized sports journalism. Before *SportsCenter*, the only televised daily sports news was a 2- to 3-minute segment on late-night local news, usually limited to scores, highlights, and news related to local teams. *SportsCenter* offered a content-rich alternative, with scores, highlights, and news on a national scope, plus an entertaining blend of irreverence and humor. In 1987, ESPN introduced *NFL Primetime*, an hour-long show devoted entirely to NFL highlights, providing in-depth coverage that previously had not been possible on TV (Miller & Shales, 2011).

Until the 1980s, the NCAA strictly regulated all college football telecasts. Coverage of regular-season games was limited to one or two games on Saturdays on ABC (the NCAA's exclusive rightsholder). NCAA rules limited the best and most popular teams to two or three national appearances per season. In the early 1980s, ESPN and TBS secured "supplemental" cable rights to college football telecasts. Postseason bowl games were televised on various networks. Everything changed in 1981, however, when two NCAA members, the University of Oklahoma and the University of Georgia, filed an antitrust suit against the NCAA that resulted in a 1985 Supreme Court decision that NCAA control of college football television was an illegal restraint of trade (*NCAA v. Board of Regents of the University of Oklahoma*, 1984). As a result, the Big Ten and Pac-10 conferences aligned themselves with ABC, while another group of conferences formed the College Football Association (CFA) and made a deal with CBS. The CFA collapsed in the 1990s when Notre Dame signed a separate coverage agreement with NBC, leading to individual conferences signing their own deals with other networks. All of this resulted in a substantial increase in the number of games televised (Reed, 1991).

In 1993, the entire American television landscape changed profoundly, and it was sports that spurred the change. The Fox Broadcast Network, which had for years been a loose confederation of independent stations, acquired telecast rights to the NFL, outbidding the incumbent rightsholder CBS by 25%—roughly $400 million per year versus CBS's offer of $300 million. The deal established Fox as the nation's fourth broadcast network (Wulf, 1993).

Fox also acquired a number of regional sports networks during the 1990s, which provided additional financial resources for these relatively new niche cable networks. Fox unsuccessfully tried to amalgamate these regional networks into a national competitor to ESPN by producing a national news show to compete with *SportsCenter*, hosted by outspoken former *SportsCenter* anchor Keith Olbermann (Olbermann, 2011).

Other national media powers, such as Comcast, also invested in regional sports cable networks. This competition increased the rights fees paid to the teams whose games were covered on the networks, further solidifying the importance of television as a revenue stream to teams and leagues (Comcast, n.d.).

An even more significant cultural change occurred in the 1990s, when public usage of the Internet started growing at a rate of 100% per year (Internet World Stats, n.d.). The first mainstream "channel" of computer-delivered services was America Online, which grew from a startup with fewer than 150,000 subscribers in 1991 (McCracken, 2010) to a service with 20 million paying members by 2000 (CNN, 2000). By 1994, AOL was offering **multimedia** content that included news, reference, entertainment, and educational material (McCracken, 2010). Two pioneering sport-only websites, *ESPNET SportsZone* (now ESPN.com) and *SportsLine* (now CBSSports.com), both launched in 1995. The Internet-connected personal computer became the first meaningful competitor to the TV set as an electronic appliance for delivering news, information, and entertainment.

In 1995, the Walt Disney Company purchased Capital Cities/ABC, the company that owned ESPN (Fabrikant, 1995). At that time, Disney regarded ABC as the most valuable asset being acquired, but it soon became apparent that ESPN was truly the crown jewel of the transaction. Disney's deep financial pockets provided ESPN with additional working capital to fund its growth. ESPN also secured

long-term affiliate agreements with cable and DBS companies that compounded its annual subscriber fees, generating substantial revenue that allowed ESPN to acquire rights to more events for higher rights fees, thereby driving up the values of programming on an industry-wide basis (Miller & Shales, 2011).

In 1995, ESPN also staged the first Extreme Games, a collection of competitions in non-traditional "action sports," such as skateboard, bicycle, and motorcycle stunt competitions. Soon rebranded the X Games, it gave the network a television property it could own, instead of having to pay a rights fee for. The X Games also helped give a brand identity to ESPN2, which was marketed as the "hipper and hotter" version of ESPN when it was launched in 1993 (Pickert, 2009).

Technology developments continued to impact the television industry. After decades of work involving Congress, the FCC, television manufacturers, networks, and the emerging digital media industry, **high-definition television (HDTV)** established itself in the early 2000s as a force in the marketplace (Cianci, 2012). In 2003, ESPN became the first sports network to launch an HD channel (*ESPN Media Zone*, n.d.). The rest of the industry quickly followed suit (TVB, 2012). The enhanced picture quality and wider screen dramatically enhanced the experience of watching sports on TV.

The first **digital video recorder (DVR)** was introduced in 1999 (TiVo, n.d.). It allowed individuals to record TV programs. Like the video cassette recorders (VCRs) that first popularized in-home recording of TV programming in the 1970s and 1980s, DVRs allowed people to **time-shift** their viewing of programs, delaying it until after their live telecasts. Unlike VCRs, however, DVRs allowed viewers to skip commercials almost instantly, instead of having to fast-forward through videotape. The picture quality of digital recording, which was superior to that of the analog videotape used in VCRs, combined with HDTV to make time-shifted programming an equivalent or even superior viewing experience in comparison to live television.

Another factor spurring this time-shifting phenomenon was the growing availability of high-speed **broadband** Internet connectivity. In the 1990s, most people connected to the Internet via relatively slow "dial-up" phone lines. New fiber-optic cable allowed video signals to be **streamed** without the need for traditional television networks (Hayes, 2013). High-speed broadband service became a lucrative new revenue source for cable companies, allowing them to further leverage the investments they already had made in installing high-speed wiring in most American homes for cable TV (NCTA, n.d.).

The easier it became to time-shift viewing of entertainment programming, the more valuable live sport programming became. By the end of the first decade of the 2000s, sport events became recognized as the only "DVR-proof" television programming. Because the inherent drama is based on the uncertain outcome of live games, and scores and information about games were readily available via the Internet, social media, and mobile devices, it was difficult to avoid learning a score or outcome before watching a recording of the event (Deninger, 2012).

During the 2011–2012 television season, the five most-watched programs were NFL games (topped by Super Bowl XLVI), and 22 of the 25 most-watched programs were sport related (TVB, 2012). As a result, sports rights fees paid by telecasters grew at unprecedented rates (Ourand, 2011).

In 2011, the NFL renewed all of its network agreements for an average increase of 60% over previous deals. Each of the NFL's three broadcast rightsholders—Fox, NBC, and CBS—agreed to pay more than $1 billion per year for 9 years (Hiestand, 2011). ESPN agreed to pay even

more—$1.9 billion per year—for *Monday Night Football*, because the NFL was able to leverage the provision in ESPN's affiliation agreements requiring that its lucrative **subscriber fees** be reduced if the network were to lose NFL game coverage rights (Sandomir, 2011b).

Across the sport broadcasting industry, other rightsholders also reaped major fee increases. For example, the growth in rights fees accelerated so drastically that in 2010 the Atlantic Coast Conference (ACC) more than doubled its previous rights fees and then tried to renegotiate the deal 4 months before it took effect because other conferences had signed even more lucrative agreements in the meantime (Ourand, 2011).

Sports programming also affected the value of other sports-related assets. In 2012, the Los Angeles Dodgers were sold for $2.15 billion, a six-fold increase in franchise valuation since the previous sale of the team in 2004 for $371 million (Gurnick, 2012). The new Dodgers owners promptly monetized their new asset by selling the team's cable rights for $8.5 billion over 25 years (Minami, 2013) to Time Warner, which announced plans to make the Dodgers the centerpiece of a new regional sports network, SportsNet LA (Gurnick, 2013).

The flow of money into new sports networks seemed limitless. All major professional sports leagues launched their own networks in the early 2000s—the NFL Network in 2003 (NFL, 2011), MLB Network in 2009 (MLB, n.d.), NBA TV in late 1999 (NBA, n.d.), and NHL Network in 2007 (Brady, 2007). Four of the major college conferences followed suit, led by the Big Ten in 2007 (Big Ten, 2007) and followed in rapid-fire fashion by the Pacific-12 Conference in 2011 (Facer, 2011), the Southeastern Conference in 2013 (ESPN.com, 2013), and the Atlantic Coast Conference in 2016. The University of Texas established the first network devoted to a single college athletic program when it formed the

Longhorn Network in association with ESPN in 2011 (Staples, 2011). In 2012, NBC rebranded the Versus network (acquired in the 2009 Comcast–NBC merger) as NBC Sports Network (Sandomir, 2011a). The following year, News Corporation launched Fox Sports One (Fox Sports, 2013).

However, disruption was lurking just beneath the surface. Beginning with the launch of Apple's iPhone in 2007, "smartphone" mobile devices capable of viewing video grew from a novelty to a staple, with nearly 3 billion users worldwide by 2016. In 2008, the average adult American accessed digital content via a mobile device 20 minutes per day; by 2016, that usage rate had increased tenfold, to more than 3 hours per day (Kleiner Perkins, 2017).

In 2011, Netflix changed its business model from mail-order DVD rentals to a video streaming service (Pepitone, 2011). This emulated the formula of the Hulu subscription service launched in 2008 (Hulu, 2008). Netflix's subscriber base quintupled during the next five years, to almost 100 million subscribers paying fees that accounted for almost 30% of all U.S. home entertainment revenue by 2017 (Kleiner Perkins, 2017). In 2011, Amazon launched a video streaming service as an additional feature of its Amazon Prime service (Stevens, 2011). Apple's iTunes Store acquired rights for pay-per-view streaming of entertainment content, including a deal with the Walt Disney Company in 2010 (Ourand, 2017).

In 2010, total U.S. subscribers to cable- and satellite-delivered television services declined for the first time ever (Ramachandran, 2012). The term **cord-cutting** entered the lexicon of the media industry, amid growing reports that U.S. consumers were terminating their services consisting of traditional cable and DBS "bundles" of television networks in favor of the proliferating and less-expensive alternatives (Manjoo, 2014).

By 2014, "cord-cutting" pressure was being felt throughout the sports media industry, even at ESPN. As the network prepared to negotiate what would be a nine-year extension to its rights agreement with the NBA, senior executives within the company warned that ESPN's subscriber base was eroding, potentially affecting the network's long-term ability to keep paying big increases for telecast rights (Ourand, 2017). After peaking in 2011, ESPN's base of paying subscribers decreased by 13 million during the next five years. After years of earning steady profits, ESPN's operating income started becoming a quarterly source of bad news for its parent company, the Walt Disney Company (Drape & Barnes, 2017).

In addition to the decline in subscribers and viewership, ESPN faces a fundamental change in viewer habits. In the 1980s and 1990s, *SportsCenter* became the network's hallmark program because it was the place where sports fans tuned for breaking sports news and highlights. In the age of Twitter and other instant-access media accessible via mobile devices, news and highlights are available on-demand, instead of at the scheduled times of *SportsCenter*.

ESPN has responded to the changing marketplace by investing in new technology and revising its business model. In August 2017, Disney acquired a controlling stake in BAMTech, the digital media company spun off from Major League Baseball's Baseball Advance Media, and launched a direct-to-consumer app (Brown, 2017). Disney's CEO, Robert Iger, has acknowledged publicly that ESPN ultimately will shift from distributing its programming via cable and satellite distributors to a "direct consumer" model (Castillo, 2017).

Nevertheless, any fundamental decline in the revenue stream flowing through the sports media ecosystem could have profoundly unsettling ripples for the entire sport industry. Less revenue means that existing broadcast (e.g., CBS, NBC, Fox) and cable (e.g., ESPN, FS1, CBS Sports Network) networks will have fewer dollars to pay in rights fees to leagues and conferences. That would result in decreased revenues to the rightsholders, which are used to pay player salaries and service debt on facilities (ranging from stadiums to training facilities), unless new revenue streams can be tapped. New partners such as Amazon, Verizon, and Twitter have all paid significant rights fees in recent years to telecast NFL games (Wertheim, 2017).

The Business of Sport Broadcasting

The standard sport broadcasting business model is that a telecaster pays a rights fee to the organizer of a game or event, and then the telecaster produces the telecast, arranges for its distribution to the public, and recoups its fees and expenses by selling advertising in the game telecast and network distribution rights to cable and DBS operators.

Rights Fees

Negotiations

The legal presumption is that a home team controls the broadcasting rights to its games. When the team is a member of a league or conference, its television rights usually are ceded to the larger organization, which negotiates on behalf of all members. In most professional and college team sports, national television rights are controlled by the league or conference, though individual teams retain radio rights and some local television rights. For individual sports, such as tennis tournaments and boxing matches, the event organizer controls the television rights.

The key business terms in a rights agreement include the amount of the rights fees, the territory in which the telecast can (or must) be distributed, the length of the deal, the process for selecting particular games for telecast, copyright ownership, sponsorship rights, the number of commercial units to be included in the telecast, procedures for pre-empting coverage in the event of inclement weather or other unforeseen circumstances, the telecast distribution means (e.g., over-the-air television, cable/DBS, "over-the-top" systems, and "TV Everywhere"; a secondary issue is whether a rightsholder will have the exclusive right to televise the game or must share exclusivity with other distribution "platforms"), and whether the telecaster will have the first right to negotiate a renewal of the agreement before the rightsholder conducts competitive bidding for future rights on the open market.

Value

Traditionally, the amount of rights fees that broadcasters were willing to pay was determined primarily by how much money they could make by selling advertising spots in the game programs. However, rights-fee value components have grown increasingly complex. Cable-delivered networks such as ESPN, TBS, and FS1 can charge higher subscription fees to their cable/DBS distributors by having highly rated sports programming, ranging from NFL football to the NCAA Final Four to Big Ten football. Fox outbid CBS for NFL telecast rights in the 1990s by including in its rights-valuation formula the increased revenues it could attract from local broadcast television stations in local affiliation fees, due to the presence of NFL football telecasts on those stations. DIRECTV pays the NFL for its *Sunday Ticket* coverage of the NFL, involving a channel showing only scoring drives and **out of market** telecasts of all league games (supplementing the game telecasts available only in the local team markets); this rights fee is based on both the fee charged to purchasers of the package and the value of the competitive advantage that *Sunday Ticket* provides to DIRECTV over its cable and DBS competitors. Another NFL rightsholder, Verizon, pays the league only for the right to stream NFL game telecasts to its wireless subscribers. New marketplace entrants such as Amazon may bid on future major league rights based on whether such programming increases the value of subscription services consisting of both video programming and unrelated services, such as Amazon Prime.

The National Football League receives the largest rights fees of any American sports organization, reflecting the reality that NFL game telecasts are consistently the highest-rated sports programs. NASCAR fans (according to studies conducted by market research companies) are especially likely to purchase the products advertised on NASCAR race telecasts, making advertisers willing to pay a premium for such loyalty. As a general rule, sports TV audiences are disproportionately male and young, in comparison to the general population, so sellers of products appealing to this demographic will pay a premium for their ads to run in programs watched by especially large proportions of their **target markets**.

The popularity of a network's programming also helps determine the subscription fees it can charge to cable and DBS operators. Since 1992, broadcast networks have been able to charge fees to cable and DBS systems for the appearance of the networks on those distribution systems, and the value of such **retransmission consent** fees depends in part on the quality of the network programming.

Revenue-Sharing

The rights fees paid to leagues or conferences usually are shared equally among all member teams. Because all NFL games are subject to league-wide contracts, all TV revenue is shared equally. However, in sports where teams receive television fees from both national and local rightsholders, revenue disparities can occur. In MLB, the proceeds from its national "Game of the Week" series and postseason games are shared equally. However, most MLB games are not subject to the national agreements, leaving each team free to make its own television arrangements within its home market. Teams in large population areas earn larger rights fees for their local telecasts than teams do in smaller markets, and only 34% of those local rights fees are subject to revenue-sharing among all MLB teams. Similar disparities occur in the NBA and NHL, although each league has its own formula for sharing portions of local TV revenue, in an effort to level the playing field economically for all member clubs.

The rights fees paid to organizers of individual events such as tennis and golf tournaments and boxing matches are a primary source of funding (along with ticket sales and sponsorship revenue) for the prize money paid to competitors in the event. For a sense of the rights fees in these events, we can look to ESPN's fees paid to the U.S Open and Wimbledon tennis tournaments. ESPN has an 11-year deal with the U.S. Open that pays $75 million annually in rights fees, for a total of $825 million in rights fees. For Wimbledon, ESPN's deal is for $40 million per year for 12 years, totaling $480 million (Traina, 2017).

Production

In addition to paying a rights fee for a particular event or series, a broadcaster must pay the expenses necessary to produce the coverage. Typically, this involves setting up cameras at various locations within the playing venue, outfitting a booth in the venue's press box for the announcers describing the action, and arranging for a **remote production facility**, frequently called the "production truck" because it is configured to travel to various events.

The truck houses most of the production crew, while additional personnel, such as camera operators, are located in the stadium/ arena. All cameras and microphones are connected to the production truck. In the truck, the crew performs a vast array of tasks. Through an intercom system, they can speak directly to camera operators and announcers to request particular shots or provide them with information. The director decides which camera shots to include in the program feed, frequently making split-second decisions about the best camera angle and images of a particular play. Engineers constantly monitor the quality of the sound and pictures. Assistant producers and directors implement specific instructions they receive, such as incorporating replays into the telecast or creating graphics containing statistics or information about a team or player. The **clean feed** of the program is transmitted from the truck to a network studio, where commercial and promotional announcements are added. The finished program then is retransmitted to network **affiliates** (or, in the case of cable/DBS systems, to their local **head ends**, the master facilities where programs are received and then fed to individual subscribers).

The expenses of producing a game telecast usually are paid by the network. Rightsholders sometimes agree to reimburse the network for a portion of the production expenses. At times, a rightsholder may even agree to pay all of the production expenses or assume all responsibilities for producing the telecast, in which case the rightsholder then purchases time from a network—called a **time-buy**—at a price equivalent to the network's profit margin for producing, selling advertising for, and televising other programming at that time of day.

Advertising and Sponsorship

The advertising and promotional messages contained in a television program generate revenue to offset the costs of acquiring the programming rights and of producing the program.

Advertising

The traditional advertisement in a sport television program is a 30-second commercial message for a consumer product. These ads are shown during **commercial breaks** when there is no game action. Usually, multiple spots are grouped into a **pod** of commercials. The structure of certain sports is ideal for this format—baseball games have breaks between each half-inning, football games have time-outs after a score or a change in possession, tennis matches have rest periods after every other game, and auto races require cars to run at low speeds and not pass each other during caution flags. Other sports, such as soccer and hockey, do not have such frequent breaks, making commercial formatting more challenging.

Nevertheless, all sports alter their game-action format to some extent to accommodate commercials. For example, all NFL games are required to have five 2-minute commercial breaks per quarter. If you ever wondered why an NFL game shows commercials after a touchdown, then has a kickoff, followed by yet another commercial break, it is due to the need to get all five of those breaks in during every quarter. In 2017, networks began experimenting with running short commercial spots, some as short as 6 seconds long, during pauses in game action shorter than traditional commercial breaks. This new practice was a prominent feature of Fox's coverage of the 2017 World Series (Crupi, 2017).

These **commercial formats** contain advertising breaks for both national commercials, sold by the networks (or equivalent independent production company), and local advertisements, which are sold by local stations or cable systems. The operating agreements between networks and affiliates/distributors guarantee a certain amount of local advertising per hour.

The price of advertisements is calculated on the basis of the number of people watching the telecast. This is why **ratings**, which measure the size of the program audience, are vital to the economics of television. A program watched by 2.5 million people can charge 10 times more for ad units than a program watched by 250,000 people, although the demographics of a particular program audience also affect prices. It is more efficient for companies selling products appealing primarily to men (such as shaving and grooming products, beer, and automobiles) to advertise on sport programs instead of on programs targeting a female audience. Advertising agencies invest heavily in audience research to determine where to run particular ads.

Ratings

The rating is the percentage of households having at least one television set that are tuned to a particular program. The Nielson Company, the leading audience-measurement company in the nation, estimates there were 115.6 million TV households in 2013. This means that an audience of 1.156 million people for a particular show would equate to a 1.0 rating. A companion measurement to a program rating is its **share**, which is the percentage of television sets actually in use at a particular time that are tuned to a show (Nielsen Media Research, n.d.). Networks and advertisers have recently developed ways to measure the total audience watching a program, including digital streaming as well as traditional broadcasting and cable/satellite viewership (Lovinger, 2017).

Sponsorship

Sponsorship is a form of financial support to an event or a telecast, either cash or in-kind goods or services, in exchange for public recognition that generates commercial exposure for the sponsor at times other than during a commercial unit. Sponsorships can be sold either by an event organizer or by the broadcaster.

Event organizers can sell the naming rights to the event itself. Most of the golf tournaments on the PGA Tour, for example, are now named for "title sponsors"—what used to be "The Phoenix Open" is now "The Waste Management Open." Other events retain their traditional name, but have a "presenting sponsor"—for example, "The Memorial Tournament—Presented by Nationwide Insurance." Networks can insist that the sponsor purchase advertising units in the telecast as a condition of referring to the sponsor on the air.

Depending on the terms of its contract with a rightsholder, a broadcaster may be able to sell sponsorships. *The Gillette Cavalcade of Sports* was a long-running series that personified a telecast title sponsorship (IMDB, n.d.a). Depending on the terms of its contract with a rightsholder, a broadcaster also can sell sponsorships. "ESPN College GameDay—Built by the Home Depot" is a modern example of a telecast presenting sponsorship.

Some companies engage in **ambush marketing**, seeking television exposure for products or brands without paying any fees to the telecaster or event organizer. This frequently involves a company paying players to wear products bearing logos that compete with those of companies that sponsor an event, or by placing a billboard in a location within the range of cameras covering the game that cannot be controlled by the event organizer. For example, the Citgo energy company has long maintained a sign on the roof of a building near Fenway Park that is visible to spectators and television viewers every time a home run is hit over the "Green Monster" wall in leftfield (Associated Press [AP], 2017).

Distribution

Broadcast Networks

Traditional broadcast television and radio networks are composed of various stations in cities throughout the nation. These affiliates are required to air all (or almost all) programming provided to them by their networks. These agreements, as well as rules established by the FCC, regulate the number of programming hours that can be provided by networks. At times when no network programming is provided, affiliates are free to televise whatever programming they choose.

Broadcast affiliates usually have limited rights not to "clear" a particular program—that is, not to show a network program in the local market. If the affiliate chooses not to show the program, that decision is usually made because the station does not believe it will generate good ratings, meaning that the station can make more money by acquiring independently produced programming and selling all advertising on a local basis. The contracts between networks and their affiliates require affiliates to clear a minimum percentage of network programming.

Syndication

Not all sport programming is distributed on networks. Independent producers can acquire rights, create programs, and **syndicate** them; that is, they can sell the programs to stations not affiliated with networks or to network affiliates for telecast at times when they are not obligated to show network programs.

Cable Networks

Until the 1970s, the signals of almost all television stations were transmitted over public airwaves and received by people having their own antennae. Cable television networks, in contrast, have a "closed signal path" that can be accessed only by cable/DBS systems. Those systems have agreements with the cable networks to distribute their programming, for which they pay the networks monthly fees for each subscriber that has the right to receive each particular network, ranging from a few cents to $7.21 for ESPN (the most expensive cable network) (Traina, 2017). The cable/DBS companies also pay retransmission consent fees to broadcast networks for the right to show the networks' programming on their systems.

Cable/DBS systems, in turn, sell packages of television networks to the public. Various networks are divided into **tiers**, or groups of networks, that are marketed to customers at different fees. "Basic Service" or "Lifeline Service" usually includes the broadcast networks and a handful of local stations and is the lowest-priced package. Next in order is "Expanded Basic," which is composed of an array of highly rated cable networks, including channels specializing in entertainment, sports, news, and other popular programming genres. Additional tiers contain more specialized networks, such as a "sports tier," which includes various regional sports networks and networks devoted to specific sports, or "premium" services such as commercial-free movie networks. Although consumers can select which tiers to subscribe to, they cannot choose which networks to include in the various tiers. Cable/DBS companies decide which networks to bundle into particular tiers, although many cable networks make it a contractual requirement that they be included in a specific tier; Expanded Basic is where most networks want to be, because it usually is the tier with the largest number of subscribers.

Digital Networks

The emergence of broadband Internet as a means of distributing and viewing audio–video material now enables new networks to transmit programming without the need to be packaged on a tier by a cable/DBS systems. The ESPN3.com network pioneered this new genre of **digital networks**, which is increasingly referred to as **over-the-top (OTT) networks**. Such offerings may be composed of one network or a "skinny bundle" of multiple networks, which includes fewer networks than the traditional "cable bundle" of 100 or more networks.

Pay-Per-View

A limited number of sports programs, usually championship boxing matches and other fighting-oriented sports and exhibitions, are distributed on a **pay-per-view** basis. Instead of televising the event on commercial television and amortizing the costs by advertising sales, a pay-per-view program is distributed on a special channel on cable/DBS systems that is accessible only to consumers who pay a specified fee to watch the program. In this model, there is no advertising in the telecast; instead, the sales revenue is shared by the cable/DBS operators, the event promoter, and, in the case of boxing matches, the fighters themselves.

Regionalization

Networks provide programming to their affiliates on either a national, regional, or local basis. For example, every NFL football game is televised into the home markets of the participating teams (except for home games when all stadium tickets are not sold, in which case there is a **blackout** of the game in the home market to encourage future ticket sales). Other sports, such as the NBA, authorize "split-national" telecasts, showing a game between two eastern teams to its audience in that half of the country and a different game between two western teams to its West Coast audience, in an effort to maximize total viewership by taking advantage of regional and local fan interests. Coverage patterns are controlled by rightsholders in consultation with their telecasting partners.

Local telecasts, which are arranged for by individual teams, usually can be shown only in the participating teams' home territories. This limitation protects teams in weaker, smaller markets from having their local television revenues and exposure overwhelmed by bigger, more famous teams. The need for this protection is illustrated by the fact that, at the height of the Yankees–Red Sox rivalry in 2003–2004, game telecasts between those two teams received higher ratings in Los Angeles than did games involving the Dodgers or Angels in the Los Angeles area. Any fans of out-of-town teams now can pay a fee to acquire out-of-market coverage of game telecasts not available locally.

The Pac-12 Network has adopted an innovative regional coverage model. It has established a series of seven networks: one for a national audience, plus six regional networks focusing their programming on the geographic affinities of a region within the conference territory. The regional networks focus on Arizona (the home of conference members University of Arizona and Arizona State), Oregon (Oregon and Oregon State), Northern California (California and Stanford), the Rocky Mountains (Colorado and Utah), Southern California (USC and UCLA), and Washington (Washington and Washington State).

TV Everywhere

Both traditional over-the-air and cable networks as well as digital networks are expanding their coverage patterns by offering "TV Everywhere" availability. In this model, a network is "streamed" to a mobile device for **out-of-home viewing**, but typically only to viewers who have a paid subscription to a cable or satellite distribution service. The viewer must enter log-in credentials to access the out-of-home stream.

Radio

Most radio stations continue to operate on the traditional over-air model, although satellite-delivered radio has been available on a subscription basis since the early 2000s.

Highlights and Ancillary Rights

The conclusion of a game telecast does not mean an end to its commercial value. Game telecasts, like all television programs, are protected by **copyright** law. A copyright is literally the right to copy an original work that is in tangible form; songs, movies, books, webpages, video games, and game telecasts are examples of artistic works that cannot be used commercially without the permission of their creators.

When a game ends, its results can be reported by anyone as news—but video highlights can be included in a news report only with the permission of the owner of the game footage. Traditionally, permission has been limited to a handful of plays on newscasts during the 2 days following the conclusion of the game.

Until the 1980s, ownership of game telecast copyrights was seldom a deal point in rights negotiations. Networks were the legal owners of the copyrights because they produced the game telecasts using their own equipment and personnel. But with the proliferation of programs such as *SportsCenter*, *NFL Primetime*, *College GameDay*, and even entertainment programs such as *The ESPYs*, all of which rely heavily on highlights, plus emerging technology allowing on-demand highlight streaming on the Internet, the value of postgame footage rights has increased. The omnipresence of mobile devices has also created a new market for on-demand highlight streaming on sites operated by television networks, independent websites, and leagues/conferences themselves, further increasing the value of highlights.

Rightsholders now routinely insist on new rights agreements that own game telecast copyrights (permitted under the work-for-hire doctrine of copyright law). Those new agreements also frequently require networks to transfer copyright ownership of the game telecasts produced under prior agreements to leagues and conferences. Rightsholders such as NASCAR and the International Olympic Committee (IOC) were so intent on acquiring such copyrights that they made an assignment of those rights a prerequisite to negotiations with networks for new agreements.

By owning telecast copyrights and controlling highlight usage, rightsholders have created new opportunities to monetize those assets. This model also allows them to more effectively control their images. As a condition of granting a license for use of highlights, a rightsholder can insist on having the right to approve the content of the program containing its footage. This is a powerful way to prevent an unflattering portrayal of a league, team, or player. For example, the 2004 World Series highlight video contains no references to a controversial play in the sixth game of the American League Championship Series, when Alex Rodriguez of the Yankees knocked the ball out of the glove of Red Sox pitcher Bronson Arroyo during a close play at first base. The play triggered a lengthy argument when Rodriguez was first called safe, and then out, ruining a potential series-altering rally by the Yankees. By exercising its right to keep footage of the play out of the video, MLB seems to have chosen to sanitize the controversy.

International Sport Coverage

As the world economy undergoes globalization, American sport organizations and broadcasting companies are expanding their presence in foreign markets. Their international counterparts are doing the same in the United States.

International Sport Programming in the United States

American television networks regularly acquire rights to show international sport programming in the United States. The most valuable international property remains the Olympic Games. NBC has had the telecast rights to this event since 1988. In 2011, NBC outbid its rivals with a $4.38 billion offer to cover the 2014, 2016, 2018, and 2020 Games. In 2014, following its success in Sochi, Russia, NBC forged a private deal with the IOC for $7.75 billion for the Olympic rights in 2022–2032 (Sandomir, 2014). Other international sport events regularly shown on U.S. cable and broadcast networks include the Wimbledon, Australian Open, and French Open tennis tournaments; the British Open golf championship; the European Tour golf series;

the Tour de France bicycle race; Formula One auto racing; and the world figure skating and gymnastics championships.

It is international soccer, however, that has made the biggest impact in recent years on the U.S. television market. As recently as 1978, the Fédération Internationale de Football Association (FIFA) World Cup tournament received no American television coverage. In 1994, the event was held in the United States for the first time, with ABC and ESPN providing extensive coverage. Since then, the rights fees for the event have mushroomed. Fox and Telemundo agreed in 2011 to pay a reported $1 billion for the English- and Spanish-language rights to the 2018 and 2022 World Cups—more than twice what ESPN and Univision paid for the 2010 and 2014 tournaments (AP, 2011). In addition, the English Premier League (EPL) has recently received significantly increased rights fees in the United States from NBC.

New networks are using soccer as an entrée to establish a business presence in the United States. beIN Sport, owned by the Qatar-based Al Jazeera chain of networks, debuted in the United States in 2012. Its programming mix features rights to several well-regarded international soccer leagues, including La Liga (Spain), Ligue 1 (France), and Serie A (Italy) (Davis, 2012).

Commissioner Don Garber of Major League Soccer (MLS) expressed concern about a glut of soccer on American television (Peck, 2013). Garber's comments came amid public speculation about whether increased U.S. television coverage of foreign soccer would help or hurt MLS. The best future benchmark of this influence will be the amount of rights fees that MLS receives during its next round of negotiations for U.S. television rights (Smith, 2013). The current deal with ESPN is for $38 million annually for 8 years totaling $304 million (Traina, 2017).

U.S. Sports Programming Internationally

The telecasting of American sports internationally occurs by a variety of transactions. Many professional leagues and organizations, such as the NFL, the NBA, the Augusta National Golf Club (host of the Masters), and the U.S. Tennis Association (which operates the U.S. Open) negotiate rights agreements with networks on a country-by-country basis. Other rightsholders utilize agents to secure international television coverage. The agents negotiate rights fees on behalf of their clients and receive a percentage of the fees as payment for their services.

Foreign-Language Sports Networks in the United States

To serve the growing Hispanic population in the United States, both ESPN and Fox operate domestic Spanish-language sports networks. Fox Sports en Espanol debuted in 1996 and was rebranded Fox Deportes in 2010. ESPN Deportes was launched in 2004. The programming of these channels is specifically targeted to Hispanic audiences, instead of merely being Spanish-language **simulcasts** of English-language stations.

The American Spanish-language broadcast networks Univision and Telemundo both include sports in their respective programming mixes. Univision owns the Univision Deportes network, and Telemundo operates Telemundo Deportes in association with NBC Sports. In 2012, ESPN debuted the first-ever Spanish-language spot (featuring New York Yankees star Robinson Cano) in its famous "This Is SportsCenter" advertising campaign for telecast on the main ESPN channel.

Current Issues

Even at a time of unprecedented success, the sport broadcasting industry faces important challenges.

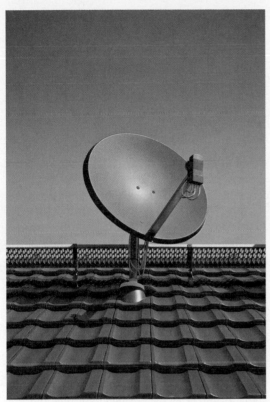

© jbk_photography/iStock/Thinkstock

Market "Bubble"?

Rights fees increased dramatically during the early 2000s. For example, the NFL's most recent TV deals with CBS, ESPN, Fox, and NBC in 2011 represented a 60% increase in fees over the previous deals (Hiestand, 2011). That same year, the Pac-12 tripled its national rights fees and the NHL secured nearly that same percentage increase (Ourand, 2011). Throughout the decade of the 2010s, sports rights fees continued to rise.

This trend has raised questions about whether there is a growing **bubble** in sports media rights. A marketplace bubble occurs when prices rise steeply in a short time, followed by sudden decrease in value when the marketplace "corrects" itself. Two famous recent bubbles were the "dot.com bubble" in 2000, in which stock values of Internet companies rose

sharply and then crashed, and the "housing bubble" of 2007–2008, when residential real estate prices fell sharply after a years-long escalation. Both bubbles resulted in recessions to the American economy and bankrupted many companies and homeowners.

Revenue growth for the traditional television networks was mixed in the 2010s. ESPN's well-publicized decreases in subscriber revenue were offset by growth of retransmission consent fees payable to traditional over-the-air networks. At the same time, the role of new marketplace entrants such as Amazon and Netflix in future sports rights negotiations is largely uncertain.

Bundling

Throughout the 1990s and early 2000s, traditional cable and DBS operators relied on a "big bundle" of networks—both sports and non-sports in nature—as their primary consumer offering. As these "Expanded Basic" bundles grew bigger and more costly, they attracted widespread public criticism about the impact of these costs on consumers' monthly cable bills (Thompson, 2013). One particularly vociferous critic has been U.S. Senator John McCain. In 2013, McCain introduced federal legislation to encourage cable operators to offer cable channels on an **à la carte** basis instead of **bundling** them into tiers and charging subscribers for an entire tier containing channels that subscribers never watched (Flint, 2013).

By 2015, however, it was a combination of consumer choice and technology, not legislation, that disrupted the big bundle. New "skinny bundles" delivered "over-the-top" (via the Internet instead of a DBS satellite or a cable set-top box) were offered at lower prices and containing fewer networks. ESPN announced plans to launch its own direct-to-subscriber product in 2018 (Rappaport, 2017).

Audience Fragmentation

The more choices available to people, the fewer people are likely to choose any particular offering. This kind of **fragmentation** is a seemingly endless trend in television. There are two forms of television audience fragmentation. The first form is the availability of more television networks, each catering to a specialized segment of the public. In 1979, for example, ESPN was considered a niche network because it offered only sport programming; now it is considered more of a general-interest network in comparison to other channels specializing in such content as college sports (ESPNU), one particular sport (NFL Network, Golf Channel), one league (Big Ten Network, Pac-12 Network), and even one team (YES, n.d.).

The second form of fragmentation is the availability of video games, social media, and on-demand entertainment programming services as alternatives to live television. Recent studies suggest that young people are watching less TV due to these alternatives (Marketing Charts, 2013). Electronic gaming (eSports) is projected to be a $1.5 billion-dollar industry by 2020, and it appeals primarily to younger demographics (Dunn, 2017). The potential for this new genre of sport-related entertainment to dilute interest in traditional sports is demonstrated by the fact that professional sport team owners are becoming eSports investors (Ungar, 2017) and the NCAA has been considering regulating collegiate-level eSports competitions (Darcy, 2017).

The overall effect of fragmentation may be to force television advertisers to focus on targeted opportunities instead of the increasingly outdated mass-market strategies (Morgan, 2012).

Career Opportunities

Although sports media are heavily based on technology, this field remains a people-driven business that offers a wide array of career opportunities. There are two fundamental types of jobs at networks: business-related jobs and production-related jobs.

Business-related jobs tend to be more strategic in nature. Programming jobs relate to the acquisition and exploitation of rights—identifying rightsholders, analyzing the value of rights and whether particular programming is compatible with the network's other content, negotiating with rightsholders, scheduling the network's programming, and administering the working relationship with rightsholders. Sales jobs involve the sale of advertising and sponsorship for particular programs or sports or the sale of network distribution rights to cable/DBS operators. Job titles for junior positions tend to be "associate," "assistant," and "coordinator," and then advance to "manager" and "director," with executive-level positions carrying the title of "vice-president" or "senior vice-president," or other modifiers. For example, an associate program planner would be a junior job for someone working on program scheduling. A research coordinator would gather statistics and other data related to ratings and demographics for use primarily in advertising sales. A director of finance would supervise the personnel who are responsible for the accounting of costs and expenses related to a company's business operations. A vice-president of programming would have management responsibilities for all or a significant part of the programming decisions made by a network.

© Ryan McVay/Photodisc/Thinkstock

Production-related jobs involve the creation of programs—producing and directing telecasts, operating cameras, recording highlights, mixing in music and other production elements, researching statistics, and transmitting program signals through the maze of satellites and fiber-optic cables that result in the program being available for viewing. A production assistant would be a junior position for someone responsible for a particular aspect of program production, such as operating a videotape machine or carrying a sideline microphone. A replay supervisor would oversee all available camera feeds for selection of the best views of a play for replaying highlights. An associate producer would oversee and troubleshoot designated elements of the event production, supervising various assistants while being subject to the control of the producer. A program engineer would be responsible for ensuring that the program feed is produced according to the network's quality standards and transmitted from the production facility for "uplinking" to a satellite or to fiber-optic cable. The coordinating producer has overall control for planning and executing the creation of a program.

Most rightsholders employ staffs to manage their relationships with networks, ranging from negotiating rights agreements to regulating the access that production crews have to stadiums to factoring TV-related considerations into the creation of playing schedules. Many individual teams also employ staff members to manage TV-related matters. Titles could range from a vice-president of broadcasting to a media relations coordinator.

Sport programming is so important to cable companies and other content distributors that they employ staffs to analyze the industry and work directly with sport-related networks on matters of mutual interest. With sports playing an increasingly important role in the business of cable/DBS companies, job titles can be as lofty as senior vice-president and general manager for oversight of all sport-related operations.

Advertising agencies employ specialists in sports media, who analyze program ratings, audience demographics, and market trends to maximize the effectiveness of advertising and sponsorship in particular programming. Similarly, sport marketing companies seek opportunities for clients to engage in promotional programs and other strategic alignment with sport events and telecasts. Job titles can include "account executive," for a relatively junior position at an advertising agency working on the business of a particular client, and "special events coordinator," for someone responsible for all travel and hospitality details of an agency for a trip to a big event such as the Super Bowl to entertain clients.

A portion of the business of sport-related consumer product companies, such as Nike, includes a media strategy for purchasing advertising, arranging for product placement to gain on-air exposure, and analyzing other marketing and promotional opportunities. A director of marketing would work on the management team responsible for implementing these objectives.

Companies such as Major League Baseball Advanced Media personify the new industry-wide emphasis on technology in sports media, which has created a wealth of new tech-centric job opportunities, ranging from software development to alternative distribution and marketing.

There are also independent companies that work on everything from representing leagues in negotiating rights agreements to producing telecasts. These organizations vary in size from sole proprietorships to multinational corporations.

In an era when media rights can involve billion-dollar fees, there is a need for specialized lawyers, accountants, and financiers to properly structure a variety of transactions, ranging from writing and negotiating contracts to coordinating with a network's bank on how to structure payments of large rights fees.

Case Study 17-1

The Dominance of ESPN

ESPN has been a dominant force in sports television since the 1980s. It controls programming rights to an unparalleled portfolio of major sports properties in the United States, including the NFL, NBA, MLB, Southeastern Conference (SEC), Atlantic Coast Conference (ACC), College Football Playoffs, the Masters, Wimbledon, U.S. Open Tennis, the Little League World Series, and more. It operates eight domestic television networks, including ESPN, ESPN2, ESPNEWS, ESPNU, and the SEC Network. Its ESPN website is among the most-viewed sport-related websites in the United States, and its other digital assets include ESPNDeportes.com, FiveThirtyEight.com, TheUndefeated.com, and ESPN3. It owns and operates the X Games, the best-known action sports competition in the world. Its *30 for 30* movie and documentary series has been acclaimed for high-quality content (including winning the 2016 Academy Award for Best Documentary Film). In 2017, its parent company, the Walt Disney Company, purchased 22 regional sports networks from Fox.

Despite all of its success and market power, ESPN recently has been beset by a number of challenges. Between 2013 and 2017, the network lost approximately 12 million of its 100 million subscribers, worth an estimated $1 billion in annual revenue. In 2015, average ratings on the ESPN network declined 7% from 2014, then dropped another 11% in 2016. Ad revenue for ESPN's flagship *SportsCenter* program declined by nearly 25% in 2016 (Berg, 2017).

At the same time, ESPN started a new nine-year rights agreement with the NBA that nearly tripled its annual rights fee obligation,

to $1.4 billion per year (Lombardo & Ourand, 2014). It telecast the first year of the new College Football Playoff at a fee of $608 million per year (*Sporting News*, 2012). Its annual $1.9 billion rights-fee payments to the NFL are more than one-third higher than those paid by CBS, Fox, and NBC (Jackson, 2017).

Although ESPN reportedly is still profitable (Ozanian, 2017), the company laid off 550 workers, representing more than 13% of its domestic workforce, from 2015 to 2017 (Duffy, 2015; Thompson, 2017). The company also came under fire for statements by its on-air announcers that were regarded as political instead of sport-related (Draper, 2017), and it has been the target of claims of sexual harassment (Reimer, 2017).

Questions for Discussion

1. Identify the effects of the various marketplace changes and risk factors identified in this chapter on ESPN, and rank those potential effects on ESPN.

2. Based on ESPN's business model as of 2017—a $7.25 per month subscription fee, paid by 88 million cable/DBS subscribers, producing 75% of ESPN's revenue—construct an alternative model (including existing revenue sources as well as new sources) to generate equivalent revenue.

3. If other networks besides ESPN also incur revenue losses that result in less revenue being available for rights-fee payments, what would be the consequences for the sports industry?

Resources

Because the sport broadcasting industry changes so rapidly, people who work in the industry—and those who want to—must keep abreast of the latest news and trends. Although many of the details of the broadcasting business are theoretically confidential, the trade press has cultivated sources in the industry who often are glad to share news about the latest contracts, advertising packages, and demographic trends.

The most widely read industry news publications are *Broadcasting & Cable, SportsBusiness Journal/SportsBusiness Daily, MediaWeek, AdWeek, Multichannel News, Variety*, and *Advertising Age*. As their titles suggest, each covers the industry from a different perspective. All are available online, and many produce print editions. Many of these companies also produce annual directories and summaries. Almost every media organization, ranging from networks to research firms such as Nielsen and SNL Kagan, maintains an information-rich website.

Network public relations offices are often helpful if contacted directly.

ABC Sports (see ESPN)
c/o ESPN
47 W. 66th Street
New York, NY 10023
212-456-7777

beIN Sport
7291 NW 74th Street
Medley, FL 33166
305-777-1900
www.beinsports.com/us/

Big Ten Network
600 W. Chicago Avenue
Chicago, IL 60610
312-665-0700
www.btn.com

CBS Sports
51 W. 52nd Street
New York, NY 10019
212-975-5100
www.cbssports.com

ESPN (also ABC Sports)
ESPN Plaza
935 Middle Street
Bristol, CT 06010
860-766-2000
www.espn.com
www.espn.com/nba/abcsports/television

Fox Sports
10201 W. Pico Boulevard
Los Angeles, CA 90064
310-369-2762
www.foxsports.com

The Golf Channel
7580 Golf Channel Drive
Orlando, FL 32819
407-355-4653
www.golfchannel.com

MLB Network
1 MLB Network Plaza
Secaucus, NJ 07094
201-520-6400
http://m.mlb.com/network

NBA TV
c/o Turner Sports
One CNN Center
Atlanta, GA 30303
404-827-1700
www.nba.com/#/

NBC Sports Group
1 Blachley Road
Stamford, CT 06902
203-356-7000; 203-357-0202
http://www.nbcsportsgrouppressbox.com

New England Sports Network (NESN)

480 Arsenal Street, Building 1

Watertown, MA 02472

617-536-9233

https://nesn.com

NFL Network

10950 Washington Boulevard, Suite 100

Culver City, CA 90232

310-840-4635

www.nfl.com

NHL Network

c/o NBC Comcast

NBC Sports/Comcast Sportsnet

1 Blachley Road

Stamford, CT 06902

203-352-2806

www.nhl.com/info/network

Pac-12 Networks

360 Third Street

San Francisco, CA 94107

415-580-4200

http://pac-12.com/networks

Root Sports Northwest

3626 156th Avenue SE

Bellevue, WA 98006

425-641-0104

https://northwest.rootsports.com

TBS Sports

One CNN Center

Atlanta, GA 30303

404-827-1700

www.turner.com/pressroom/united-states/turner-sports

Telemundo Deportes

Telemundo Center

2350 NW 117th Place

Miami, FL 33182

305-884-8200

www.telemundodeportes.com

The Tennis Channel

2850 Ocean Park Boulevard, Suite 150

Santa Monica, CA 90405

310-392-1920

http://thetennischannel.com

Univision Deportes

605 Third Avenue

New York, NY 10158

212-455-5200

www.univision.com/deportes

Yankees Entertainment and Sports Network (YES)

805 Third Avenue

New York, NY 10022

646-487-3600

http://web.yesnetwork.com/index.jsp

Key Terms

à la carte, affiliates, ambush marketing, blackout, broadband, broadcasting, broadcasting rights, bubble, bundling, clean feed, commercial breaks, commercial formats, copyright, cord-cutting, demographic, digital networks, digital video recorder (DVR), direct broadcast satellites (DBS), Federal Communications Commission (FCC), fragmentation, high-definition television (HDTV), head ends, master antenna, multimedia, networks, out of market, out-of-home viewing, over-the-top (OTT) networks, pay-per-view, penetration, pod, primetime, ratings, remote production facility, retransmission consent, revenue-sharing, rights fees, rightsholders, Roone Arledge, Pete Rozelle, share, simulcasts, sponsor, sponsorship, streamed, subscriber fees, symbiotic relationship, syndicate, target markets, television markets, tiers, time-buy, time-shift, trashsports

References

ABC Sports Online. (2003, January 15). History of ABC's *Monday Night Football.* Retrieved from http://espn.go.com/abcsports/mnf/s/2003 /0115/1493105.html

Ampex. (n.d.). Ampex history. Retrieved from http://www.ampex.com/news/history.html ?start=30

Associated Press (AP). (2011, October 22). FIFA confirms Fox, Telemundo get U.S. World Cup rights. Retrieved from http://usatoday30. usatoday.com/sports/soccer/worldcup /story/2011-10-21/fox-telemundo-us-tv -rights-2018-2022-world-cup/50856226/1

Associated Press (AP). (2017, March 16). A deal has been reached to save Boston's iconic Citgo sign. Retrieved at http://fox61 .com/2017/03/16/a-deal-has-been-reached -to-save-bostons-iconic-citgo-sign/

Barnouw, E. (1966–1970). *A history of broadcasting in the United States* (Vols. 1–3). New York, NY: Oxford University Press.

Berg, M. (2017). Don't blame Jemele Hill for ESPN's ratings problem. Retrieved from https://www.forbes.com/sites/maddieberg /2017/10/10/dont-blame-jemele-hill-for -espns-ratings-problem/#4d844406ae36

Big Ten. (2007, July 20). Big Ten Network to officially launch August 30th. Retrieved from http://www.bigten.org/genrel/070207aaa.html

Brady, S. (2007). NHL Network launches in the U.S. Retrieved from http://www.cablefax .com/360AM/25974.html

Brown, M. (2017). Disney accelerates purchase of BAMtech and announces streaming service with ESPN. *Forbes.* Retrieved from https:// www.forbes.com/sites/maurybrown/2017 /08/08/disney-accelerates-purchase-of -bamtech-espn-disney-will-see-new-digital -streaming-media-apps/#7e20bf584a5d

Carter, B. (2002, December 7). Edgar Scherick, producer of television and movies. Retrieved from http://www.nytimes.com/2002/12/07 /arts/edgar-scherick-78-producer-for -television-and-movies.html

Carter, B. (n.d.). Rozelle made NFL what it is today. Retrieved from http://espn.go.com /classic/biography/s/rozelle_pete.htm

Castillo, M. (2017, October 3). Disney's CEO Bob Iger on political controversies in sports: "It's complicated." CNBC. Retrieved from https://www.cnbc.com/2017/10/03/disney -bob-iger-digital-espn-details-talks-political -controversy.html

Chad, N., & Reid, T. (1989, May 12). ABC, once the network of the Olympics, now the network of May. *Los Angeles Times.* Retrieved from http://articles.latimes.com/1989-03-12 /sports/sp-1097_1_abc-sports-production

Cianci, P. J. (2012). *High definition television: The creation, development and implementation of HDTV technology.* Jefferson, NC: McFarland.

Classic Television Database. (n.d.). Home page. Retrieved from http://classic-tv.com

CNN. (2000, January 2). AOL: $2.5b in holiday sales. Retrieved from http://money.cnn .com/2000/01/03/technology/aol/

Comcast. (n.d.). Comcast Sportsnet information. Retrieved from http://www.comcastsportsnet .com

Crupi, A. (2017, November 20). T-Mobile says its 6-second World Series ads were a home run. Retrieved from http://adage.com/article/media /tmobile-six-second-ads-world-series/311361/

Cutting the cord. (2009, August 13). *The Economist.* Retrieved from http://www.economist.com /node/14214847

Darcy, K (2017, October 23). College eSports is the next big thing in varsity athletics. Retrieved from http://www.espn.com/college-sports /story/_/id/21113602/the-next-big-thing -collegiate-athletics-esports

Davis, J. (2008). *Rozelle.* New York, NY: McGraw-Hill.

Deninger, D. (2012). *Sports on television: The how and why behind what you see.* London, UK: Routledge.

Digital TV Europe. (2013, June 3). Ericsson predicts 60% annual mobile video growth. Retrieved from http://www.digitaltveurope

.net/61942/ericsson-predicts-60-annual
-mobile-video-growth/

DIRECTV. (n.d.). DIRECTV history. Retrieved
from http://www.directv.com/DTVAPP
/content/about_us/company_profile

Douglas, S. (1987). *Inventing American
broadcasting: 1899–1922*. Baltimore, MD:
Johns Hopkins University Press.

Drape, J., & Barnes, B. (2017, April 26). ESPN
layoffs: The struggling industry giant sheds
on-air talent. *New York Times*. Retrieved
from https://www.nytimes.com/2017/04/26
/sports/espn-layoffs.html

Draper, K. (2017, November 29). ESPN is laying
off 150 more employees. *New York Times*.
Retrieved from https://www.nytimes
.com/2017/11/29/sports/espn-layoffs.html

Duffy, T (2015). ESPN layoffs begin tomorrow:
350 employees, six-figure earners. Retrieved
from http://thebiglead.com/2015/10/20/espn
-layoffs-begin-tomorrow-350-employees-six
-figure-earners/

Dunn, J. (2017, Mar. 27). Competitive video
gaming will be a $1.5 billion industry by 2020,
researchers say. *Business Insider*. Retrieved
from http://www.businessinsider.com/esports
-popularity-revenue-forecast-chart-2017-3

Dunning, J. (1998). *On the air: The encyclopedia
of old-time radio*. Oxford, UK: Oxford
University Press.

Early Television Museum. (n.d.). Home page.
Retrieved from http://www.earlytelevision.org

Economy in NFL history. (n.d.). Retrieved from
http://www.shmoop.com/nfl-history
/economy.html

Eisenmann, T. T. (2000, July 10). Cable TV: From
community antennas to wired cities. Retrieved
from http://hbswk.hbs.edu/item/1591.html

ESPN Media Zone. (n.d.). ESPN, Inc. fact sheet.
Retrieved from http://espnmediazone.com
/us/espn-inc-fact-sheet/

ESPN.com. (2013, May 2). SEC Network to
broadcast 24/7. Retrieved from http://espn
.go.com/espn/story/_/id/9235260/sec-espn
-announce-sec-network-2014

Evensen, B. J. (1996). *When Dempsey fought Tunney:
Heroes, hokum, and storytelling in the Jazz Age*.
Knoxville, TN: University of Tennessee Press.

Fabrikant, G. (1995, August 1). The media
business: The merger; Walt Disney to acquire
ABC in $19 billion deal to build a giant for
entertainment. *New York Times*. Retrieved
from http://www.nytimes.com/1995/08/01
/business/media-business-merger-walt
-disney-acquire-abc-19-billion-deal-build
-giant-for.html?pagewanted=all&src=pm

Facer, D. (2011, July 28). Utah Utes football:
Pac-12 creates its own TV network. Retrieved
from http://www.deseretnews.com/article
/700166468/Utah-Utes-football-Pac-12
-creates-its-own-TV-network.html

Fierce Wireless. (n.d.). Mobile video traffic:
Alleviating the capacity crunch. Retrieved
from http://www.fiercewireless.com/special
-reports/mobile-video-traffic-alleviating
-capacity-crunch

Flint, J. (2013, May 9). John McCain introduces
Television Consumer Freedom Act of 2013.
LA Times. Retrieved from http://www.latimes
.com/entertainment/envelope/cotown/la-et-ct
-mccain-cable-20130509,0,2224732.story

Florio, M. (2009, May 16). The NFL declares
its dominance over baseball. NBC Sports.
Retrieved from http://profootballtalk
.nbcsports.com/2009/05/16/the-nfl-declares
-its-dominance-over-baseball/

Forsyth, K. S. (2002). History of the Delta Launch
Vehicle. Retrieved from http://kevinforsyth
.net/delta/satcom.htm

Fox Sports. (2013, March 5). Fox announces Fox
Sports1 network. Retrieved from http://msn
.foxsports.com/other/story/FOX-Sports
-announces-FOX-Sports-1-network-030513

Fullerton, H. S. (1915, October 19). Nothing
but luck saved the Phillies. *New York Times*.

Futterman, M. (2012, March 29). $2 billion
Dodgers price tag shatters records. *Wall
Street Journal*. Retrieved from http://online
.wsj.com/article/SB100014240527023034047 0
4577308483250633906.html

Gelston, D. (2008, December 5). Army–Navy, instant reply, Tony Verna, 45 years later. *Farther Off the Wall with Tom Hoffarth*. Retrieved from http://www.insidesocal.com/tomhoffarth/2008/12/05/army-navy-insta/

Grant, A. E., & Meadows, J. H. (2013). *Communication technology update and fundamentals*. Boca Raton, FL: CRC Press.

Gruver, E. (1997). *The American Football League: A year-by-year history, 1960–1969*. Jefferson, NC: McFarland.

Gurnick, K. (2012, March 28). Dodgers sold to Magic Johnson's group. Retrieved from http://losangeles.dodgers.mlb.com/news/article.jsp?ymd=20120327&content_id=27685944

Gurnick, K. (2013, January 28). Dodgers to launch network with Time Warner TV deal. Retrieved from http://mlb.mlb.com/news/article.jsp?ymd=20130128&content_id=41215548&c_id=l

Guthrie, M. (2012). CBS Sports' Sean McManus: How my dad covered the Munich Massacre. *Hollywood Reporter*. Retrieved from http://www.hollywoodreporter.com/news/olympics-2012-cbs-sports-sean-mcmanus-munich-massacre-353669

Hayes, D. (2013, January 14). Nielsen study reveals broadband growth, narrowband decline. Retrieved from http://www.cedmagazine.com/news/2003/01/nielsen-study-reveals-broadband-growth,-narrowband-decline

Head, S., Sterling, C., & Schofield, L. (1994). *Broadcasting in America* (7th ed.). Boston, MA: Houghton Mifflin.

Hiestand, M. (2011, December 14). New NFL TV deals go up 60%. Retrieved from http://content.usatoday.com/communities/gameon/post/2011/12/new-nfl-tv-deals-bonanza/1#.Uf_WoRblNcR

History.com. (n.d.). May 28, 1957: Baseball owners allow Dodgers and Giants to move. Retrieved from http://www.history.com/this-day-in-history/baseball-owners-allow-dodgers-and-giants-to-move

Howell, E. (2013, February 12). Telstar: Satellite beamed 1st TV signals across the sea. Retrieved from http://www.space.com/19756-telstar.html

Hulu. (2008, March 12). Hulu press release. Retrieved from https://web.archive.org/web/20080318113552/http://www.hulu.com/press/launch_press_release.html

IBIS World. (2013). Global Internet service providers: Market research report. Retrieved from http://www.ibisworld.com/industry/global/global-internet-service-providers.html

IMDB. (n.d.a). *Gillette Cavalcade of Sports*. Retrieved from http://www.imdb.com/title/tt0268788/

IMDB. (n.d.b). *The Huntley–Brinkley Report*. Retrieved from http://www.imdb.com/title/tt0275133/

Internet World Stats. (n.d.). Internet growth statistics. Retrieved from http://www.internetworldstats.com/emarketing.htm

Jackson, E. (2017, June 30). Why ESPN is still well-positioned to keep NFL rights in 2022 and beyond Retrieved from https://www.cnbc.com/2017/06/30/espn-is-well-positioned-to-keep-nfl-rights.html

Karp, A. (2013, July 9). ESPN Q2 viewership drops sharply, while NBC Sports Network sees audience gains. Retrieved from http://www.sportsbusinessdaily.com/Daily/Issues/2013/07/09/Research-and-Ratings/Q2-viewership.aspx

KDKA. (2010, April 1). KDKA firsts. Retrieved from http://pittsburgh.cbslocal.com/2010/04/01/kdka-firsts/

Keller, R. (1982). Sport and television in the 1950's: A preliminary survey. Retrieved from http://library.la84.org/SportsLibrary/NASSH_Proceedings/NP1982/NP1982v.pdf

Kindred, D. (2006). *Sound and fury: Two powerful lives, one fateful friendship*. New York, NY: Free Press.

Kleiner Perking. (2017). Internet Trends 2017: Code conference.

Lombardo, J., & Ourand, J. (2014, October 6). ESPN, Turner will pay a combined $24b in new nine-year NBA media rights deal. *SportsBusiness Daily*. Retrieved from

http://www.sportsbusinessdaily.com/Daily
/Issues/2014/10/06/Media/NBA-media.aspx

Loup, R. (2001, January 22). The AFL: A football
legacy. Retrieved from http://sportsillustrated
.cnn.com/football/news/2001/01/22
/afl_history_1/

Lovinger, D. (2017, December 4). Time for
industry to embrace Total Audience Delivery.
SportsBusiness Journal. Retrieved from http://
www.sportsbusinessdaily.com/Journal
/Issues/2017/12/04/Opinion/Lovinger.aspx

MacDonald, J. F. (2009). Sports and television.
Retrieved from http://www.jfredmacdonald
.com/onutv/sportstv.htm

Major League Baseball (MLB). (n.d.). About MLB
Network. Retrieved from http://mlb.mlb
.com/network/about/

Manjoo, F. (2014, Feb. 15). Comcast vs. the cord
cutters. *New York Times.* Retrieved from https://
www.nytimes.com/2014/02/16/business/media
/comcast-vs-the-cord-cutters.html

Marketing Charts staff. (2013). Are young people
watching less TV? (Updated Q2 2013 data).
Retrieved from http://www.marketingcharts
.com/wp/television/are-young-people
-watching-less-tv-24817/

Marvin, G. (2013, April 12). Mobile video
views surge 300%; tablets fuel growth and
engagement. *Marketing Land.* Retrieved from
http://marketingland.com/adobe-mobile
-video-views-rise-300-tablets-see-fastest
-growth-highest-completion-rate-39586

Maule, T. (1959). The greatest football game
ever played. Retrieved from http://
sportsillustrated.cnn.com/vault/article
/magazine/MAG1133692/index.htm

McCracken, H. (2010, May 24). A history of AOL,
as told in its own old press releases. Retrieved
from http://technologizer.com/2010/05/24
/aol-anniversary/

Meserole, M. (2002, December 6). Arledge created
Monday Night Football. Retrieved from http://
www.espn.com/classic/obit/arledgeobit.html

Meyers, C. B. (2011). The problems with sponsorship
in U.S. broadcasting, 1930s–1950s: Perspectives

from the advertising industry. *Historical Journal
of Film, Radio, and Television, 31*(3), 355–372.

Miller, J. A., & Shales, T. (2011). *Those guys have all
the fun.* Boston, MA: Little, Brown.

Minami, C. (2013, June 13). Dodgers, MLB reach
tentative agreement on cable deal, per report.
Retrieved from http://www.truebluela.com
/2013/6/13/4429002/dodgers-mlb-reach
-tentative-agreement-on-cable-deal

National Basketball Association (NBA). (n.d.).
NBA history. Retrieved from http://www.nba
.com/history/

National Football League (NFL). (n.d.). History.
Retrieved from http://www.nfl.com/history
/chronology/1869-1910

*NCAA v. Board of Regents of the University of
Oklahoma,* 468 U.S. 85 (1984).

NCTA. (n.d.). Cable's ongoing evolution.
Retrieved from http://www.ncta.com
/who-we-are/our-story

Nielsen Media Research. (n.d.). Television
audience measurement terms. Retrieved from
http://www.nielsenmedia.ca/English
/NMR_U_PDF/TV%20Terms.pdf

Ohio History Central. (n.d.). Powel Crosley, Jr.
Retrieved from http://www.ohiohistorycentral
.org/w/Powel_Crosley_Jr.

Olbermann, K. (2011, August 1). How I was hired—
and fired—by Rupert Murdoch. *The Guardian.*
Retrieved from http://www.theguardian.com
/commentisfree/cifamerica/2011/aug/01
/rupert-murdoch-keith-olbermann

Oracle Education Foundation. (n.d.). Retrieved
from http://library.thinkquest.org/27629
/themes/media/md60s.html

Ourand, J. (2011, June 6). How high can rights
fees go? *SportsBusiness Daily.* Retrieved from
http://www.sportsbusinessdaily.com/Journal
/Issues/2011/06/06/In-Depth/Rights-Fees
.aspx

Ourand, J. (2013, May 6). Outside of big live
events, is TV Everywhere going nowhere?
SportsBusiness Daily. Retrieved from http://
www.sportsbusinessdaily.com/Journal/Issues
/2013/05/06/Media/Sports-Media.aspx

Ourand, J. (2017, June 26). Taking the pulse of ESPN. *SportsBusiness Daily*. Retrieved from http://www.sportsbusinessdaily.com/Journal/Issues/2017/06/26/Media/ESPN-main.aspx

Ozanian, M. (2017, February 8). The rise and fall of ESPN [Graphic]. *Forbes*. Retrieved from https://www.forbes.com/sites/mikeozanian/2017/02/08/the-rise-and-fall-of-espn-graphic/#8eb5d6346044

Peck, B. (2013, April 27). MLS commissioner thinks there's "way too much soccer on television." Retrieved from http://sports.yahoo.com/blogs/soccer-dirty-tackle/mls-commissioner-thinks-way-too-much-soccer-television-050024816.html

Pepitone, J. (2011, July 12). Netflix hikes prices for DVDs + streaming. *CNN Money*. Retrieved from http://money.cnn.com/2011/07/12/technology/netflix_unlimited_dvd/index.htm

Pickert, K. (2009, January 22). A brief history of the X Games. *Time*. Retrieved from http://content.time.com/time/nation/article/0,8599,1873166,00.html

Pittsburgh Athletic Co. v. KQV Broadcasting Co., 24 F. Supp. 490 (W.D. Pa. 1938).

Pro Football Hall of Fame. (n.d.). Rams team history. Retrieved from http://www.profootballhof.com/teams/los-angeles-rams/

Ramachandran, S. (2012, August 7). Evidence grows on TV cord-cutting. *Wall Street Journal*. Retrieved from https://www.wsj.com/articles/SB10000872396390443792604577574901875760374

Rappaport, D. (2017, August 8). Disney to launch its own ESPN streaming service. *Sports Illustrated*. Retrieved from https://www.si.com/tech-media/2017/08/08/disney-watch-espn-streaming-service

Rauscher, A. (n.d.). February 5, 1963. The Beatles in America: We loved them yeah, yeah, yeah. Newseum. Retrieved from http://www.newseum.org/news/2009/02/the-beatles-in-america-we-loved-them--yeah--yeah--yeah.html

Reed, W. F. (1991). All shook up. Retrieved from http://sportsillustrated.cnn.com/vault/article/magazine/MAG1140740/1/index.htm

Reimer, A. (2017, December 14). New ESPN sexual harassment accusations name anchor John Cubbigross and analyst Matthew Berry. WEEI. Retrieved from http://www.weei.com/blogs/alex-reimer/new-espn-sexual-harassment-accusations-name-anchor-john-buccigross-and-analyst

Rische, P. (2012, October 31). NBC Sports betting big on soccer with acquisition of Barclays English Premier League. *Forbes*. Retrieved from http://www.forbes.com/sites/prishe/2012/10/31/nbc-sports-betting-big-on-soccer-with-acquisition-of-barclays-english-premiere-league/

Rovell, D. (2012, November 20). News Corp acquires stake in YES. ESPN.com. Retrieved from http://www.espn.com/new-york/mlb/story/_/id/8654665/news-corp-acquires-49-percent-stake-yes-network

Sandomir, R. (2011a, August 1). Versus renamed again. *New York Times*. Retrieved from http://www.nytimes.com/2011/08/02/sports/versus-renamed-again.html

Sandomir, R. (2011b, September 8). ESPN extends deal with N.F.L. for $15 billion. *New York Times*. Retrieved from http://www.nytimes.com/2011/09/09/sports/football/espn-extends-deal-with-nfl-for-15-billion.html

Sandomir, R. (2014, May 7). NBC extends Olympic deal into unknown. *New York Times*. Retrieved from https://www.nytimes.com/2014/05/08/sports/olympics/nbc-extends-olympic-tv-deal-through-2032.html

Schexnayder, C. J. (2009, December 22). The 1927 Rose Bowl: Alabama vs. Stanford. Retrieved from http://www.rollbamaroll.com/2009/12/22/1197979/the-1927-rose-bowl-alabama-vs

Shannon, R. (2010, February 9). USA vs. USSR, 1962: The greatest track meet of all time. *Bleacher Report*. Retrieved from http://bleacherreport.com/articles/342578-usa-vs-ussr-1962-the-greatest-track-meet-of-all-time

Smentek, S. (2011, June 1). Media experts say audience fragmentation is affecting advertiser reach and agency resources. Retrieved from https://www.comcastspotlight.com

/about/blog/media-experts-say-audience-fragmentation-affecting-advertiser-reach-and-agency-resources

Smith, C. (1995). *The storytellers: From Mel Allen to Bob Costas: Sixty years of baseball tales from the broadcast booth.* New York, NY: Macmillan.

Sporting News. (2012, November 21). ESPN reaches 12-year deal for new college football playoff TV rights. Retrieved from http://www.sportingnews.com/ncaa-football/news/4333600-college-football-playoff-espn-tv-rights-12-years-500-million-bcs

SportsBusiness Daily. (2012, February 29). Four sports channels among top 10 for cable net monthly subscriber fees. Retrieved from http://www.sportsbusinessdaily.com/Daily/Issues/2012/02/29/Research-and-Ratings/Sub-fees.aspx.

Staples, A. (2011, July 21). Texas' Longhorn Network sparking another Big 12 missile crisis. Retrieved from http://sportsillustrated.cnn.com/2011/writers/andy_staples/07/21/longhorn-network-big-12/index.html

Stephens, M. (n.d.). History of television. *Grolier Encyclopedia.* Retrieved from http://www.nyu.edu/classes/stephens/History%20of%20Television%20page.htm

Stevens, T. (2011, February 22). Amazon launches Prime Instant Video, unlimited streaming for Prime subscriber. *Engadget.* Retrieved from https://www.engadget.com/2011/02/22/amazon-launches-prime-instant-videos-unlimited-streaming-for-pr/

Television Obscurities. (2013, December 22). Color adoption slow. Retrieved from http://www.tvobscurities.com/articles/color60s/

Thompson, D. (2013, April 2). Mad about the cost of TV? Blame sports. *The Atlantic.* Retrieved from http://www.theatlantic.com/business/archive/2013/04/mad-about-the-cost-of-tv-blame-sports/274575/

Thompson, D. (2017, May 1). ESPN is not doomed. *The Atlantic.* Retrieved from https://www.theatlantic.com/business/archive/2017/05/espn-layoffs-future/524922/

TiVo. (n.d.). TiVo history. Retrieved from http://www3.tivo.com/jobs/questions/history-of-tivo/index.html

Todayinsport.com. (n.d.) Today in World Series history (Part 2). Retrieved from http://www.todayinsport.com/baseball/baseball-championships/world-series?p=2

Traina, J. (2017, June 26). Here's what ESPN pays for most of its sports rights. *Sports Illustrated.* Retrieved from https://www.si.com/extra-mustard/2017/06/26/espn-sports-rights-cost

TVB. (2012). Local media marketing solutions. Retrieved from http://www.tvb.org/media/file/TV_Basics.pdf

TVhistory.tv. (2001–2013). Number of TV households in America. Retrieved from http://www.tvhistory.tv/Annual_TV_Households_50-78.JPG

Twentieth Century Sporting Club, Inc. v. Transradio Press Service, Inc., 300 N.Y.S. 159 (1937).

Ungar, K. (2017, August 8). Why investment from traditional sports is so important to eSports in 2017. Retrieved from https://venturebeat.com/2017/08/08/why-are-traditional-sports-investing-in-esports-now/

Wallenstein, A. (2013, June 3). Top Wall Street analyst: Pay TV "cord-cutting is real." *Variety.* Retrieved from http://variety.com/2013/digital/news/top-wall-street-analyst-pay-tv-cord-cutting-is-real-1200491763/

Wertheim, J. (2012). When Billy beat Bobby. *Sports Illustrated.* Retrieved from http://sportsillustrated.cnn.com/vault/article/magazine/MAG1197984/index.htm

Wertheim, J. (2017, May 9). The reckoning: When rights-fee bubble bursts, college sports will be changed forever. *Sports Illustrated.* Retrieved from https://www.si.com/college-football/2017/05/09/espn-layoffs-media-rights-bubble-college-sports

Wulf, S. (1993). Out foxed. *Sports Illustrated.* Retrieved from http://sportsillustrated.cnn.com/vault/article/magazine/MAG1138126/index.htm

YES. (n.d.). About the YES Network. Retrieved from http://web.yesnetwork.com/about/

Chapter 18

Dan Covell

The Sporting Goods and Licensed Products Industries

Learning Objectives

Upon completion of this chapter, students should be able to:

1. Estimate the size and scope of the sporting goods and licensed products industry.

2. Appraise the historical development of the sporting goods and licensed products industries, with a particular emphasis on how leagues and players associations came to establish properties divisions and licensing programs.

3. Differentiate between licensed and branded products.

4. Assess the steps in the licensing process and the role that licensing plays in generating revenue for licensors and licensees.

5. Identify the career opportunities available in the sporting goods and licensed products industries, and discuss the skills needed to succeed in them.

6. Explain the importance of innovation in producing and selling products.

7. Illustrate how the concept of expert usage, exhibited through product endorsements, helps overcome the risk factors that customers assess when making a purchase decision.

8. Analyze the role of global sourcing, particularly in the sport apparel and footwear industries, and explain how this practice may create an ethical dilemma for manufacturers.

Introduction

This chapter presents information on two related segments of the sport industry: **sporting goods** and **licensed products**. According to Hardy (1997), an analysis of sport products reveals their triple commodity nature: the activity or game form, the service, and the goods. Hardy defines *sporting goods* as the physical objects necessary for the game form. The development and sale of such goods serve as the focus of this chapter.

The sporting goods industry has a long history and encompasses equipment, apparel, and footwear. Licensed products—clothing or products bearing the name or logo of a popular collegiate or professional sport team—have been around for a comparatively short period of time and comprise a specialized subset of the sporting goods industry. The following data outline the scope of these industries, as compiled in 2015 by the Sports and Fitness Industry Association (SFIA), the trade association of leading industry sports and fitness brands, suppliers, retailers and partners:

- Total sports apparel sales grew 4% to $34.1 billion, up from $32.8 billion the previous year. Fitness apparel sales grew 13.3% to $394 million, up $47 million from $347 million in 2013.
- Total sports equipment sales grew 2.7% to $22.8 billion, led by firearms, fishing, camping, golf, and football products.
- In the fitness equipment category, consumer exercise equipment sales grew 4.7% to $3.75 billion, with treadmills continuing to be the best-selling exercise equipment category by a large margin.
- Total athletic footwear shipments reached $14.48 billion, an increase of 4.3% from the previous year. Running footwear continues to dominate as a category leader, with $4.3 billion in 2014 shipments, followed by

the kids, classics, basketball, and skate/surf categories. Approximately 93 million people in the United States bought athletic shoes in 2015 (Statista, 2015).

Additional data show that approximately one-fourth of all sporting goods equipment sales in the United States are handled by sporting goods stores like Dick's Sporting Goods and Bass Pro Shop. The biggest sporting goods retailer in terms of revenue, however, is Walmart, with $9.6 billion in revenue from sporting goods sales in 2014. Approximately 14% of sporting goods equipment is sold through online channels, which is the distribution channel with the highest growth in market share. Despite the growth in online sales, nearly 105 million people shopped for sporting goods at a sporting goods store in 2015. Nike and adidas are the market leaders among sporting goods manufacturers, with about $30.6 billion and $18.5 billion in worldwide revenues, respectively. Other major sporting goods manufacturers with at least $1.5 billion in revenue are VF Corporation, Puma, Asics, Jorden, New Balance, Amer Sports, and Under Armour (Statista, 2015).

So how do these issues impact sport organizations? Consider the case of Under Armour (UA). As the football team's special teams captain (and a business major) at the University of Maryland in 1995, Kevin Plank, the founder and CEO of UA, saw teammates suffer from heat stress during practice and wondered whether their sweat-soaked T-shirts contributed to their maladies. In response, Plank developed a performance undershirt that wicked moisture away from the skin. He initially financed the company with $20,000 of his own money, $40,000 spread on five credit cards, additional funds from family and friends, and a $250,000 loan from the U.S. Small Business Administration. Plank could not convince large manufacturers to back him, so he took to selling directly to team equipment managers out of the trunk of his car. In 1996, he booked $17,000 in sales and made a deal with an Ohio apparel manufacturer ("Call in your orders by noon," said plant owner Sal Fasciana, "and we'll make and ship the product by the end of the day"). Plank established official supplier agreements with Major League Baseball (MLB), Major League Soccer (MLS), the National Hockey League (NHL), USA Baseball, and the U.S. Ski team, and developed new product lines such as "LooseGear" and "Performance Grey" products (McCarthy, 2008).

Over time, Under Armour became the fastest-growing sport apparel and footwear brand in the world. In 2011, the company's estimated valuation was $1 billion, with revenues of $1.4 billion and 3% of the total U.S. athletic apparel market (Oznian, 2011). In terms of brand strength, according to writer Daniel Roberts (2011), the interlocking UA company logo "is becoming as recognizable as the Nike swoosh;" in contrast to Nike's "deification" of individual athletes, "UA's brand identity was always about the team" (p. 1). UA signed apparel and footwear agreements with several National Collegiate Athletic Association (NCAA) Division I athletic programs, including Plank's alma mater the University of Maryland (a deal signed in 2009 that was worth $17.5 million), Auburn University, and Boston College. In fact, some dubbed the 2011 Bowl Championship Series (BCS) National Championship Game (Auburn University versus the University of Oregon, the pet athletic department of Nike founder Phil Knight) as UA versus Nike (Roberts, 2011). In 2014, UA announced the most lucrative deal yet in college athletics, entering into a 10-year, $90 million contract with the University of Notre Dame (Rovell, 2014). The Irish had been outfitted by adidas prior to signing with UA. Another big move occurred at the end of 2016, when UA signed a 10-year uniform partnership with MLB. That deal, which is set to begin with the 2020 MLB

season, gives UA exclusive rights for a 10-year period to provide MLB teams with all their on-field uniforms, including jerseys that will feature the company's **branding**, as well as base layer and game-day outerwear gear, and training apparel for all 30 teams (Kell, 2016).

These environmental factors and related tactics by footwear and apparel manufacturers are examples of the market impact of sporting goods and licensed products. The remainder of the chapter examines the specifics of these related segments, and explores how the functional areas of sport management impact these segments.

History of Sporting Goods and Apparel

Sporting Goods

The French economic philosopher J. B. Say (1964) coined the term **entrepreneur** to describe those persons who created ideas for better uses of existing technology. The early sporting goods industry in the United States was replete with entrepreneurial innovation. As early as 1811, George Tryon, a gunsmith, began to carve out a niche with people interested in sport. After expanding into the fishing tackle business, Tryon's company became a major wholesaler of sporting goods east of the Mississippi River. In the late 1840s and 1850s, Michael Phelan and John Brunswick each had established production of billiards equipment. Brunswick, a Swiss immigrant, established billiard parlors across the United States and by 1884 had merged with his two largest competitors, creating a $1.5 million operation that was larger than the businesses of all of his competitors combined. The company moved into bowling in the 1890s. Hillerich and Bradsby began in 1859 as a wood-turning shop in Louisville, Kentucky, and expanded to baseball bat production in 1884. Former professional baseball player George Wright, along with partner H. A. Ditson, operated Wright and Ditson in the late 1880s (the company was later bought by Albert G. Spalding, but continued to operate under the original name). In 1888, Rawlings began operations in St. Louis, promoting itself as offering a "full-line emporium" of all sporting goods (Thorn, 2011).

In the early twentieth century, cities across the United States sustained multiple sporting goods shops filled with the latest equipment and apparel, including Brine Sporting Goods (which first opened in Cambridge, Massachusetts, in 1867), Oshman's Dry Goods (opened in Richmond, Texas, in 1919), Maurice's Sporting Goods (opened in Chicago, Illinois, in 1923), and Dunham's Sports (opened in Waterford, Michigan, in 1937). Even teen clothing retailer Abercrombie & Fitch started out as an elite sporting goods retailer, when founder David Abercrombie started selling high-end camping gear in New York before expanding into women's clothing in 1910 (Lieber, 2016).

But it was Albert G. Spalding who best typified the early sporting goods entrepreneur. Spalding, a standout professional baseball pitcher in the late nineteenth century, parlayed his baseball reputation and a loan of $800 into a sporting goods manufacturing giant based on selling to the expanding middle class in the United States. Also the owner of the Chicago White Stockings of the National League, Spalding adopted technological advances to manufacture bats, baseballs, gloves, uniforms, golf clubs, bicycles, hunting goods, and football equipment. Many other manufacturers also focused on the production of sporting goods, but Spalding understood that he had to create and foster the markets for these products as the newly affluent middle class sought to find activities to fill their leisure time. Spalding produced guides on how to play and exercise, promoted grassroots sport competitions, and gained credibility with consumers by claiming official supplier status with baseball's National League. Spalding's connection with the National League helped establish the value of endorsements and licensing connections, which eventually would become industry staples—as in the case of Kevin Plank at Under Armour, discussed earlier in this chapter (Levine, 1985).

Spalding also created a profitable distribution system in which the company sold directly to retailers at a set price, with the guarantee that retailers would sell at a price that Spalding set. This technique created stable markets for Spalding goods and eliminated price cutting at the retail level (Levine, 1985).

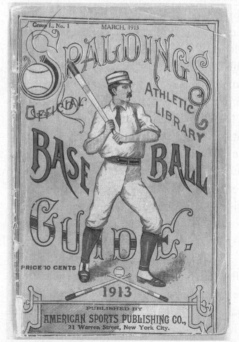

Courtesy of Library of Congress, General Collections [LC-USZC4-6145 DLC]

The twentieth century saw continued developments in the industry as consumer demand kept on growing. In 1903, Harvard football coach Bill Reid devoted many pages in his diary to his efforts in working with local merchants to design and manufacture pads to protect his players (Smith, 1994). The Sports and Fitness Industry Association (formerly the

Sporting Goods Manufacturers Association) was founded in 1906 as intercollegiate football leaders and athletic equipment manufacturers sought to make the sport safer and less violent. In the 1920s, a number of famous sport personalities began to endorse sporting goods products, including Knute Rockne, Honus Wagner, and Nap Lajoie.

The 1940s saw a retrenchment in spending on sporting goods, but after the Korean War ended in the 1950s and prosperity returned to the country, spending on sporting goods increased. Tennis greats Fred Perry and Jean Rene Lacoste (Izod) helped launch the fashion-sportswear segment in the 1950s. In the 1960s, imported products arrived in greater numbers in the U.S. market, especially Japanese baseball products. The 1970s also brought increased recognition of product liability and the injuries associated with sports equipment. This recognition increased concern for risk management on the part of teachers, coaches, and administrators. As the industry moved through the 1980s and 1990s, market growth continued as products and consumer demographics became more diverse (O'Brien, 2002).

In the middle of the twentieth century, German footwear and apparel manufacturer adidas established a strong international presence. Founded in the 1920s by Adolph "Adi" Dassler (the source of the company's name) as an expansion of a family shoe business, the firm made strong inroads through the production of soccer cleats and track spikes. Dassler established his products, in part, by convincing U.S. track Olympian Jesse Owens to wear his spikes in the 1936 Berlin Summer Olympic Games. Adi's brother, Rudolf, would later go on to found Puma after a falling out between the two brothers. The two companies competed for international market share for the remainder of the century, with adidas ultimately prevailing, in part through its close partnership with Fédération Internationale de Football

Association (FIFA, soccer's international governing body) (Smit, 2008).

In the 1980s and 1990s, the industry experienced the emergence of several industry giants, most notably Nike and Reebok. Nike, the brainchild of Phil Knight, began as an offshoot of Knight's original Blue Ribbon Sports. The Nike name came from one of Knight's colleagues in 1971. By 1980, Nike was pulling in $269 million annually and had replaced adidas as the United States' top sneaker maker. Although Nike temporarily lost its top ranking to Reebok in 1986, the advent of the "Air Jordan" and "Bo Knows" marketing campaigns in the late 1980s propelled Nike back to the top, and Nike was a $2 billion company by 1990 (Katz, 1993). During the third quarter of fiscal year 2003, Nike claimed global revenues of $2.4 billion ($1.3 billion in the United States), with a net income of $125 million. In 2012, Nike reported fiscal revenues of $24.1 billion (Nike, 2012). Eventually, adidas countered Nike's ascendance by purchasing Reebok in 2005 for $3.8 billion, in part to gain control over Reebok's licensing agreements with the National Football League (NFL) and the National Basketball Association (NBA) (Smit, 2008).

Licensed Products

Baseball historian Warren Goldstein (1989) noted that many early baseball teams (such as the Cincinnati Red Stockings in 1869) got their names from their distinctive apparel and that uniforms created a sense of apartness and defined who was a player and who was not. This affinity for uniforms was already a long-standing tradition, as Roman historian Pliny the Younger noted in 109 CE that fans of chariot racers would cheer for the contestants whose clothing they liked best. "Such mighty charms," wrote Pliny, "such wondrous powers reside in the color of a paltry tunic!" (Thorn, 2011, p. 144).

Licensed apparel sales are based on the notion that fans will purchase goods to draw them closer to their beloved organizations and athletes. Writer Bill Simmons (2004) described the early days of buying player-specific licensed products this way: "Fans bought them because they wanted to dress like players on the team. Not only were we supporting our guys, but the player we chose became an expression of sorts" (p. 12).

The sports apparel industry, however, was slow to realize the financial potential of such connections. In 1924, sportswriter Francis Wallace observed displays and neckties in the colors of what he termed the aristocracy of the gridiron in the shops while walking down Fifth Avenue in Manhattan: Army, Harvard, Notre Dame, Princeton, and Yale. In 1947, University of Oregon Athletic Director Leo Harris and Walt Disney agreed to allow Oregon to use Disney's Donald Duck image for the university's mascot.

Although these were some early steps toward the development of licensable properties, the University of California–Los Angeles (UCLA) is generally credited with being the first school to enter into a licensing agreement with a manufacturer, when its school bookstore granted a license to a watch manufacturer in 1973. The NCAA formed its properties division to license championship merchandise in 1975, but it does not administer licensing programs for member schools. Significant revenue growth began in the late 1980s, when the University of Notre Dame, which began its licensing program in 1983, experienced growth of 375% from 1988 to 1989. Collegiate licensed product sales totaled $100 million in the early 1980s. In 1995, sales reached $2.5 billion. The peak for licensed sales of major college and professional licensed products was 1996, with sales of $13.8 billion. That figure had slipped to $11.8 billion by 2001 (Hiestand, 2002; Nichols, 1995; Plata, 1996; Sperber, 1993).

© Christopher Penler/Shutterstock, Inc.

The licensing programs in professional sport leagues are administered by a for-profit branch of the league, generally referred to as a **properties division**. Properties divisions approve licensees, police trademark infringement, and distribute licensing revenues equally among league franchises. Properties divisions usually handle marketing and sponsorship efforts as well. The NFL was the first professional league to develop a properties component in 1963, under the leadership of then-commissioner Alvin "Pete" Rozelle. The first license was granted to Sport Specialties. David Warsaw, the founder of the company, had worked with Chicago Bears owner George Halas in the 1930s selling Bears merchandise, and later developed licensing agreements with the Los Angeles Dodgers and the Los Angeles Rams (Granelli 1996). By the late 1970s, each NFL team's licensing share was believed to be nearly $500,000 annually.

MLB followed with the creation of its properties division (MLB Properties) in 1966, although many teams with strong local sales were reluctant to give up their licensing rights to the league. Indeed, some teams were loath to share their marks with licensees because of their perceptions that such actions would cheapen the product. George Weiss, general manager of the New York Yankees, recoiled at the notion of licensing agreements, saying, "Do you think I want every kid in this city walking around with a Yankees cap?" (Helyar, 1994, p. 70). NHL

Enterprises began formal league-governed licensing in 1969, and NBA Properties initiated its activities in 1982 (Lipsey, 1996).

Players unions also administer licensing programs. The Major League Baseball Players Association (MLBPA) was the first to enter into such an agreement in the late 1960s when then–Executive Director Marvin Miller entered into a two-year, $120,000 pact with Coca-Cola to permit the beverage manufacturer to put players' likenesses on bottle caps. Such royalties helped fund the emerging union's organizing activities. Miller also negotiated a comprehensive agreement with trading card manufacturer Topps Company in 1968. Topps was permitted to continue manufacturing trading cards bearing player likenesses for double the player's previous yearly fees (from $125 to $250), and it paid the union 8% on annual sales up to $4 million and 10% on all subsequent sales. In the first year, the contract earned the MLBPA $320,000 (Helyar, 1994).

Industry Structure

Sporting Goods

The Sports and Fitness Industry Association, the industry trade association for the sporting goods industry, defines the sporting goods industry as being comprised of the manufacturers of sporting goods equipment, athletic footwear, and sports apparel, as well as manufacturers of accessory items to the sport and recreation market (SFIA, 2017). **Sporting goods equipment** includes fitness products as well as sport-specific products for golf, soccer, tennis, in-line skating, and so on. In recent years, participation rates in sport and physical activities have remained constant, as have the accompanying sales of sporting goods equipment. The second segment is **athletic footwear**, which is defined as branded and unbranded athletic shoes for casual wear or active usage, outdoor/hiking sports boots, and sports sandals. The third segment is **sports apparel**.

Broadly defined, it encompasses garments that are designed for, or could be used in, active sports.

© Glenn Bloomquist/iStock/Thinkstock

Sporting Goods Trade Associations

Within the industry, a number of **trade associations** for sporting goods professionals have been established. One of these, as previously mentioned, is the Sport and Fitness Industry Association. SFIA is the self-described "premier trade association for more than 1000 sporting goods and fitness brands, manufacturers, retailers, and marketers in the industry." SFIA's stated purpose is "to support our member companies and promote a healthy environment for the sporting goods industry by providing access to insight, information, influence and industry connections" (SFIA, 2017, para. 6). The sporting goods industry employs more than 375,000 people and generates $150 billion in domestic wholesale sales (SFIA, 2017).

Licensing

The manufacturers of licensed products (i.e., the **licensees**) include well-known companies mentioned previously, such as adidas, Nike, and Under Armour; prominent electronics and video game manufacturers Electronic Arts and Sony; and smaller firms such as Artcarved (jewelry), Mead (stationery), and Topps (trading cards and memorabilia). Licensees pay teams and leagues (i.e., the **licensors**) for the right to manufacture products bearing team and school names, nicknames, mascots, colors, and logos. If these names and logos are registered with the U.S. Patent and Trademark Office, they are referred to as **trademarks**. A trademark is defined under the Federal Trademark Act of 1946 (the Lanham Act) as "any word, name, symbol, or device or combination thereof adopted and used by a manufacturer or merchant to identify his goods and distinguish them from those manufactured or sold by others" (Lanham Act, 15 U.S.C. § 1051–1127, 1946, p. 1). The law defines trademark infringement as the "reproduction, counterfeiting, copying, or imitation, in commerce of a registered mark and bars companies that do not pay for the right to use these trademarks from manufacturing products bearing those marks" (Lanham Act, 15 U.S.C. § 1051–1127, 1946, p. 1).

Licensing enables schools and teams to generate brand recognition and interest and to increase their revenues with very little financial risk. The licensees assume the risk by manufacturing the product, and then pay the licensor a fee, called a **royalty**, for the use of specific trademarks on specific products. A royalty is a certain percent depending on the type of merchandise. For example, the royalty fees for video games which use a logo may be higher than the royalty fees for toys. Wholesale costs are those paid by the retailer, not the price paid by consumers. Licensees use the established images and popularity of sport teams to boost their sales.

Collegiate Sport

Some NCAA Division I schools administer their own licensing programs. The benefit of self-maintenance is that schools can retain a greater portion of sales revenues. The remainder of Division I Football Bowl Subdivision (FBS) schools, like the smaller pro leagues and many Football Championship Subdivision (FCS)

schools, enlist the services of independent licensing companies to manage their programs. The Collegiate Licensing Company (CLC), formed in 1981, recently purchased by sport marketing company IMG and now known as IMG College, negotiates licensing agreements on behalf of approximately 200 colleges and universities, bowls, conferences, the Heisman Trophy, and the NCAA. Client colleges pay a portion of the royalties (usually 50%) to CLC for its efforts. According to Pat Battle, senior corporate vice president of IMG College, by 2008 the retail market for collegiate merchandise had grown to more than $3.5 billion in annual sales, with apparel accounting for 62%, and with less than 20% of those sales taking place on college campuses (Covell & Walker, 2016). Recently, total revenues from collegiate licensing are estimated at $209 million on $3.88 billion of retail sales (Heitner, 2015).

Career Opportunities

A number of career opportunities exist in these segments, ranging from entrepreneurship based on an idea for a specific product to employment with firms such as Callaway, Russell, Under Armour, or New Balance. Sporting goods stores are another employment option, including locally owned single-unit stores; large chains, such as Champs Sports or Dick's Sporting Goods; and niche retailers, such as Lids, which specializes in the sale of licensed and branded headwear. The potential career opportunities that exist in the licensing industry include employment with league licensing departments, collegiate licensing offices, and licensees, as well as with retail sales outlets and product manufacturers.

Large companies, such as footwear and apparel manufacturer New Balance, establish divisions for each product line, such as basketball, tennis, cross-training/fitness, and children. New Balance has created a niche in the highly competitive footwear market by providing customers with footwear with extensive width sizing; it has done this, the company states, through a commitment to domestic manufacturing (the company employs more than 4,000 workers and maintains manufacturing facilities in Massachusetts and Maine) and leadership in technological innovation. In 2004, the company acquired lacrosse equipment manufacturer Warrior, and by 2011 the company reported worldwide sales of $2 billion (Martin, 2012). New Balance has staff positions in manufacturing, research and development, sales and marketing, and promotions.

Application of Key Principles

Management

As long as society, the economy, and technology remain somewhat stable or change only slowly, management in many industries has time to make the adjustments necessary to maintain and improve performance. Rapid change is the rule in the sporting goods and licensed products industries, however, and industry managers face new challenges brought on by a changing environment. These include intense competition and new performance standards that every management team must now achieve—namely, those based on competition, quality, speed, flexibility, innovation, and sustainable growth (Covell & Walker, 2013).

Innovation is a key performance standard impacting sporting goods and licensed products, and according to industry experts it is a critical factor not just for success, but for survival. As noted earlier in the chapter, entrepreneurs such as Albert Spalding and John Brunswick significantly altered those industries through the creation of new products and services to meet the needs and wants of consumers. When combined with continual improvements in equipment and related products, one sees countless examples of entrepreneurial efforts

throughout the history of sport management. Some famous innovators were featured in Chapter 1 on the history of sport management.

Earlier in the chapter. the remarkable path of development and growth experienced by apparel and footwear manufacturer Under Armour was described. Recently, however, multiple company missteps have called into question the ability of company management to respond to environmental changes. In 2017, founder Kevin Plank said of recently elected U.S. President Donald Trump: "To have such a pro-business president is something that is a real asset for the country." The next day, one of the company's most highly paid endorsers, NBA star Stephen Curry, responded to the assertion that Trump that was an "asset" by saying, "I agree with that description, if you remove the 'et.'" The two-time NBA MVP said that he was not opposed to Plank collaborating with Trump, but had some concerns about UA adopting what he saw as Trump's values. "Are we promoting change? Are we doing things that are going to look out for everybody?" Curry said. "And not being so self-serving that it's only about making money, selling shoes, doing this and that. That's not the priority. It's about changing lives. I think we can continue to do that." When asked if he would go so far as to leave Under Armour if he did not like the company's direction, Curry said, "If I can say the leadership is not in line with my core values, then there is no amount of money, there is no platform I wouldn't jump off, if it wasn't in line with who I am." After additional backlash, including a "#BoycottUnderArmour" hashtag on social media, the company issued a statement that sought to downplay the issue: "We engage in policy, not politics" (Bieler, 2017, p. 1).

Numerous NBA players and coaches—most notably, San Antonio Spurs head coach Gregg Popovich—have roundly criticized Trump as well. Popovich, a graduate of the U.S. Air Force Academy and a former intelligence officer in eastern Europe, described Trump's actions thusly: "It's got to do with the way one individual conducts himself. It's embarrassing. It's dangerous to our institutions and what we all stand for and what we expect the country to be. But for this individual, he's at a game show and everything that happens begins and ends with him, not our people or our country" (Amick, 2017, para. 1). If the leadership of Under Armour continues to be at odds with many of its major clients and stakeholders, the company will no doubt suffer.

Finance

The End of Traditional Retail

The future of Under Armour also now looks even more bleak because of the company's over-reliance on the traditional retail environment for sales. In early 2017, the seemingly unending growth story for UA took a different turn when the company's shares plummeted more than 25% after the company reported disappointing 2016 holiday sales and issued an underwhelming sales target for the coming year. In addition, the company announced that its chief financial officer was stepping down due to "personal reasons." Plank listed a number of woes that hurt UA during the key holiday season, including the recent bankruptcies of sports apparel retail companies like Sports Authority and City Sports, which hampered UA's ability to get stock onto shelves. These issues affected UA more than Nike and adidas because 85% of UA's revenues come from the North American market, and UA relies on traditional retailers far more as well. UA also relied more on apparel than footwear sales than its main rivals.

In a presentation to investors and shareholders, Plank stated: "I want to be clear, our growth story is intact. . . . What you won't hear from us today are excuses" (Kell, 2017, para. 3). He went on to say that while 2017 revenue would increase by about $600 million from 2016, operating income would decline

by $100 million to about $320 million because the company wanted to continue to invest in the brand through strategic initiatives such as the MLB apparel deal mentioned earlier. Some investors questioned this brand strategy because those moves are not likely to fuel big sales growth anytime soon, while others asked whether UA should adjust and focus on fewer more core focused strategies (Kell, 2017).

But UA's distribution problems will not be easily addressed. As recently as 2015, U.S. sporting goods stores were bringing in as much as $48 billion in annual revenue, up from $39.8 billion in 2012. In mid-2016, however, Sports Authority decided to liquidate its assets instead of restructure. A company spokesperson said it was "pursuing a sale of some or all of the business" (Lieber, 2016, para. 4) and the company began auctioning off its assets. Earlier that year, East Coast–based City Sports filed for bankruptcy and closed 8 of its 26 stores. Likewise, Vestis Retail Group, the parent company of Eastern Mountain Sports, Bob's Stores, and Sport Chalet, filed for bankruptcy. With $500 million in liabilities, that company planned to close 56 stores, including all 47 Sport Chalet locations. Brent Sonnek-Schmelz, who owns the Soccer Post retail chain, admitted to the *Philadelphia Inquirer* newspaper that the sporting goods industry "is in a state of upheaval" (Lieber, 2016, para. 5).

The causes of this retail meltdown are several. According to journalist Chavie Lieber, the marketplace is congested with brands and retailers like Lululemon jumping into the "athleisure" clothing category. Five years ago, companies like Sports Authority and Eastern Mountain Sports were in a position to capitalize on this trend, say industry experts, by either stocking up-and-coming fitness brands or creating lines of their own. Instead, Sports Authority thought it could succeed through store expansion only, opening 35 new stores a year beginning in 2012. This effort ultimately failed to help the company hold onto its position in the marketplace (Lieber, 2016).

In addition, all of the old-line "big box" sporting goods stores stock items from the major footwear and apparel makers. In contrast, adidas and Nike have shifted from being primarily wholesale companies to powerful retail sellers. Greg Thomsen, the managing director of adidas's outdoor division, summarized the switch this way: "It's hard for sporting goods stores when their number one brand also becomes their number one competitor" (Lieber, 2016, para. 1).

Ultimately, the drift to online purchasing might be the biggest issue for the old-line brick-and-mortar retail stores. "The lines between wholesale and retail faded from black and white to gray to nonexistent," said Greg Baldwin, vice president of merchandising at sporting goods chain Schuylkill Valley Sports, which has 16 stores located in Pennsylvania and New Jersey. "I now compete with 90 percent of my suppliers via e-commerce, physical stores, or a combination of the two. The importance of the retailer as a pipeline to the consumer has been greatly diminished" (Lieber, 2016, para. 2). Not only have Nike and adidas sites edged these brick-and-mortar retailers out of the market, but websites like Amazon have made significant inroads into the sporting goods realm. Indeed, a recent report notes that more than 16% of all U.S. households have a membership for Amazon Prime, a paid service that provides free shipping and access to video and music streaming. "A chain like Sport Chalet can only carry so many of our items," adidas's Thomsen explains. "We know the walls in their stores can't carry every piece of adidas, but a company like Zappos can hold every one of our items, and so a new generation of shoppers who wants that kind of selection is just going to go straight there" (Kim, 2016; Lieber, 2016, para. 2).

Ultimately, the key to survival for sporting goods retailers is to offer something e-commerce cannot. "Retailers in general have a huge advantage over Amazon in that they have physical stores and they are able to actually raise an emotional response," says one industry expert. "These stores need to understand the opportunity and leverage that because they have way more to offer. Once they think in those terms, competing with Amazon becomes a different type of exercise." One remaining retailer, Dick's Sporting Goods, has seen the handwriting on the virtual wall and has developed stronger partnerships and created in-store shops like a trend-focused "Nike Field House" and a dedicated "Under Armour All-American" section in its stores (Lieber, 2016, para. 3).

Marketing

Endorsements

The heart of the sporting goods industry, as Albert Spalding first demonstrated, is the concept that expert usage helps overcome the risk factors customers assess when deciding on a purchase. Spalding sold consumers on the fact that his ball was the one used by the best baseball league in the world, conveying the message to buyers that if it was good enough for the best, it was good enough for them. Thus, the concept of endorsements in sport was born.

Today, this concept continues to play a major role in the industry. Most athletic footwear companies spend large amounts of money to win star athletes' endorsements. Consider the case of professional golfers and their selection of on-course apparel for competitions. For years, the looks sported by golfers on the PGA Tour were dismissed by many as staid and boring. Recently, however, an increasing number of PGA pros are wearing more flamboyant ensembles, with designers such as Ralph Lauren pushing its players like Davis Love III and Webb Simpson to wear bright pink pants (actually termed "Bubblicious" by the maker), paired with pastel striped shirts. Clothing companies often script the outfits for their golfers at major tournaments. "They tell me, 'Look, we sell more pink pants whenever you wear the pink pants,'" said Love. "Frankly, I'm not a fan of yellow or pink pants, but if they give them to me—and they do—I wear them. I figure they know better than me" (Macur, 2011, p. Y6). Dustin Johnson, however, draws the line at wearing orange. Why? "I don't like orange," he explained (Macur, 2011, p. Y6). When Rickie Fowler (outfitted by Puma), who made orange his signature color—an homage to his collegiate alma mater, Oklahoma State University—heard Johnson's remark, he said: "I've got to talk to him about that. Everybody needs some orange, man" (Macur, 2011, p. Y6). A writer for *Golf Digest* defends the approach this way: "People have to dress their personality . . . and there's nothing wrong with that" (Macur, 2011, p. Y6). British golfer Ian Poulter, who once wore pants with the Union Jack British flag design, summed up his sartorial choices this way: "I wanted to liven up golf. . . . What I always say is, 'Look good, feel good, play good'" (Pennington, 2012, p. D7).

The issue of dress has also been a topic of interest in women's golf. In 2017, the leadership of the Ladies Professional Golf Association (LPGA) informed players that their skirts must not be too short as to see the "bottom area" and that sports tops must not be too low-cut. In an email sent to all players, the LPGA stated its regulation as follows: the "skirt must be long enough to not see your bottom area (even if covered by under shorts) at any time, standing or bent over." Players will be given a $1,000 fine for an initial violation, which doubles with each subsequent offense. Many top LPGA players criticized the ruling, including Britain's top golfer Charley Hull, who expressed concern that such hidebound rules demonstrate the sport's overreliance on tradition and will deter younger players from participating in the sport. "A couple of weeks ago I, along with all the girls on the LPGA Tour, received an email

explaining that as part of the new dress code, plunging neck lines, leggings and revealing skirts are now banned. I don't wear any of them, so it doesn't really affect me. But I think it's a shame, as many people label golf old fashioned and we need to move away from that. Golf needs to be more original and athletic. If you look at most golfers, I don't think they look that good. If the clothes were cool, more people would play and watch it" (Paul, 2017, para 1). If Hull is correct, the LPGA's punitive measures could end up costing tour players endorsement revenues.

Ethics

Manufacturer, Licensee, and Professional League Conduct

One of the most basic forms of global commerce occurs when a business turns to a foreign company to manufacture one or more of its products. This practice is called **global sourcing**, because the company turns to whatever manufacturer or source around the world will produce its products most cheaply. Companies that engage in global sourcing take advantage of manufacturing expertise or lower wage rates in foreign countries, and then sell their products either just in their home market or in markets around the world. Global sourcing is common in the clothing and footwear industries. For example, companies in countries such as Mexico, China, and Malaysia have much lower production costs because workers are paid much lower wage rates than are workers in the United States. The foreign producer or source manufactures the product to a particular company's specifications and then attaches the company's label or logo to the product. Nike, Reebok, Benetton, and Banana Republic are examples of companies utilizing a great deal of global sourcing.

Many sport apparel and shoe manufacturers have come under fire for paying unfairly low wages and having unsafe working conditions in their overseas operations, particularly in Asian nations. One consumer advocacy group sued Nike, saying that its claims about the fairness of its global sourcing practices were false; the U.S. Supreme Court opted to have the case heard in California state court (Greenhouse, 2003).

Industry giants adidas, Nike, and Puma have been universally and repeatedly criticized for paying low wages and treating workers poorly. The most recent case involved evidence of managers in Bangladeshi sweatshops verbally and physically abusing workers. At one supplier for Puma, two-thirds of workers claimed they had been beaten or slapped, and women working for Nike and adidas reported sexual harassment incidents. Workers for all three companies also had to work illegally long hours for less than the established minimum wage (about $1.50 per day), with some working for as little as 12 cents per hour (Chamberlain, 2012).

All three companies dispute the claims or promise to address the concerns. A Nike spokesperson told *The Guardian* that the company "takes working conditions in our factories very seriously. All Nike suppliers must adhere to our code of conduct . . . we will get back to you as soon as someone . . . has made an assessment" (Chamberlain, 2012, p. 1).

In part to help address the perception of its lack of social responsibility, industry giant adidas has opted to provide free design resources and financial support to U.S. high schools looking to drop Native American mascots, nicknames, or images. For decades, many interest groups have decried the use of such images, citing the practice as hostile or abusive. In 2005, the NCAA prohibited 19 of its member institutions with such nicknames from hosting Association championship events, and by 2016 all 19 had altered images or obtained tribal permission for use (Covell & Walker, 2016). Many states, including most recently California, Colorado, and Oregon (the state in which adidas's North American operations are headquartered)

have also passed laws that ban the use of such mascots and images by public schools.

According to the group "Change the Mascot," approximately 2,000 schools across the United States still have or use such images and nicknames. Said the head of adidas's global brands, the company wanted to "offer up our resources to schools that want to do what's right . . . our intention is to help break down any barriers to change—change that can lead to a more respectful and inclusive environment for all American athletes." Officials with adidas stated that the company is not in the position to force schools to change, and merely wanted to help schools that wanted to change but lacked the resources to do so.

In response to the initiative, then-President Barack Obama told an audience of Native American youth conference attendees: "What they're saying is one of the top sports companies in the world, one of the top brands in the world, is prepared to come and use all their expertise to come up with something that's really going to work and that the entire community can feel proud of and can bring people together and give a fresh start." Obama added, in a reference to the NFL's Washington Redskins: "I don't know if Adidas made the same offer to a certain NFL team, here in Washington. But they might want to think about that as well." In response, a Redskins spokesperson attempted to deflect attention from the Washington team:

> The hypocrisy of changing names at the high school level of play and continuing to profit off of professional like-named teams is absurd. Adidas make [sic] hundreds of millions of dollars selling uniforms to teams like the [NHL's] Chicago Blackhawks and the [NBA's] Golden State Warriors, while profiting off sales of fan apparel for the [MLB's] Cleveland Indians,

Atlanta Braves and many other like-named teams. It seems safe to say that Adidas' [sic] next targets will be the biggest sports teams in the country, which won't be very popular with their shareholders, team fans, or partner organizations.

One of the pro league teams mentioned—the Cleveland Indians—may, at the urging of MLB, now be close to moving on from its "Chief Wahoo" logo. The team adopted the "Indians" nickname in 1915 to honor Louis Sockalexis, a member of the Native American Penobscot tribe in Maine who played for Cleveland Spiders in 1897, and who is recognized as the first Native American to play in the National League (Society for American Baseball Research, 2017). At the outset of the 2017 season, MLB Commissioner Rob Manfred applied pressure and expressed his "desire to transition away from the Chief Wahoo logo," while an MLB spokesperson stated that the league had outlined "specific steps in an identified process and are making progress. We are confident that a positive resolution will be reached that will be good for the game and the club" (Waldstein, 2017, p. B10).

The move, which would be applauded by many, would likely upset some fans, as evidenced by the comments of one, who said: "Chief Wahoo is the Cleveland Indians . . . I don't think it's hurting anybody"; another angrily accosted a man protesting the mascot at game early that season, yelling, "It's a caricature. Get over it" (Waldstein, 2017, pp. B10, B14). The team's senior vice-president of public affairs attempted to defuse the issue, stating that the team "understands the sensitivities of the logo, those who find it insensitive and also those fans who have a longstanding attachment to its place in the history of the team" (Waldstein, 2017, pp. B10, B14). Under the leadership of former team president Mark Shapiro, the team has for

several years gradually reduced the visibility of the logo on its uniforms (opting to replace it on one version of its caps with a simple block "C," which had been used on caps as early as 1902) and throughout its home park. Said Shapiro, who has since moved on to a similar position with the Toronto Blue Jays, "I think there will be a day, whenever that is, that the people that are making decisions [in Cleveland] decide that Chief Wahoo is no longer fitting" (Waldstein, 2017, pp. B10, B14). The stance of the commissioner would seem to indicate that the team's ownership is not making that day come quickly enough. It was announcd in early 2018, however, that the Indians will remove the Chief Wahoo logo from caps and jerseys in 2019 (Siemaszko, 2018).

Legal Issues

Theft and Sports Collectibles

At Super Bowl LI in 2017 in Houston, Texas, following the miraculous comeback by the New England Patriots, who defeated the Atlanta Falcons 34–28 in overtime, a curious side story emerged from the winning team's locker room. Patriots quarterback Tom Brady, who had just accepted his third Super Bowl MVP award, was at his locker looking through a duffle bag that contained gear he had given an equipment manager prior to accepting the award. "Where's my jersey?" Brady exclaimed, "It was right here; I know exactly where I put it" (Belson, 2017a, p. 1). The jersey had been stolen. Soon after, it was learned that a similar theft of a Brady jersey had occurred after Super Bowl XLIX, as well as a helmet thought to belong to Denver Broncos linebacker Von Miller, MVP of Super Bowl 50, immediately following that game in 2016 (Belson, 2017a).

All three items were recovered several weeks after Super Bowl LI by personnel from the Federal Bureau of Investigation (FBI), police from Houston, and officials in Mexico. The items were in the possession of Mauricio Ortega, a newspaper editor from Mexico City who had a media credential for the event. The investigation, aided by footage from a security camera near the locker room, uncovered the fact that Ortega had taken the items from team locker rooms following each game. Both jerseys were recovered and returned to Brady soon thereafter (Belson, 2017a).

While this sleuthing saga had a happy ending for the quarterback many acknowledge to be the greatest in NFL history, its outcome was an atypical one. Over the past few years, Ken Belson of *The New York Times* reported, the Brady theft, along with that of the trophy for the 1903 Belmont Stakes thoroughbred horse race and the World Series rings of former New York Yankees catcher and Baseball Hall of Famer Yogi Berra, had become "part of what experts believe is a spike in purloined . . . sports-related memorabilia that together are worth millions of dollars" (Belson, 2017b, p. D1). The vast majority of these heists go unsolved. As Belson noted, the market for rare sports collectibles, many of which are now authenticated and licensed by professional league and players association properties divisions, is now worth $1 billion per year. Nevertheless, approximately $100 million in fraudulent items, mostly autographs, are exchanged annually (Belson, 2017b).

Part of the rise in thefts, according to an expert with JSA (a company that verifies the legitimacy of memorabilia), is due to the recent realization of the worth of such objects. "There's a lot of theft [from museums], with people even breaking into homes to take this stuff" (Belson, 2017b, pp. D1, D4). Five trophies recently stolen from the National Museum of Racing in Saratoga Springs, New York, are thought to be worth collectively $500,000. Complicating the issue is the fact that many museums do not monitor or inventory their holdings regularly and often fail to discover thefts until long after they have

occurred; even then, they may not report the thefts to law enforcement (Belson, 2017b).

In the rare instances the crimes are solved, investigations are often aided by thieves' attempts to resell stolen items online or through auction houses that seek to verify the provenance of items put up for bid. This was the case with the Brady jerseys, when Ortega contacted Dylan Wagner, a Seattle, Washington, teenager, with a photo of the Brady 2015 Super Bowl jersey. That Ortega had the jersey struck Wagner as odd, but the jersey had never been reported as stolen. When Wagner asked Ortega how he obtained the item, Ortega said he would tell him later. When Wagner learned that Brady's jersey from Super Bowl LI had gone missing, he alerted investigators and shared with them his communications with Ortega. As this example indicates, while stealing items might be achievable, moving the stolen goods for money is far more difficult. A former FBI agent who now works tracking such stolen items emphasizes the importance of verification in the selling process, either by leagues or by companies: "There is no secondary market for things that don't have good title" (Belson, 2017b, p. D4). After recovering the items, Brady was unwilling to press charges against Ortega, saying, "I'm just happy I was able to get it back. . . . My reaction then wasn't heartbroken. I thought, at the end of the day, it was a jersey" (O'Connor, 2017, p. 1).

Summary

This chapter considers two significant segments of the sport industry: sporting goods and licensed products. Three product categories make up the sporting goods industry segment: equipment, athletic footwear, and apparel. Several trade associations assist sporting goods professionals, the largest of which is SFIA.

The licensed products industry continues to generate significant revenues. Teams and leagues earn a certain percentage of sales, called royalties, on items bearing logos. Leagues and players associations administer licensing programs on the professional level. Colleges may administer their own licensing programs or may enlist the services of organizations such as IMG College to perform these activities on their behalf.

Individuals are needed to work in many capacities in both the sporting goods and licensed products industries. These areas cut across many other segments of the sport industry, including professional sports, intercollegiate athletics, recreational sports, and the health and fitness industry. Wherever there is a need for equipment to play a sport or a need for the right clothing to announce that a person is a fan of a particular team, the sporting goods industry and the licensed product industry become pivotal.

Case Study 18-1

The Challenges of Entering a New Market

New Balance (NB), the privately held footwear and apparel manufacturing company headquartered in Brighton, Massachusetts, has deliberately inched its way up in sales and growth in the past decades. NB benefited from the running boom of the 1970s, with sales growing from $200,000 annually to $80 million, and has found a niche with middle-aged and older consumers who were more concerned with performance than fashion. Many consumers rate the company's products as particularly high in comfort.

Following a few failed attempts at taking on Nike and becoming a flashy and "cool" brand to attract a bigger share of the market, former NB chair and CEO Jim Davis said a lesson was learned: "If we try to be like everyone else, if we try to stress fashion over quality or marketing over performance, we won't be successful" (Reidy, 2005, p. E4). This sustainable approach to growth has allowed NB to retain its core market, and NB's annual sales are approaching $4 billion. NB has made great strides into the baseball cleats market over the past several years in part through endorsement deals with MLB stars and sponsorship agreements with organizations like the Boston Red Sox.

However, another recent effort to try and play the hip game fell flat when NB tried to break into the soccer market with one of its subsidiary brands, Warrior, which is known much more as a lacrosse and hockey brand. With cleated products curiously called "Murder Hole" and "Glory Hole," the launch failed.

Although only 29 years old, Bronwen Morrison is an industry veteran. When she first came out of her undergraduate sport management degree program, she took a job with Liberty Sports Group, where she had interned while in college, and managed the launch of the "Beckster," a skateboarding shoe targeted toward the market's smaller grassroots users where smaller niche companies tend to dominate. The shoe was a modest success, so much so that Morrison, when spotted wearing a throwback 1976 San Diego Padres jersey at the sporting goods Super Show in Atlanta, was asked to head the creation of a line of throwback-inspired urban fashion clothes for women by Trey Luce, creator and owner of Thugstaz. The line, dubbed "Hugstaz," was also a solid market success and put the line in positive competition with similar products by other urban fashion companies. Bronwen then went on to work at the apparel retail chain Lululemon Athletica (which describes its products as "yoga-inspired athletic apparel"), helping the company create a product line targeted toward men.

Her next professional challenge brought her back to the footwear market—specifically, to NB, to increase sales for the company's "Minimus" line of minimal running shoes. While that trend has flattened out, NB has asked Bronwen to turn her efforts to New Balance Football, the rebooted attempt by NB to step into the soccer market.

One established connection to the international soccer market is NB's annual uniform and apparel deal at a cost of $35 million per year with English Premier League club Liverpool F.C. That EPL club is owned by John Henry, who is also the principal owner of the Red Sox. But unlike going after the baseball market, which means competing more directly with the like-sized Under Armour, chasing the soccer shoe market means trying to match the resources of adidas (which spends more than $1.6 billion alone in a uniform and apparel deal with Real Madrid) and Nike (which spends more than $1.3 billion alone in a uniform and apparel deal with Barcelona) (Brennan, 2016). Since NB can't outspend adidas and Nike, Bronwen has to take a different approach.

Questions for Discussion

1. Explain how Bronwen can begin to identify a main target market group for NB Football's cleat market.

2. Explain how NB should use both traditional and nontradtional retailers to help sell this new product line.

3. Explain how NB can employ specific social media platforms to support this sales effort.

4. Explain whether NB should continue to pursue endorsements and sponsorships to support this sales effort.

5. Identify and explain any concerns about manufacturer conduct that NB can promote as a part of this sales effort.

Key Terms

athletic footwear, branding, entrepreneur, global sourcing, licensed products, licensees, licensors, properties division, royalty, sporting goods, sporting goods equipment, sport apparel, trade associations, trademarks

References

Amick, S. (2017, May 14). Spurs coach Gregg Popovich criticizes "embarrassing" Trump. *USA Today*. Retrieved from https://www.usatoday.com/story/sports/nba/spurs/2017/05/14/san-antonio-spurs-gregg-popovich-criticizes-embarrassing-president-donald-trump/101688934/

Belson, K. (2017a, March 20). F.B.I. recovers Tom Brady's missing Super Bowl jerseys in Mexico. *New York Times*. Retrieved from https://www.nytimes.com/2017/03/20/sports/football/tom-brady-super-bowl-jersey-stolen.html

Belson, K. (2107b, May 15). Legacies secure, but trophies and rings are another matter. *New York Times*, pp. D1, D4.

Bieler, D. (2017, February 8). Steph Curry bluntly disagrees with Under Armour CEO calling Trump an "asset." *Washington Post*. Retrieved from https://www.washingtonpost.com/news/early-lead/wp/2017/02/08/steph-curry-bluntly-disagrees-with-under-armour-ceo-calling-trump-an-asset/?utm_term=.7745a371d7b1

Brennan, A. (2016, June 22). Who's winning the latest sports brand war: Adidas who's pitch perfect or Nike boxing out the NBA? *Forbes*. Retrieved from https://www.forbes.com/sites/andrewbrennan/2016/06/22/whos-winning-the-latest-sports-brand-war-adidas-whos-pitch-perfect-or-nike-boxing-out-in-the-nba/#59c714c33d20

Chamberlain, G. (2012, March 3). Olympic brands caught up in abuse scandal. *The Guardian*. Retrieved from http://www.guardian.co.uk/business/2012/mar/03/olympic-brands-abuse-scandal?INTCMP=SRCH

Covell, D., & Walker, S. (2013). *Managing sport organizations: Responsibility for performance* (3rd ed.). New York, NY: Routledge.

Covell, D., & Walker, S. (2016). *Managing intercollegiate athletics* (2nd ed.). Scottsdale, AZ: Holcomb Hathaway.

ESPN. (2015, November 5). Adidas offers to help eliminate Native American mascots. Retrieved from http://www.espn.com/moresports /story/_/id/14057043/adidas-offers-help -eliminate-native-american-mascots

Goldstein, W. (1989). *Playing for keeps: A history of early baseball*. Ithaca, NY: Cornell University Press.

Granelli, J. (1996). David Warsaw, sport merchandsing pioneer, dies at 83. *Los Angeles Times*. Retrieved from http://articles.latimes .com/1996-04-03/local/me-54553_1_david -warsaw

Greenhouse, L. (2003, June 27). Nike free speech case is unexpectedly returned to California. *The New York Times*, p. A15.

Hardy, S. (1995). Adopted by all the leading clubs: Sporting goods and the shaping of leisure. In D. K. Wiggins (Ed.), *Sport in America* (pp. 133–150). Champaign, IL: Human Kinetics.

Hardy, S. H. (1997). Entrepreneurs, organizations, and the sports marketplace. In S. W. Pope (Ed.), *The new American sports history* (pp. 341–365). Champaign, IL: University of Illinois Press.

Heitner, D. (2015, April 3). March Madness makes millions for burgeoning collegiate licensing business. *Forbes*. Retrieved from https://www .forbes.com/sites/darrenheitner/2015/04/03 /march-madness-makes-millions-for -burgeoning-collegiate-licensing-business /#4536d3d25d35

Helyar, J. (1994). *Lords of the realm*. New York, NY: Random House.

Hiestand, M. (2002, August 19). Sports gear so out of style it's in style. *USA Today*, p. 3C.

Katz, D. (1993, August 16). Triumph of the swoosh. *Sports Illustrated*, pp. 54–73.

Kell, J. (2016, December 5). Here's why the MLB deal is huge for Under Amour. *Fortune*. Retrieved from http://fortune .com/2016/12/05/under-armour-signs -mlb-deal/

Kell, J. (2017, January 31). Here's why shares of Under Armour are plummeting today. *Fortune*. Retrieved from http://fortune .com/2017/01/31/under-armour-sales-soften/

Kim, E. (2016, September 26). Amazon's Prime membership is eating into Costco and Sam's Club territory. *Business Insider*. Retrieved from http://www.businessinsider.com /amazons-prime-membership-hurting -costco-and-sams-clubs-2016-9

Lanham Act, 15 U.S.C. § 1051–1127 (1946).

Levine, P. (1985). *A. G. Spalding and the rise of baseball: The promise of American sport*. New York, NY: Oxford University Press.

Lieber, C. (2016, May 18). The death of the great American sporting goods store. *Racked*. Retrieved from http://www.racked.com/2016 /5/18/11692166/sports-authority-bankruptcy -dicks-sporting-goods-modells

Lipsey, R. (Ed.). (1996). *Sports market place*. Princeton, NJ: Sportsguide.

Macur, J. (2011, June 19). The fairway as runway. *New York Times*, p. Y6.

Martin, E. (2012, May 3). New Balance wants its tariffs. Nike does not. *Bloomberg Businessweek*. Retrieved from http://www .businessweek.com/articles/2012-05-03/new -balance-wants-its-tariffs-dot-nike-doesnt

McCarthy, M. (2008, December 9). Under Armour is making a run at Nike. *USA Today*, p. 1C.

Nichols, M. A. (1995, April). A look at some of the issues affecting collegiate licensing. *Team Licensing Business*, 7(4), p. 18.

Nike. (2012). Nike reports fiscal 2012 fourth quarter and full year results. Retrieved from https://news.nike.com/news/nike-inc -reports-fiscal-2012-fourth-quarter-and -full-year-results

O'Brien, G. (2002, June). Elements of style: A smashing shirt. *GQ*, p. 61.

O'Connor, I. (2017, May 15). Surpassing Michael Jordan as ultimate GOAT is Tom Brady's last challenge. ESPN. Retrieved from http://www .espn.com/nfl/story/_/id/19360436/nfl -new-england-patriots-qb-tom-brady-last -challenge-surpassing-nba-hall-famer -michael-jordan-ultimate-goat

Oznian, M. (2011, October 3). The *Forbes* Fab 40: The world's most valuable sports brands. *Forbes*. Retrieved from http://www.forbes.com /sites/mikeozanian/2011/10/03/the-forbes-fab -40-the-worlds-most-valuable-sports-brands-3

Paul, O. (2017, August 2). Golfers upset over LPGA fines for dressing too sexy. *New York Post*. Retrieved from http://nypost.com/2017/08/02 /golfers-upset-over-lpga-fines-for-dressing -too-sexy/

Pennington, B. (2012, July 9). Daring from tee to green: The clothes, not the shots. *New York Times*, p. D7.

Plata, C. (1996). Ducks & dollars. *Team Licensing Business, 8*(6), 38.

Reidy, C. (2005, August 4). New Balance plots independent strategy. *Boston Globe*, p. E4.

Roberts, D. (2011, October 26). Under Armour gets serious. *CNN Money*. Retrieved from http:// fortune.com/2011/10/26/under-armour -gets-serious/

Rovell, D. (2014, January 21). Under Armour signs Notre Dame. Retrieved from http://espn. go .com/college-football/story/_/id /10328133 /notre-dame-fighting-irish-armour-agree -most-valuable-apparel-contract -ncaa-history

Say, J. B. (1964). *A treatise on political economy*. New York, NY: Sentry Press.

Siemaszko, C. (2018). Cleveland Indians will remove Chief Wahoo logo in 2019. Retrieved from https://www.nbcnews.com/news/sports /cleveland-indians-will-remove-chief-wahoo -logo-2019-n842196

Simmons, B. (2004, December 20). The sports guy. *ESPN Magazine*, p. 12.

Smit, B. (2008). *Sneaker wars: The enemy brothers who founded Adidas and Puma and the family feud that forever changed the business of sport*. New York, NY: Ecco.

Smith, R. A. (Ed.). (1994). *Big-time football at Harvard, 1905: The diary of coach Bill Reid*. Champaign, IL: University of Illinois Press.

Society for American Baseball Research. (2017). Louis Sockalexis. Retrieved from https://sabr .org/bioproj/person/2b1aea0a

Sperber, M. (1993). *Shake down the thunder: The creation of Notre Dame football*. New York, NY: Henry Holt.

Sports and Fitness Industry Association (SFIA). (2017). Who we are. Retrieved from https:// www.sfia.org/about/overview

Statista. (2015). Sportswear/sporting goods companies ranked by worldwide revenue in 2015. Retrieved from https://www. statista.com/statistics/241885/sporting -goods–sportswear-companies-revenue -worldwide/

Thorn, J. (2011). *Baseball in the Garden of Eden: The secret history of the early game*. New York, NY: Simon & Schuster.

Waldstein, D. (2017, April 13). Baseball urges Indians to phase out caricature. *New York Times*, pp. B10, B14.

© Shutterstock, Inc. / Danilo_Vuletic

Part V — Lifestyle Sports

Chapter 19 Recreation and Golf Club Management

Chapter

19

Tara Mahoney

Recreation and Golf Club Management

Learning Objectives

Upon completion of this chapter, students should be able to:

1. Describe how, within the extensive and diverse recreation industry, all organizations strive to provide activities that offer personal and social benefits to individuals during their leisure time.

2. Differentiate between activities that involve active performance (direct participation) and those in which the consumer is primarily a spectator (indirect participation).

3. Discuss the history of recreation and leisure activities in the United States as well as trends in recreation participation and some of the reasons for those trends.

4. Describe the golf and country club industry, including the differences between public and private clubs as well as between private equity and non-equity clubs.

5. Analyze the market drivers that influence the demand for golf and country club services, as well as the role that market segmentation plays in industry performance.

6. Assess the career opportunities available in the recreation and golf club industry and describe the skills and professional preparation necessary to succeed in each of them.

7. Debate future trends and current issues of importance in the recreation and golf club industries.

Introduction

An interest in recreation is integral to the lives of most people in the United States, from childhood through adulthood. Whether the arena is indoors or outdoors, people seek to be involved directly or indirectly with recreational activities for a variety of reasons, including fun, excitement, relaxation, social interaction, physical or mental challenge, and lifestyle enhancement.

The roots of involvement with organized recreation may begin in childhood with Little League baseball or softball. Continued participation can be nurtured through involvement in Young Men's Christian Association (YMCA) aquatics programs and summer camp experiences. In adulthood, people explore enjoyable activities such as the thrill of whitewater kayaking and spending summer vacations with families in state or national parks. Through retirement, a person can embrace a range of "masters" activities, such as "70-plus" ski clubs or hockey teams, which encourage lifelong participation in an activity.

The recreation industry in the United States is extensive and diverse, although the various segments usually share a common mission. Organizations strive to provide activities that offer personal and social benefits to individuals during their leisure time. A characteristic of recreation that sets it apart from other segments of the sport industry is that there is often **direct participation** by people through active performance in an activity, such as sea kayaking classes, mountain bike racing, or fishing with a certified guide. However, **indirect participation** by spectators may also occur in recreation and contributes to the economic base—a strategy effective in the tourism industry, which seeks to promote recreation-based events such as triathlons that draw spectators to a particular region.

© Fuse/Thinkstock

Another significant component of the recreation industry encompasses golf courses and country clubs, which attract an estimated 80 million players on more than 30,000 golf courses throughout the world. In fact, the National Golf Foundation's "Golf Around the World" report indicates there are now golf courses in 208 of the 245 countries in the world (Matuszewski, 2017; National Golf Foundation, 2017). In the United States, approximately 24 million people play golf on more than 15,000 courses (Heitner, 2016). Few sports leave as distinctive an imprint on the landscape as golf courses and country clubs. In addition, golf is one of the few sports where the playing field is not standardized, but differs from course to course and even from day to day. During the last quarter of the twentieth century, the number of golfers increased four times faster than the nation's population, from 10 million golfers to more than 30 million (Napton & Laingen, 2008). Since then, golf courses and clubs have been challenged by economic and societal changes that have impacted demand and forced industry professionals to reevaluate their management and marketing practices.

Golf courses and country clubs come in two major forms: public and private. This distinction is important. Private courses, especially country club facilities, outnumbered public courses until 1960. These private courses were popular because the game had evolved from being played solely by social elites in the US, who had brought golf here from Scotland in the late 1800s. The evolution of the country club and the development of more public access courses and facilities created a period of rapid growth and a coming of age for the modern era of golf and club management. The game and its management for the general public at both private and public facilities are now considered to be in a mature phase of the game's life cycle (Breitbarth, Kaiser-Jovy, Dickson, 2018).

Golf courses throughout the United States have developed into business operations that require managers who have a broad understanding of the golf industry. These managers must also recognize and understand the impact of a range of current issues. Declining demand, changes in lifestyles and family expectations, the need for sustainability, and technological advances have all changed the industry. Decreased participation rates and the closure of approximately 500 golf courses during the last decade have also forced managers and industry leaders to think differently about how these businesses are operated (Mona, Beditz, & Steranka, 2011). A number of programs have been initiated in an attempt to develop more golfers of all ages, abilities, and ethnicities. Golf 2.0, The First Tee, Women's Golf Month, the National Alliance for Accessible Golf, and Tee It Forward are examples of programs that aim to make golf more accessible and enjoyable.

History

In the nineteenth century, leisure time emerged as a result of the urbanization and industrialization of U.S. society. Technological innovations in factories made work more monotonous and prompted citizens to seek diversions in their non-working hours. The recreation movement sought to address social issues affecting a population faced with a 66-hour workweek (6 days a

week, 11 hours a day). Public attitudes toward work and leisure changed from a more Puritan ethic, which valued work over play, to a perception of recreation as important to the growth and health of the individual and as a means to improve community well-being.

By the end of the nineteenth century, the recreation movement had created formal organizations via local clubs and national associations devoted to recreation and committed to developing standards for activities. Organizations such as the American Canoe Association, established in 1880, began to shape not only recreational participation through the development of instructional guidelines, but also competition rules for races and regattas. Early in the twentieth century, interest in recreation continued to accelerate with the establishment of well-known organizations such as the Boy Scouts (founded in 1910) and the Girl Scouts (founded in 1912).

A phenomenon unique to the United States emerged during this time, as organized summer camps for children began to proliferate. In the nineteenth century, the camping movement often focused on gatherings of a religious nature for adults. Concerned about the effects of urbanization on children, advocates developed the first fresh-air camps in the latter half of the 1800s to allow urban children to travel to the country. By the early 1900s, the camping movement had gained momentum and attracted numerous children to these popular outdoor experiences. Today, specialty camps for sports and recreational activities are a popular part of the mix. The American Camping Association (ACA, 2017) reported that an estimated 14,000 camps existed nationwide in 2017, serving 14 million children and adults and employing 1.5 million adults, making it a $18 billion industry.

Following World War II, the expanding U.S. economy promoted a broadening of the scope of the recreation industry. This economic growth led to the creation of local parks and recreation departments, the establishment of armed forces recreation to improve the morale of soldiers and their families, and the emergence of commercial recreation enterprises such as the ski industry. The federal government also approved legislation that created the National Wilderness Preservation System; the National Wild and Scenic Rivers System; the National Trails System, a system of National Recreation Areas; and the Land and Water Conservation Fund, which provides matching grants to state and local governments for the purpose of acquiring and developing public outdoor recreation areas. Today, growing numbers of people are participating in outdoor recreation in the United States, especially women and older adults.

One of the most prominent subsets of the recreation industry is golf, which is estimated to be a $70 billion industry. More than 24 million people in the U.S. play 465 million rounds of golf at approximately 15,200 facilities annually (Heitner, 2016). The game of golf originated with the Scottish players and founders of the Royal and Ancient Golf Club of St. Andrews, Scotland. Construction of facilities for the sport evolved quickly in the United States. Napton and Laingen (2008) documented four major periods of golf course construction and development from 1878 through 2000. The game was first introduced to the U.S. market in Yonkers, New York, with the Apple Tree Gang, where the first small, three-hole course was built, also named St. Andrews. In 1895, the United States Golf Association (USGA) was formed and contributed greatly to the transformation of golf from a purely recreational game to a competitive sport. From 1878 to 1919, the growth of new golf courses and country clubs was concentrated primarily in *golf club villages* located on urban fringes. During this time, 962 courses were built, mostly private country clubs (Napton & Laingen, 2008). In 1914, the Club Managers Association of Boston was formed.

At the same time in New York, a similar organizational effort among club managers was taking place. These organizations ultimately formed the **Club Managers Association of America (CMAA)** and the **Professional Golfers' Association (PGA)** (Morris, 2002). Today, almost 30,000 golf professionals are members of the PGA (PGA, 2017a).

Many new golf courses were built in the 1920s following World War I, but this growth spurt was slowed by the worldwide economic depression from 1929 to the early 1940s and then later by World War II. Construction of the classic Augusta National golf course occurred in Georgia in 1932, setting a new standard in golf course design (Napton & Laingen, 2008). Golf was well positioned for a dramatic growth period corresponding with the increase in leisure time and affluence of the 1950s and 1960s. During these two decades, an upwardly mobile, wealthy growing population wanted to leave behind the Great Depression, memories of war, and the polluted and decaying central cities, in favor of open areas of land and the game of golf. During this period, 5,558 new golf courses were built (Napton & Laingen, 2008). The 1970s and 1980s saw a maturation and subsequent saturation of the golf and country club market and a slowdown in the number of new course builds. Professional golf tours such as the PGA Tour, featuring popular players including Jack Nicklaus and Arnold Palmer, began to enjoy larger crowds.

The boom period of the 1990s saw additional growth that rivaled the gains of the 1960s. An important difference between the boom periods of the 1960s and the 1990s, however, was the type of courses that were built. The courses built in the 1960s were generally affordable public courses, whereas those built in the 1990s were mostly courses with expensive daily fees or where play was limited to those living in private gated communities. This shift negatively impacted the growth rate of golf. Later, from 2000 to 2008, many private clubs were converted to public facilities. A large number of these facilities were converted to a management contract, meaning that they were taken over by large golf management companies such as American Golf. From 2005 to 2010, 713 golf courses (18-hole equivalents) closed for business; although the decline has since slowed, golf remains a cluttered marketplace (Mona et al., 2011; Statchura, 2017).

Segments of the Recreation Industry

The recreation industry offers people a wealth of opportunities for participation across its many segments. Consumers can find many intriguing activities to suit their needs. Competent recreation professionals are needed to staff the various types of industry organizations, and those interested in this field would be wise to explore the variety of options in what has become a very competitive job market. The industry is so diverse that it can appear fragmented because it is divided into a myriad of professional associations specific to certain activities. The categories presented in the next few sections are meant to explore the major segments of the recreation industry, and the prospective employee should realize that a particular recreation field may fit into two or three of the basic segments.

Community-Based Recreation

The term **community-based recreation** implies that participants are united by a common interest in recreation at the local level. Local parks and recreation departments and community agencies such as the YMCA, Young Women's Christian Association (YWCA), Jewish Community Centers, Girls and Boys Clubs, and Girl and Boy Scouts offer general community recreation services. Some agencies may target specific ages through youth centers or senior centers. Parks and recreation departments are supported through a mix of local property tax monies and user fees from participants. Many of these programs are no longer free to the public, given the increased competition for budgetary support among all municipal services (e.g., fire and police departments). As a result, recreation managers are becoming increasingly creative in soliciting private sponsorships from local companies for special programs, as part of an effort to keep program costs low for the public. To support their programs, agencies such as the YMCA, Jewish Community Centers, and Boys and Girls Clubs often rely on a greater mix of funding sources including user fees and memberships, private donations (such as from the United Way), grant programs from public and private sources, and in-house fundraising events.

Public Recreation

Public recreation reaches beyond the local level to those programs supported by state and federal agencies. State forest and parks departments, the National Park Service (NPS; a division of the U.S. Department of the Interior), and the National Forest Service (a division of the U.S. Department of Agriculture) manage recreational opportunities on public lands. Interest in national forests and parks remains high, and the number of visits to the 390 areas in the national park system and the 155 national forests has exploded in recent years. The National Park Service recorded nearly 331 million visits to national parks, seashores, monuments, and historic sites in 2016, an increase of 7.72% from the previous year (NPS, 2017a; Reynolds, 2017). This high use continues to affect a system beleaguered by federal budget constraints. The National Park Service is also grappling with policy issues concerning vehicle congestion, recreational vehicle access, a deteriorating infrastructure, control of visitor volume and duration, and it has identified the need to conduct a comprehensive study of public use of the park system (Lee, 2003). In both 2000 and 2008, this federal agency conducted a Comprehensive Survey of the American Public to better inform its decisions regarding the previously mentioned challenges, among various other ongoing research projects (NPS, 2017b).

© Photos.com

Military Recreation

The U.S. Department of Defense maintains extensive **military recreation** programs through branches of the armed services. Although their overriding mission is to promote the fitness and military readiness of their personnel, the armed services also seek to provide an array of recreational opportunities for families on bases in the United States and abroad as a means of improving overall morale and a sense of community. Facilities include, but are not limited to, ski areas, marinas, recreation centers, fitness centers, youth centers, golf courses, and bowling centers. The military is also creating new programs for enlisted personnel and veterans with disabilities who have returned from the country's recent wars and occupations, such as the Wounded Warriors Project at Fort Carson, Colorado.

Since 1948, the armed services have also supported the training of athletes for the Olympic Games and other major international competitions. More than 400 active-duty personnel have achieved Olympic status as a result (Quigley, 2004), including 18 service-member athletes in the most recent 2016 Rio Olympic Summer Games (Wells, 2016); another 34 Team USA members competing at the 2016 Rio Paralympic Games were military athletes (Heintz, 2016) and 18 military athletes represented Team USA at the 2018 PyeongChang Winter Paralympic Games (USOC, 2018).

Military recreation organizations face the same challenges as other government-funded recreation programs. Recent decreases in appropriated funds have challenged the armed services to maintain program quality and improve their economic performance.

Outdoor Recreation

Outdoor recreation attracts those who enjoy natural environments in different seasons, and people's increasing passion for the outdoors continues to expand this already large segment of the industry. The Outdoor Industry Association (2017) reported that nearly half of all people in the U.S. participated in at least one outdoor activity, with more than 144 million people in the United States participating annually. Spending on outdoor recreation falls primarily into two categories: outdoor recreation product sales (e.g., gear, apparel, footwear) and trips and travel-related spending (e.g., accommodations, transportation, and entertainment). This booming industry has created more than 6.1 million jobs and sustains economic growth in many rural economies. Running, jogging, and trail running top the list of popular activities, with 32 million participants (Outdoor Industry Association, 2017).

The outdoor industry is highly diverse, with a mix of for-profit and nonprofit ventures in each subcategory. Activities include, but are not limited to, skiing and snowboarding, boating (e.g., rafting, canoeing, kayaking, and sailing), golf, summer camps, backpacking and camping, natural resources management, and tourist travel. Adventurous programs modeled after Outward Bound are also popular among people seeking challenging outdoor experiences.

Campus Recreation

Campus recreation includes any recreational activity provided by colleges or universities, ranging from exercise facilities and fitness programming to club and intramural sports and coordinated outdoor recreation activities. With the goal of inspiring wellness through collegiate recreation, the National Intramural-Recreation Sports Association (NIRSA, 2017) includes more than 4,500 recreation professionals providing recreational opportunities for approximately 8.1 million students. Three out of four college students participate in some form of campus recreation. Additionally, of those students, 80% participate in campus recreational activities at least once a week (Forrester, 2014).

Additionally NIRSA (2017) offers excellent resources for students, including a student leadership team, a mentoring program, and beneficial career resources. The goal of many campus recreation programs is to teach students about the benefits of recreation and to encourage participation in a variety of contexts with the hope that students will continue to be active into later adulthood. Organizations such as NIRSA and the Association for Experiential Education (AEE) aim to provide educational trainings and host activities to develop prospective leaders in the recreation field or other areas.

Therapeutic Recreation

The **therapeutic recreation** field uses recreational activities as a means to improve a participant's physical, emotional, and mental health. The activities can be offered as part of an overall treatment or rehabilitation program that may have evolved from medical care at a hospital, rehabilitation center, psychiatric facility, or nursing home. In addition, therapeutic recreation services are offered through park and recreation departments, independent living centers, schools, community mental health agencies, specialty recreation organizations, and social services agencies. Such services may also include programs for individuals who may be at risk of entering or are already in the judicial system. The programs vary widely, from hospital-based cardiac rehabilitation, for which recreation is used to improve physical fitness, to wilderness camps sponsored by states' divisions of youth services that seek to change the behaviors of court-referred youth.

Therapeutic recreation organizations often seek personnel with experience in recreation, counseling, or social work. Most important, they need employees whose specific skills and experience match the needs of a designated population, such as trained chemical dependency counselors. Therapists who do not have specialized training in recreational activities such as ropes/challenge courses or water sports work in conjunction with other recreation professionals who can offer that leadership. As the U.S. population continues to age, prospective employees should explore the opportunities available in adult day care, outpatient programs, psychiatric rehabilitation, and physical rehabilitation, especially services for people with disabilities.

Segments of the Golf and Country Club Industry

The two major categories of clubs where recreational activities such as golf, tennis, or other sports are pursued are public clubs and private clubs. These venues differ in terms of access, membership, operation philosophy, profit motive, market orientation, and organizational structure.

Public Clubs

A **public club** is like any typical business that is open to the public. Some of these clubs compete aggressively for members or business sponsorships in a public setting. Individuals and members are welcome to play or use the facilities if they can pay the required course fee. Some people are members, but the club is largely a public facility, welcoming participants from nearly all backgrounds to play golf and enjoy the club's offerings. Public golf facilities are typically just golf courses with very limited services. Some offer additional revenue-producing facilities, such as tennis or swimming, and a limited food and beverage outlet. A number of public facilities have banquet areas to support golf outings. Many public courses are owned and operated by cities, counties, or states as a public service to the residents of the area (Kelley, 2018).

Public clubs that are privately owned for-profit enterprises also exist, with many providing high-end daily fee, resort, and destination experiences that are open to all socioeconomic classes to enjoy. In fact, until recently one of the fastest-growing concepts in the golf sector was the high-end, daily-fee public course. Public health clubs, day spas, and health spas, including many large hotel chains that have club concepts in their operations, now operate in this market. Luxury resorts, time-share community club concepts, and hotels are replicating the *club experience* and compete aggressively for this business.

Private Clubs

A **private club** restricts its membership and may be either a private for-profit entity or a private nonprofit entity. **Private exclusive clubs** go one step further by restricting membership to only those persons who are invited to join or become members by a vote of the current existing membership. Although money may be an important factor in why a person joins a private country club, it is not the sole reason. Compatibility and like-mindedness with the membership are equally important.

A private club can be defined as follows:

1. The club is not open to the public.

2. A member or an individual must be accepted by the rest of the membership before he or she can join. Once accepted, the new member usually must pay an initiation fee and then continuing monthly membership dues. Some clubs also have minimum spending requirements for members (e.g., members must spend a certain amount of money each month or year in the club's food and beverage outlets).

3. The club has a standard meeting place, typically a clubhouse, that is critical to its operation.

4. It is a place where comingling of social, recreational, or educational purposes occurs (Premier Club Services, 2010).

A *public accommodation club* or *private for-profit club*, in contrast, is open to the public, may have special membership plans, may advertise and compete readily for the public to use and enjoy its facilities, and typically does not restrict the number of potential users except in case of capacity issues. Private exclusive clubs are eligible for tax breaks and have restrictions on how they may compete in the public marketplace. For example, private exclusive clubs may not advertise their services (Premier Club Services, 2010).

People join private clubs for a variety of reasons. Some like the exclusive atmosphere of the club and see membership as a statement of social position or social class. Others join because of the recreational facilities, because the club is convenient for their types of interests, or because it is part of or close by their neighborhood. Others view club membership as a way to get ahead in business, because people in their professions are also members or because their clubs give them an impressive place to entertain clients. Some people, typically called **legacy members**, join clubs because their parents and grandparents were club members; that is, club membership is a family tradition. Others simply enjoy the personal recognition and service they receive at a private club.

Restrictions are placed on which types of clubs can accept corporate memberships. Exclusively private, nonprofit clubs do not accept corporate memberships. Only individuals and families can be members.

Private clubs are built for a variety of reasons. U.S. clubs that began in the nineteenth century or earlier were often started by a small group of individuals who decided to each put up a sum of money to buy a piece of land or an existing building and began the club for purely social reasons. Modern-day private clubs are built by developers (residential, resort, and free-standing facilities) as a way to help them sell homes, attract visitors, or target high-level playing communities. In such instances, the club and its golf course are the centerpiece of a housing development, and individuals who buy the homes surrounding it are either automatically members or have the option to become members. A resort type of course may also be one of several centerpiece attractions to draw people to a vacation destination.

The unique environment of a signature-designed golf course and the historic setting of the facility are all part of the major appeal for club members. Private clubs tend to have the best clubhouse furnishings in a state-of-the-art golf facility as well as impressive, well-kept grounds designed especially for playability. Most offer other recreational facilities as well. Furthermore, the goal of most private clubs is to provide a level of service that is rarely found elsewhere and creates an enduring impression, which is intended to maintain the individual's membership for a lifetime.

Today, all of a private club's facilities face competition from public and resort facilities. Clubs are also restricted in some of the services they can provide to their members due to tax regulations and other competitive advantages. Even so, there is demand for private clubs and the typical food service and recreation options they offer. Competitors for a club's food and beverage outlets include high-end gourmet restaurants, corporate chain restaurants, sports bars, and even fast-food restaurants. Private clubs typically have multiple food outlets, ranging from fine dining rooms to casual pubs or grill rooms, snack bars at the pool complex, and quick-service outlets on the golf course or in mobile units roaming the course.

Current Trends

Trends in Recreation Participation

An appreciation of the outdoors is central to the lifestyle of people in the United States, and recent trends in participation support the enduring value of outdoor recreation. Approximately 144 million people in the U.S. (48.6% of the population) participated in one or more outdoor activities in 2016, an increase of nearly 10 million from a decade ago (Outdoor Industry Association, 2017).

The 2017 Outdoor Foundation Survey on Outdoor Recreation and Participation reported the top outdoor recreation activities for people age 25 years and older. Running, jogging, and trail running remain at the top of the list, followed by fishing, hiking, bicycling, and camping (Outdoor Industry Association, 2017). Activities such as stand-up paddle boarding, cross-country skiing, and BMX biking saw significant growth rates over the past three years, indicating participation trend interests among consumers. Interest in extreme sports continues to grow among people of various ages, along with some long-lasting favorites, such as skateboarding, and newer activities, such as paintball. Over the past three years, the recreational activities with the greatest growth rate among individuals have been stand-up paddle boarding, cross-country skiing, and BMX bicycling (Outdoor Industry Association, 2017).

Recreation sport managers will need to be aware of the changing demographics of their consumers. Between 2000 and 2050, the U.S. population is expected to increase in size from 310 million to 439 million (U.S. Department of Commerce, 2010). The Hispanic population was responsible for 32% of the nation's population growth from 1990 to 2000, and for 39% of that growth from 2000 to 2010. This segment of the population is expected to account for 45% of total population growth from 2010 to 2030 and 60% from 2030 to 2050 (Cheeseman-Day, n.d.). Not only will the recreation industry need to respond to the needs of a more diverse population, but it must also address the impact of demographic shifts on recreation areas near cities.

Participation rates vary greatly by activity, and a newcomer to the recreation field would be wise to examine demographic trends in the specific area being served. As national demographics shift with regard to both age and ethnicity, managers will be faced with the challenging task of altering recreation facilities and programs to meet participants' needs. Overall, participants in the future are more likely to be women, older, more racially and ethnically diverse, and to come from urban areas. These factors will shape the industry in the coming years as recreation managers modify the strategies used in designing facilities, marketing programs, and hiring staff to deliver recreational opportunities responsive to this changing population.

Trends in the Golf Industry

Depending on the source and method of data collection, estimates of the number of golf facilities in the United States vary. The latest statistics indicate there are 15,372 golf courses and country club facilities (establishments primarily engaged in operating golf courses, except miniature golf) in the United States (Associated Press, 2015), making this a $70 billion industry (Heitner, 2016). Golf participation in the United States was hit by the recession in the late 2000s, but has now stabilized at approximately 23.8 million golfers (Statchura, 2017).

While the participation rate for 2016 was 1.5% lower than it was in 2015, golf industry experts are hopeful due to other notable statistics found in the National Golf Foundation's annual report on participation. First, the number of beginner golfers increased almost 14% to 2.5 million people in 2016, which represented an all-time high. Second, the number of "committed golfers" increased for the first time in five years to 20.1 million. Third, the number of non-golfers interested in playing the sport was 12.8 million, double what it was five years earlier. Finally, the number of junior golfers was similar to the number in the previous year, at 2.9 million (Statchura, 2017).

Interestingly, the annual golf participation survey measured a new category called "off-course participation" to capture those people utilizing driving ranges, simulators, and entertainment facilities such as TopGolf. This segment grew 11% from 2015 to more than 20 million participants in 2016. Of those individuals, 8.2 million never played on a traditional course (Statchura, 2017). As technology continues to become a pervasive aspect of our lives, it is important to note the influence it may have on sport participation and the evolution of the golf and country club industry.

Market Drivers

Market demand in the golf and country club industry is influenced by a number of factors, also known as *market drivers*:

- Participation and access to playing partners.
- Number of courses and types of courses available to the playing public and private club members.

- Condition of the course and the playing experience.
- Demand for quality experiences and services.
- Price to play a round of golf.
- Available time to play a full 18-hole round of golf.
- Seasonal play and weather patterns.

Golf participation is a key driving factor in the demand for golf. As more people play, more facilities and services are needed, more equipment is purchased, and more soft goods (e.g., balls, shoes, clothing) are consumed. The growth in recent years in the number of junior, women, and minority golfers also cannot be overlooked, because these trends may influence current and future demand for the game and facilities. The social nature of golf and the need for access to playing partners is an important element for many players. Clubs that promote leagues and socially focused programs can assist players in finding appropriate playing partners (Hatami, 2013).

The number and type of golf courses and country clubs available for participation also influences demand. Differing demographics, geographic locations, and income levels impact the choices made by golfers in selecting courses to play. Likewise, the overall condition of golf courses affect how regularly people play. As competition for the consumer has increased, clubs are striving to provide quality conditions and services to gain a competitive edge. This has directly led to golf course condition improvements. There is increased demand from the golfing public for course beauty and action similar to what they have observed on televised PGA or LPGA tournaments. The latest golf course maintenance technology improvements have enhanced overall course design, layout, and playing conditions. These factors have contributed to a general demand for high-quality courses over the past few decades, which has challenged superintendents who must manage the costs of golf course maintenance (Williams, 2012).

Similarly, the ability to afford and be associated with a high-quality or unique, long-standing exclusive club influences membership demand. With this type of demand comes the status of being associated with a country club, especially a prestigious club with a waiting list. This status will influence overall demand for membership. Indeed, although membership in a country club may include both negative and positive connotations, the demand for these private exclusive, unique golf services, courses, and experiences has increased strongly over the past two decades. The long-standing tradition of country club membership that drove the evolution of the country club cannot be underestimated (Perdue, 2013).

The cost of playing a typical round of golf often affects demand. If fee increases are too rapid or too high, people may reduce their playing volume, trade down to lower-cost alternatives, or simply seek different recreational pursuits. For example, the economic downturn in the late 2000s had a significant negative effect on the golf industry and led many courses to offer discounts to entice more people to play. This was seen as an unusual practice at that time—but as competition among clubs has increased in recent years, more discount offers and packages have become available.

Additional factors affecting demand include the popularity of other sports such as tennis and exercise activities; the availability of fitness centers at country clubs and more full-service facilities; the amount of leisure time available to people who play golf and other activities; the impact of weather on participation; the latent demand factor, or desire, to increase sport participation and fitness levels; and the success of U.S. golfers on the professional golf circuit (i.e., the "win on Sunday, play on Monday" syndrome) (Mona et al., 2011).

The seasonal use of clubs and the opportunity to play throughout the year varies substantially across various regions of the United States. Generally, usage of country club and golf facilities declines during the first (January to March) and fourth (October to December) quarters of the year in northern regions, when colder temperatures and shorter days reduce the demand for golf. Usage may also decline in southern regions when temperatures become too hot to play due to extremely high heat indices, humidity, threat of thunderstorms, and overall heat stress conditions. Typically, country clubs generate a greater share of their yearly revenues in the third and fourth quarters, which includes end-of-the-year tournaments, the holidays, and the year-end party season. In turn, firms usually generate a disproportionate share of their revenues and cash flows in the second, third, and fourth quarters of each year and have lower revenues and profits in the first quarter (Perdue, 2013).

In many areas, golf demand is affected by nonseasonal and severe weather patterns. Periods of extremely hot, cold, or rainy weather in a given region can be expected to reduce golf-related revenue. Droughts and extended periods of low or reduced rainfall may affect the availability and cost of water needed to irrigate golf courses and to keep fairways, tee boxes, and especially greens in optimal playing conditions. Optimal playing conditions require turf grass to maintain a stable growing cycle to retain the color and speed to carry the golf ball across playing surfaces. This requires significant amounts of water, fertilization, and maintenance. Conversely, too much rain, floods, and high winds or violent storms may reduce or interrupt golfing opportunities.

Career Opportunities

The recreation field offers individuals excellent opportunities to work indoors and outdoors in pleasant surroundings, enjoy a healthy

Table 19-1 Typical Recreation Positions
Activity director (cruise ships, senior centers)
Aquatics director
Aquatics specialist (town summer programs, YMCAs, YWCAs)
Armed forces recreation leader
Camp counselor
Camp director
Facilities manager (bowling, marinas, rafting)
Guide (river, fishing, hunting)
Instructor (skiing, swimming, canoeing, kayaking, scuba diving, wilderness)
Naturalist
Outdoor travel/tour leader
Park ranger
Park superintendent
"Pro" (golf, tennis)
Program director
Recreation director (town, community center)
Recreation therapist
Retail manager
Youth coordinator

lifestyle, and introduce others to the benefits of participation at any age and ability level. A number of common positions exist at recreation organizations, whether public or private, for-profit or nonprofit (**Table 19-1**). Recreation consumers, particularly those willing to pay a fee for participation, are increasingly savvy customers who expect a high degree of professional service in instruction and overall service delivery. From the moment they contact an organization to inquire about recreation programs and services, customers often seek to be reassured that they will obtain an educational, enjoyable, and safe experience. Some recreational activities can be very exciting, offering higher degrees of risk than other activities. After all, the challenging nature of outdoor sports such as whitewater kayaking or rock climbing is the very element that intrigues participants. Recreation professionals have a responsibility to deliver these programs with a high degree of skill and to manage them with an eye to providing acceptable degrees of risk.

The management team of a golf club comprises a group of highly skilled and trained professionals. This was not always the case. In the past, members of the club often tried to manage and operate the club or course on their own. However, due to the size of the clubs and a lack of volunteers, more clubs have hired staff and handed the day-to-day operations over to professional management teams who are specialists in a variety of skill areas. **Table 19-2** highlights the types of positions available in golf course and country club operations.

Because their members own them, private equity clubs can operate as the members desire, but many of these clubs, along with non-equity clubs and public clubs, now typically employ professional managers and industry specialists. The preferred organizational management structure employs a management team endorsed by the CMAA that is composed of club professionals; department heads; certified professionals in food and beverage management (including chefs, cooks, and bartenders); sport-related professionals (golf, tennis, and aquatics professionals); grounds and golf course superintendents; building and engineering technicians/specialists; and other specialty staff members who report to a general manager (CMAA, 2017; Perdue, 2013).

Strategies for Entering the Recreation, Golf Management and Club Operations Field

Recreation Management Professional Preparation

Recreation managers are always seeking effective instructors, leaders, or guides who can create and execute programs, deliver excellent instruction tailored to the participants' needs, and provide leadership in challenging situations. A recreation manager wants people-oriented employees who know how to communicate well with the public, who work well with a diverse population of customers and staff, and who are responsible individuals committed to delivering quality programs and services. A recreation agency is often a small, lean operation that also needs employees who bring business skills to the workplace. As recreation professionals move into managerial positions, they may need to supervise programs and staff, monitor program risk-management concerns, create innovative marketing campaigns, develop and administer budgets, act as liaisons with public and private agencies, and develop alternative sources of funding beyond user fees.

Table 19-2 Typical Golf and Country Club Industry Positions
Aquatics director
Banquet or event manager
Clubhouse manager
Controller
Department managers
Executive chef
Golf course superintendent
Golf professional
Grounds crew
Membership director
Spa director
Tennis professional

Finding a recreation job requires a general understanding of all segments of the industry and a sense of where expansion in this highly competitive industry is occurring or is likely to occur. A prospective employee should analyze the specialized instructional and managerial skills necessary in specific areas of interest. A multifaceted approach should be adopted to successfully obtain a recreation position:

1. *Participate in a variety of activities.* Explore both popular and relatively uncommon activities (such as backpacking, scuba diving, sailing, or rock climbing). Share your interests and hobbies during interviews, whether they include music, travel, or other useful experiences. Employers and clients want to see staff with active experience in a variety of interesting undertakings.

2. *Develop general instructional and programming skills.* Working with a wide variety of ages, genders, abilities, and types of programming is helpful, particularly for those individuals who aspire to an administrative position as a coordinator or director. Recreation managers seek employees with tangible skills. A useful strategy is to obtain training and hands-on experience through internships, cooperative education, summer employment, and volunteer opportunities.

3. *Refine skills in several specific programming areas.* Recreation is becoming increasingly specialized, and prospective employers may want an employee with a set of skills unique to a specific activity. Obtaining specific training and certification from a designated national governing body, such as the Professional Ski Instructors of America, the American Red Cross, or the American Canoe Association, may be necessary. First aid and emergency preparedness skills are essential parts of this training.

4. *Consider associated skills that can strengthen a resumé.* A versatile candidate also offers a base of knowledge and skills useful to a business office, including marketing, accounting, public relations, business computer applications, writing, knowledge of legal issues, and computer-aided promotional design. Academic programs enable a prospective candidate to develop this more extensive background.

Two approaches to professional preparation exist in the recreation field. The recreation skills approach provides shorter, more intensive preparation in a particular area, often resulting in certification. The other approach is to select an academic program of one, two, or four years duration at a college or university, which provides a broader knowledge base. Of course, not every prospective employee will have a recreation or outdoor recreation degree. Other related, useful degrees include sport management, environmental science and forestry, social work, business, early childhood education, criminal justice, environmental education, and public administration.

The skills approach enables a person to obtain training and experience through organizations such as the National Outdoor Leadership School (NOLS) or Outward Bound, two of the largest outdoor organizations that provide specialized leadership development. A candidate might also participate in the certification processes offered by national governing bodies such as the American Canoe Association or Professional Ski Instructors of America. Other nationally recognized agencies also provide training: Project Adventure, for example, teaches people to use structured activities on challenge/obstacle courses in environments ranging from summer camps to corporate training and development. Project Adventure provides a short-term, focused program at a lower cost (compared to other training avenues) and develops an individual's instructional and leadership skills in one specific activity.

Academic programs at colleges and universities offer a broader base of knowledge through expanded curricula for bachelor's and master's degrees. Individuals who seek to advance to managerial positions in program development or general administration would be wise to seek a master's degree. These programs vary in their alignments within the institution, and such alignments may give the curriculum a unique flavor. For instance, they may be housed in schools of health, physical education, recreation, or education as well as in departments of sport management, forestry and natural resources, regional planning, or travel and tourism. Interested students would be wise to establish a foundation of knowledge through general courses and select a focus in a particular segment that provides deeper knowledge and skills.

Golf and Club Operations Professional Preparation

The club management field provides opportunities for career development and advancement for those individuals who choose to pursue the club management career path. This is largely achieved by following the path to become a certified club manager (CCM).

Students may begin their career path by accumulating certification points while still in school. They may seek work or summer internships with independent, stand-alone, private nonprofit clubs as one entry path into club management. On the sport professional side, students who have a passion for sports such as golf, tennis, or racquetball, among others, may pursue positions as assistant professionals who teach and direct these sports for the membership. The PGA (golf), U.S. Tennis Association (USTA; tennis), and American Red Cross (swimming) offer career paths for those who

love these sports and would like to teach them as part of their career. Those wanting to work outdoors may pursue a career as a golf course superintendent. Students may find an internship involving turf and course grounds and recreational facilities maintenance; certification would then be obtained through the Golf Course Superintendents Association of America (GCSAA).

Educational preparation for careers in club management is available from college and professional associations. Because success in this field requires an understanding of business and club management skills and sport professional concepts, degree programs in club management in a hospitality program, sport management, and exercise science or professional golf management are particularly relevant. These areas of study may be viewed as complementary, and colleges that offer courses in each of these professional areas provide the best opportunity for the widest choices and preparation for the club management field.

Courses in turf management, plant and soil sciences, pest management, and grounds maintenance are essential for people destined for a career in golf course turf management. Anyone seeking entry through the clubhouse side of the industry must take management courses in club, events, food and beverage services, and banquet management, plus related hospitality management courses. A background in business and club management can prepare a person to face the myriad of managerial, legal, marketing, accounting, and financial issues involved in the successful operation of a golf or country club.

Beyond earning a college degree in the previously mentioned fields, a person on the club management career track can connect with the CMAA, the PGA, or the USTA for advanced educational opportunities and certification programs. CMAA offers the appropriate education training for entry-level managers to advance in a club management career as well as the certified club manager (CCM) program.

Students wishing to pursue a career in the golf side of the business as a golf professional may pursue a golf management degree at one of the 20 Professional Golf Management (PGM) programs located at various universities across the United States. The PGA Golf Management University Program is a four- to five-year college curriculum for aspiring PGA professionals that requires 600 hours of work experience. Four specifically designed golf internships are offered. Current college students may also become PGA professional members by starting their careers as registered apprentices and going through the PGA Professional Golf Management (PGA PGM) program. This program provides the opportunity to acquire the knowledge and skills necessary for success in the golf industry through extensive classroom studies and internship experiences. The PGA claims a 100% job placement rate for those who complete the University Program (PGA, 2017b).

Students seeking a career in the turf management side of the business can gain a turf management degree by completing courses in agronomy, plant science, soil science, and turf management at an agricultural college or university. To become a golf course superintendent, a student must master agronomy and turf grass management practices; possess a working knowledge of golf facility construction principles, practices, and methods; and have a thorough understanding of the rules and strategies of the game of golf.

Other positions in golf course maintenance operations include assistant golf course superintendent, equipment manager, and assistant equipment manager. Students interested in learning more about the golf maintenance side

of the industry should become involved with the GCSAA by visiting the association's website (www.gcsaa.org) or becoming involved with a local university student chapter.

Current Issues for Recreation, Golf and Club Management

The traditional roots of the recreation industry continue to shape the modern profession. The value of recreation programming is still judged in terms of its ability to improve health and well-being. Managers will need to monitor shifting demographic trends to adequately respond to the continuing financial constraints facing the recreation industry.

A fundamental shift in financing recreation has occurred as federal, state, and local governments have reduced their proportionate shares of recreation budgets. Public recreation now competes for funding in an economic climate overshadowed by a rising federal deficit, the emergence of state tax reform initiatives, and constrained local budgets. The recreation professional is often faced with the task of finding alternatives to government funding or user fees to support recreation services.

Park and recreation officials at local, state, and federal levels face challenges that include deteriorating park and recreation infrastructures; increasing crime in these venues; and declining federal, state, and local tax resources. Professionals must determine creative methods for capital development while simultaneously controlling operating expenses and establishing spending priorities in light of reduced budgets. Recreation managers must also strategize how to keep parks and recreation areas safe from vandalism, crime, gangs, and substance abuse so they do not develop a negative image that prevents citizens from enjoying them. They must advocate for the essential role that public recreation plays in promoting individual and community health and well-being (National Recreation and Park Association, 2010).

Since 2000, the golf industry has faced a number of challenges owing to the economic downturn and an oversupply of golf courses brought about by the building boom of the 1990s. Even with course closures, the supply of golf courses continues to exceed demand, which is a positive development for golfers but a rather problematic issue for the golf industry. The golf industry must also respond to changes in social structure and lifestyles, including an increased focus on families, that have had an impact on the demand for golf. More women golfers, increased diversity, and a focus on health-related benefits of sport must be considered as well. Today's golfers have less time, more choices, and different priorities, so the challenge for the industry is to address these issues and find ways to increase participation in golf ("Golf's 2020 Vision," 2012).

In 2012, the PGA of America began to promote a comprehensive, industry-wide initiative, **Golf 2.0**, that focuses on player development and seeks to boost golf participation by targeting specific groups with tailored programs. The program is seen as a long-term plan that will build participation levels toward a goal of 40 million golf players by 2020 and will be based on three key strategies: (1) retain and strengthen the golfing core, (2) engage lapsed players, and (3) drive new players. In support of retaining and strengthening the golfing core strategy, the Golf 2.0 program encourages PGA professionals to get to know their customers better, recognizing what is important to them and nurturing these customers to make sure they keep coming back. Lapsed golfers, particularly women, families, and seniors, are seen as high-value market segments that should be the focus of targeted programs

designed to reengage them as frequent participants. Attention to new golfers and programs designed to reach the "other 84%"—those individuals who do not currently play golf—are also highlighted as part of this initiative. Other underlying elements of Golf 2.0 are based on the need to provide increased professional development, education, and training to PGA professionals so that they can improve their skills in marketing and managing relevant facilities and programs that highlight the value of golf in today's world (Golf 2.0, 2013).

Numerous programs have been developed in an attempt to attract the next generation of golfers. The First Tee program has more than 200 chapters around the United States that are focused on introducing children to golf. Get Golf Ready is an adult-oriented player development program that provides a five-lesson package designed to get new people into the game. Tee It Forward is another industry initiative that encourages golfers to play from the tee that is most suited to their ability. This approach makes the game more fun for the average golfer and speeds up the pace of play. "Take Your Daughter to the Course Week" and "Women's Golf Month" are other programs that are designed to bring more girls and women to the game of golf (National Golf Course Owners Association [NGCOA], 2017). Starting New at Golf (SNAG, 2017) is an international golf development program that utilizes modified equipment so that the basic skills can be learned in a fun environment.

Golfers and potential golfers younger than the age of 35 have also received attention from golf industry professionals, who would like to strengthen participation rates among this group, often referred to as the "next generation." Lifestyle and cultural values are important when marketing to this group. They expect personalized experiences and respond well to flexible programs that offer a more varied golf experience, such as "Play and Pay by the Hour" or "Fast Golf." The Lake of the Ozarks Resort in Missouri implemented an hourly rate in 2017 in an effort to reach golfers pressed for time, or those who want the flexibility to play as much or as little golf as they choose (Sens, 2017).

Sustainability and the Environment

As the number of visitors to public lands increases, recreation professionals have a responsibility to monitor and control use of those areas to prevent destruction of natural resources and enhance participant safety. Improved **environmental awareness** is necessary, as instructors, guides, and managers need to abide by the increasingly strict regulations that control public use and educate recreation participants about those guidelines. Users must understand the recommended environmental practices for minimizing impact on trails, rivers, and camping areas, particularly in high-traffic locations, and must abide by the restrictions in group numbers levied by federal and state agencies. Leaders need to minimize conflicts among diverse users, such as hikers, mountain bikers, skiers, snowshoers, snowmobilers, and users of personal watercraft and off-road vehicles.

Managers also need to conduct activities in accordance with recognized safe practices so as to minimize accidents and rescues. Although client safety itself is an issue, cost is a concern as well. The public cannot afford to underwrite the costs of rescues, which increase as the total number of visitors in the outdoors escalates.

Finally, the importance of sustainability cannot be overemphasized. Managers need to consider how sustainable or "green" practices for facilities can promote ethical use of natural resources, such as the National Ski Areas Association's (2017) Sustainable Slopes project, which has been endorsed by almost 200 ski areas.

Indeed, sustainability and environmental stewardship are important issues for many businesses. The golf industry has been considering these issues when building and managing new courses for many years now. Managing existing courses within the context of supporting a sustainable environment requires modifying existing practices in many areas. Developers of new golf courses must be aware of federal guidelines designed to protect the environment from the very beginning of the design process. Today's courses are adopting policies to conserve and protect water resources, reduce pollution, conserve energy, and protect the natural habitat. In 2012, the International Golf Federation published a statement on sustainability that was subsequently adopted by allied golf associations from 150 countries around the world, including the United States (**Box 19-1**). This statement clarifies essential principles and practices of sustainability in the context of the golf industry in the United States.

Audubon International (n.d.) offers the Audubon Cooperative Sanctuary Program, which recognizes the efforts of individual golf clubs/courses in managing their properties in an environmentally responsible manner. Courses that meet specific criteria related to wildlife and habitat management, water conservation, environmental planning, and chemical reduction can be designated as Certified Audubon Cooperative Sanctuaries. This program began in 1991 and has steadily grown to include 2,300 courses in the United States and 36 countries worldwide. Complete details of the program can be found on the Audubon International website (https://www.audubon international.org/acspgolf).

Box 19-1 Shared Principles on Sustainability

Adopted in 2012 by the World Golf Foundation, PGA Tour, Ladies Professional Golf Association (LPGA) Tour, PGA of America, National Golf Course Owners Association, Golf Course Superintendents Association of America, American Society of Golf Course Architects, and Golf Course Builders Association of America.

To help the game realize these important goals, our professional members will:

- Design, construct, and manage environmentally responsible golf courses in an economically viable manner
- Commit to continual improvement in the design, development, construction, and management of golf courses
- Provide ecological and economic benefits to communities
- Provide and protect habitat for wildlife and plant species
- Recognize that every golf course must be developed and managed with consideration for the unique conditions of the ecosystem of which it is a part

- Provide important green space benefits
- Use natural resources efficiently
- Respect adjacent land use when planning, constructing, maintaining, and operating golf courses
- Create desirable playing conditions through practices that preserve environmental quality
- Support ongoing research to scientifically establish new and better ways to design, construct, and manage golf courses in harmony with the environment
- Document outstanding development and management practices to promote more widespread implementation of environmentally sound golf
- Educate golfers and developers about the principles of environmental responsibility and promote the value of environmentally sound golf courses

Courtesy of We Are Golf. Shared Principles of Sustainability. Retrieved from https://golf2020.com/sustainability/shared-principles/

Summary

The complexity of modern life is likely to promote a continuing need for enjoyable, safe, and challenging recreational activities as a diversion for the public and as a partial solution to social problems. Just as lifestyles have become more complex in the United States, so has the nature of the recreation profession. Industry professionals face numerous challenges as they seek to provide quality recreational experiences for diverse participants.

Increasing government regulation, particularly in the area of safety, means professionals must be aware of and comply with new laws, policies, and procedures. As specific industry segments mature, employees will be held to higher and higher standards of training and performance. These challenges require employees to bring a broad range of skills to their positions and to continue their education so they can deliver quality experiences that meet the current standards in the field. The reward is involvement in enriching experiences that enhance the recreation employee's life and can affect social change.

Golf courses and country clubs are significant business enterprises operating throughout the United States that provide diverse experiences and opportunities for golfers of all ages. The golf industry is expected to rebound from recent declines in participation, and new initiatives are currently being implemented to make the game more appealing and accessible to a diverse golfing population. Managers in the industry must recognize that the traditional structure of the golf enterprise is now evolving into a new model that provides flexibility, is more relaxed, and meets the needs of changing demographics. Families, women, and minorities are expected to become more active and will drive the demand for facilities and programs that address their expectations.

Future golf professionals must prepare for the complexities of this environment by developing the skills needed to be successful. It is not enough to be an active or strong golfer—business skills are needed, as well as specific knowledge of specialty aspects of the field. The recently implemented Golf 2.0 program highlights the professional development of existing professionals, especially in areas related to management and marketing. In a competitive marketplace, these skills are as important as

understanding how to run a member tournament or staff the driving range.

Golf industry professionals must also ensure that they are involved in professional organizations and continue to stay ahead of changes that may impact their business. Current lifestyle changes and trends may challenge existing practices or provide opportunities to expand into new areas. In 2016, golf became an Olympic sport for the first time in more than 100 years. How might this kind of attention contribute to new business opportunities? How might a club take advantage of the attention the sport received both before and during the Olympic Games? This is just one example of how external events may impact golf business operations and provide new and exciting opportunities if golf managers are prepared to take advantage of them.

Case Study 19-1

Collegiate University Embracing Technology

Collegiate University recently finished construction of a $56 million student recreation center. Prior to construction of the facility, the director of campus recreation, Aaron Burgoon, surveyed the student population to better understand their wants and needs for the facility. The administration aimed to take everyone's opinion into consideration and design a facility that would become the epicenter of campus life and fulfill the recreational needs of the student population. Although the benefits of the recreation center would reach faculty, staff, alumni, and the greater community, student participation was the major goal of the facility.

Highlights of the 8,000-square-foot state-of-the-art facility include the following:

- 3 pools
- 8 racquetball courts
- A 6-court gymnasium

- A quarter-mile elevated track
- A 40-foot rock-climbing wall
- 3 multipurpose rooms
- 200 pieces of cardiovascular equipment
- 100 weight machines
- More than 20,000 pounds of free weights

Student membership fees for the facility are incorporated into the student activity fee and are included in tuition. Faculty, staff, alumni, and community members pay approximately $50 per month to use the facility.

Collegiate University was excited to unveil the new facility at the beginning of the 2016–2017 school year. Considering that the primary goal for the facility was to engage the student population in recreation participation, Aaron, as the director of campus recreation, collected baseline participation data for the facility and programs throughout the first year. He knew that the national average for participation in recreational opportunities on campus was approximately 75% (NIRSA, 2013) and was very disappointed to see that after the first academic year of operation, only 40% of students at Collegiate University had used the recreational facility and programming.

To address this problem and make changes for the 2017–2018 year, Aaron held a focus group meeting at the end of the school year with 50 of his student employees. The student employees provided very insightful feedback, making statements such as "Everyone knows the facility is here, but no one really understands what we have to offer," "Many students do not read their university email," and "A lot of people are afraid to participate alone." Aaron assessed the information he gained through the focus groups, along with the initial survey data he had from the facility.

Through his analysis, Aaron realized that one of the major factors associated with student participation had to do with communication. The facility itself met all of the needs of the student population, yet if students did not know what was offered and when, they would not attend. After doing more research, Aaron realized that the vast majority of students were on some, if not many, social media platforms. He recognized that embracing social media might be a cost-effective and efficient way to reach his target student population. Considering that Aaron was nearing retirement and had yet to embrace technology and social media into his lifestyle, he once again sought the assistance of his student employees.

Put yourself in the shoes of one of the student employees hired by Aaron and answer the following questions.

Questions for Discussion

1. How can the recreation center use technology and social media to better communicate with the student population? Which platforms would you use? Which types of messages would you send through each platform? Why? Identify specific messages that you could potentially use.

2. In addition to raising awareness about the recreation center, how else could the facility use social media? What else could the recreation center do to embrace technology (in addition to the social media platforms previously addressed)? Explain.

3. Create an event that the recreation center could organize that would both embrace technology and aid in the goal of increasing student participation.

4. What are your recommendations to Aaron on how to assess the recreation center's use of technology? How could you tell if your social media efforts were truly helping to increase student participation rates?

Case Study 19-2

To Host or Not to Host?

Casco Bay Country Club (CBCC) is considered one of the premier golf clubs in Maine. It features a scenic golf course; a sophisticated, state-of-the-art clubhouse; and a beautiful swimming pool complex and tennis facilities. The golf course is a nationally renowned 18-hole Donald Ross–designed course in a scenic oceanside setting. The course was also the first in Maine to become a Certified Audubon Cooperative Sanctuary, highlighting the club's commitment to the environment. The club is a private

(continues)

To Host or Not to Host? (*Continued*)

501(c)(7) organization that was established in 1890 and currently has 300 members. It hosts numerous events for its members, including member tournaments and guest events, as well as weddings, banquets, family gatherings, and corporate meetings.

The board of directors and the golf planning committee are considering a proposal to bid on hosting the USGA U.S. Senior Amateur Men's Championship in 2020. This event brings together 156 qualifying golfers from across the country for a weeklong tournament that begins with two rounds of match play and culminates with the top 64 golfers advancing to match play. Qualifying tournaments are held nationwide, and in 2014 more than 2,000 amateur golfers participated. Hosting a USGA event requires clubs to meet basic golf facility requirements with regard to course length/yardage, the driving range, club house capabilities, parking capacity, and so on. It also requires the host club to provide a host hotel with special rates, accommodations for USGA officials, a welcome dinner, and other events during the week.

CBCC General Manager Charlie Lowton and Head Golf Professional Nancy Canning both support the proposal based on the potential benefits and exposure that the club can expect to receive. Charlie and Nancy believe that this event will bring additional prestige and recognition to the club. It would be the first USGA event to be hosted in the state since 1976, and only 13 such events are held around the United States each year. Hosting the event is also likely to have a positive impact on the demand for membership at the club.

The club will incur some costs that need to be fully assessed. Costs for hosting the event will be incurred in the following categories (unless sponsors are secured): housing of officials, the welcome dinner, a champions reception, transportation for officials, meals for golfers, gift packets, and any necessary course and/or facility improvements.

The board of directors agrees that this is a prestigious event and acknowledges that hosting it would further enhance the club's image. The board does, however, have other concerns that need to be addressed before a final decision is made. First, the club's membership is already at capacity, and a waiting list for new members exists, which may diminish the value of hosting the event in terms of its impact on membership recruitment. Second, the golf course will be out of commission to members for the week of the tournament and for two additional days prior to the event and one day after. Third, because the event will be held in September, members would lose access to potential tee times during some of the best playing times in the Maine golf season. Finally, members would have to vacate the locker rooms during this time and have limited access to certain areas of the clubhouse.

Charlie and Nancy plan to get feedback from the members prior to the board meeting and are hopeful that the board will see this as an exciting opportunity for the Casco Bay Country Club. They are also preparing a presentation to inform the board of the details of this undertaking. The board will need to make a decision quickly and send a formal invitation to the USGA declaring the club's interest in hosting this prestigious event.

Questions for Discussion

1. Which information should be gathered from the membership prior to the meeting with the board of directors?

2. If you were preparing this presentation for the board, what five key points would you make to open your remarks?

3. What are the most significant benefits to the club in hosting this event?

4. Which areas are likely to be most costly and time consuming in managing the USGA event?

5. How would you manage the additional work that will come with the event?

6. How would you measure success after the event has been completed?

Resources

American Camp Association (ACA)
5000 State Road 67 North
Martinsville, IN 46151
765-342-8456
www.acacamps.org

American Golf Corporation
6080 Center Drive, Suite 500
Los Angeles, CA 90045
www.americangolf.com

American Recreation Coalition (ARC)
1225 New York Avenue NW, Suite 450
Washington, DC 20005
202-682-9530
www.funoutdoors.com/arc

Association for Experiential Education (AEE)
3775 Iris Avenue, Suite 4
Boulder, CO 80301
303-440-8844
www.aee.org

Club Managers Association of America (CMAA)
1733 King Street
Alexandria, VA 22314
703-739-9500
www.cmaa.org

ClubCorp USA, Inc.
3030 Lyndon B. Johnson Freeway,
Suite 600
Dallas, TX 75234
972-243-6191
www.clubcorp.com

Ladies Professional Golf Association (LPGA)
100 International Golf Drive
Daytona Beach, FL 32124
386-274-6200
www.lpga.com

National Golf Course Owners Association (NGCOA)
291 Seven Farms Drive, Suite 2
Daniel Island, SC 29492
843-881-9956
www.ngcoa.org

National Golf Foundation (NGF)
1150 S. US Highway One, Suite 401
Jupiter, FL 33477
561-744-6006
www.ngf.org

National Intramural-Recreation Sport Association (NIRSA)
4185 SW Research Way
Corvallis, OR 97333
541-766-8211
https://nirsa.net/nirsa/

National Park Service (NPS)
1849 C Street, NW
Washington, DC 20240
202-208-6834
General information: www.nps.gov/index.htm
Job information: www.nps.gov/aboutus/workwithus.htm

National Recreation and Park Association (NRPA)
22377 Belmont Ridge Road
Ashburn, VA 20148
703-858-0784
http://www.nrpa.org

Professional Golfers Association (PGA)
100 Avenue of the Champions
Palm Beach Gardens, FL 33418
561-624-8400
www.pga.com/home/

Troon Golf
15044 N. Scottsdale Road, Suite 300
Scottsdale, AZ 85254
480-606-1000
www.troongolf.com

United States Golf Association (USGA)
P.O. Box 708
Far Hills, NJ 07931
908-234-2300
www.usga.org

World Golf Foundation
1 World Golf Place
St. Augustine, FL 32092
904-940-4000
www.worldgolffoundation.org

Key Terms

campus recreation, Club Managers Association of America (CMAA), community-based recreation, direct participation, environmental awareness, Golf 2.0, indirect participation, legacy members, military recreation, outdoor recreation, private club, private exclusive clubs, Professional Golfers Association (PGA), public club, public recreation, therapeutic recreation

References

American Camping Association. (2017). Facts and trends. Retrieved from https://www.acacamps.org/press-room/aca-facts-trends

Associated Press. (2015, March 11). U.S. gold courses in steady decline. Retrieved from http://www.espn.com/golf/story/_/id/12461331/number-us-golf-courses-steady-decline-says-report

Audubon International. (n.d.). About the Audubon Sanctuary Program for Golf. Retrieved from https://www.audubon international.org/acspgolf

Breitbarth, T., Kaiser-Jovy, S., & Dickson, J. (2018). *Golf business and management: A global introduction.* New York, NY: Routledge.

Cheeseman-Day, J. (2011). *Population profile of the United States.* Retrieved from https://csrd.asu.edu/sites/default/files/pdf/Population%20Profile%20of%20the%20United%20States.pdf

Club Managers Association of America (CMAA). (2017). CMAA: Who we are. Retrieved from http://www.cmaa.org/template.aspx?id=216

Forrester, S. (2014). The Benefits of Campus Recreation. Corvallis, OR: NIRSA.

Golf 2.0. (2013). PGA. Retrieved from http://pdf.pgalinks.com/golf20/Golf2.0_PlayerDev_Playbook.pdf

Golf's 2020 vision: The HSBC report. (2012). Retrieved from http://golfnetworkadmin.gamznhosting.com/site/_content/document/00017543-source.pdf

Hatami, D. (2013, April 1). Thoughts from the industry golf show. *HVS Global Hospitality Report.* Retrieved from http://www.hvs.com/article/6272/thoughts-from-the-golf-industry-show-part-1-of-3/

Heintz, M. (2016). 34 US veterans to participate in 2016 Paralympic Games. U.S. Department of Veterans Affairs. Retrieved from http://www.blogs.va.gov/VAntage/30610/34-u-s-veterans-to-participate-in-2016 paralympic-games/

Heitner, D. (2016, May 8). The state of the golf industry in 2016. *Forbes.* Retrieved from https://www.forbes.com/sites/darrenheitner/2016/05/08/the-state-of-the-golf-industry-in-2016/#8f2912c33a6e

Kelley, B. (2018, January 8).The different types of golf courses. ThoughtCo. Retrieved from https://www.thoughtco.com/the-different-types-of-golf-courses-1563526

Lee, R. F. (2003). *Public use of the national park system 1872–2000.* Washington, DC: National Park Service.

Matuszewski, E. (2017, May 26). Golf's global reach: Just how many of the world's

245 countries have courses? *Forbes*. Retrieved from https://www.forbes.com/sites /erikmatuszewski/2017/05/26/golfs-global -reach-just-how-many-of-the-worlds-245 -countries-have-courses/#73fa8cf418e3

Mona, S., Beditz, J., & Steranka, J. (2011, May 10). *The latest and greatest. Industry reports*. Paper presented at the 2011 Golf 20/20 Forum, St. Augustine, FL.

Morris, R. R. (2002). In Martin J. (Ed.), *Club Managers Association of America: Celebrating seventy-five years of service, 1927–2002*. (English trans.). (1st ed.). Virginia Beach, VA: Donning Company.

Napton, D. E., & Laingen, C. R. (2008). Expansion of golf courses in the United States. *Geographical Review, 98*(1), 24–41.

National Golf Course Owners Association (NGCOA). (2017). NGCOA player development. Retrieved from http://www .ngcoa.org/pageview.asp?doc=312

National Golf Foundation. (2017, May). R&A releases report on global golf supply: Courses now in 208 countries. Retrieved from http:// ngfdashboard.clubnewsmaker.org /Newsletter /rhxsoksqvwy?a=1&p=2418447&t=410813

National Intramural-Recreation Sports Association (NIRSA). (2017). About NIRSA. Retrieved from https://nirsa.net/nirsa/about/

National Park Service (NPS). (2017a). Annual summary report. Retrieved from https://irma .nps.gov/Stats/SSRSReports/National%20 Reports/Current%20Year%20Monthly%20 and%20Annual%20Summary%20Report%20 (1979%20-%20Present)

National Park Service (NPS). (2017b). Social science: Current efforts. Retrieved from https://www. nature.nps.gov/socialscience /research.cfm

National Recreation and Park Association. (2010). Why parks and recreation are essential public services. Retrieved from http://www .nrpa.org/uploadedFiles/nrpa.org/Advocacy /Resources/Parks-Recreation-Essential -Public-Services-January-2010.pdf

National Ski Areas Association. (2017). NSAA sustainable slopes annual report 2016. Retrieved from http://www.nsaa.org /media/276021/SSAR2016.pdf

Outdoor Industry Association. (2017). Outdoor foundation: Outdoor recreation participation topline report. Retrieved from https://outdoorindustry.org/wp-content/ uploads /2017/04/2017-Topline-Report_ FINAL.pdf

Perdue, J. (2013). *Contemporary club management* (3rd ed.). Upper Saddle River, NJ: Pearson Education.

Premier Club Services. (2010). Your club and the law. Club Managers Association of America. Retrieved from http://www.cmaa.org /WorkArea/linkit.aspx?LinkIdentifier=id &ItemID=37396

Professional Golfers' Association (PGA). (2017a). Directory. Retrieved from https://www.pga .org/directory

Professional Golfers' Association (PGA). (2017b). What is the PGA Golf Management University Program? Retrieved from https://www.pga .org/articles/what-pga-golf-management -university-program

Quigley, S. (2004, August 13). Military athletes have proud Olympic history. Retrieved from http://archive.defense.gov/news/newsarticle .aspx?id=25521

Reynolds, C. (2017, March 1). National parks saw a record setting number of visitors last year. Were they too much of a good thing? Retrieved from http://www.latimes.com /travel/la-tr-nps-crowds-20170228-story.html

Sens, J. (2017, January 10). Missouri course experiments with the novel pay-by-the-hour greens fees. Retrieved from http://www.golf .com/tour-and-news/missouri-course -experiments-novel-pay-hour-green-fees

Starting New at Golf (SNAG). (2017). SNAG's history and philosophy. Retrieved from http://www.snaggolf.com/home /snags-history-philosophy/

Statchura, M. (2017, April 22). The NGF's annual golf participation report uncovers favorable trends for the game's future. *Golf Digest*. Retrieved from http://www.golfdigest.com /story/the-ngf-annual-golf-participation -report-uncovers-favorable-trends-for-the -games-future

U.S. Department of Commerce. (2010). *The next four decades: The older population in the United States 2010–2050*. Washington, DC: Author.

USOC. (2018). 2018 U.S. Paralympic team announced. Retrieved from https://www .teamusa.org/News/2018/February/26/2018 -US-Paralympic-Team-Announced

Wells, M. (2016, August 9). 18 military service members participating in the 2016 Rio Olympics. *Military 1*. Retrieved from https://www.military1.com/off-duty /article/1625555014-18-military-service -members-participating-in-the-2016 -rio-olympics/

Williams, B. (2012, February 10). How do you measure up? *Golf Course Industry*. Retrieved from http://www.golfcourseindustry.com /gci0212-state-of-industry-report.aspx

© Shutterstock, Inc./ Danilo_Vuletic

Part VI

Career Preparation

Chapter 20 Strategies for Career Success

Chapter 20

Mary A. Hums and
Regina G. Presley

Strategies for Career Success

Learning Objectives

Upon completion of this chapter, students should be able to:

1. Assess the realities of employment opportunities in the sport industry.

2. Recognize the importance of gaining skills and experience in the sport industry by volunteering and doing sport internships.

3. Assess the personal goals, skills, characteristics, and abilities that will set them apart from others competing for jobs in the sport industry.

4. Design a personal job search strategy and career plan.

5. Evaluate the role of informational interviews and developing a professional network as part of an overall career development program.

6. Compose an effective cover letter, resumé, and reference list.

7. Develop an effective "elevator pitch" to sell skills to potential employers.

8. Take the steps necessary to prepare for a successful job interview.

9. Identify the factors that make for a successful job candidate.

10. Recognize that landing a job in the sport industry is often the result of being more prepared than the other candidates.

Introduction

As a future sport management professional, it is important to consider your "dream job" in the industry. Jobs in the sport industry are highly competitive and challenging to obtain. As a student pursuing a possible career in sport, perhaps you aspire to a job such as General Manager of the Miami Heat, Director of Stadium Operations at SunTrust Park, Athletic Director at the University of Oregon, Marketing Director for the U.S. Olympic Committee, or Social Media Manager for the San Antonio Spurs, to name a few possibilities. New jobs are always emerging as well, as sport managers now work in areas such as data analytics, advanced social media, and technology operations in venues and stadiums. Just recently, the Philadelphia 76ers advertised a Director of Gaming position that focused on experience with the global eSports market. With the skill sets you bring to the industry, you have the potential to be among the new leaders in some of these emerging areas. Some of your supervisors may still come from a time when social media did not even exist and will need to rely on your skills in that area to improve the organization. Recent graduates have much to offer as the sport industry continues to evolve. All different types of sport management jobs are attainable with appropriate knowledge of the industry, assessment of personal strengths and weaknesses, a clear set of goals, and a realistic approach to marketing that most valuable asset—your skills.

The Reality of a Career in Sport Management

People are drawn to the sport management profession for a great number of reasons. The most common reason is a love and passion for sport. While that asset is certainly important, it will not be enough to land a job in the sport industry. It is essential that you set yourself apart from other candidates, and a love and passion for sport will not make you unique among the pool of applicants. Prospective employers look for people who want to work in the business of sport and have the determination and drive to get there. It is important to love your job, but it is also important to understand that the love of the game, especially from a fan's perspective, will not be enough.

The reality of working in the sport industry can be a challenge for some to accept. Those seeking careers in the sport industry share some common misconceptions related to the business environment. Many believe a degree in Sport Management guarantees an opportunity to work in the industry. Although an undergraduate degree in Sport Management can be very helpful for students seeking work in youth, college, professional, and other sport fields, it is not the only factor employers consider when hiring. The number of Sport Management programs in the country is growing, with more than 300 colleges and universities currently offering Sport Management as a major at either the undergraduate or graduate level. All of the graduates of these programs are likely to seek employment in the sport industry. In addition, students graduating with degrees in management, marketing, public relations, communications, or exercise science, as well as many from MBA programs and law schools, may be vying to land jobs in the field. People currently working in industries outside of sport, such as advertising, banking, law, or financial services, are increasingly considering career changes into the sport industry, showcasing the transferable skills, such as sales or merchandising, they acquired in those other industries.

A few examples will amply illustrate the demand for jobs in the industry. On average, 450 to 550 internship and job openings are posted each year at the Professional Baseball Employment Opportunities (PBEO) Job Fair, which is held in conjunction with the Winter

Baseball Meetings (PBEO, 2013). Typically, 500 to 600 people attend this event. When the New Orleans Hornets had an opening for a community relations position with an annual salary of $25,000, the opening drew 1,000 applications in 1 week (Helyar, 2006). Positions with the organizing committee for the Chicago 2016 Olympic and Paralympic Games bid drew thousands of applications, and once the bid was awarded to Rio de Janeiro, those working for the bid committee found themselves unemployed (Chicago Press Release Services, 2009). The large volume of job applicants has caused a number of sport organizations to incorporate electronic databases and websites to gather job applicant information. Obviously, competition for jobs is intense, and a Sport Management degree will not assure anyone of a job in the industry.

It is important to note that the sport industry is quite broad. People most frequently think about working in either professional sport or intercollegiate athletics, likely because that is what we see most often being broadcast and this part of the sport industry drives the most conversation. In reality, a myriad of employment opportunities exist in health and fitness, facility management, higher education, recreational sport, sport for people with disabilities, youth sports, nonprofit agencies, entrepreneurial businesses, and other areas. Also, the more willing a person is to relocate, the better the chance he or she has of finding employment.

A Sport Management degree does offer several benefits. First, it is important that those entering the field learn the business principles that apply to the sport industry. Taking a business marketing class, for example, provides groundwork in basic marketing concepts. Sport marketing is inherently different from traditional marketing because the sport product is unpredictable, inconsistent, subjective, and perishable. A sport marketer has very little, if any, control over the core product (especially on the field). A degree in Sport Management will provide a solid understanding of the business aspects that are applicable in the industry. A Sport Management degree also gives a student working knowledge of the industry, as classes are geared specifically toward sport. Students are immersed in industry-specific knowledge, constantly learning about current issues and current events in sport. Students also stay up-to-date by reading current sport publications or websites such as *Street & Smith's SportsBusiness Journal, Athletic Business*, or insidethegames.biz.

Many Sport Management degree programs assist with initial access to the sport industry through **internship** opportunities with sport organizations. Internships provide hands-on learning experiences, giving students the chance to gain valuable work experience as well as the opportunity to meet people working in the industry. Building a professional **network** is key in establishing your career in sport. In addition, a good number of Sport Management academic programs have professors who have come to academia after working in the industry and who actively maintain industry ties, giving students another way to access a network of sport industry professionals. The importance of networking is discussed later in this chapter.

Finally, when working on a Sport Management degree, students learn about opportunities to develop a winning resumé. Sport Management programs often stage campus or community events such as 3-on-3 basketball tournaments, golf tournaments, road races, or sport symposiums. These programs also routinely receive requests from sport organizations such as their university's athletic department or local sport commission for event volunteers. Students should take advantage of as many opportunities as possible to separate themselves from other candidates. Having a variety of experiences on a resumé will indicate the job candidate's commitment to success in the field. By comparison, individuals who do not major in Sport Management may not necessarily have access to the networking, resources, or resumé-building opportunities provided in specific Sport Management programs.

As mentioned earlier, in sport, it is essential to build a strong industry network. The people with experience in the industry will likely be the ones offering the jobs. The old adage, "It's not what you know, it's who you know," holds true in most industries; in sport, however, the saying is "It's not what you know, and it's not who you know, but it's *who knows you*." Having a degree in Sport Management is simply not enough. In the sport industry, as much or perhaps more than in just about any other industry, people hire someone because of personal knowledge of the applicant or a personal recommendation from someone else. The ability to be acknowledged by others in the industry as an essential employee will be one of the primary ways to get a job in sport. Years ago, people would network by gathering large databases of business cards and collecting the names and contact numbers of as many individuals as possible (Misner, 2012). Today, networking includes connecting with professionals in person by attending conferences, social events, and sport expos, as well as by building a reputable social media presence. Professional networking sites such as LinkedIn or Teamwork Online have gained traction in the industry and are essential to helping grow and build a network. The importance of building a strong sport industry network cannot be overstated.

Sport Management students and sport managers need to actively work to expand their networks to include all types of industry connections. It is easy and comfortable for people to build networks with others like themselves, but it is also important to expand one's contacts across age ranges, gender, race, disability, national origin, or sexual orientation, as well as across a variety of other industry segments, to grow a successful network. This open-mindedness will help to promote diversity in the sport workforce—a critical step to success for new and innovative organizations that seek to be successful in an increasingly international and multicultural sport industry.

As important as it is to build a diverse network, it is equally as important to consider the variety of positions available in the industry. When people hear the term *sport management*, the jobs that most often come to mind are in professional sport or college sport. Many students have an interest in these two areas and forget about all the other industry segments available in the field. The limited number of jobs in professional and college sport are related to the low turnover in professional sport positions and the size of many of the sport offices. A minor league baseball team, for example, has a small staff—perhaps as few as 10 to 25 full-time employees. In college sport, funding constraints may pose a barrier to hiring additional staff. State universities are especially susceptible to this problem, because state lawmakers make decisions about where limited state funding will go. If the state legislature cuts the amount of money available to a university, the cutbacks will be felt throughout all areas of the institution, including athletics. This makes it difficult for college and university athletic departments to create new positions. To make up for this shortfall in full-time paid personnel, however, college and university athletic departments offer graduate assistantships and internships, which can prove invaluable opportunities for those trying to enter the field to gain experience.

New students entering the sport industry are well advised to look beyond professional and college sport for job opportunities. Among the multibillion-dollar segments of the sport industry today are sporting goods and apparel, marketing agencies, recreational sport, eSports, health and fitness, and the nonprofit sector, to name a few. It is essential to recognize the vast opportunities in all the different segments of the sport industry.

Each segment provides unique opportunities to grow within the organization. One common misconception is that jobs in the sport world will be glamorous and exciting. The reality is decidedly harsher. For example, a typical work schedule for an event coordinator in Major League Baseball (MLB) is 60 to 70 hours per week, including late nights and long weekends. When people go out to be entertained, they come to the place where the sport manager is hard at work. Although it is exciting to work games or events, a sport manager very seldom—if ever—gets to see any of the action of the game or event itself.

In addition, salaries—especially starting salaries—tend to be low in the sport industry, although there is potential for increased earnings as you move up in the industry. There is high demand to work for a sport, team, or organization that is loved by many. Each job opening receives a high number of applicants, which drives starting salaries down. Demand for the jobs far outweighs the supply. According to Belson (2012), be prepared for starting salaries around $35,000, although some jobs will pay even less.

As you consider some of the barriers and realities of finding your place within the sport industry, it is equally as important to learn the steps in a successful career search in sport. As a student, you will likely gradually transition into an internship to gain experience and eventually transition into the job search to find your future career. The steps in preparing yourself, finding a job, and landing the dream career will require a focus on resumé writing, recognizing accomplishments, developing skills, and interview preparation.

Career Preparation

Finding a job—any job—is a difficult, time-consuming, and challenging process. Currently, you are focused on gaining education to prepare for a career, but it is still essential to consider the importance of career preparation during college. To prepare yourself for a future career in sport, you must begin early in your collegiate experience. Most importantly, it is vital that you have a plan to prepare for your future in the sport industry. Figure 20-1 illustrates the various phases of the career preparation process and provides details to help guide you in your future internship and job search.

Step 1. Self Reflection

One of the most important considerations when preparing for any career is knowing and understanding the skills you will bring to an organization. It is essential that you have the ability to analyze your skills, abilities, interests, and preferred workplace environment. Identifying and developing new skills is what will make you marketable in the industry. It can be challenging to assess personal abilities, but clearly identifying skills and being able to articulate those skills will help you obtain both an internship and eventually a job.

One way to review your skills is to write down your top three accomplishments—for example, being awarded the most valuable player honor, being made the captain of the hockey team, being named the top sales person in a fundraising campaign, or making the dean's list for three consecutive semesters. Each of these accomplishments requires some very specific skills, such as time management, leadership, effective communication, customer service, or even expertise in sales. All of these are skills identified in a reflection of self. A common goal will be to identify your strengths and weaknesses, and then to determine how those strengths set you apart from others seeking the same position. A variety of instruments are available to help you with exercises that clarify your strengths and weaknesses, but you alone will need to clearly understand the skills you possess and consider how those skills will

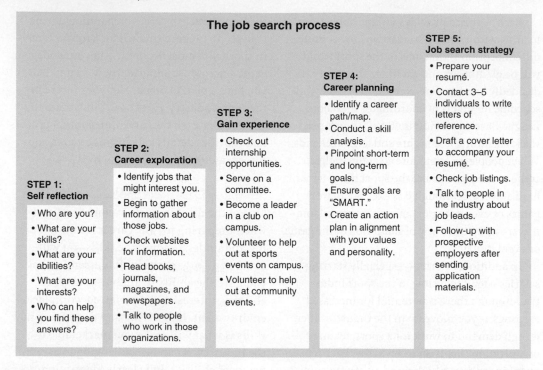

The job search process

STEP 1:
Self reflection

- Who are you?
- What are your skills?
- What are your abilities?
- What are your interests?
- Who can help you find these answers?

STEP 2:
Career exploration

- Identify jobs that might interest you.
- Begin to gather information about those jobs.
- Check websites for information.
- Read books, journals, magazines, and newspapers.
- Talk to people who work in those organizations.

STEP 3:
Gain experience

- Check out internship opportunities.
- Serve on a committee.
- Become a leader in a club on campus.
- Volunteer to help out at sports events on campus.
- Volunteer to help out at community events.

STEP 4:
Career planning

- Identify a career path/map.
- Conduct a skill analysis.
- Pinpoint short-term and long-term goals.
- Ensure goals are "SMART."
- Create an action plan in alignment with your values and personality.

STEP 5:
Job search strategy

- Prepare your resumé.
- Contact 3–5 individuals to write letters of reference.
- Draft a cover letter to accompany your resumé.
- Check job listings.
- Talk to people in the industry about job leads.
- Follow-up with prospective employers after sending application materials.

Figure 20-1 The Job Search Process

make you an asset in any workplace. Think of yourself as a "brand," and consider how would you describe yourself to sell your strengths, skills, and abilities.

Another consideration is doing a self-assessment regarding your personality traits and characteristics. This exercise can help you identify the type of position that will make the most sense for you in the long term. A variety of self-assessment tools are available to assist you in understanding how personality and character traits will play a role in a specific career. Some examples of personality traits or characteristics that can enhance a person's success in the sport industry include ambition, initiative, determination, willingness to learn, motivation, responsibility, confidence, creativity, and organization, to name a few. The ability to recognize the traits and characteristics that set you apart will help separate

you from others competing for the same internship or job.

Step 2. Career Exploration

Exploring internship opportunities, careers, and jobs in sport, although time consuming, can prove to be valuable for the future. The sport industry is unique in that most employers are seeking applicants with some type of work or volunteer experience. It is important to explore the variety of roles and positions in the industry as you begin your search. Doing research on positions with favorite teams and in locations that are familiar is a great way to start the search. When reviewing job or internship descriptions, it is helpful to review the "qualifications" and "responsibilities" sections to further understand what sport employers are seeking. The more informed you are, the better prepared you will be to make a decision about your own career. It can also be helpful to read professional journals, magazines, newspapers, online resources, and books that are related to your area of interest. Some additional advice includes following and connecting with sport managers on social media. This research will help you articulate how you can "fill the need" that employers in sport are seeking to meet.

Another way to explore a career and gain industry knowledge is to seek out those working in the field. One effective means of expanding your understanding of an industry, an organization, or a particular job or department is to speak to someone who is already there. The information you gain from an **informational interview** can serve as a foundation for making future career decisions, while simultaneously building a valuable network of professional connections. An informational interview with relatives, friends, acquaintances, alumni, or someone you have never met can provide great knowledge about the steps needed to gain experience or enter the field. Alumni are sometimes an overlooked resource; however, they can be valuable in the job search process. Alumni or graduates of other Sport Management programs are typically very interested in helping new professionals achieve their sport industry goals. Communicating with these industry employees can be a valuable way to determine which career path might be the most appropriate and fitting for your future.

The Informational Interviewing Process

- Prepare for an interview by asking questions related to the interviewee's career trajectory.
- Conduct your interview at the interviewee's place of business, if possible.
- Dress appropriately. This is a business meeting, so wear business attire.
- Be professional and articulate in your presentation.
- Observe the setting, the overall culture of the organization, and the relationships among the employees.
- Bring copies of your resumé and business cards (if you have them—and you should have them).
- While there, ask yourself if you would be comfortable working in this environment.
- Get business cards from each person you meet.
- Send a personally written thank-you note immediately afterward. It can be handwritten if your handwriting is legible; otherwise, it should be typed. Email is also acceptable if you have been communicating that way. Remember: Appropriate grammar is expected in an email—not the abbreviations used in text messaging, tweets, or chat conversations!
- Keep accurate notes of your interviews, as you may need to refer to them later.
- Remember to connect with these resources on social media to build your network.

Step 3. Gain Experience

In sport, one of the most important factors in obtaining a position, internship, or job is to figure out how to separate yourself from others competing for the same role. Many of your classmates will become part of your network—but also become your competition in a job hunt. It is well known that with experience comes marketability. Gaining some industry

© Jaimie Duplass/Shutterstock, Inc.

experience makes you a stronger candidate for employment. As a student, you will have numerous opportunities to experiment with different segments of the sport industry, gain new skills, and improve your current skills. One of the best ways to gain experience is to take advantage of volunteer opportunities. In some cases, you can earn college credit while experimenting with different positions in the industry. Volunteering also provides a means to make valuable connections with people working in professional sport franchises, marketing agencies, health clubs, facilities, sports commissions, sporting goods companies, and even your university athletic department. In some cases, volunteer work can be demanding and offers little or no pay, but remember that you are gaining essential skills to prepare you for your future career. The more volunteer experiences you accrue during college, the greater the possibility that an internship might lead to permanent employment.

Many organizations offer opportunities to volunteer for one-time events. These one-time or once-a-year events can provide unique skills that will set you apart from other applicants. Organizations such as the Professional Golfers' Association (PGA), the Ladies Professional Golf Association (LPGA), the U.S. Tennis Association (USTA), the Special Olympics, the National Wheelchair Basketball Association (NWBA), and local sports commissions are always seeking volunteers to assist in reoccurring events.

Some students take the initiative and create their own volunteer opportunities by communicating with professors or asking sport professionals if any opportunities exist. Remember: All experience is valuable. Gaining knowledge and experience with on-campus sport or non-sport organizations can still offer opportunities to develop valuable skills like leadership, public speaking, communication, and programming. In addition, participating in student government associations, fraternities, sororities, or other non-sport activities will build the experience and confidence needed to be successful in all industries, including sport.

Job shadowing is also an effective way to gain valuable experience in the sport industry. A job shadow provides the opportunity to learn and view a sport position or career first hand. Some of the benefits of job shadowing include identifying specific daily tasks, ability to compare careers, building confidence and knowledge of the industry, developing a more diverse network, and improving communication skills. Participating in job shadowing can be valuable to assist students who are unsure of the area in the sport industry where they would like to work. Participating in a job shadow at a variety of organizations allows students to personally experience a sport manager's daily work and observe the culture and climate of a specific organization. A job shadow experience can also lead to internships and additional networking possibilities.

Step 4. Career Planning

As a student, you likely have a current plan of completing your degree and graduating from college. In addition to getting the degree, it is important to develop a career plan for the first few years after graduation and to establish some longer-term goals for the future. One easy first step is to write down your "dream job" in the sport industry. This will help you identify a career path or career map to get to your final outcome. Once you identify the dream job, you can then work backward by listing the steps it will likely take to achieve the position. For example, if your dream job is to work as the director of athletic academic advising at Syracuse University, you may have to work as an athletic advising intern at first and plan to gain additional skills to move up the athletic advising ladder. It will be helpful to plan to do an internship in the specific area as well.

Clearly identifying goals and considering other necessary skills to be successful in each position is essential. For example, experience in mentoring or tutoring would assist you in getting a job in athletic academic advising. Doing an effective analysis of the skills and qualifications needed for your dream job will help you establish a plan of action to obtain both those specific skills and eventually the job. **Figure 20-2** represents the possible goal setting and career track of a student seeking a "dream job" of director of athletic academic advising. Each of the positions included in the figure will help you on the path to obtaining the final destination you call your "dream job."

In the career planning process, it is important to identify both short-term and long-term goals. Goal setting is the process of writing down

personal objectives and actions needed to achieve a specific plan. Goal setting will help guide your decisions and future actions, and is a key process in planning a future career. When creating your goals, it is a good idea to follow the SMART acronym. SMART stands for *Specific*, *Measurable*, *Achievable*, *Realistic*, and *Timely*.

- Specific: By writing down the dream job, you have already identified a *specific* goal.
- Measurable: You want to develop goals for which there is a *measurable* outcome— for example, to increase your professional network by 100 new contacts. You can measure your progress toward this goal by creating a LinkedIn account and increasing the connections on your professional profile.
- Achievable: Be sure to identify goals that are *achievable*. This is the place where it is important to "keep your feet on the ground." For example, if you are not

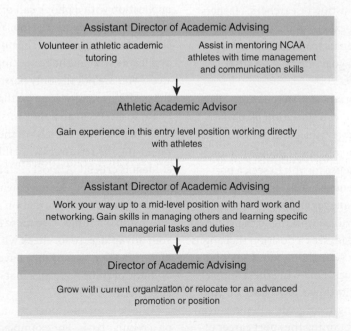

Figure 20-2 Goal setting and career track for achieving a Director of Athletic Academic Advising position

interested in going to law school, then a goal of becoming a sport lawyer would not be achievable.

- Realistic: You want to be able to *realistically* achieve the goals that you set. It is helpful to set both short-term and long-term goals to assist in recognizing and accomplishing your goals.
- Timely: Your goals should be *timely*; that is, you want to be able to set concrete deadlines and benchmarks to achieve these goals. For example, you might plan to complete your required coursework in three years and start an internship in your senior year.

Having the ability to check the goals off and set new goals will give you a sense of accomplishment and help you develop effective leadership skills. Following the SMART system of goal setting will greatly assist you in planning and preparing for your future career. In the past, the SMART goals system has been shown to be helpful in assisting researchers, teachers, mentors, public speakers, and a variety of other industry professionals to obtain and achieve effective results in goal setting (O'Neill & Conzemius, 2006).

Another important step in the career planning process is to create an action plan that aligns with your core values and personality. For example, if you are not a "people person," it does not make sense for you to seek a position working in venue suite sales or ticket sales. Such a position manages and handles customer relations, so you will be working with people on a daily basis. Instead, seek a position that aligns well with not only your abilities and goals but also your core values. Following these simple steps to create, write down, and check off your short-term and long-term goals will put you on the path toward obtaining the sport career of your dreams.

Step 5. Job Search Strategies

The process of finding a job requires time, energy, and thoughtful preparation. Now that you have a clearer picture of your skills, abilities, and goals, you are in a position to begin writing an effective resumé and accompanying cover letter. These documents should reflect the preparation you have done already and demonstrate the skills you will bring to any sport organization. It is also essential that you showcase your ability to work in a professional workplace.

The job hunt will take time, commitment, and attention to detail. Thus, it is important that you have a plan and "work" at finding a job. Make sure you keep a well-documented journal of your job search activities, especially if you are applying for many jobs in different areas. If you are called for an interview, you will need to be able to read and review the job description and qualifications before engaging in the conversation. Follow up after you submit each application with a phone call or an email within a week of applying for the job. You can be persistent, but keep in mind the number of other applicants who might be seeking the job as well—you are not the only person applying for the position—and recognize that the employer needs to attend to all applicants.

When looking for jobs in the sport industry, reviewing the resources available to you as a student is crucial. Almost certainly, your college or university Sport Management program will routinely send out information about job and internship openings. Use these connections to your advantage. Also, check with your departmental faculty, as they may have connections or know of some openings that are not publicly advertised.

Check team and sport organization websites on a regular basis. For example, *NCAA News*, which lists openings in intercollegiate athletics, is available online. Organizations such as Nike, the U.S. Olympic Committee, the National Basketball Association (NBA), and the International Paralympic Committee also list job and internship opportunities online. Traditional job websites such as Monster.com or Jobs.com may also have a limited selection of sport-related jobs. Although a number of websites and Twitter accounts provide information specifically about job opportunities in the sport industry, remember that these are often not free services, and there will be a cost associated with using them. Some sport-related job websites include TeamWork Online (www.teamworkonline.com), JobsInSports.com, WomeninSports.com, and SportsRecruitment.com.

You can also find out about jobs by attending a career fair sponsored by your school or a local sport organization. For example, Sports and Entertainment (2018) hosts an annual career fair that includes numerous sports employers, and the Tennessee Titans (2017) host an annual event for local sport employers.

Finally, your university's career services office may have a jobs database listing employment opportunities with employers that may be particularly interested in students from your school.

Other Sources of Information

Professional journals, websites, relevant books, and industry publications are valuable sources of career information, especially on current trends and plans for the future. Many of these resources have been discussed in previous chapters, such as *Street & Smith's SportsBusiness Journal*, which is required reading for any sport management student and professional. Know the sources for your particular industry segment of interest, whether it is college athletics, professional sport, event management, facility management, marketing, health and fitness, or recreational sport.

Most industry segments have an association that provides support for the profession and usually for students as well. For example, the National Intramural-Recreational Sports Association (NIRSA) is the professional organization for campus recreation. The National Association of Collegiate Directors of Athletics (NACDA) serves this purpose in intercollegiate athletics. The National Federation of State High School Associations (NFSHSA) provides information for people working in scholastic sport. These associations provide valuable connections, current relevant information, and sometimes job postings. Some have student memberships, which is a convenient way to begin your professional affiliations.

Developing a Personal Brand

Image and Presence

As a student, you are already letting people know about you. Your work ethic in the classroom, your ability to take initiative, and your attention to detail are all characteristics that you present to others. Each day, you are marketing yourself and building your personal brand image. Identifying what sets you apart in the industry is one of the most important aspects of career preparation. Indeed, building your personal brand is essential for learning and developing self-awareness and consideration of what you will be known for in the industry.

Your personal brand is what others see and how the world perceives you (Smale, 2015). Your own perception is not always the reality that others see. You already have a clear brand, whether you are aware of it or not. This brand image is how others perceive you, what they think of your abilities, and what they perceive as your best or worst assets. A common exercise to determine your brand image is to write down 10 words that describe what others think of you. What would your mother, girlfriend/boyfriend, professors, or friends say about you? What would your coach, advisor, or supervisor say? All of these words *are* your personal brand image. It may be good, it may be bad, but it already exists. It is important to know how others perceive you so that you can showcase your strengths and recognize how to work to alleviate your weaknesses.

Another important step in building your brand is to develop a strong social media presence. As you work through college, into an internship, and eventually into a job, your ability to market yourself online will become a key component of a successful job hunt. It is important to actively work to increase your positive presence on social media. Consider using LinkedIn for your professional networking.

If you have your own website or an account on a social network such as Facebook, Twitter, Foursquare, Instagram, or Pinterest, make sure the information you post there presents an image that you want a prospective employer to see. There is no way to be sure exactly who is looking at your online profile. You might imagine that if you allow only your "friends" to have access, your information is secure—but the reality is that there are always ways to find personal information online. For example, government agencies can access your profile under the auspices of the Patriot Act.

Understand the ramifications of posting questionable material (and make sure you have a clear understanding of what questionable material includes). What is funny or cute to friends may leave a very different (and negative) impression on potential employers. Oftentimes, even if the material is intended only for friends, it can be viewed by anyone with Internet access. If you are in a photo that someone else posts with your name on it, you can or will come up in an Internet search. In a recent poll conducted by Harris Interactive, 37% of hiring managers used

social networking sites to screen applicants, and an additional 11% said they intended to start doing so. The majority of employers said they were looking to see if the candidates presented themselves professionally. Potential red flags to employers include provocative photos, discussions of alcohol/drug use, complaints about former employers, and poor writing ("37 Percent of Employers," 2013). The only one way to ensure that no one has access to potentially damaging information or photographs online is to not post that material online in the first place.

Writing an Effective Resumé

Before you begin to write your **resumé**, make a list of your previous jobs, accomplishments, volunteer experiences, honors, awards, and extracurricular activities. Evaluate your activities relative to your career goals. Also on this list, describe in detail the specific skills you gained from each experience. It is essential to add transferrable, quantifiable, and actionable skills to your resumé. You want to be able to articulate these skills to prospective employers by demonstrating your significant contribution to the organization or experience. Present yourself as a potential employee, not "just a student."

Tips to Effectively Communicate and Present Your Experiences and Skills

- All experience is important. Be sure to acknowledge your accomplishments, activities, internships, and jobs.
- Use the language of the industry when appropriate. Look over the job qualifications and try to match up the language used in the posting with the language used in your resumé. Each industry has its own vocabulary, including acronyms, that may be specific to it. Using these terms demonstrates your knowledge of the industry.
- One of the most common complaints from industry professionals is that students think they have industry knowledge

when they actually do not. Make sure you accurately portray the level of knowledge you have. You do not want to "over-promise and under-deliver" on your job skills. For example, if you add math skills on the resumé, be sure you could correctly solve a linear algebra equation; if not, it might better to leave this skill off the resumé.

- Convey the skills that you can bring to the organization. It is important to consider the duties associated with a past position, but simply listing your duties or responsibilities is insufficient to demonstrate whether you can fulfill the organization's need. Simply stating duties such as "answered phones and greeted customers" will not be enough. Use action words to describe your experience—for example, "managed and assisted customers in telephone and email communications while acting as the face of the organization to ensure quality customer satisfaction."
- It is always helpful to quantify your skills when appropriate. This means reporting monetary amounts, percentages, and numbers. How many participants were part of the event you organized? How many additional corporate sponsors participated this year because of your efforts? How much money was raised? Figures give the reader a clearer picture of the depth and breadth of your experience—for example, "assisted in three fundraising events and secured $10,000 of additional sponsorship activations."
- Demonstrate the value you brought to the organization or the environment: What did you do that no one else provided? These can be personal attributes, such as time management, decision making, work ethic, leadership, or problem solving. Be specific with examples of what these attributes looked like in action.

- Be sure to consider all your skills that are transferrable to other organizations. Think of skills that you can take from one organization or position to the next. Common transferrable skills include communication, public speaking, customer relations, conflict management, sales knowledge, or computer (software, applications, and platform-specific) skills.
- Have a clean, clear, and concise resumé that highlights your skills and is presented in a format that directs the reader to specific information. It can be useful to use a template to assist in organizing your skills and experiences on this document, although a template is not required.

Resumé Outline

When it is time to write up your resumé, it helps to have an outline in mind. The following suggestions will give your resumé an organized approach that prospective employers will find helpful.

1. *Heading: Name, Address, Telephone Number, Email Address.* You want to be easy to reach, while also presenting a professional image. Your heading should be clear and easy to read. The heading can be in a block format or a line format to save space. Provide a phone number where you will get messages if you are not available and an email address that you will check regularly. Be sure to set up a professional-sounding email address and voicemail message. What professional image do you convey to a potential employer if your email address is partygirl@myschool.edu or studboy@school.com, or if your voicemail message sounds like you just woke up?

2. *Education.* Include the college or university you are attending or have graduated from, along with your degree, major, and minor. Do not include high school information.

If your university grade-point average (GPA) is strong (3.75 or higher), you should include it. If it is average, it is recommended that you leave it off. After all, you are trying to give the impression that you are "the best" and an average GPA will not send this message. Be sure to include the degree you are seeking and your anticipated graduation date, so the reader will know when you may be available for work as a permanent employee. Under the education section, you will also want to include any national or international student-exchange experience, academic awards, or honor societies. Listing the courses taken is optional, but not preferred, as you want the organization to think of you as an employee, not a student. The exception to this recommendation is if you are applying for an internship that requires academic credit. In this case, it might be relevant to list some classes that align with the internship position.

3. *Experience.* The experience section can be written in several ways. As noted earlier, experience working in sport is very important when applying for a sport position. In particular, volunteer sport-event experiences might be more relevant to the position than your retail or fast-food job. The experience you want the organization to recognize is the experience that is most relevant to the job for which you are applying. Experiences can be grouped to ensure the employer focuses on those most relevant to your career goals, such as under the headings "Sport Experience" and "Other Experience." By using this format, you can highlight all the sport industry activities in which you have participated (excluding varsity and intramural athletics). Be sure to list experiences in reverse chronological order; that is, list your most recent experiences first.

4. *Accomplishments, Honors, and Awards.* Include major accomplishments, honors, and awards demonstrating the qualities an employer looks for in a potential employee (e.g., captain of the student debate team, salesperson of the month for three consecutive months, hiked the entire Appalachian Trail). Each accomplishment addressed in your self-assessment should be considered for this section of the resumé. This heading should include a minimum of two entries. The placement of this section depends on the types of accomplishments, honors, or awards listed.

5. *Skills.* A skills section is one of the most important parts of the resumé, yet the element that people overlook the most often. If you offer a skills section, it should identify the specific skills you bring to the organization. Also, if you have skills that set you apart from others, such as the ability to speak different languages, knowledge of specific computer programs (e.g., Dreamweaver, Adobe, InDesign), or expertise with other specific computer packages and systems (e.g., desktop publishing, Web design, ticketing systems), and particularly if you have advanced skills, be sure to add them here.

6. *Activities.* These activities may be organized by the school, the local area, or the region (e.g., athletics, student government, band member, sport association memberships, leadership). They are independent of the things you do by yourself (e.g., reading, playing music, fitness), which are more like hobbies and should not appear on your resumé.

Final Resumé Tips

- Use a template to help get you started. As your skills and experiences grow, a template may not be needed. A clean format will help draw the reader's eye directly to your skills.

- Use clear headings, ALL CAPS, **bold**, underline, or *italics* to draw the eye of the reader. Also use bullet points to highlight skills.
- Organize information logically.
- Use a simple, easy-to-read font, 10 to 12 points in size.
- Tailor the information to the job you are seeking.
- Pay attention to spelling, punctuation, and grammar. Making even one spelling error may mean the employer will not consider you any further.
- Have several people proofread your resumé.
- Consult several professionals (career services, faculty, friends) to review your resumé and make comments and suggestions. The resumé is a "living" document and can and will be ever-changing as your experiences change.
- Typically, a resumé for someone just graduating with an undergraduate degree is one page. A resumé can be two pages, but the information on the second page must be important enough for the reader to turn the page. Therefore, one-page-only resumés are strongly encouraged.
- Today, most resumés will be uploaded to a database or emailed to a hiring manager. Be sure to be professional in all email communications related to a possible job, including how you address the individual to whom you are sending the email. While communication is getting less formal, this is not so with the job search. Address people as "Mr. Jenkins" or "Ms. Sullivan." Do not start emails to prospective employers with informal greetings like "Hi Tyler" or "Hi Sarah." Even during informal communications with a network professional,

always maintain a professional manner. You may submit your resumé by copying and pasting the document into the body of the email or by submitting it as an attachment. Use caution, however, because not all email programs can read attachments. The same is true for the cover letter. Resumés submitted as Word documents are easier for employers to access but also may be modified by others. If you choose to submit your application materials in PDF format, they will have a higher level of security, but may present a barrier to being read.

- Remember, the goal in submitting your resumé is to get an interview. The goal of the interview is to get the job.

Several examples of entry-level one-page resumés are presented in **Figures 20-3, 20-4**, and **20-5**. These documents provide good examples of how the information in this chapter can be utilized to create a winning resumé. You can also visit a variety of websites or search Word templates for additional examples and suggestions for resumé writing.

The Cover Letter

Each resumé must be accompanied by a **cover letter**. This document must also be professional and informative without being identical to your resumé. There is no one model for a particular job application. Each letter should address the specific concerns of the organization to which you are applying. Consequently, you should expect to thoroughly research each organization and, after careful analysis, write a letter that demonstrates your value to the prospective employer.

The cover letter should be written using a formal business letter format. Structure your one-page letters of application to consist of three or four paragraphs:

- *Paragraph 1:* Describe the position for which you are applying and explain why

JOSHUA P. JOHNSON
123 Flexnor Way • Louisville, KY 40000 •
Phone: (303) 123-4567 • joshuajohnson@aol.com

EDUCATION

University of Cincinnati   **Cincinnati, OH**
Bachelor of Science: Business   Expected Graduation 2020
Dean's List, Honor Roll

WORK EXPERIENCE

Sports Academy Inc.

Associate   *Summer-Fall 2015*
- Managed stock and coordinated sport merchandise
- Assisted customers with point-of-sale service
- Trained 10 new employees on register and customer management

Runza's

Kitchen Crew   *Summer-Fall 2014*
- Worked a variety of kitchen positions from fryer to buns
- Assisted in the coordination and completion of all service orders
- Trained new employees on several kitchen positions and end of shift close procedures

SPLASH CITY USA

Grounds Crew   *Summer 2012*
- Assisted with customer questions and customer services
- Worked with daily clean-up of grounds, tables, restrooms and children's area
- Learned to work in a team environment

VOLUNTEER EXPERIENCE

Ironman Kentucky
- Assisted with registration of athletes and day-of-event operations   2012–2015

National FastPitch Coaches Association
- Assisted with coordination of events and management of coaches and players
  during 2-day event   2012–2013

Food Bank of the Rockies
- Assisted with coordination of delivery of food and supplies to at-risk population   2012–2013

Mountain City High School

Science Assistant   **2012–2013**
- Assisted faculty in organizing files and forms for students

Plainview Academy K-8

Track Manager   *2011–2012*
- Assisted in organizing files and forms for student-athletes
- Helped manage and time daily track & field and soccer practices

ACTIVITIES

Alpha Chapter of Rho Kappa   **2011–2012**
- Active member of Social Studies Honor Society

Varsity Band
- Participated in Junior Varsity band and marching band   2011–2012
- Participated in Varsity marching band   2012–2013

Figure 20-3 Sample Resume #1

BRANDON L. PARKS
123 West Avenue Apt. 23 • brandonlparks@texas.edu • 45 Stonybrook Drive •
Denver, CO 12345 • (807) 321-0000 • Oxford, IL 54321

EDUCATION

University of Texas,   **Anticipated Graduation May 2018**

Bachelor of Science in *Sport Administration*
Minor: *Business Administration*

PROFESSIONAL EXPERIENCE

University of Texas Athletics   **August 2015–Present**

Sports Information Intern

- Provide support with promotion, publicity, and game day responsibilities for 23 NCAA sports
- Execute multimedia post-game responsibilities, including shooting and editing coach and player press conferences
- Serve as a liaison for video highlights to be posted through digital platforms
- Produce athletic publications such as game programs and media guides
- Monitor Texas Athletics' social media sites (i.e. Twitter)

SPORT RELATED EXPERIENCE

Oxford High School   **March 2012–June 2014**

Sophomore & Varsity Baseball Manager

- Deciphered plays to track in statistic application and scoring book
- Recorded film of players to enhance on-field performance
- Attended games and practices to assist with statistics

SPORT EVENT EXPERIENCE

KFC Yum! Center   **October 2016**

Minnesota vs. Miami NBA Preseason Game

- Distributed statistics to team benches and front office executives
- Transcribed coaches pre-game and post-game interviews

Cardinal Arena   **December 2015**

NCAA Women's Volleyball First & Second Rounds

- Transcribed post-game statements from teams
- Delivered statistics to the scorer's table and media

HONORS & LEADERSHIP

Sport Studies Student Association, **University of Texas**   *October 2015–Present*

University of Texas Kappa Sigma Fraternity   *September 2014–Present*

Scholarship Chair

- Monitor the grades of the Chapter
- Record the required study hours of 100+ members
- Help struggling members find assistance from excelling peers

National Scholars Award, **University of Texas**   *August 2014–Present*

2 Semesters Dean's List, **University of Texas**   *December 2014–April 2016*

North Suburban Conference All-Academic, **Oxford High School**   *June 2014*

Figure 20-4 Sample Resume #2

JOHN SAMPLE

8300 Example Drive • Louisville, KY 40222 •
Phone: (303)-593-6049 • E-Mail: jjsample@louisville.edu

EDUCATION

University of Louisville   **Louisville, KY**
Bachelor of Science, Sport Administration   Graduation 2018

RELEVANT WORK & VOLUNTEER EXPERIENCE

Lakeside State Park   **Louisville, KY**

Recreational Aide   *05/2016–09/2016*

- Provided friendly service to park visitors everyday
- Assisted in keeping the Activities Building and the park itself clean
  and presentable for park visitors
- Set up sporting events weekly and took hundreds of dollars in for said events
- Handled hundreds of dollars weekly
- Kept gardens tidy through yard work
- Helped solve problems with customers everyday, in person and over the phone.

Hoop Stars Academy Basketball   **Louisville, KY**

Volunteer Assistant Coach   *10/2015–Present*

- Volunteer assistant coach for the 6th grade boys basketball team
- Assisted the head coach in practices and games
- Kept score book periodically for Whitefield's middle school basketball league

NWBA National Tournament   **Louisville, KY**

Volunteer   *04/2017*

- Assisted with checking 90+ teams into tournament
- Kept time and score for multiple games at both the adult and youth level

SKILLS

- Great oral communicator with coworkers, customers, and bosses
- Responsible hard-worker who takes pride in his work and pays attention to detail
- Eager and enthusiastic to learn and take on new and exciting challenges
- Extremely confident in the work place
- Manages time well and is exceedingly prompt
- Able to work in a team exceptionally well
- Proficient in Microsoft Word and PowerPoint
- Proven Leader

ADDITIONAL WORK EXPERIENCE

SuperStores USA   **Louisville, KY**

Store Associate   *09/2016–Present*

- Provide great customer service
- Handle thousands of dollars in transactions daily
- Check customers out at a pace of 1,100+ items per hour
- Operate electronic pallet jacks
- Stock store shelves

Figure 20-5 Sample Resume #3

you think you are a good fit for the position. It is important to mention the specific position, as many organizations may be filling several positions at once. For example, you might say: "Please accept my cover letter and enclosed resumé for your open position of Assistant to the Director of Events with the Las Vegas Raiders. I fit the needs of the position based on my experience working in my university's football events for the past three years." Demonstrate your knowledge of the organization. By including a reference to the company, you form a positive connection from the start.

- *Paragraph 2:* Discuss your strongest qualifications that match the position as you understand it. Provide concrete evidence or specific examples of how you can fill the needs of the organization. Discuss your experience as it relates to the specific job description. Use examples when applicable.
- *Paragraph 3 (optional):* Reinforce the qualifications presented in your resumé, but do not repeat them exactly. Show your strong writing skills. This is a good opportunity to show your soft skills and your personality.
- *Paragraph 3 or 4:* Thank the reader for his or her time and consideration. Request an interview. Mention that you will call after a specific period of time (one week is about right) to discuss an appointment, and follow up accordingly.

Always generate your own unique job search correspondence. This is an opportunity to demonstrate your value to the employer, your professionalism, and your strong writing abilities. Be sure to address the letter to a specific individual by using his or her appropriate business title and address. Some job opening postings will ask you to send your materials to the human resources office, and there will be no specific person's name listed. If this is the case, when you send your materials, you should address the person

as "Dear Hiring Manager" or "Dear Internship Director"; avoid using "Dear Sir" or "To Whom It May Concern." Adapt your letter for each situation, and always be able to offer specific examples to confirm the main points of your experiences. Finally, always produce error-free copy. As with your resumé, one spelling mistake in a cover letter can mean the employer will no longer consider your application.

Use the cover letter to enhance your resumé, not restate it. If the job search is a marketing campaign, then this letter is an integral part of that endeavor. You are the product, and, unlike the sport product, you want to be positively predictable. You do have total control over the product—that is, how you present yourself. Show this quality in your application package by making it professional and confident.

The "Elevator Pitch"

In the course of looking for employment in the sport industry, there will be times when you will meet potential employers or influential people in an informal setting. When they find out you are a job seeker and ask you about yourself, it is important to be prepared with an answer that is professional, is focused, and projects confidence about you and your experiences. A 30-second to 1-minute conversation, sometimes referred to as an "elevator pitch," is a clear, concise, carefully planned, and well-practiced description about your skills that can be told in the amount of time it might take to ride an elevator with someone between floors. Collamer (2013) suggests an elevator pitch should clearly describe your job target and effectively articulate the confidence that makes you a great candidate for a possible position. To effectively write a successful elevator pitch, you must consider the following questions:

Who are you?
Briefly describe who you are and how you got here. Keep it simple and brief.

What makes you unique? What do you have to offer? Which special skills do you possess that are special to this industry? What is your specialty?

Discuss what makes you special, unique, or different. Which specific qualities, skills, or abilities set you apart from others? Find the need and fill the need. Provide an example of at least one success. For example, if you know this organization is falling short in its ability to bring families to the ballpark, you might highlight your experience and ability to increase sales of family 4-packs from a previous position.

What do you have that your competition does not? What is your competitive advantage?

Each of us has a special skill that makes us unique. Briefly discuss who you are competing against and what sets you apart. In the job hunt, success is your competitive advantage. Simply being a Sport Management major and having sales experience might not be enough; instead, you need to effectively communicate how you are *different* and why you have an advantage over others. Do you have a better work ethic, a key network connection, excellent social media knowledge, recruiting experience, or programming or software skills?

Many researchers have offered a variety of tips and tricks that can help you develop the most effective elevator-pitch presentation (Allawos, n.d.; Collamer, 2013; Klaff, 2011). As each pitch situation may be different, a variety of formats may be effective. Many believe the elevator pitch can be the most effective and useful tool to sell yourself in the industry.

Successful "Elevator Pitch"

The following are characteristics of a successful "elevator pitch":

- *150–250 words or 60 seconds:* The pitch should be no longer than 60 seconds.

- *A "hook":* Open your pitch by getting some attention with a "hook"—that is, a statement or question that piques the interest of the listener. For example, "Did you know that in 2016, 68% of student-athletes reported sending 10 or more snaps a day on SnapChat?" (DeShazo, 2016).

- *Finding the need and filling the need:* Find the organization's need and explain how you (with your skills and experience) fill that need. For example: "Most college athletic programs need help teaching student-athletes to effectively use social media platforms. With my extensive knowledge working with college students and athletic departments on the use, measurements, and analytics of social media, I can help increase student-athletes' understanding of changing media platforms and how to present themselves in a professional manner."

- *Passion:* Be sure you are energetic and passionate, and show interest in this potential career. Sport employers are seeking energy and dedication from applicants, and this is a chance to let your personality shine. The pitch offers a great opportunity to present your personality, creativity, and positive attitude in addition to showcasing your skills and abilities.

- *The "ask":* At the end of your pitch, you must make a request or an *ask* to connect again. For example: "When can we get together to discuss how I can become the next social media professional at your organization?"

Collamer (2013) suggests the following nine steps will be effective for developing a successful elevator speech:

1. Clarify your job target.

2. Put it on paper.

3. Format it.

4. Tailor the pitch to them, not you.

5. Eliminate industry jargon.

6. Read your pitch out loud.

7. Practice, practice, practice (then solicit feedback).

8. Prepare a few variations.

9. Nail it with confidence.

A well-prepared and practiced elevator pitch can help you articulate your skills and develop a clear understanding of how you "fit" into the industry. It is not likely that you will be riding an elevator with a sport industry executive, but you will be asked about what value you bring to the organization. Having this clear description of yourself prepared in advance will help you clearly explain the advantages you have over other candidates in the applicant pool. You will always be prepared and professional.

Pitch Example 1

Did you know the latest NCAA APR scores showed overall improvement in Division I baseball, football, and men's and women's basketball from the previous year? To keep this upward trend, you need me in your athletic department. I know here at your school you strive for your student-athletes to not only perform their best on the field, but also excel in the classroom. I would be able to provide your student-athletes with opportunities for community outreach, preparation for graduation, assistance with progress toward their degree, and career planning. Over the past two years, I have had experience in academics specifically by being a teaching assistant, working as a student orientation counselor, and working as an intern in athletic compliance. If I could have 30 minutes of your time, I would like to share more about these experiences and discuss how I can help grow your athletic department to continue the upward trend of strong academics among student-athletes.

Pitch Example 2

Did you know that nearly three-quarters of today's hiring managers claim recent graduates are not prepared to sell their skills in the job market (Pianin, 2014)? My name is Regina Presley, and I am excited to tell you about how I have helped hundreds of students transition from college into the workforce by developing a "resumé that sells." I have worked in education and training for the past 20 years, and have spent many of those years evaluating, reviewing, and training students to build their personal brand. I'm sure you will agree there is a growing need for graduates who possess the strong skills they present on their resumé and in an interview. My goal is to focus on customizing each student's career aspirations to help identify the ABCs—accomplishments, brevity, and competence (skills)—that will set him or her apart from the crowd. With my proven method of teaching resumé success, your students will be guaranteed to obtain better careers with higher incomes in a shorter amount of time. So, when would you like to get together to further discuss how I can help your students achieve their dream jobs?

References

You should always assume that employers will want to check your **references** before they make you a job offer. Most employers will want to speak to one to three references; therefore, your list should include three to five people. Include each person's name, organization, title, address, email, and telephone number. Your references should be able to speak articulately and comfortably about you. If someone seems uncomfortable with the idea of doing a verbal interview, give the person an "out" by suggesting that perhaps he or she would prefer to write a letter instead. It is not just what your references say, but how they say it that makes the difference.

As an undergraduate, your references should include faculty members, advisors, coaches, and previous or current employers. Unless they specify otherwise, potential employers are typically not interested in personal references. Choose people who know you well enough to address your true abilities to perform the job successfully and who will speak highly of your skills. At various events, you may briefly meet prominent people in the sport industry who say to you, "Let me know how I can help you in the future." Avoid the temptation to put a "big name" on your list if that person truly does not know your daily work ethic. Name-dropping can potentially backfire, costing you more than it helps you.

You should have conversations with all the people who will serve as your references, so make an appointment to see them or speak to them on the phone. You want your references to have a good idea of the work you are seeking and why you are qualified for the position. They should also have a sense of your personality, your goals, and your strengths and weaknesses as they apply to the job.

Make sure your references have a copy of your current resumé and keep them informed of your career progress. They should have an expectation that someone will be calling about you—the employer's contact should not come as a surprise. It is also important that you tell your references whether you receive an offer and if you accept it.

Employers check references only if they are seriously considering making an offer. References do have an influence on the outcome, so choose yours wisely. Also remember that the sport industry is a small network of people, many of whom know each other even if they work in different industry segments. It is common for potential employers to go "off the list" to talk to someone they know whom you did not include on your references list. This possibility

is important to remember as you are entering the industry. You want to make sure that all people in the industry will speak highly of you for future job possibilities.

The Job Interview

The job **interview** is your opportunity to demonstrate to a prospective employer that you are the best candidate for the position. It is also a chance to learn more about the organization, the position, and opportunities for advancement—in short, to determine whether you are interested in continuing to pursue employment with the organization. The keys to an effective interview are threefold: interview preparation, the interview, and the follow-up.

Preparation

Preparation for the interview is critical. Just as a football team practices for many hours during the week to be successful in the 3-hour game on Saturday, so, too, must you prepare. To present a clear picture of who you are and what you have to offer, you must take time to assess yourself. Be honest with yourself. Evaluate the person you are, your skills, and your characteristics, and determine what sets you apart. Be familiar with your strengths and weaknesses and be able to articulate them when asked. You should be able to discuss your strengths with confidence and identify at least one weakness. You also want to speak about how you plan to overcome this weakness. For example, you might say, "One of my weaknesses is procrastination. I have been working to correct this by making lists, prioritizing tasks, and managing my personal time more efficiently." By assessing yourself honestly, you will be able to explain how you will be a great employee.

It is also important that you research the position and the organization. It is common for an employer to ask if the interviewee knows the mission of the organization. To be able to answer this question, you must have done some research on the organization, job, and position. Simply knowing the statistics of the team or the players is not enough to impress the organization. You want to make sure you can articulate how you fit into the role of a business-oriented job. Here are some potential information sources to research organizations:

- Make use of the Internet, which is a prime information source for almost every industry. Most sport organizations have their own home page. It is also possible to use the Internet to gather valuable information regarding the competition.
- Read newspapers and professional journals.
- Follow the organization and/or its executives on Twitter.
- Talk to someone who currently works for the organization. Perhaps that person had the job for which you are applying or worked with the person who did.
- Speak to clients, customers, and competitors.

In addition to reviewing your skills and researching the organization, you should practice answering interview questions. Many interviewers will ask very similar questions. The more you prepare, the better you will perform in the interview. A simple Internet search of the most commonly asked interview questions will help you prepare. It is also advised that you practice with a friend, family member, or career advisor. Again, the practice of speaking out loud about your skills and experience will greatly benefit you in the actual interview.

The Interview

During the actual interview, you are always being observed. For this reason, it is important to present a positive and professional attitude throughout the entire interview process. The best predictor of future performance is past performance in a similar situation. Interviewers

are looking not just for particular skills, but for the personal attributes of a successful professional. What is it an employer wants to know about a candidate that is relative to the job? Characteristics of a successful employee include oral and written communication skills, adaptability, ability to learn, critical thinking, initiative, creativity and innovation, integrity, interpersonal skills, ability to work with diverse populations, decisiveness, leadership, planning and organizing, sensitivity, time management, stress tolerance, tenacity, and high standards of performance.

Interviews are limited in time, so it is essential to be clear about your skills and abilities. Remember the old cliché: "You get only one chance to make a first impression." As in any new relationship, the first goal is to establish a good rapport.

- Dress appropriately. Appropriate attire for an interview is a suit. The sport industry may seem like a casual industry, but it is important to present yourself in the best possible way. It is better to be overdressed than underdressed.
- Arrive at least 10 minutes early and relax while you are waiting to meet with the interviewer(s).
- Shake hands firmly and smile, making eye contact with each person you meet.
- Engage in conversation, but be careful not to talk too much. It is often hard when nervous to not speak incessantly.
- Be friendly, warm, courteous, and interested.

One common interview method is known as behavioral interviewing. During a behavioral interview, the interviewer will ask questions probing for examples of specific, relevant behaviors. Questions may be phrased to extract the most telling response from the interviewee.

Here are some sample questions from a behavioral interview:

- We have all experienced times when we felt overwhelmed in a class or a project. Tell me about a time when you have felt overwhelmed or burdened by a project or assignment. How did you handle the situation?
- What would you identify as the biggest achievement of your college career? What did you do to contribute to that achievement?
- Tell me about a time that you managed a conflict with a former employee, supervisor, or another student. How did you manage the situation so you could continue to work with that person?

In each of these examples, the interviewer is asking the interviewee to describe a specific situation or task, the action that took place, and the outcome or consequence of that action. Quality responses should not include feelings or opinions, but rather statements of fact about your actual behavior in the situation and your ability to produce a positive result. Spend some time identifying specific situations you have encountered in the past, and you will be prepared for most of the questions you are asked. If the employer asks a theoretical question such as "Describe your strengths and weaknesses," you can still respond with a situation demonstrating the strengths you want to showcase or describing how you make accommodations for your weaknesses.

In addition to questions you can answer using the behavioral format, be ready for some of the old standards: "Tell me about yourself" or "How would your friends describe you?" Be honest. When answering interview questions, honesty is the best policy. Also, take advantage of these open-ended questions to discuss the skills and unique abilities that set you apart. It is not only what you say that impresses an interviewer, but also how you conduct yourself. The recruiter is trying to find out how well you know yourself and how comfortable you are with who you are.

Again, the best predictor of future performance is past performance in a similar situation. Be prepared with anecdotes demonstrating your behaviors in a positive light. Think of specific events or examples in which you overcame obstacles, managed conflict, or had to think outside of the box. Each of these examples will help you effectively communicate your abilities. Remember, examples speak volumes. Think of one of two examples that help demonstrate what the interviewer is asking.

© Dmitriy Shironosov/Shutterstock, Inc.

Once the actual interview begins, concentrate on communicating effectively:

- Listen attentively. Restate the question if you are unsure what the interviewer is actually asking.
- Answer questions directly, providing examples. Try not to overexplain.
- Make good eye contact with the interviewer.
- Talk openly about yourself, your accomplishments, and your goals.
- Maintain a positive, interested demeanor.
- Ask appropriate questions. Demonstrate interest in, and knowledge of, the organization. More than 60% of employers surveyed

in a recent article in *The Wall Street Journal* said that "applicants ought to be more familiar with the company and industry, and must ask better questions in interviews" (Gee, 2017, para. 5).

- Prepare at least five questions that you plan to ask the interviewers. This is a good opportunity to get information about the position and the organization, and asking questions also shows interest in your future with the business.
- Make certain you have a clear idea of the position for which you are interviewing.
- Always get a business card or a means of connecting with the interviewer later.

Illegal Questions

U.S. law prevents employers from asking certain questions in interview situations. Interviewers must limit themselves to gathering information that will help them decide whether a person can perform the functions of a particular job. Therefore, questions seeking more personal information—for example, marital status, sexual orientation, national origin or citizenship, age, disability, or arrest record—do not have to be answered. The decision to answer or not is made by the interviewee. Although most interviewers will not ask these questions, you should think about how you will respond if the situation arises. If you feel particularly uncomfortable, discuss this issue with a career counselor on your campus or one of your sport management faculty members before your first interview.

Follow-Up

The follow-up to an interview is an indication of your interest and maturity. As part of the follow-up, do the following:

- Assess the interview. Were all your questions answered? Was there anything you could have presented more clearly? It is common to send an email asking additional follow-up questions that were not discussed. This is a good way to keep the lines of communication open.
- Write a thank-you note immediately, reinforcing your interest and qualifications for the position. An email note is acceptable, thanking the person for his or her time and consideration of you for the position. A handwritten note is more memorable.
- Call the interviewer if you have something to add or if you have additional questions. This action shows you are enthusiastic, persistent, and interested.
- Call the sport organization if you have not heard from someone there in the time the interviewer indicated you would hear back.

If you are well prepared, aware of your competencies and areas requiring development, understand the type of work environment you would prefer, and believe you have the necessary skills and abilities, you will have a successful interview. When qualifications of competing candidates are relatively equal, interviewers are inclined to hire people who have been honest and straightforward. Be yourself.

What Makes a Successful Candidate?

A successful candidate exhibits certain traits and skills. Some of these include the following:

- *Preparation:* Knowledge of and interest in the employer and the specific job opening.
- *Personal or soft skills:* Confidence, adaptability, flexibility, maturity, energy, drive, enthusiasm, initiative, and empathy.
- *Goal orientation:* Ability to set short- and long-term goals.
- *Communication skills:* Written and oral, including listening and nonverbal communication skills.
- *Organizational skills:* Teamwork, leadership, problem identification and solving, critical thinking, and time management.

- *Experience:* Ability to articulate the relevance of previous experience to the position for which you are interviewing.
- *Professional appearance:* Business suits for men and women alike. Remember, some people have allergic reactions to perfumes and colognes, so it is best not to use them prior to your interview. Tattoos? Show them at your own risk. They may not matter to some people, but they will to others.
- *Cross-cultural awareness:* Multiple languages, international or intercultural experience.
- *Computer skills:* Website development, statistical packages, word processing, spreadsheets, social media, and desktop publishing.

Summary

Finding a job in the sport industry can be a challenging task, but the results can be rewarding. This chapter presents information about the realities of looking for a job in the sport industry and speaks honestly about the difficult challenges that exist when you are trying to break into sport management. This chapter, while highlighting some of the barriers you will face, also gives you some proven tools to use that can help you along the way. Incorporating the techniques included in this chapter, such as networking, informational interviewing, resumé and cover letter writing, preparing an elevator pitch, and interviewing skills, will help increase your marketability in the sport industry.

Recommended Activities

1. Describe the career preparation process and the steps to take to begin planning for a career in the sport industry.

2. Make a list of your strengths and a list of your weaknesses. It can also be useful to do a SWOT (strengths, weaknesses, opportunities, threats) analysis to review what might be an opportunity in the industry and what may be a threat to student success. Be sure to identify how you will overcome the weaknesses and ideally turn them into strengths.

3. Make a list of skills. These can be soft skills, such as dependability, hard work, and dedication, or hard skills, such as ability to speak two languages or knowledge of the InDesign and Dreamweaver software programs.

4. Make a list of your accomplishments. For each accomplishment, discuss the skill(s) or professional strengths gained from the experience. For example: Senior Vice President of Delta Kappa Phi—gained skills in leadership, motivation, and organization.

5. Write down both your short-term goals and your long-term goals, and discuss how you plan to achieve these goals.

6. Research three internships or jobs in the sport organization or industry segment where you intend to work. Look at the qualifications and requirements for the positions. Identify which of these you possess and make a list of the ones you still need to obtain.

7. Research resumé templates. Print out three of these templates, and discuss with a classmate what you like and dislike about those formats.

8. Plan and schedule an informational interview with a person in a job you may seek in the future. Develop 10 questions that you would ask this professional to prepare for the interview. Write up a one-page paper summarizing the interview with this sport industry professional.

9. Prepare an elevator pitch for a specific job highlighting your skills and abilities and present it to the class.

10. Write a practice cover letter for a specific internship or entry-level job opening.

11. Do a mock interview with a classmate. Do an Internet search for common interview questions. Write out the 10 questions most commonly found in your search and ask

them of a classmate. Have him or her ask you 10 additional questions. Compare and contrast your answers.

12. Write a cover letter, resumé, references, and thank-you letter. Do a peer review of another student's work and make suggestions about how he or she could use the content in this chapter to improve these documents.

Key Terms

cover letter, informational interview, internship, interview, network, references, resumé

References

37 percent of employers use Facebook to pre-screen applicants, new study says. (2013, April 20). *Huffington Post*. Retrieved from http://www.huffingtonpost.com/2012/04/20/employers-use-facebook-to-pre-screen-applicants_n_1441289.html

Allawos, M. (n.d.). The 30 second elevator pitch. Retrieved from http://www.allawosandcompany.com/images/the_30_second_elevator_pitch.pdf

Belson, K. (2012, February 29). Studying to release your inner George Costanza. *New York Times*. Retrieved from http://www.nytimes.com/2012/03/01/education/learning-sports-management-in-graduate-school.html

Chicago Press Release Services. (2009, October 14). Chicago 2016 Olympic bid team now unemployed, in search of new jobs. Retrieved from http://chicagopressrelease.com/news/chicago-2016-olympic-bid-team-now-unemployed-in-search-of-new-jobs

Collamer, N. (2013, February 4). The perfect elevator pitch to land a job. *Forbes*. Retrieved from http://www.forbes.com/sites/nextavenue/2013/02/04/the-perfect-elevator-pitch-to-land-a-job/

DeShazo, K. (2016). 2016 social media use of student athletes [Infographic]. Retrieved from http://www.fieldhousemedia.net/2016-social-media-use-of-student-athletes-infographic/

Gee, K. (2017). Where college seniors are falling short. *Wall Street Journal*. Retrieved from https://www.wsj.com/articles/where-college-seniors-are-falling-short-1493118000?mod=e2fb

Helyar, J. (2006, September 16). Failing effort. Retrieved from https://www.wsj.com/articles/SB115813093294561776

Klaff, O. (2011). *Pitch anything: An innovative method for presenting, persuading and winning the deal*. New York, NY: McGraw-Hill.

Misner, I. (2012, November 23). A new definition of networking. Retrieved from https://www.entrepreneur.com/article/225067

O'Neill, J., & Conzemius, A. (2006). *The power of SMART goals*. Bloomington, IN: Solution Tree Press.

Pacers Sports and Entertainment. (2018). Pacers Sports & Entertainment Career Fair, Monday, February 5. Retrieved from http://www.nba.com/pacers/careerfair

Pianin, E. (2014). The surprising reason college grads can't get a job. *Fiscal Times*. Retrieved from http://www.thefiscaltimes.com /Articles/2014/01/29/Surprising-Reason -College-Grads-Can-t-Get-Job

Professional Baseball Employment Opportunities. (2013). Get started in Nashville and launch your baseball career at the 19th annual PBEO Job Fair. Retrieved from http://www.pbeo .com/12_job_fair.aspx

Smale, T. (2015, September 23). 5 steps to build your personal brand. Retrieved from https: //www.entrepreneur.com/article/250924

Tennessee Titans. (2017). Tennessee Titans Sports Industry Career Fair. Retrieved from http:// www.titansonline.com/tickets/career-fair.html

Glossary

absolutism   The belief that moral precepts are universal, that is, applicable to all circumstances.

account executive   An executive who coordinates all of the marketing and sponsorship activities for sport properties. This person, also called a sports marketing representative, will be involved with an agency's corporate clients by servicing their needs and leading sales and marketing efforts.

activation   The commitment of financial resources in support of a company's sponsorship through promotion and advertising that thematically includes the sport property's imagery.

administrative law   The body of law created by rules, regulations, orders, and decisions of administrative bodies.

affiliate   A local or regional broadcaster or station that carries some or all of the programming of the network.

aftermarketing   Customer retention activities that take place after a purchase has been made; the process of providing continued satisfaction and reinforcement to individuals or organizations who are past or current customers.

Age Discrimination in Employment Act (ADEA)   A 1967 law that prohibits employment discrimination on the basis of age.

agency   A relationship in which one party (the agent) agrees to act for and under the direction of another (the principal).

agent   A party acting for and under the direction of another (the principal).

a la carte   To select options individually.

ambush marketing   A strategy that involves placement of marketing material and promotions at an event that attracts consumer and media attention, without becoming an official sponsor of that event.

Americans with Disabilities Act (ADA)   A 1990 law that has as its intent the prevention of discrimination against people with disabilities in employment, public services, transportation, public accommodations, and telecommunications services; it protects employees with disabilities at all stages of the employment relationship.

analytics center of excellence (ACE)   A centralized structure that implements sport analytics into an organization where all analytics personnel are grouped together fulfilling tasks across multiple departments.

ancillary revenue   Proceeds from the sale of food and beverage, merchandise, parking charges, ticket fees, and sponsorships.

antitrust law   The body of state and federal law designed to protect trade and commerce from unlawful restraint, monopolies, price fixing, and price discrimination.

arenas   Indoor facilities that host sporting and entertainment events; they are usually built to accommodate one or more prime sports tenants.

Arledge, Roone   An executive at ABC TV who was responsible for the development of sport broadcasting so that it appealed as entertainment to an audience beyond hard-core fans.

assets   Things that an organization owns that can be used to generate future revenues, such as equipment, stadiums, and league memberships.

Association for Intercollegiate Athletics for Women (AIAW)   A governance organization for women's athletics, established in 1971, that emphasized the educational needs of students and rejected the commercialized men's athletics model. It became effectively defunct in 1982.

athletic footwear   Branded and unbranded athletic shoes for casual wear or active usage, outdoor/hiking sports boots, and sport sandals.

back-end   Computer tools that usually consist of a server, an application, and a database. These tools power the data management functions of a given project.

balance sheet   A financial statement that shows the assets, liabilities, and owners' equity of an organization.

barnstorming tours   The travel and appearances at events of star athletes and teams to promote the popularity of a particular sport.

benefit selling   A sales approach that involves the promotion and creation of new benefits or the promotion and enhancement of existing benefits to offset existing perceptions or assumed negatives related to the sport product or service.

Big Ten Conference   An athletic conference formed in 1895 by college and university faculty representatives (under the name Intercollegiate Conference of Faculty Representatives) to create student eligibility rules for football. The athletic conference has a 100-year tradition of shared practices and policies that enforce the priority of academics and emphasize the values of integrity, fairness, and competitiveness in all aspects of its student-athletes' lives.

blackout   A sporting contest is not televised in the home market if the game itself is not a sellout. This practice is used to encourage future ticket sales.

bona fide occupational qualification (BFOQ)   An employment qualification that, although it may discriminate against a protected class (i.e., sex, religion, or national origin), relates to an essential job duty and is considered reasonably necessary for the normal operation of a business or organization and therefore not illegal.

bonds   Financial instruments typically issued by large corporate entities or governments that allow the borrower to borrow large dollar amounts, usually for a relatively long period of time.

booking director   A person responsible for scheduling events for a facility.

Boras, Scott   Founder of the corporation that bears his name and an innovator in baseball representation. He is known for his free-market philosophy, the use of data in negotiations, his level of preparation, and his knowledge of the game and rules.

box office director   A person responsible for the sale of all tickets to events as well as the collection of all ticket revenue.

branding   The cumulative view, beliefs, and associations of consumers and others about a brand. It evokes the idea that a consumer is not just purchasing a product or a service, but also the impression of that product or service.

breach   The breaking of a promise in a contract.

broadband   High-speed Internet connectivity that is supported by fiber-optic cable.

broadcasting   To transmit through signals by way of radio or television.

broadcasting rights   The property interest possessed under law that allows an entity to broadcast sound and/or images of an event.

bubble   Occurs when prices rise steeply in a short time, followed by a sudden decrease in value when the marketplace "corrects" itself.

budgeting   The process of developing a written plan of revenues and expenses for a particular accounting cycle; the budget specifies available funds among the many purposes of an organization to control spending and achieve organizational goals.

bundling   Packaging various options together so the customer pays one price for all of the options.

business analytics   A subset of sports analytics, which is applied to strategic initiatives such as ticket pricing, customer relationship management, social media marketing, or facility financing.

business development   A business function focused on strategy, creating strategic partnerships, and relationships with suppliers and customers. This function focuses on strategic deal-making with a goal of increasing sales, attracting new clients, and expanding a company's long-term business success or scope.

business intelligence   A term to describe projects rich in data storage, analysis, and operations.

campus recreation   Includes any recreational activity provided by colleges and universities, ranging from exercise facilities and fitness programming to club and intramural sports and coordinated outdoor recreation activities.

capacity   The ability to understand the nature and effects of one's actions.

Carnegie Reports of 1929   Documents by the Carnegie Foundation that examined intercollegiate athletics and identified many academic abuses, recruiting abuses, payments to student-athletes, and commercialization of athletics. These reports pressured the NCAA to evolve from a group that developed rules for competition into an organization for overseeing all aspects of intercollegiate athletics.

cash-flow budgeting   Accounting for the receipt and timing of all sources and expenditures of money.

cause-related marketing effort   An event sponsored by a corporation for the purpose of generating money for a particular cause.

clean feed   A video signal that does not have added graphics and text.

Club Managers Association of America (CMAA)   Organization composed of club professionals, department heads, and certified professionals in food and beverage management (including chefs, cooks, and bartenders); sport management professionals (golf, tennis, and aquatics professionals); grounds and golf course superintendents; building and engineering technicians/specialists; and other specialty staff members who report to a club's general manager.

club   Sport management structures composed of a limited number of members who organize events, standardize rules, and settle disputes.

club system   A sport development system whereby young athletes move up within the same club.

coaches   People who instruct or train players in the fundamentals of a sport and direct team strategy.

code of conduct   Statements of a company, business, organization, or profession that explicitly outline and explain the principles under which it operates and provide guidelines for employee behavior; also called code of ethics.

code of ethics   Statements of a company, business, organization, or profession that explicitly outline and explain the principles under which it operates and provide guidelines for employee behavior; also called code of conduct.

collective bargaining agreement (CBA)   A legal agreement between an employer and a labor union that regulates the hours, wages, and terms and conditions of employment.

commercial breaks   Breaks in play during a sport contest to allow for commercial advertising (e.g., all NFL games are required to have five 2-minute commercial breaks per quarter).

commercial formats   Advertising breaks provided for national commercials, sold by the networks, and local advertisements, sold by local stations or cable systems.

Commission on Intercollegiate Athletics for Women (CIAW)   A governance organization for women's athletics created in 1966; forerunner of the Association for Intercollegiate Athletics for Women (AIAW).

Commission on Sport Management Accreditation (COSMA)   A specialized accrediting body launched by NASSM and NASPE that promotes and recognizes excellence in sport management education in colleges and universities at the baccalaureate and graduate levels.

commissioner   The administrative head of a professional sport league.

communication skills   Oral and written skills for presenting facts and information in an organized, courteous fashion.

community-based recreation   Recreational activities at the local level, such as those offered by community agencies and local parks and recreation departments.

competitive balance   The notion that the outcome of a competition is uncertain, and thus provides greater entertainment value for spectators.

competitive balance tax   A tax on teams that exceed a preset threshold on team salary spending for a given year. Teams whose payrolls exceed the threshold will be taxed and often the tax rate increases based on the number of previous consecutive years that a team has qualified for the tax.

concerts   Musical events.

conference realignment   A school wanting to join a conference or change conference affiliation. An issue that occurs periodically, effectively changing the landscape of college athletics.

conference rules   Standards set forth by particular conferences that require member institutions to abide by, in addition to NCAA regulation.

conflicts of interest   Situations in which one's own interests may be furthered over those of the principal to whom one owes a fiduciary duty (e.g., the athlete being represented by the agent).

consideration   The inducement to a contract represented by something of value, such as money, property, or an intangible quality.

constitutional law   The body of law developed from precedents established by courts applying the language of the U.S. Constitution and state constitutions to the actions and policies of governmental entities.

contests   Competitions that award prizes based on contestants' skills and abilities; a purchase may be required as a condition of entering the competition.

contract   A written or oral agreement between two or more parties that creates a legal obligation to fulfill the promises made by the agreement.

convention centers   Facilities built and owned by a public entity and used to lure conferences and business meetings to a particular municipality.

convocations   An assembly of people for a specific purpose (i.e., graduation, speaking engagement).

copyright   The right to copy an original work that is in tangible form, such as songs, movies, books, webpages, video games, and sports game telecasts.

Corcoran, Fred   The architect of the professional golf tournament.

cord-cutting   When people refuse to subscribe to cable TV and instead watch television by using an over-air antenna for live viewing of broadcast networks and by subscribing to services such as Hulu and Netflix for cable-distributed programming.

corporate governance model   A model of league leadership in which owners act as the board of directors, and the commissioner acts as the chief executive officer.

corporate ownership   The ownership of a team by a corporation.

correlation   Two variables have a statistical relationship to each other.

coupons   Certificates that generally offer a reduction in price for a product or service.

cover letter   A document accompanying a resumé that introduces yourself and demonstrates your value to the prospective employer.

cross-ownership   Ownership of more than one sport franchise.

cross-promotion   A joining together of two or more companies to capitalize on a sponsorship or expand its scope.

crowd management plan   A document that assesses the type of event, surrounding facilities and/or environment, team or school rivalries, threats of violence, and details emergency contingencies, taking crowd size and seating configuration, and the use of security personnel and ushers into consideration.

Curt Flood Act   This act granted Major League Baseball players, but not minor leaguers, the legal right to sue their employers under the Sherman Act. It confirmed that baseball's exemption from federal antitrust laws applies to business areas including the minor leagues; the minor league player reserve clause; the amateur draft; franchise expansion, location or relocation; franchise ownership issues; marketing and sales of the entertainment product of baseball; and licensed properties.

customer relationship management (CRM)   The implementation of relationship marketing practices that involves creating a database usually of demographic and psychographic information of current and prospective customers.

data centralization   The second step in data management where all organizational data are stored in a central location.

data integration   The third step in data management where data are merged to maximize value to the organization.

data management   Managing available data and cleaning the data appropriately by using a three-step process consisting of data standardization, data centralization, and data integration.

data standardization   The first step in data management where all information and data are organized in a common format with a standard set of definitions.

debt   An amount of money that an organization borrows.

decentralized structure   One of the typical structural methods in which sport analytics are implemented into the day-to-day processes of an organization. In this method, individual analytics employees are embedded into each department of the sports organization to help address the needs of those departments separately.

decision making   A process of gathering and analyzing information so as to make a choice on how to pursue an opportunity or solve a problem.

de Coubertin, Pierre   Founder of the modern Olympics.

default   Occurs when a borrower is unable to repay a debt.

defendant   The person or organization against whom a lawsuit is brought.

delegation   Assigning responsibility and accountability for results to employees.

demographic   Related to the statistical characteristics of a group of people (i.e., age, income, gender, social class, or educational background).

descriptive analytics   Uses data aggregation and data mining to provide insight into the past and shed light on what has happened.

digital networks   The transmission of programming via broadband Internet without the need to be packaged on a tier by cable/DBS systems.

digital video recorder (DVR)   Consumer electronics device or application software that records digital video to a storage device so that it can be replayed at a later time.

direct broadcast satellite (DBS)   Satellite television broadcasts intended for home reception.

direct (e)mail   A method of communication that uses material sent directly to a specific target audience either via mail or e-mail.

direct participation   Active performance of an activity.

disaffirm   To opt out of a contract.

diversity   Any differences between individuals, including age, race, gender, sexual orientation, disability, education, and social and economic background, that affect how people perform and interact with each other.

Division I   A subgroup of NCAA institutions that, in general, supports the philosophy of competitiveness, generating revenue through athletics, and national success; these institutions offer athletic scholarships.

Division II   A subgroup of NCAA institutions that, in general, attracts student-athletes from the local or in-state area, who may receive some athletic scholarship money but usually not a full amount.

Division III   A subgroup of NCAA institutions that does not allow athletic scholarships, and that encourages participation in athletics by maximizing the number and variety of opportunities available to students; the emphasis is on the participants' experience rather than that of spectators.

due process   The right to notice and a hearing before life, liberty, or property may be taken away.

duty of care   A legal obligation that a person acts toward another as a reasonable person would in the circumstances. This duty arises from one's relationship to another, a voluntary assumption of the duty of care, or from a duty mandated by law.

dynamic ticket pricing   Takes into account the cost of a game on the secondary market—like StubHub—in the lead-up to a single game.

eduselling   An evolutionary form of selling that combines needs assessment, relationship building, customer education, and aftermarketing in a process that originates at the prospect-targeting stage and progresses to an ongoing partnership agreement.

emotional intelligence   The ability of workers to identify and acknowledge people's emotions and, instead of having an immediate emotional response, to take a step back and allow rational thought to influence their actions.

empowerment   The encouragement of employees to use their initiative and make decisions within their areas of operations, and the provision of resources to enable them to do so.

end users   Teams, leagues, media research companies that use analytics to solve problems or answer questions about their various businesses.

enforcement   An area within the NCAA administrative structure, created in 1952, that deals with enforcing the NCAA's rules and regulations.

entertainment district   A designated area of a city that has a critical mass of unique properties, e.g. sport stadia, movie theaters, restaurants, to attract people to the city.

entrepreneur   A person who creates an idea for a better use of existing technology.

environmental awareness   Knowledge of the regulations that control public use of lands, and the responsibility to monitor and control human relationships with natural environment use to prevent destruction of natural resources.

Equal Pay Act (EPA)   A 1963 law that prohibits an employer from paying one employee less than another on the basis of sex when the two are performing jobs of equal skill, effort, and responsibility and are working under similar conditions.

equal protection   The Fourteenth Amendment guarantee that no person or class of persons shall be denied the protection of the laws that is enjoyed by other persons or other classes in like circumstances in their enjoyment of personal rights and the prevention and redress of wrongs.

ethical decision making   Requires decision makers to consider how their actions will affect different groups of people and individuals.

ethical dilemma   A practical conflict involving more or less equally compelling values or social obligations.

ethical reasoning   The process of making a fair and correct decision; it depends on one's values or the values of the organization for which one works.

ethics   The systematic study of the values guiding decision making.

evaluating   A functional area of management that measures and ensures progress toward organizational objectives by establishing reporting systems, developing performance standards, observing employee performance, and designing reward systems to acknowledge successful work on the part of employees.

event director   A person involved in planning, organizing, and executing projects, celebrations, sporting contests, etc. Management of the show from start to finish may involve dealing with ushers, security, and medical personnel, show promoters, patrons, and coping with crises that may occur.

event marketing   The process of promoting and selling a sport or special event; it encompasses nine areas: sales of corporate sponsorship, advertising efforts, public relations activities, hospitality, ticket sales, broadcasting, website development and management, licensing/merchandising, and fund-raising.

expenses   The costs incurred by an organization in an effort to generate revenues.

facility financing   The methods by which a stadium or facility receives financing, such as tax-exempt bonds, public financing through tax dollars, or private financing.

faculty athletics representative (FAR)   A member of an institution's faculty or administrative staff who is designated to represent the institution and its faculty in the institution's relationships with the NCAA and its conference.

family events   Products geared toward the toddler and through the "tween" markets. Often these are acts produced from television or movie programs that are run on mainstream television or theaters, such as Sesame Street Live or Disney On Ice.

fan identification   The personal commitment and emotional involvement that customers have with a sport organization.

Federal Communications Commission (FCC)   Federal agency that regulates interstate and international communications by radio, television, wire, satellite, and cable.

fiduciary   A person who is invested with rights and powers to be exercised for the benefit of another person.

fiduciary duties   Obligation to act in the best interest of another party.

five-tool analytics   A tool to assess prospective analytics professionals' ability to add value to the industry. The tool analyzes an individual's ability to ask the right questions, collect the correct data, understand statistics sufficiently to model the data properly, interpret the data, and communicate findings.

Football Bowl Subdivision (FBS)   A category of Division I institutions that are large football-playing schools; they must meet minimum attendance requirements for football. Formerly known as Division I-A.

Football Championship Subdivision (FCS)   A category of Division I institutions that play football at a level below that of Division I-A; they are not held to any attendance requirements. Formerly known as Division I-AA.

fragmentation   With the emergence of more TV networks and other outlets for entertainment programming, an audience's attention is no longer focused on a few outlets, but split toward many separate outlets.

franchise free agency   A strategy in which team owners move their teams to cities that provide them newer facilities with better lease arrangements and more revenues.

franchise rights   The privileges afforded to owners of a group of sport teams.

freestanding inserts   Separately printed advertising or coupon sections that are inserted into a newspaper.

freestanding sport management firm   A full-service sport management firm providing a wide range of services to the athlete, including contract negotiations, marketing, and financial planning.

front-end   A team app or league website delivering the benefits of a more connected sport experience to the user.

full-service agencies   Sport marketing and event management agencies that perform a complete set of agency functions.

Gantt chart   A tool that shows the activities, tasks, and events that need to occur when managing an event. This graphical illustration assists in organizing and tracking activities.

gate receipts   Revenue from ticket sales.

globalization   The process by which companies or organizations operate on an international scale resulting in enhanced cultural, economic, and political interactions.

global sourcing   The use of whatever manufacturer or source around the world that will most efficiently produce a company's products.

Golf 2.0   A comprehensive, industry-wide initiative that focuses on player development and increased golf participation by targeting specific groups with tailored programs.

governing bodies   Groups that create and maintain rules and guidelines and handle overall administrative tasks.

grassroots programs   Activities and events that target individuals at the most basic level of involvement, sport participation.

gross negligence   Occurs when a defendant acts recklessly, when a person knows that the act is harmful but fails to realize it will produce the extreme harm that results.

head ends   In broadcasting, the master facilities where programs are received and then fed to individual subscribers.

health and wellness   An increase in focus within collegiate athletic departments on training regimes, nutrition, injuries including concussions in football and women's soccer, and mental health concerns in student-athletes.

high-definition TV (HDTV)   Television broadcast that has a resolution substantially higher than standard-definition television.

hospitality   Providing a satisfying experience for all stakeholders in an event (participants, spectators, media, and sponsors).

Hulbert, William   The "Czar of Baseball"; he developed the National League of Professional Baseball Players.

human relations movement   Management theory focusing on the behavior and motivations of people in the workplace.

human rights   Basic rights that all people are entitled to regardless of race, gender, national origin, disability, religion, or language among others. These include the right to education, freedom of expression, the right to work.

hybrid structure   A blending of two methods used to implement sport analytics into a sport organization. The two methods that are blended are analytics center of excellence (ACE) and decentralized structure.

impasse   A breakdown in negotiations.

income   The difference between revenues and expenses, also called profit.

income mismanagement   A form of unethical behavior by a sports agent that consists of mishandling a client's money, whether by incompetence or criminal intent.

income statement   A summary of the revenues, expenses, and profits of an organization over a given time period.

independent contractor   A worker who is not under the employer's supervision and control.

indirect participation   Participating in an activity as a spectator.

inertial movement analysis   Sensor technology that is placed on the back of an athletes uniform that provides data on the athletes power, acceleration, and speed metrics, as well as mid-workout reviewing capabilities for constant improvement.

information systems   One of the three basic components of a sport analytics program. The other two are data management and predictive models.

informational interviewing   Asking questions of someone employed in a particular career or organization in an effort to expand one's understanding of that industry, organization, or career.

in-house agencies   Separate departments or divisions within a major corporation that deal with event management.

initiative   Going beyond one's formal job description to help the organization.

injunction   An order from a court to do or not to do a particular action.

in-kind sponsorship   Benefits given to a newspaper, magazine, radio station, or television station in exchange for a specified number of free advertising spots or space, rather than money.

inside sales   Used by the majority of professional sport teams and typically involves a 9- to 12-month sales training program that focuses on taking people with little or no sales experience and training them in professional development and sales strategies.

integrated marketing   Long-term strategic planning for managing functions in a consistent manner.

intellectual property   Refers to creations of the mind.

intercept interviews   Interviews in heavy-traffic areas (such as malls) that utilize visual aids and assess the interviewee's reaction to the visual aids. Also called pass-by interviews.

Intercollegiate Athletic Association of the United States (IAAUS)   The forerunner of the National Collegiate Athletic Association (NCAA); formed in 1905 by 62 colleges and universities to formulate rules making football safer and more exciting to play.

Intercollegiate Conference of Faculty Representatives   An athletic conference formed in 1895 to create student eligibility rules for football that emphasize the priority of academics. Also called Big Ten Conference.

Intercollegiate Football Association   An athletic association formed in 1876 and made up of students from Harvard, Yale, Princeton, and Columbia who agreed on consistent playing and eligibility rules for football.

interest   Money that is paid for the use of money lent, or principal, according to a set percentage (rate).

International Association of Venue Managers (IAVM)   The professional trade association for the facility management field.

International Olympic Committee (IOC)   A nongovernmental, nonprofit organization that is the legal and business entity; entrusted with the control, development, and operation of the modern Olympic Games.

International Paralympic Committee (IPC)   The organization that governs the Paralympic Games, where the world's elite athletes with physical disabilities compete.

internship   A job position in which students or graduates gain supervised practical experience.

interview   A formal meeting between an employer and a prospective employee to evaluate the latter's qualifications for a job.

invasion of privacy   An unjustified intrusion into one's personal activity or an unjustified exploitation of one's personality.

judges   Individual contractors employed to supervise athletic competitions. Also called officials.

judicial review   Evaluation by a court that occurs when a plaintiff challenges a rule, regulation, or decision.

Knight Commission   A commission created in 1989 by the Trustees of the Knight Foundation, composed of university presidents, CEOs and presidents of corporations, and a congressional representative, to propose a reform agenda for intercollegiate athletics.

labor exemption   An exception that states that terms agreed to in a collective bargaining agreement are immune from antitrust scrutiny during the term of the agreement.

Lanham Act   A federal law that governs trademarks and service marks and gives protection to the owner of a name or logo.

law practice only   A type of sport management firm that deals only with the legal aspects of an athlete's career, such as contract negotiation, dispute resolution, legal representation in arbitration or other proceedings, and the preparation of tax forms.

leading   A functional area of management that is the "action" part of the management process; it involves a variety of activities, including delegating, managing differences, managing change, and motivating employees.

league   A profit-oriented legal and business entity organized so that teams can compete against each other, but also operate together in areas such as rule making, broadcasting, licensing, and marketing.

"league think"   A term coined by NFL Commissioner Pete Rozelle to describe the need for owners to think about what was best for the NFL as a whole rather than what was best for their individual franchises.

LEED certification   A gold standard for facilities that helps operators identify green building design, construction, operation, and maintenance. LEED stands for Leadership in Energy and Environmental Design.

legacy members   People who join clubs because their parents and grandparents were club members and club membership is a family tradition.

legality   Concept that the subject matter of a contract cannot violate laws or public policy.

legitimate interest   Refers to a reason for upholding the use of separate-gender teams.

liabilities   The sum of debts that an organization owes.

licensed merchandise   Items bearing the logo or trademark of a sport organization; their sale generates a royalty (percentage of the net or wholesale selling price) for the sport organization. Also called licensed products.

licensed products   Items bearing the logo or trademark of a sport organization; their sale generates a royalty (percentage of the net or wholesale selling price) for the sport organization.

licensees   The manufacturers of licensed products.

licensors   Teams and leagues that own the rights to logos, names, and so forth.

local/civic venues   Typically located in towns or small cities, these locations offer small capacity.

lockout An economic weapon used by management in which they do not allow the employees to work during a labor dispute. If the employees are not working, they are not earning a salary. It may therefore, force them to agree to the employer's terms in negotiation.

luxury tax A fee that a team incurs when it exceeds a set payroll threshold.

managing change Effectively implementing change in the workplace and being aware of employees' natural resistance to change.

managing technology Being familiar with technology and using it to one's advantage.

marketing director A person involved with analyzing and purchasing media (e.g., TV, radio, print, billboards), coordinating promotions, and designing marketing materials (e.g., brochures, flyers).

marketing fund A pool of money that is set aside from the profits of other shows. The concessionaire and the venue director each agree to a certain share of the percentage of sold goods, and they use the pool to help invest in future programs.

marketing mix The controllable variables a company puts together to satisfy a target market group, including product, price, place, and promotion.

Mason, James G. Co-inventor, with Walter O'Malley, of the idea of a sport management curriculum.

master antenna The emergence of cable television services in the 1940s through the selling of access to an appliance store owner's antenna which provided a clearer picture on their TVs.

McCormack, Mark Founder of IMG (International Management Group) who invented the modern sports agency. He built IMG from one client in 1960 to a global sports, entertainment, and media company with 2,200 employees in 70 offices in 30 countries at the time of his death in 2003. IMG at the time billed itself as the world's largest, most diverse, truly global company dedicated to the marketing and management of sport and leisure lifestyle.

member conferences Groupings of institutions within the NCAA that provide many benefits and services to their members. Conferences have legislative power over their member institutions in the running of championship events and the formulation of conference rules and regulations.

membership model A trend in the sport ticket sales landscape that involves replacing traditional season ticket plans with a "membership program" whereby season tickets are supplemented by other benefits such as experiential awards, exclusive merchandise, and even the ability to vote on franchise initiatives.

metrics A standard of measurement such as earned run average (ERA) or wins above replacement (WAR) in baseball.

metropolitan facilities Venues located in large cities with very large capacities, such as Madison Square Garden in New York, The Wells Fargo Center complex in Philadelphia, and the Staples Center in Los Angeles.

military recreation Recreational programs offered by the armed services for military personnel and their families on bases in the United States and abroad.

modern Olympic Games An international athletic event, started in 1896, based on ancient Greek athletic games.

monopoly A business or organization that faces no direct competition for its products or services, and as a result possesses high bargaining power.

morality Concerned with the values guiding behavior; a specific type of ethical issue.

moral principles Virtues or moral precepts.

morals   The fundamental baseline values dictating appropriate behavior within a society.

motivation   The reasons why individuals strive to achieve organizational and personal goals and objectives.

multicultural marketing   Sport sponsorship strategies to more effectively target ethnic groups, particularly the Latino and Asian communities who historically have represented only a small percentage of the sport spectator base in the United States.

multimedia   Content that includes various programming including news, entertainment, educational material, etc.

mutual assent   A requirement by a valid contract involving an offer by one party and an acceptance by another.

naming rights   A source of revenue for sport organizations by providing the opportunity to sell the title of its arena or stadium, the practice facility, or the team itself.

National Association of Intercollegiate Athletics (NAIA)   An athletic governance organization for small colleges and universities, founded in 1940.

National Association of Professional Baseball Players (NAPBP)   A group of professional baseball teams formed in 1871; any ball club that was willing to pay its elite players could join.

National Collegiate Athletic Association (NCAA)   A voluntary association that is the primary rule-making body for college athletics in the United States. It oversees academic standards for student-athletes, monitors recruiting activities of coaches and administrators, and establishes principles governing amateurism.

National Federation of State High School Associations (NFHS)   A nonprofit organization that serves as the national coordinator for high school sports as well as activities such as music, debate, theater, and student council.

National Junior College Athletic Association (NJCAA)   An athletic association founded in 1937 to promote and supervise a national program of junior college sports and activities.

National Labor Relations Act (NLRA)   A 1935 law that establishes the procedures for union certification and decertification and sets forth the rights and obligations of union and management once a union is in place.

National Labor Relations Board   An independent federal agency vested with power, from the National Labor Relations Act, to safeguard employees' rights to organize and to determine whether to have unions as their bargaining representative. The agency also acts to prevent and remedy unfair labor practices committed by private sector employers and unions.

National League of Professional Baseball Players (NLPBP)   The successor to the National Association of Professional Baseball Players; formed in 1876, it was a stronger body in which authority for the management of baseball rested.

national youth league organizations   Organizations that promote participation in a particular sport among children and are not affiliated with schools.

NCAA National Office   The main office of the National Collegiate Athletic Association, located in Indianapolis, Indiana; it enforces the rules the NCAA membership passes and provides administrative services to all NCAA committees, member institutions, and conferences.

negligence   An unintentional tort that occurs when a person or organization commits an act or omission that causes injury to a person to whom he, she, or it owes a duty of care.

network   People who know you and can serve as a reference for you during the job search process.

networks   The predominant national organizations where most programming occurs (e.g., the traditional Big Three included ABC, CBS, and NBC although more national and regional networks have emerged).

niche sports Sports that are unique and appealing to a distinct segment of the market, whether defined by age demographics, such as the Millennial Generation or Generation Y (the teenagers and 20-somethings of today), or socio-economic class, as is seen with sailing and polo's appeal to those with higher incomes.

non-equity clubs Nonmember owned clubs.

nonschool agencies Organizations that are not affiliated with a school system.

North American Society for Sport Management (NASSM) An organization that promotes, stimulates, and encourages study, research, scholarly writing, and professional development in the area of sport management, in both its theoretical and applied aspects.

not-for-profit A classification of an event or organization; most often, these events focus on raising money for a charitable enterprise.

officials Individual contractors employed by schools or leagues to supervise athletic competitions.

off the record Remarks made to the media that are not meant to be published or broadcast.

Ohio University The first university to establish a master's program in sport management, in 1966.

Olympic Movement The celebrations of sport that take place every 4 years in the summer or the winter. The governing bodies of this international sport system include the International Olympic Committee (IOC), the International Sports Federations (IFs), and the National Olympic Committees (NOCs).

O'Malley, Walter Co-inventor, with James G. Mason, of the idea of a sport management curriculum. Also owner of the Brooklyn and Los Angeles Dodgers from 1943 until his death in 1979.

operations director A person who supervises facility preparation for all types of events, and coordinates, schedules, and supervises the numerous changeovers that take place as one event moves in and another moves out.

organizational behavior A field involved with the study and application of the human side of management and organizations.

organizational politics The use of power or other resources outside of the formal definition of a person's job to achieve a preferred outcome in the workplace.

organizing A functional area of management that focuses on putting plans into action by determining which types of jobs need to be performed and who will be responsible for doing these jobs.

out-of-home viewing A network is "streamed" to a mobile device for viewing, but typically only to viewers who have a paid subscription to a cable or satellite distribution service.

out-of-market Fans of out-of-town teams now can pay a fee to acquire coverage of game telecasts not available locally.

outdoor recreation Type of activities that take place in natural environments (e.g., camping, canoeing, golfing, etc.).

outsourcing Relying on the expertise of external consulting companies or firms to handle the sales and management of the licensing, sponsorship, and broadcasting rights for a sport organization, team, college, or university.

over-the-top (OTT) networks The use of broadband Internet as a means of distributing and viewing audio–video material which enables new networks to transmit programming without the need to be packaged on a tier by cable/DBS systems.

over-the-top viewing Watching content by using broadband Internet and watching on a network such as ESPN3 as opposed to watching on a cable TV or satellite system.

overly aggressive client recruitment A form of unethical behavior by sports agents that includes such behaviors as paying athletes to encourage them to sign with agents early and promising athletes things that may not be achievable.

owners' equity   The amount of their own money that owners have invested in the firm.

Paralympic Movement   The international sport system—that includes the International Paralympic Committee (IPC), international federations, national governing bodies, and national Paralympic committees—that organizes the summer and winter Paralympic Games for athletes with physical, vision, or intellectual disabilities.

participative decision making   A decision-making process that includes employees or members of an organization.

pass-by interviews   On-site interviews in heavy-traffic areas (such as malls) that utilize visual aids and assess the interviewee's reaction to the visual aids.

pay-per-view   A program that is distributed on a special channel on cable/DBS systems and only accessible by consumers who pay a specified fee to watch the program.

penetration   Describes the number/percentage of people or households receiving a particular product or service.

people skills   Knowing how to treat all people fairly, ethically, and with respect.

personal selling   Face-to-face selling.

physical therapists   Individuals who treat the ailments and injuries of the members of an athletic team. Also called trainers.

plaintiff   The person or organization that initiates a lawsuit.

planning   A functional area of management that includes defining organizational goals and determining the appropriate means by which to achieve those desired goals.

player migration   The increased globalization of sport has resulted in athletes crossing country borders.

player performance analytics   A subset of sport analytics which is applied to the areas of scouting, player development, and the statistical analysis of in-game strategy.

pod   A grouping of multiple TV commercial spots. They fit well with many sports due to their natural commercial breaks between innings, periods, halftimes, quarters, etc.

podcast   A series of digital audio files that can be downloaded through online syndication.

point-of-sale/point-of-purchase marketing   Display materials used by marketers to attract consumers' attention to their product or service and their promotional campaign at the retail level.

Power 5 conferences   Conferences that are recognized under the 2014 NCAA Division I restructuring and comprise the Atlantic Coast Conference (ACC), Big 12, Big Ten, Pac-12, and Southeastern Conference (SEC).

predictive analytics   Uses statistical models and forecasting techniques to understand the future and answer the question, "What could happen?"

predictive models   One of the three basic components of a sport analytics program, as applied to teams, leagues, and a variety of sports industry stakeholders. The other two are data management and information systems.

premium seating   Personal seat licenses, luxury suites, and club seating.

premiums   Merchandise offered free or at a reduced price as an inducement to buy a different item or items.

primetime   During hours of the day, evening hours, when most people are at home and can watch TV.

principal   (1) The original amount that an organization borrows. (2) One who authorizes another to act on his or her behalf as an agent.

private club   A place where people hold a common bond of special interests, experiences, backgrounds, professions, and desires for coming together in a standard meeting place to gather for social and recreational purposes; not open to the public.

private exclusive clubs   A specific type of private club restricting membership to only those who are invited to join or become a member by a vote of the current existing membership.

private schools   Institutions that do not receive government assistance. In the United States, they were the first schools to provide athletic participation opportunities.

private sector   Nongovernment population.

Professional Golfers Association (PGA)   An organization comprised of more than 28,000 golf professionals who work at golf courses and country clubs.

professional tournaments   Sporting events that are sponsored by community groups, corporations, or charities; players earn their income through prize money and endorsements.

profits   The difference between an organization's revenues and expenses.

Progressive movement   An early twentieth-century social and political movement that believed in social improvement by governmental action and advocated economic, political, and social reforms.

project management   An approach that helps organize and oversee all of the details and aspects of an event from start to finish.

promotion   When a team finishes the season at the top of its league, it is moved up to the next higher league.

properties division   A for-profit branch of a league that administers the league's licensing program; such divisions approve licensees, police trademark infringement, and distribute licensing revenues.

proximity marketing   A form of location-based advertising powered through data-based profiles, where communication with a consumer is timely, relevant, and personal.

psychographic   Related to the preferences, beliefs, values, attitudes, personalities, and behavior of an individual or group.

public club   An accommodation facility welcoming participants from nearly all types of backgrounds to play golf and enjoy the offerings of the club.

public ownership   When something is owned by stockholders via shares that can be freely traded on the open market.

public policy   Pertains to a service important to the public.

public recreation   Activities or opportunities offered at the state and federal level, such as state and federal forest and parks departments.

public relations (PR) or communications director   A person who works with the media, including TV and radio news directors, newspaper editors, and reporters, to establish or promote a person, corporation/manufacturer, or product.

public school   A free tax-supported school controlled by a local governmental authority.

rating   The percentage of television households in the survey universe that is tuned in to a particular program.

rational basis   Lowest standard of review in a discrimination case and focuses on any basis other than race, religion, national origin, or gender. Examples include economic or social background, sexual orientation, physical or mental disability, or athletic team membership.

references   People who know you well enough to speak on your behalf.

refugees   People who are displaced from their home countries by wars, occupations, political unrest, or natural disasters.

registration system   A system for registering participants in events and collecting and disseminating the appropriate information.

relationship marketing   Aims to build mutually satisfying long-term relations with key parties (e.g., customers, suppliers, and distributors) in an attempt to earn and retain their business.

relativism   The belief that what is moral depends on the specific situation.

release of liability   Contract that parties sign after an injury occurs, by which a party gives up the right to sue later (usually in return for a financial settlement).

relegation   When a team finishes the season at the bottom of its league, it is moved down to the next lower league.

religious events   Encompass mass worship.

remote production facility   Houses most of the production crew and frequently called the "production truck."

reserve clause   A clause in a player's standard contract that gives a team the option to renew the player for the following season.

reserve list   A list of players that was sent to each team in Major League Baseball; the teams had a gentleman's agreement not to offer contracts to any player on this list, thus keeping players bound to their teams.

reserve system   A restrictive system used to limit a free and open market so that owners retain the rights to players and control salary expenditures.

resumé   A short summary of one's career and qualifications prepared by an applicant for a position.

retention marketing   Sport organizations that recognize the importance of keeping past or existing customers develop aggressive plans to provide continued satisfaction to customers.

retransmission consent   Broadcast networks charge fees to cable and DBS systems for the appearance of the networks on those distribution systems.

return on investment (ROI)   The expected dollar-value return on the financial cost of an investment, usually stated as a percentage.

return on objectives (ROO)   An approach sport organizations or teams use to evaluate the success of sport sponsorships by measuring the success of an activity's intentions (such as measuring the generation of more positive attitudes toward a brand).

revenue sharing   A system in which each team receives a percentage of various league-wide profits.

revenues   The funds that flow into an organization and constitute its income.

rights fee   A type of arrangement in which the network pays the rightsholder a fee, and is responsible for all costs and expenses associated with producing the game(s) or event(s) for television, sells all of the advertising time itself, and retains all the revenue.

rightsholder   The person or entity that owns or controls the rights to an event.

risk   The uncertainty of the future benefits of an investment made today.

risk management   Protecting a business or organization from anything that could possibly go wrong and lead to a loss of revenues or customers; developing a management strategy to prevent legal disputes from arising and to deal with them if they do occur.

rival leagues   Competition for established leagues.

Rooney Rule   NFL rule named for Steelers owner Dan Rooney that requires teams with coaching openings to interview minority coaches during the search process.

royalty   A fee paid to the licensor for the use of specific trademarks on specific products.

Rozelle, Alvin "Pete"   A commissioner of the National Football League (NFL) and shrewd promoter of the league who is largely credited with building the NFL into the model professional sport league. While commissioner, he increased shared broadcasting and marketing revenues, restructured the revenue sharing system, and negotiated the merger of the American Football League into the NFL.

sabermetrics   The empirical, analytical study of baseball.

salary cap   A financial mechanism that limits team payroll to a percentage of league revenues, thereby preventing large market teams from exploiting their financial advantage to buy the best teams.

sales inventory   The products available to the sales staff to market, promote, and sell through a range of sales methodologies.

sales promotion   A short-term promotional activity that is designed to stimulate immediate product demand.

sampling   Giving away free samples of a product to induce consumers to try it.

school athletic director   An administrator of a school athletic program whose responsibilities include risk management, researching and purchasing insurance, handling employment issues, ensuring gender equity, and fund-raising.

scientific management   The idea that there is one best way to perform a job most efficiently that can be discovered through scientific studies of the tasks that make up a job, and the belief that managers can get workers to perform the job in this best way by enticing them with economic rewards. Also known as Taylorism.

script   A specific, detailed, minute-by-minute schedule of activities throughout an event's day, including information on (a) the time of day and the activities taking place then, (b) the operational needs (equipment and setup) surrounding each activity, and (c) the event person or persons in charge of the various activities.

seasonal events   Events that take place during a specific time frame.

secondary meaning   Trademarks that use common words can be difficult to protect; however, these names can be protected if the company has strengthened the terms through advertising and media to lead the public to identify the producer or product with the trade or service mark.

segmentation   Identifying subgroups of the overall marketplace based on a variety of factors, such as age, income level, ethnicity, geography, and lifestyle.

self-governance   System in which leagues organize themselves.

senior women's administrator (SWA)   The highest-ranking female administrator involved with the conduct of an NCAA member institution's intercollegiate athletics program.

share   One way to measure a television program's rating is to determine what percentage of television sets are tuned in to a show at a particular time.

simulcast   The broadcast of programs or events across more than one medium.

single entity   A term used to determine that a team is an independently owned and managed business.

single-entity structure   A model of league ownership in which the league is considered an independent entity to avoid antitrust liability and to create some centralized fiscal control.

soccer-specific stadium (SSS)   Facilities built solely for soccer teams have become the legacy of soccer investor, Lamar Hunt, owner of the Columbus Crew. His stadium in Columbus, Ohio, was the first venue of its size to be built in the United States and has fueled growth for this type of facility.

social media   Usage of various platforms (e.g., Twitter, Facebook, Snapchat, etc.) as a way of marketing, branding, and communicating.

specialized agency   A sport marketing and event management agency that limits the scope of services performed or the type of clients serviced.

sponsor   A person or organization that provides funding or support for an event or broadcast in exchange for commercial exposure or financial gain.

sponsorship   The acquisition of rights to affiliate or directly associate with a product or event for the purpose of deriving benefits related to that affiliation.

sport analytics   The management of structured historical data, the application of predictive analytic models that utilize that data, and the use of information systems to inform decision makers and enable them to help their organizations in gaining a competitive advantage.

sport apparel   Garments that are designed for, or could be used in, active sports.

sport events   Games or tournaments in facilities that typically take place on a seasonal basis and can be scheduled up to 8 months in advance.

sport law   The application of existing laws to the sport setting.

sport management firm affiliated with a law firm   A type of arrangement in which a freestanding sport management has a working relationship with a law firm so that each entity can fill a void by providing the services the other does not offer.

sport management structures   Building blocks that help managers organize and run sports; they are conceived and evolve in response to broad social changes or to address specific issues within a segment of the sport industry.

sport marketing and event management agencies   A business that acts on behalf of a sport property (i.e., a person, company, event, team, or place).

sport property   An athlete, company, event, team, or place.

sporting goods   The physical objects necessary to play a sport.

sporting goods equipment   Fitness products and sport-specific products.

sports agent   A person who acts as a representative of an athlete or coach to further the client's interests.

sports event managers   Personnel who administer, promote, and operate any type of events related to sport.

sports marketing representative   A person who coordinates all of the marketing and sponsorship activities for sport properties, which include sporting events run by the agency firm and the athletes represented by the firm.

stadiums   Outdoor or domed facilities that provide sites for sports teams and other nonsport events, such as outdoor concerts.

standard player contract   An individual contract used by a league for its professional athlete employees in which all terms are standardized except for the time period and salary.

state actor   A private entity that is so enmeshed with a public entity that the private entity is considered a governmental one for purposes of subjecting the private entity to the rights protected by the U.S. and state constitutions.

state associations   Nonprofit groups that have a direct role in organizing state championships and competitions in athletics and activities and are the final authority in determining athlete eligibility.

statutes   Legislatively created laws codified in an act or a body of acts collected and arranged according to a particular theme or session of a legislature.

streamed   Broadcasting of video signals through usage of fiber-optic cable without the need for traditional television networks.

strict scrutiny   First standard of review in a discrimination case. Applies where one discriminates on the basis of race, religion, or national origin.

student-athlete services An area of responsibility within a collegiate athletic department that addresses the academic concerns and welfare of student-athletes, overseeing such areas as academic advising, tutoring, and counseling.

subscriber fees Additional revenue that cable networks earn from the money individuals pay to receive cable television in their homes.

sweepstakes A game of chance or luck in which everyone has an equal chance to win; purchase may be required to enter.

symbiotic relationship A relationship that is mutually beneficial such as the sports industry and the broadcast media business relationship that produces valuable, compelling programming content that has become an essential element of the worldwide sports industry.

syndicate The selling of programs by independent producers to stations not affiliated with networks or to network affiliates for telecast.

target market A group of consumers to whom a product is marketed.

telemarketing Sales efforts conducted over the phone.

television markets Group of counties or cities geographically identified as consisting of a large number of television households.

territorial rights Rules that limit a competitor franchise from moving into another team's area without league permission or without providing compensation.

theaters Public assembly facilities that are primarily used for the presentation of live artistic entertainment; they are usually constructed by universities, public entities, and private (usually nonprofit) groups.

The Olympic Partner Program (TOP) A sponsorship program established by the International Olympic Committee in which corporations pay millions of dollars for status as an official Olympic sponsor for a 4-year period and are granted exclusivity in a sponsorship category.

therapeutic recreation Recreational activities that are offered as a means to improve a participant's physical, emotional, and mental health.

ticket rebate Part of the surcharge that the consumer must pay when they purchase a ticket to an event. This is an additional fee that is structured based on the ticket price and returned to the facility or venue as a result of the sale.

tiers Groups of networks that are marketed to customers at different fees.

time-buy A type of rights arrangement in which the organizer buys time on the network and, subject to the network's quality control, is responsible for production of the event and handling sales.

time-shift The ability, provided through DVR, to watch programs after their live telecasts.

Title IX A comprehensive statute aimed at eliminating sex discrimination in any educational program or activity that receives federal funding.

Title VII of the Civil Rights Act A statute that specifically prohibits any employment decision, practice, or policy that treats individuals unequally due to race, color, national origin, sex, or religion; it covers employers with 15 or more employees.

TOP program A sponsorship program established by the International Olympic Committee in which corporations pay millions of dollars for status as an official Olympic sponsor for a 4-year period and are granted exclusivity in a sponsorship category. Also called The Olympic Partner Program.

tort An injury or wrong suffered as the result of another's improper conduct.

tournament operations Pre-event, actual event, and postevent activities for staging an event.

trade associations   Organizations dedicated to promoting the interests of and assisting the members of a particular industry.

trade shows   Multiple-day events held annually in the same location.

trademark   A word, name, or symbol used by a manufacturer or merchant to identify and distinguish its goods from those manufactured and sold by others.

trainers   Individuals who treat the ailments and injuries of the members of an athletic team.

transfer fees   In professional soccer in the international setting, the fees paid for the rights to a player when that player moves from one team to another. The team acquiring the player pays this to the team the player is leaving.

trashsports   Entertainment that advertises itself as sport but that has no real sporting significance.

uniform player contract   An individual contract used by a league for its professional athlete employees in which all terms are standardized except for the time period and salary.

universal design   A new concept which extends the Americans with Disabilities Act and makes facilities more accessible for all people.

university venues   Colleges and universities can host events at their stadiums, arenas, and theaters.

unreasonable searches and seizures   Searches and seizures conducted without probable cause or other considerations that would make them legally permissible.

up-selling   Persuading an existing customer to move up to the next more expensive sales level.

value-added   The difference between the total sales revenue of an industry and the total cost of components, materials, or services purchased from other firms (and therefore outside the industry).

variable ticket pricing   Charging a premium price for tickets to events or games in greater demand.

vendors   Companies that provide solutions and services to end users.

vicarious liability   Provides a plaintiff with a cause of action to sue a superior for the negligent acts of a subordinate.

video news release (VNR)   A preproduced video piece that is edited for broadcast and includes a written story summary or press release.

volunteer management   The supervision of volunteers involved with an event; it involves two areas: (1) working with event organizers and staff to determine the areas in which volunteers are needed and the quantity needed and (2) soliciting, training, and managing the volunteers.

waivers   A contract in which parties agree to give up their right to sue for negligence before participating in an activity.

wearable analytics   Provides cutting-edge data and performance insights based on the biometric activity of the user.

youth league director   A supervisor of a youth league, whose responsibilities may include hiring, supervising, and evaluating coaches; coordinating nearly all facets of contest management, including the hiring and paying of officials and event staff; setting league training and disciplinary policies; determining league budgets; overseeing all associated fund-raising; determining and verifying game scheduling and athlete eligibility; transmitting relevant publicity; and handling public relations.

zero-base budgeting   Reviewing all activities and related costs as if the event were being produced or occurring for the first time; previous budgets and actual revenues and expenses are ignored.

Index

Note: Page numbers followed by *f* and *t* indicate material in figures and tables, respectively.